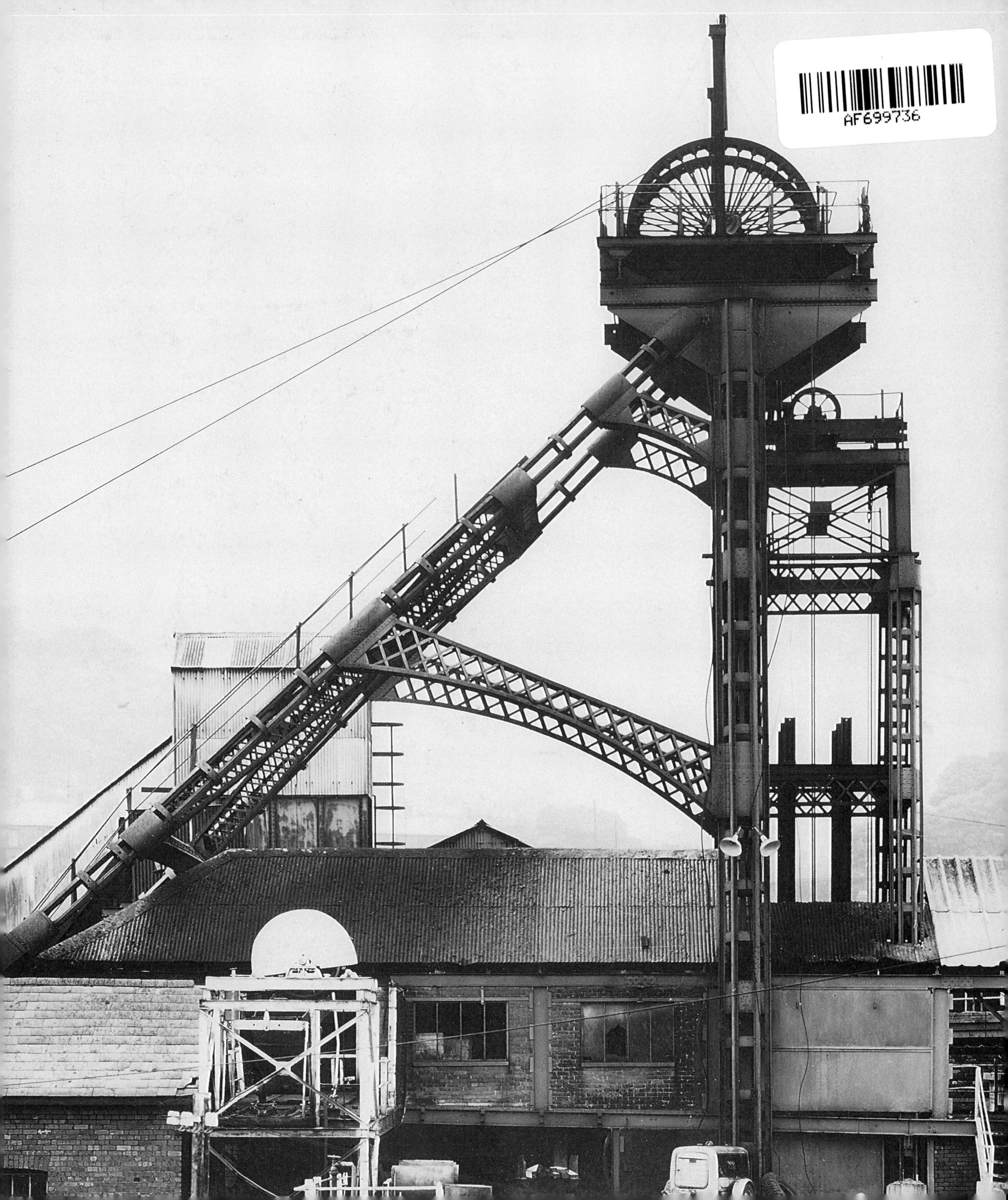

PHOTOGRAPHY TRANSFORMED

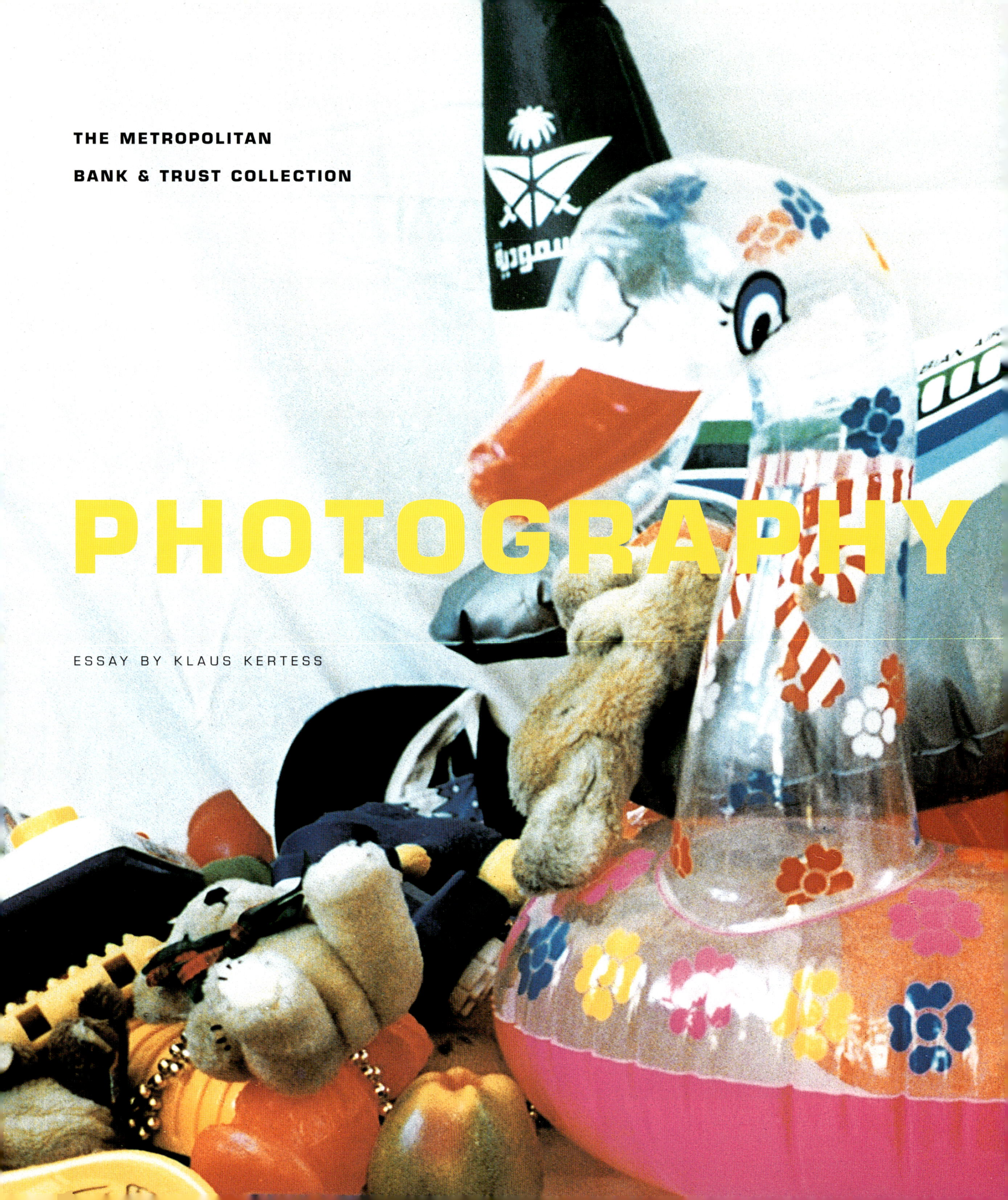

THE METROPOLITAN

BANK & TRUST COLLECTION

PHOTOGRAPHY

ESSAY BY KLAUS KERTESS

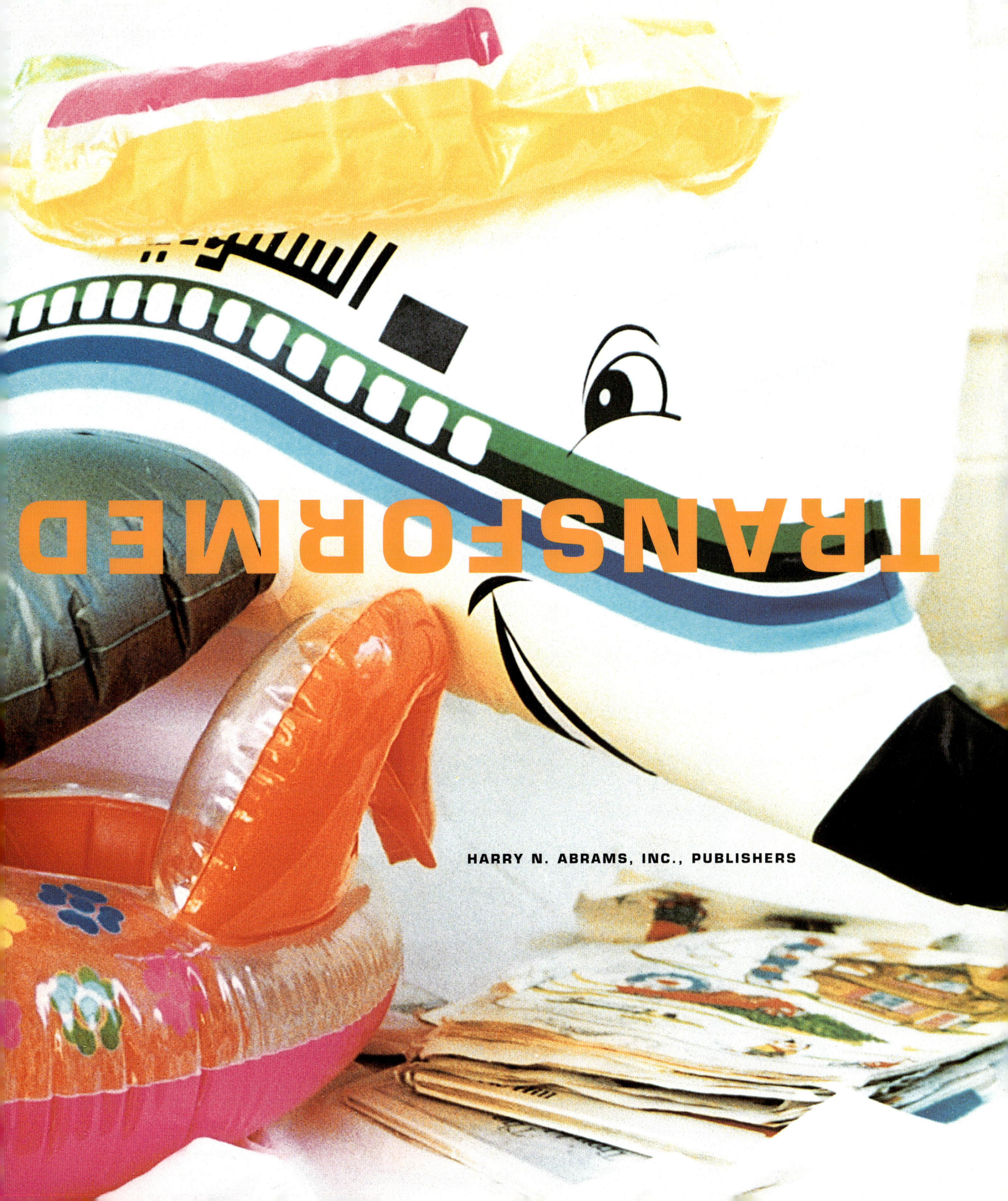

TRANSFORMED

HARRY N. ABRAMS, INC., PUBLISHERS

Editor's note

All artworks illustrated in this volume are part of the Metropolitan Bank & Trust collection. Works illustrated in the essay and the plate sections are not repeated in the collection section, but are referenced by page number in the index of artists. Works consisting of multiple images (diptychs, triptychs, installations, etc.) have been reproduced according to the directions of the artists, when those were available. In some cases, individual images were selected to represent a multi-image work or installation and are referred to as "details."

Endpapers: Bernd and Hilla Becher. *Winding Towers* (details). 1983. Installation: nine gelatin silver prints, 61½ × 49½ inches

Pages 2–3: Andrea Zittel. *Untitled (Project with Gavin and Lucy)* (detail). 1992. Installation: twenty-four chromogenic process prints mounted to aluminum, each paired with framed text panel, dimensions varied

Page 6: Thomas Struth. *Musée d'Orsay 2, Paris, 1989.* 1990. Chromogenic process print, face mounted to plexiglass, 89½ × 73½ inches

Page 264: Rosemarie Trockel. *Yvonne* (detail). 1997. Suite of ten iris print video stills on rag paper, 6¾ × 9 inches each

Project Director: Eric Himmel
Editor: Deborah Aaronson
Designer: Russell Hassell

Library of Congress Cataloging-in-Publication Data

Kertess, Klaus.
Photography transformed : the Metropolitan Bank & Trust collection essay / by Klaus Kertess.
p. cm.
1. Photography, Artistic. 2. Metropolitan Bank & Trust (Cleveland, Ohio)—Photograph collections. 3. Photograph collections—Ohio—Cleveland. I. Metropolitan Bank & Trust (Cleveland, Ohio) II. Title.
TR654 .K439 2002
779'.074771'32—dc21
2001004936

Published in 2002 by Harry N. Abrams, Incorporated, New York

Printed and bound in Japan

10 9 8 7 6 5 4 3 2 1

ABRAMS

Harry N. Abrams, Inc.
100 Fifth Avenue
New York, N.Y. 10011
www.abramsbooks.com

Abrams is a subsidiary of

LA MARTINIÈRE GROUPE

CONTENTS

7 Foreword

8 Multiple Exposure
Klaus Kertess

34 Plates

223 The Collection

262 Index and Photograph Credits

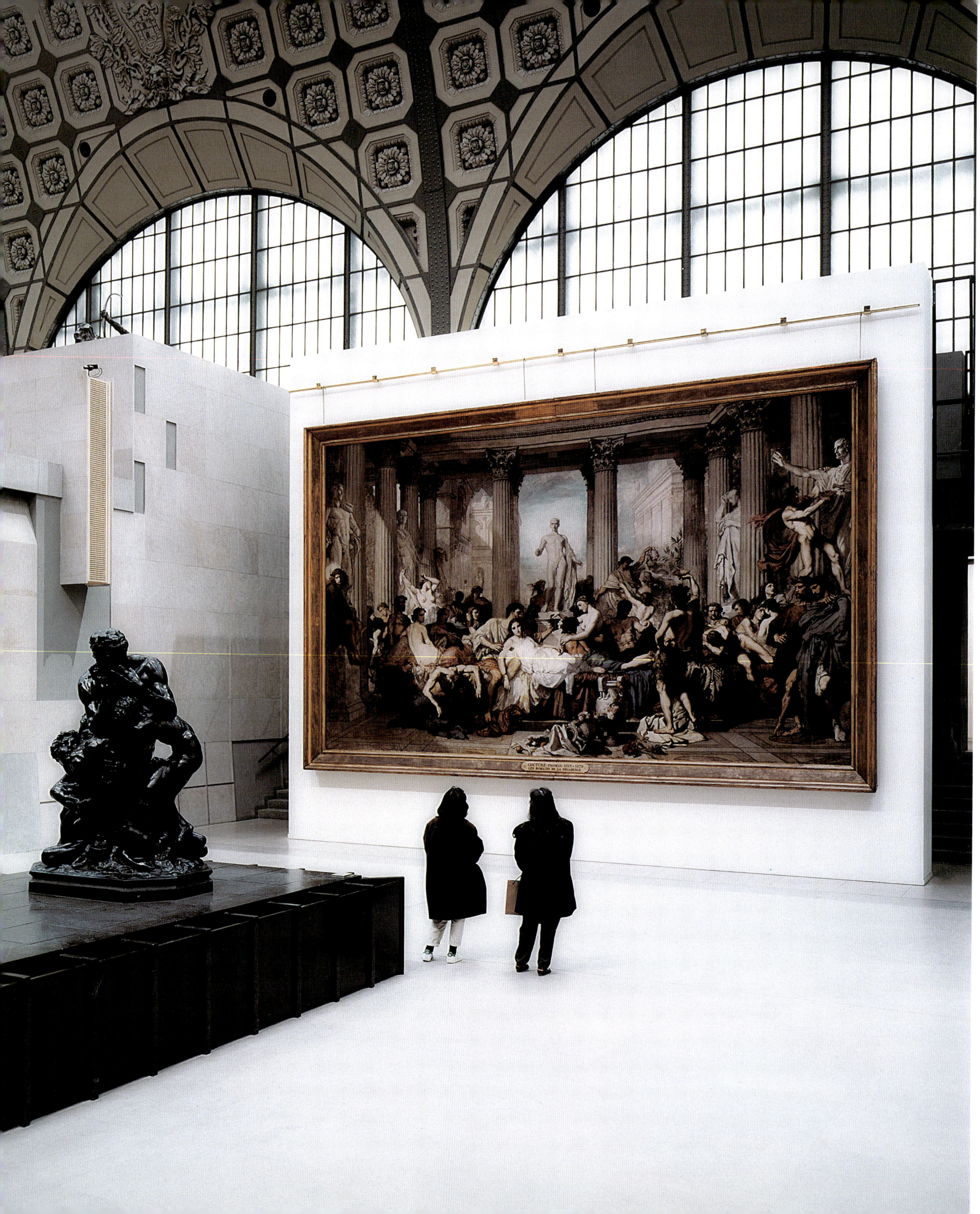
COUTURE THOMAS 1815 · 1879
LES ROMAINS DE LA DÉCADENCE

FOREWORD

Twenty years ago, I began to collect contemporary art. My growing collection became a central part of my life and provided me with a great deal of pleasure as my knowledge of the field increased. In the early 1990s, I decided to create a separate collection of contemporary artist-based photography for Metropolitan Bank & Trust, a community bank located in Cleveland, Ohio, where I serve as Chairman. I believed that a corporate collection would not simply decorate the walls of the bank's headquarters and regional offices, but, more importantly, would offer aesthetic pleasure and intellectual stimulation to the bank's employees and clients, and to the broader cultural community of northeast Ohio. This plan culminated in the recent opening of Metropolitan's new headquarters building, designed by the architectural firm of Skidmore, Owings & Merrill LLP, on whose walls the collection was given an ideal setting.

From the outset, I have been assisted by Barbara Gladstone, a New York gallerist, in the assembling of Metropolitan's collection. Together we decided to make contemporary photography the exclusive focus of the bank's collection. Although recently the field of contemporary photography has become an area of intense interest on the part of museums and private collectors, and a "hot" market as a result, this was not the case when Barbara and I first began our efforts. At that time, no collection of artists' photography of this scope existed. Metropolitan's collection represents a decade of seeking out the most important work produced by an international group of artists who use photography as their prime medium, as artists in the past used painting or sculpture.

This book, along with an exhibition of selections from Metropolitan's collection at the Cleveland Museum of Art, mounted to celebrate this publication, bring me special pleasure since both projects will introduce the collection to a wide audience. I have been assisted by many individuals to whom I would like to express my appreciation and gratitude. Going back to my early days as a collector, I was inspired and assisted by the enthusiasm and knowledge of Jack Bolton, a New York art advisor. In more recent years, Barbara Gladstone's efforts to bring to my attention works of the highest quality from around the world were essential to my endeavors. Along with her friendship, the knowledge I have gained from Barbara is of great value to me. Diane Upright, a private art dealer, has also provided me with wonderful academic insight into the entire world of art history, as well as her friendship, advice, and support. I would like to thank Katharine Lee Reid, Director of the Cleveland Museum of Art, and the museum's Photography Curator, Tom Hinson, for making the public exhibition a reality. I am also grateful to Klaus Kertess for his perceptive essay that serves as the introduction to this book. Finally, this publication owes its existence to Eric Himmel at Harry N. Abrams, who greeted the project with enthusiasm and has ably seen it through to completion.

Robert M. Kaye, *Chairman, Metropolitan Bank & Trust*

MULTIPLE EXPOSURE

KLAUS KERTESS

In the last half of the twentieth century, we came to see the world as photography; photography no longer documented our reality so much as it created our reality. We live for and in photo opportunities. Entertainment, news, and surveillance define each other—and all depend upon the eye of one form of camera or another. From photography we accept illusions and deceptions we long ago denied painting. It has even come to be that many people know painting (and sculpture and architecture) primarily through photography. Stop and think what world you would know without photography.

Since the 1950s, photography has moved from forming a minor tributary navigated primarily by specialists (in 1970, only one photography gallery existed in New York) to becoming a powerful current in the art world's mainstream. Much of this increased interest was created by the first generation to grow up under television's light. Even the definition of photography has expanded to include work referred to as "photography based," meaning not only photographs, but also film and/or video stills, and digital photography created by artists not schooled as, nor desirous of being labeled as, "fine art photographers." Just as sculptors like Donald Judd and Carl Andre could all but order their work by phone, many a photo-based artist has never dipped fingers into developer and some don't even hold the camera responsible for the images they create.

The vast collection that this essay circles around primarily, but not exclusively, celebrates the photo-based work. Included in this territory are performers, painters, sculptors, filmmakers, and video artists, as well as artists referring to themselves as "photographers"—most of them adventurers in their medium or media. The camera thrown in the air and the negativeless photograph variously recur, as does the blurring of distinctions between photography and painting, sculpture, and performance—and the distinction between photo-based art and fine art photography. Pioneering works created earlier in the twentieth century by August Sander, Walker Evans, Man Ray, and Dziga Vertov set precedents for, and frequently influenced, many of the works to be discussed here.

The 1950s ushered in a giddy rise in consumerism and a swelling tide of mass-media imagery; television made advertising an intimate participant in middle-class domesticity. Artists like Jasper Johns and Robert Rauschenberg treated the apocalyptic hangover of World War II and the metaphysical Sturm und Drang of Abstract Expressionism with a bromide of the vernacular. In the early 1960s, Rauschenberg and Andy Warhol became the first major painters to make photo-based work, both, to very different ends, employing the commercial technique of silkscreen. While photography had previously played an important role as adjunct to painting, from Degas's snapshot-like compositional cropping to Francis Bacon's fascination with the blur of newsprint reproductions and his acknowledgment of Muybridge as a major influence, until the end of the twentieth century, photography and painting had never previously been so totally conflated.

In the early 1950s, Rauschenberg together with his then wife Susan Weill exposed large sheets of blueprint paper to light from above, often combining a nude model with various still-life objects. These life-size, fugitive images literally and figuratively foreshadowed the joy in combinative play and compositional brilliance of Rauschenberg's later silkscreened paintings that employ a fractured narrative mix of images taken from print media and his own photographs. This negativeless, light-exposing technique was initiated in the mid-nineteenth century by William Henry Fox Talbot with ephemeral images of plants he gathered in his book *The Pencil of Nature*. In the 1920s, Laszlo Moholy-Nagy and Man Ray separately turned this technique into X rays of Modernism. Man Ray's rayographs transformed Dada disjunctions into a witty poetry of light that looked forward to Rauschenberg and succeeding generations of artist/photographers.

Throughout his career, Rauschenberg has also taken conventional photographs, exhibiting a penchant for urban and rural surfaces bristling with signs, graffiti, and other reflections of time's patination. The fragmentation they document with their faultless framing, such as the partial side of a truck seen through a window in *Untitled (Fort Myers, Florida)* (1980), often looks like found Rauschenberg paintings. His love of graphic fragments and rural imagery call to the earlier work of the master American photographer Walker Evans—although Rauschenberg prefers close-ups that frame compositions even more abstract than Evans's. The first great photographs Evans shot (1936–38) documented the drought and poverty of the rural South for the Farm Security Administration. Low key, matter-of-fact, and visually mesmerizing, Evans's work made moot the difference between documentation and art, in ways paralleling Rauschenberg's later desire to work in the gap between art and life.

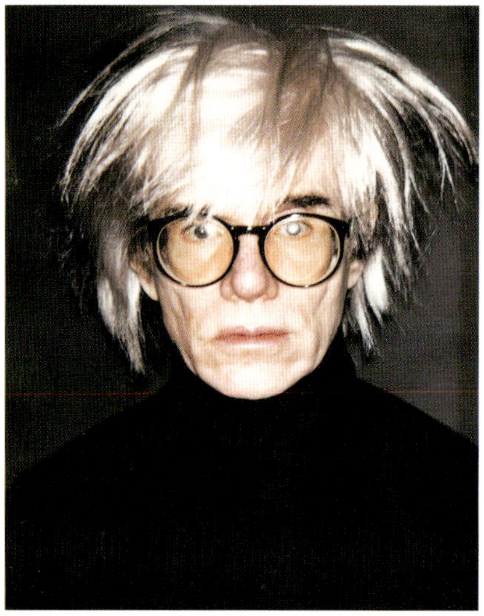

ANDY WARHOL
Untitled (Self-Portrait). 1986. SX 70 Polaroid photograph, $4\frac{1}{4} \times 3\frac{1}{2}$ inches

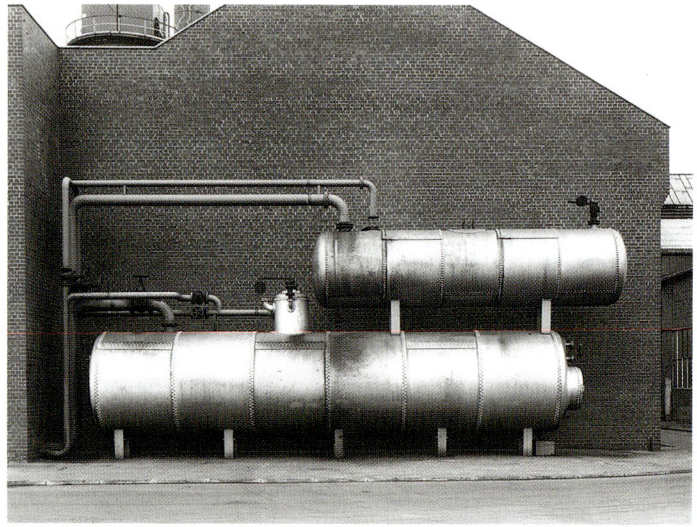

BERND AND HILLA BECHER
Coal Mines and Steelplants (Coal Mine "Minister Stein" Dortmund, Ruhr) (detail). 1988. Installation: four unique gelatin silver prints, 34×43 inches

Unlike Rauschenberg, whose iconography often included one or another surrogate for everyman, and who showed a preference for humble detritus and stuffed farm animals, Warhol was obsessed with glamor, especially the old-time glamor of Hollywood that perhaps saw its last fluorescence in Elizabeth Taylor and Marilyn Monroe in the 1960s. Passive/aggressive, worshiper/fabricator of fame, and artist/promoter, Warhol inverted and converted mass-media images into icons of exclusivity and vice versa. He reinvented the long-lapsed art of portraiture, turning his subjects into mass-producible images—endowing their faces with product identity. Photo-booth portraits became his studies and Polaroids his drawings. In his many self-portraits, his silver-sprayed wig identified him more readily than his bland features and pasty skin; indeed, even in person he looked like a walking black-and-white photograph. We see him here in a late Polaroid *Untitled (Self-Portrait)* (1986), the Svengali of consumerism and fame.

Note has been made of Rauschenberg and Warhol because their engagement and experimentation with photography provided the foundation for many of the artists more fully represented in this collection, which focuses on the succeeding generations from the mid-1960s to the present. Rauschenberg and Warhol propelled photography into a broader context, as well as reinventing genres of narrative, still life, and portraiture that had been more frequently seen in fine art photography's realm than in that of late modernism's. And they alarmed the ordinary and the banal into beauty.

The depersonalization of the hand-made mark and concomitant desire for an anonymous (often machine-made) surface, as well as the tendency to treat subject matter as neutral, even documentary, information laid out on a grid or in simple geometric configuration that pervaded so much work referred to as Minimalist in the 1960s, proved readily compatible with various aspects of photography's nature. Indeed some photographers were practicing their severe dignities before the word Minimalism was coined. The German couple Bernd and Hilla Becher started collaborating on their program of industrial archaeology in 1959, and they continue today to inventory with obsessive thoroughness and detail the vanishing architecture of European (and occasionally American) industrialization: water towers, gas tanks, blast furnaces, working men's houses, cooling towers, mineheads, blast furnaces, cone silos, winding towers, and more, and more. Their books include meticulously compiled information on their subjects; the one devoted to framework houses includes the street name and number, year of construction, as well as the name and profession of the owner of each of the houses. The Bechers's chosen subject is always photographed under a cloudless sky, in diffuse light without shadow, frontally, and with minimal perspectival distortion in as shallow a space as the structure permits—heightening the stark geometric clarity and economy of the architecture. When exhibited, the variants of each subject are hung in a grid. Whether immediately recognizable, like the tanks of the *Coal Mines and Steelplants* or more alien like the *Blast Furnaces, Heads,* each series is at once neutral, clear, cold, and mysterious—not unlike one of Judd's wall-hung, metal progressions of the mid-1960s. The Bechers's painstaking research and execution not only maximize each subject's presence, but make it resonate with a muscular and pensive poetry.

The "neutrality" of the Bechers's archival pursuits relates to aspects of Minimalism while also looking back to an earlier twentieth-century archivist, perhaps even more obsessed, the great German photographer August Sander who, in the 1920s, began to document mankind. He divided the German population into "archetypes" such as craftsmen, peasants, women, and artists, and photographed them as frontally and neutrally as possible. His all-inclusive ethos clashed with Hitler's exclusiveness, and Sander fell into obscurity until after his death in 1964. The Bechers kept the tradition of Sander alive and passed it on to a younger generation of German photographers currently gathering more and more acclaim.

Like the Bechers, the Dutch artist Jan Dibbets is preoccupied with architectural structure and geometric measure. However, he is less concerned with the camera's role as historical preservationist than he is with extending and merging the measured, spatial clarities and/or optical researches of Dutch forebears, such as Pieter Saenredam, Johannes Vermeer, and Piet Mondrian, with the monocular vision of his camera's lens. For some forty years, he has analyzed and made lyrically concrete his explorations of how we construct our visual intelligence. In his *Perspective Correction* works done in the late 1960s, Dibbets drew a distorted rectangular shape on a wall, or on his studio floor, or on a patch of grass in a configuration that would appear as a square when photographed. This imposition of a geometric figure onto the receding space of a photograph seems to subvert the one-point perspectival vision of the camera; the conundrum of illusion then slowly turns into an illusion of a conundrum. In such works as *Panorama Bloemendaal* (1971), Dibbets divides the panoramic seascape into sequential units of time/light as the consecutive shots (sometimes from dawn to dusk) are arrayed on a grid and turn the sea (and the seeing) into units of shadowy polyphony. Or we might encounter an almost real-scale photograph of a window taken at just such an angle that its perspectival distortion threatens to turn the wall it is hung on into an illusion (*Ten Windows* series), or interior window shutters that appear to beat like wings against the light, or the geometric clarity and necessity of a photographic sequencing that opens radially like the petals of a flower or spirals like a snail—always giving a new shape to time.

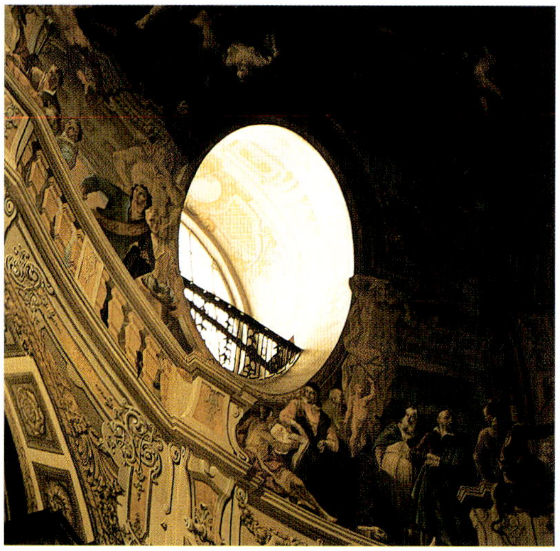

JAN DIBBETS
Ten Windows (Il Soissons 1989) (detail). 1997. Sequenced suite of ten chromogenic process prints, $21\frac{1}{2} \times 21\frac{1}{2}$ inches each

Repetition and/or seriality, the self-evident, the seen, and the ordinary pervaded the art of the 1960s, whether in Pop works like Warhol's painting *210 Coca-Cola Bottles,* or in the Minimalist Dan Flavin's monuments built out of readymade fluorescent light fixtures, or in the photographic works discussed above. The artist/theorist Dan Graham wrote about and explored Pop's dependence on the context of media, and Minimalism's dependence on the context of the gallery, and he himself created photo-based work solely dependent upon its reproduction in an art magazine. His many photographs of dull, serial housing, as banally executed as their subject, such as *Entrance with One White and One Yellow Door; Two Home House*; *Staten Island, N.Y. 1978*

(1978), sought to explore the social context of architecture. Edward Ruscha, on the other hand, in both his paintings and his photographs, with laid-back, deadpan humor, celebrated the implacable banality of so much American architecture, and turned his paintings of words into celebratory still lifes of our logocentric culture. His 1962 photographs in the series *Gasoline Stations* embrace the ubiquity of the ordinary that would later become so much a part of architectural theorizing by architects such as Robert Venturi. Ruscha's gasoline stations, as well as his 1966 fold-out book (some nine yards worth), *Every Building on Sunset Strip,* were almost instantly declared monuments of Pop Art.

The involvement of Rauschenberg, Claes Oldenburg, Alan Kaprow, and others in real-time, brilliantly nonsensical "happenings" in the mid-1960s, together with the often related, ordinary-movement-based choreographies of such artists as Yvonne Rainer and Trisha Brown, and the subsequent emphasis on process and dematerialization of the art object in the late 1960s, as well as the introduction of more portable video cameras, all introduced a new performative aspect into art, and gave the camera, as witness, an indispensable role.

The remote landscape, so often romanticized in mid-nineteenth-century painting, reappeared at the end of the 1960s as the site for monumental earthworks by Robert Smithson and Michael Heizer, and in records of journeys undertaken by Englishmen Hamish Fulton and Richard Long. Artist and explorer became interchangeable terms as did picture postcard, documentation, and art artifact; drawing became walking became sculpture and vice versa. Long has sometimes left a fragile trail or circle of leaves or twigs or stones encountered and/or excavated on his journey; sometimes he has annotated his walk with an evocative text, often he has just walked. The photographs of these activities, such as those documented in *Dartmoor Circle Along a Two Day Walk* (1992), are assigned no less weight as sculpture than the stones frequently gathered from a walk site and later piled in a circle; both might be displayed together in a gallery or museum. Text, but no materials from the site, accompanies Fulton's photographed quests for the picturesque, such as his *Ringdom Gompa Ladakh Northern India July 1978* (1978), taken in northern India.

Staying closer to their London home, Gilbert and George tread out to tea or to a park in their tightly buttoned and vested suits and sent sepia-toned and Victorian-texted photo missives documenting their genteel journeys to their avant-garde mailing list. Then in 1971 they beguiled us as living sculptures—bodies painted gold, attired in their signature suits, revolving jerkily like windup toys and singing "Underneath the Arches." After 1970, their multipaneled photo works acquired the scale, color, and transparency of stained-glass windows. Their roles as guileless and unflappable Victorian innocents have moved through fragmented tableaus ranging from such enigmas as *Night View* (1978), to politically fraught and more explicitly scatological subjects. Relentlessly cheerful, their barbed charm is as formally surprising as it is iconographically.

Perhaps no one played more presciently in the late 1960s than Bruce Nauman as he sought to give literal and figurative body to his restless thoughts about how to make art without relying on paint and brush, and what the social role of the artist might be. After starting off with almost-painting-like fiberglass pieces, in the mid-1960s he turned his attention to everyday actions and accidents performed, and inconsequential spaces encountered, in his studio—making wax impressions of his knees (and titling it *Wax Impressions of Knees of Five Famous Artists*) or creating casts of the space under his chair, exploring the edges where boredom meets creativity, where inconsequence becomes visceral, and where narcissism becomes art. His experience of Man Ray's retrospective at the Los Angeles County Museum of Art in 1966 fueled his interest in performance and photographic mediums. The movie camera as main protagonist and generator of zany action seen in Man Ray's riotous Surrealist movie *Emak Bakia* (1927) particularly impressed Nauman as he began to record his own actions with a still camera, or a movie camera, or a video camera, or with holography. Manipulating his face like silly putty in his photographic *Studies for Holograms (a–e)* (1970), Nauman continued the deadpan explorations of his body as medium that he had initiated in his earlier photograph *Self Portrait as a Fountain* (1966), with its punning bow to Duchamp's readymade urinal, *Fountain* (1917). Critical to the art of the late 1960s, the performative, whether a neutral record of material procedures or the movements of the artist's body as sculptural medium, transformed Jackson Pollock's choreography of body as brush into a theater (often absurdist) of the everyday. Some of Nauman's actions were called Body Art, as were those of his East Coast peer, Vito Acconci.

As smitten with the high jinks play of Dada and Surrealism as was Nauman, and as wary of aesthetic conventions, John Baldessari has made a career of juggling joyously with found images of the ordinary, constantly asking what is required of an activity in order to call it "art." In 1969, he took Minimalism's suppression of the artist's touch one step further and exhibited a group of paintings bearing his name, but made by commissioning others to paint them. In his myriad photo-based assemblages, Baldessari juxtaposes words and images in punning or nonsensical pieces that undermine and redirect our need for "meaning." For the works in his *Blasted Allegories (Colorful Sentences): Worried Appeal Cycle* series (1978), Baldessari set up a

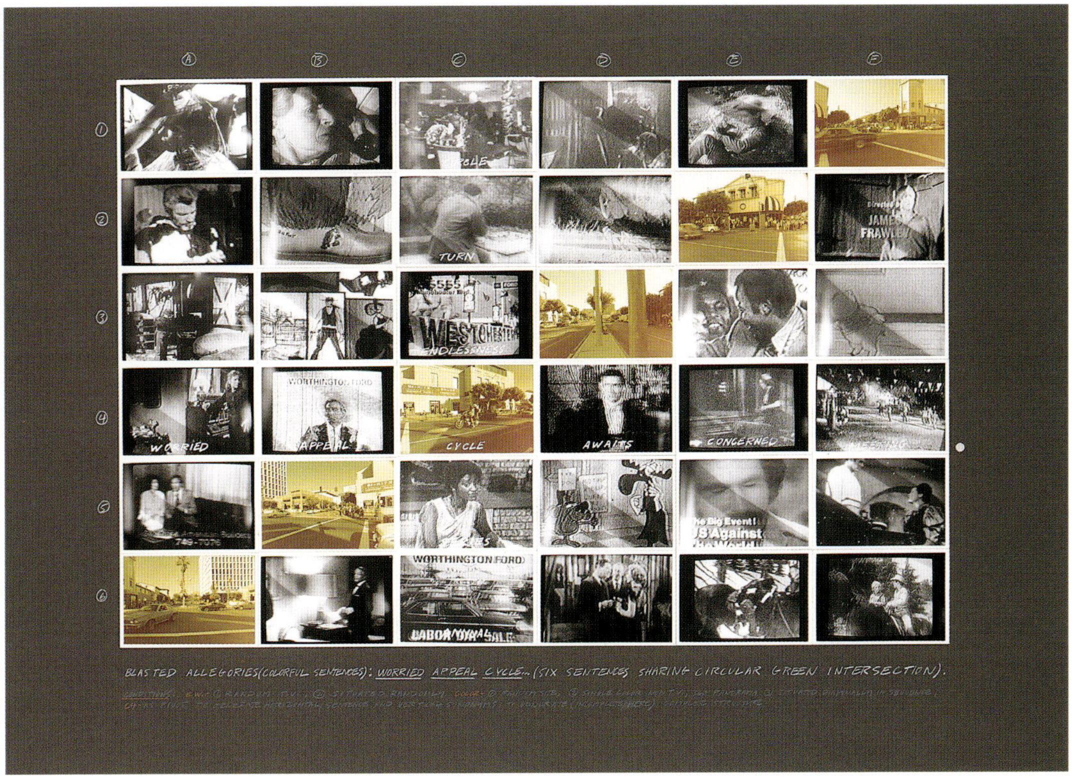

JOHN BALDESSARI
Blasted Allegories (Colorful Sentences): Worried Appeal Cycle. **1978. Thirty-six gelatin silver and chromogenic process prints, mounted on board with colored pencil text, 31¾ × 41 inches**

camera in front of a television; the camera was equipped with a timer to take a picture every ten minutes and was periodically fitted with one of a series of color filters. Subsequently, each image was labeled with the first suitable word thought of by Baldessari or one of his friends, and was then filed in alphabetical order determined by its color (black and white, full color, or the single color produced by the red, orange, yellow, blue, green, or violet filter). Each color was also assigned a meaning, e.g., "blue" connotes "psychological." Baldessari then invented a theme for each work and turned to his new dictionary to execute it. Like all good art, the resulting work can be read in numerous ways, is multivalent in its referentiality and associativeness, refuses to surrender completely to verbalization, is visually clear and conceptually complex.

Although Nauman deeply admired de Kooning, he couldn't find his own place with a paint brush. Baldessari preferred found images to painted ones. Yet all the while, other artists continued to paint—some compellingly. Among the noteworthy painters, a number were, and continue to be, engaged in a dialogue with photography. Gerhard Richter, who today glides with alarming suaveness from photography to photo-based painting to visceral painterly abstraction, first established himself in the 1960s as a maker of grisaille paintings based on found photographs. A unifying blur resulted from Richter dragging a brush across a still-wet painting; as he developed, this

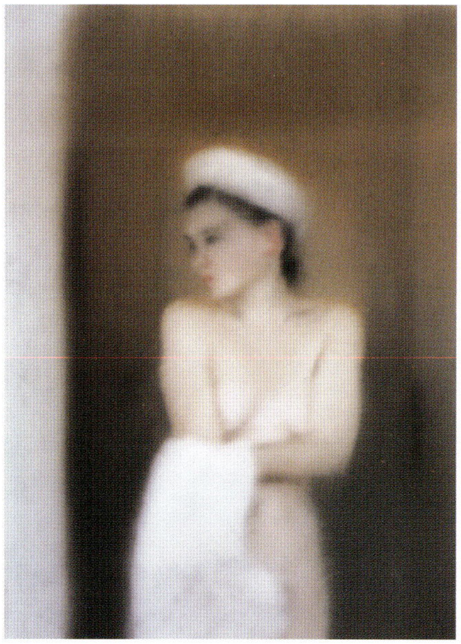

GERHARD RICHTER

K.L. Badende (Bather). 1996. Chromogenic process print, 20¾ × 14¾ inches

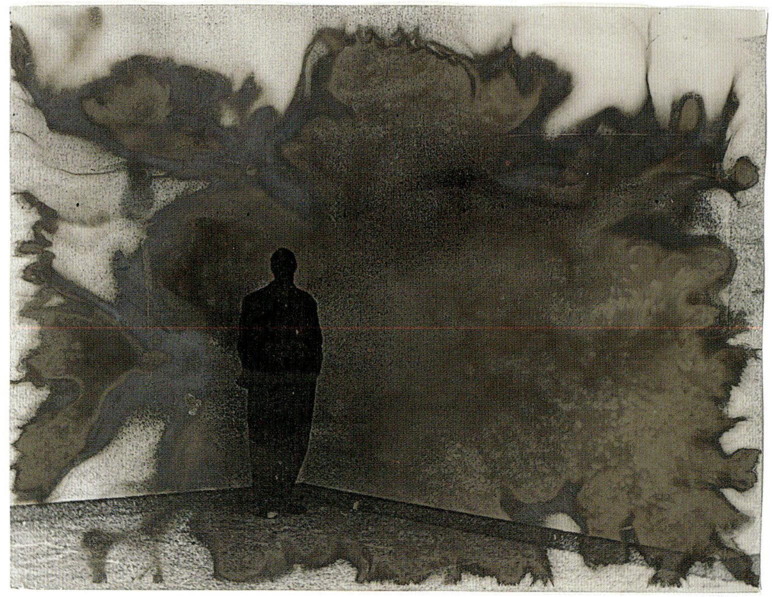

SIGMAR POLKE

Biennale de Venise (2). 1986. Unique gelatin silver print with manipulated chemistry, 9⅜ × 11⅞ inches

blurring ever more subtly veiled his images in uncertainty—whether in triple-exposed self-portrait photographs splattered with paint (1990), or gray paintings of clouds (1970), or the Baader-Meinhof gang (1987), or the "double-exposure" blur created in his abstract paintings by cloaking his gestural strokes with a paint-filled spatula. Photography and painting become penumbral mirrors of each other; both reflecting a fragile awareness of awareness. In reproduction, only the caption can assure us that an image of a bather *K.L. Badende (Bather)* (1996) is not a painting but a photograph.

Richter's friend Sigmar Polke has proved to be the Merlin of painting—and of photography. Starting with a quirky Pop mix of dot-screen grids and comic book drawing in the mid-1960s, his paintings quickly evolved into a dizzying, disjunctive mix of techniques, materials, and images—quaintly patterned fabric, gestural strokes, a silkscreened image from some medieval tome, and an image of nuclear war might all vie for attention or dissolve into abstraction within a single painting. He at once mocked and elevated painting's transformative power, its alchemy. The more literal liquid transformations employing minerals and chemicals that have preoccupied

Polke since the 1980s perhaps took their cue from his liquid daring in the darkroom. In the 1970s he began manipulating negatives with developing solution, overpainting developed images or partially destroying them. In 1971, working under the influence of LSD, he created a series of hallucinatory images: of figurines, a sleeping head, a naked body submerged in a tub, the film stock itself—all in various stages of being photographed or developed. He might manipulate the developing solution to parallel the distress of the homeless on the Bowery (1973), or to simulate the magic torpor of an opium den (1975), or paint delicate throngs of gold and colored calligraphic marks over photographs made in Afghanistan (1974). He could also induce negativeless wonders of luminescence by laying pieces of uranium on unexposed photo paper for a week and then developing the paper (1982). For the Venice Biennale in 1986, Polke created a huge painting that reacted to the humidity level of the exhibition space. Before the work was hung, he created a series of photographs in the space that paralleled the transformational aspects of the painting. The space of the photographs is alternately inhabited by apparitions of a swirling spume of smoke, a shower of light, something amoeba-like engorging the space, a shadowy colossus turning a corner, a tiny figure, and more—all bred in the dark room (*Biennale de Venise [Venice Biennale] (2),* 1986). That tiny figure is the self-portrait of an artist making more magic in the darkroom than almost anyone since Man Ray.

Chuck Close began employing photography as a model for his painting in 1968, to depersonalize the vagrant acts of his hand and to avoid subjective choice making—as artists like Sol LeWitt chose simple geometries to objectify their making. Close took frontal photographs of himself or a friend, gridded them off, and set about painting a head some nine feet high, one square of the grid at a time, with barely a thimble full of paint, using such tools as a razor blade, an electric eraser, and sandpaper—professing to employ a technique akin to a paint-by-numbers set. Obsessively and "objectively" he sought to translate the view of the lens into paint, from the hard focus on the eyes to the blurring of the hair and the tip of the nose. The vast size of the head requires a view from afar to resolve photographically; close-up the viewer's eyes get lost in a gridded maze. When he turned from black and white to color, Close simulated the color printing process of layering color separations—painting the image in its entirety layer upon layer, red, yellow, and then blue as is indicated in the photo study *Nat (Five Color States)* (1971). Transparent layers of watercolor mimed the transparency of photographic color separations and fused into modulations of full color. Close has given stunning faces to Minimalist strategies of making, and new meaning to the idea of the Protestant work ethic.

Together with the achievements of such forebears as Warhol and Rauschenberg, the ideas embodied by the generation that includes the Bechers, Dibbets, Nauman, Baldessari, Richter, and Polke have reverberated into the new millennium. However, by the 1980s, so many aesthetic tributaries emerged that no mainstream could still be recognized. Labels like "postmodernism" and "multiculturalism" lost their meaning, sometimes as quickly as they were coined. The siren songs of mass media and fashion; a desire for a more explicit engagement with narrative; issues of race, gender, and sex growing out of the 1960s political upheaval; the high-tech shrinking of our globe; renewed interest in autobiography, myth, and the revival of beauty's possibility, and more flow in and out of each other in dizzying speeds that mandate a kind of zigzagging chronicle back and forth across the last three decades. The wreckage of drug addiction, surreal fabulism, and highly aestheticized hermeticism can all lay equal claims on our attention.

The camera is, of course, ideally suited to conspire in the blurring of fiction and nonfiction, art and reality, now so ubiquitously cultivated by television's light. Recently, the cinema verité of filmmakers of the late 1960s like Shirley Clarke has been absorbed into a larger culture. The "reality based" television programming, so popular today, was initiated in 1973 with the PBS documentary, *An American Family*, that documented, amongst much else, the changes wrought on the subjects by their documentation. The dismantling of the borders between memoir, biography and/or autobiography, and the invented, long ago initiated by Proust, then taken over by steamy tabloids, was resumed by literate hands such as those of Norman Mailer and Truman Capote in the 1970s. In the 1920s and 1930s, the 35mm camera made possible mobility, speed, and spontaneity, which permitted photographers like Henri Cartier-Bresson to more closely document "reality". In Paris, Brassaï (Gyula Halász) brought his camera into a brothel (1932); in New York, Walker Evans concealed his camera while photographing in the subway (1938–41). Lisette Model's love of her 35mm camera, and desire to get close to the harsher realities she sought out on the street, as well as her profound visual acuity, paved the way for photographers such as Diane Arbus, Peter Hujar, and Nan Goldin. By the 1970s, the photographer was found more and more often on both sides of the lens, conflating the "I" and the eye of the camera that today pervades the art world in myriad manifestations.

Larry Clark's book of photographs, *Tulsa* (1971), invited us into his junkie's world with coolly framed directness. At the same time, a group of artists including Nan Goldin, David Armstrong, the late Mark Morrisroe, and Jack Pierson were photographically recording themselves and friends having sex and posing and having sex in the demimonde of Boston, at another kind of

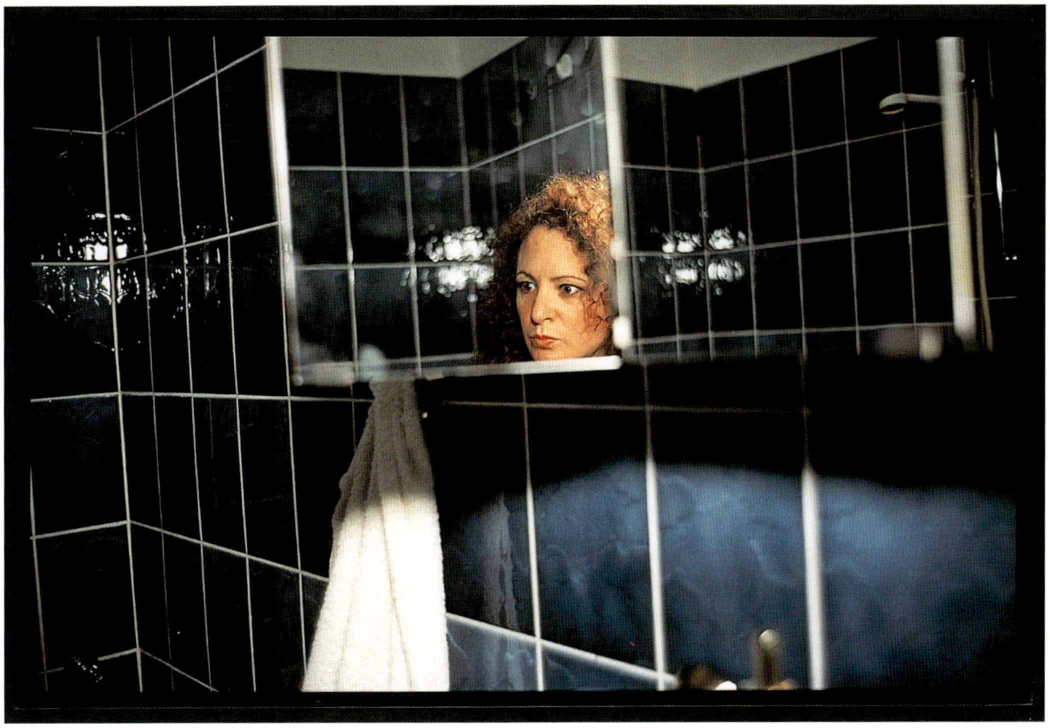

NAN GOLDIN
Self-Portrait in My Blue Bathroom, Berlin.
1991. Silver dye bleach process print in artist's frame, 28$^{3}/_{8}$ × 41 inches

tea party. First in black and white and, after 1973, in luscious color, Nan Goldin charted her friendship with David Armstrong and assorted drag queens. With compassion and growing visual assurance, in 1978, Goldin began celebrating what would be the last round of New York's downtown bohemian life before AIDS and big money demolished it in the 1980s. Herself an AIDS activist, she memorialized her afflicted friends and, with raw confessional candor, recorded the physical abuse she occasionally suffered at the hands of lovers, as well as her recurring stays in detox clinics. Relentlessly she studied herself in the camera as her moody *Self-Portrait in My Blue Bathroom, Berlin* (1991) attests. Photographs of Goldin with a black eye became one of the monograms of the 1980s, along with the lush dishevelment of her interiors, the pre- and postcoital embraces of many of her subjects, and the dreamy, wasted gazes which fed the hungry eyes of countless fashion photographers.

Born in 1953, one year Goldin's senior, the Parisian photographer Patrick Faigenbaum has created a kind of surrogate autobiography as discreetly distant as Clark's and Goldin's works are brazenly upfront. The loss of his father early in his life, and the disappearance of many of his relatives in the Holocaust, catalyzed the creation of a photographic family as firmly and historically grounded as Faigenbaum's forebears were precariously nomadic. With unabashed refinement and a mastery of silvery light, he systematically made portraits of the nobility of Florence, Rome, and Naples—obsessively exploring portraiture's traditional role of ensuring family continuity and power not only to his subjects but (transitively) to himself. Not at all defensive about being a "straight" photographer as some of his American peers are, Faigenbaum meticulously prints his matte photographs. The superb composition and play of pearlescent light surrounding the little girl lost in inspection of her hands, celebrated in *Untitled* (1994–96), harkens back to eighteenth-century Dutch genre painting, especially to Vermeer, as does the combination of restraint and intimacy.

The younger Catherine Opie's lush Cibachrome portraits often hover somewhere between mug shot and Hollywood publicity still. She has recorded the gender theatrics of her lesbian tribe, as well as some male sisters, with insistence, warmth, humor, and another kind of glamor. Drag kings in butch regalia, frequently mustached and/or pierced and tattooed are likely to greet us forthrightly, as do the faces (one of them Opie's) in the close-up, cropped double portrait *Bo and Chicken* (from the *Being and Having* series) (1991). The legacy of the women's movement and gay liberation has empowered artists like Opie to add a kind of down-home directness to the refined gender bending of their Duchampian forebear Rrose Sélavy. Opie conflates role play as reality, role play as politics, and role play as art.

To stand in front of a camera, no matter how spontaneously or casually, is to be frozen in time—to act autobiographically artificial. Conversely, the artificial acts of making, no matter how abstractly and impersonally constructed, carry, in some form, the unique imprint of the maker. Shades of the self-performative, from the overtly autobiographical to the self-suppressed, mythological transformation, have played prominent roles in the art of the last thirty years—albeit roles of extremely varying intent. The austere, self-reflexive acts performed by artists such as Nauman and Acconci in the late 1960s have acquired ever more narrative complexity, and the medium of photography, from still images to digitalized motion, has facilitated this vast panoply of performance. The growing desire to revive "extra-artistic" narrative, referentiality, and use of metaphor that marks so much of art since the early 1970s, and that had so often been rejected in late modernism, has ever more frequently found fulfillment in photography's illusion of veracity. And the multiplicity of technological advances in all realms of photography may well have given its various manifestations the pliability and accessibility of tubes of paint. If we factor in the fast pace, so pervasive in our culture, and the degree to which we depend on photographic imagery to delineate the parameters of our lives, perhaps we can understand why so many viewers are

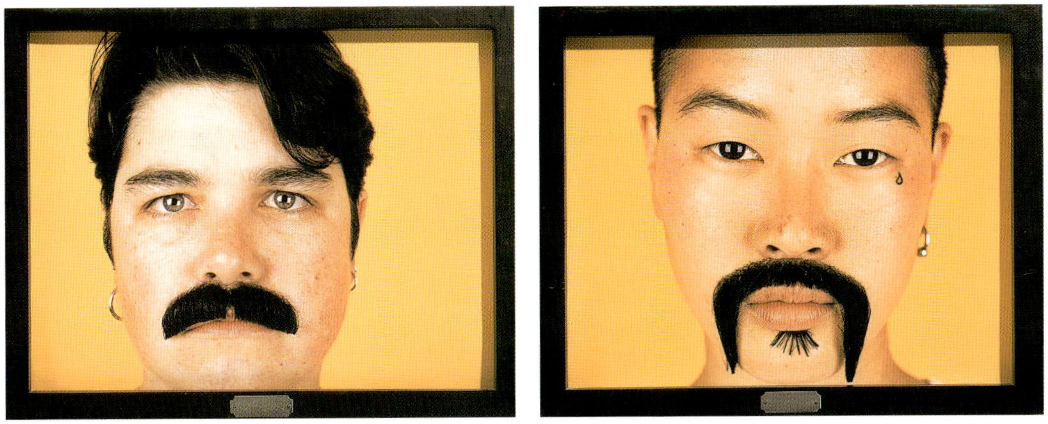

CATHERINE OPIE
Bo and Chicken. From the *Being and Having* series. 1991. Diptych: chromogenic process prints with engraved plaques on artist's frames, 17¼ × 21¼ inches each

more willing to suspend disbelief in front of a photographic illusion than they are in front of a painted illusion. Has there been anything too fabulous, too glamorous, too gory, too sublime, too minute, or too grand for the camera to reveal?

Few artists have so successfully reproduced themselves as Charles Ray and Cindy Sherman, two peers who began their mature art careers in the early 1970s—not turning themselves into photo-autobiographers but into self-fabricators, although Ray has less frequently employed a camera, and also less frequently exploited himself as subject. Simultaneously influenced by the Process Art of Richard Serra, the performative work of Acconci and Chris Burden, and Warhol's iconicization of mass consumerism, in the early 1970s, Ray embarked on a deadpan exploration of himself as sculptural object and as consumerized object. Punning on the conflation of the maker (making) and the made, so central to the Process Art of the late 1960s, as well as the body as sculptural object, Ray wedged his own body between leaning, Serra-like metal planes and photographed himself as sculpture performing and performing sculpture. He also examined himself consumed by clothes that definitely don't make the man. *All My Clothes* (1973) reduces Ray to generic blandness both through his sixteen-fold Polaroid repetition and the utter banality of his clothes—more a victim of mass production than Warholian icon. This infinitely reproducible self would reappear and be extended in a remarkable group of Ray's sculptures, beginning in 1990 when he had a mannequin molded, based on himself, which he dressed in his casually, unobtrusive clothes (*Self*).

While Ray has turned his self into an infinitely reproducible genericomic consumerized model, Cindy Sherman has multiplied her self into a kaleidoscope of womanhood. With acute directorial skill, countless cosmetics and prosthetics, and ever-growing confidence in her medium, she has turned herself again and again into photographic reproductions of acted representations of dreams, nightmares, reveries, and quotidian actualities. Childhood combinative play and role play, so critical to our development and to the making of art, literally and figuratively consume her. After exploring female roles in various film genres (in her seminal black-and-white *Film Stills*, 1977–80), Sherman created a series of "centerfolds" in 1981, including *Untitled #85* (1981), all horizontally formatted, representing various phases of female reverie, expectation, and vulnerability, packing more suspense into a still than many a movie or television director manages in a filmed melodrama. She established herself as a virtuoso of the cinematic still and has influenced several successive generations of photographers. At once exposing and reveling in artifice, Sherman has as readily explored the poses of fashion as she has the utter, visceral abjectness of a plague, or the rarefied sublimation of Old Master paintings—as can be seen in one of her *History Portraits* where she becomes a balding man à la Hans Holbein (*Untitled #214,* 1989). These works at once appropriate and undermine the notions of master and masterpiece that have historically been claimed by male artists.

One male artist seemingly still willing to assume the role of master is Jeff Koons, who has as unabashedly and narcissistically exploited himself as he has exploited sentimentality, banality, and mass culture. Like Ray, Koons's hands-off fabrications often conflate art and mass reproducibility, but Koons prefers brash excess and self-veneration to Ray's sly deadpan and self-effacement. In the four *Art Magazine Ads,* photographs he created announcing his 1989 exhibition, Koons gleefully and tastelessly revives the romance of artist as shaman, depicting himself as retriever of paradise and bearer of erotic power, as the savior of the physical world, as enlightened teacher in front of a blackboard emblazoned with "Banality as Savior" and "Exploit the Masses," and as humble servant of the masses, cheek to cheek with a pig "Ushering in Banality." His high-end slickness rivals major advertising campaigns in its interchangeability of product and promotion. Several years later, Koons would depict himself disporting with his porn-star wife in photo-silkscreened pastorales that could outdo the anesthetized hype of any cruise ship line.

The product perfection honed by Koons's various assistants became a hallmark of the 1990s. Photographs as perfectly manicured as Mariko Mori's nails in *Mirage (Miko no Inori,* 1997*)* are frequently more elaborately styled than a *Vogue* fashion shoot. Science fiction, Buddhism, Chanel, and obvious expense have been invested in Mori's elaborate, dreamy, and exotic video installations of herself performing as a model-cum-goddess, drifting through something like the mirage of a fashion show or an MTV video for a spaced-out techno tune. Like many of her video artist peers, Mori exhibits stills of her videos, which might readily be seen together with fabricated stills from an imaginary movie by an artist such as Sherman.

These self performers have been discussed together not because they form a cohesive group, but to give some idea of the wealth of narrative play so prominent in the art created since 1970—and to introduce a fragment of narrative scaffolding to the disparate artistic intentions charted in this collection and essay. While the exploration and reconfiguration of the role of woman is a concern shared by Goldin, Sherman, Opie, and Mori, their individual work separates into intentions ranging from the documentary to a purely fabricated fabulism. One might as readily employ engagement with mass culture or "straight" versus "staged" photography as narrative scaffolding to describe their intentions.

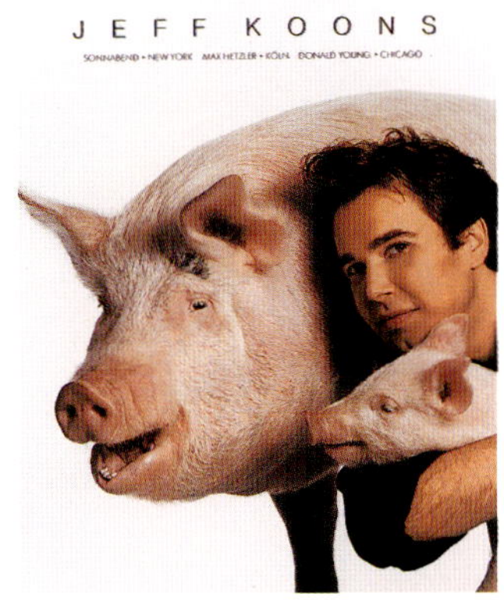

JEFF KOONS
Art Magazine Ads **(detail). 1989. Portfolio of four offset lithographs plus one cover page, $35\frac{5}{8} \times 28$ inches each**

Matthew Barney, one of the youngest artists represented here, has perhaps traveled furthest from the spartan strictures of early 1970s Process Art into a purely metaphorical realm, moving his person from a simple art-making tool into a complex series of protagonists, fully absorbing the autobiographical into the mythical. Barney began with Pollockian choreographies, tethering his body and swinging from the ceiling, from wall to wall, leaving body-trajectory marks on a pad affixed high on the wall. Chris Burden, Nauman, and Barry Le Va influenced his early extreme mark-making. Very quickly, however, drawing extended into wrestling, driving, tap dancing, and ultimately into the movements of the reproductive system as Barney developed a shifting cosmology of organic interdependencies. Magic, football, biotechnology, biology, Greek mythology, The Church of the Latter Day Saints, Stephen King, rock 'n' roll, and more, much more, have been seamlessly and mysteriously interwoven in Barney's visceral poetry as he has moved from performing simple acts of process to becoming a multiplicity of makers, including a satyr and Houdini, and stepping en route into various sexes. His five-part *CREMASTER* epic may well become the signature of the millennial decade, just as the Robert Wilson and Philip Glass collaboration *Einstein on the Beach* marked the 1970s.

Barney's directorial and sculptural pyrotechnics spill over into the various combinations of stills taken from his *CREMASTER* series. His meticulously made-up and costumed characters often move with sculptural weight and deliberation; their iconic presence radiates even in the isolation of a still, as does the image of the wasp-waisted, sinister queen (bee) in the dominant image of the four that constitute *CREMASTER 2: The Queen's Exposition* (1999). The curves of the queen's figure and cascading gown are echoed in the sensuous flow of the mountainscapes that flank her image. Barney succeeds in creating still reflections of his filmic multivalence.

Stills, whether taken from a film, video, or live performance, or whether an invented moment in an implied narrative, have been fully validated as art works; distinctions between documentation as giving evidence of art, and documentation as art, have been rendered moot as more and more younger artists such as Vanessa Beecroft and Anna Gaskell direct performances to be photographed. In her 1998 piece *Show*, Beecroft orchestrated a performance previously in the province of male-dominated soft porn; she composed a display of female models, some nude, some Gucci-bikini-clad, amidst the curves of Frank Lloyd Wright's Guggenheim Museum. More recently, she subverted the masculine rituals of the military by recruiting and directing thirty-five sailors to stand for two hours in formation on the flight deck of the aircraft carrier *Intrepid*, and calling on the Navy again for her performed arrangement and photograph of *Navy Seals* (1999). Beecroft's photographs of fashion-conscious ceremonies of female empowerment exude a cosmetic confidence at a far remove from the suspenseful uncertainty pervading Gaskell's disjointed photo narratives featuring troubled young female victims and/or victimizers. The roiled innocence of the young face seen in *Beat Him When He Sneezes* (1996) pushes Lewis Carroll's Alice toward Hollywood's *Carrie*—fittingly so, as the still was long ago invented in Hollywood and, as we have seen above, impacted the work of Cindy Sherman who has, in turn, influenced Gaskell.

Lest this partial accounting of narrative's role itself becomes too narratively coherent, we should turn back to the different but simultaneous concerns of a group of artists dealing with a very different mode of documentation than the cinematic still. Extending Duchamp's readymades, conceived in the second decade of the twentieth century, and Warhol's subsequent silkscreens of Campbell's soup cans and other appropriated products, Sherrie Levine began in the late 1970s to claim another artist's work as her own by photographing Walker Evans photographs. Levine's *After Walker Evans* (1981) challenges not only the notion of originality, so crucial to the Western criterion of art, but also the equally sacrosanct notion of authenticity. The collapsing of context into art, so gleefully begun by Duchamp, had already been revived in the 1960s in works ranging from Nauman's use of ordinary movement to Joseph Kosuth's dictionary definitions as art; it was now being revisited by Levine. The context of the work's placement in a gallery or museum alone could now make it art instead of a reproduction or a forgery. The word "appropriation" marked much of the art of the 1980s and photography's inherent, infinite reproducibility made it the ideal

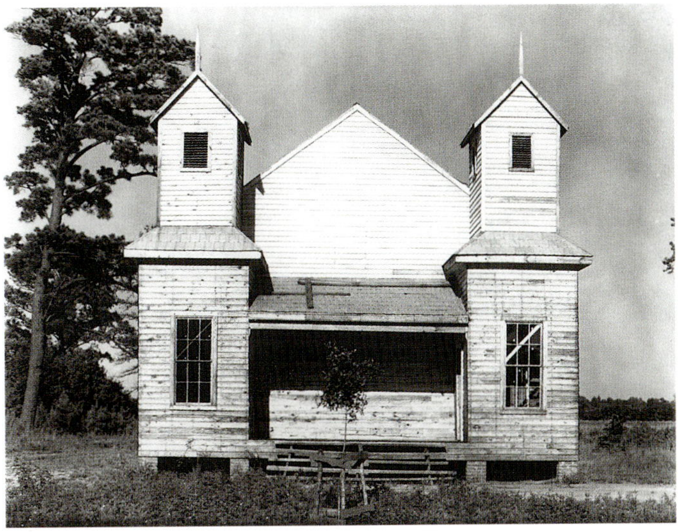

SHERRIE LEVINE
After Walker Evans. 1981. Gelatin silver print from a series, $7^{3}/_{8} \times 9^{1}/_{2}$ inches

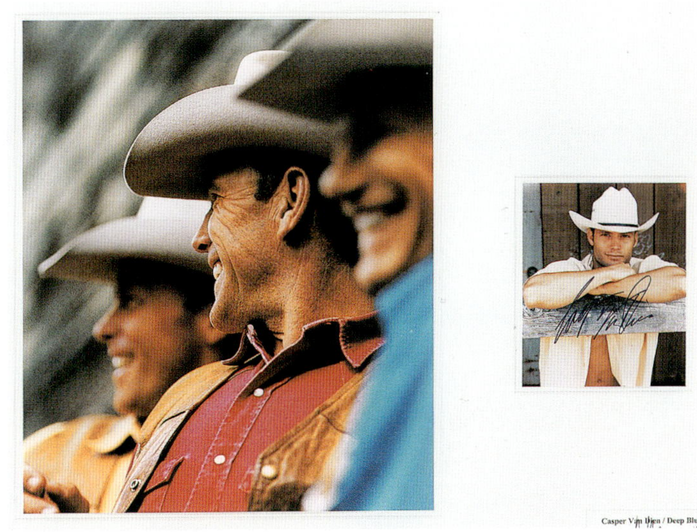

RICHARD PRINCE
Untitled (Publicity). 1999. One Richard Prince photograph and one publicity photograph, $33 \times 41^{1}/_{4}$ inches

appropriationist medium, although painters like David Salle and sculptors like Jeff Koons have also incorporated appropriated imagery in their work.

Less militant and more tongue-in-cheek than Levine, Richard Prince's appropriations have played fast and loose with the macho stereotypes still so prevalent in our culture—much the same as the stereotypes Beecroft has laid claim to for the women's side. This masculine aura is perhaps most iconically represented by the "Marlboro Man" type who has made regular appearances in Prince's work. Since the 1970s, amongst much else, he has rephotographed (and recontextualized) images he has found in magazines. In his most recent work, such as *Untitled (Publicity)* (1999), Prince arrays combinations of publicity photographs he has purchased—some of these autographed to him by the celebrity, some autographed by Prince's forged signatures. He, at once, underlines and undermines the "forged" intimacy inherent in publicity photographs and in our world of celebrity worship.

Prince's and Levine's appropriations result from very different intentions than the hands-on perfectionism seen in the works of their peers like the late Robert Mapplethorpe and Hiroshi Sugimoto. Like Prince and Beecroft, Mapplethorpe was drawn to male perfection, but his

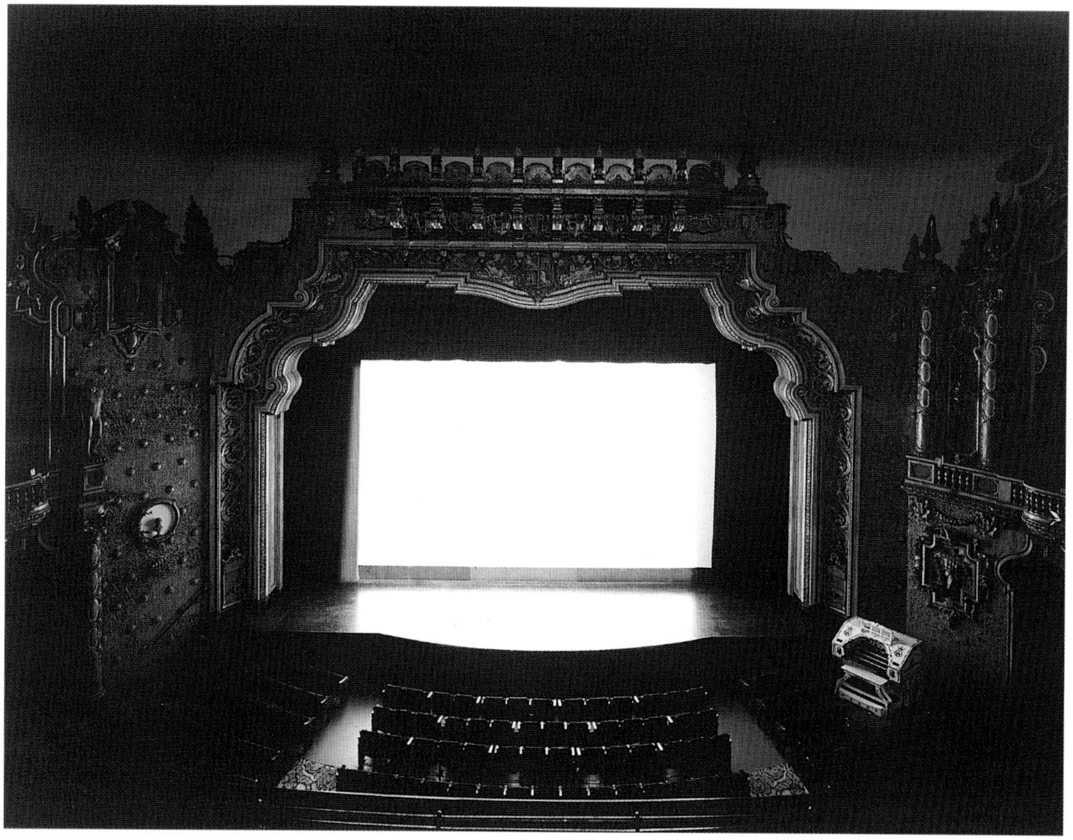

HIROSHI SUGIMOTO
Carpenter Center, Richmond. 1993.
Gelatin silver print, $16^{1}/_{2} \times 21^{1}/_{8}$ inches

representations of macho are homoeroticized and drawn from a classical tradition in photography that includes Cecil Beaton and, most importantly for Mapplethorpe, George Platt Lynes, whose obsessively stylized poses and clear, sculpting light he emulated. In one of Mapplethorpe's many still lifes from the *Flowers Portfolio* (1983), we can clearly see the same idealization and succulence embodied in his male nudes. Seldom since Georgia O'Keeffe have blossoms glistened with such seduction.

Like Mapplethorpe did, Sugimoto prefers traditional black-and-white photography techniques, but his meticulous printing and acutely focused directness transform his simple means into mysteriously luminescent stillness. Since the mid-1970s, Sugimoto has limited himself to a small, ongoing series that includes images of vintage movie theaters, seascapes, and natural history museum dioramas. He exposes his nocturnal seascapes like *Black Sea, Ozuluce* (1991) for several hours, letting the moon coat sea and sky in silver painterliness. Similarly, the glowing, white wash of the empty movie screen in his 1993 photograph *Carpenter Center, Richmond*, resulted from exposure for the duration of a full-length film. Distilled light is the subject simultaneously resolving and dissolving the compound images that comprise a single photograph. The theater becomes an analog for the interior of the camera, with the movie screen as camera lens.

More prosaically direct than Sugimoto, and totally disinterested in Mapplethorpe's worshipful idealization, the younger Rineke Dijkstra seems to have returned to a neutral nineteenth-century naturalism. Using a large-format camera, she has photographed countless adolescent girls, including many on beaches in Europe and the United States between 1992 and 1996. As in her photograph *Kolobzeg, Poland, July 23, 1992*, the girls often appear centered, but not posed in any way—formal, expressionless, and enigmatically ordinary. In their apparent vacancy and inconsequence, Dijkstra's large-format photographs have inverted the glamor of fashion photography and somehow made unformed anonymity eventful.

Mapplethorpe, Sugimoto, and Dijkstra, as well as many of the artists mentioned above such as Goldin, Opie, and Faigenbaum, are practitioners of what is frequently referred to as "straight" photography, and they are contrasted to artists creating "staged" photography such as Cindy Sherman and Anna Gaskell. In the United States, "straight" and "staged" have often designated opposing camps; but increasingly the distinctions have become blurred, especially with the growing accessibility and sophistication of digital technology.

Unquestionably Laurie Simmons stages her work as does her peer Cindy Sherman. Since the mid-1970s, with crystalline restraint and clarity, Simmons has constructed sets and tableaus for figurines, like *Walking Hourglass* (1989), which enact various clichés about female domesticity. More recently, she has fabricated adult doll houses that take their place in generic suburbia—at once playful and eerie in their pristine perfection, as is her *Pink House* (1998). Simmons's world is constructed from scratch to be photographed, whereas the German artists Peter Fischli and David Weiss have created a world in "real" space out of found objects. Their *Untitled* from the *Wurstserie (Sausage Series)* (1979) creates a fantasy out of the food most readily associated with their country—sausages: sausages as tanks, sausages as landscape, sausage people with bottle-top hats, olive-slice eyes, and ham coats performing a deli dance.

Philip-Lorca diCorcia, unlike his friend and peer Nan Goldin, prefers not autobiographical but anonymous subjects. In various ways he has literally and figuratively spotlighted the nameless.

For some years now he has set up overhead lights on crowded streets and photographed unknown people serendipitously separated from the crowd by his light and acute framing. He creates theater out of the contradictory combination of intimacy and anonymity that we all take part in on the subway, in the streets, at a disco, or in a sports arena. The young couple holding hands while crossing the street in his *Tokyo, 1998,* encourage us to enfold them in a cinematic narrative. And is this "straight" photography not "staged?"

And doesn't much of Jeff Wall's "staged" photography look "straight?" Like Jan Dibbets, Wall has set about extending painting genres into photography; but unlike Dibbets's constructed space, Wall presents us with a seamless space, no matter how many images he has montaged together. While Gilbert and George and, occasionally, Dibbets preceded him in his use of large formats, Wall's giant boxed and backlit color transparencies set the stage for several younger generations' claims on painting's exhibition space. Unlike the history painting and landscape painting he has set out to reclaim for photography, Wall's landscapes bristle with a slightly-off emptiness, or focus too much on detritus or a distant edge where industry roils nature. His complex, brilliantly staged and montaged (digitally since 1991), figurative compositions avoid climax or narrative resolution, and are often performed at the edge of the photograph's space—at the edge and on edge. And like the seventeenth-century genre paintings his compositions occasionally reflect, Wall is relentlessly committed to the everyday. His beauty often approaches the melodramatic, but, for subjects, he prefers the ordinary and always leaves us puzzling over unexplained tensions. His landscape compositions embody nature at a far remove from the grandeur of the sublime composed earlier in the twentieth century by Ansel Adams. Like the younger Dijkstra's bland adolescents, Wall's *Coastal Motifs* (1989) confounds us with the radiance of the unremarkable.

Both Wall and Cindy Sherman played a role in Gregory Crewdson's beginnings; and he, in turn, has joined in impacting younger artists like Gaskell. Like Wall's work, Crewdson's black-and-white *Hover* series, created in the mid-1990s, favors obliquely removed events, and includes such disruptions as a collapsed woman, a burning shed, or a crashed car unexpectedly ruffling the rural calm of his mises-en-scène. At the same time, Crewdson created simultaneously beautiful and repulsive color images of the "natural"—Disney mutating into Salvador Dalí decay—that relate to Sherman's *Fairy Tales* and *Disasters* (1985–89). He might spend as much as two months constructing the mesmerizing heap of butterflies seen in the sickeningly beautiful

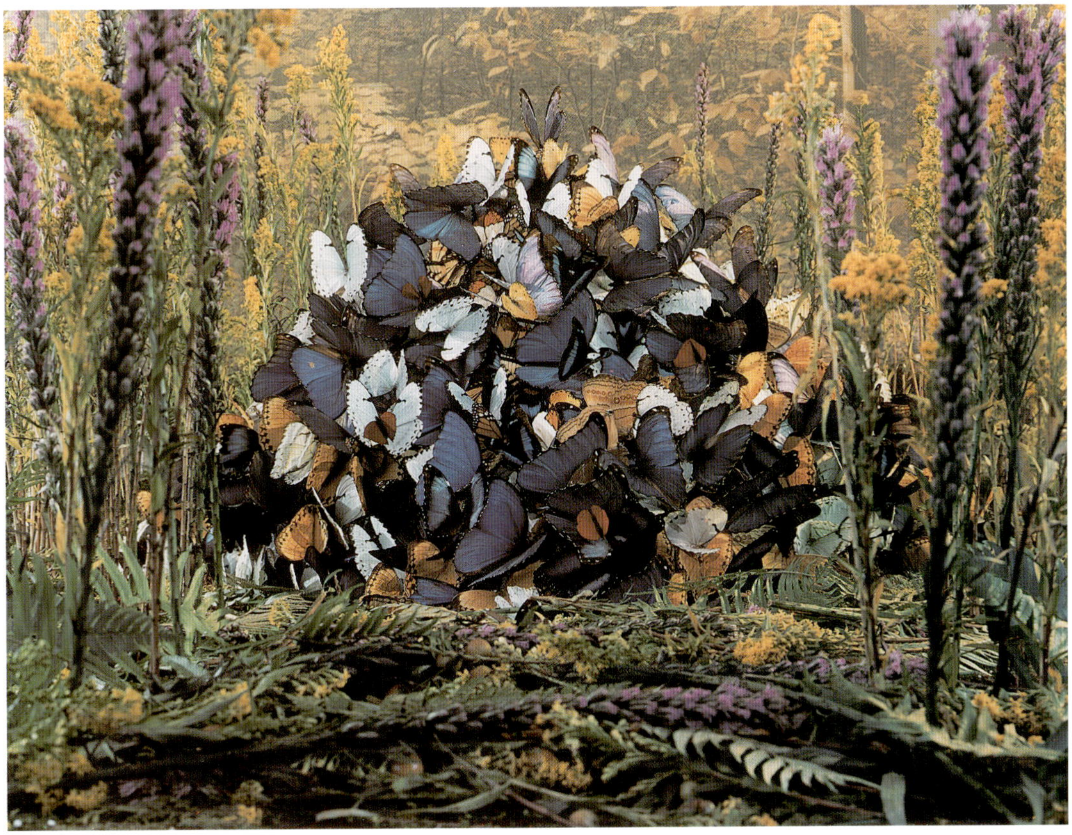

GREGORY CREWDSON
Untitled. **1994. Chromogenic process print, 27 1/2 × 37 1/4 inches**

Untitled (1994). Steven Spielberg's *Close Encounters of the Third Kind* and David Lynch's psycho-conundrums have impacted Crewdson's large-format, suburban nightmare nocturnes, like his *Untitled* works from the *Twilight* series. Hollywood accessibility and production values now play a role in art not considered in the funkier dramas of Nauman's and Acconci's 1960s.

While the photo-illusionistic Surrealism of such artists as Dalí and Yves Tanguy heralds some of Crewdson's and other fabulists' work, the more playful and formally experimental side of Dadaism and Surrealism, especially as practiced by Man Ray and Duchamp, foreshadows the camera play of artists like Doug Aitken, Wolfgang Tillmans, Steven Pippin, and James Welling. In his photographs and video installations, Aitken charts nowhere places, often propelling the viewer into inconclusiveness. He might film an impending monsoon and end the film before the storm arrives or, perhaps in homage to Dziga Vertov and Man Ray, launch his video camera into the sky with a rocket (*Inflection,* 1992). Even his conventionally created photographs, like *Passenger* (1999), directed out of an airplane window into the anonymous vastness of the sky, leave the viewer guessing in placelessness.

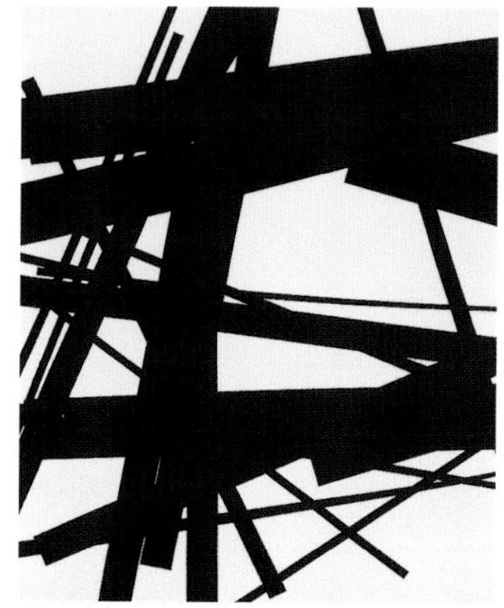

JAMES WELLING
#1. **1998. Gelatin silver print, 38½ × 26½ inches**

The German-born, London-based photographer Wolfgang Tillmans moves easily and with a light touch from the abstract to the figurative, from the beach scene of *Untitled (La Gomera)* (1997) to cameraless, fugitive wisps of color he calls "blushes," which relate to the similarly created "fumage" works made by the Surrealist Wolfgang Paalen in the 1930s. Tillmans might as readily exploit a printing mistake as a cloudburst or kids dancing at a rave, and freely juxtapose them in dialogue on a gallery wall. No less playful but more relentlessly focused in his pursuits, Steven Pippin travels his native London and the world transforming plumbing and appliances into makeshift cameras. The twelve photos in his *Laundromat–Locomotion (Walking Backwards L–L No. 04)* (1997) series, record the act of being photographed through the "lens" of a washing machine aperture. The backward walking figure gives new meaning to being washed by light. James Welling's investigations of light look back to Surrealism's more abstract experiments. He, too, has exposed photographic paper to light, but more often he highlights fragments of the everyday—tubes of fluorescent light, bulbs hanging from a ceiling, the flickering play of the sun through the branches of a tree. The mysterious tonal abstractions of his *#1* and *#25* of 1998 transmute their source into purely abstract geometrical lyrics and harken back to the concerns of early Modernists. We cannot, of course, connect these four artists in any way other than their shared interest in an experimental phase of photography's past—we cannot push them into an explanatory *ism.*

Nor can we explain (or explain away) Shirin Neshat with an *ism.* Like many artists who came to the fore in the 1980s and 1990s, she is preoccupied with issues of gender and race and, like many of those artists, she has turned to film and video to embody her intentions. Iranian-born, Neshat explores the troubled realities of feminism in Islamic culture but, at the same time, she celebrates aspects of the beauty of that culture, especially its haunting vocal tradition. Her narratives are always overlaid with universal themes of love and loss; the pared-down spatial rhythms of her still photography and films move with a grand sweep and pulsing melancholy specific only to her. Neshat's stills, such as *Stripped* (1995), of women in chadors with their unveiled hands and feet covered in Farsi script with words by Iranian feminist or pro-Islamic writers, bristle with a primordial beauty.

Lest this narrative become too insistent on multiplicity, mention must be made of a group of photographers more readily connected than those, for instance, in the cluster of autobiographers above or the aforementioned four photographers smitten with Surrealist experimentation. A remarkable group of German photographers—all born in the 1950s, all students of Bernd Becker in Dusseldorf, all self-professed chroniclers of contemporary life with a penchant for high definition and tonal variation, analytical coolness, and clear, complex, and meticulous composition—might be rounded up under *encyclopedism,* if that were not such a leaky label. More varied in their documentary pursuits than the single-minded focus and execution pursued by the Bechers, four of these artists—Thomas Struth, Thomas Ruff, Candida Hofer, and Andreas Gursky—have almost as much in common as what separates them.

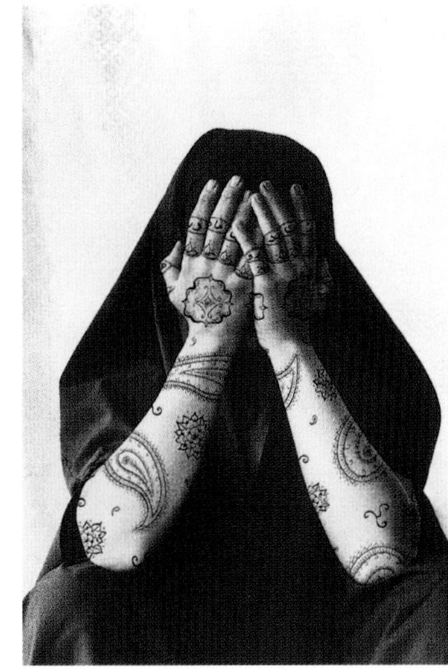

SHIRIN NESHAT
***Stripped.* 1995. Ink on gelatin silver print, 46½ × 31½ inches**

Thomas Struth began photographing in black and white in the mid-1970s, seeking a vision as objective, impersonal, and precise as the Bechers. His photographs of architecture in his native Germany neutrally reflect the upheaval and devastation of World War II. His photographs in Manhattan such as *Park Avenue (Mit Auto) (with Car), New York/Midtown, 1978* (1978), and in other cities (most recently in China), clinically chronicle the banal eclecticism and transience infusing our urban centers. He sees no less analytically when photographing more particular sights; but for the random movements and color of the foreground crowd and bright, uneven light, the clear exacting detail and absolute symmetry in his 1998 *Mailander Dom (Fassade), Mailande (Milan Cathedral [Façade], Milan)* reflect the rigors of the Bechers. Like Hofer, Ruff, and Gursky he has also recorded interior spaces where art is shown. But like many a cloud-weary Northern European, he seems to be visited by heliotropic longings that heat up and blur his analytical coolness in the light of lush flowers and unspoiled landscapes in locales like Australia—even though he assigns numbers to paradise (*Paradise 7, Daintree, Australia, 1998*).

Thomas Ruff also started by photographing buildings in a manner beholden to the Bechers, and to Walker Evans as well, but he gained his first acclaim with oversize portrait heads created in 1988–89. Vastly oversized passport photos—centered, clearly lit, meticulously detailed, pimples and all—often of teenagers. He was not documenting any categories as precise as those of August Sander earlier in the twentieth century, but rather confronting us with anonymity and an adamant insistence on the photographed. That the subject claimed less identity than the neutral image was made more insistent when Ruff began to change the "natural" eye color in some of the portraits—and still more insistent when he blended two black-and-white portraits together in his *Anders Portrat (Other Portrait) No. 109/97* in 1994–95. The young men created and seen in this series of portraits are identified only by numbers. This manipulation argues for photography as aesthetic genetics, free of personal touch and intervention. Ruff was more than willing to stretch his insistence on the illusion of the photographer's neutrality to the point where he didn't have to be responsible for the photograph. When pollution prevented him from photographing stars in Eastern Europe, he purchased negatives from the European Southern Observatory.

Clear, complex composition and meticulously focused plethora of detail conjoin with a revel in light and color in Candida Hofer's photographs, which would have made a nineteenth-century Realist painter more than a little jealous. Hofer's *National Building Museum, Washington* (1992), and *Bibliothèque Nationale de France, Paris II* (1998), turn repetitive architectural elements like columns, arches, library stacks, and architraves into rhythmic parades of sculpture. She pushes the Bechers's fastidious archival discipline into a Classicist's light, and their rigorous frontality into deep space.

Proliferation of detail is taken to hallucinatory extremes by Andreas Gursky whose ambition to create an encyclopedia of modern life is matched only by his ambition to be a player in painting's space. And, indeed, his command of scale, extreme manipulation of photography's illusionism, and ability to make photography's glossy, seamless surface play a vital part in the visuality (dare one say "physicality"?) of his work, endow his larger than large-format photographs with the surface tension and optical brio necessary for a monumental painting to justify its size. Starting in the 1980s with landscapes and groups engaged in leisure activities, he moved on to examine industrial products and producers, blowups of extreme close-ups of paintings fraught with physical agitation, close-ups of a page from a book, and a vast crowd writhing at a rave. Whether paint strokes, letters, plastic vines hanging in a hotel atrium, or people, all become generic exemplars of their species and, more often than not, all are digitally enhanced and cleaned up, like their surroundings that are more than any camera can see. Gursky's hyper-neutralization is alternately glamorous and anesthetizing; whether he is victim, victimizer or simply chronicler of mass culture remains moot. Perhaps he has reinvented pictorial formalism? The workers often depicted in his photographs of the various industrial companies and stock markets he visited in the course of the 1990s, like those seen in *Börse, Hong Kong (Hong Kong Stock Exchange)* (1994), might be technology's drones as readily as digitalized brushstrokes in a grand pictorial scheme.

Gursky's challenge to painting's space provides a fitting end to this essay's chronological and thematic zigzag through the last thirty or so years. Gursky and his various predecessors

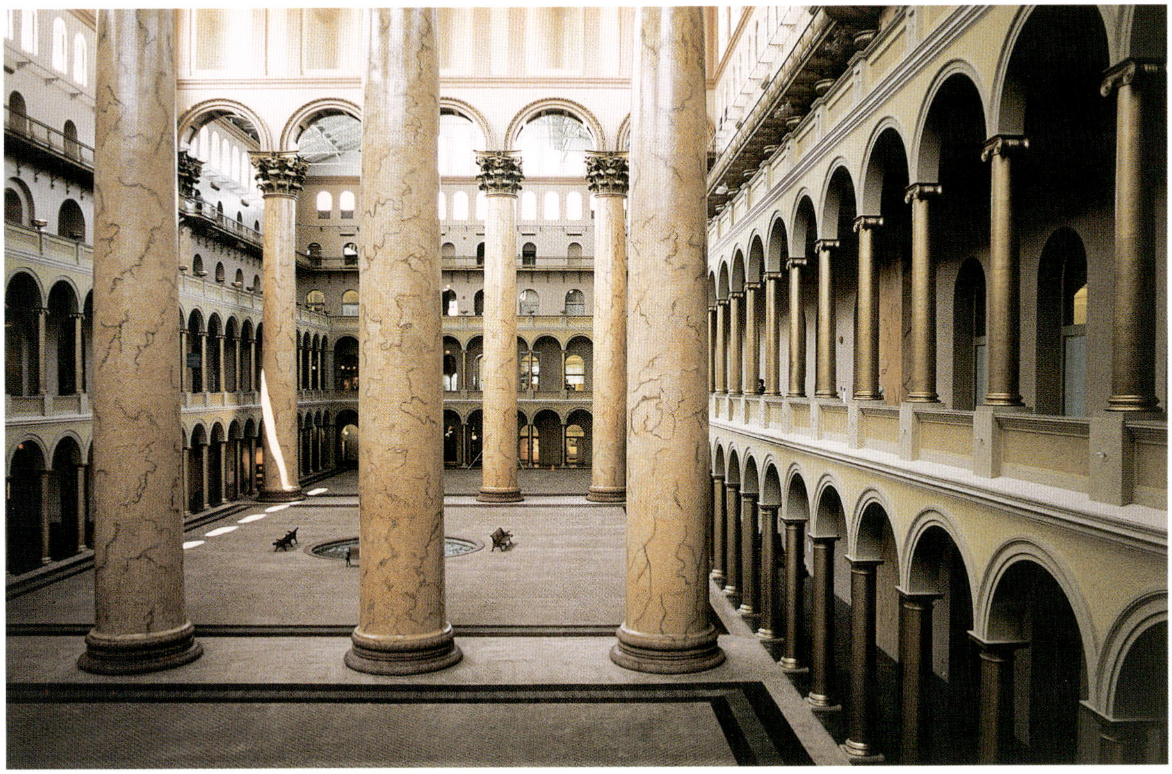

CANDIDA HOFER
National Building Museum, Washington. 1992.
Chromogenic process print, 14 × 21 inches

represented in this collection have blurred the lines between painting and photography, between photography as documentary truth and photography as illusion, and made photography not an isolated medium but one of many available to the artist. Photography has now been almost fully integrated into the artstream. Undoubtedly the issues raised by mass culture that preoccupy so many artists of all stripes have contributed to photography's integration, since the very nature of its various means, whether film or video or digital or still photography, is embedded in that culture as neither painting nor sculpture are. By focusing on artists who do not necessarily consider themselves exclusively photographers so much as visual artists employing the camera as a tool, possibly one of many tools, this collection highlights many of the artists responsible for expanding photography's context. So many artists are represented here in illustration and so few in writing; however, were all to have been called to, this essay would have dissolved in a babble of names. Needless to say, countless artists of note have not been mentioned, but hopefully enough portals were pointed to for the reader and the viewer to begin to find their own way into this rich and rewarding accumulation of work.

PLATES

The Lovers (Two Vases). 1996. Chromogenic process print with drawing in black marker on print margin, $29\frac{1}{2} \times 27\frac{1}{4}$ inches

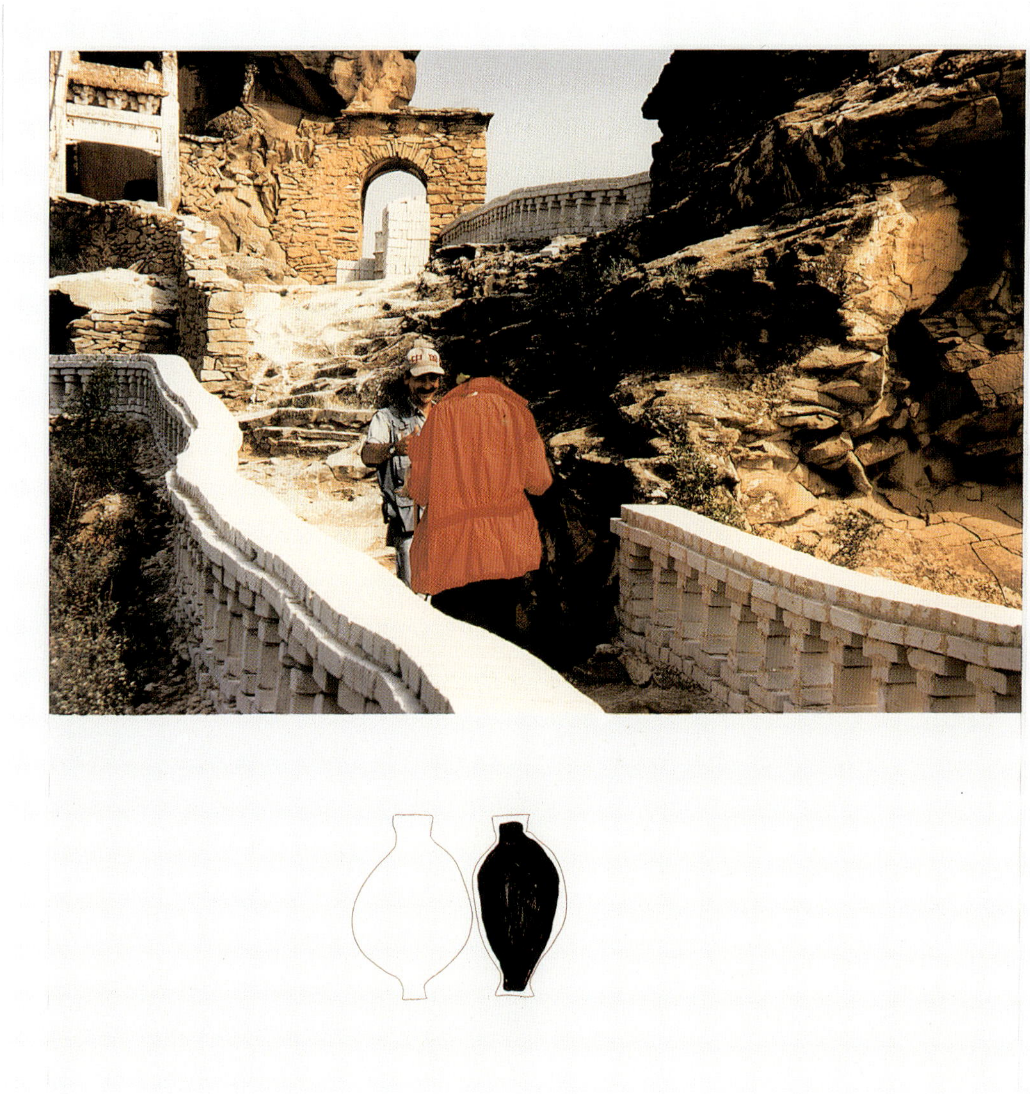

Assistant Series—Laugh. 2000. Four chromogenic process prints in hand-colored mat, 27 1/2 × 73 inches

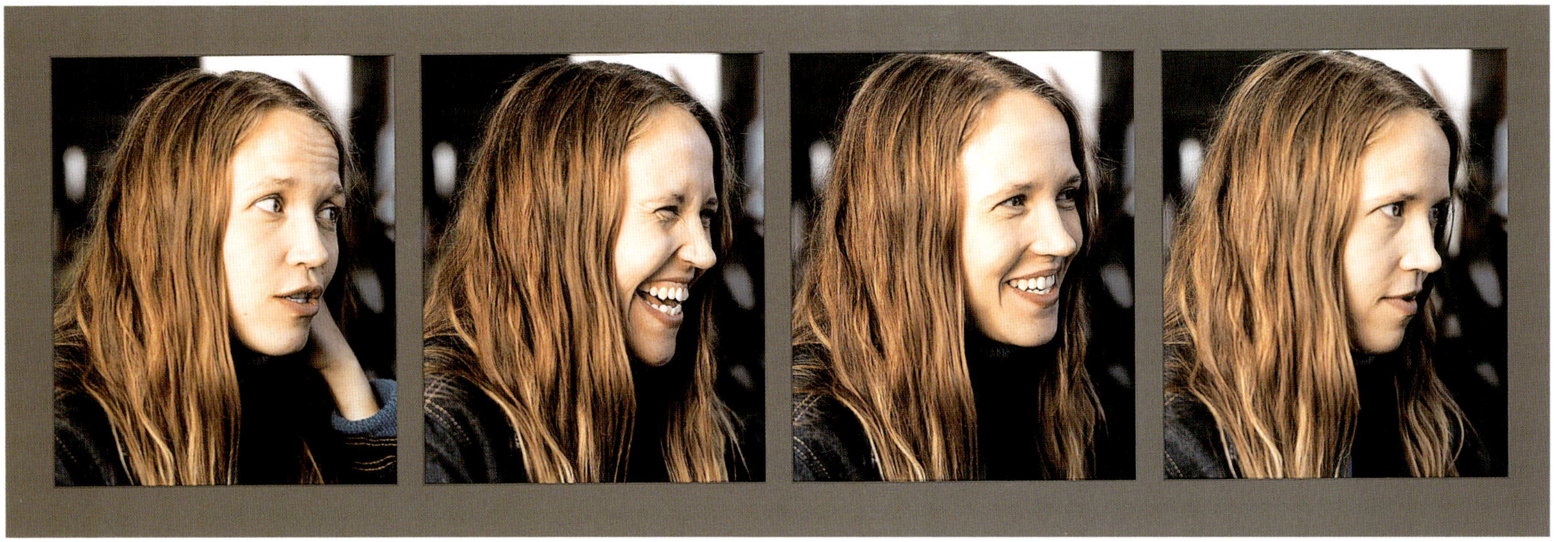

Passenger. 1999. Silver dye bleach process print, face mounted to plexiglass, 39 × 48 inches

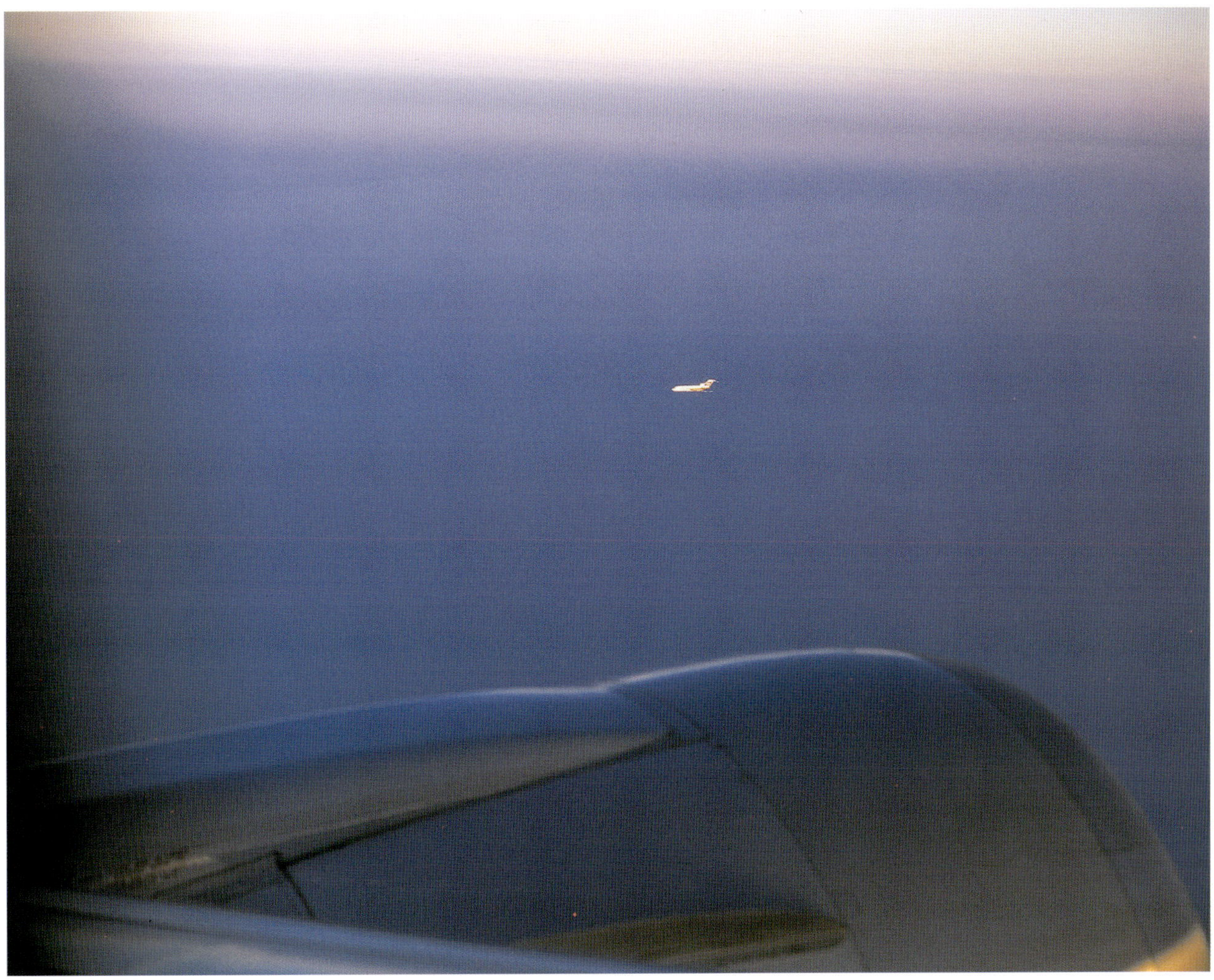

Dawn and Dusk. 1996. Diptych: 120 chromogenic process prints, $25\frac{1}{2} \times 42\frac{3}{4}$ inches

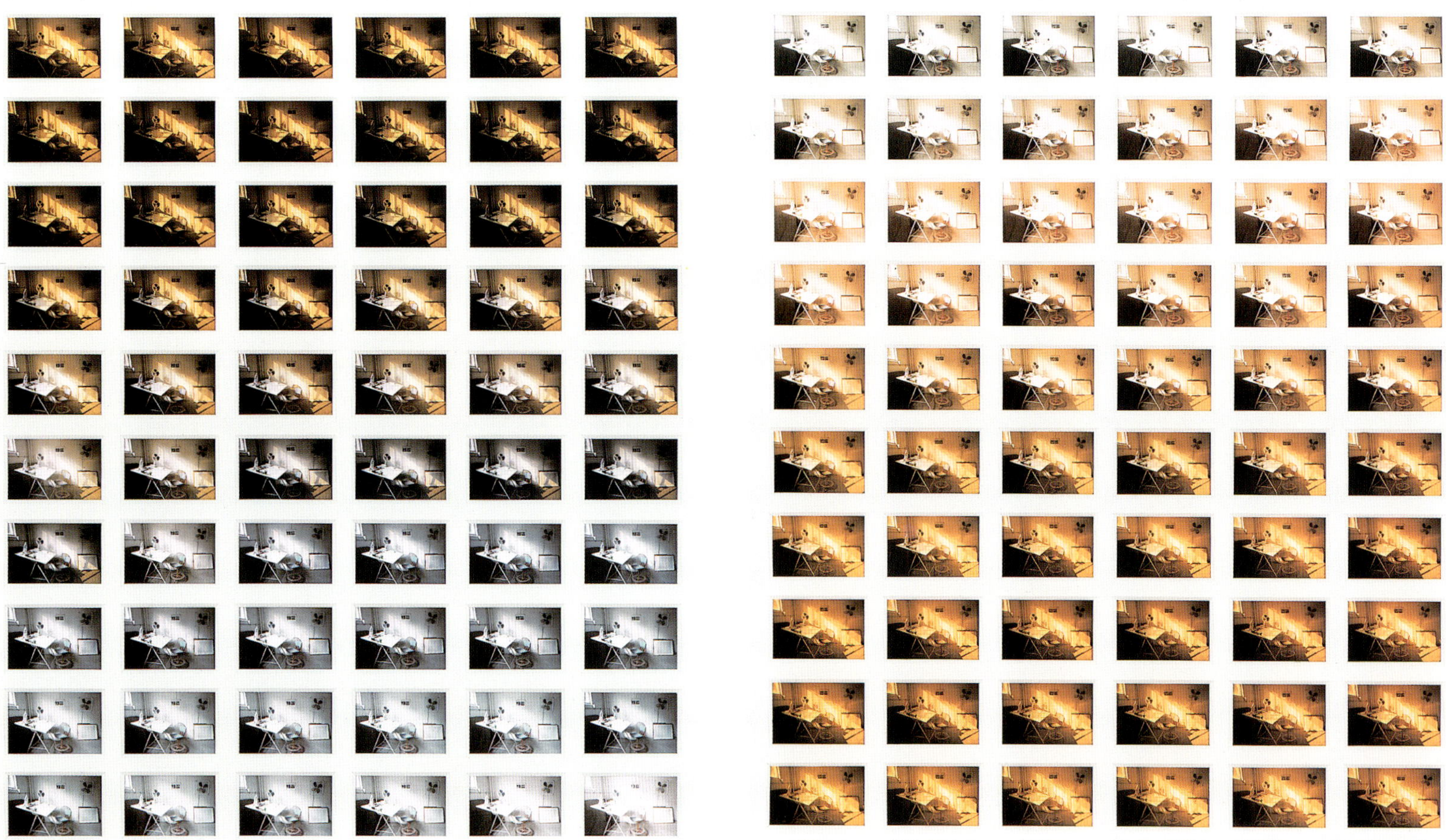

Lato Destro (Right Side). 1970. Chromogenic process print, $12\frac{3}{4} \times 9\frac{1}{8}$ inches

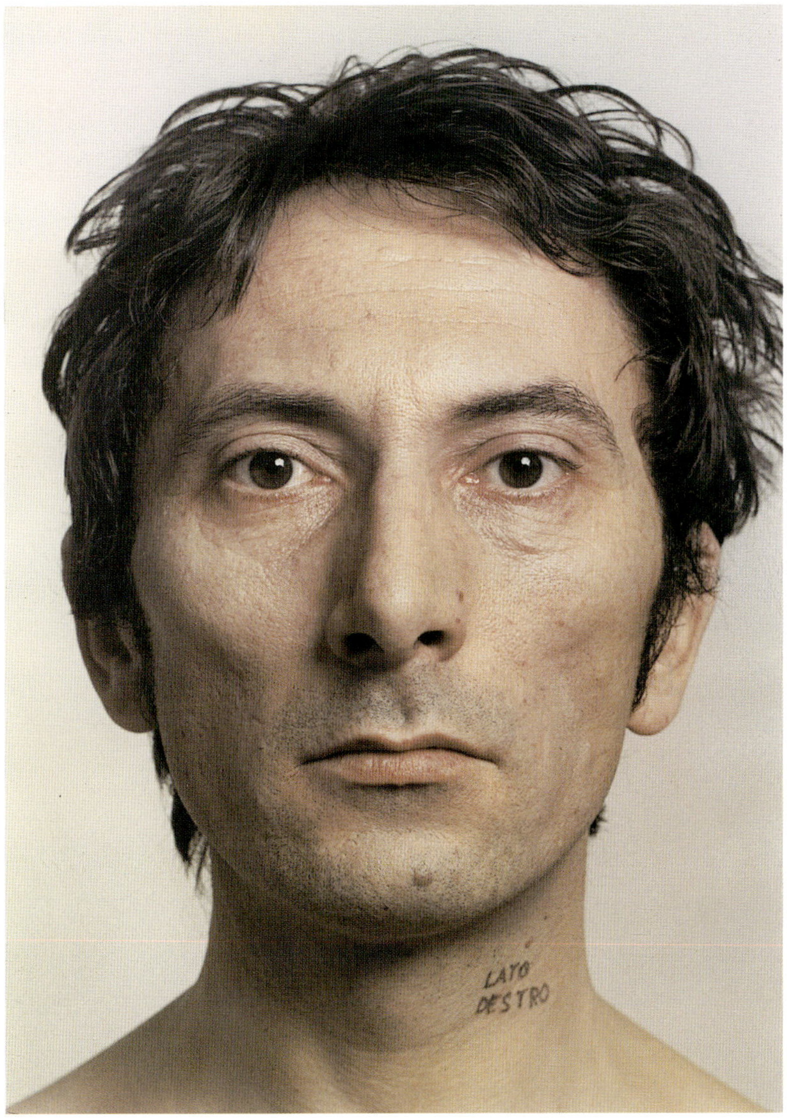

Coddle. 1999. Silver dye bleach process print and hand-carved frame, 22 × 17 inches

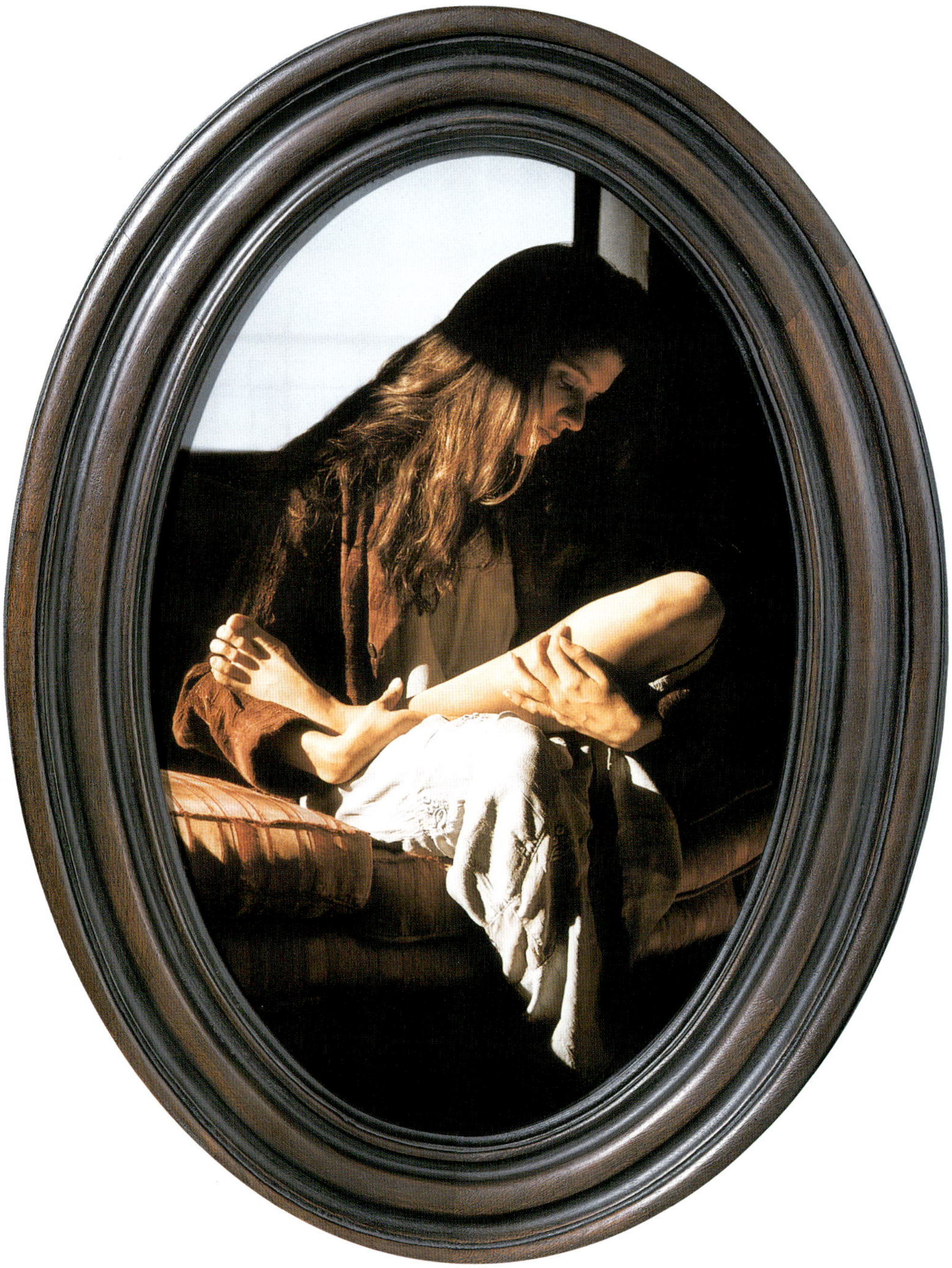

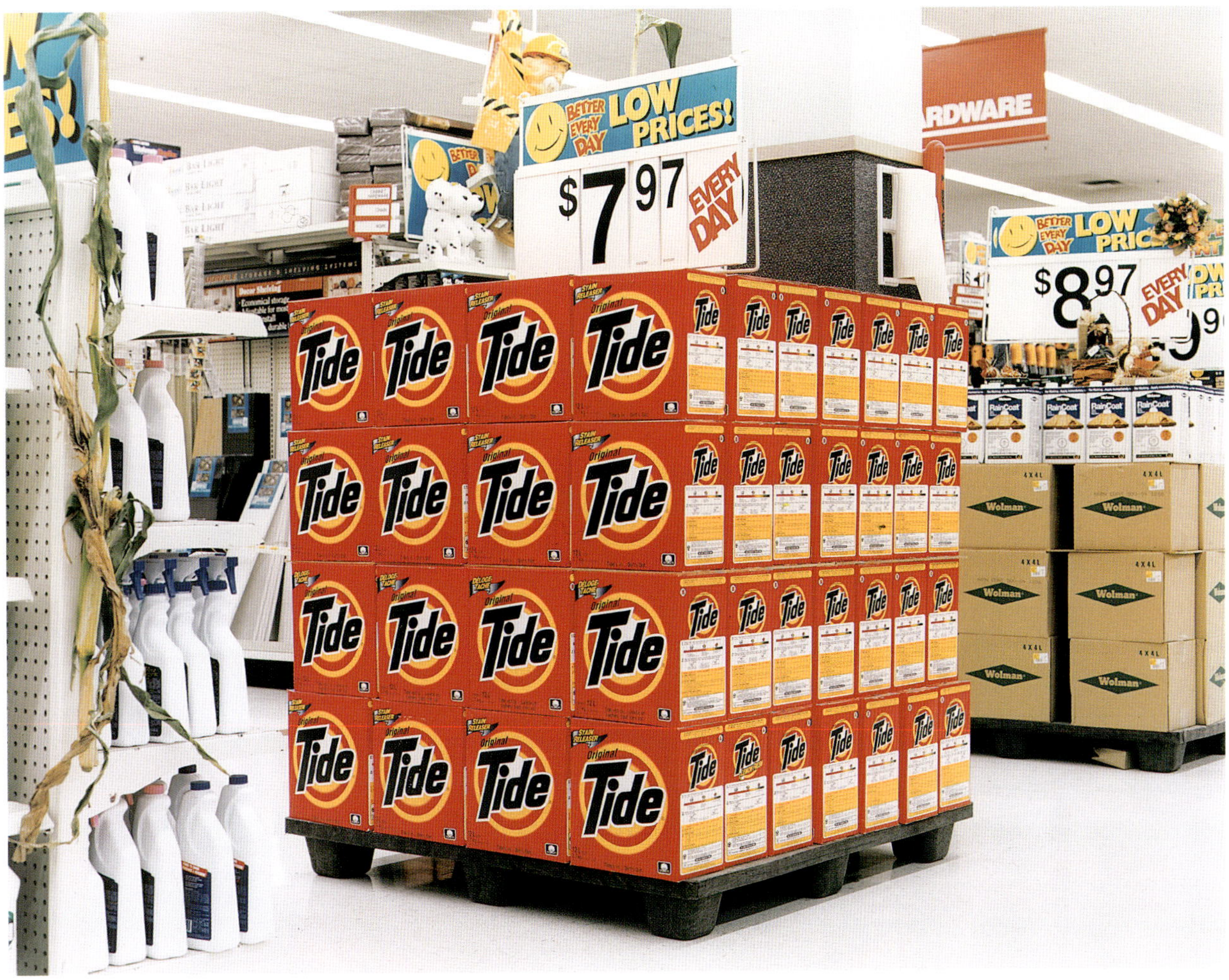

Wal-Mart Store, Burnaby, B.C. (Tide). 1996.
Chromogenic process print, 17 × 21 3/4 inches

Study #22, San Francisco. c. 1975. Unique gelatin silver print, mat board, masking tape, and ballpoint pen, 9½ × 11¼ inches

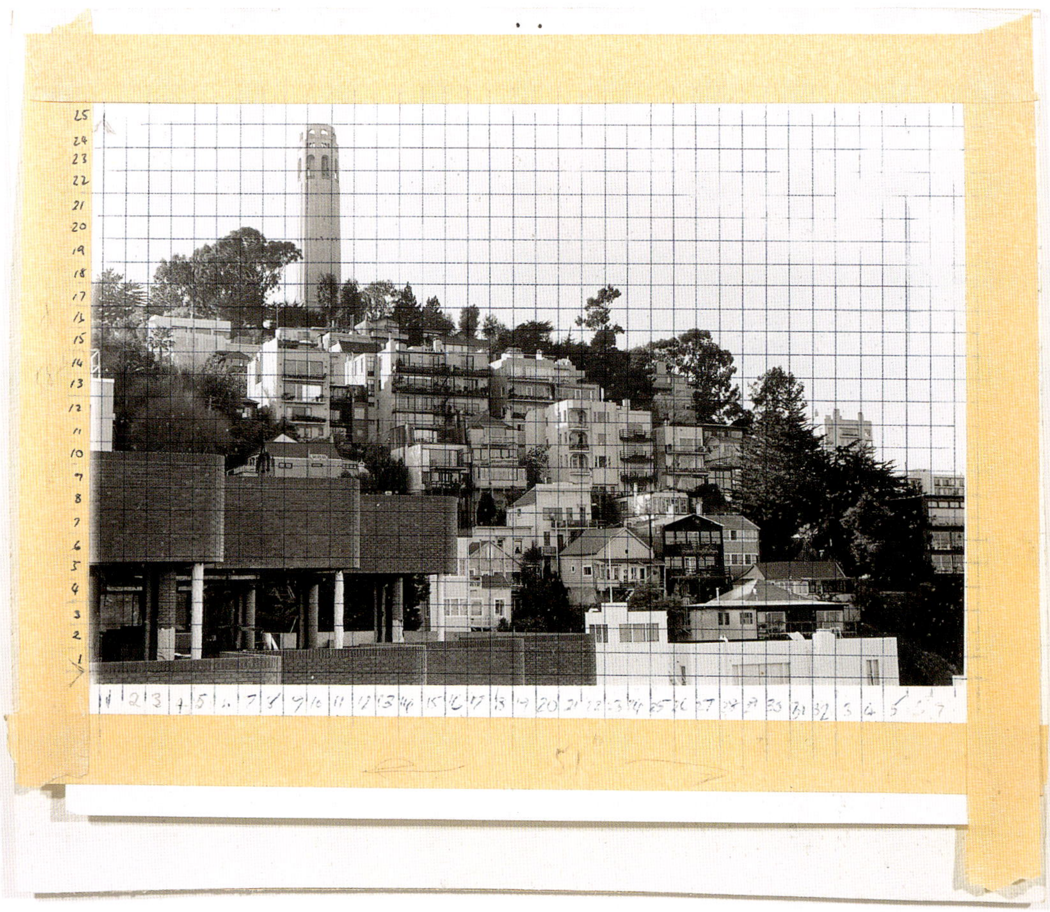

Untitled: for Felix (Oaks Bluff). 1996. Duraflex print, 48 × 44 inches

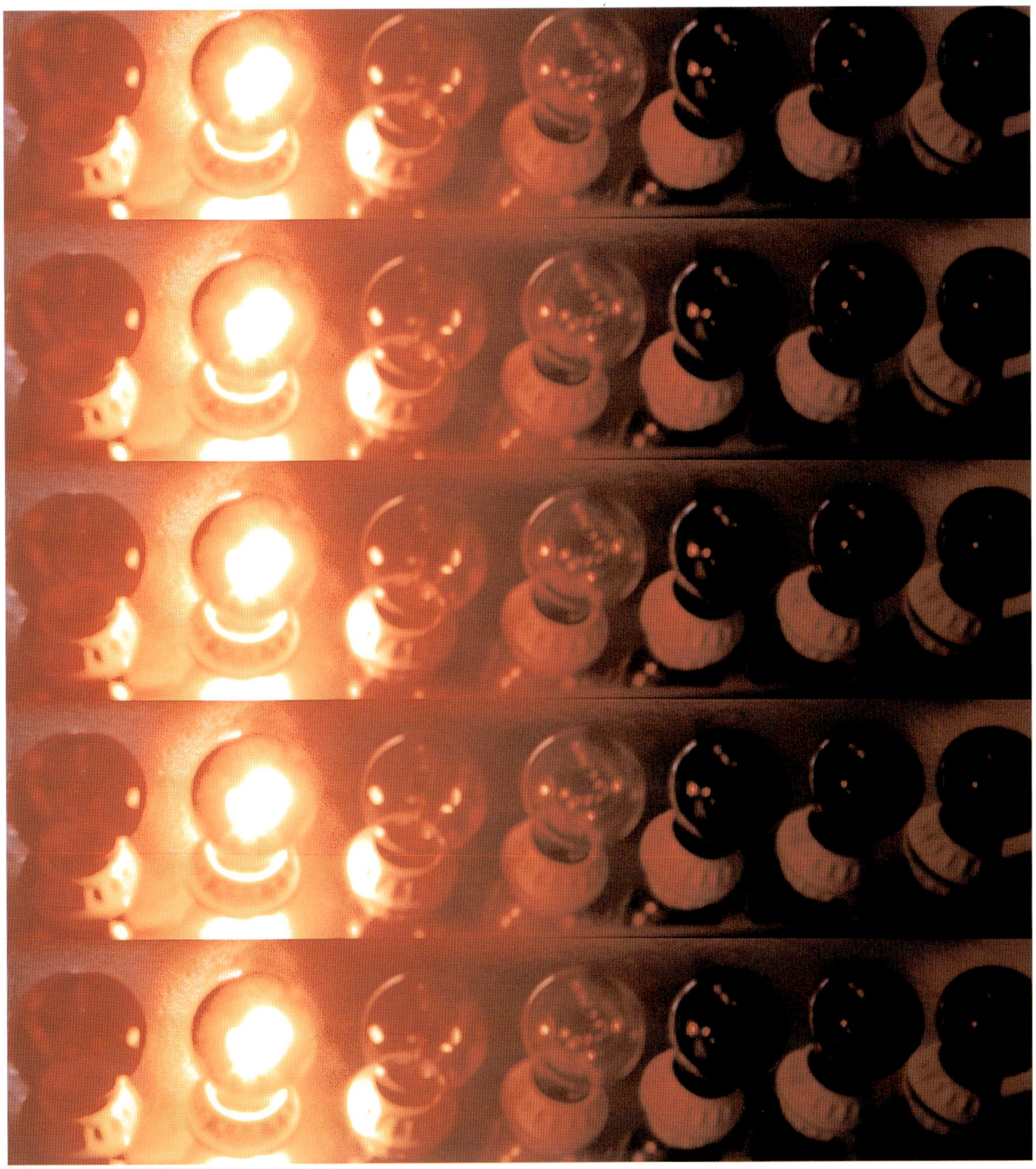

Brutus Killed Caesar. 1976. Triptych: gelatin silver prints, 9 feet $\frac{1}{4}$ inch × 8 feet 7 inches

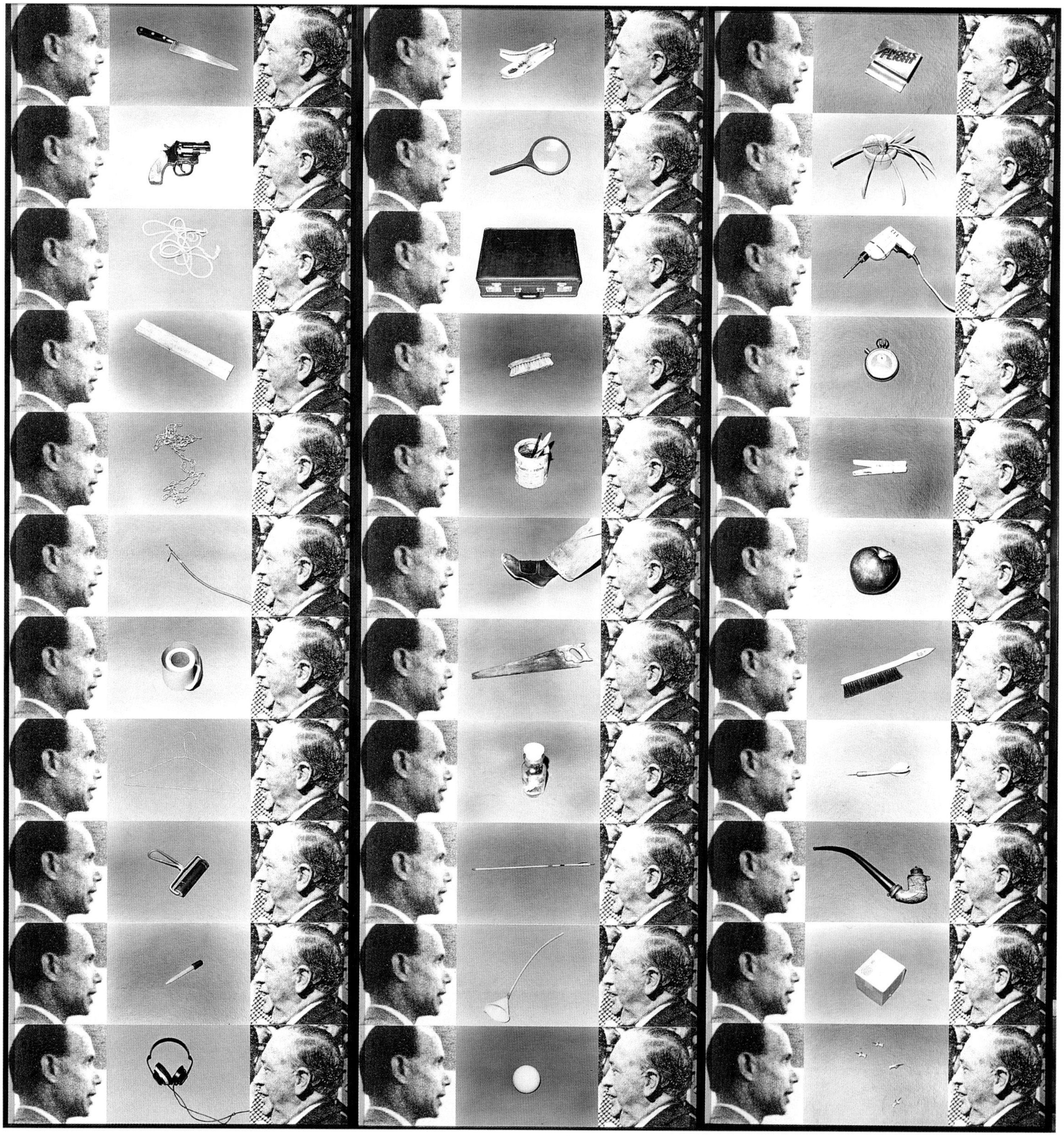

CREMASTER 1: Orchidella. 1995. Laminated chromogenic process print in artist's "self-lubricating" plastic frame, $53\frac{5}{8} \times 43\frac{5}{8}$ inches

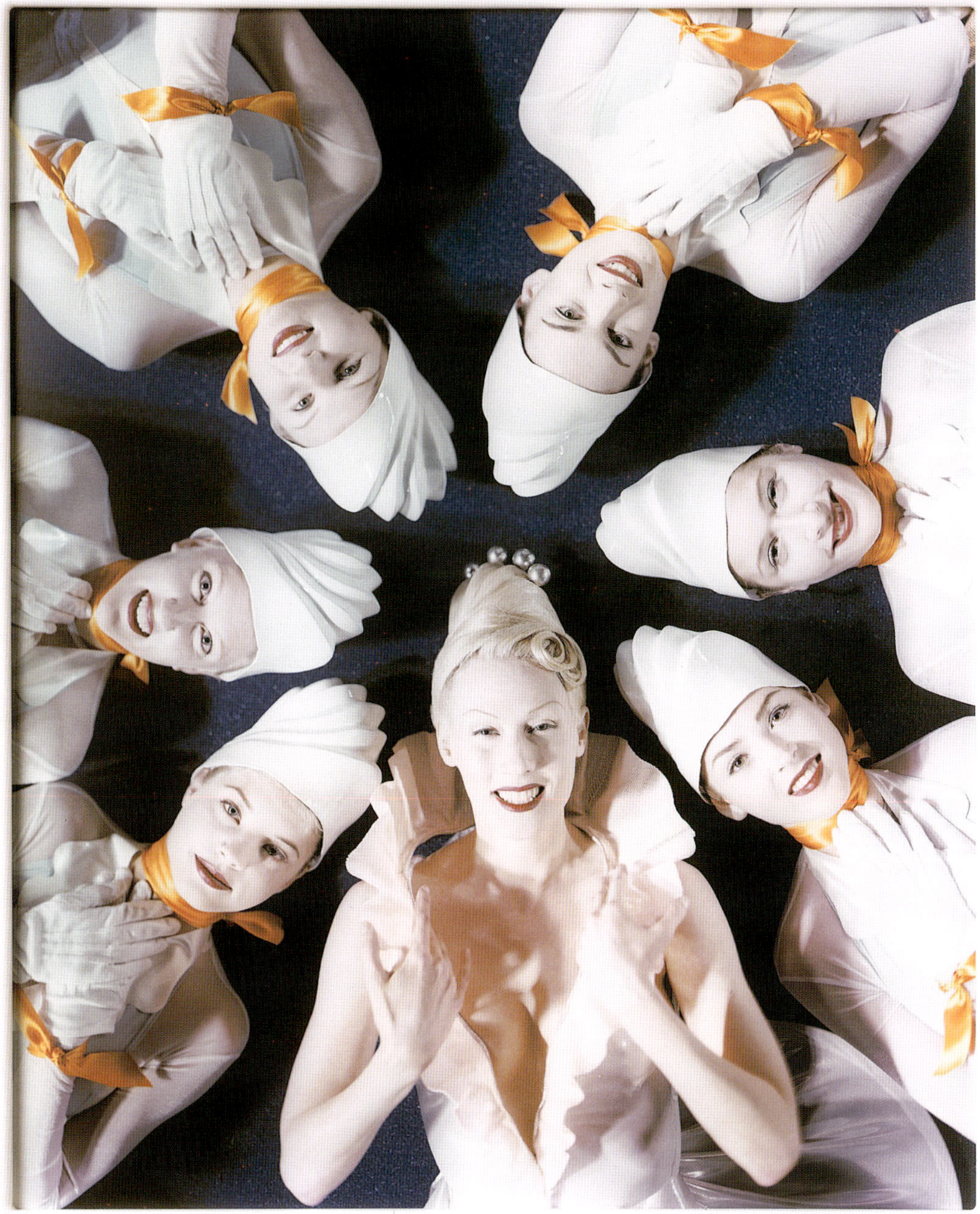

Untitled 98.7. 1998. Diptych: chromogenic process prints, 56¼ inches × 9 feet 6½ inches

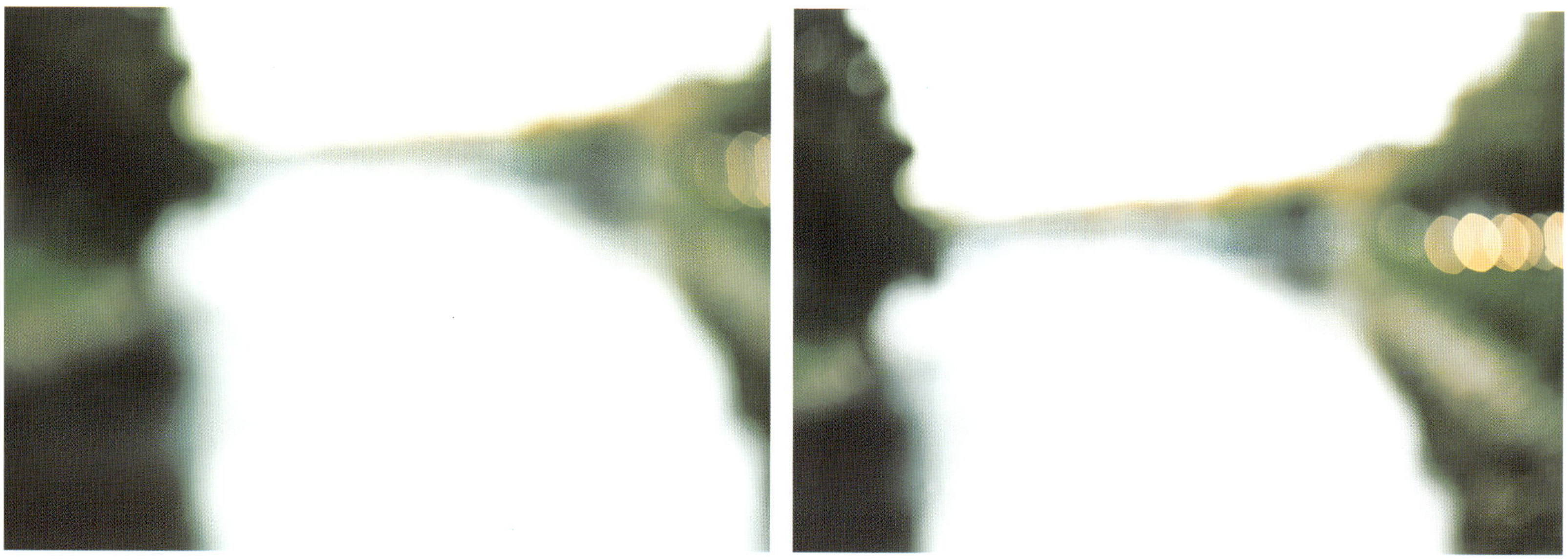

Canal 16. 1997/98. Chromogenic process print, face mounted to plexiglass, 60 × 84 3/4 inches

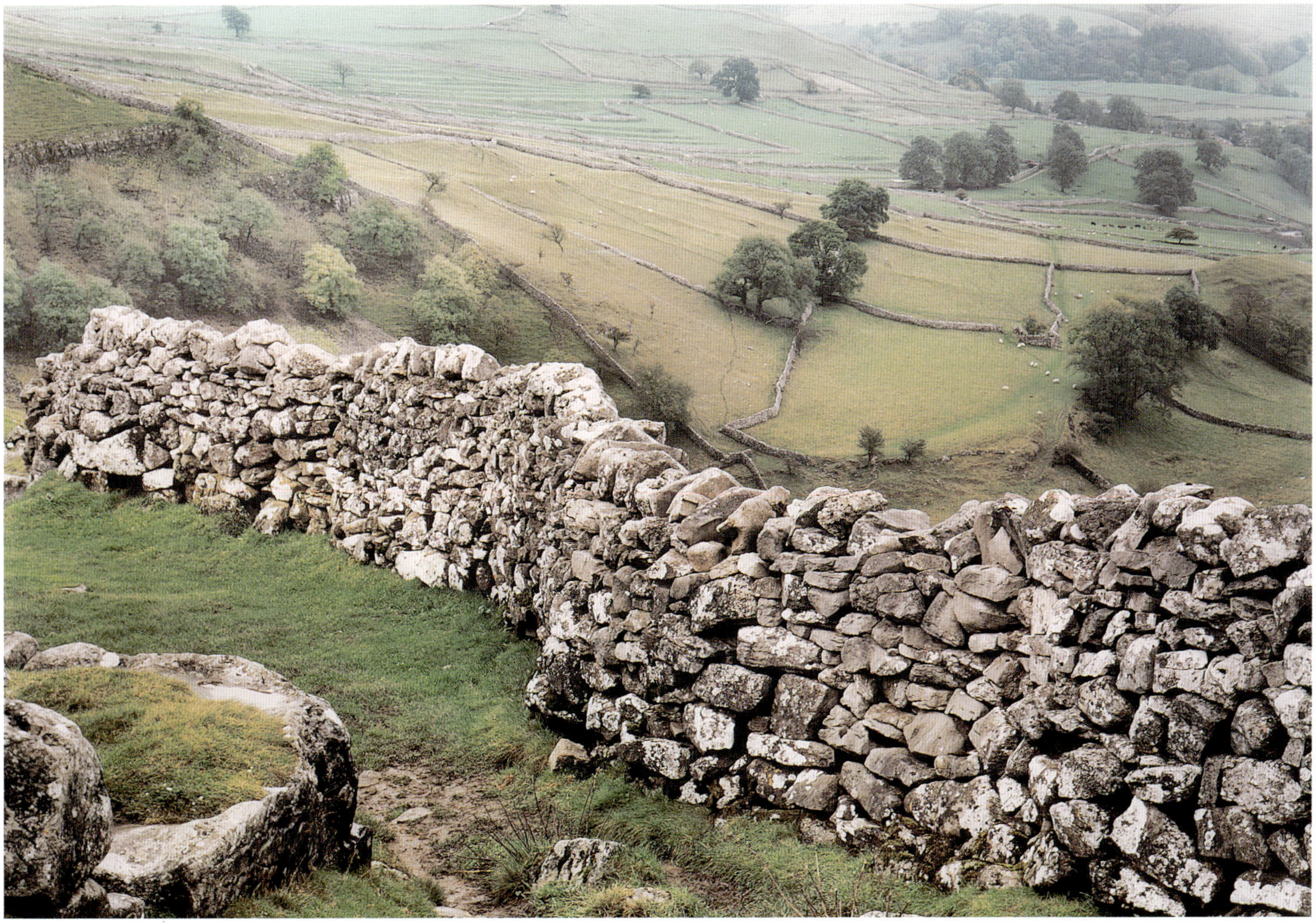

GABRIELE BASILICO

Beyrouth. 1991. Gelatin silver print, 18 × 26 inches

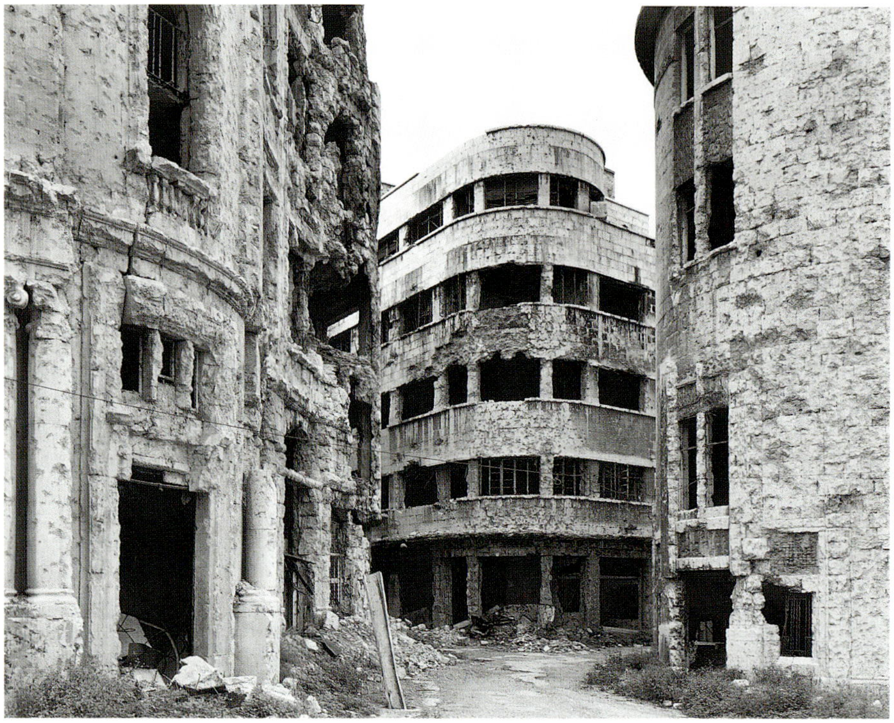

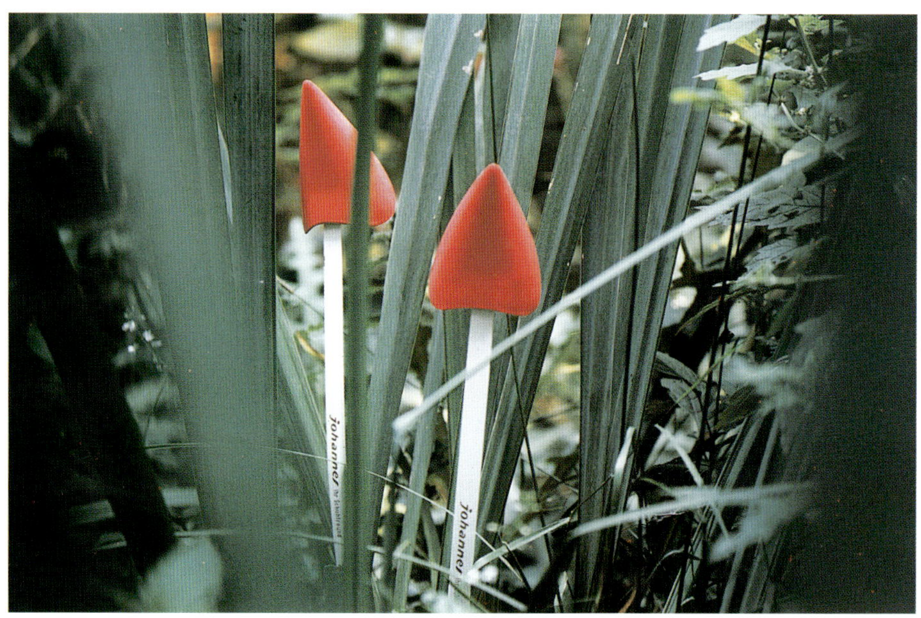

LOTHAR BAUMGARTEN

Verlorene Früchte (Wasted Fruit). 1969. Chromogenic process print, $25\frac{1}{8}$ × 32 inches

Blast Furnaces, Heads. 1996. Installation: fifteen gelatin silver prints, $68\frac{1}{4} \times 94\frac{1}{4}$ inches

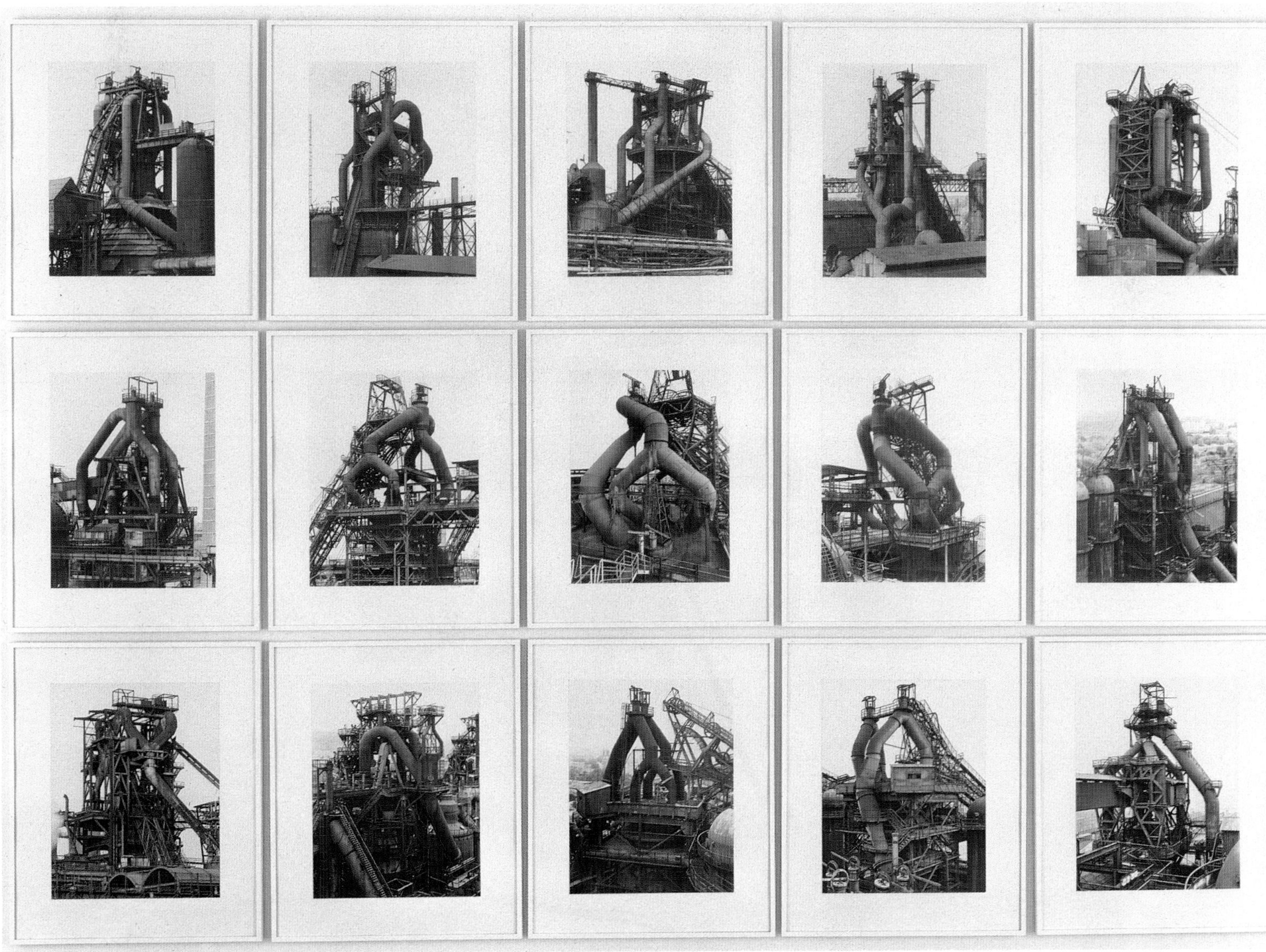

Wall Street in Cuba: Side View, Bank of Nova Scotia. 1993.
Chromogenic process print, $32^{3}/_{4} \times 27^{5}/_{8}$ inches

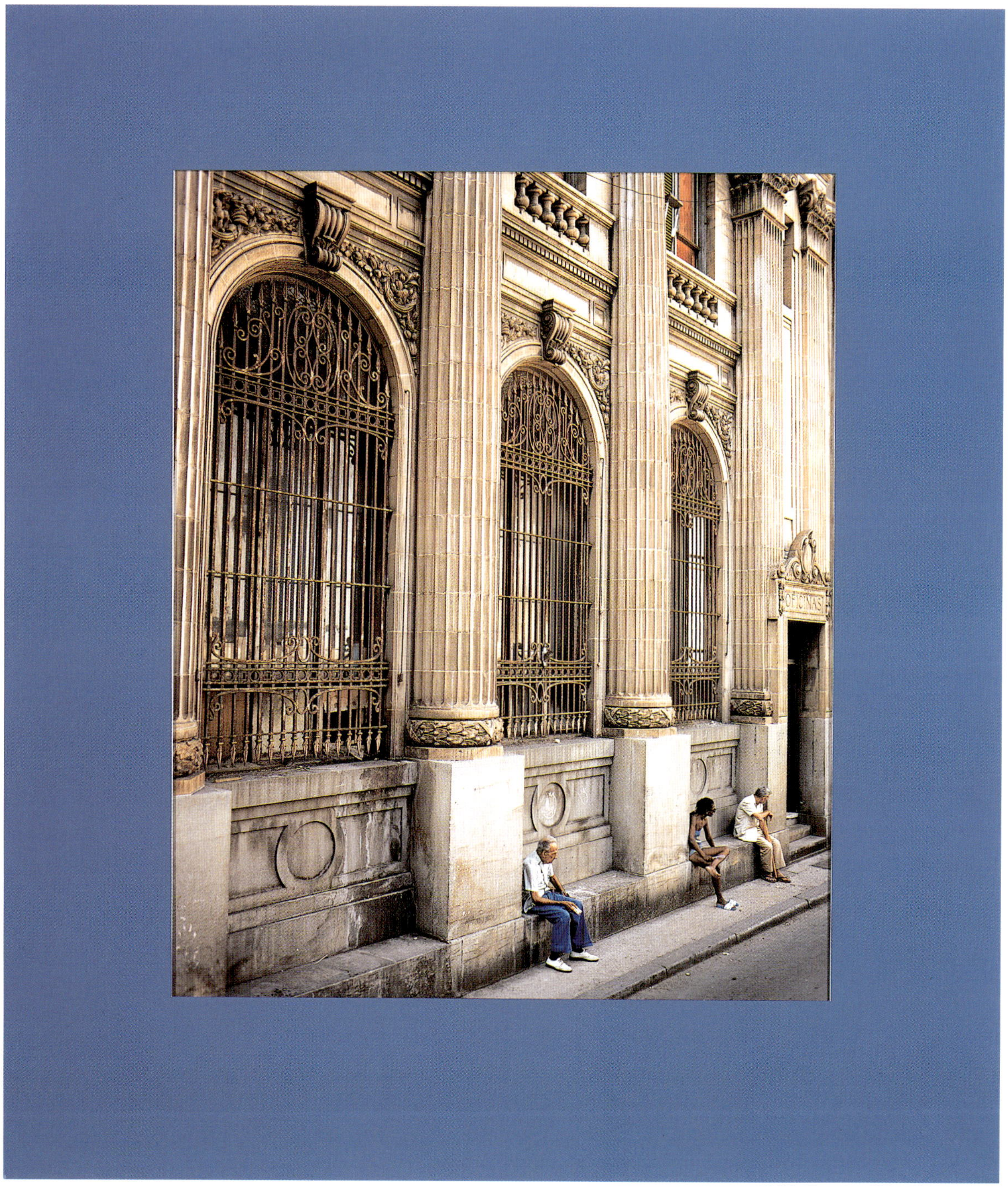

Meeting with Vox. 1996–97. Silver dye bleach process print, mounted to aluminum, 39 5/8 × 27 3/8 inches

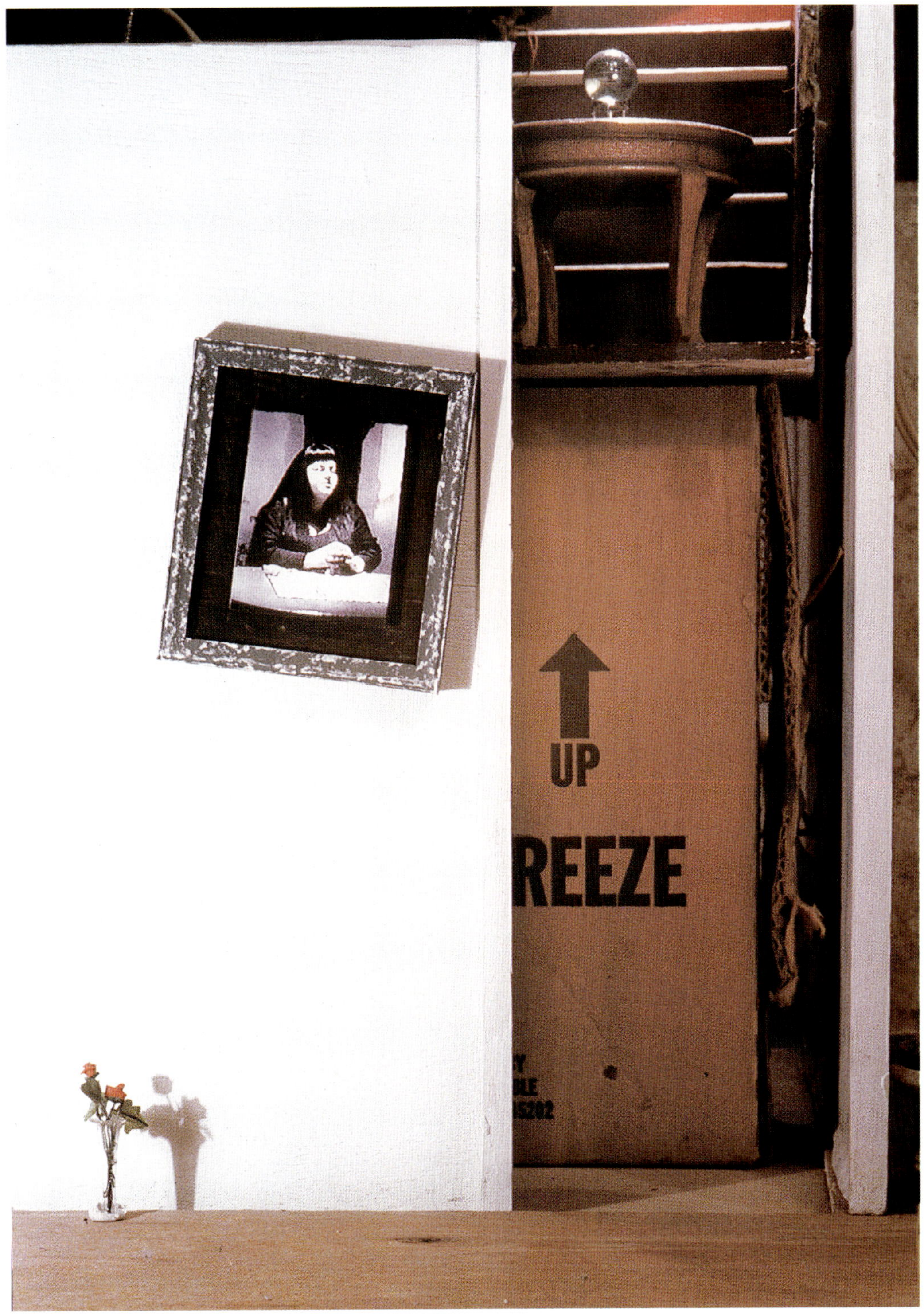

Navy Seals. 1999. Digital color print, 40 × 53¼ inches

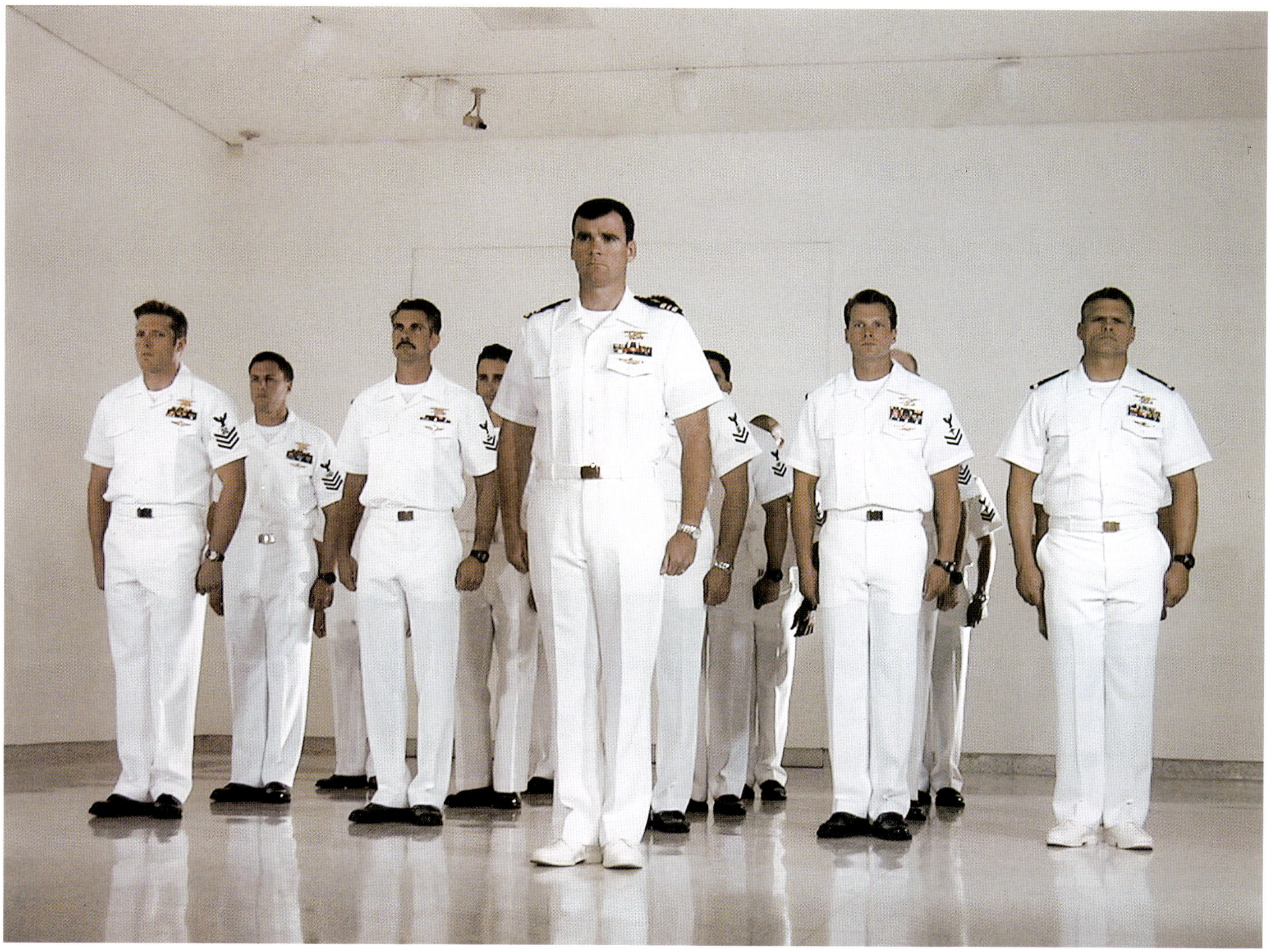

Roter Strauss/Mädchen mit Kronen (Red Bunch/Girls with Crowns). 1996. Diptych: chromogenic process prints, face mounted to plexiglass, 23 1/8 × 30 1/2 inches

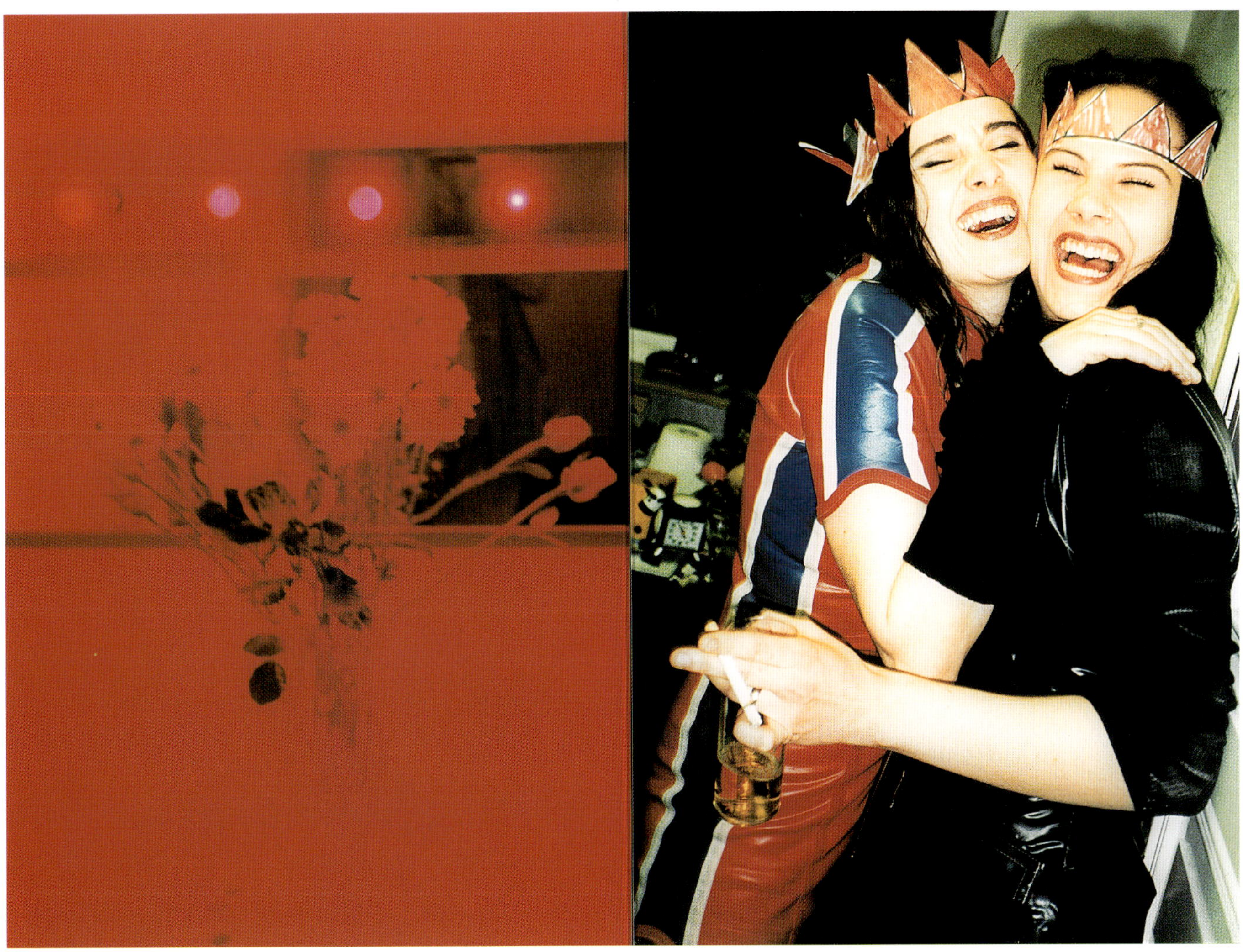

La Rivoluzione Siamo Noi (We are the Revolution). 1971.
Transfer print on polyester, $77\frac{7}{8} \times 42$ inches

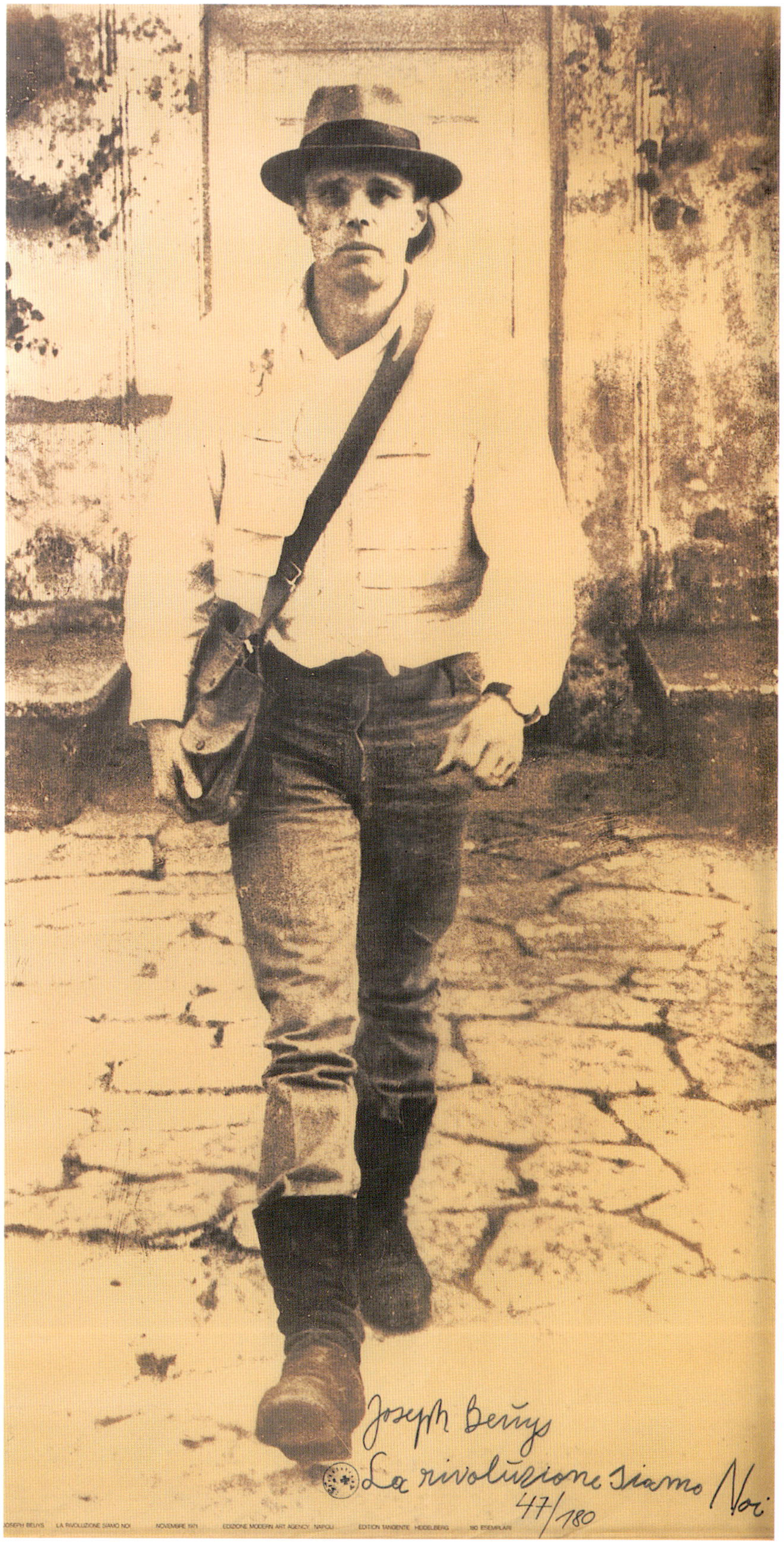

Untitled. 1995. Chromogenic process print, mounted on aluminum, 19 3/4 × 29 1/2 inches

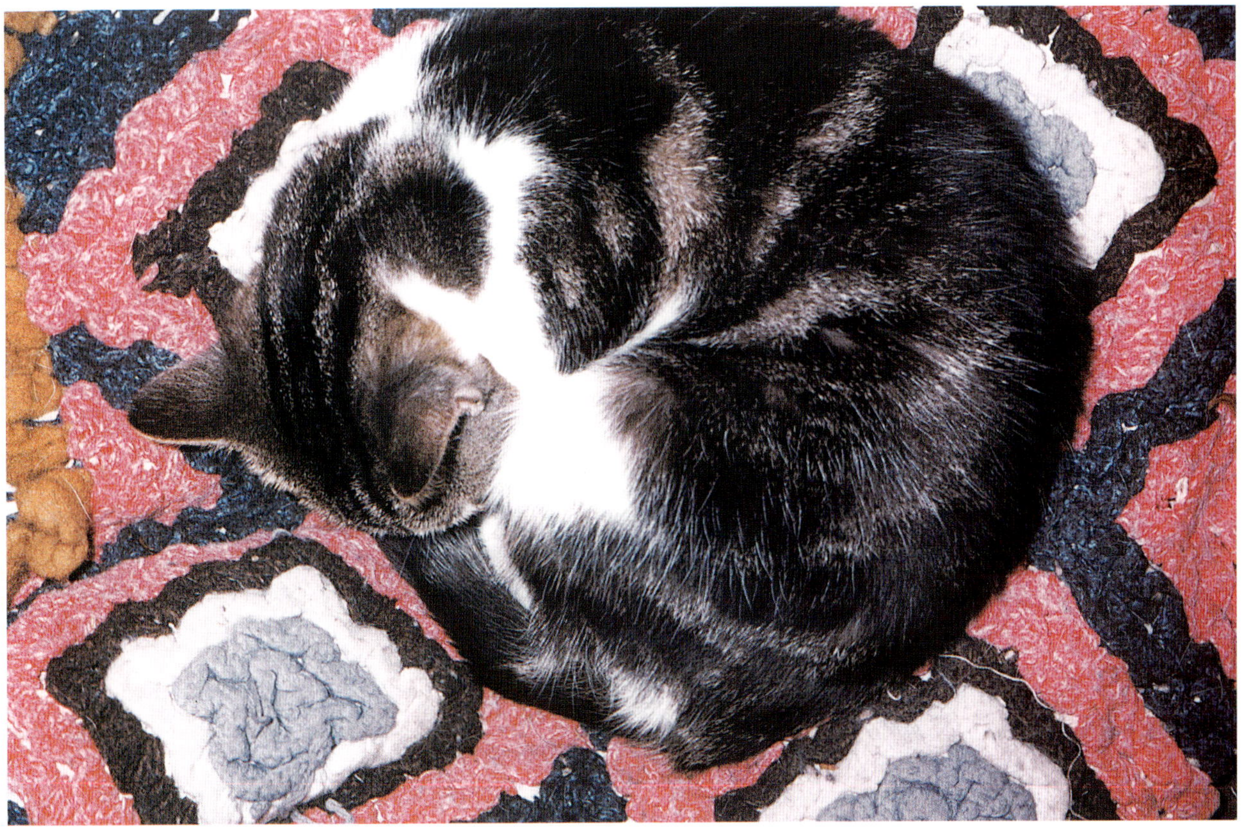

Kanal (Canal). 1999. Chromogenic process print, 61 inches × 18 feet 3/8 inches

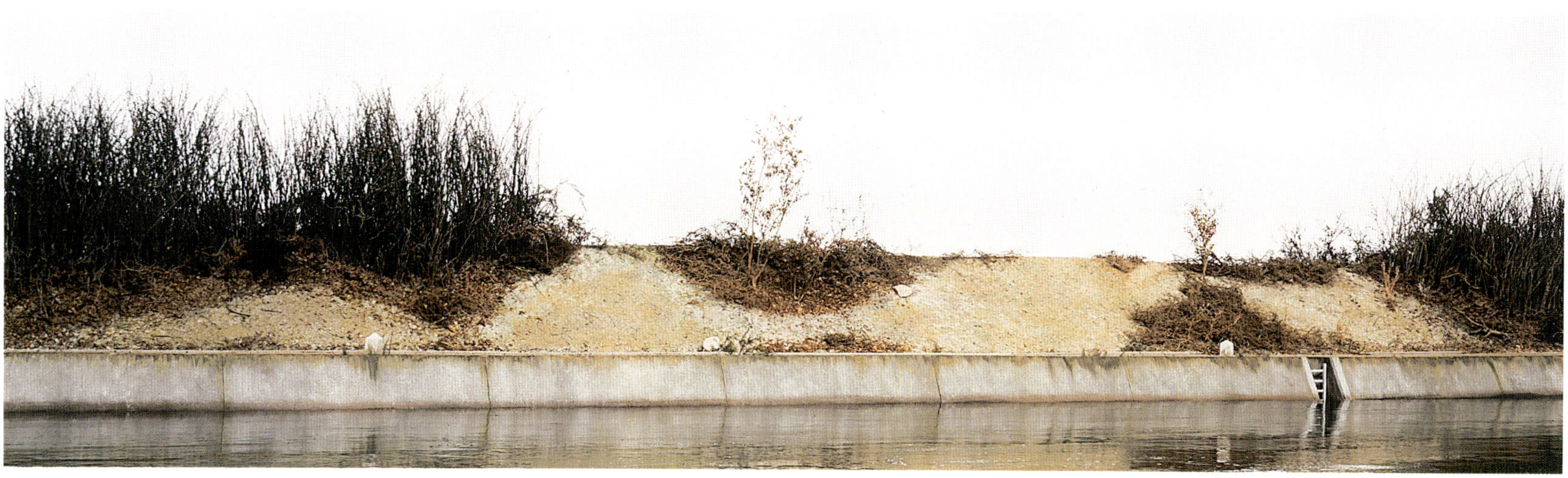

Untitled (detail). 2000. Suite of twenty-one silver dye bleach process prints, dimensions varied

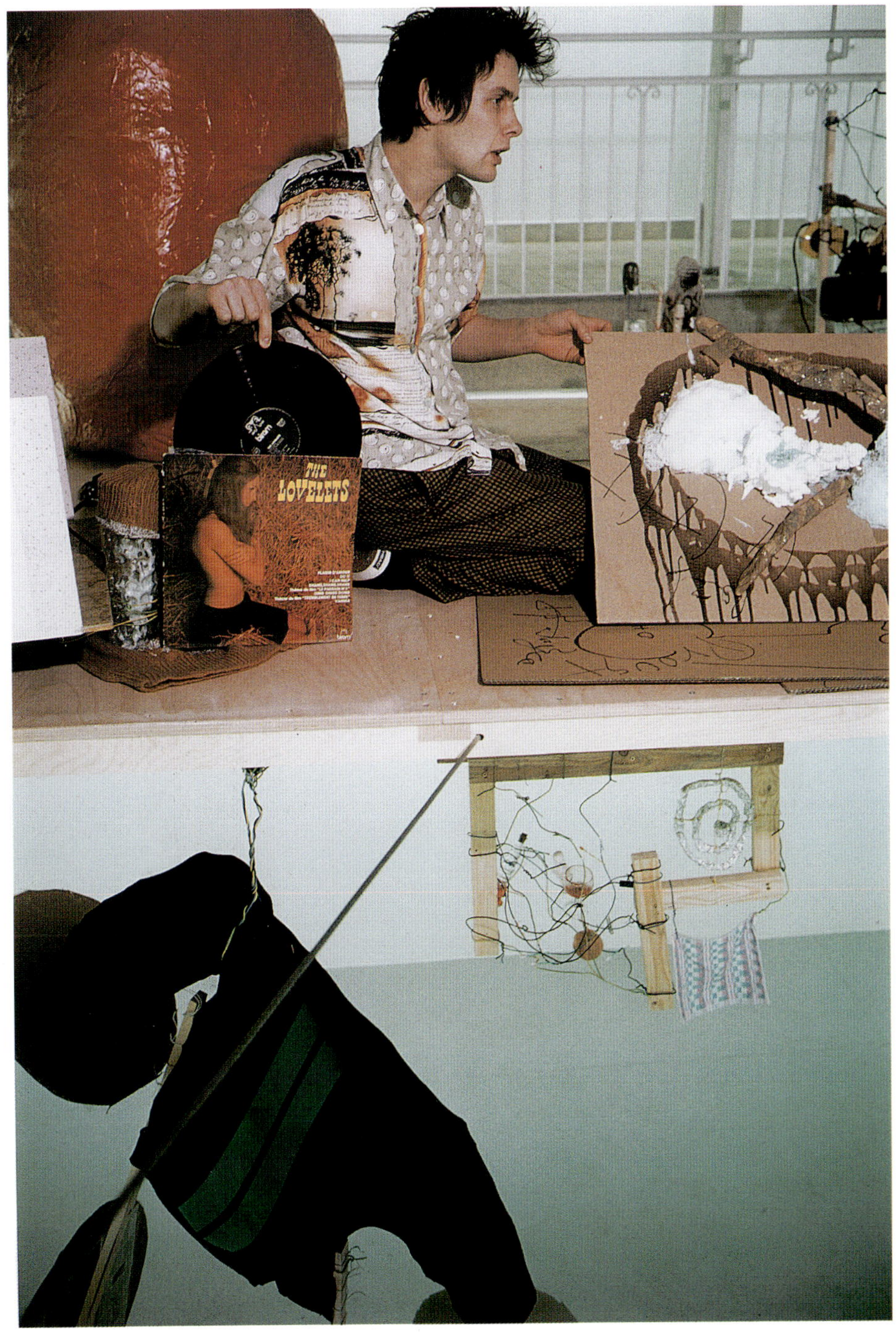

The School of Grosse Hamburgerstrasse, Berlin, 1939. 1998. Portfolio: eight photogravures on rag paper, with a title page, 25 × 19 inches each

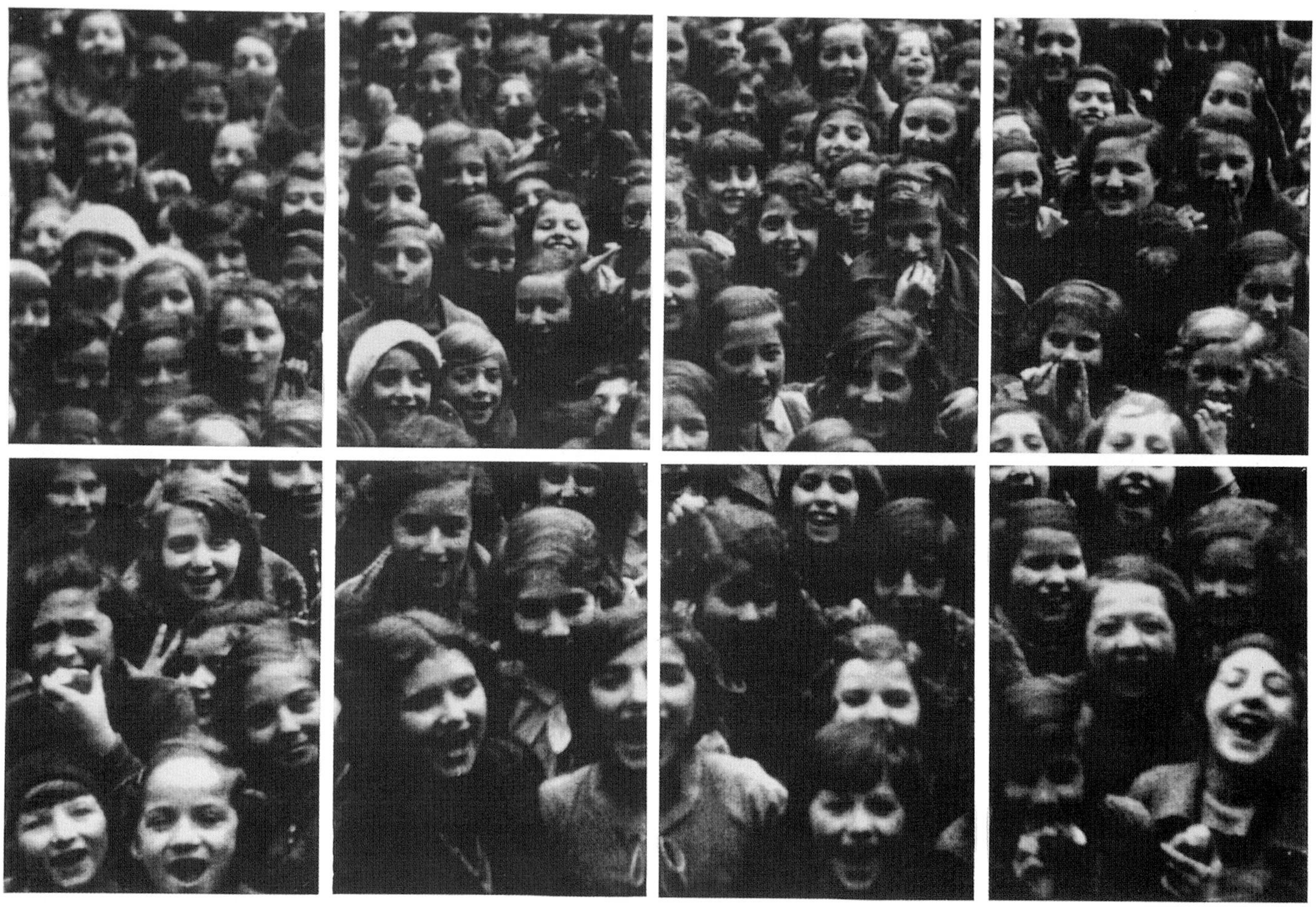

Lumières (Lights). 1990. Silkscreen on plexiglass, 73 × 55½ inches

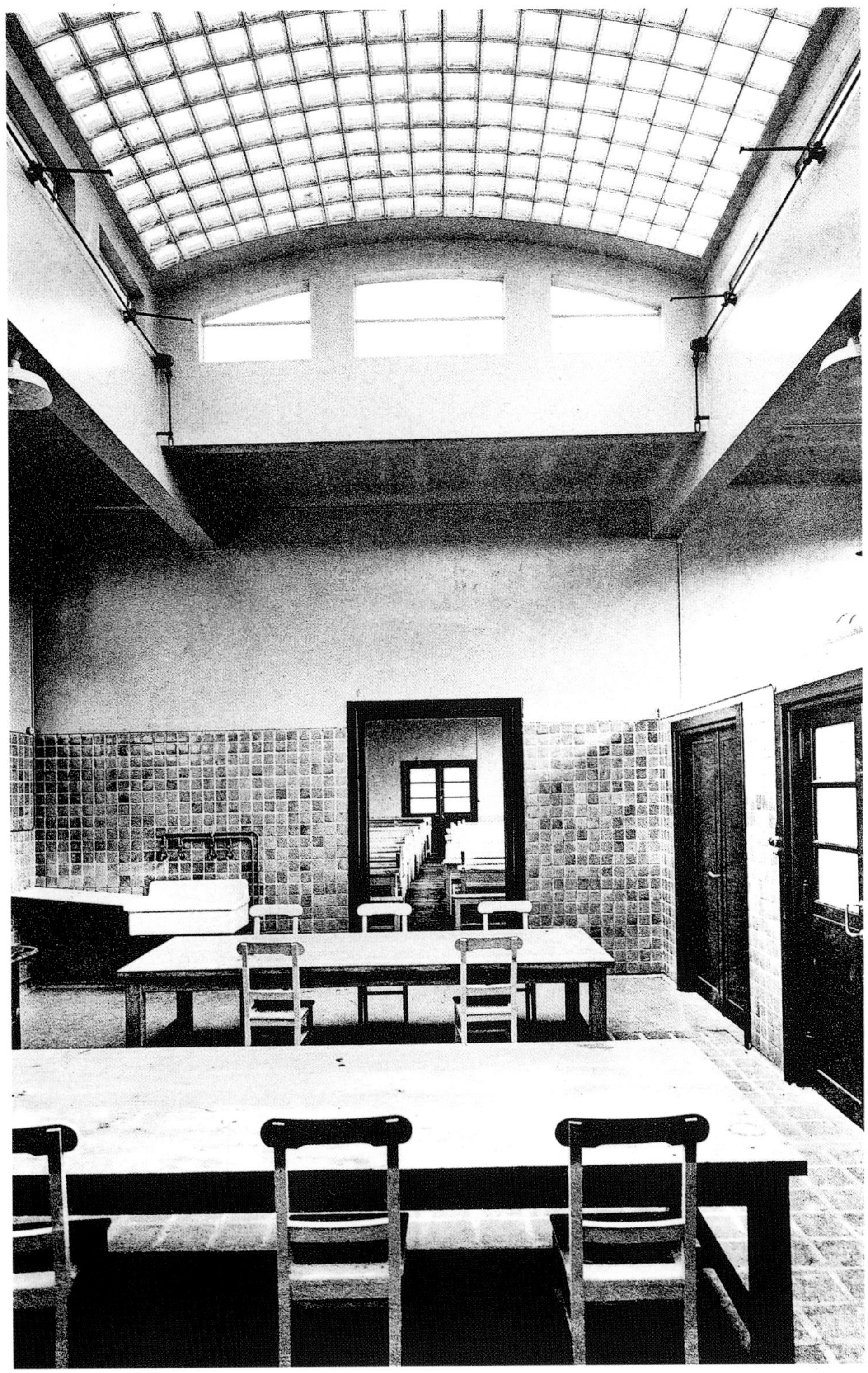

60

True Stories, The Bad Breath. 1994. Installation: two gelatin silver prints, 70 × 67 inches

I was thirty, and my father thought I had bad breath. He made an appointment for me with a doctor whom he assumed was a general practitioner. However, when I arrived at his office, I immediately realised that he was a psychoanalyst. Given the hostility my father always expressed towards this profession, I was surprised. "There must be some mistake," I said. "My father is convinced I have bad breath and he sent me to a GP." The man replied: "Do you always do what your father tells you to do?" And so I became his patient.

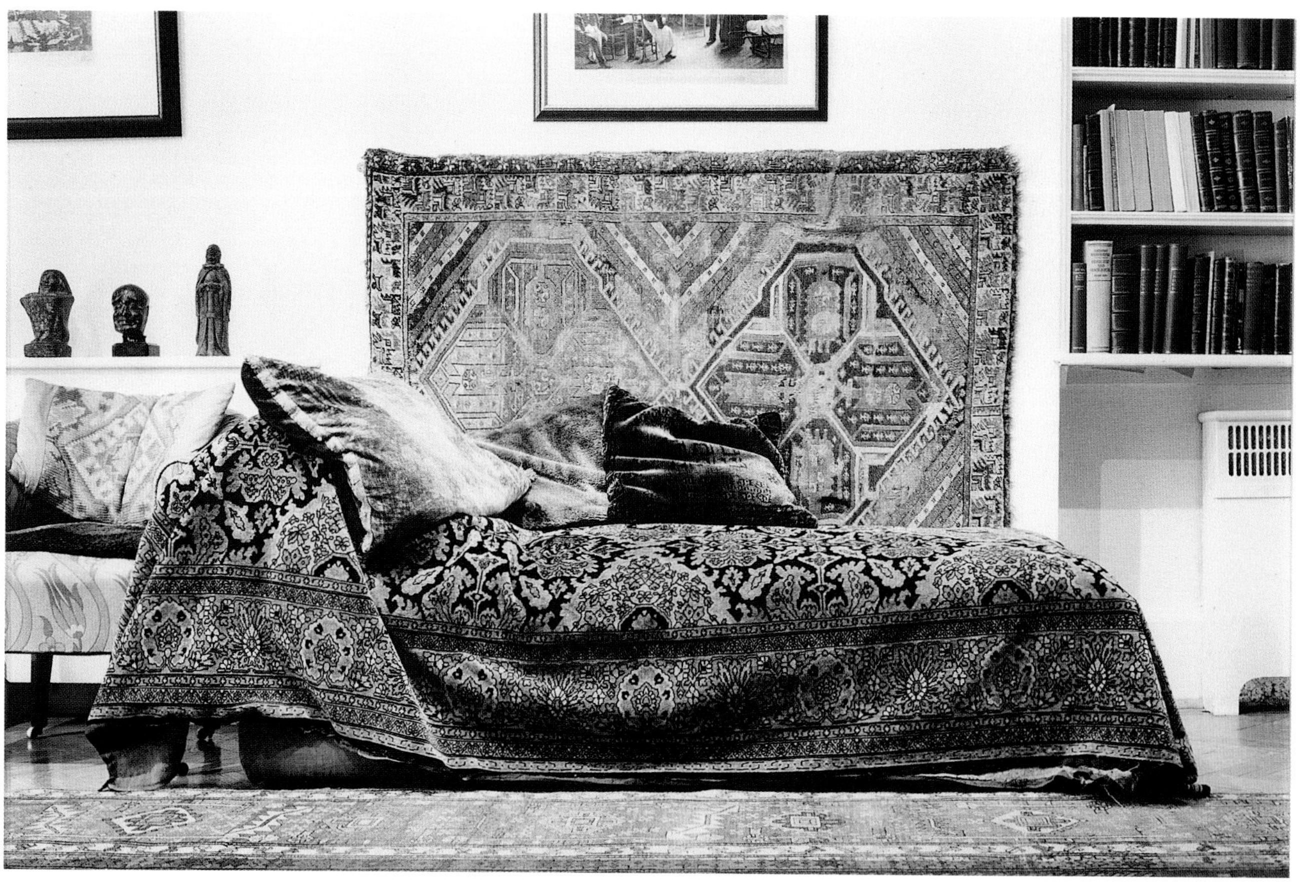

Apse. 1996. Silver dye bleach process print, 48 × 59⅝ inches

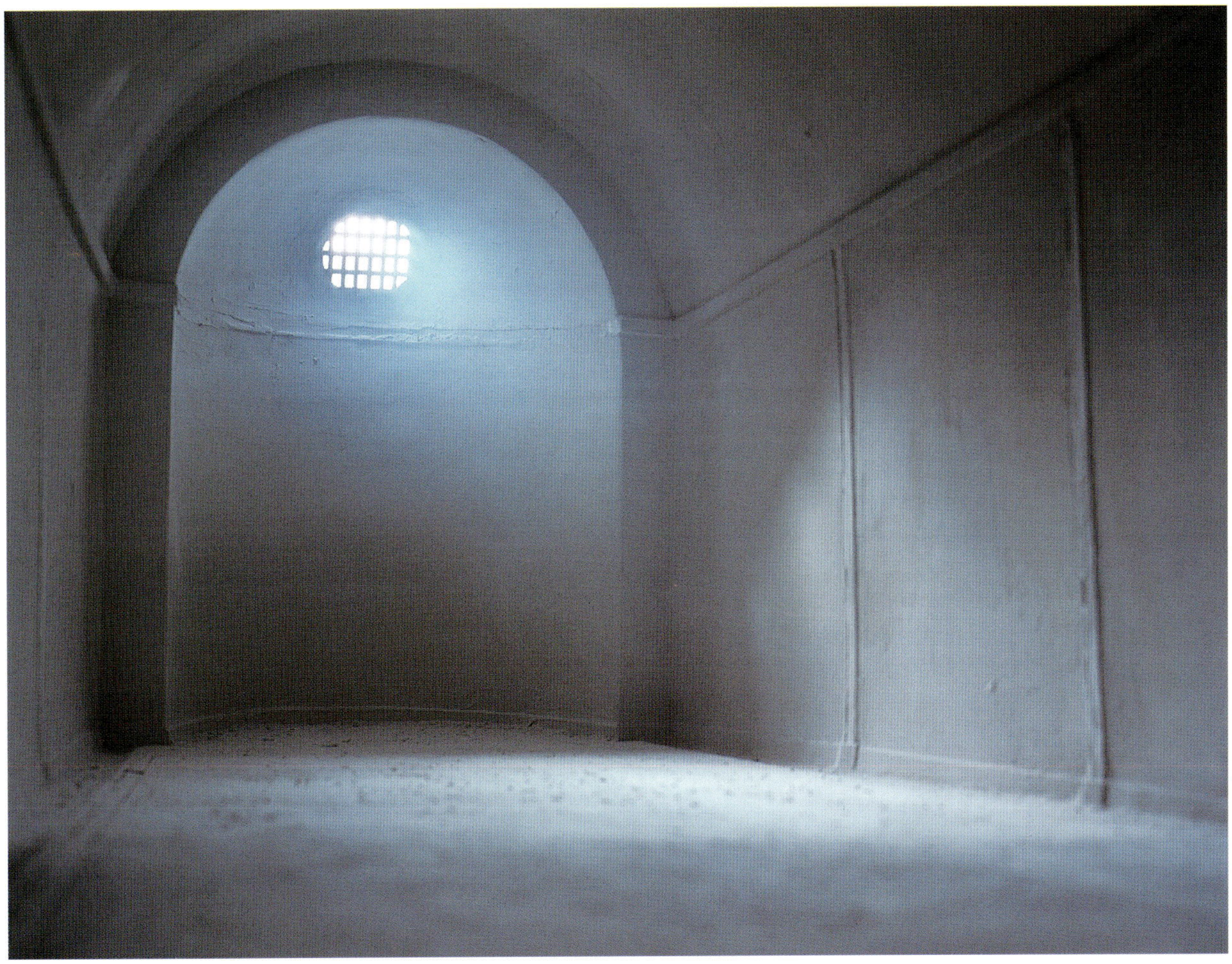

VINCENZO CASTELLA

Milano, 1998. 1998. Diptych: silver dye bleach process prints, mounted between plexiglass and Forex, $35\frac{1}{2} \times 92\frac{1}{2}$ inches

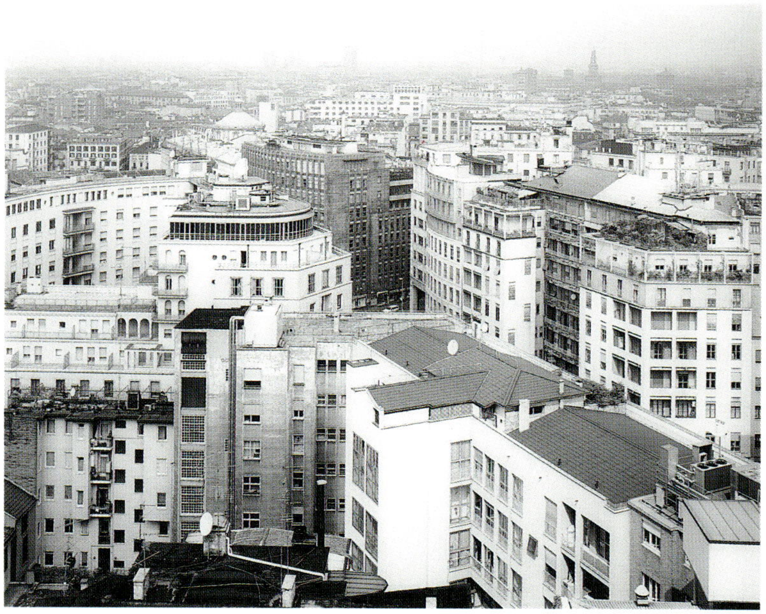

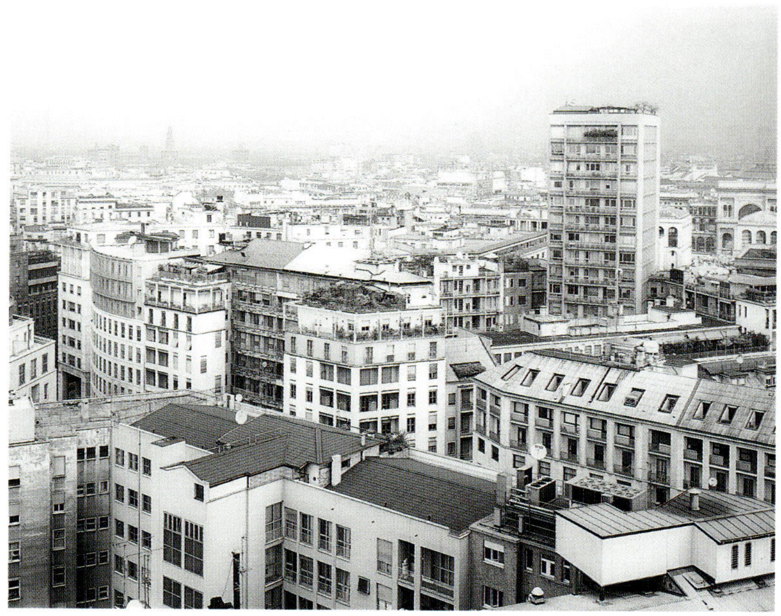

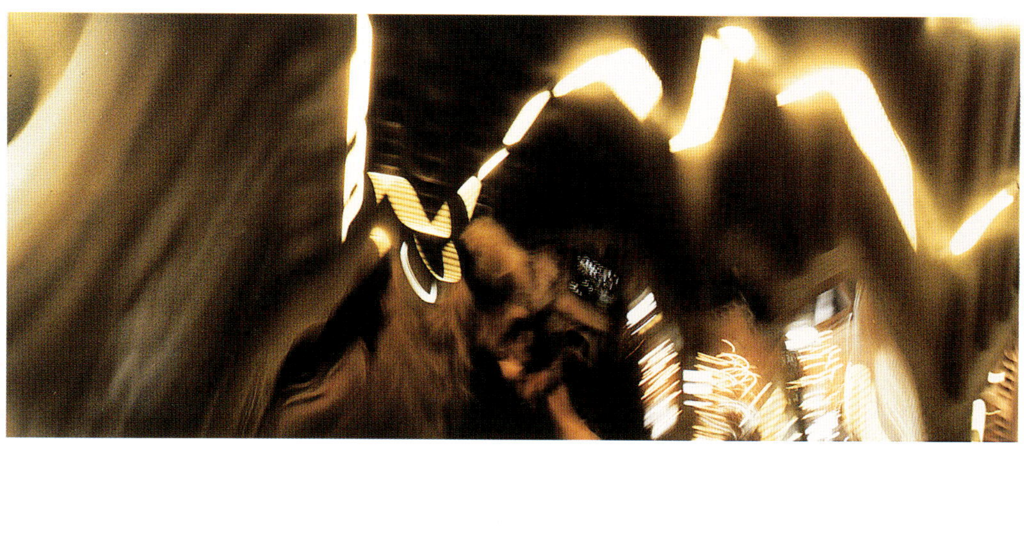

JOHN CHAMBERLAIN

Dutch Lights II. 1990. Chromogenic process print, 20×24 inches

Contemplation of a Bust. 1987. Silver dye bleach process print, face mounted to plexiglass, 72 × 48 inches

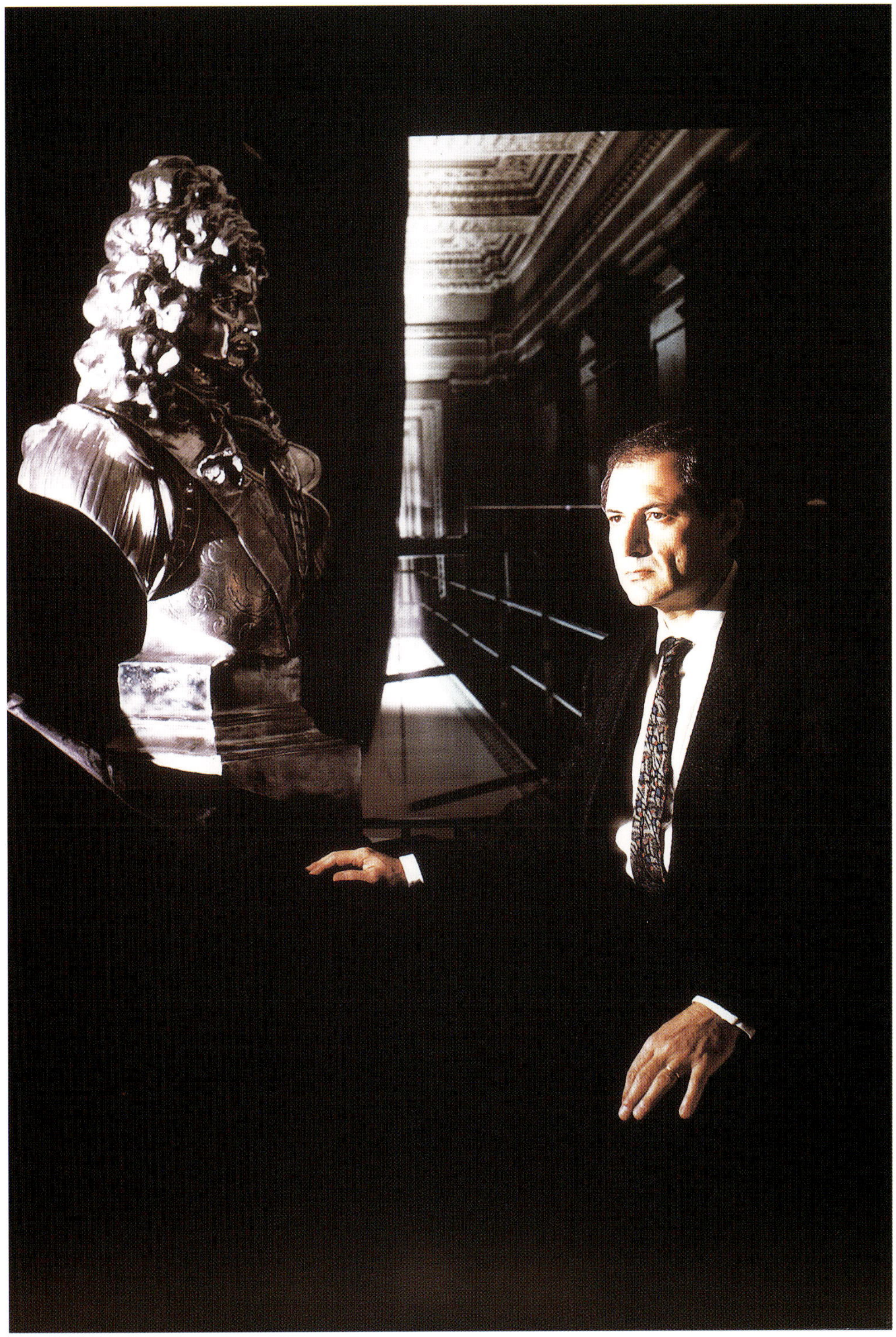

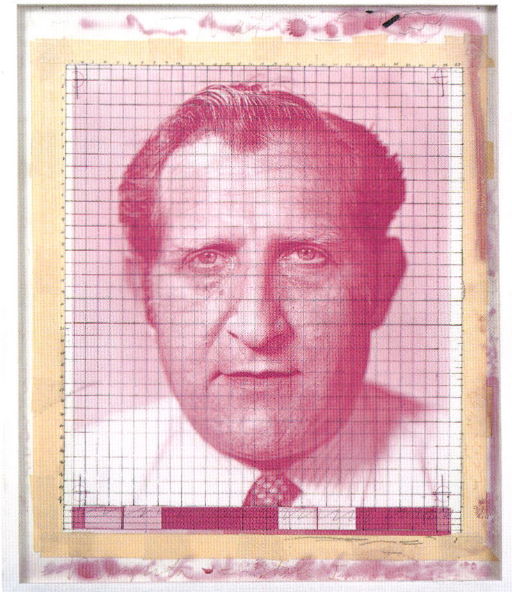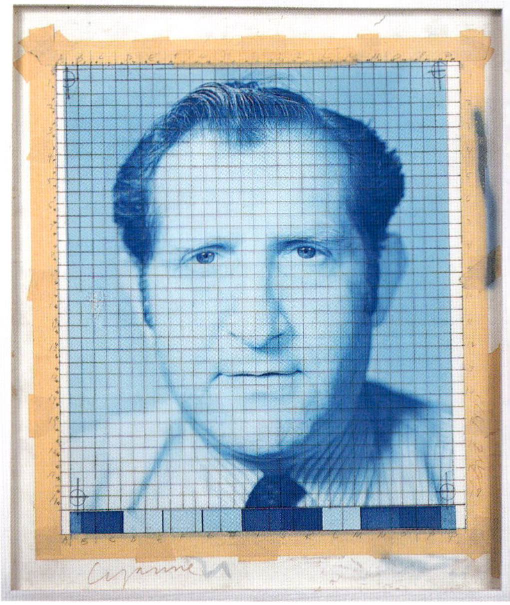

Nat (Five Color States). 1971. Sequenced suite: five dye transfer prints with acetate overlay, ink, and masking tape, $25\frac{1}{8} \times 21$ inches each

From left to right:

Nat (Five Color States)—"State One Magenta"

Nat (Five Color States)—"Cyanne" [sic]

Nat (Five Color States)—"State II Magenta + Cyanne" [sic]

Nat (Five Color States)—"Yellow"

Nat (Five Color States)—"State III Magenta + Cyanne [sic] + yellow"

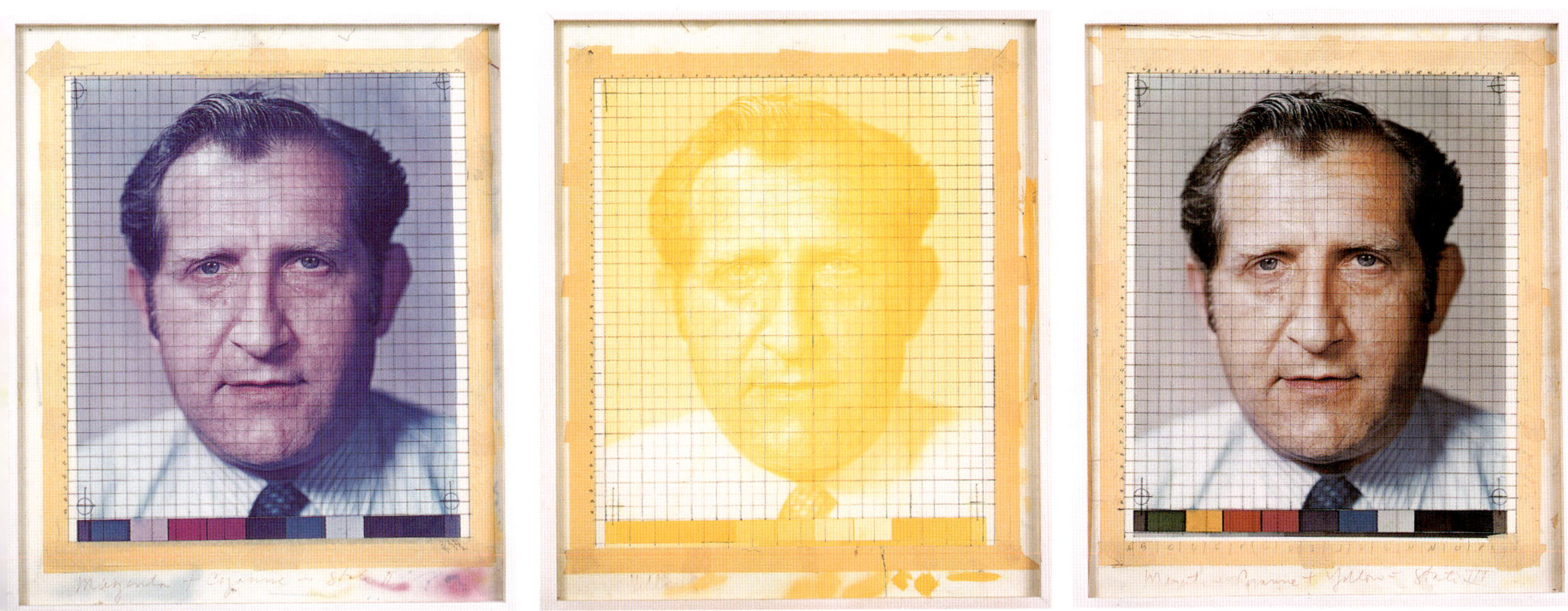

Laboratory. n.d. Gelatin silver print with text on mat, in artist's laminate frame, 43 3/8 × 50 5/8 inches

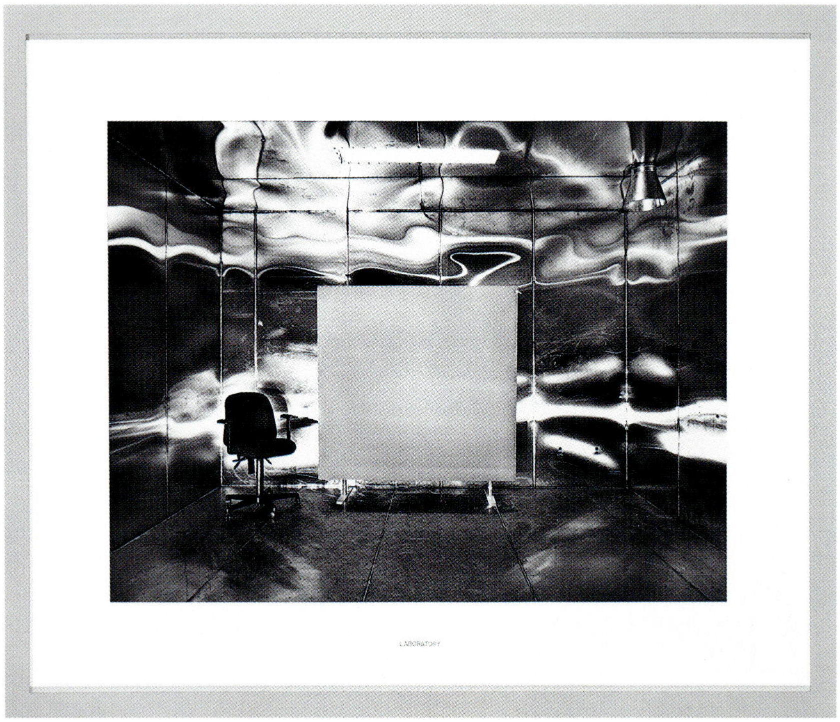

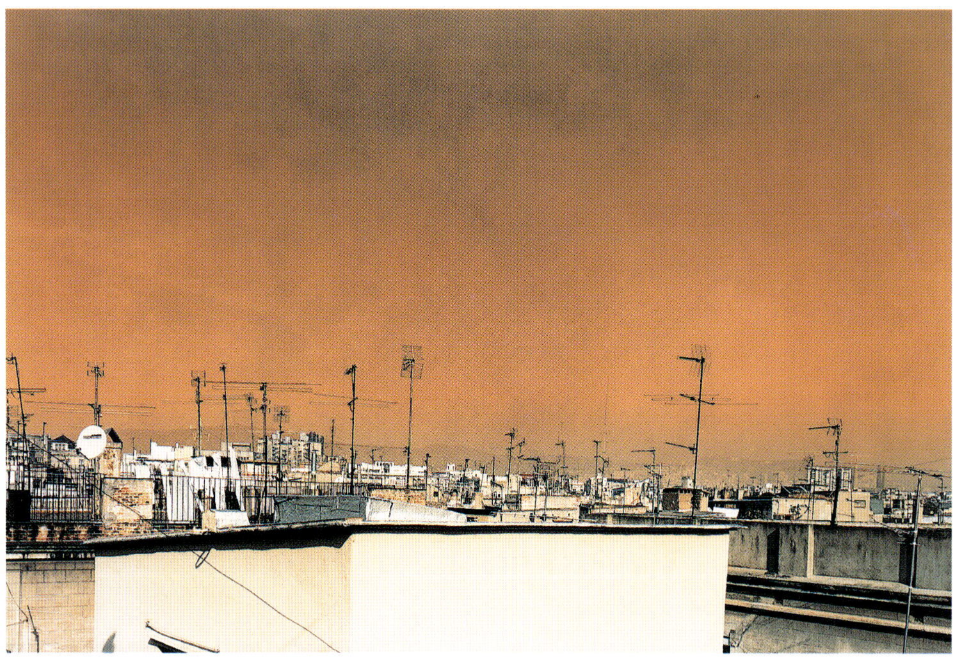

HANNAH COLLINS

True Stories III. 1998. Chromogenic process print, 69 × 92 1/4 inches

Flowers and Butterflies. 1996. Digital transparency in lightbox, 19¾ × 19¾ × 4¼ inches

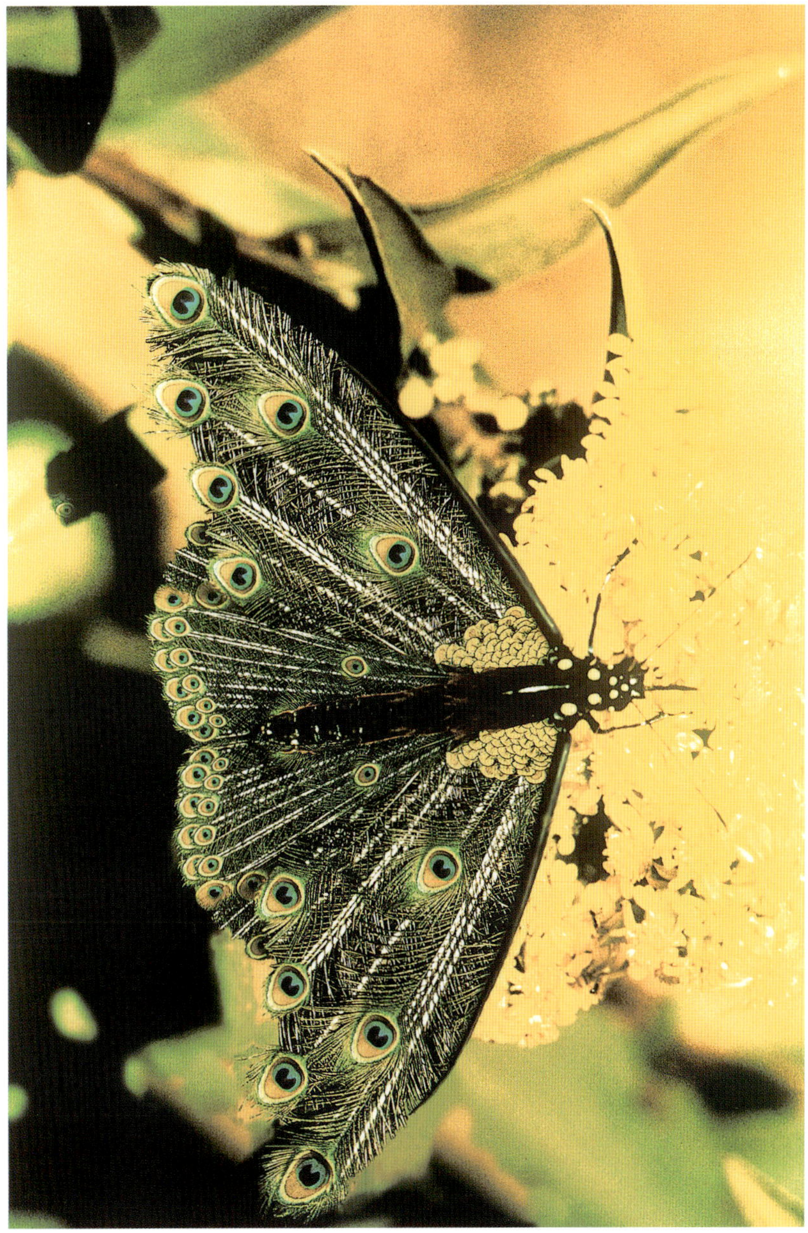

 Untitled Angel. 1975. Gelatin silver photogram, 67 × 40 inches

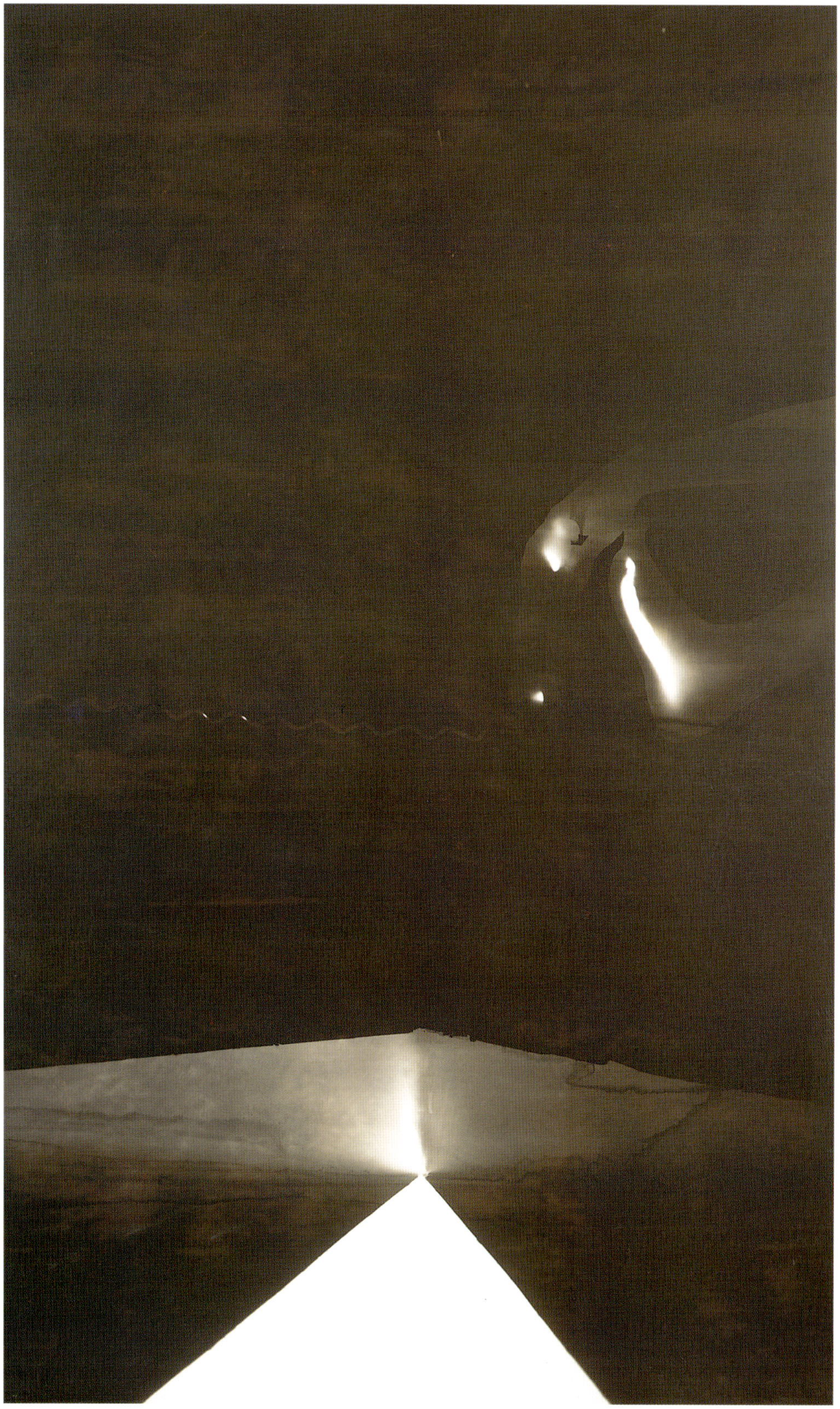

MILES COOLIDGE

Highrise, Toys-R-Us, McDonald's. From the *Safetyville* series. 1996. Chromogenic process print, face mounted to plexiglass, $32^{1/2} \times 42^{1/4}$ inches

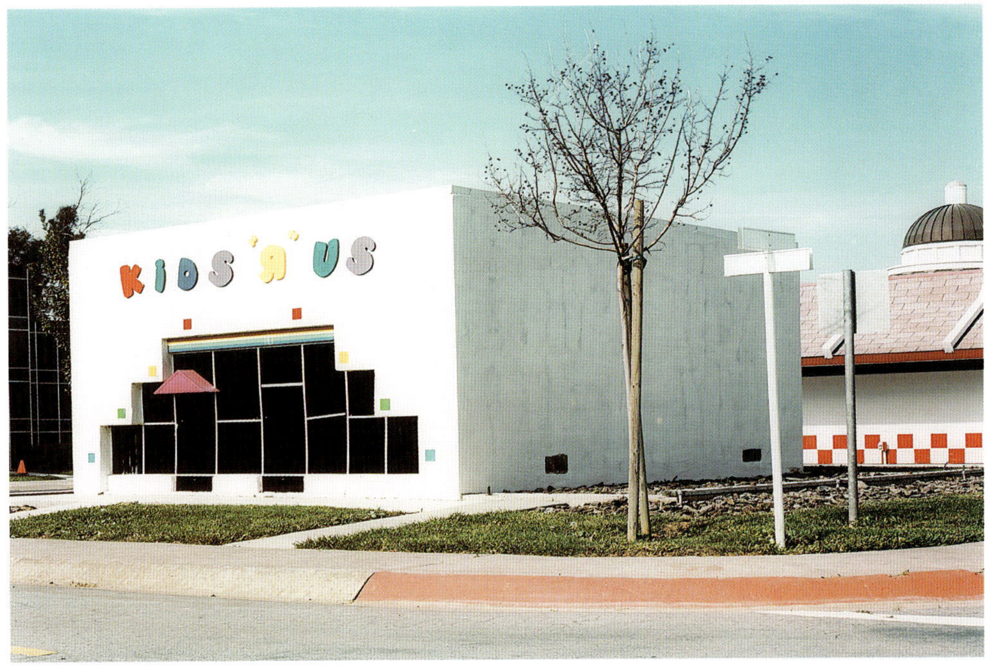

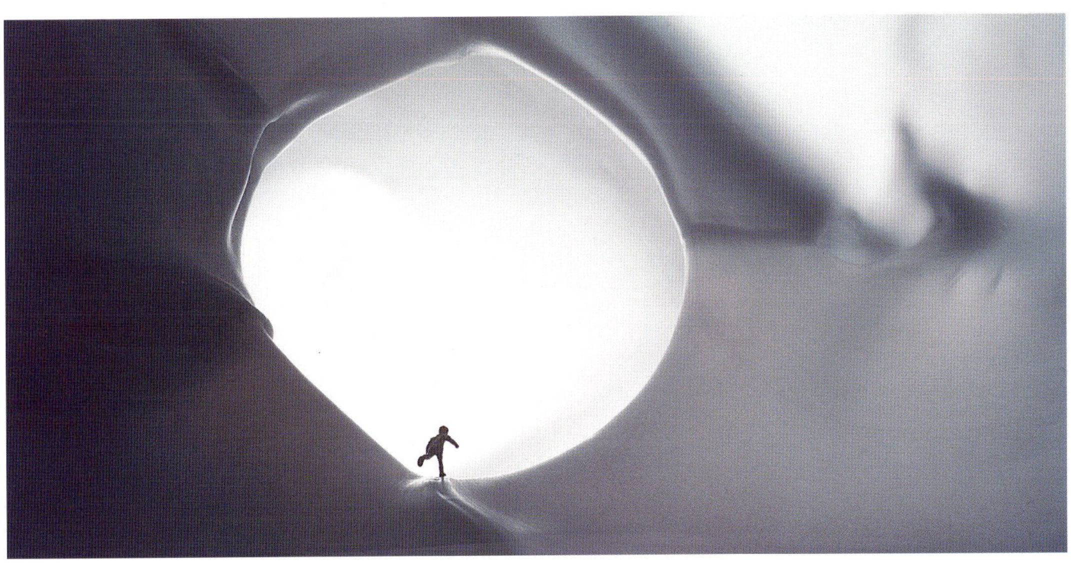

MARTINO COPPES

Sconfinamento (Boundlessness). 1995. Chromogenic process print, $28^{1/4} \times 53$ inches

Untitled. From the *Twilight* series. 1999. Laser direct chromogenic process print, $47\frac{1}{2} \times 59\frac{1}{2}$ inches

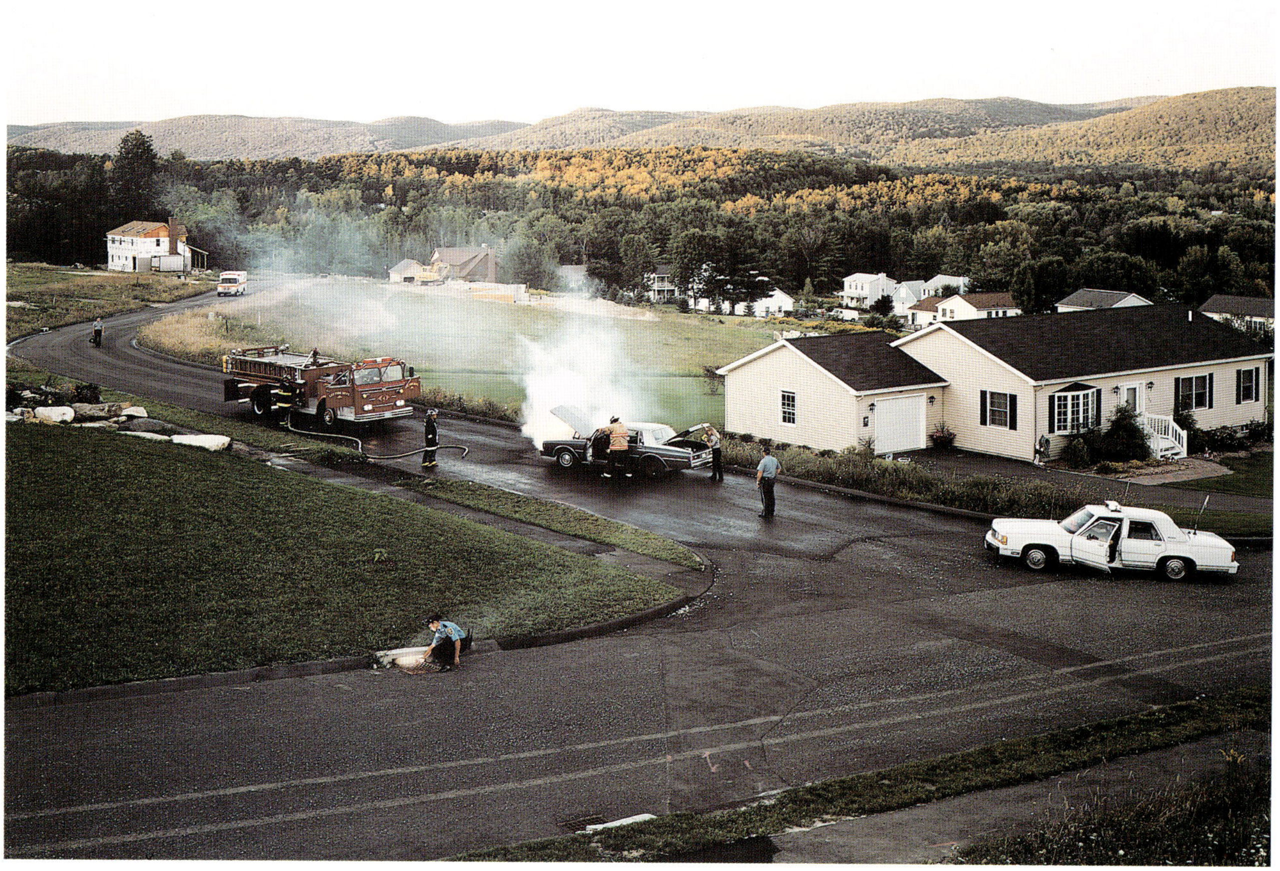

Evolution. 1978. Installation: forty-two gelatin silver prints mounted on paper with text, in artist's frames, dimensions varied

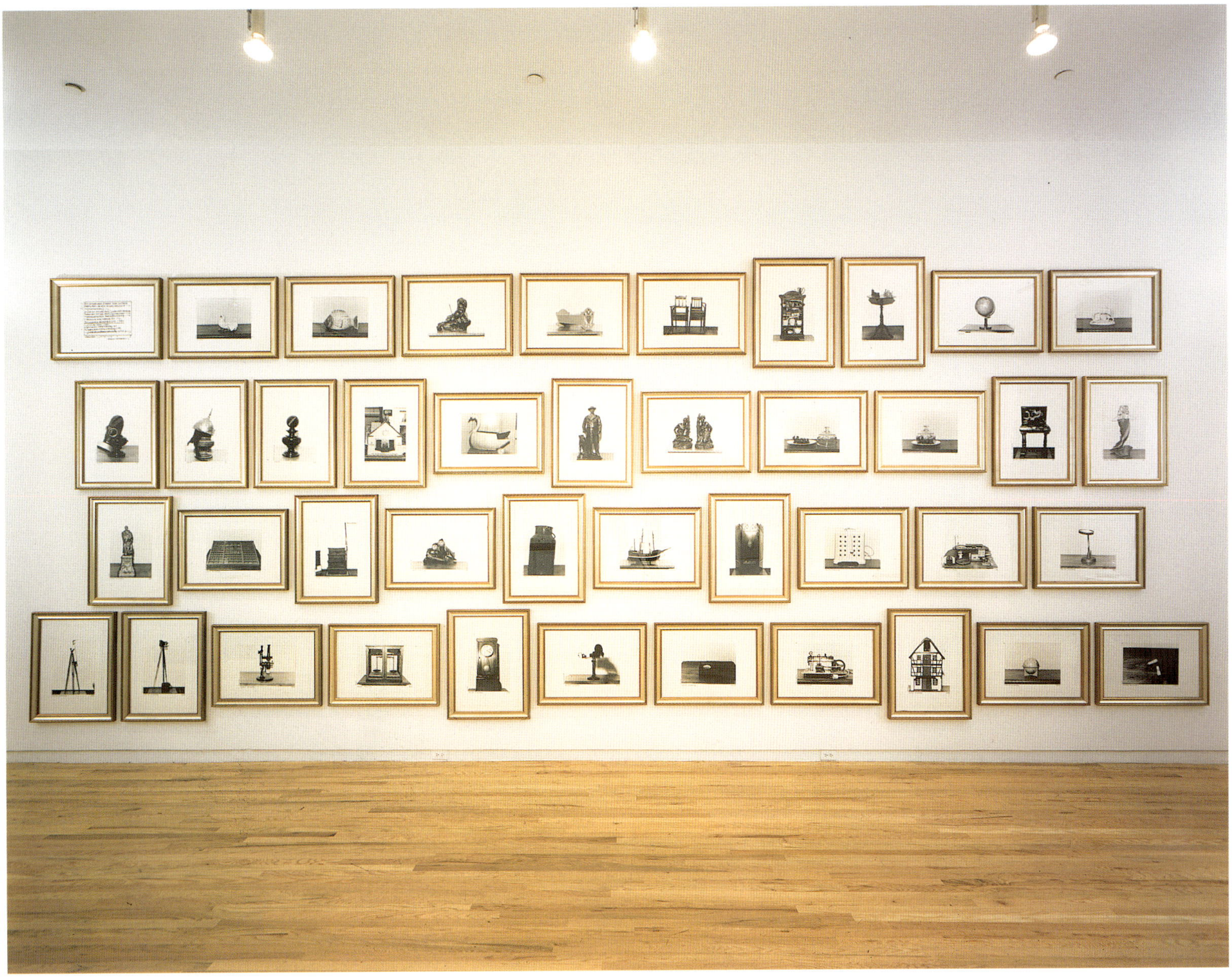

Swiss Mountain. 1996. Digital iris print, $55\frac{1}{2} \times 80\frac{5}{8}$ inches

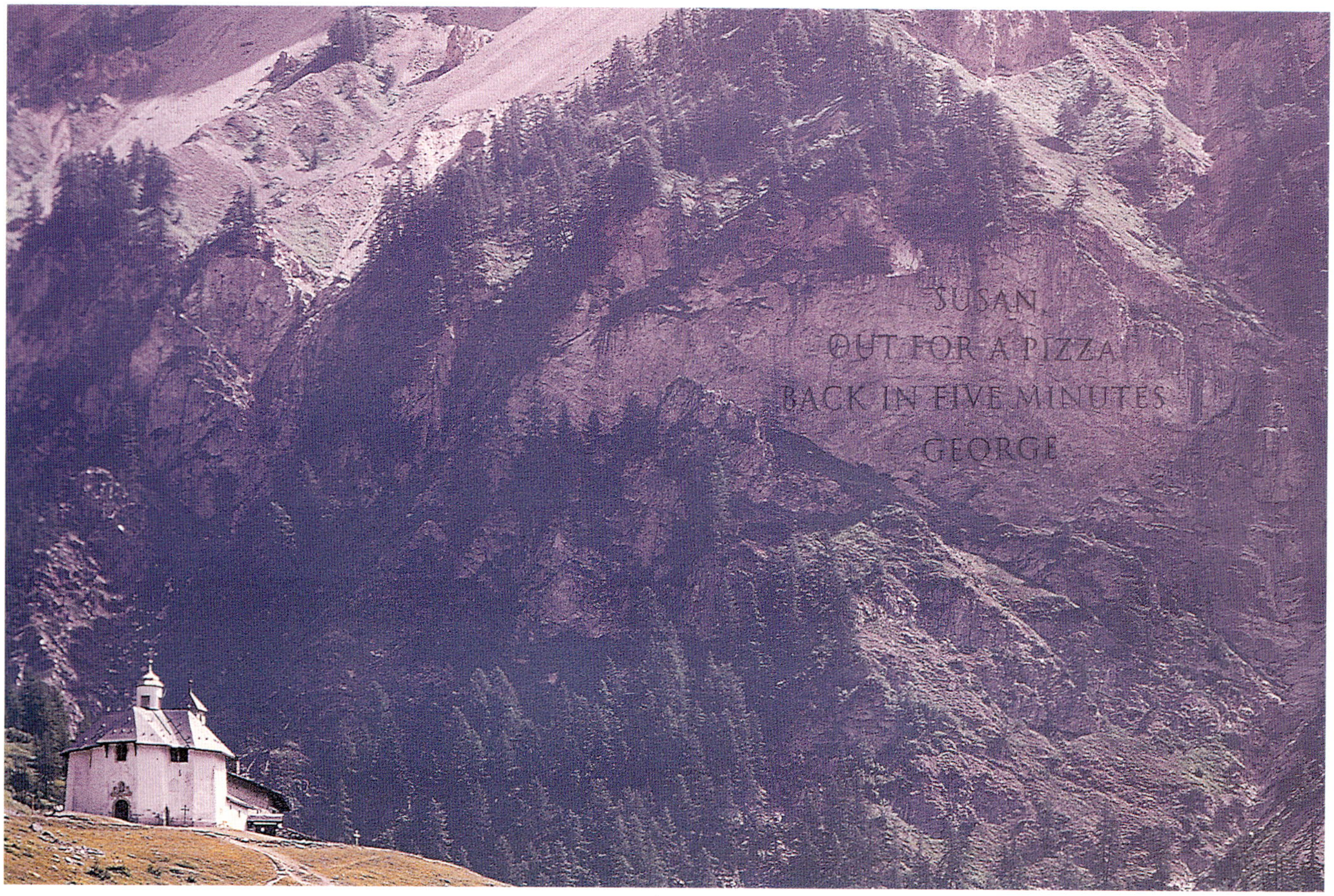

Terasse (Terrace). 1998. Chromogenic process print, face mounted to plexiglass, 72 inches × 8 feet 10 inches

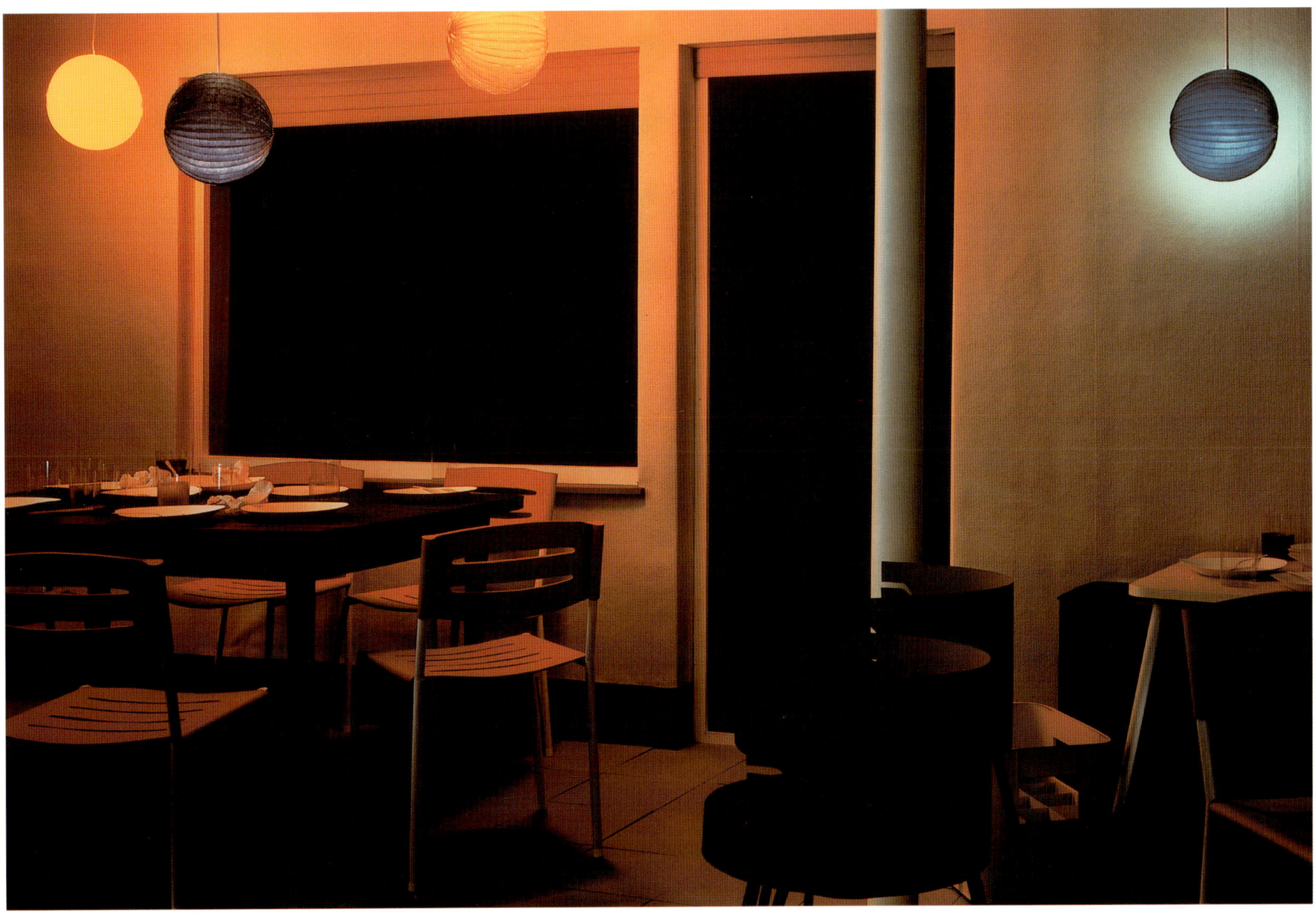

The River Taw (Leaf Fall), 3 December 1998. From the *River Taw* series. 1998. Unique dye destruction photogram, $69\frac{1}{2} \times 27\frac{3}{8}$ inches

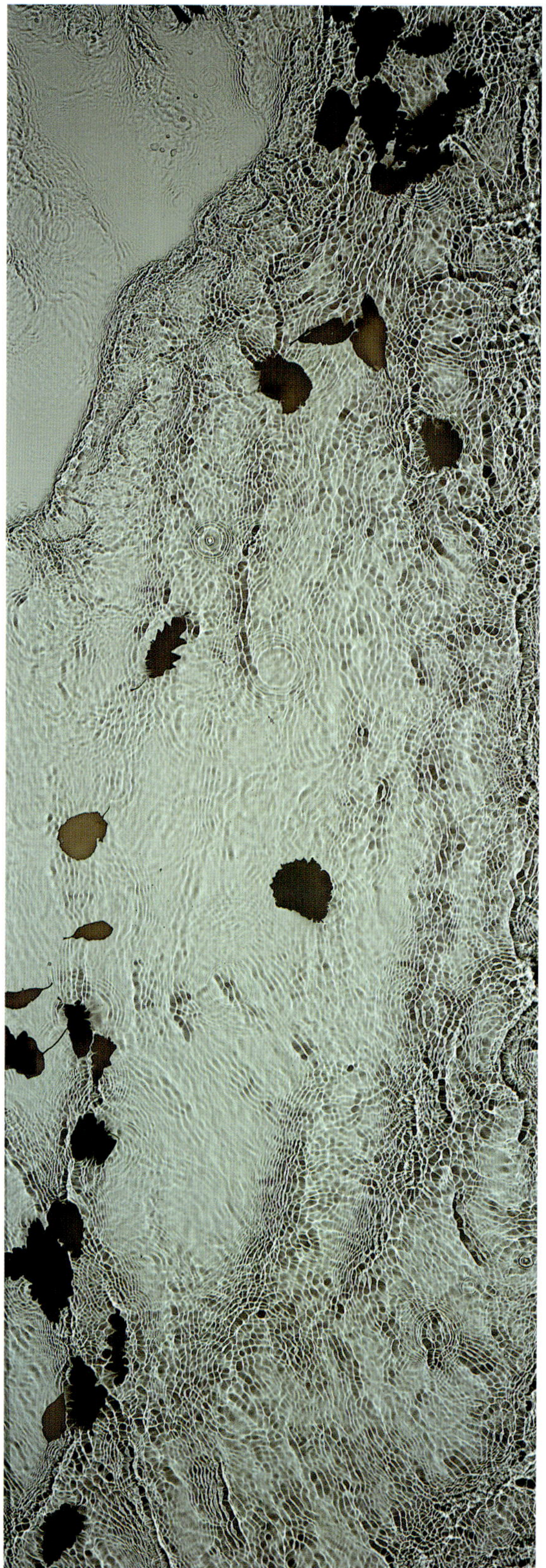

Panorama Bloemendaal (View of Bloemendaal). 1971. 144 gelatin silver prints and graphite on paper, 56 × $50^{1}/_{2}$ inches

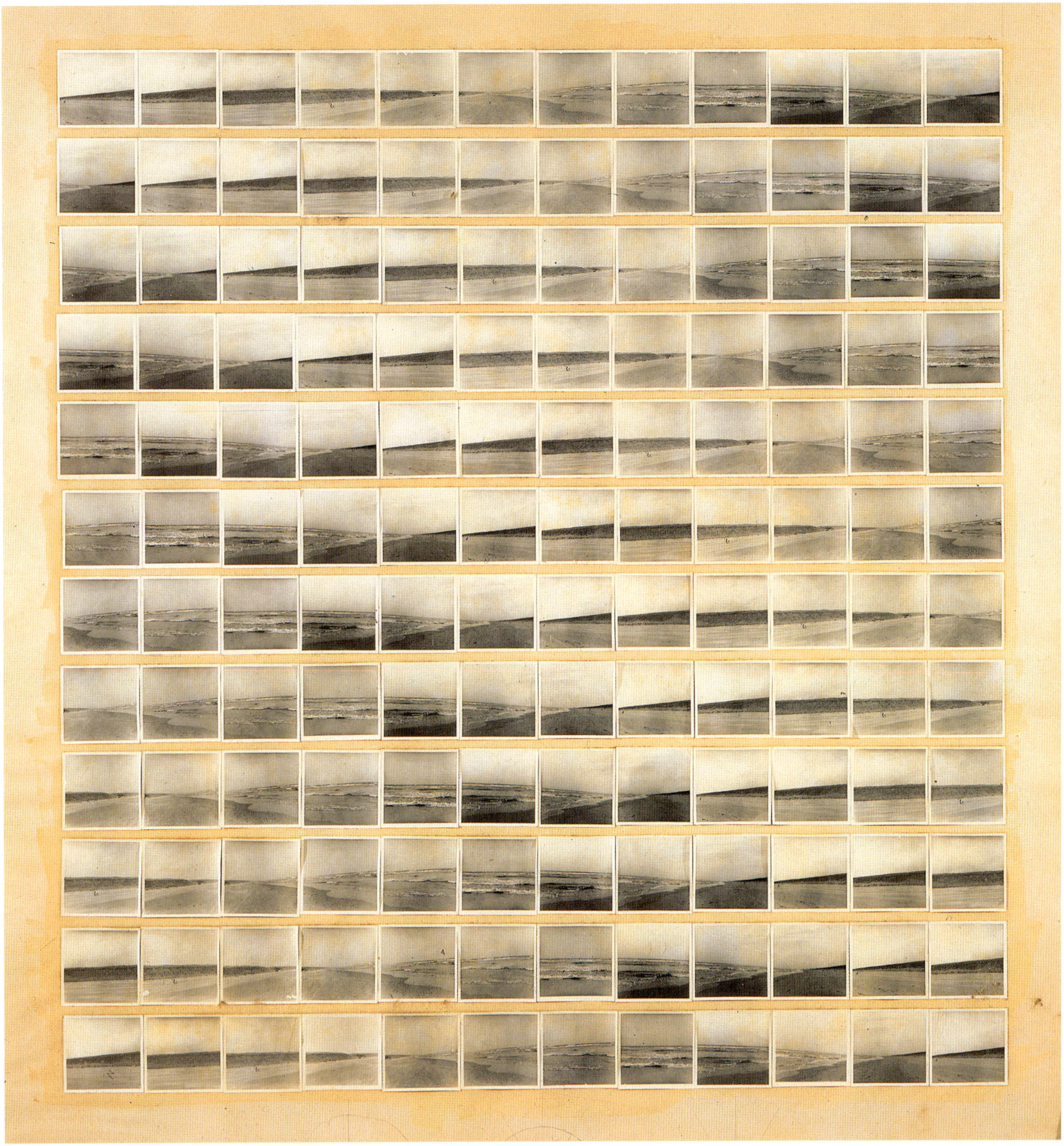

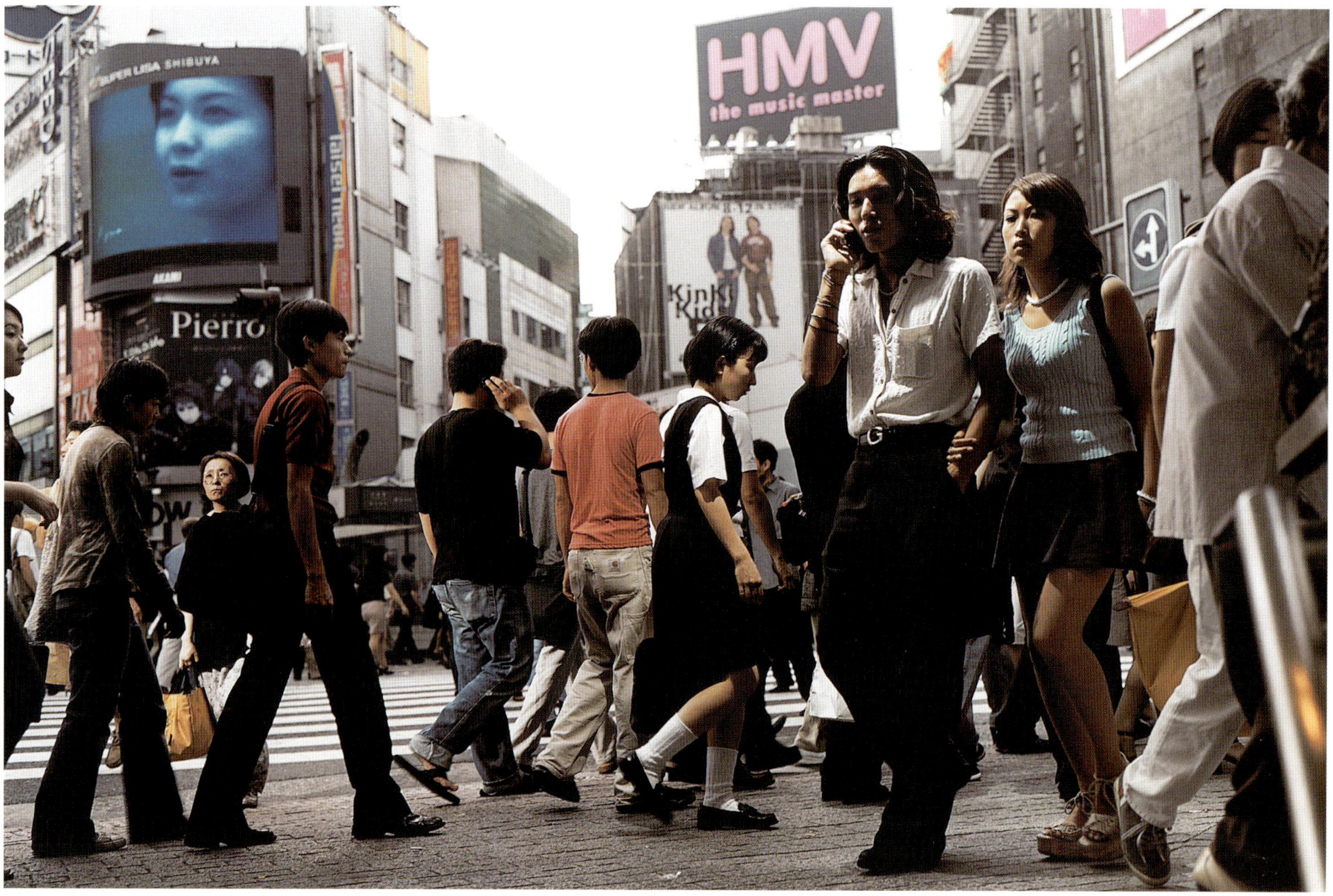

Tokyo, 1998. 1998. Chromogenic process print, $35\frac{3}{4} \times 47\frac{5}{8}$ inches

Left to right:

Almerisa, Asielzoekerscentrum, Leiden, the Netherlands, March 14, 1994. 1994

Almerisa, Wormer, the Netherlands, June 23, 1996. 1996

Almerisa, Wormer, February 21, 1998. 1998

Three chromogenic process prints from a series, 37 × 29¼ inches each

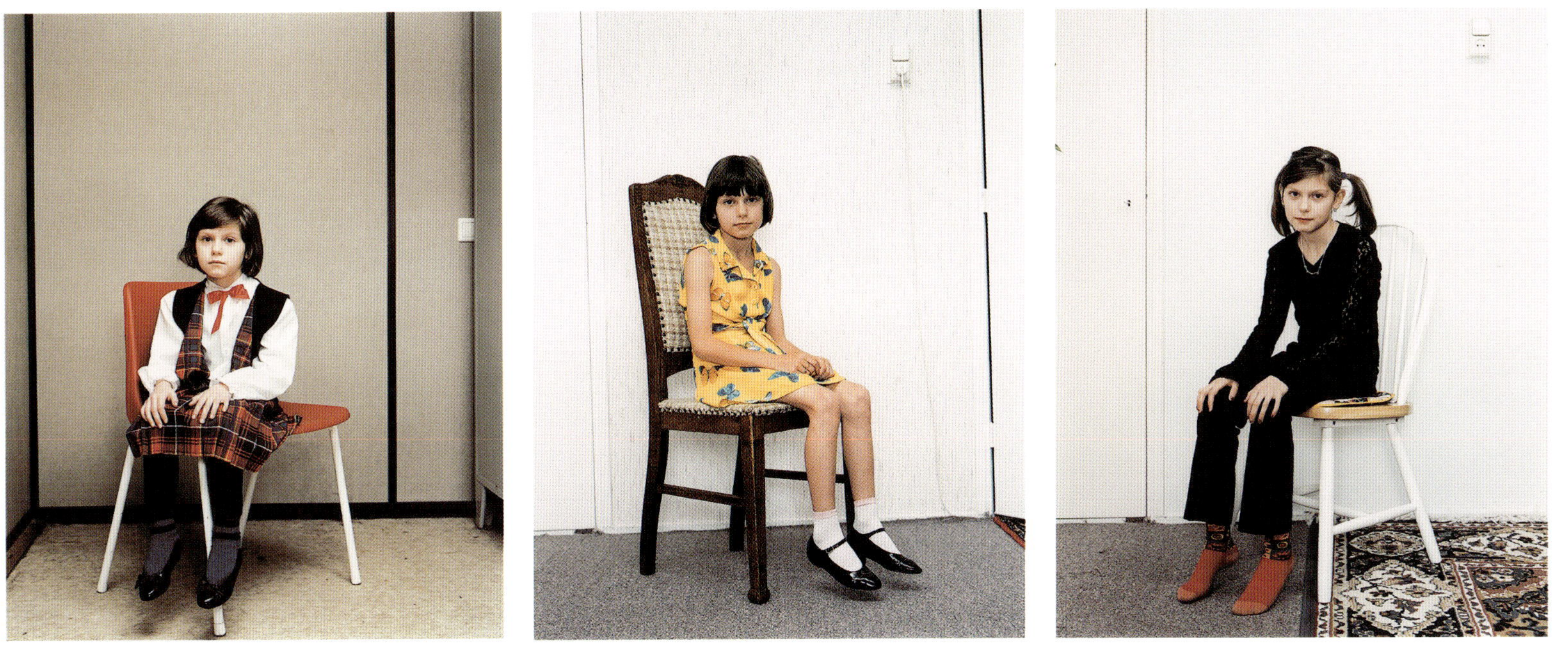

Border Road (2). 1994. Silver dye bleach process print, mounted to aluminum, $49^{1}/_{4} \times 72^{1}/_{2}$ inches

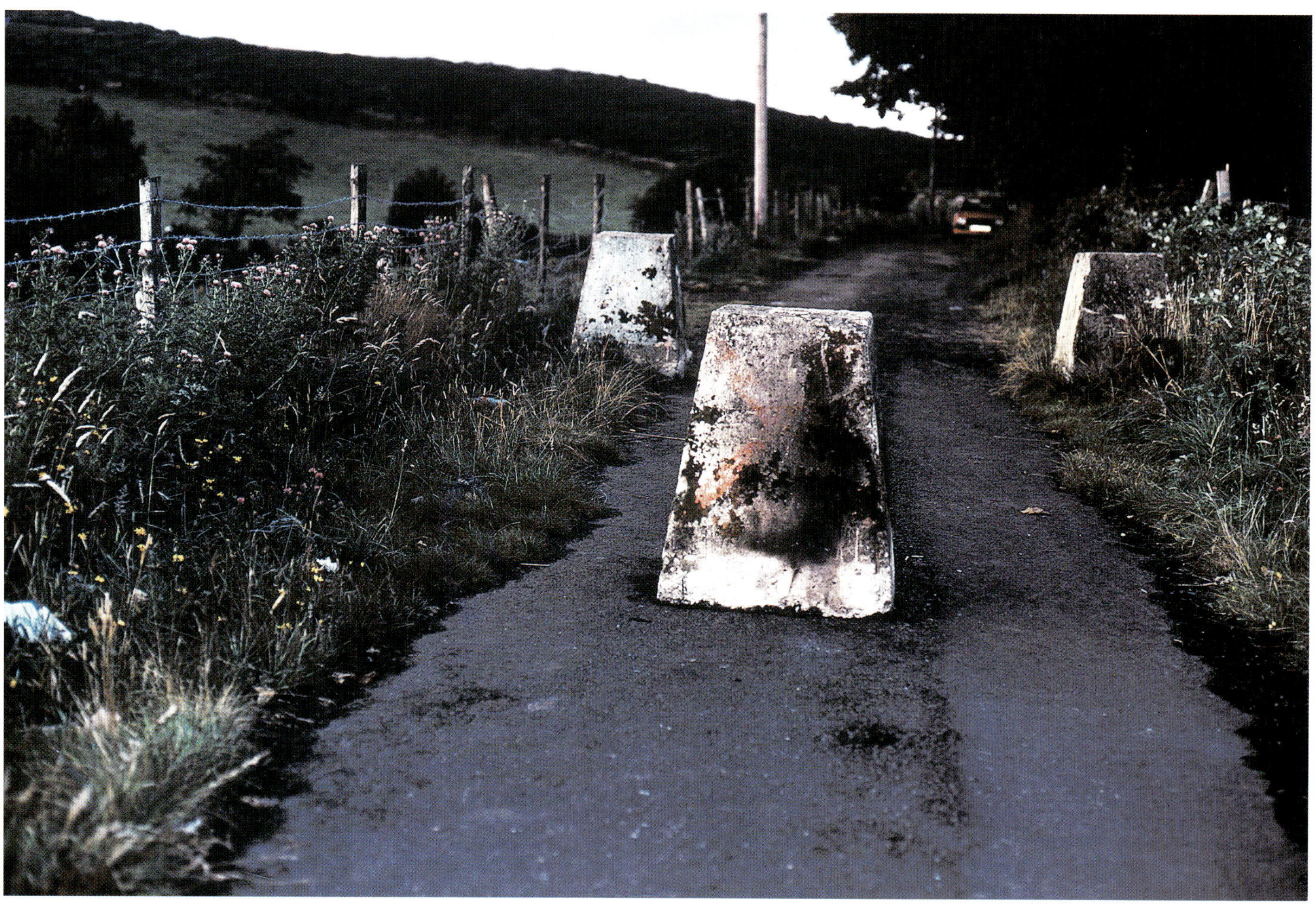

Photographs 1–9. 2000. Suite of nine chromogenic process prints, dimensions varied

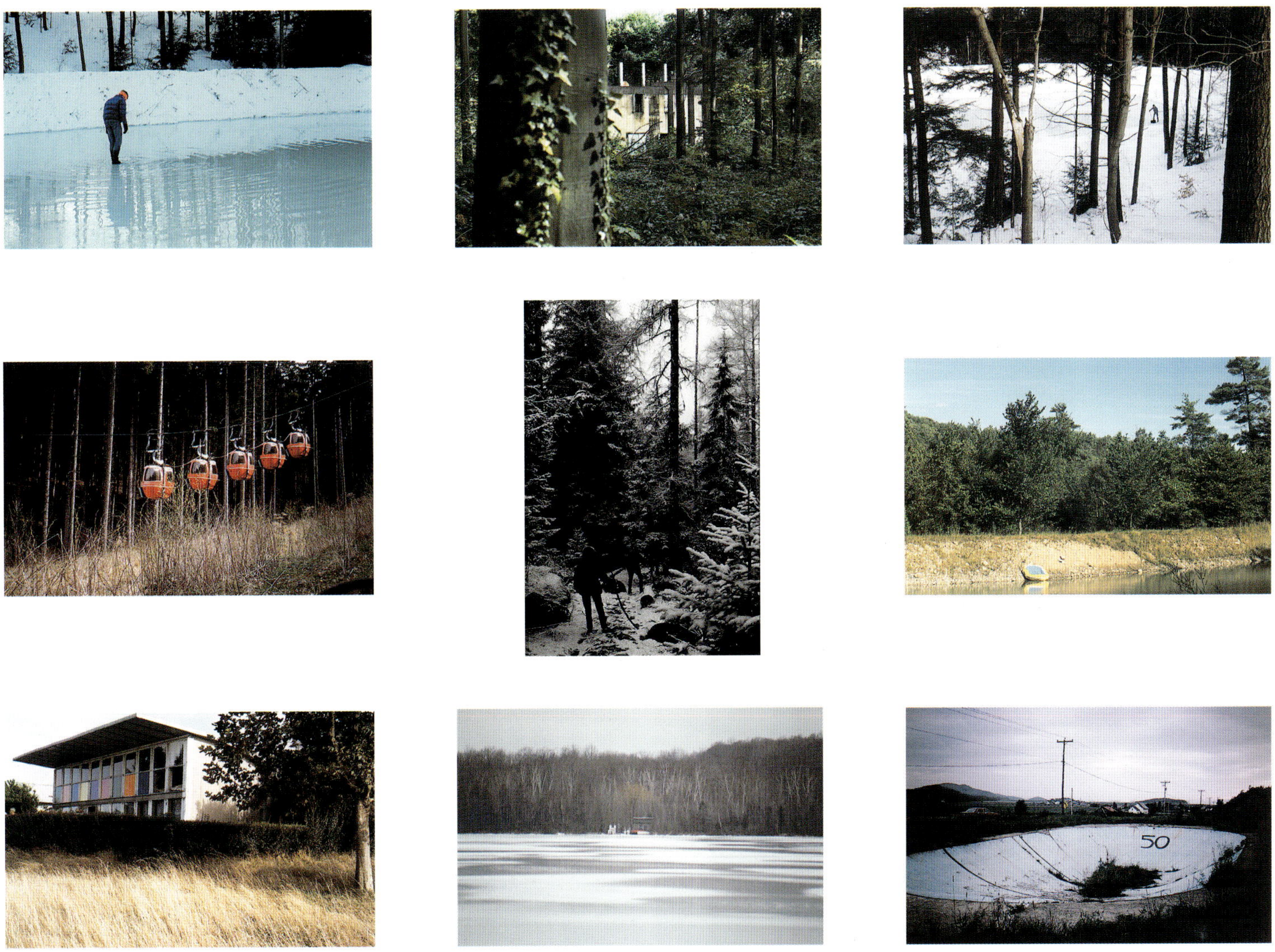

Michigan Theater. From the *Detroit* series, part I. 1997–98. From a suite of twenty-five chromogenic process prints, $17\frac{1}{2} \times 21\frac{1}{2}$ inches

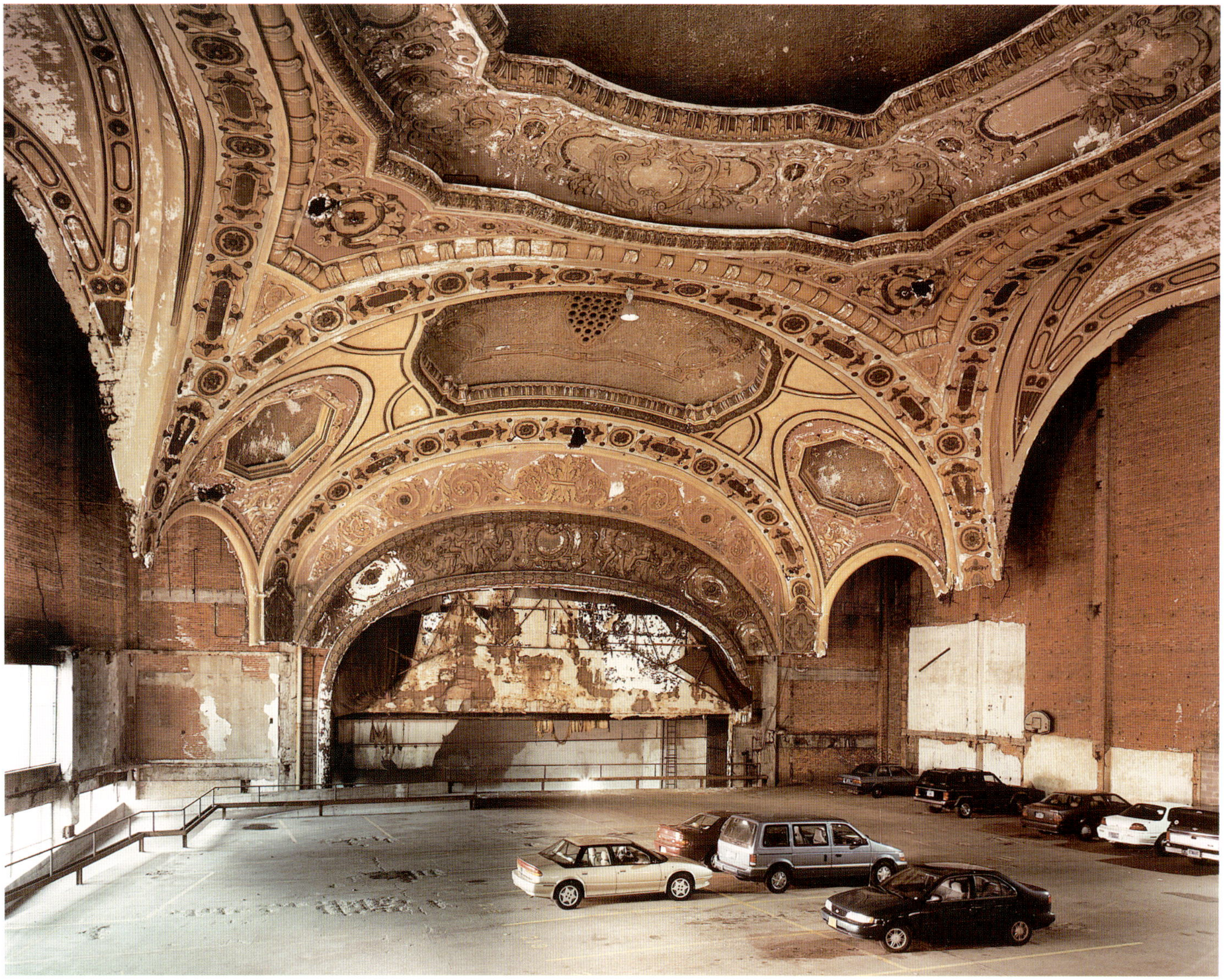

Moos Serie (Moss Series). 1999. Installation: sixteen chromogenic process prints, 32 × 56 inches

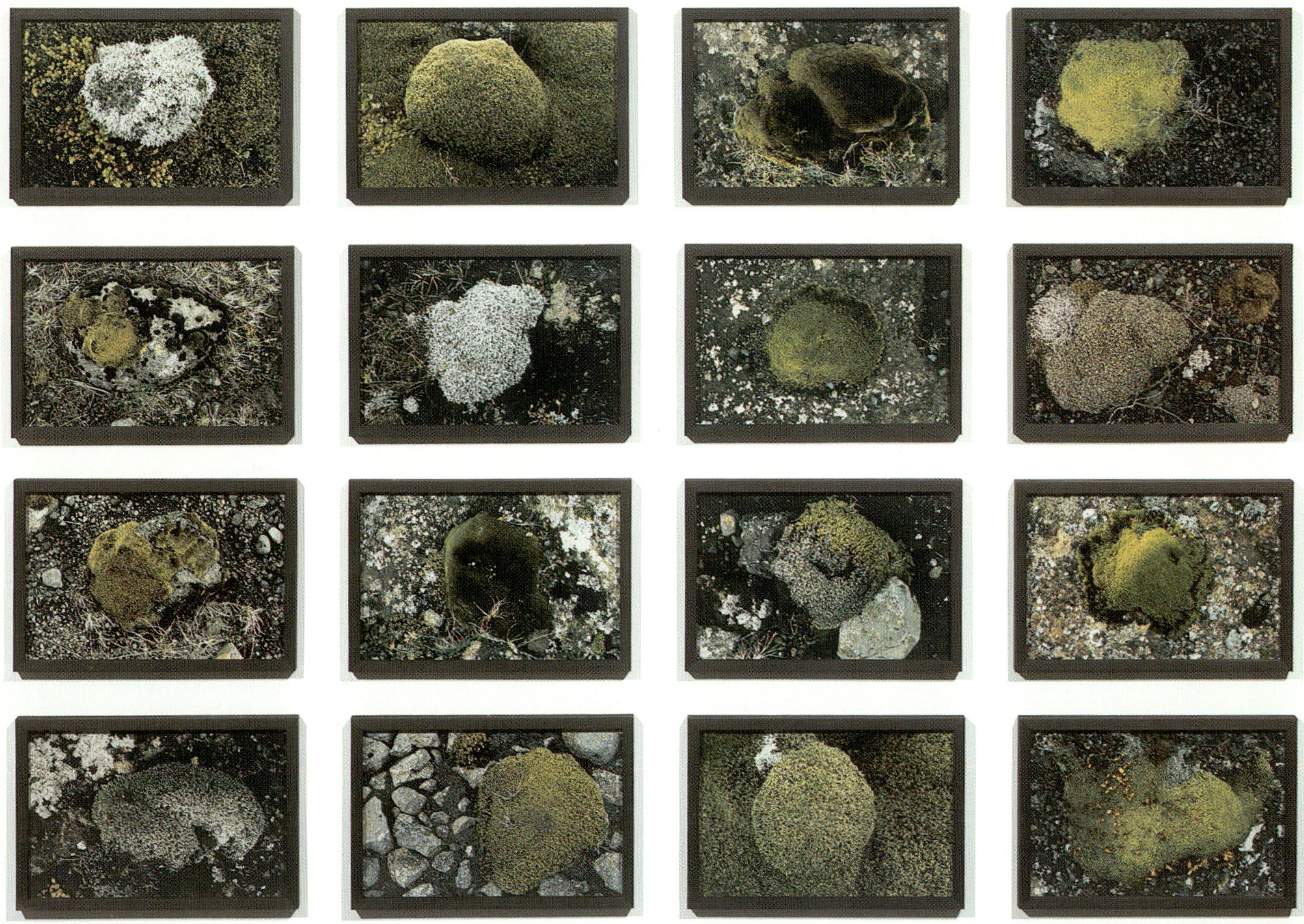

Untitled. 1988. Laminated chromogenic process print, $52^{3}/_{4} \times 62^{1}/_{2}$ inches

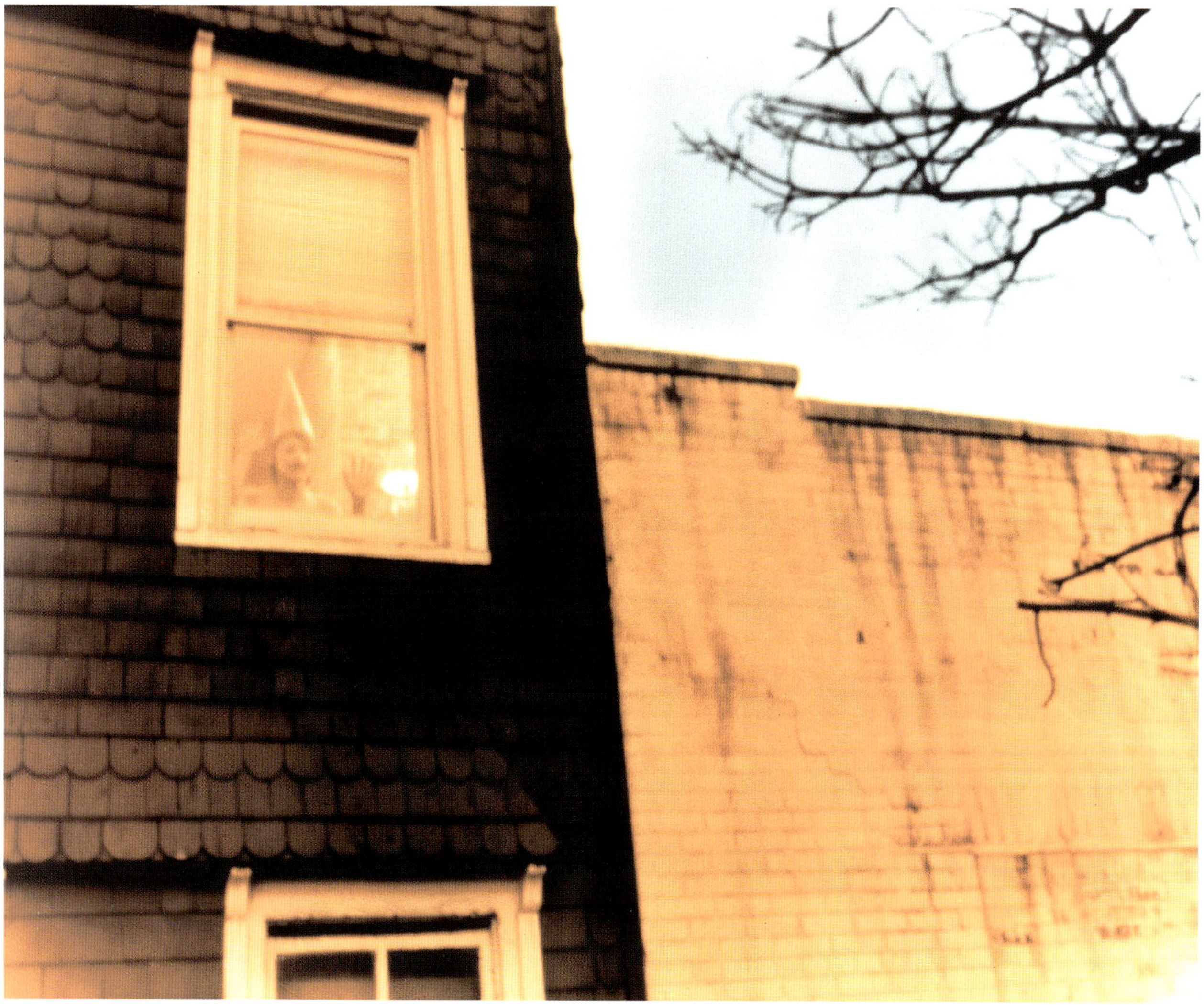

Macon, Frankreich 1996. 1996. Chromogenic process print, face mounted to plexiglass, 49 × 63⅝ inches

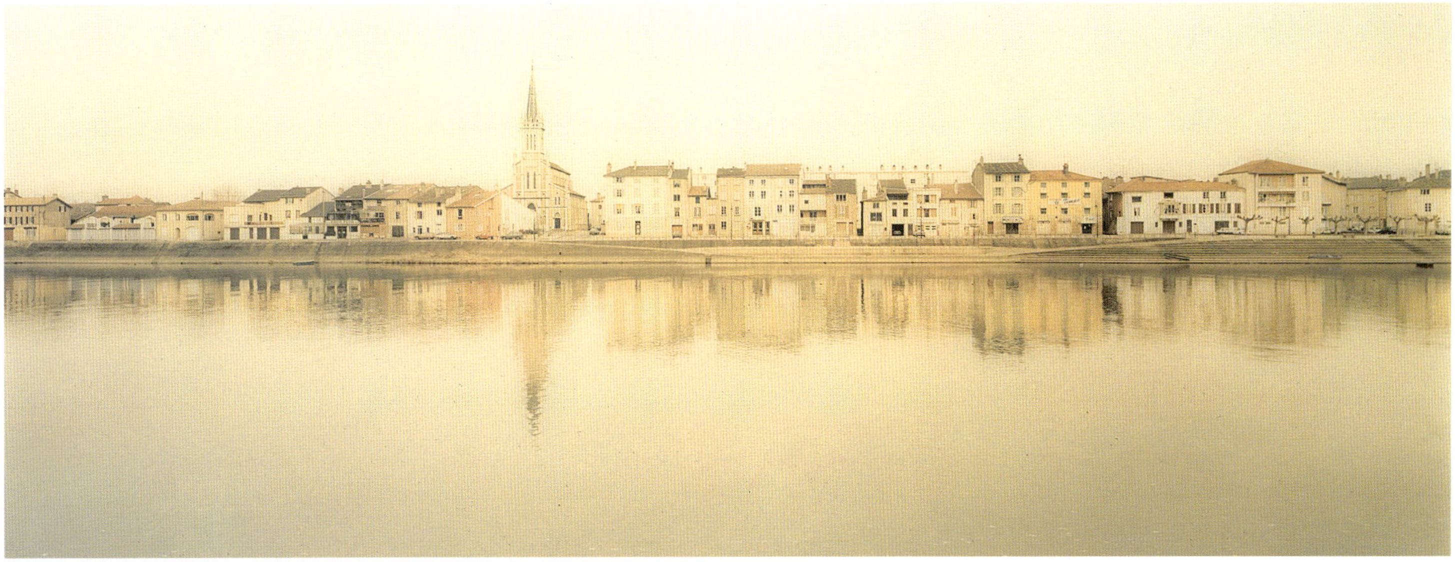

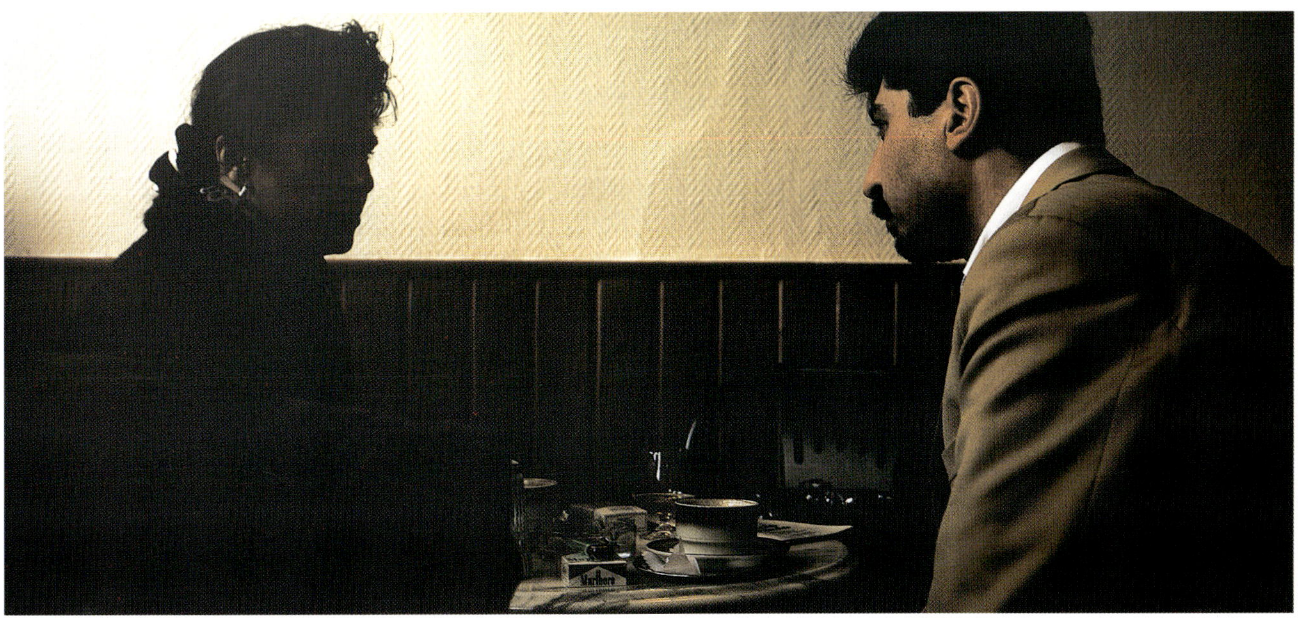

PATRICK FAIGENBAUM

Dans un café de Neuen Vahr, Bremen, 1996 (In a Café in Neuen Vahr, Bremen, 1996). 1996. Chromogenic process print, 37⅛ × 78¼ inches

ANGUS FAIRHURST

Standing Stock Still. 1998. Triptych: chromogenic process prints, 45½ × 31 inches each

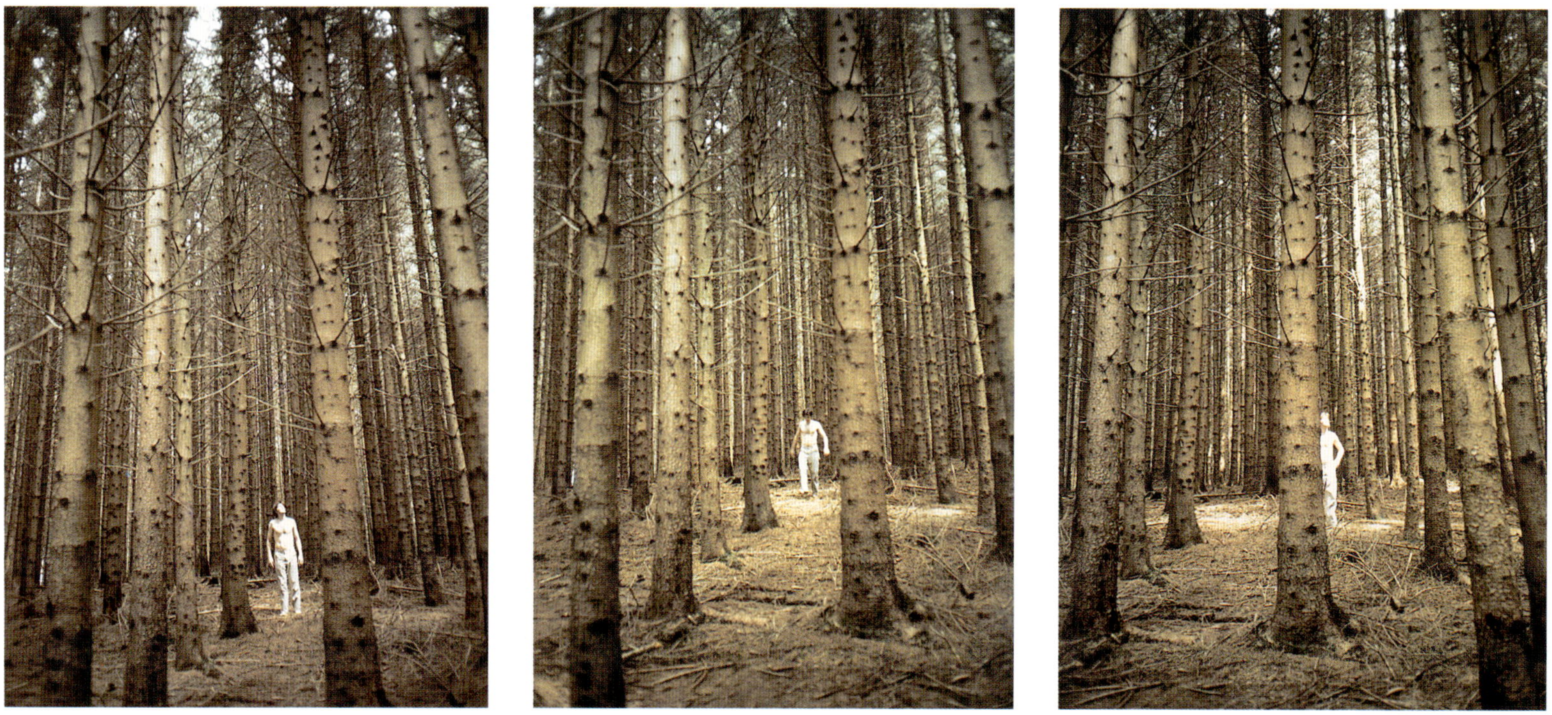

100 Years (details). 1998–2000. Six from a suite of 101 gelatin silver prints on "Baryth" paper, mounted to cardboard with paper labels, $16^{1}/_{4} \times 12^{1}/_{4}$ inches each

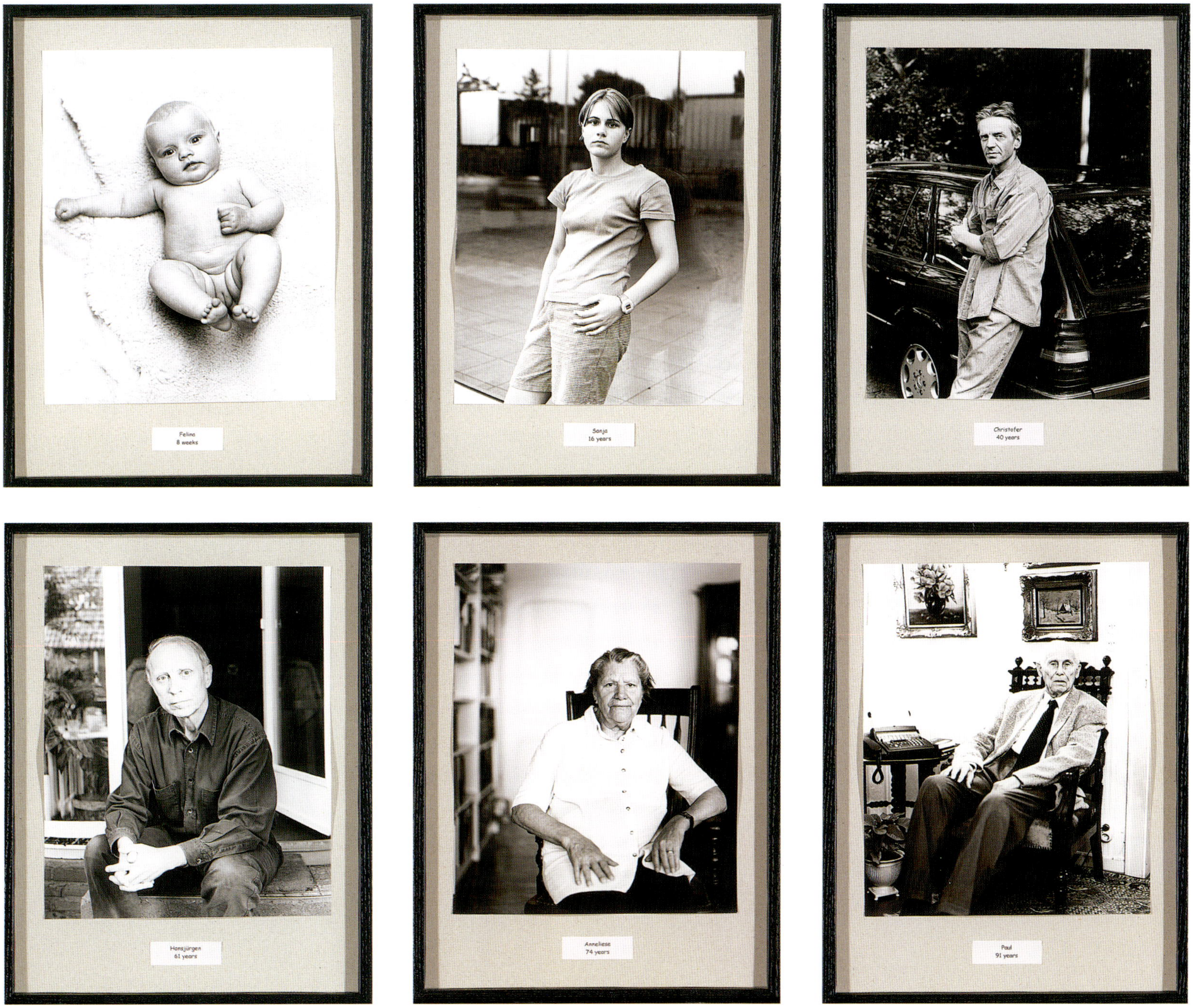

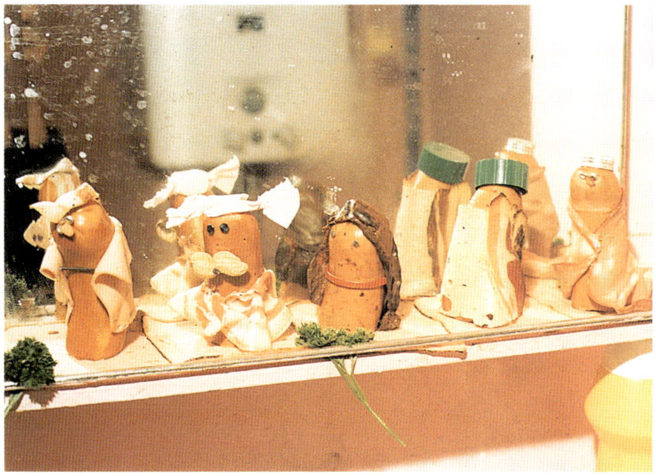
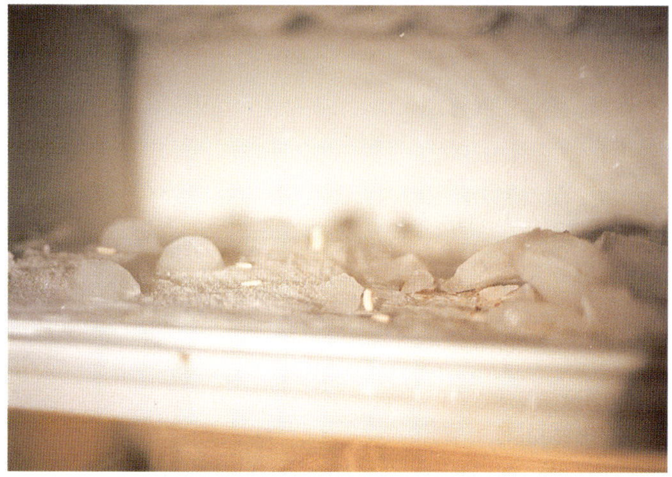
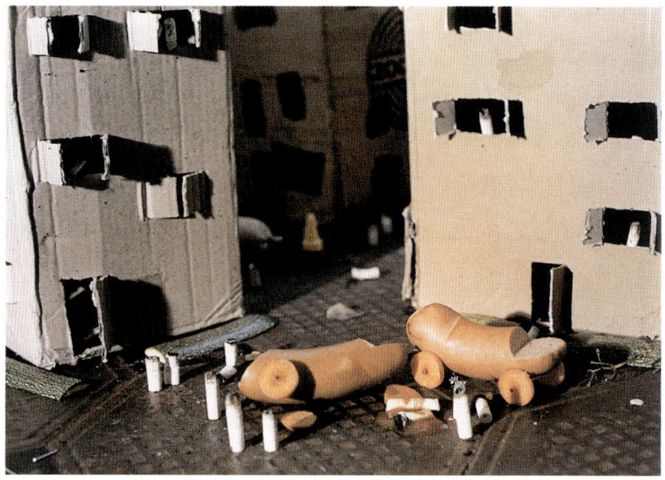
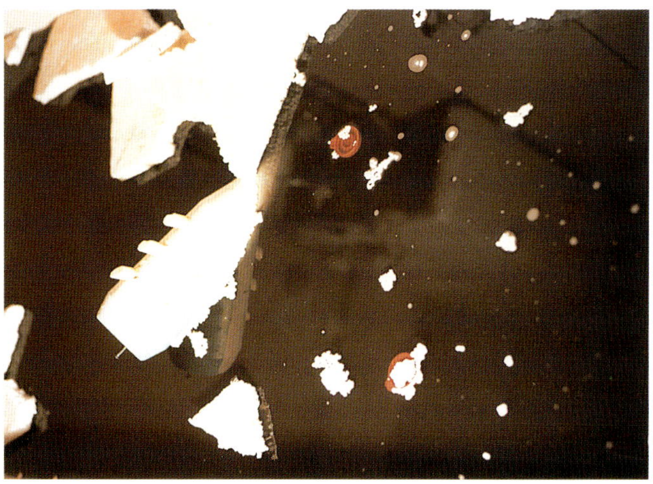
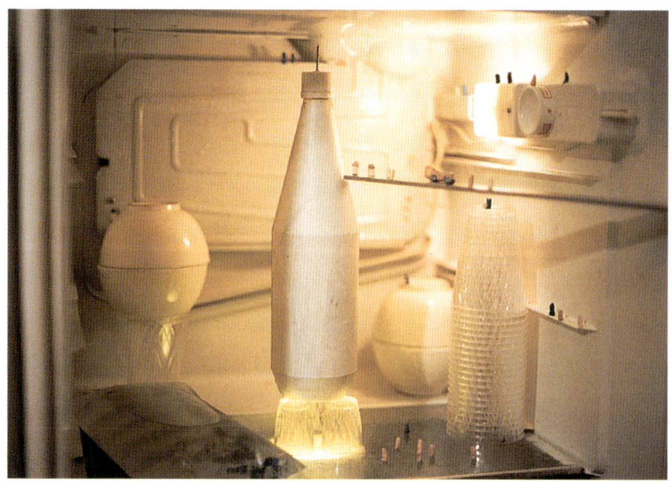

Untitled. From the *Wurstserie (Sausage Series).* 1979. Suite of ten chromogenic process prints, $9\frac{1}{2} \times 13$ inches each

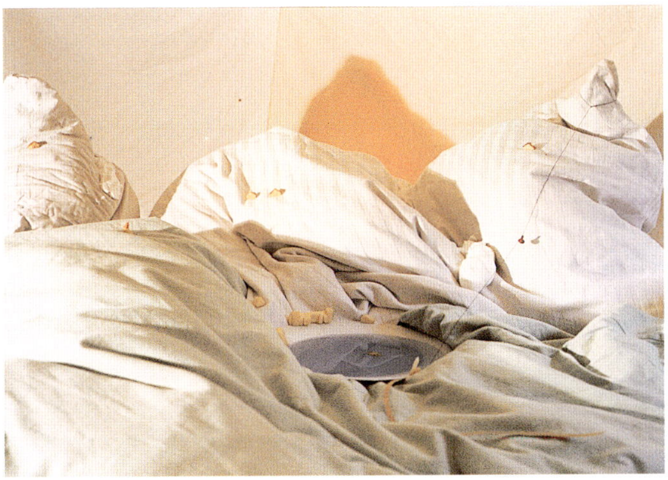

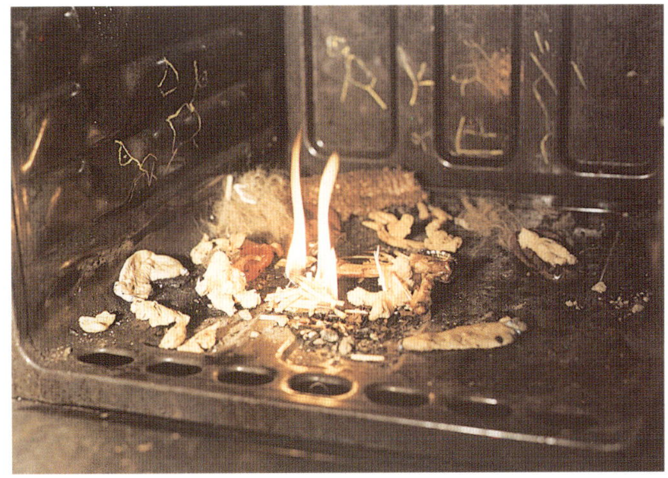

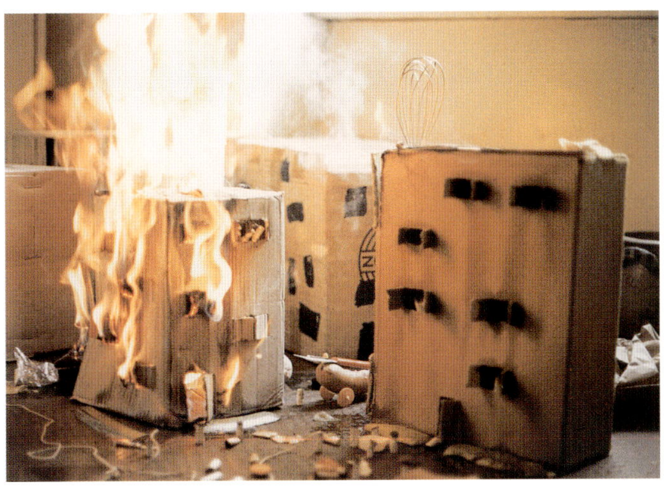

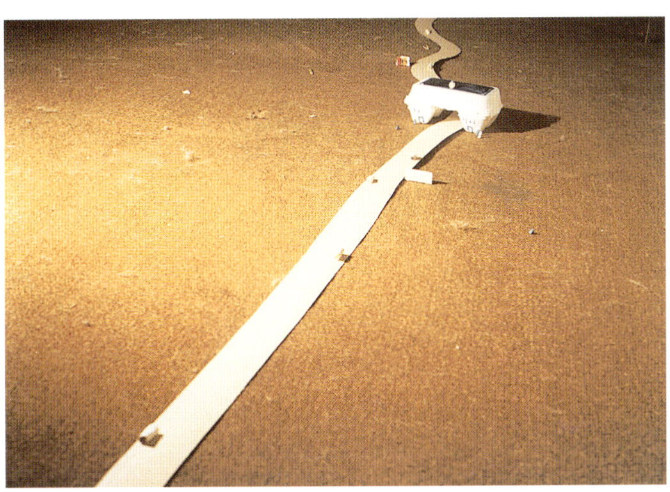

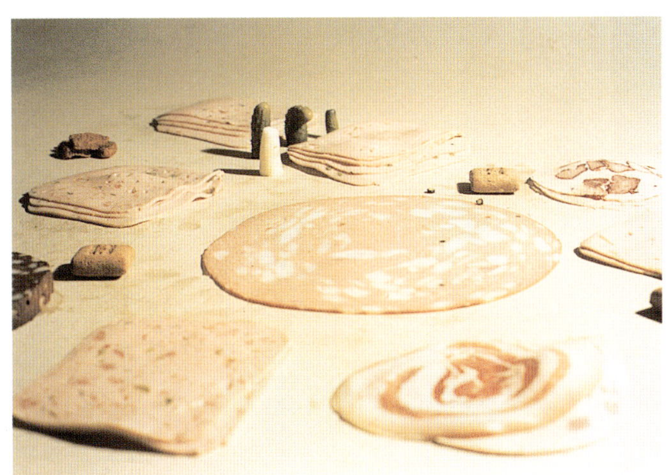

Barcelona Pavillion. 1988. Unique gelatin silver print, 9 feet $2^{7}/_{8}$ inches × $51^{5}/_{8}$ inches

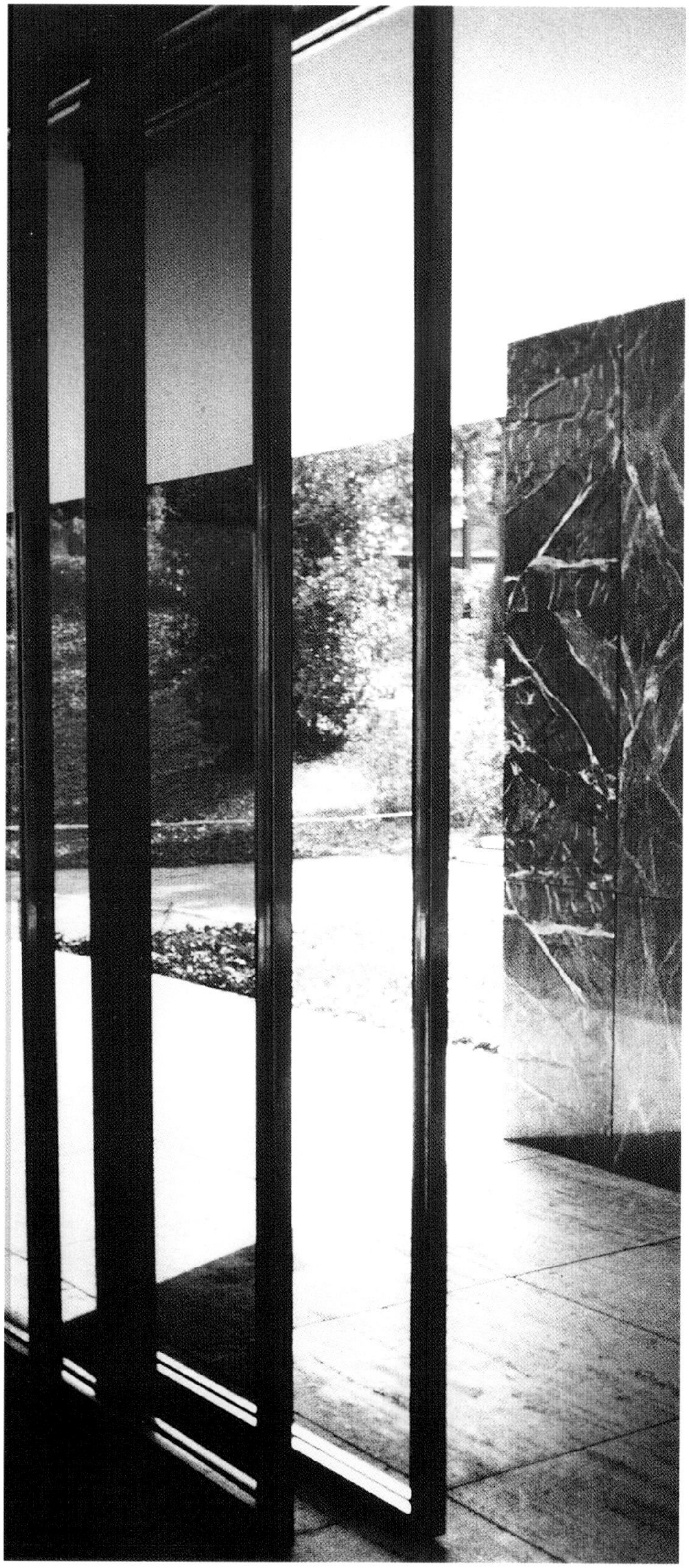

MICHEL FRANÇOIS

Untitled. 1991. Gelatin silver print, 16 × 11 inches

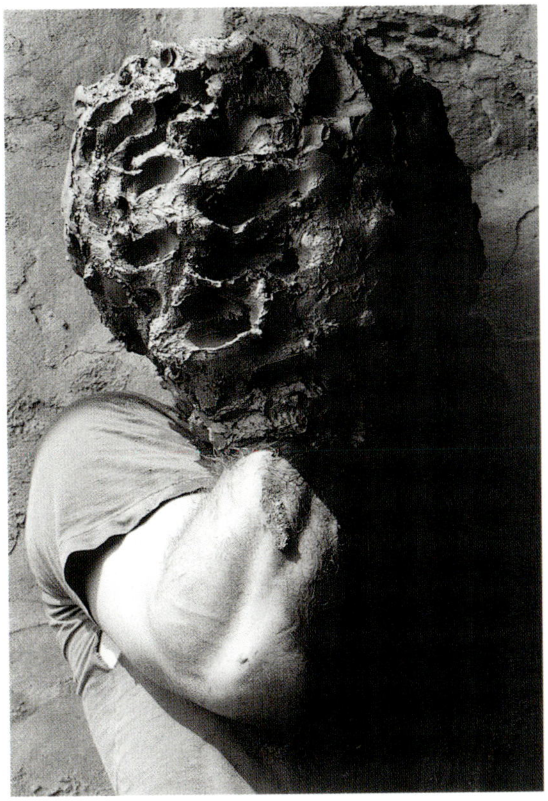

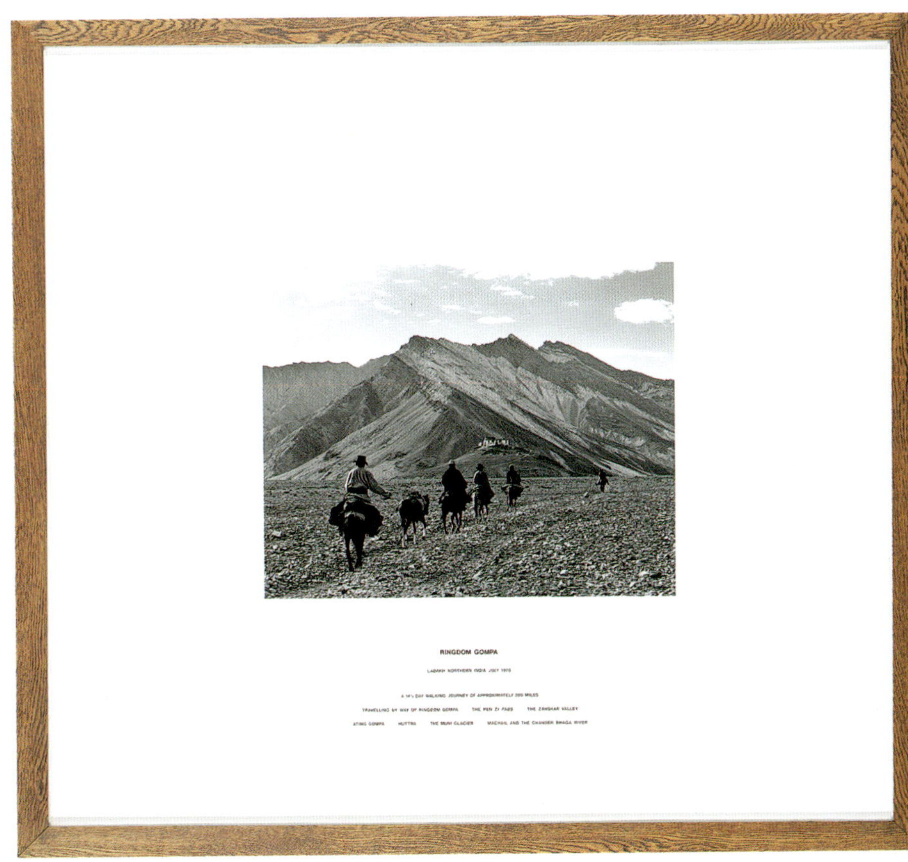

HAMISH FULTON

Ringdom Gompa Ladakh Northern India July 1978. 1978.
Gelatin silver print with text in artist's frame, 47 × 50½ inches

ADAM FUSS

Untitled. 1994. Unique silver dye bleach photogram, 43 × 33 inches

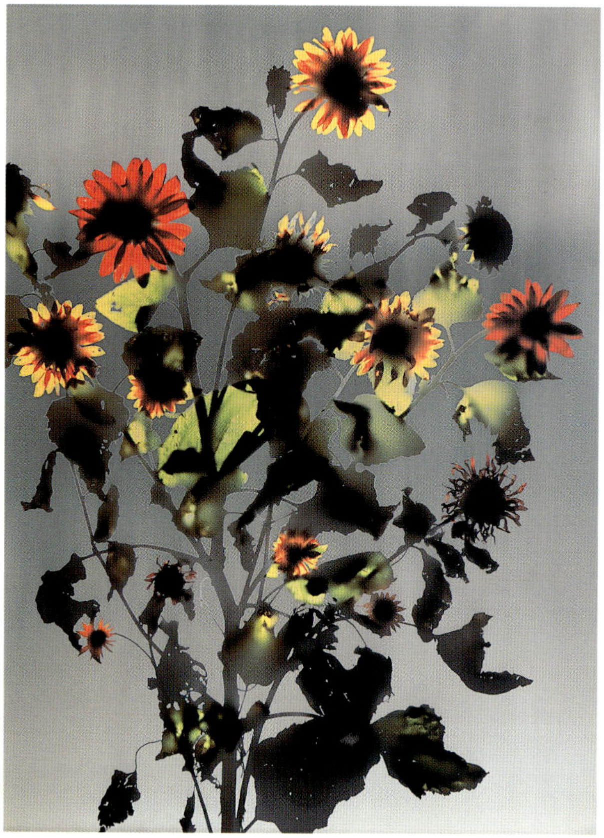

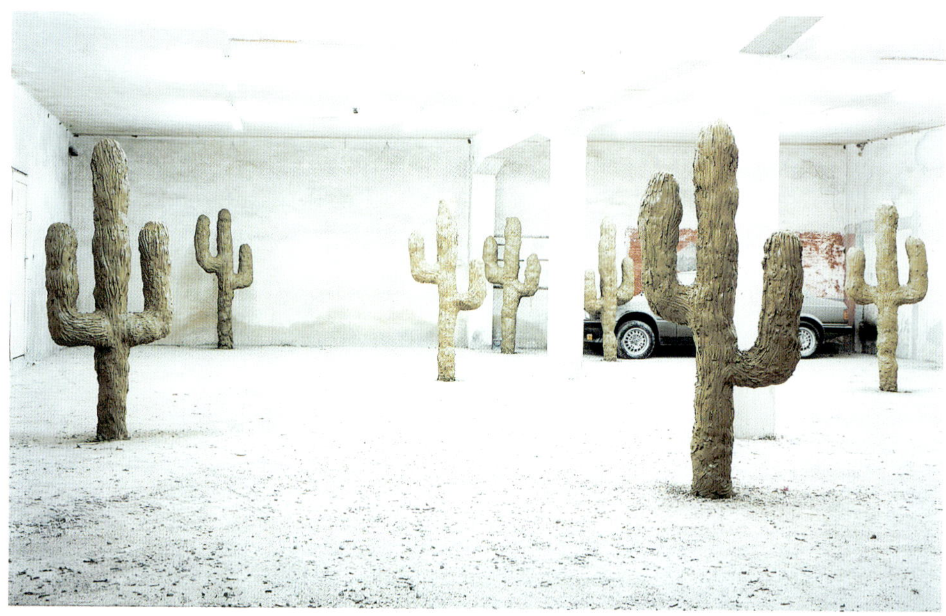

GIUSEPPE GABELLONE

Untitled. 1996. Chromogenic process print, 49 × 73 1/4 inches

About the Grandfather Clock and the Time that...(1). 1995.
Silver dye bleach process print, 19 × 18¾ inches

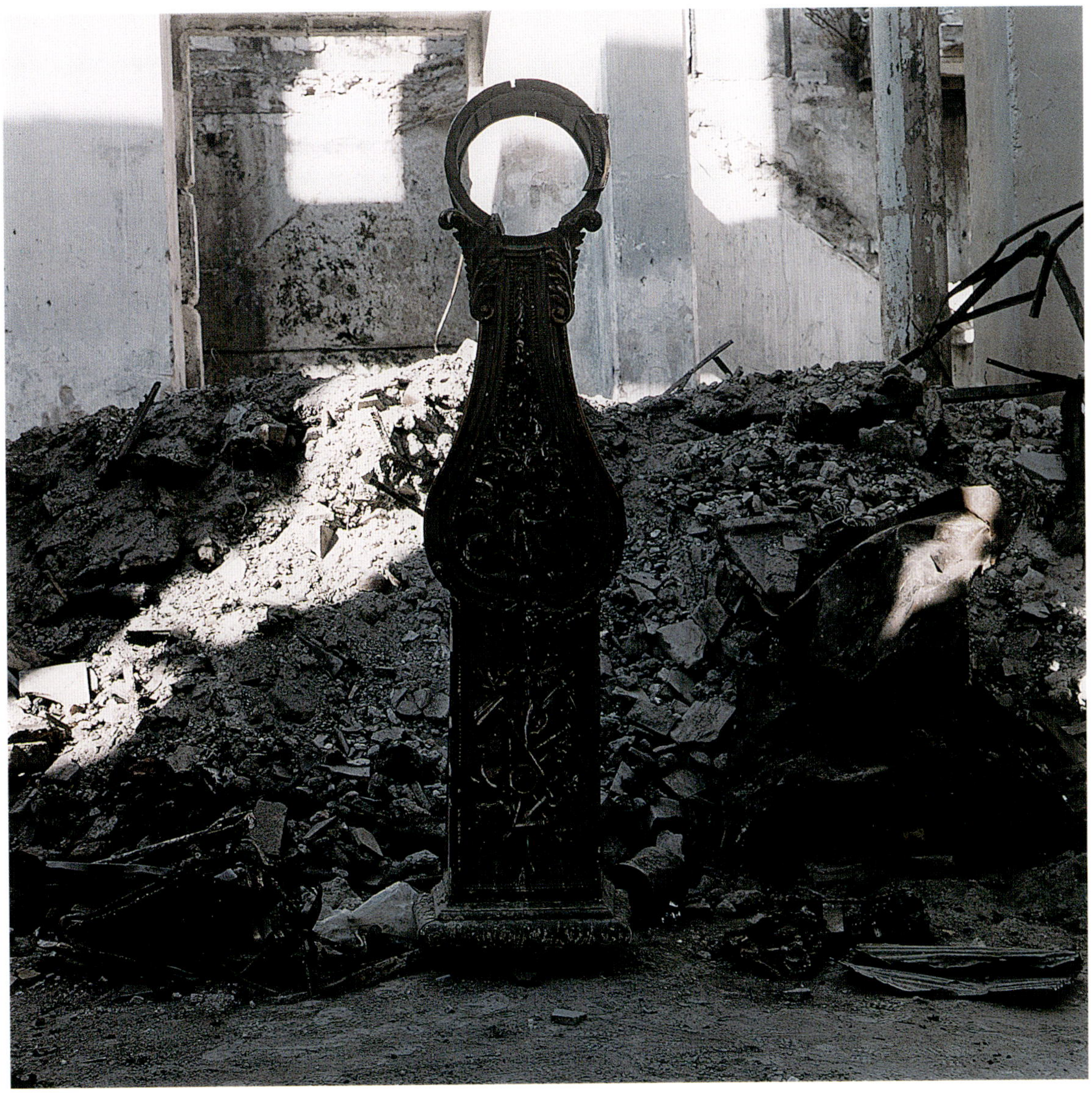

Beat Him When He Sneezes. 1996. Chromogenic process print, face mounted to plexiglass, $50^{1/8} \times 40$ inches

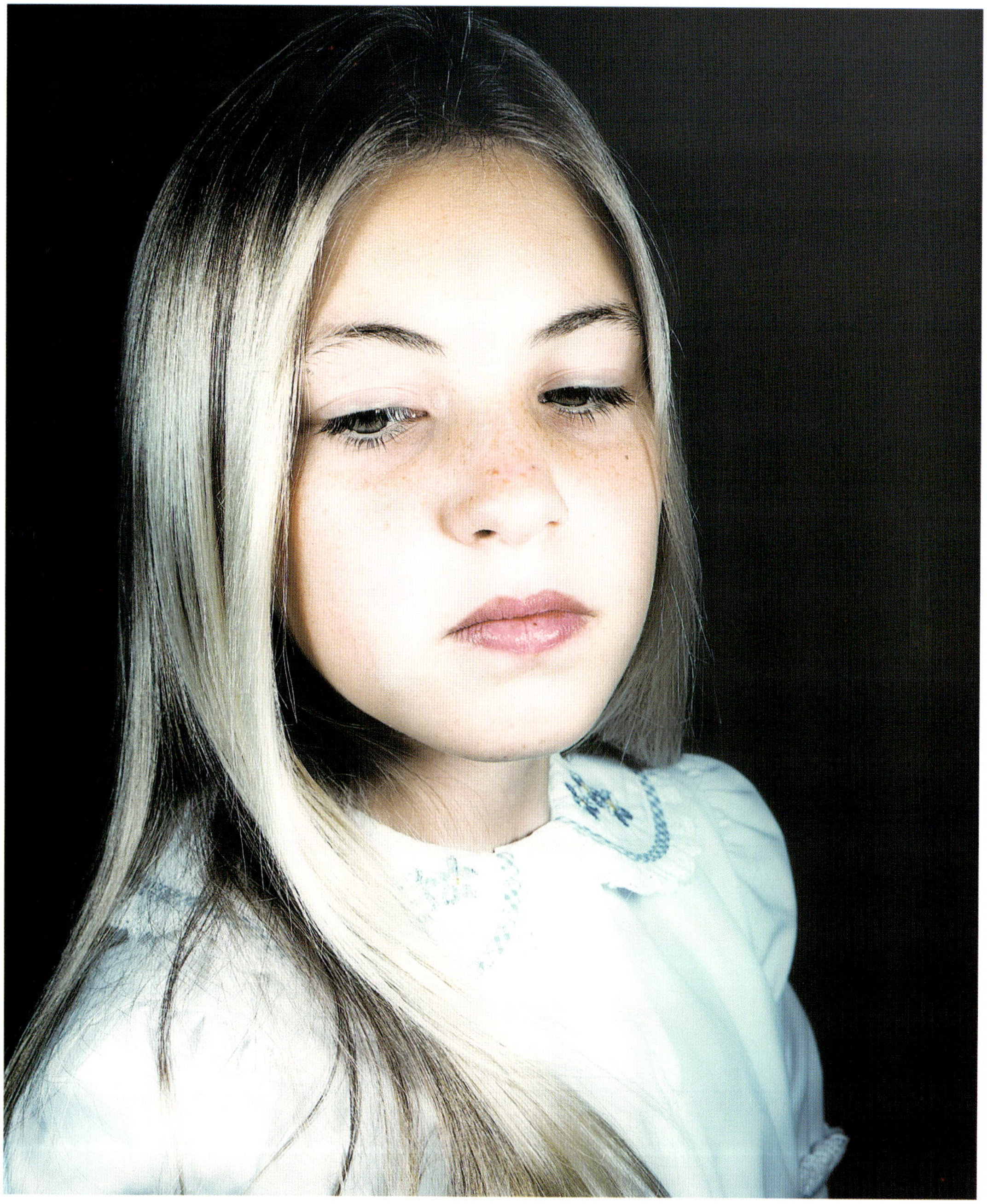

Night View. 1978. Photopiece: nine hand-colored gelatin silver prints in the artists' frames, $59\frac{1}{2} \times 47\frac{7}{8}$ inches

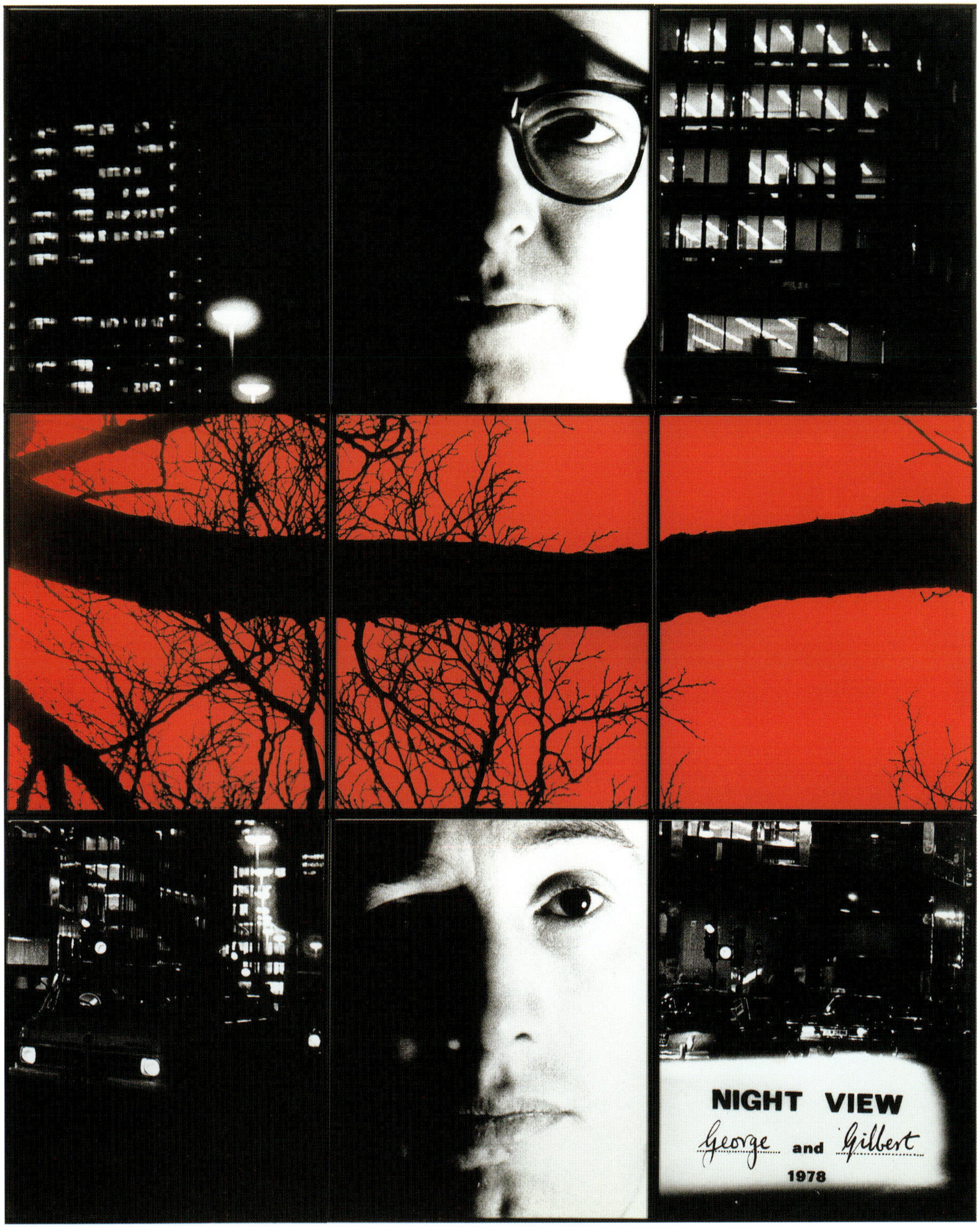

C.Z. and Max on the Beach, Truro, Ma. 1976. 1976. Silver dye bleach process print in artist's frame, $40^{7}/_{8} \times 28^{1}/_{4}$ inches

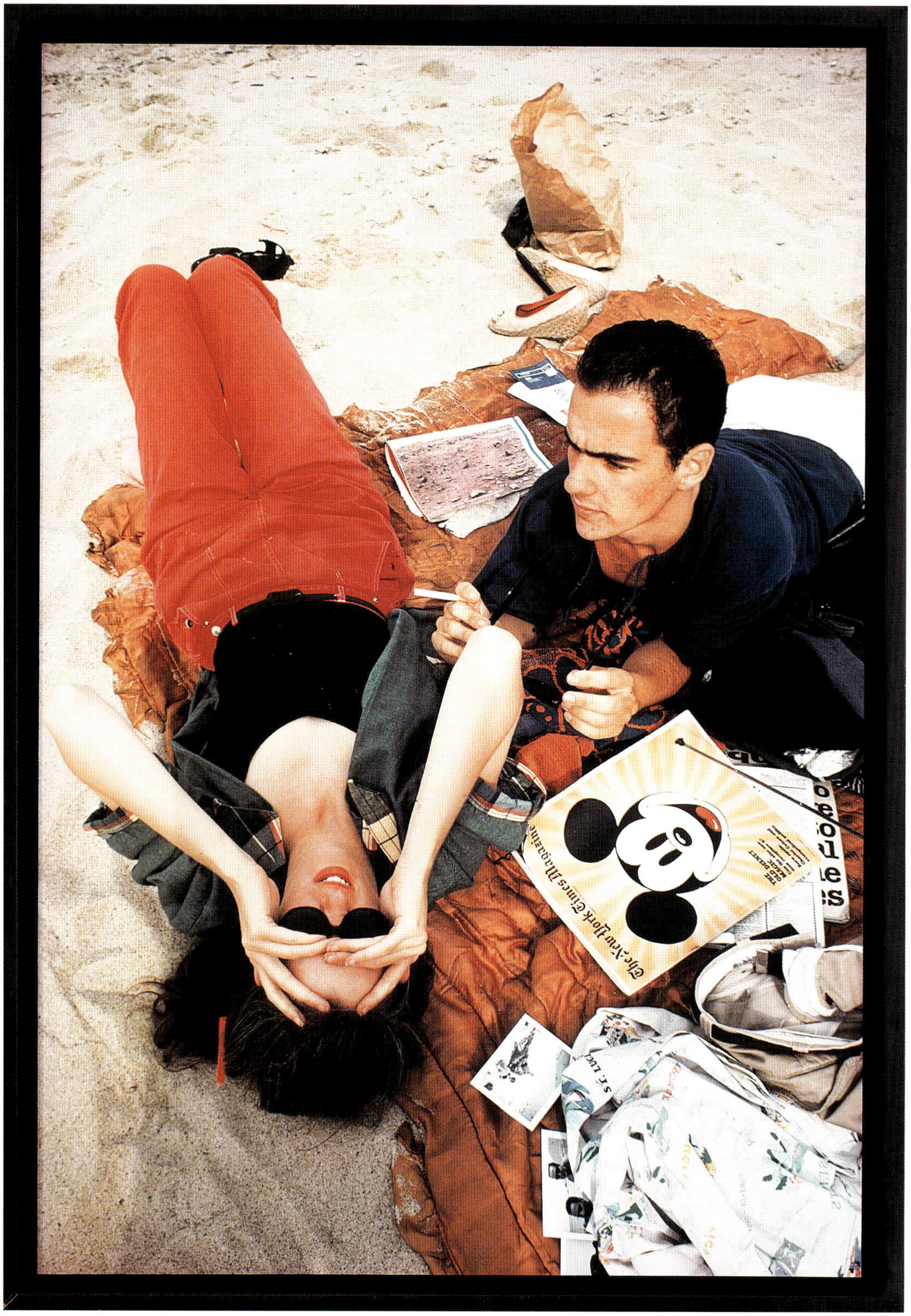

Untitled (Wall Street). 1996. Chromogenic process print, 37 × 29½ inches

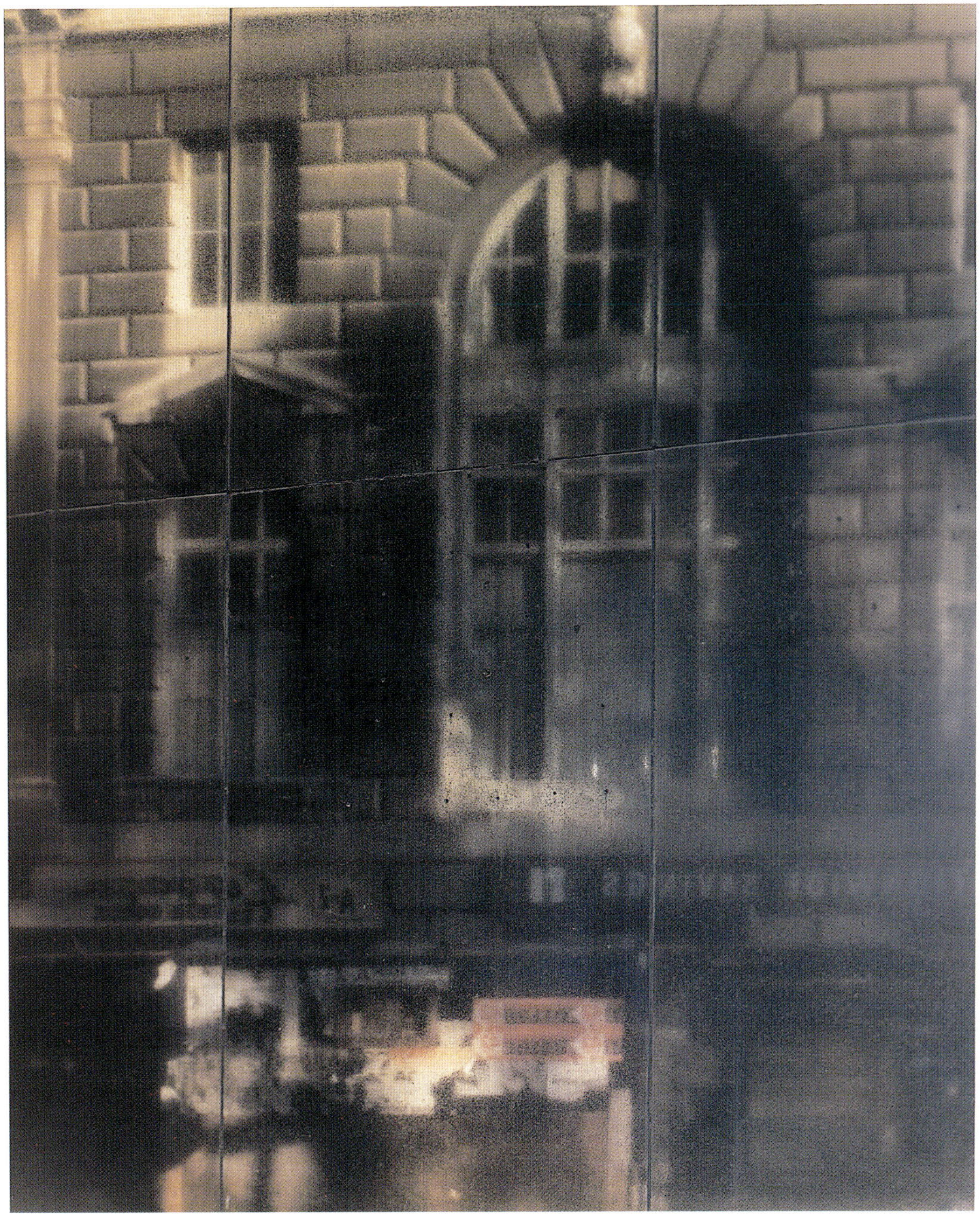

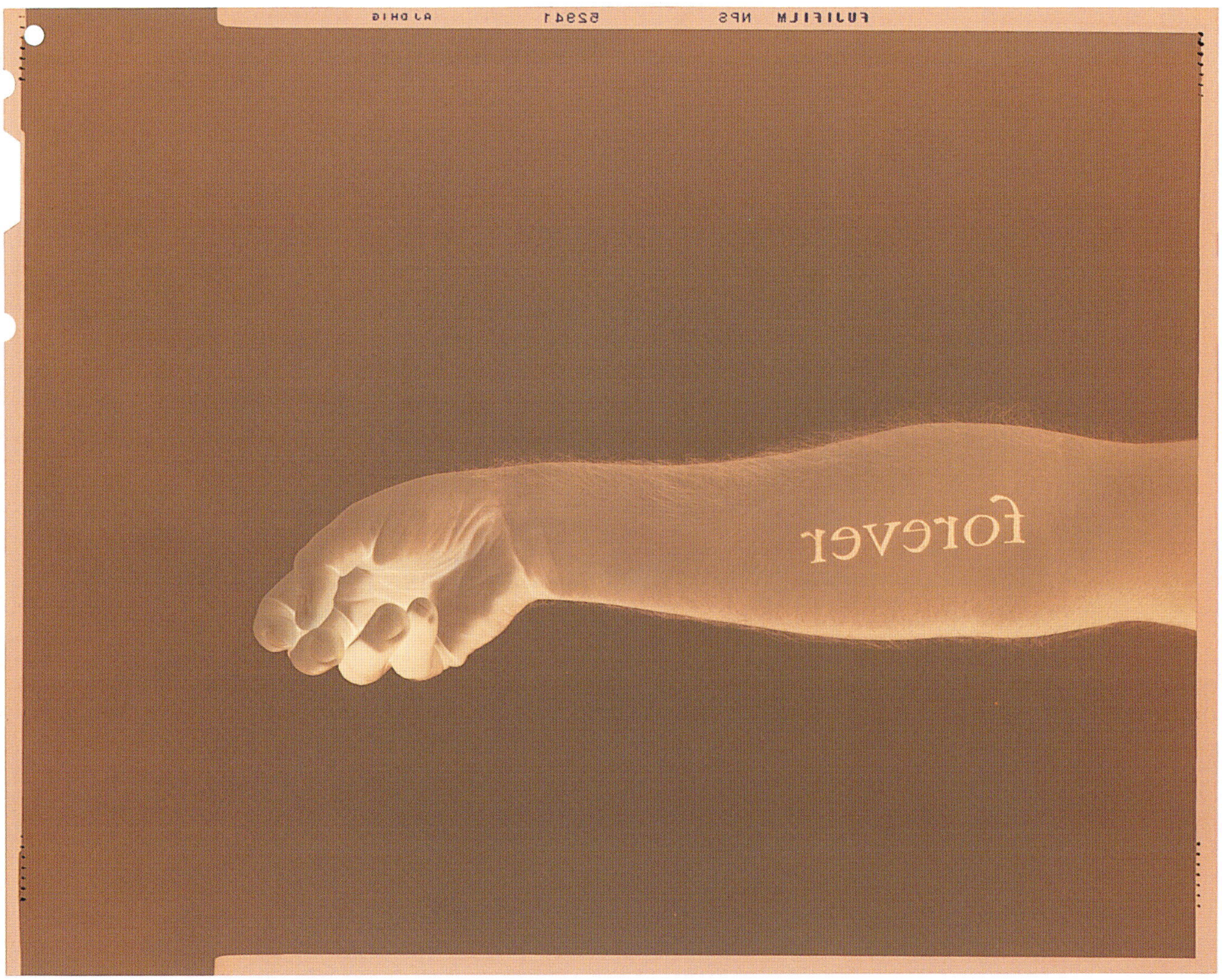
forever

Left to right:

Never Never (Black Negative Mirrored). 2000

Never Never (White Negative Mirrored). 2000

Digital chromogenic process prints, 25 × 30⅞ inches each

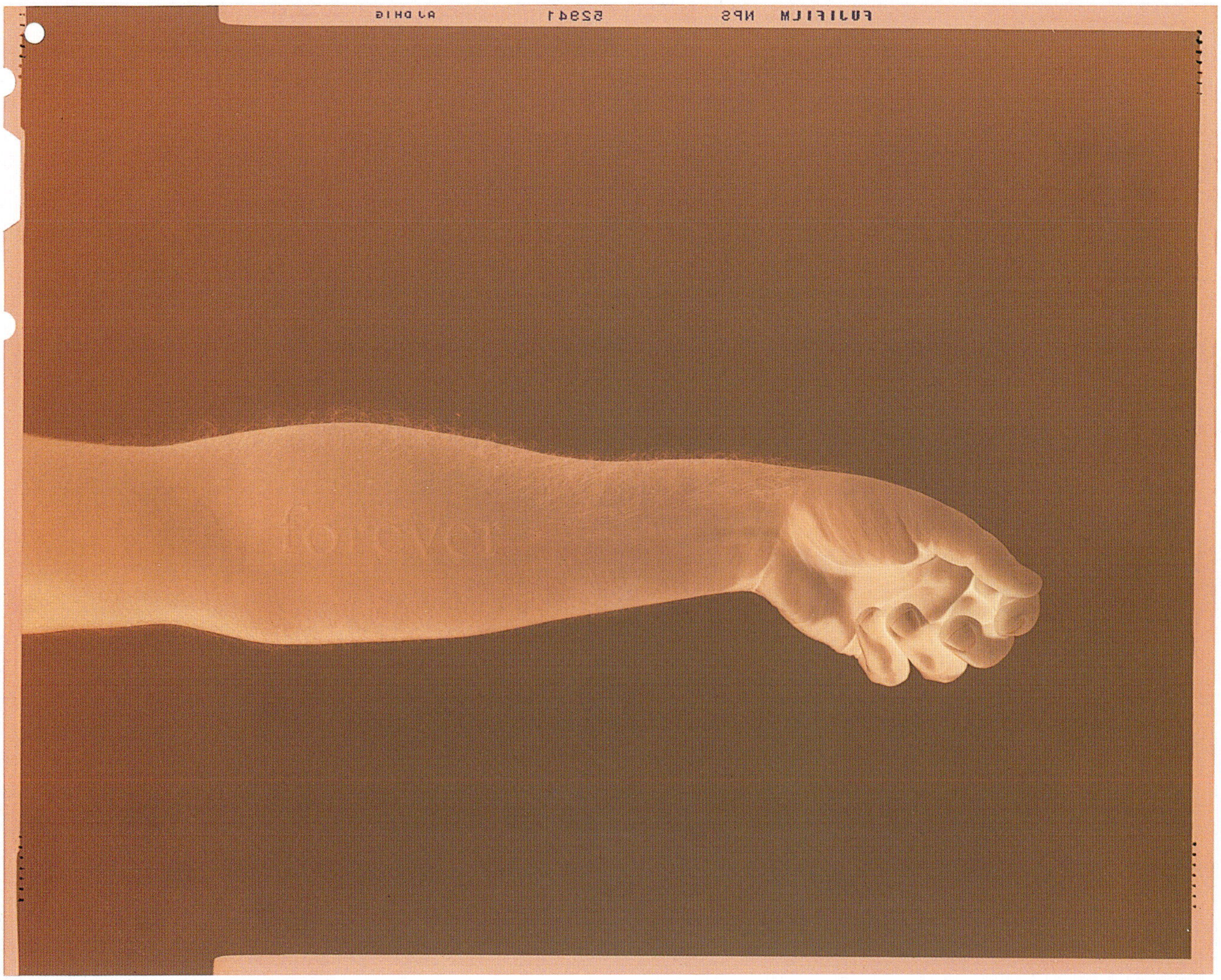

GIANFRANCO GORGONI

Robert Smithson's Spiral Jetty. 1971. Suite of nine gelatin silver prints, $41\frac{1}{2} \times 62$ inches each

98

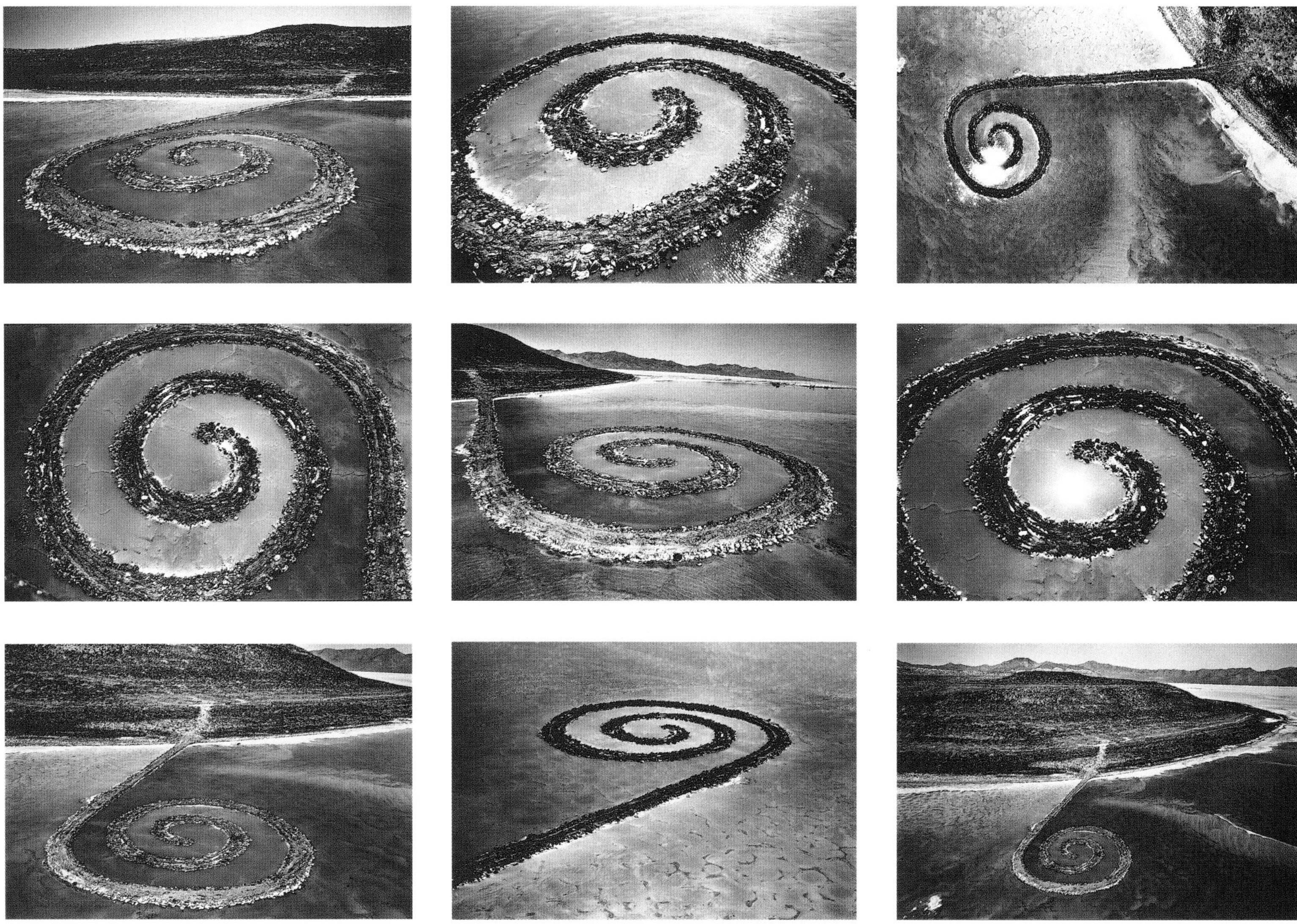

Court Steps, New York City 1966 (top). *Side Facade of Suburban House, Westfield, New Jersey 1965* (bottom). 1965–66.
Two chromogenic process prints mounted on paper, 35 × 25⅝ inches

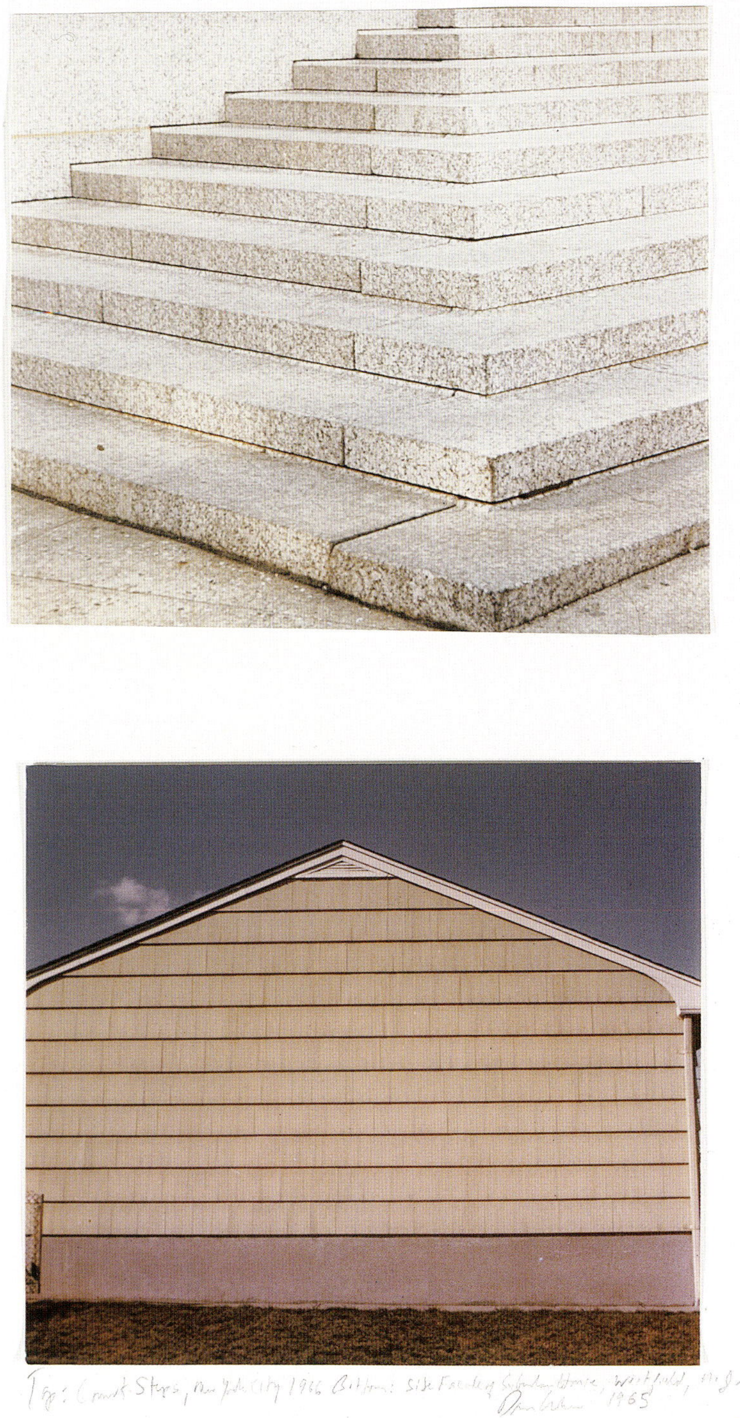

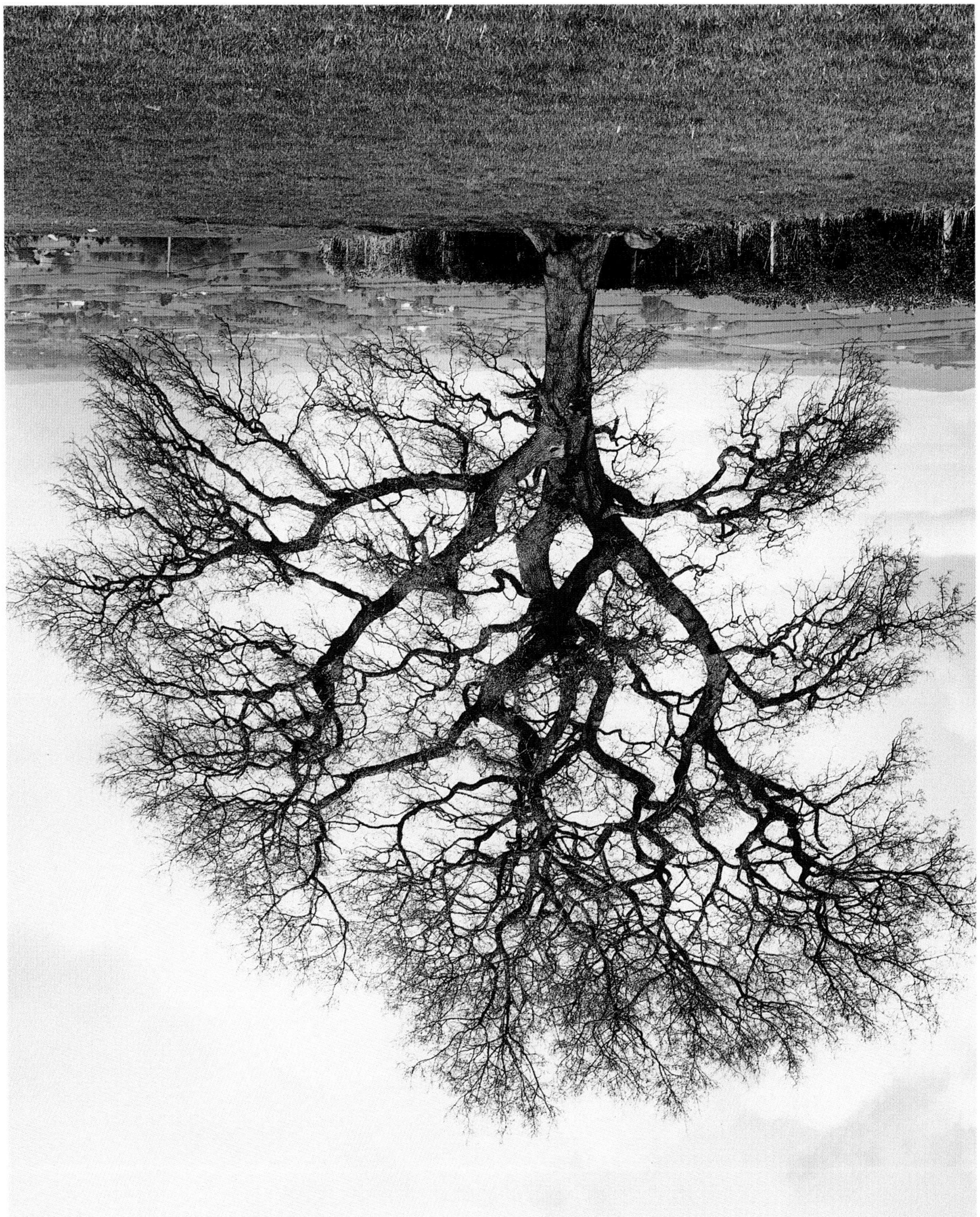

Welsh Oaks #6. 1998. Gelatin silver print, $49\frac{1}{2} \times 37\frac{5}{8}$ inches

Untitled. 1990. Chromogenic process print, $27\frac{1}{4} \times 35\frac{1}{4}$ inches

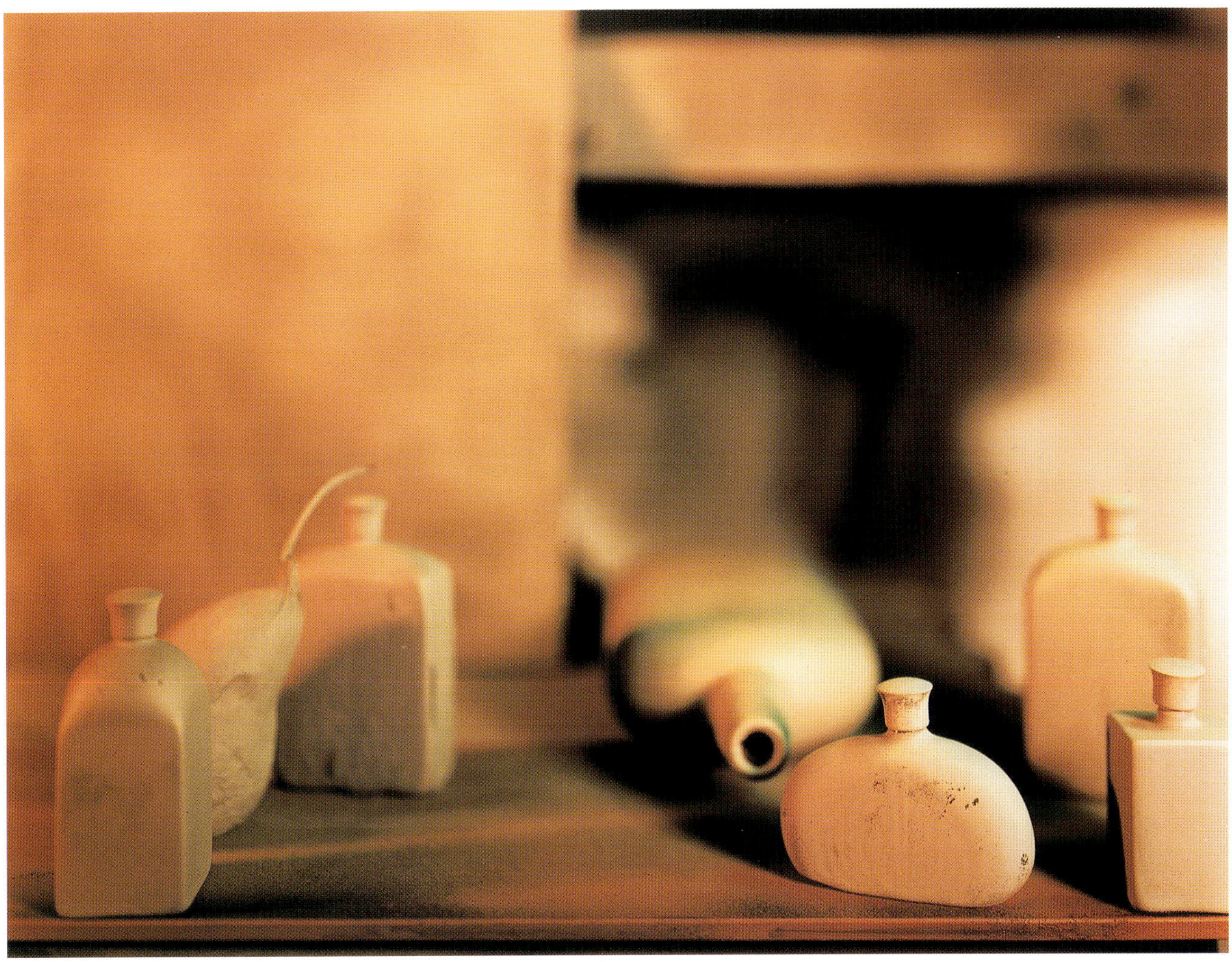

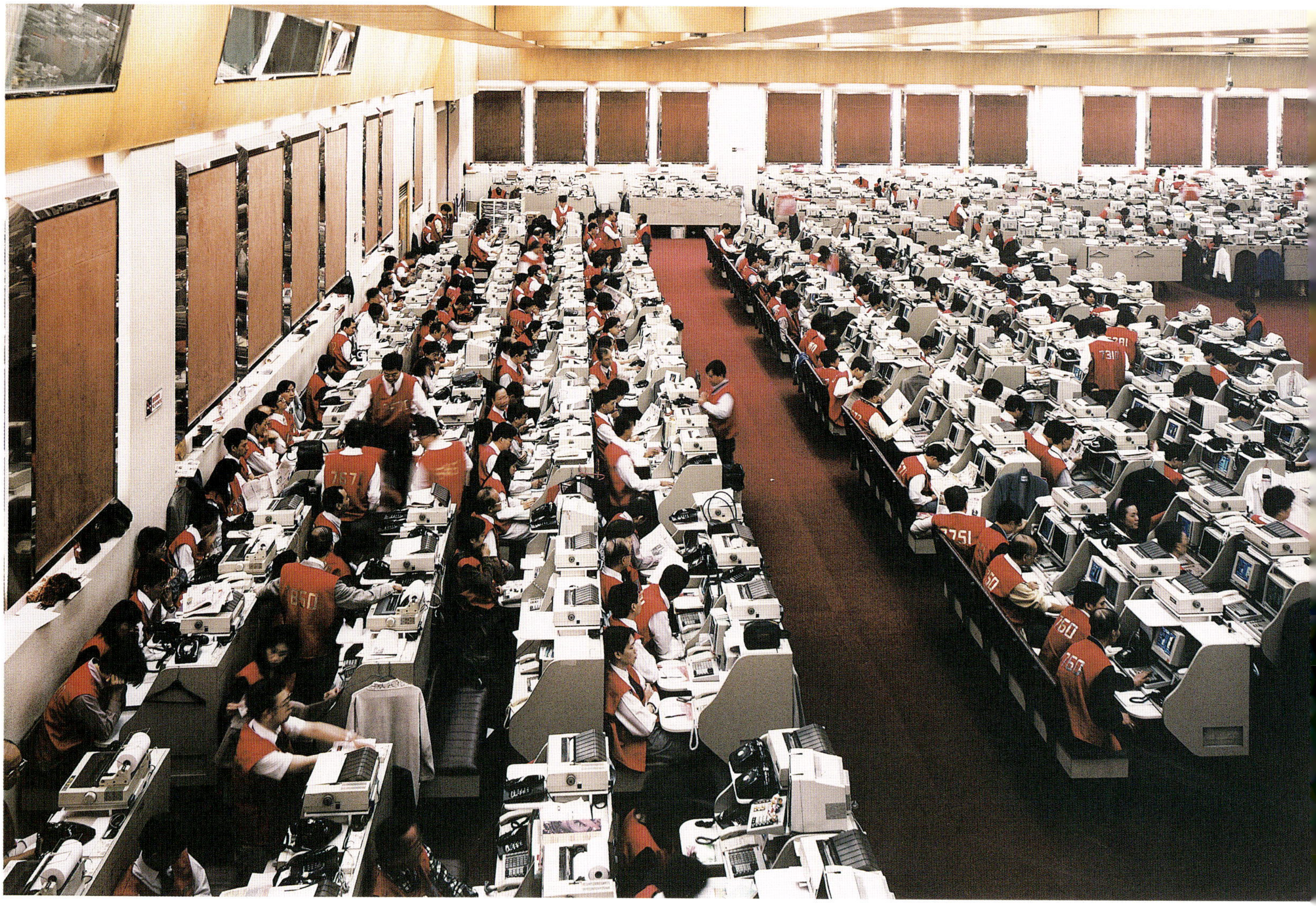

Börse, Hong Kong (Hong Kong Stock Exchange). 1994.
Diptych: chromogenic process prints, $65\frac{1}{8} \times 88\frac{3}{4}$ inches each

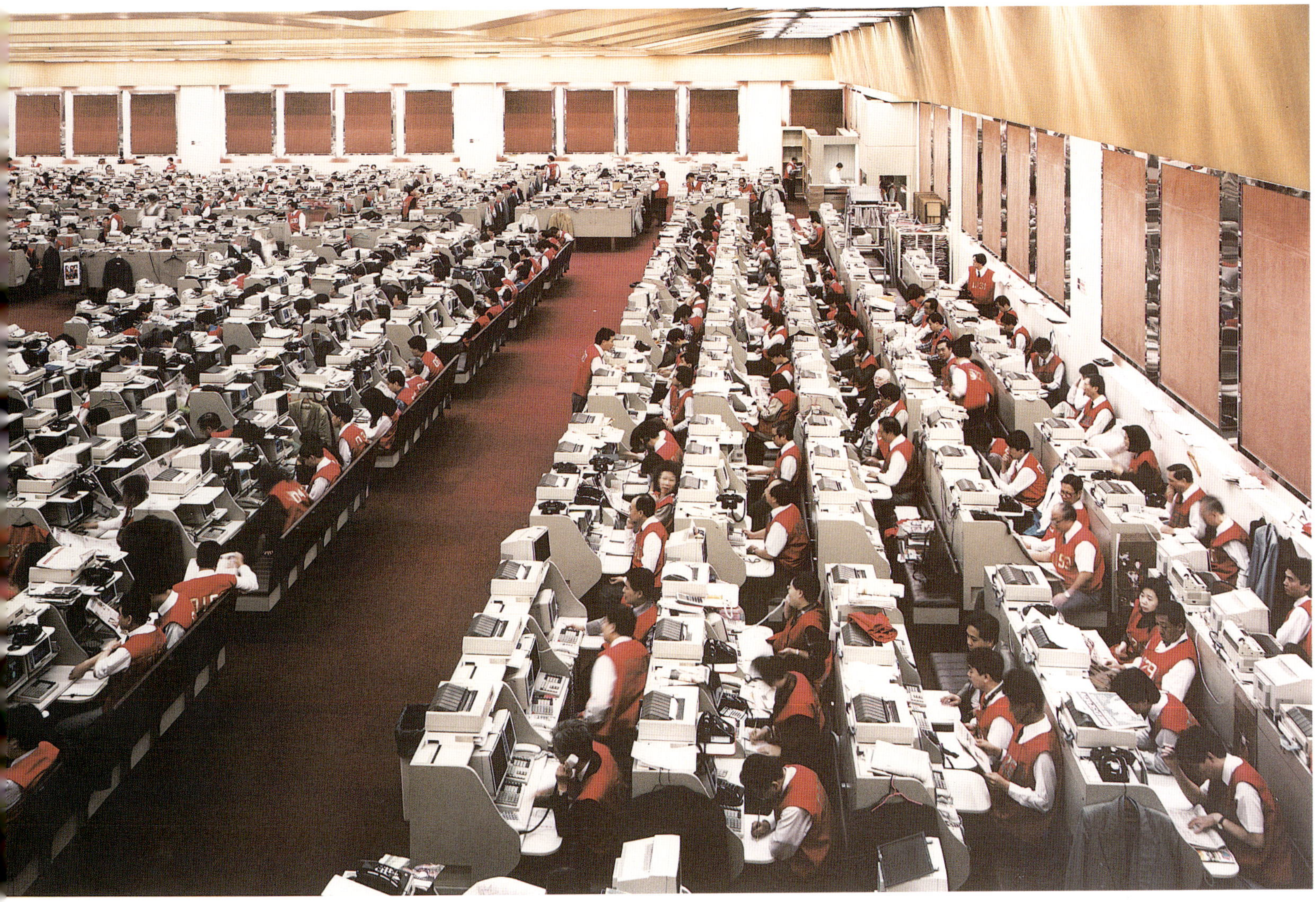

DOUG HALL

Vatican Library, Main Reading Room. 1997.
Chromogenic process print, $49\frac{3}{4} \times 62\frac{3}{4}$ inches

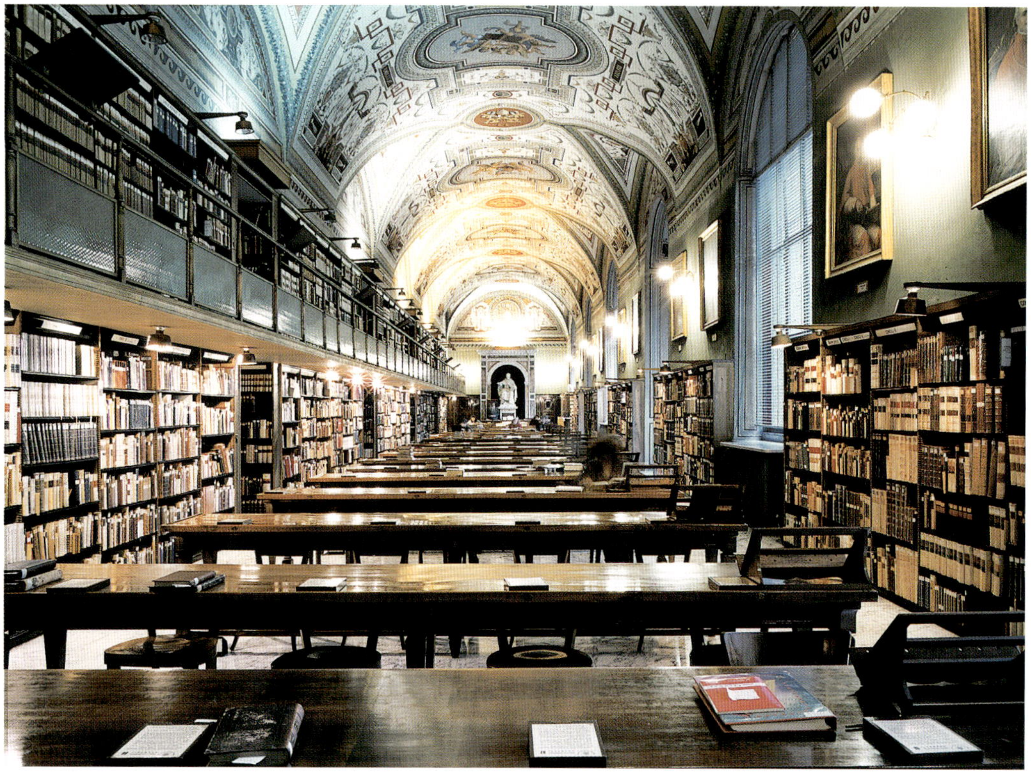

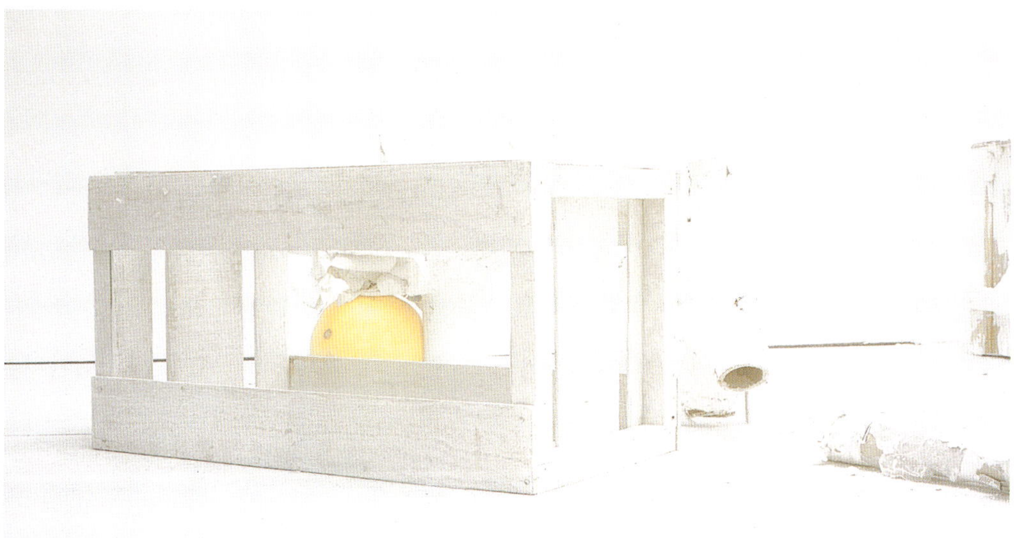

CHRIS HANSON AND HENDRIKA SONNENBERG

Fruit Bowl. 1998. Chromogenic process print, $51\frac{1}{2} \times 89\frac{5}{8}$ inches

Untitled #2237. From the *Ohio* series. 1999. Chromogenic process print, $30\frac{3}{4} \times 30\frac{3}{4}$ inches

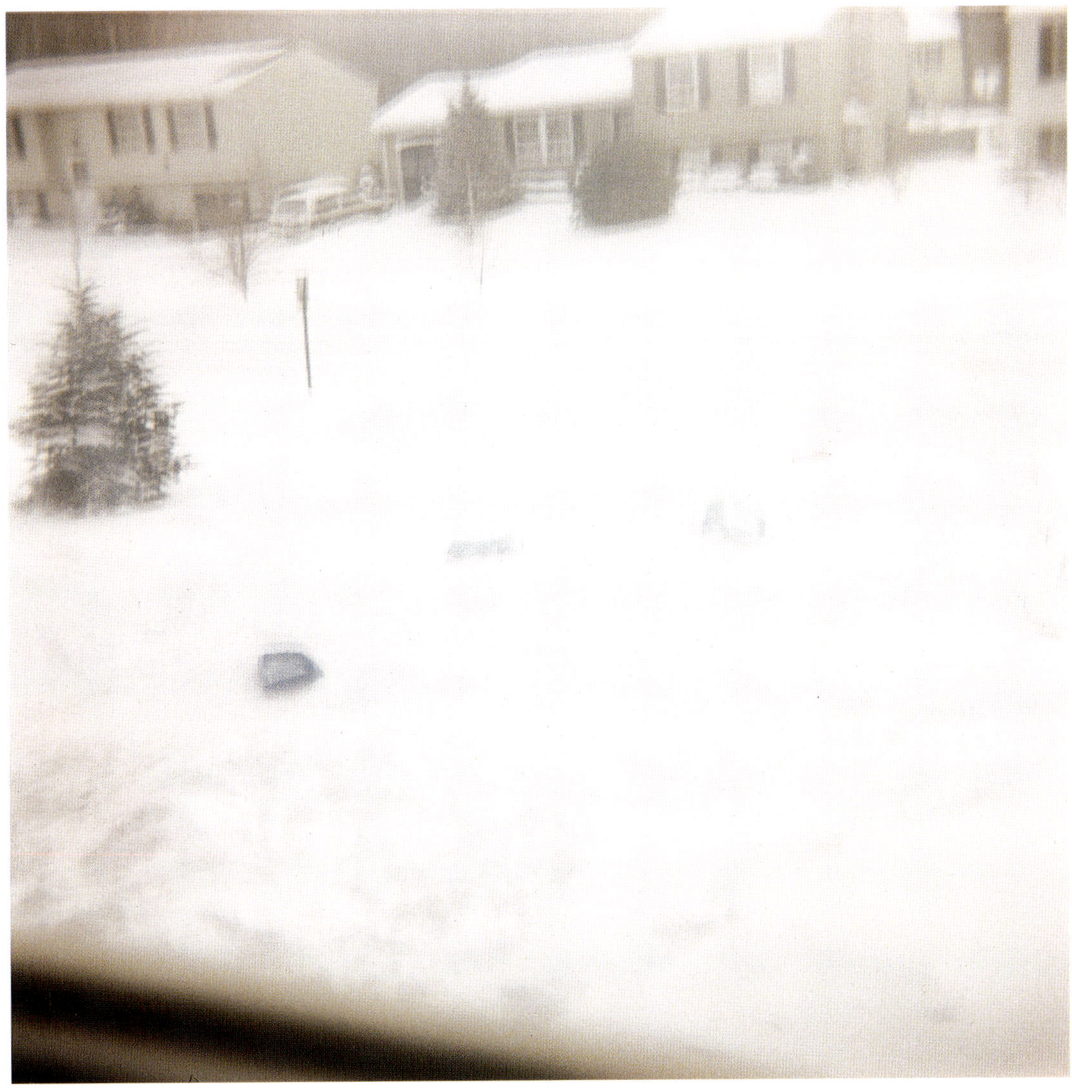

Tanja's World. 1999. Gelatin silver print, $13^1/_2 \times 21$ inches

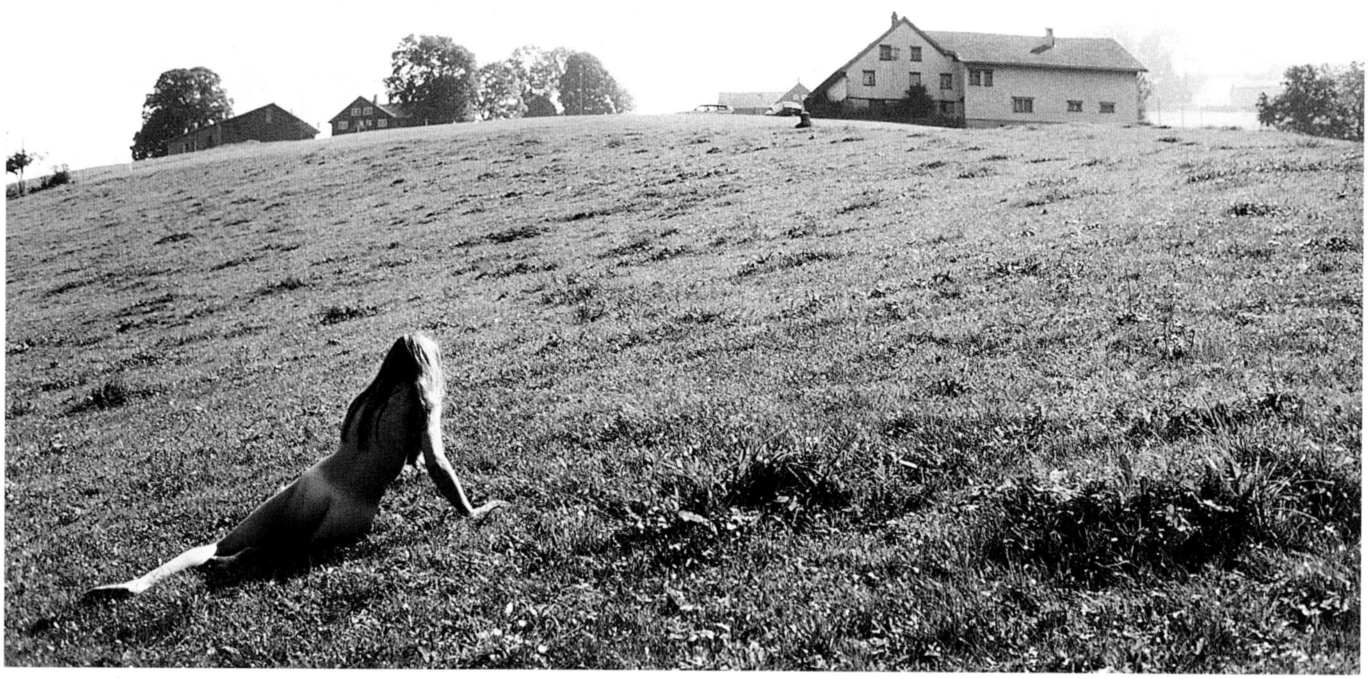

Our Simple Selves (Gray). 1995. Twenty-four mounted chromogenic process prints, $31\frac{1}{2} \times 30\frac{1}{2}$ inches

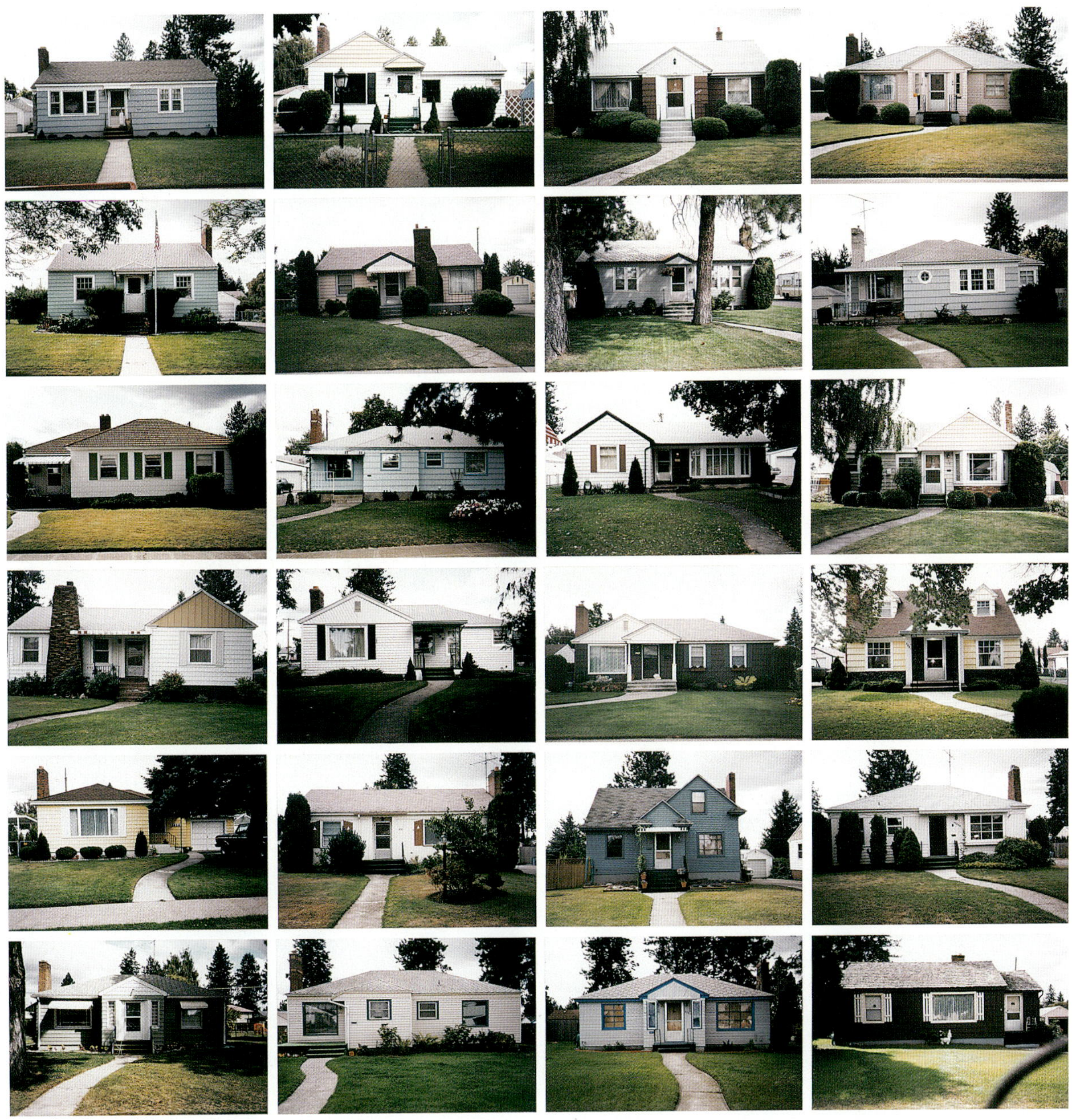

Museum für Völkerkunde, Dresden V. 2000.
Chromogenic process print, $60^{3}/_{4} \times 60^{3}/_{4}$ inches

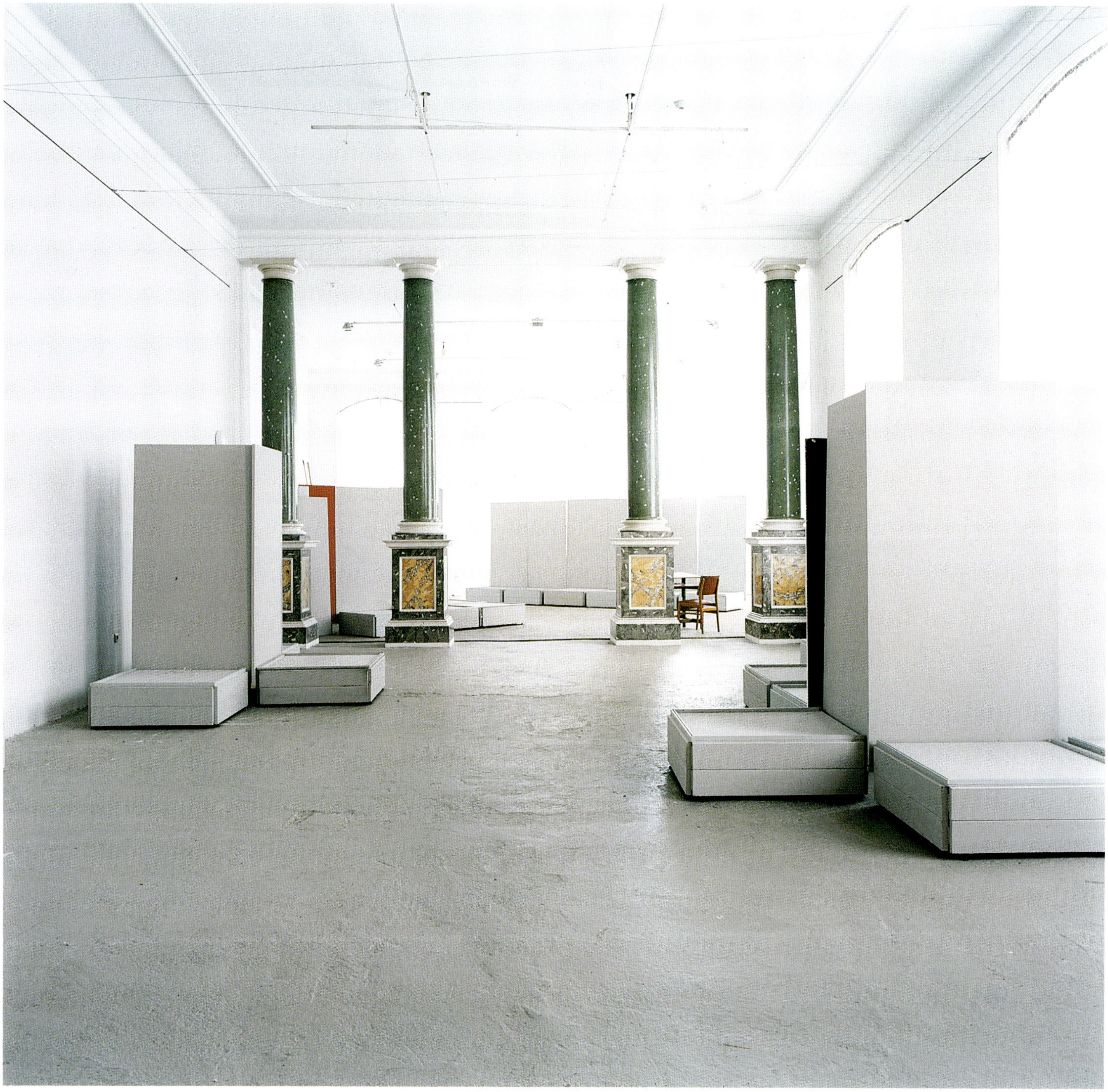

Untitled (Kitty Cats). 2000. Installation: two chromogenic process prints, $30\frac{7}{8} \times 30\frac{7}{8}$ inches each

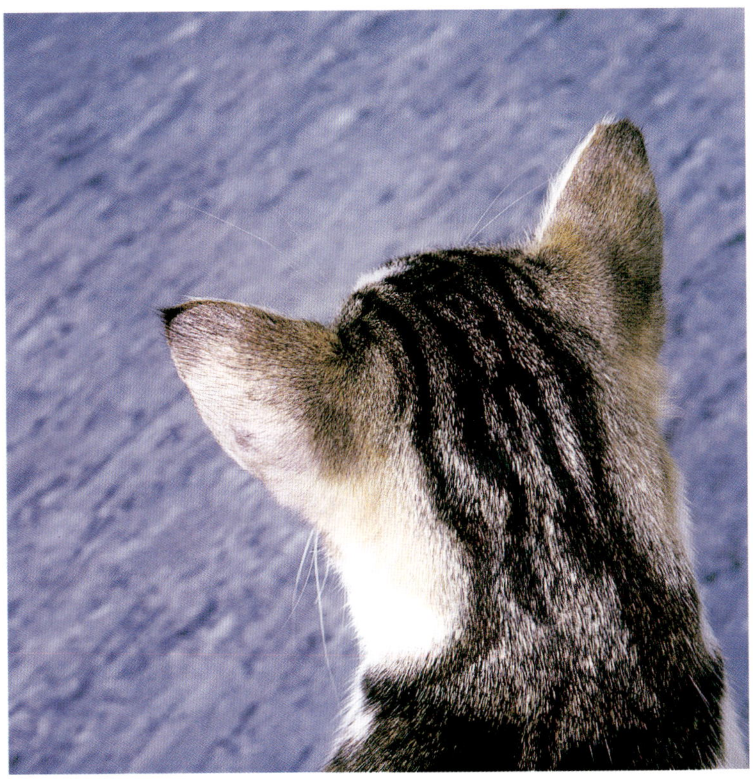

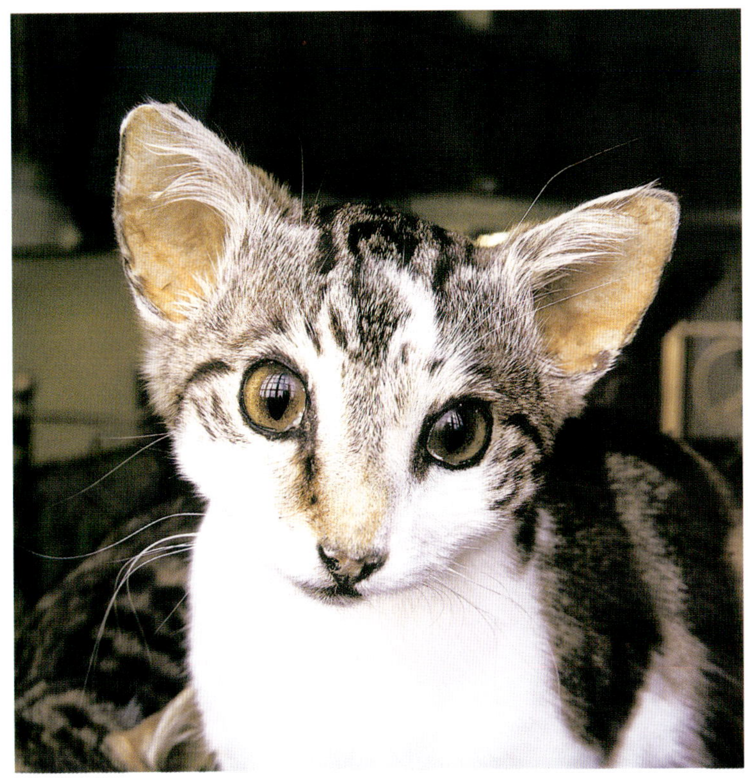

Platowska Towards Bohaterow, Stalingrado, Krakow, January 1974. 1992. Diptych: gelatin silver prints, 58 × 61½ inches each

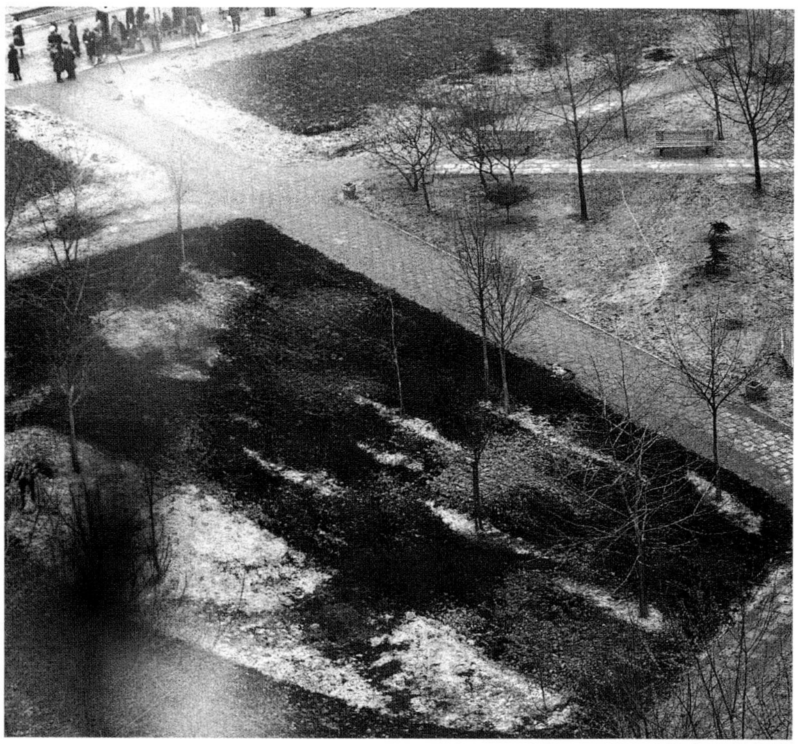

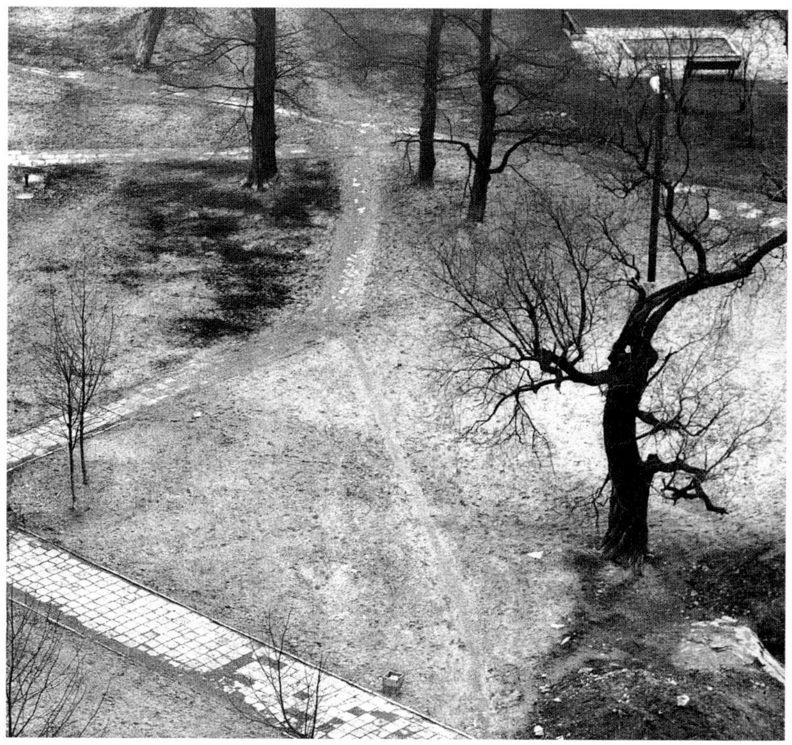

TERESA HUBBARD AND ALEXANDER BIRCHLER

Stripping. 1998. Chromogenic process print mounted to aluminum, from a suite of five, 59 × 72¾ inches

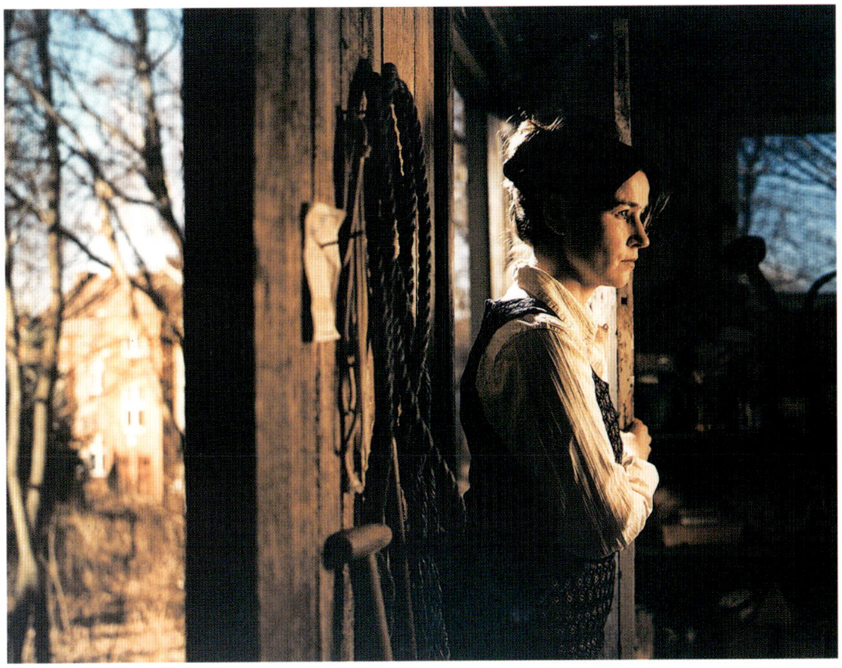

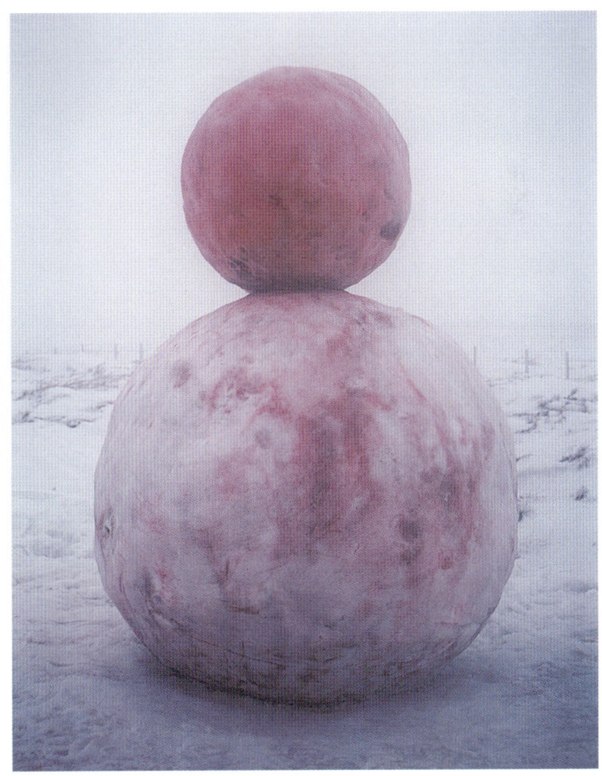

GARY HUME

Snowman. 1997. Silver dye bleach process print, 61 × 47½ inches

The Art of Squatting. 1997. Silver dye bleach process print, 59¼ × 47½ inches

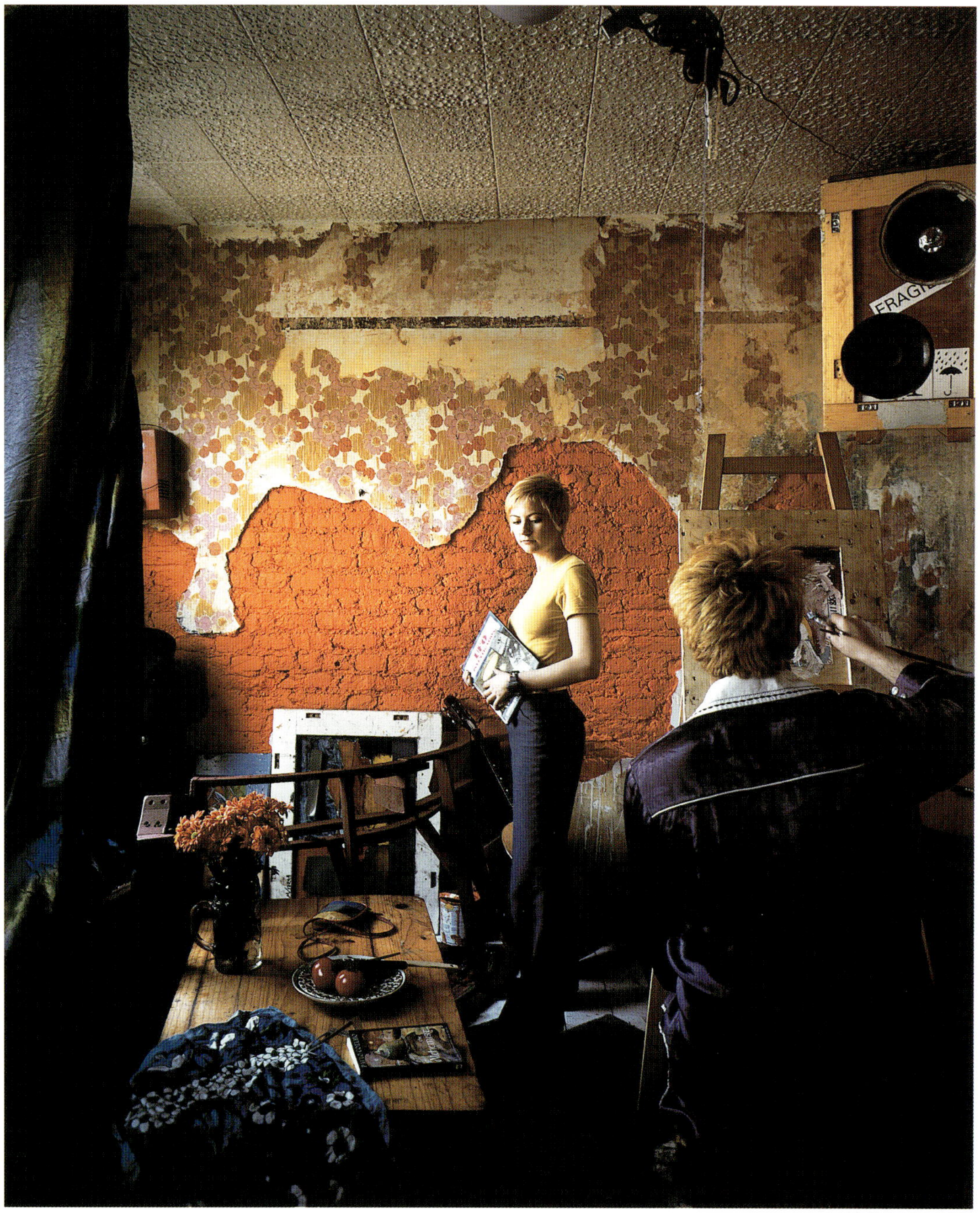

Glacier des Bossons (Bossons Glacier). 1997.
Chromogenic process print, $67\frac{1}{2} \times 81\frac{1}{4}$ inches

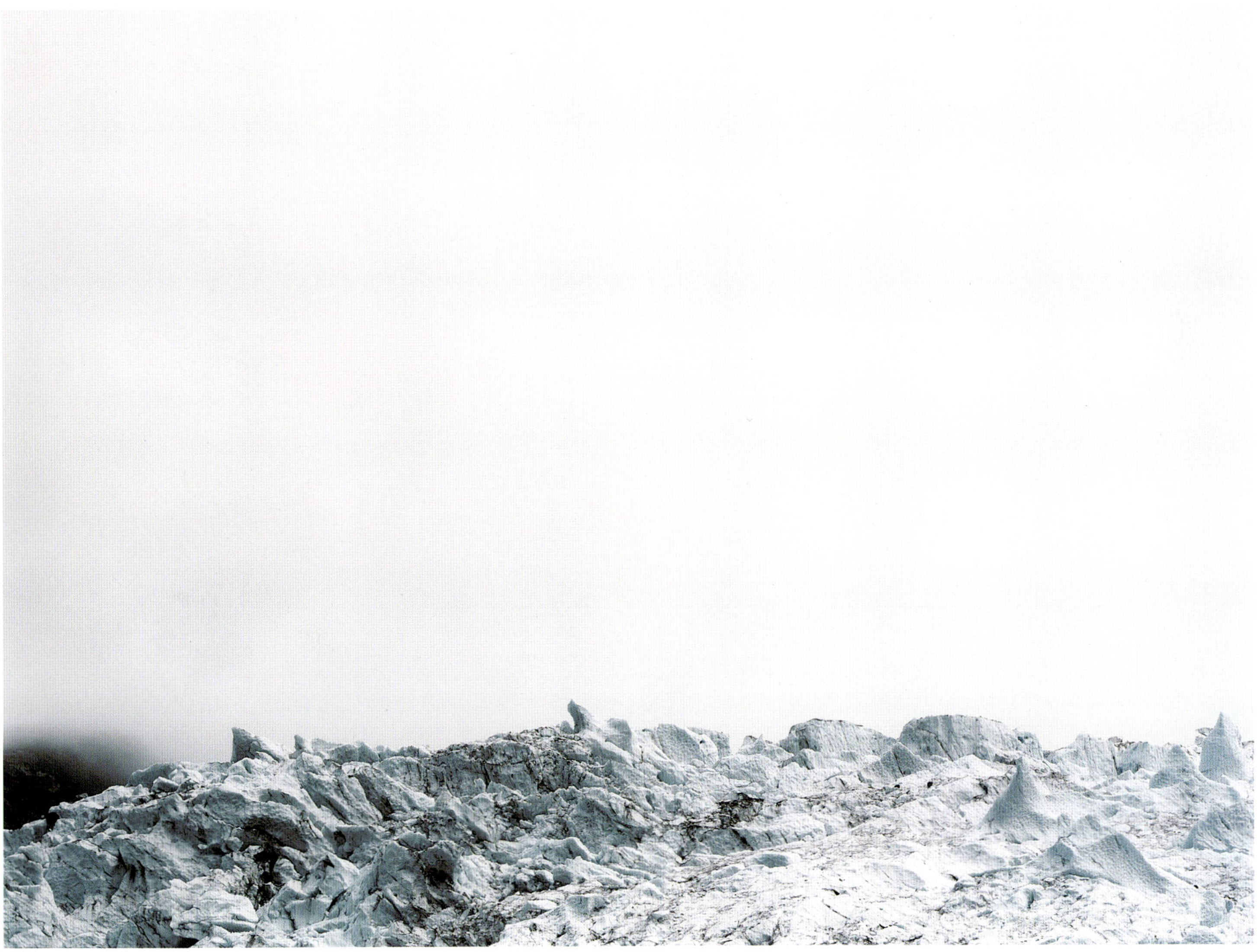

Top to bottom:

U Become Snow #1. 1998

U Become Snow #13. 1998

Two chromogenic process prints from a series, 24 3/8 × 36 1/4 inches each

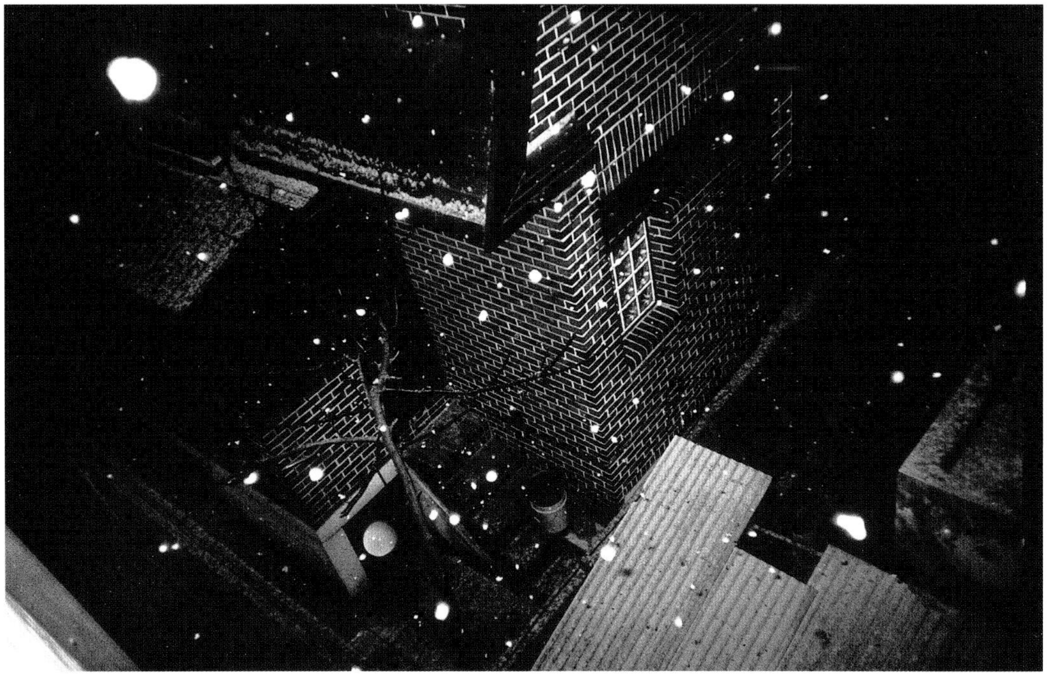

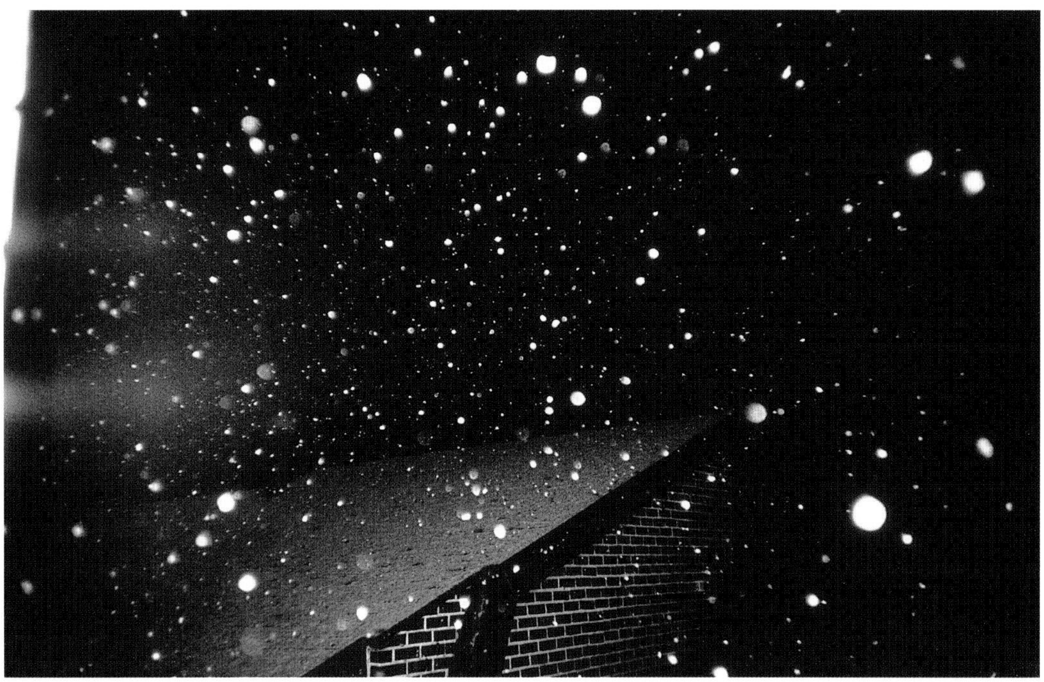

Iceland Project A. 1993. Gelatin silver print, mounted on aluminum, $44\frac{1}{2} \times 67$ inches

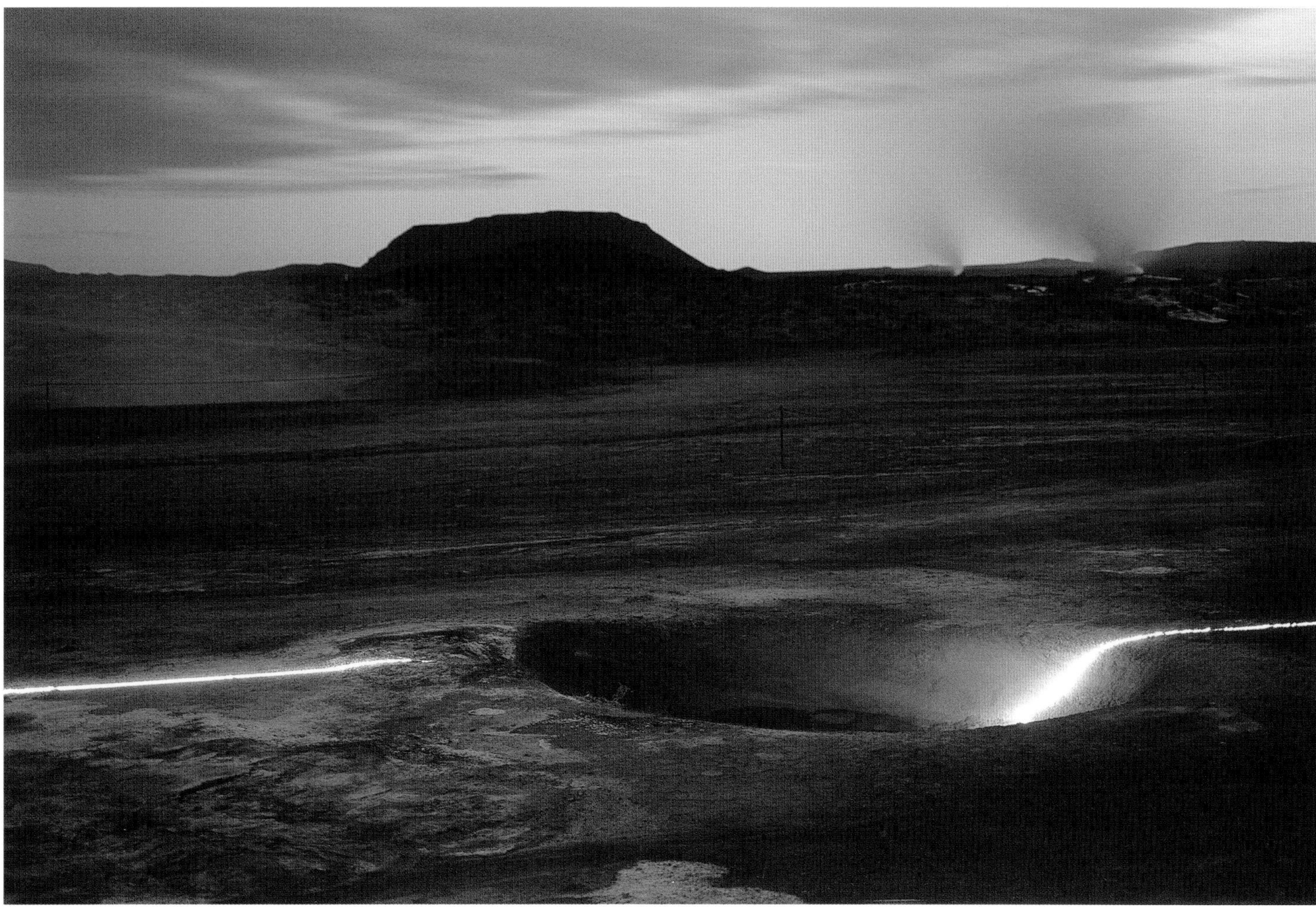

Dining Room (Francis Place) (II). 1997. Chromogenic process print, mounted to aluminum, 59 × 59 inches

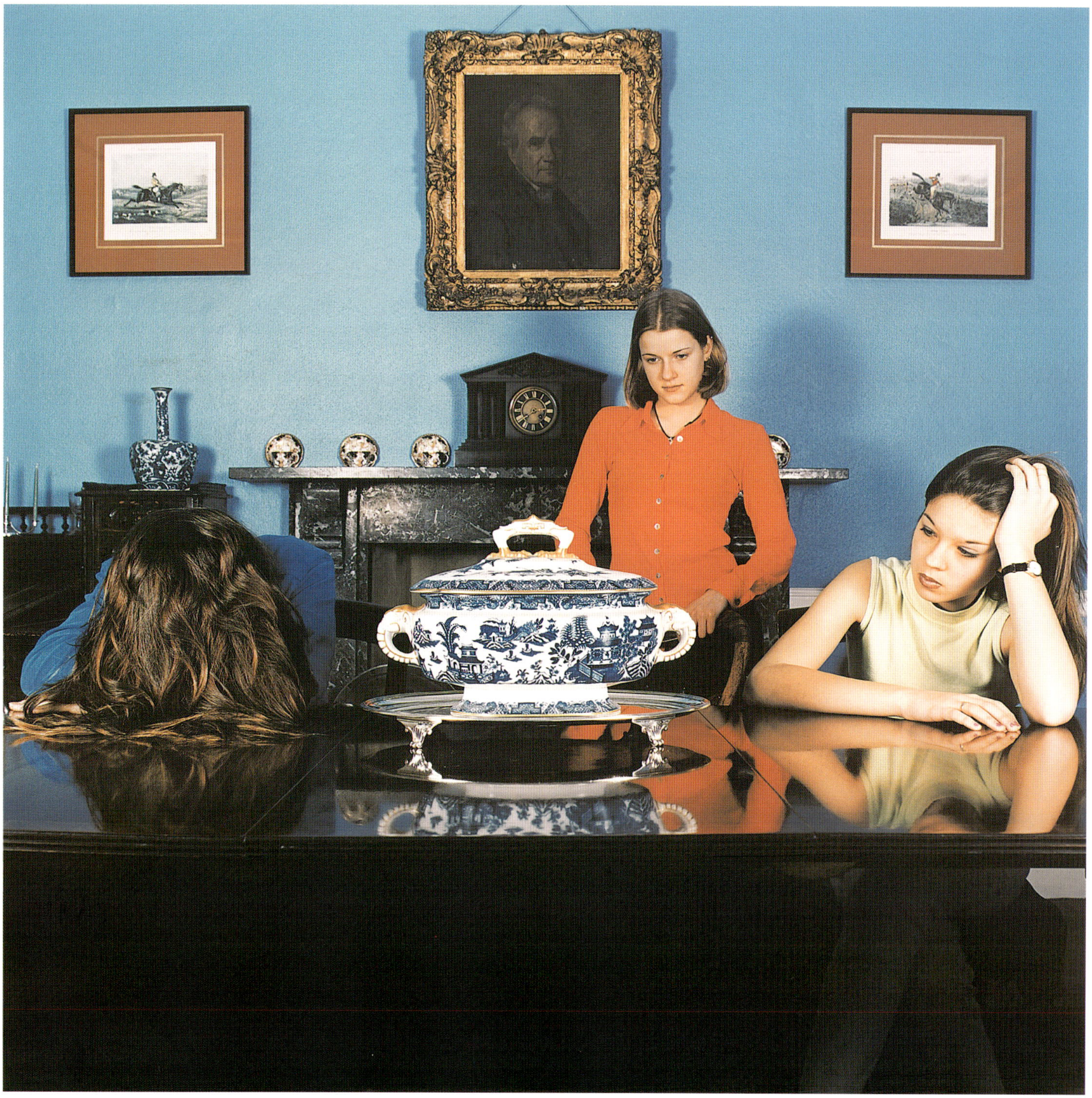

Man with Flower. 1959/1998. Gelatin silver print, $23\frac{1}{2} \times 19\frac{1}{2}$ inches

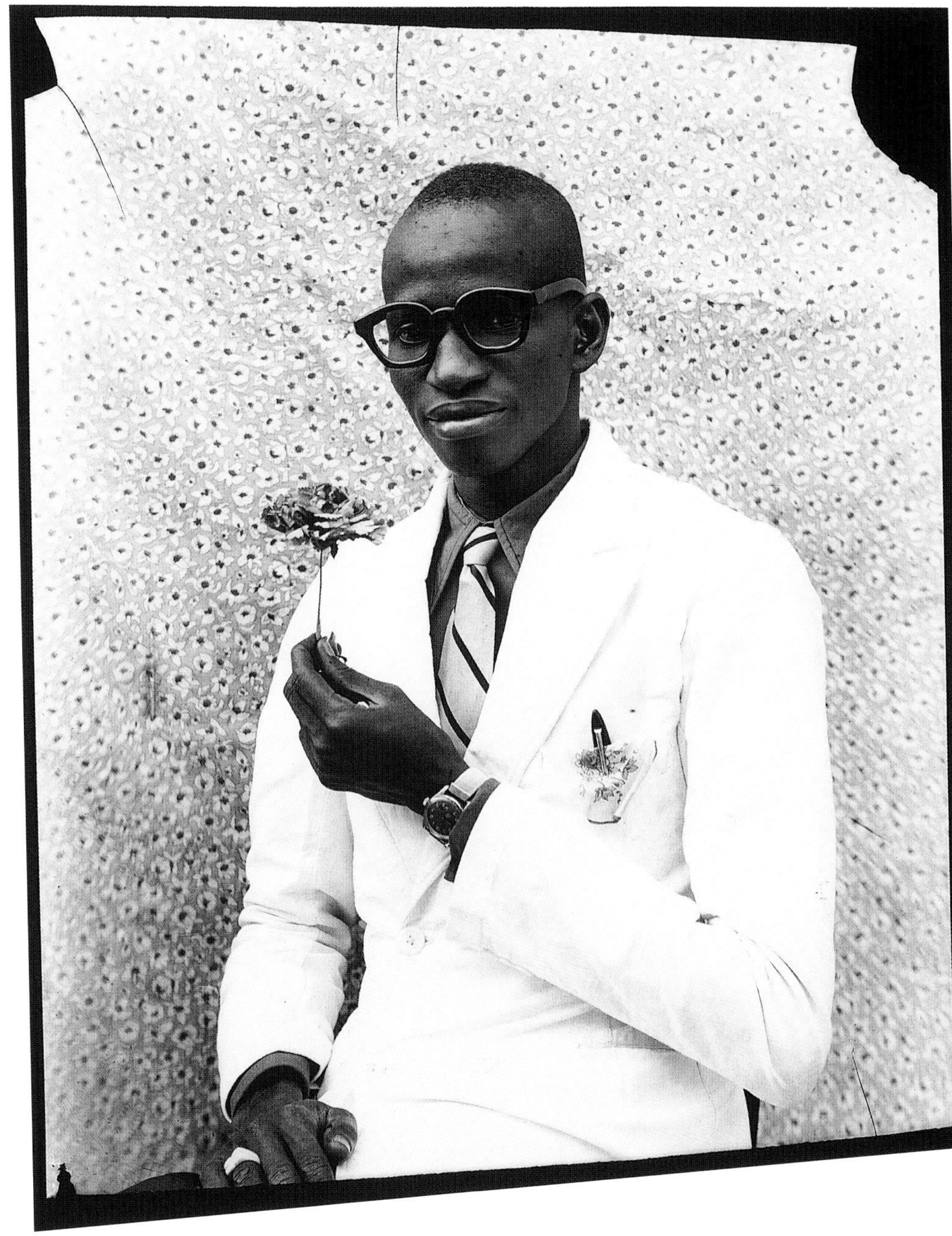

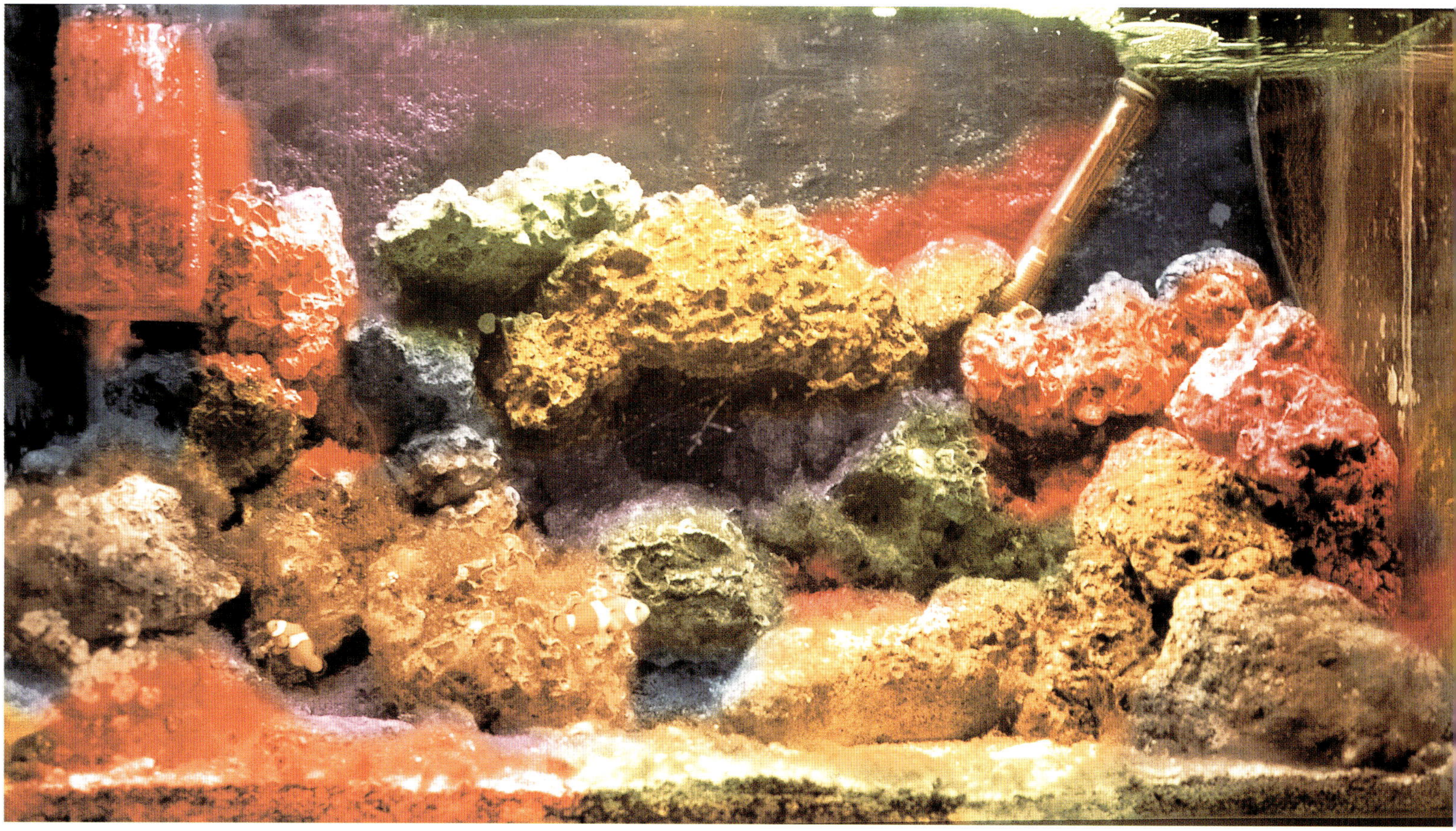

Color and Form. 1999. Diptych: chromogenic process prints, 49 × 84 1/8 inches each

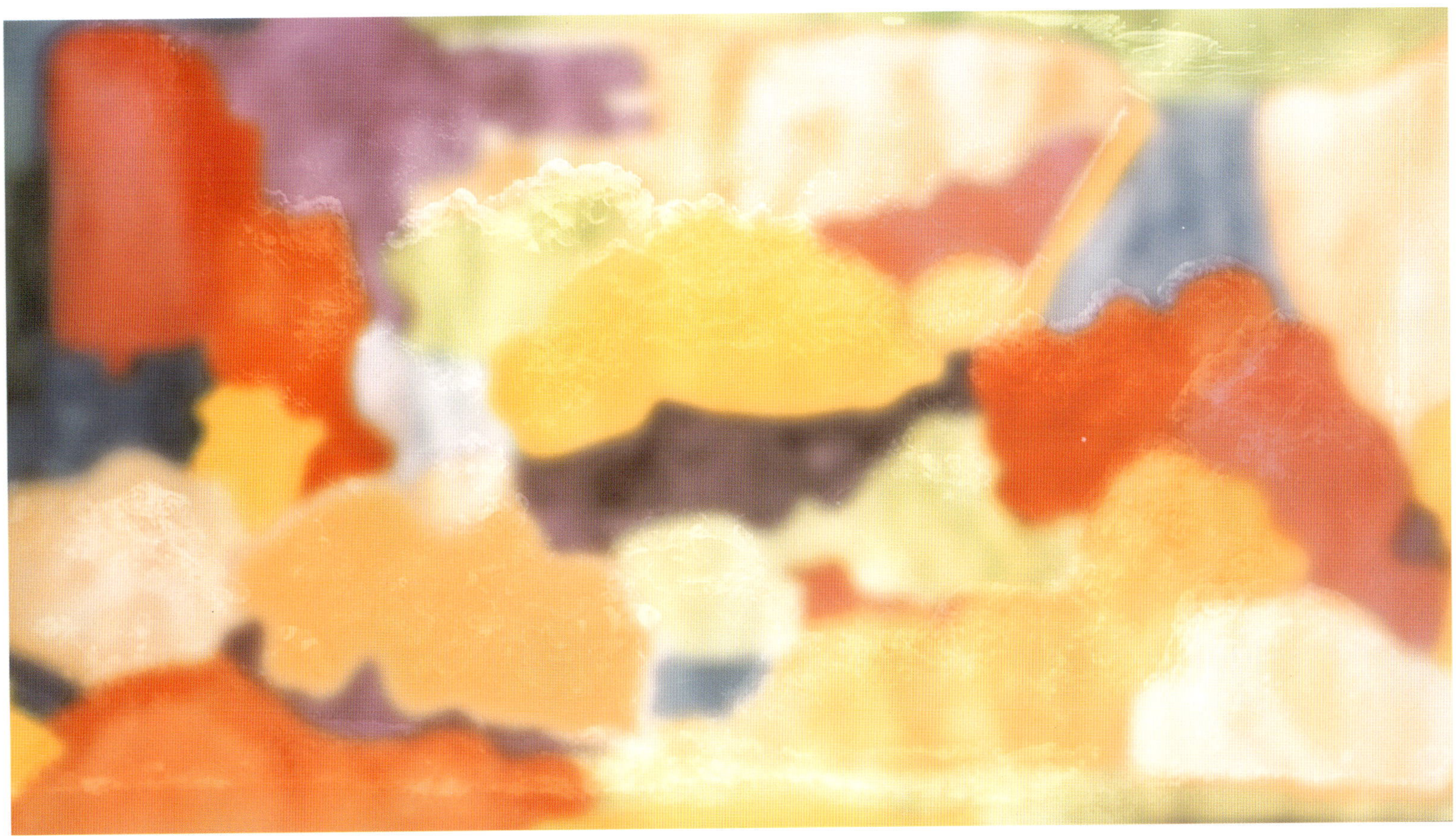

Top to bottom:

Ice Pond Fall #3. 1997

Ice Pond Fall #4. 1997

Two chromogenic process prints

from a series, 25 × 37 3/4 inches each

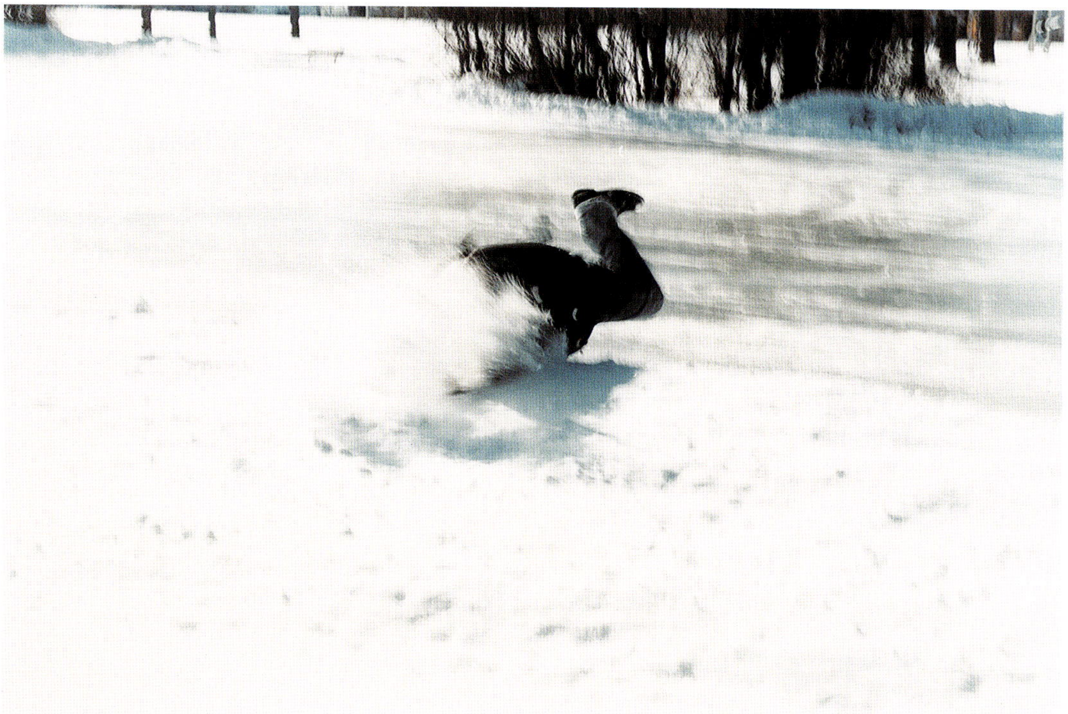

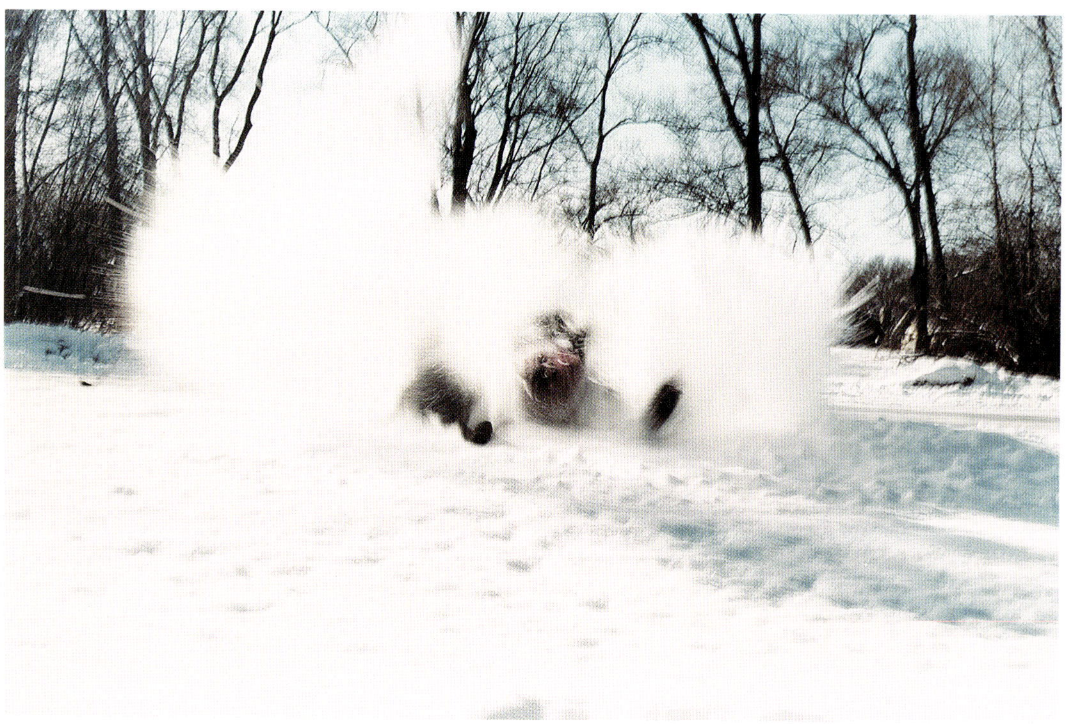

Ur. 1997. Artist's book with gelatin silver photographs and sand, mounted on chipboard pages, with canvas and heavy paint impasto, open book, $40^{3}/_{4} \times 63 \times 2$ inches

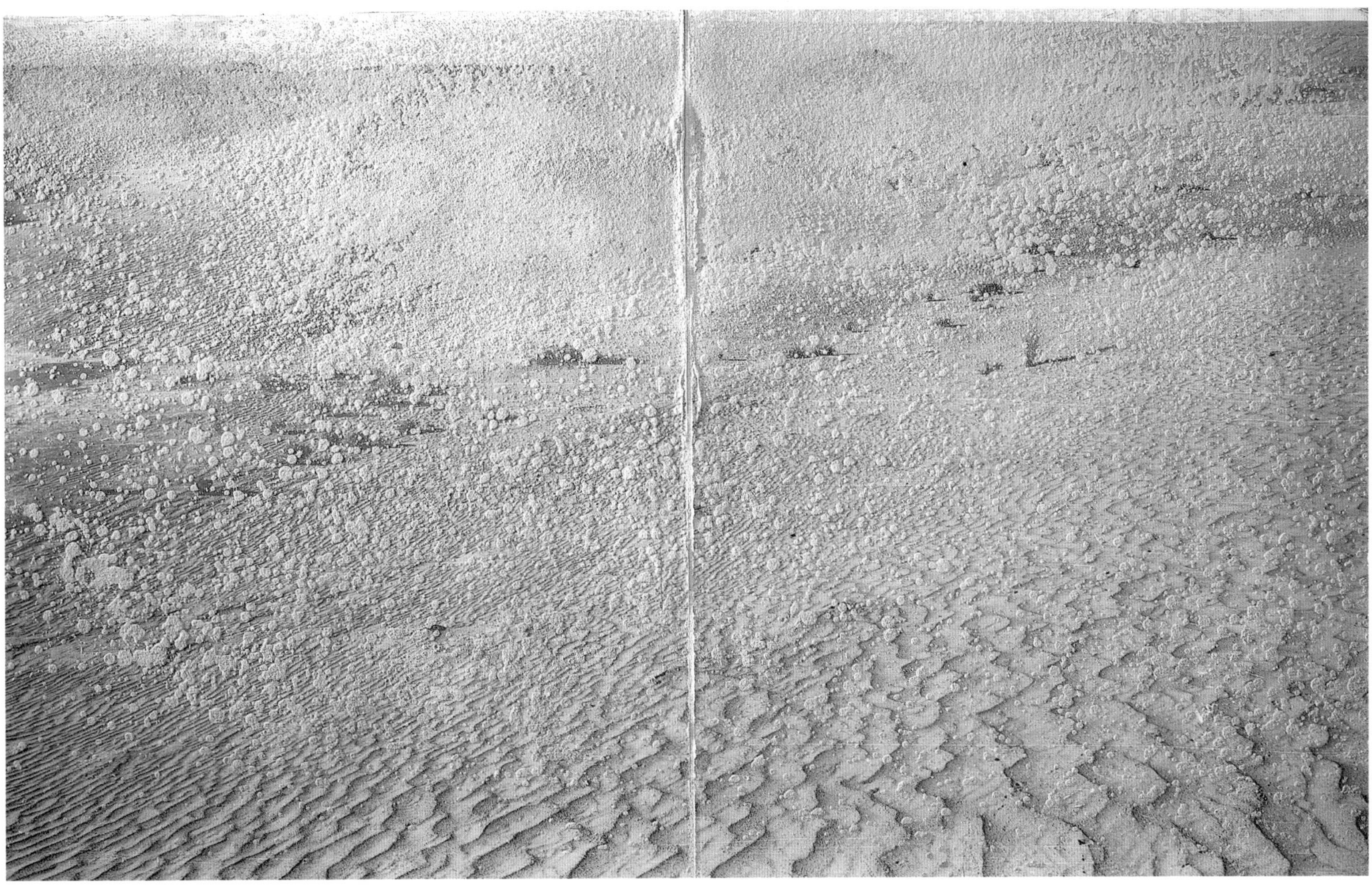

Untitled (Status Quo). From the *Heavy Burschi* series.
1989–90. Silver dye bleach process print, 49¼ × 41¼ inches

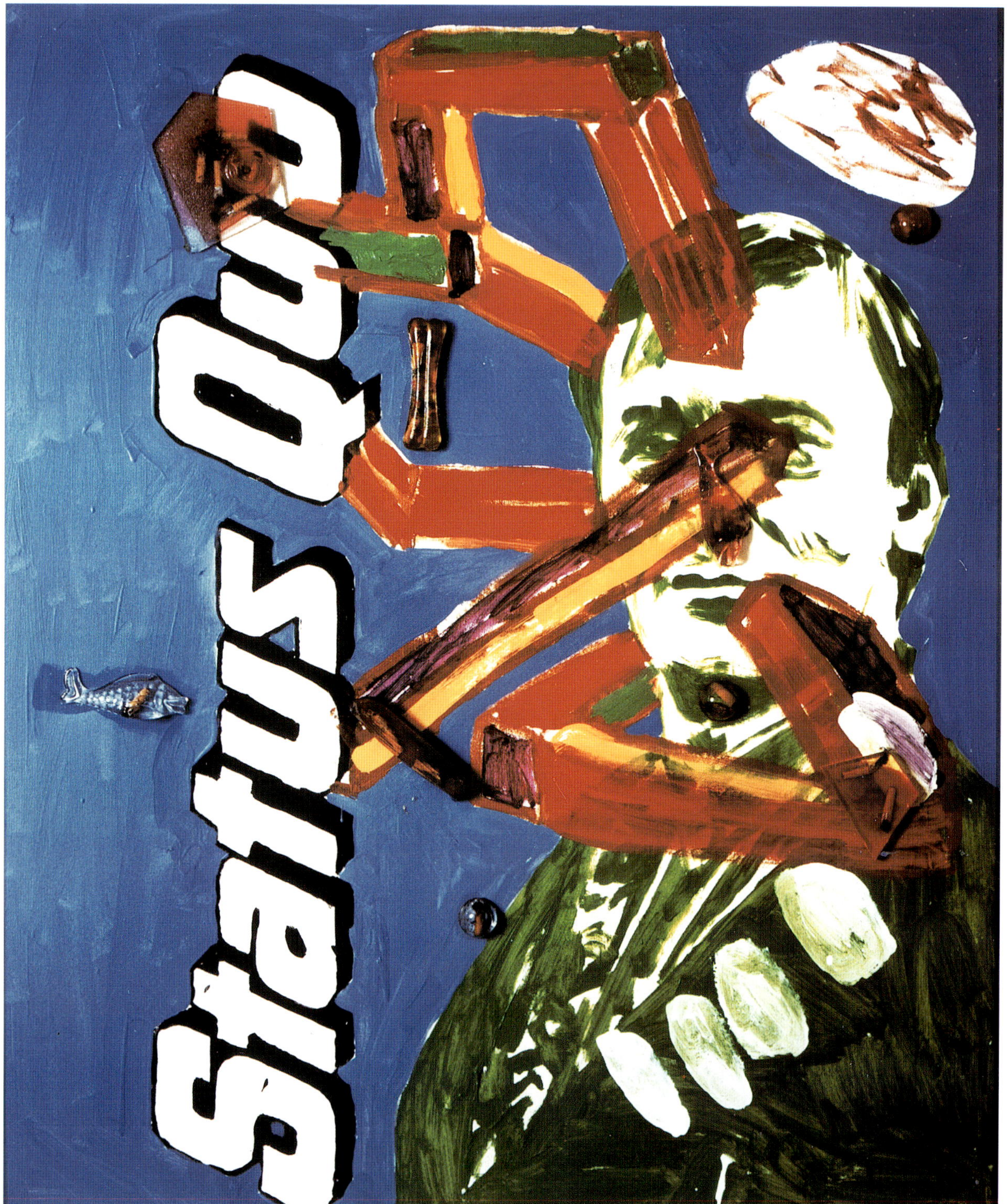

Sir Sid. 1985. Offset print, 36 × 22 inches

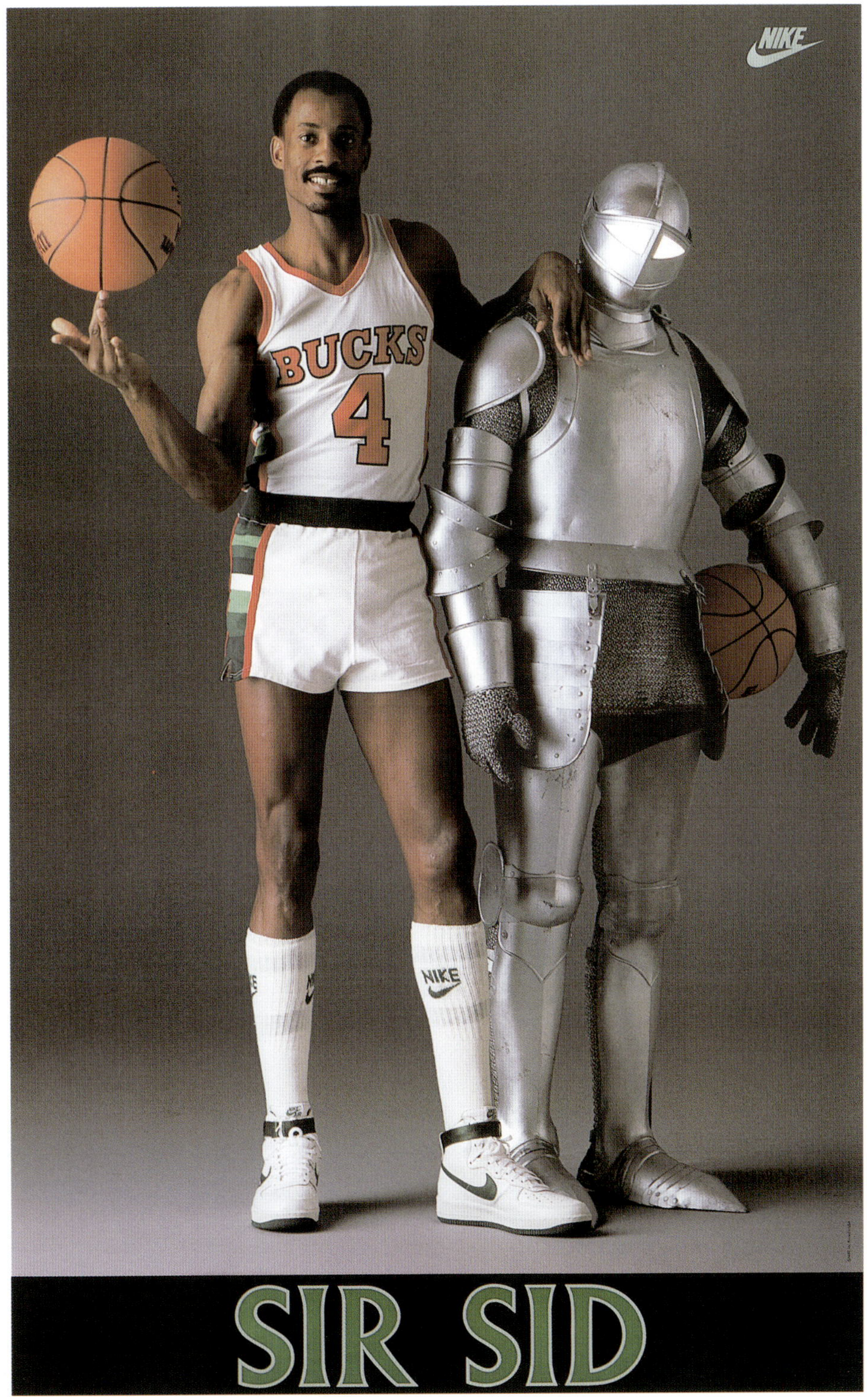

JAN KOSTER

De Kleine Bouwkolk (The Small Construction Pond).
8 October 1996. Collage: chromogenic process prints,
$44\frac{1}{2}$ inches × 8 feet 8 inches

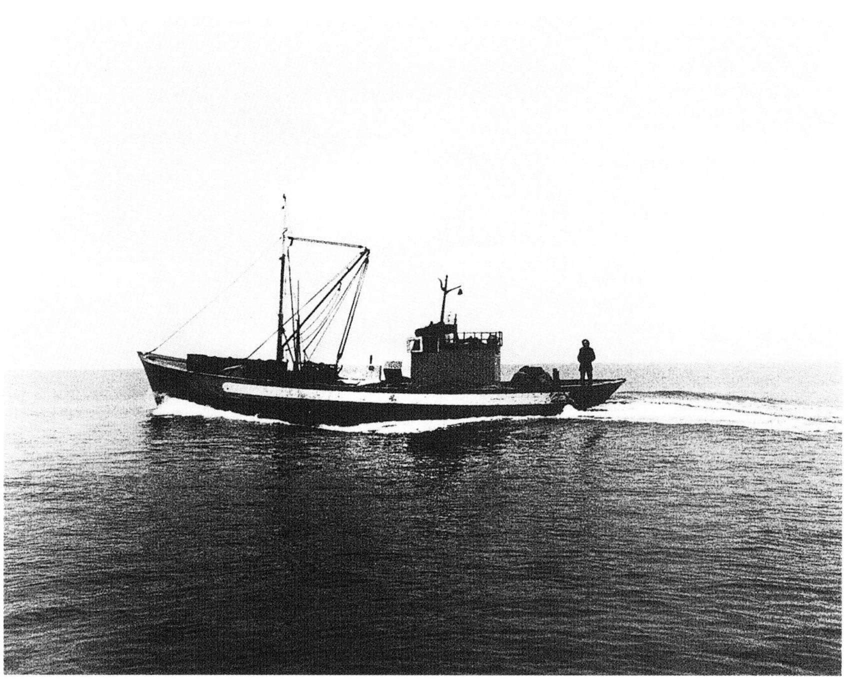

JANNIS KOUNELLIS

Il Viaggio (The Voyage). 1969.
Offset print, $26\frac{7}{8} \times 38\frac{5}{8}$ inches

Snow Angels. 2000. Laminated chromogenic process print, mounted to plastic, 30 × 40 inches

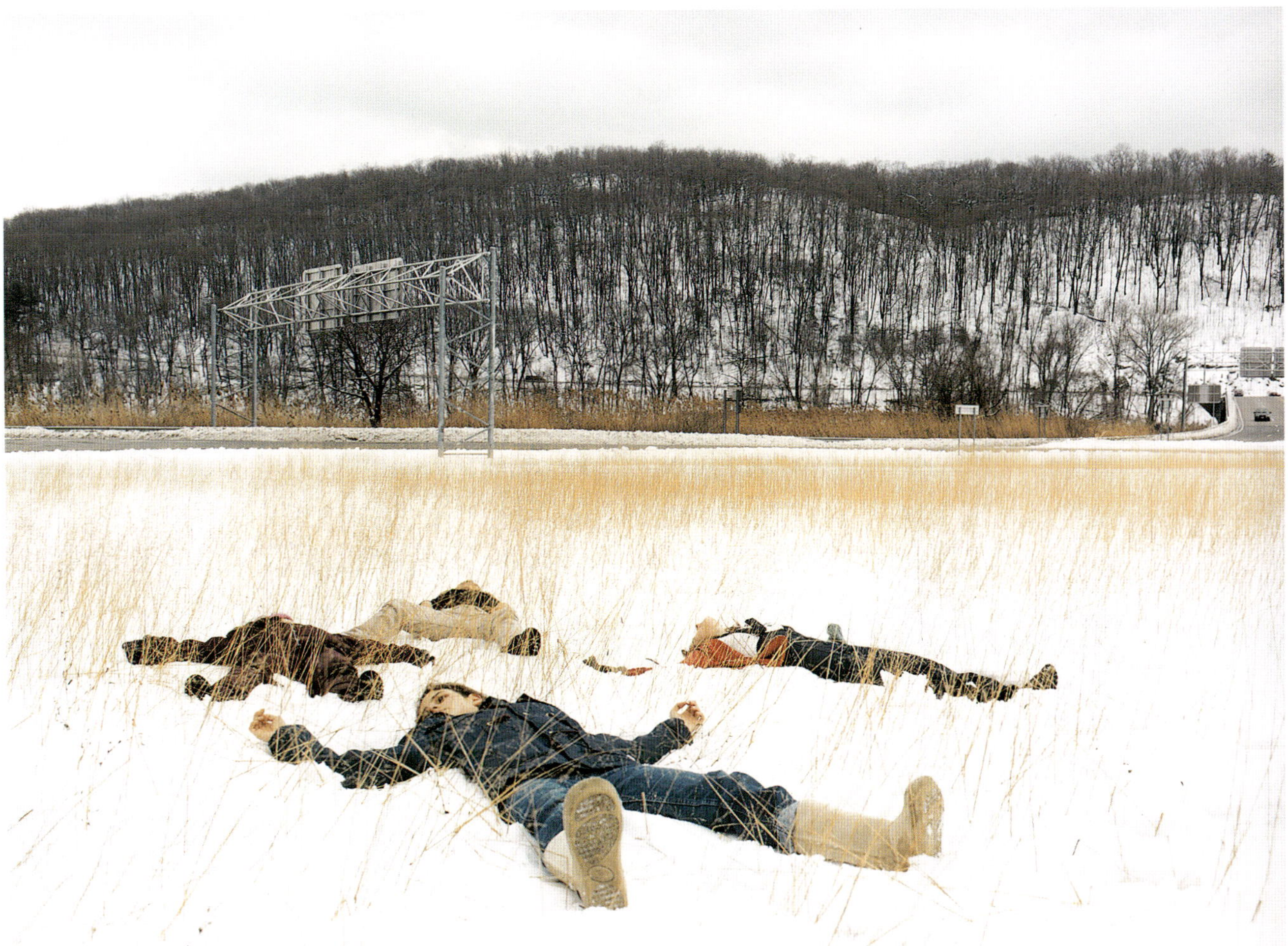

Le Balayeur (The Streetsweeper). 1996–97.
Serigraph mounted to plastic, $60\frac{3}{8} \times 47\frac{7}{8}$ inches

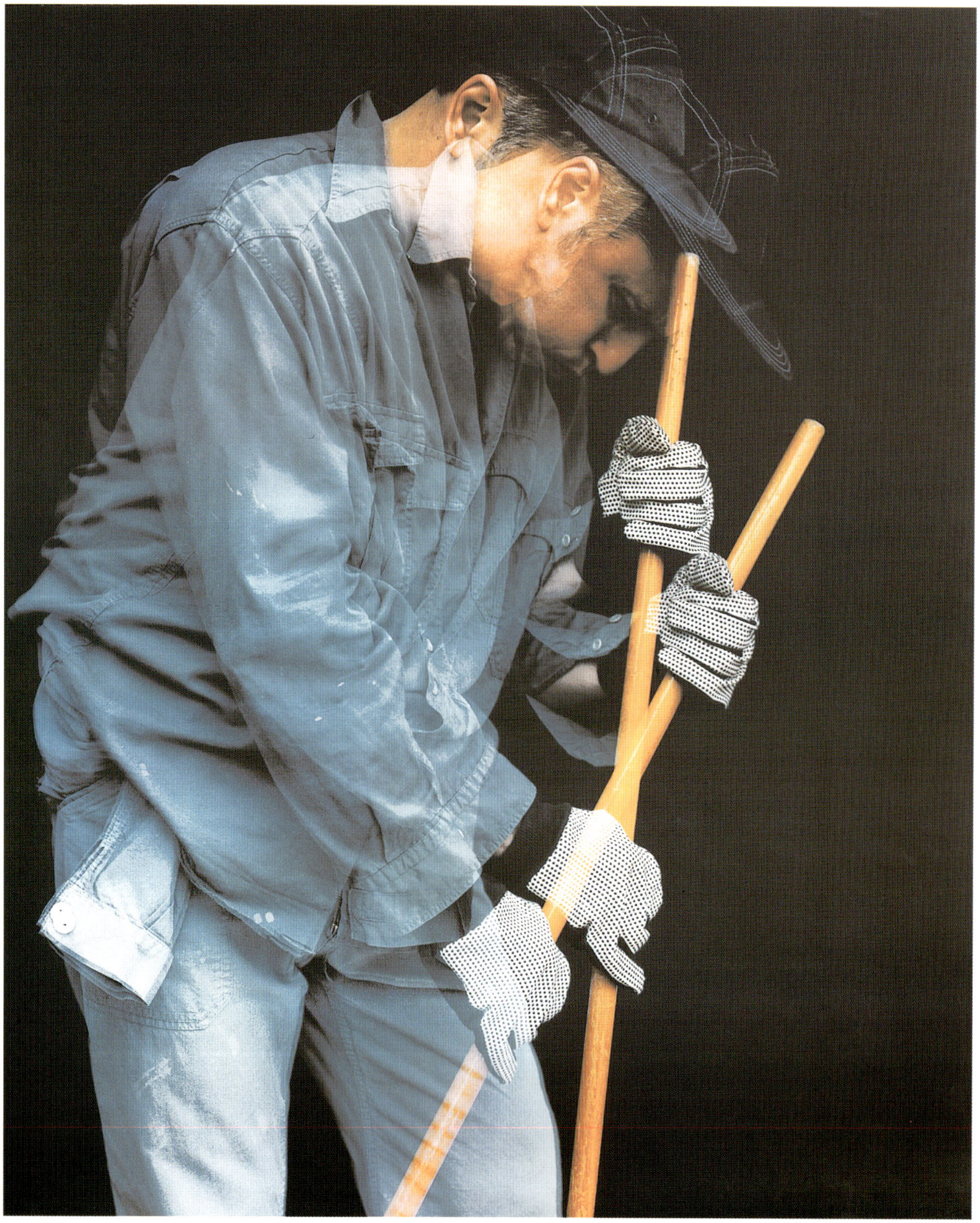

Absent Friends. 1994–95. Suite of six toned gelatin silver prints, dimensions varied

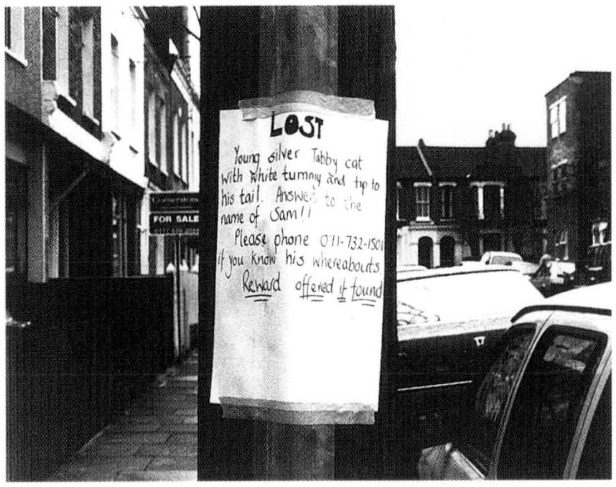

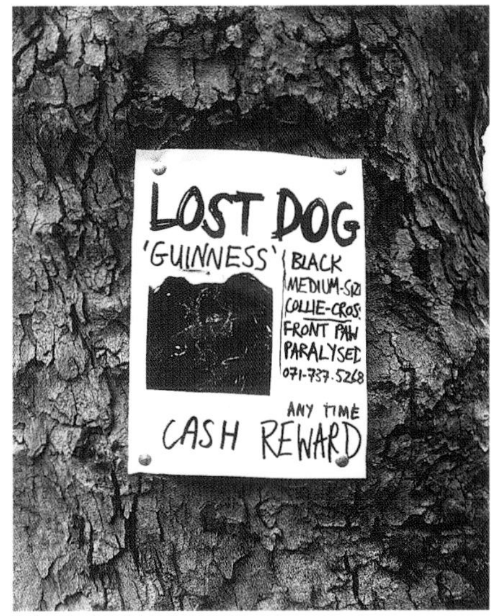

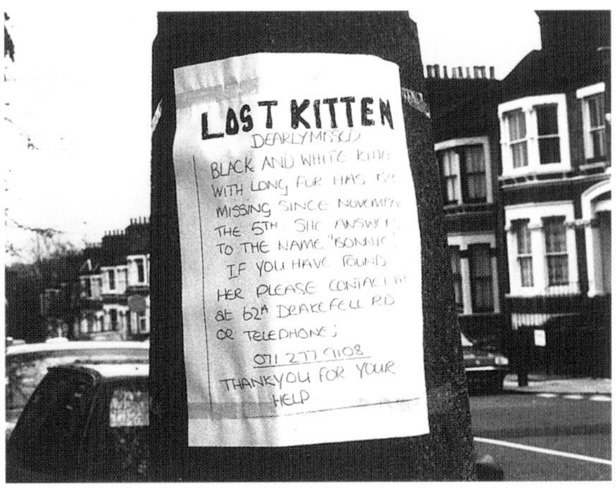

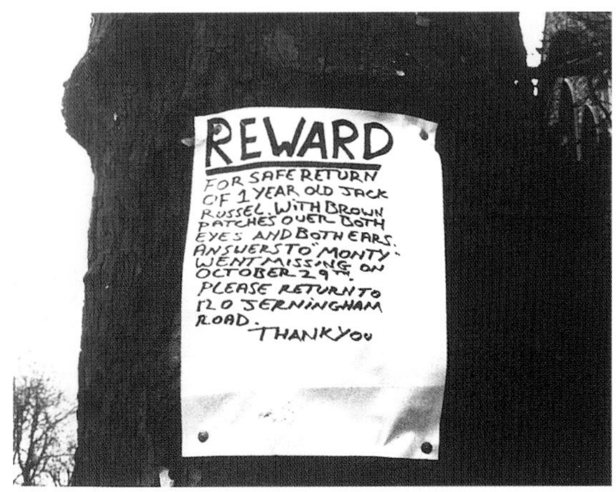

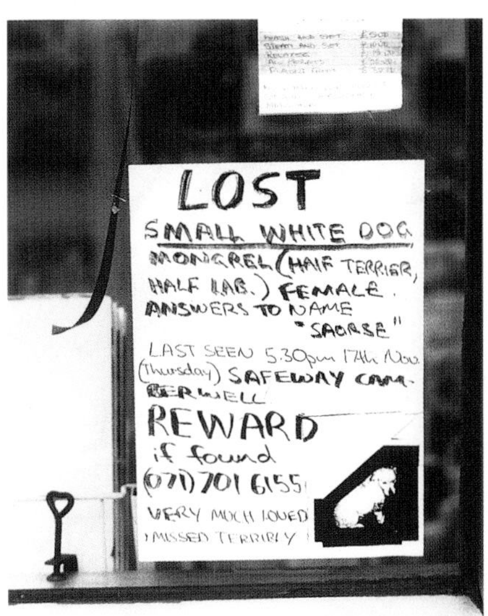

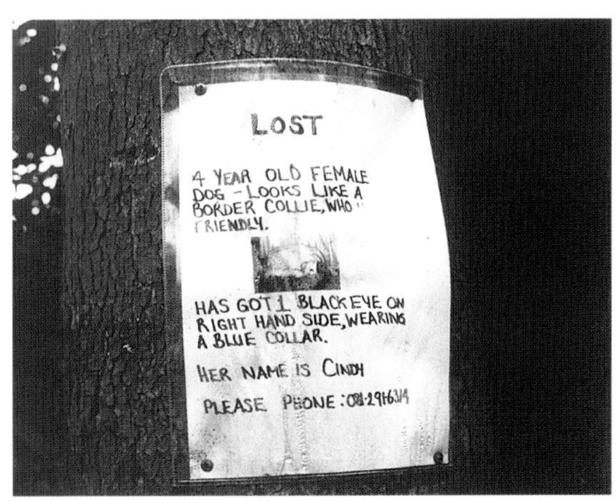

HVAC. 1996. Silver dye bleach process print, mounted to masonite, 47 7/8 × 61 3/4 inches

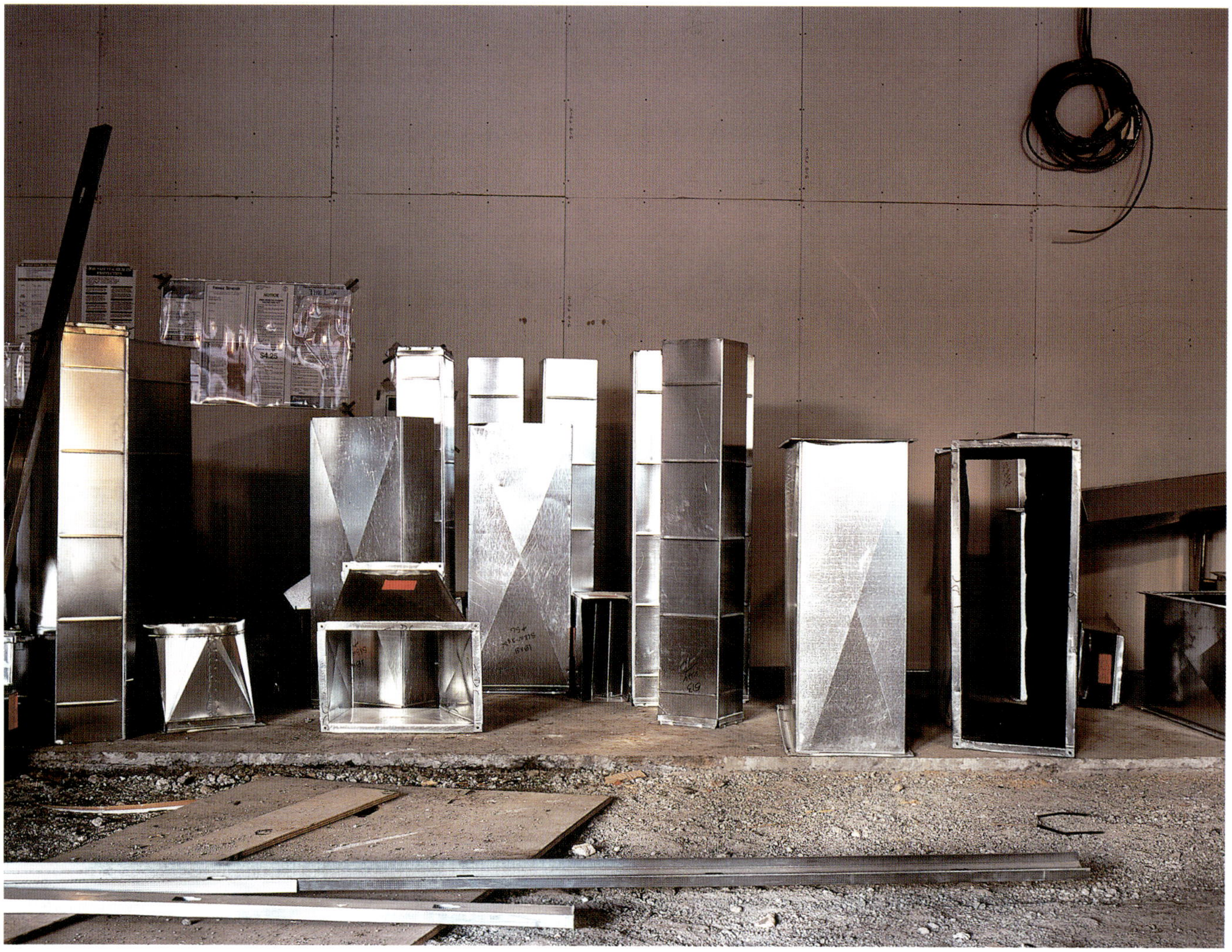

Left to right:

Extensions (b). 1970–71. Six mounted gelatin silver prints from a series, $24\frac{1}{4} \times 20\frac{1}{2}$ inches each

Extensions (c). 1970–71. Six mounted gelatin silver prints from a series, $24\frac{1}{4} \times 20\frac{1}{2}$ inches each

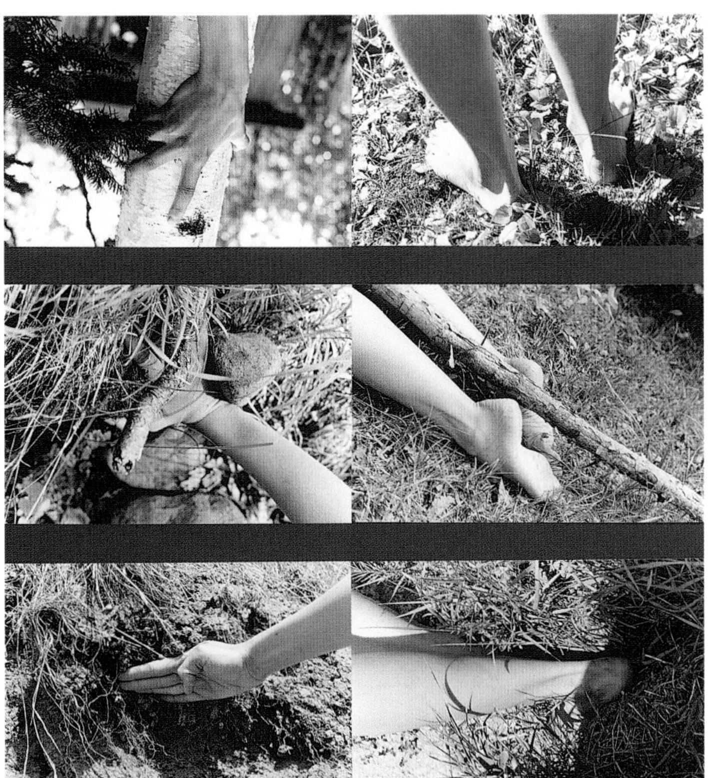

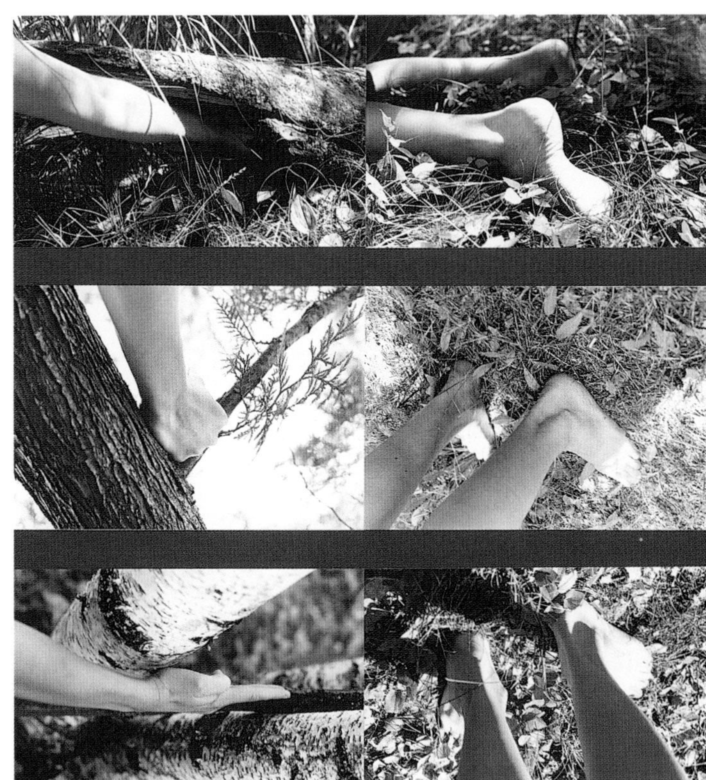

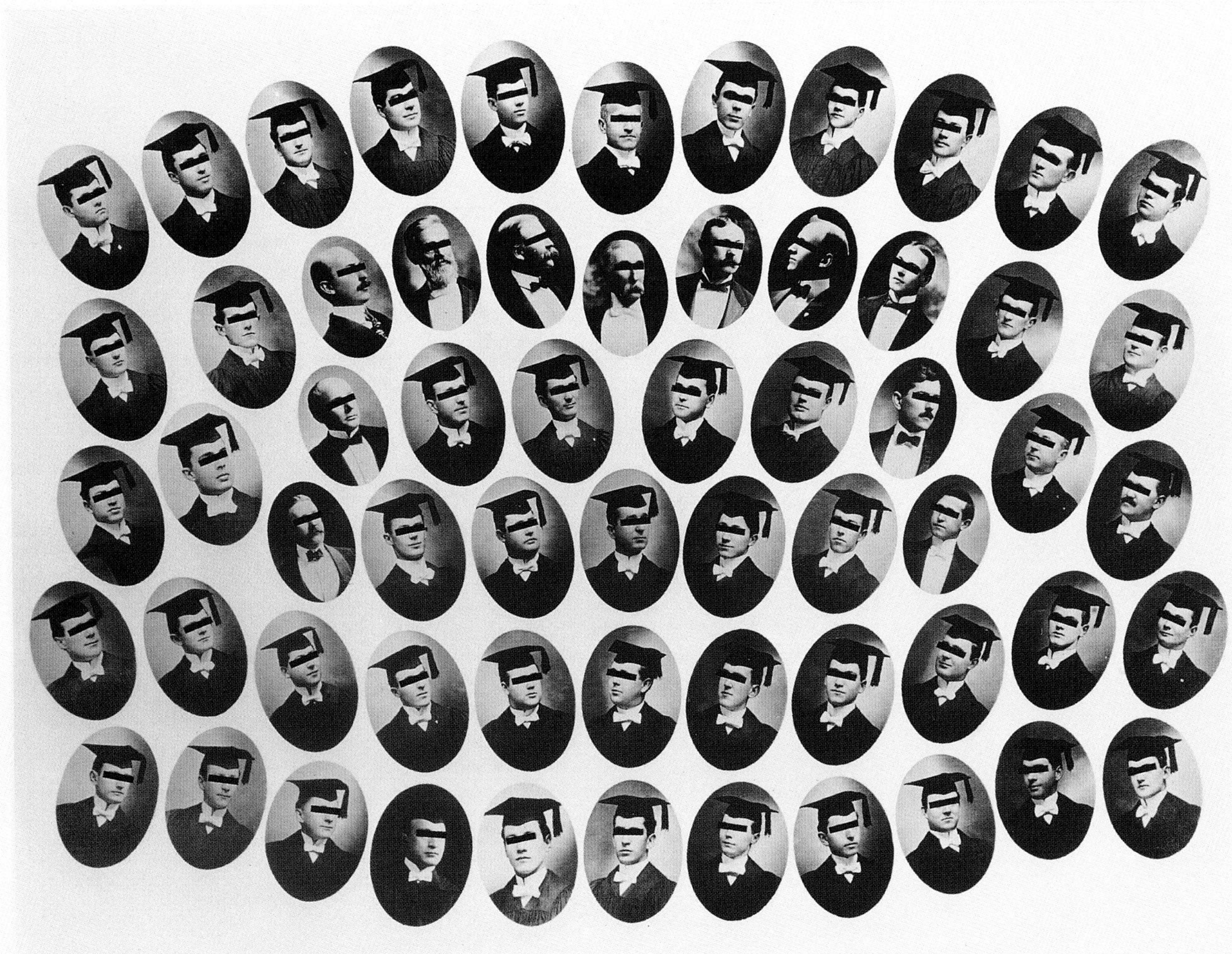

See No Evil/ Seeing Evil. 1987. Diptych: gelatin silver prints, 37½ × 48½ inches each

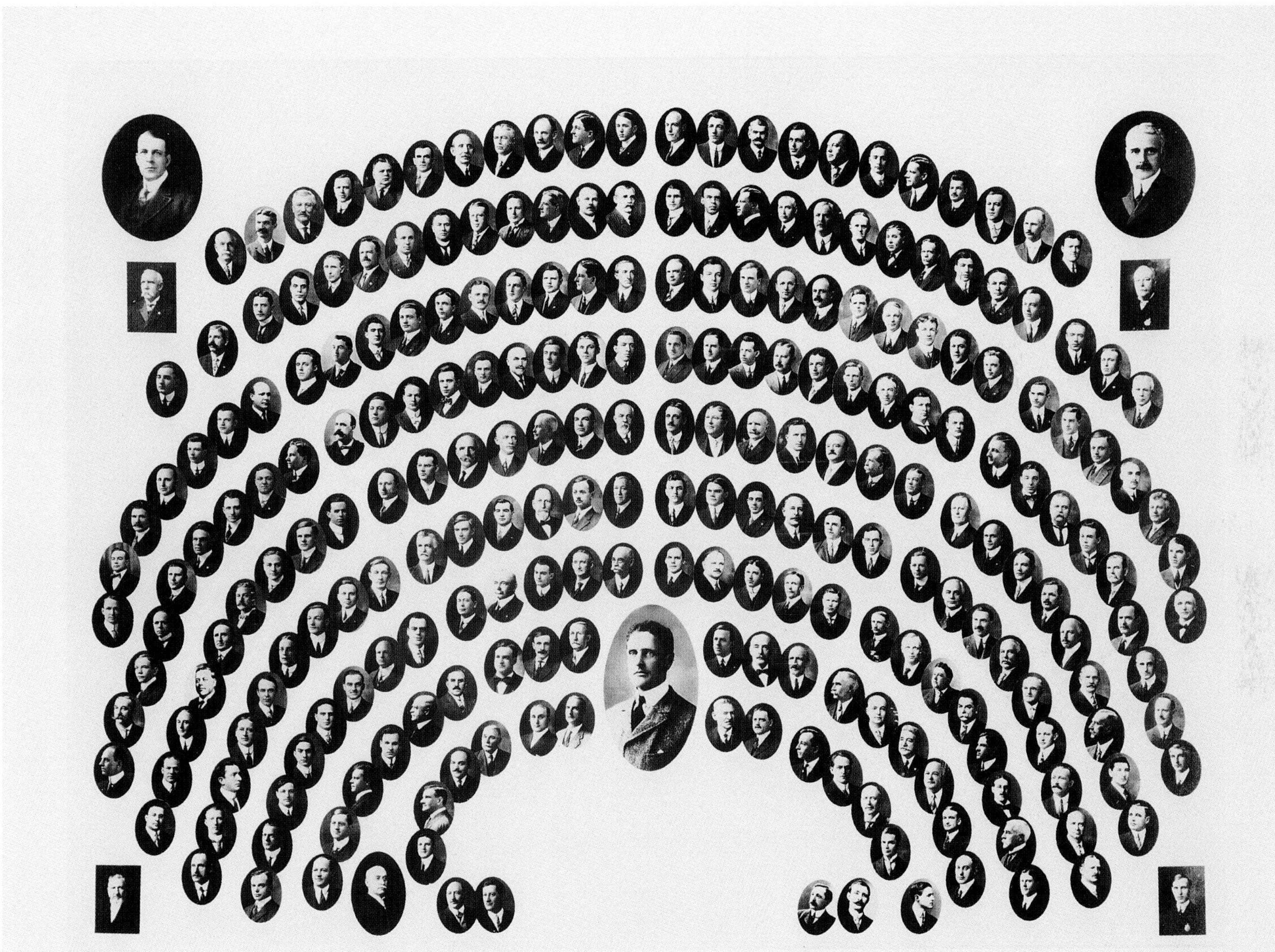

Untitled (After Walker Evans: Positive #19). 1990. Gelatin silver print in artist's plywood frame, from a series, 29 × 20½ inches

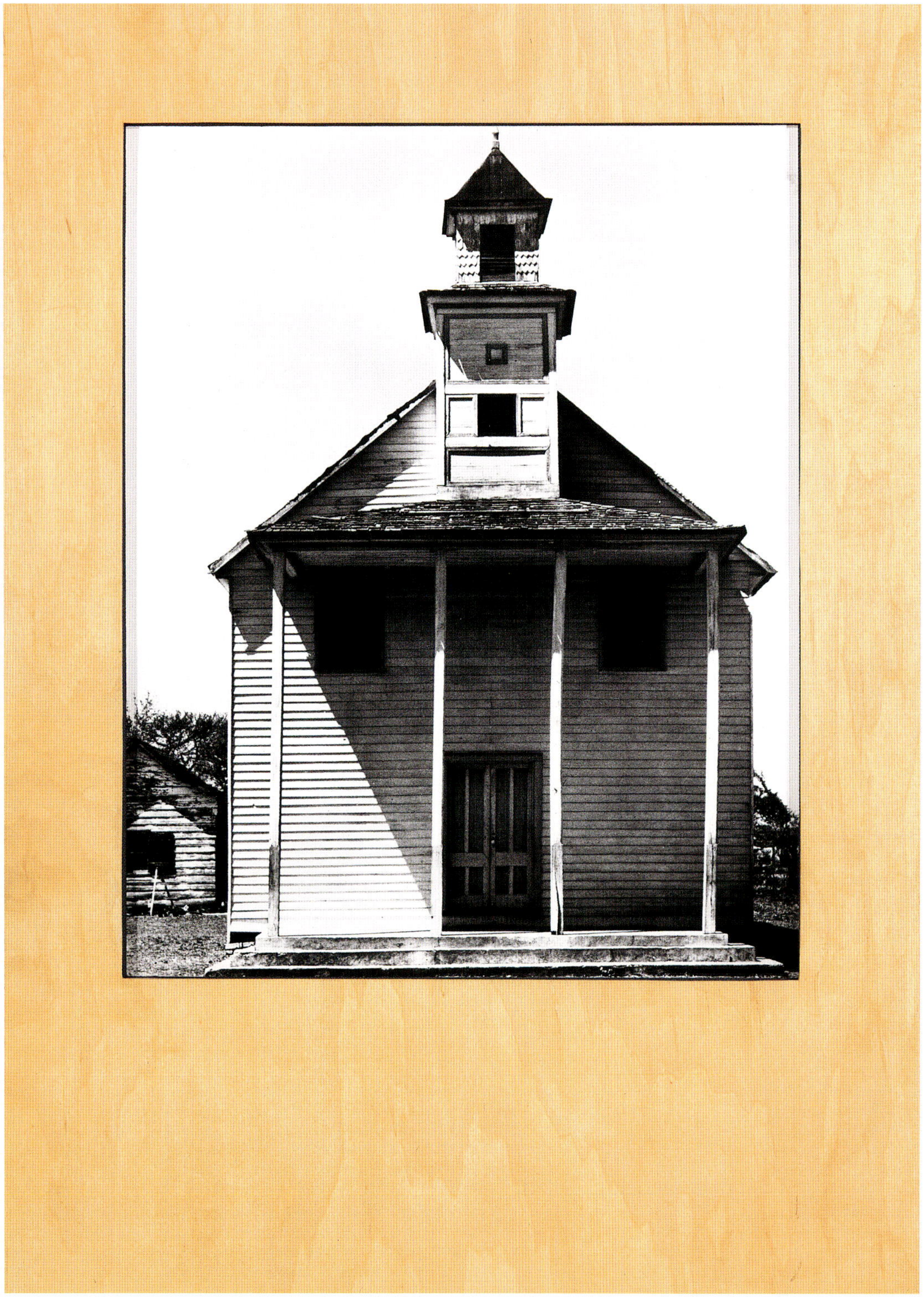

A Cube (Portfolio 2, October Magazine). 1997.
Photogravure, 12 × 12 inches

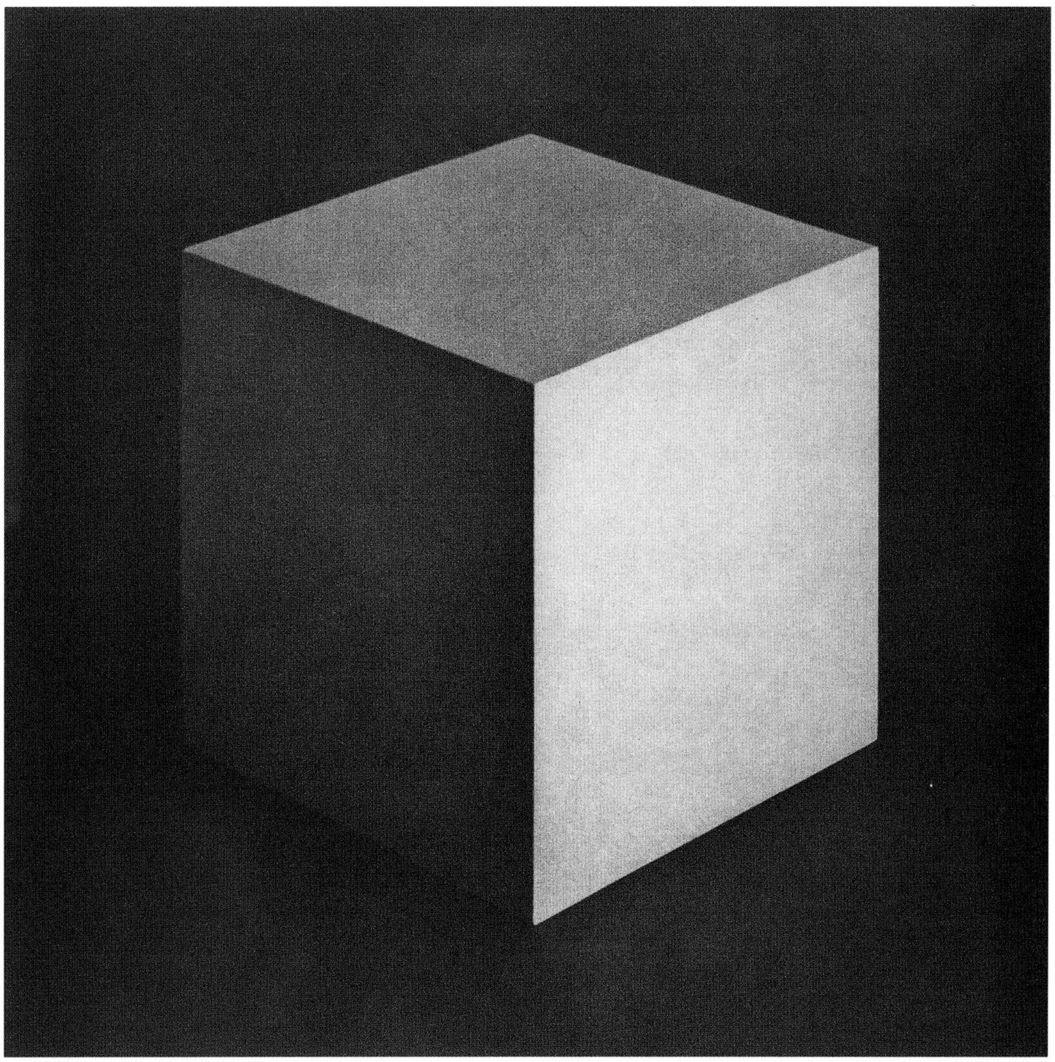

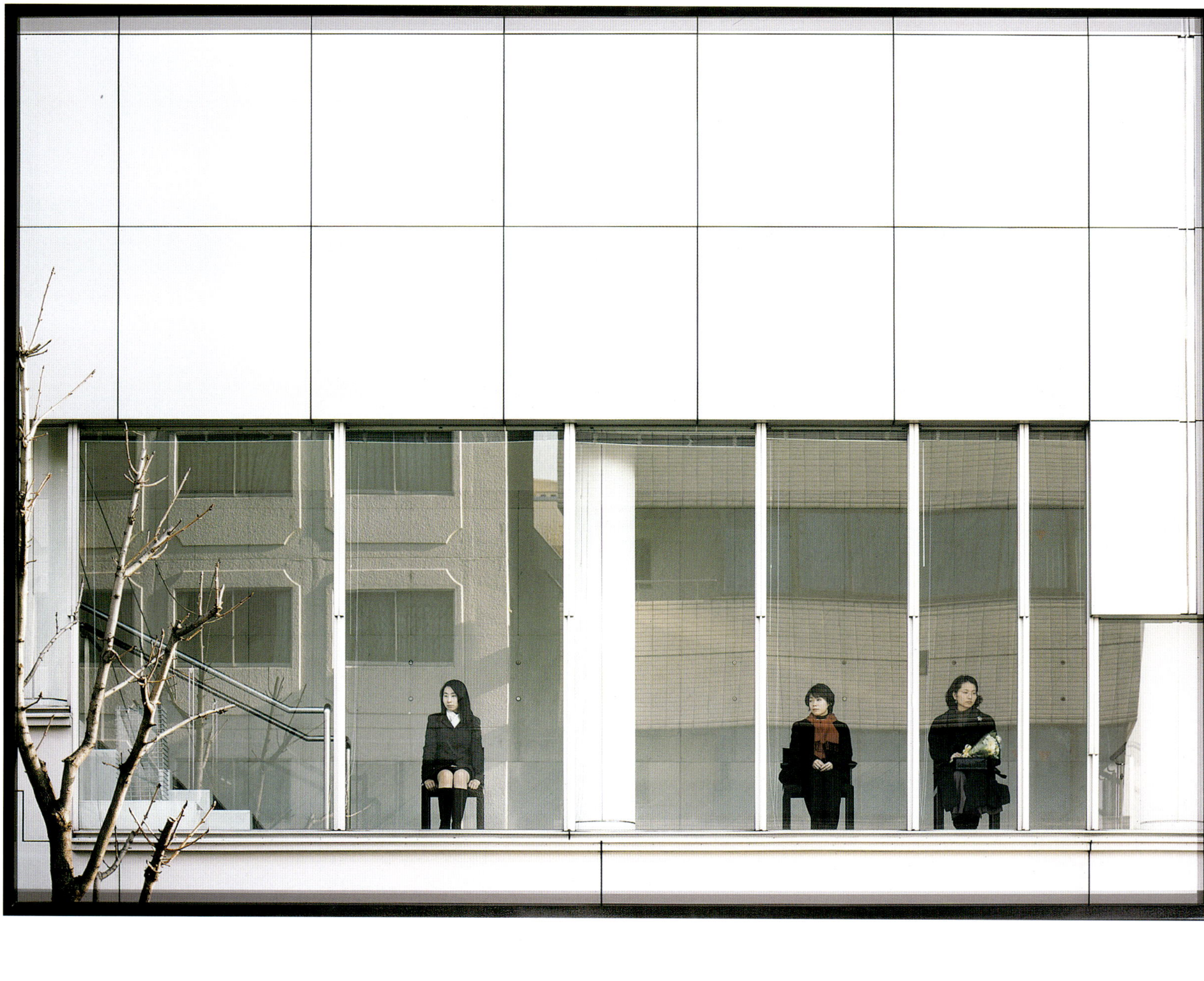

Untitled. 1997. Diptych: chromogenic process prints, 49 × 65 inches each

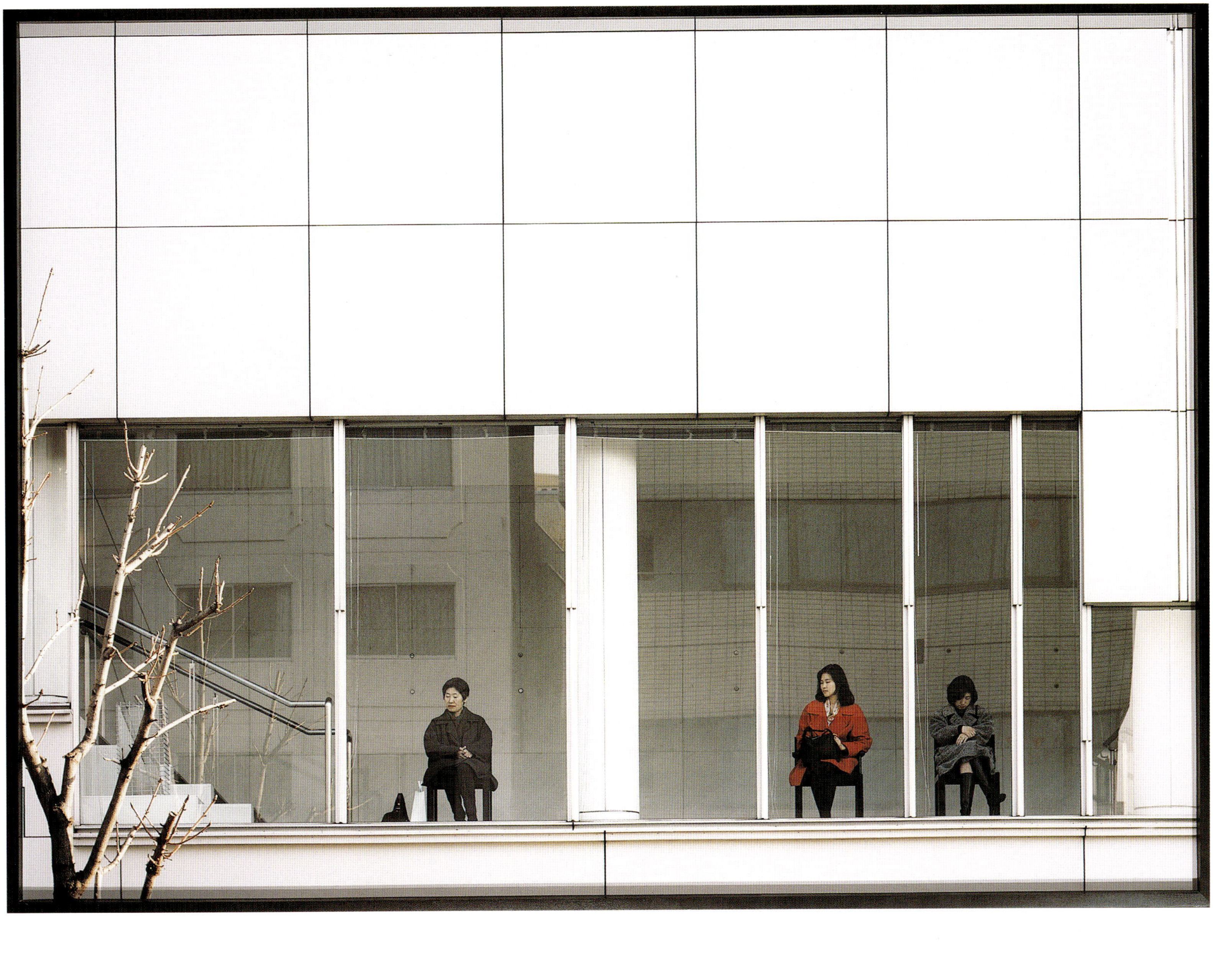

Dartmoor Circle Along a Two Day Walk. 1992. Gelatin silver print, mounted on paper, with pencil text, in artist's frame, 33 × 45 inches

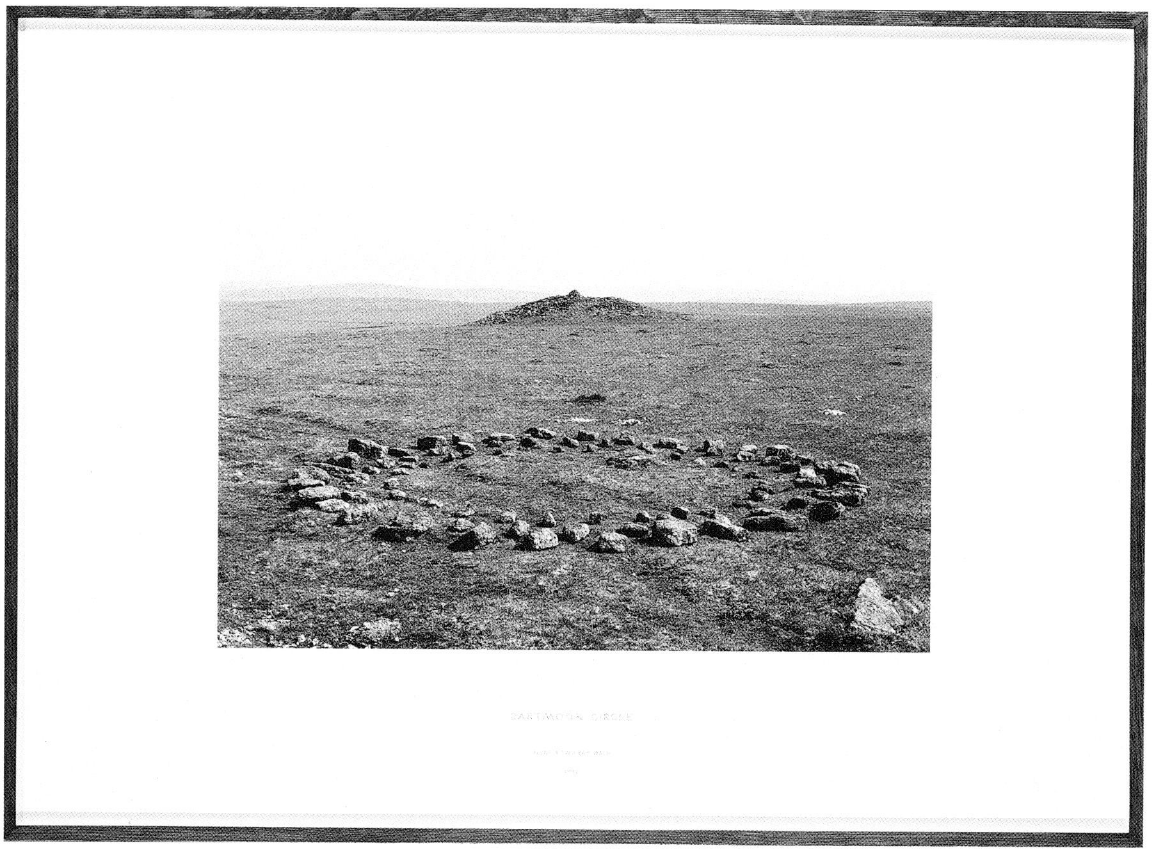

Supersensible. 1995. Gelatin silver print, $50\frac{7}{8} \times 73\frac{3}{4}$ inches

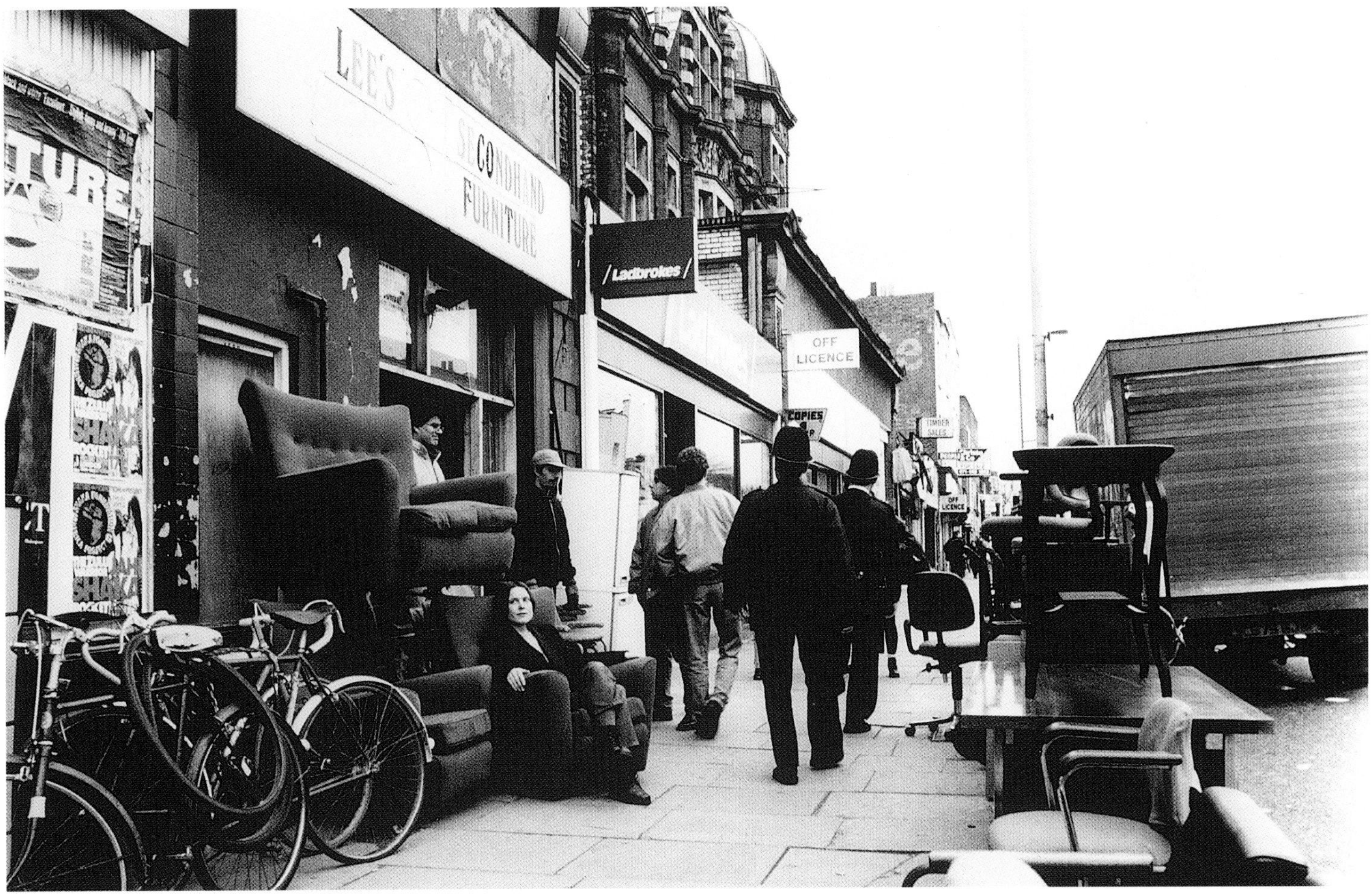

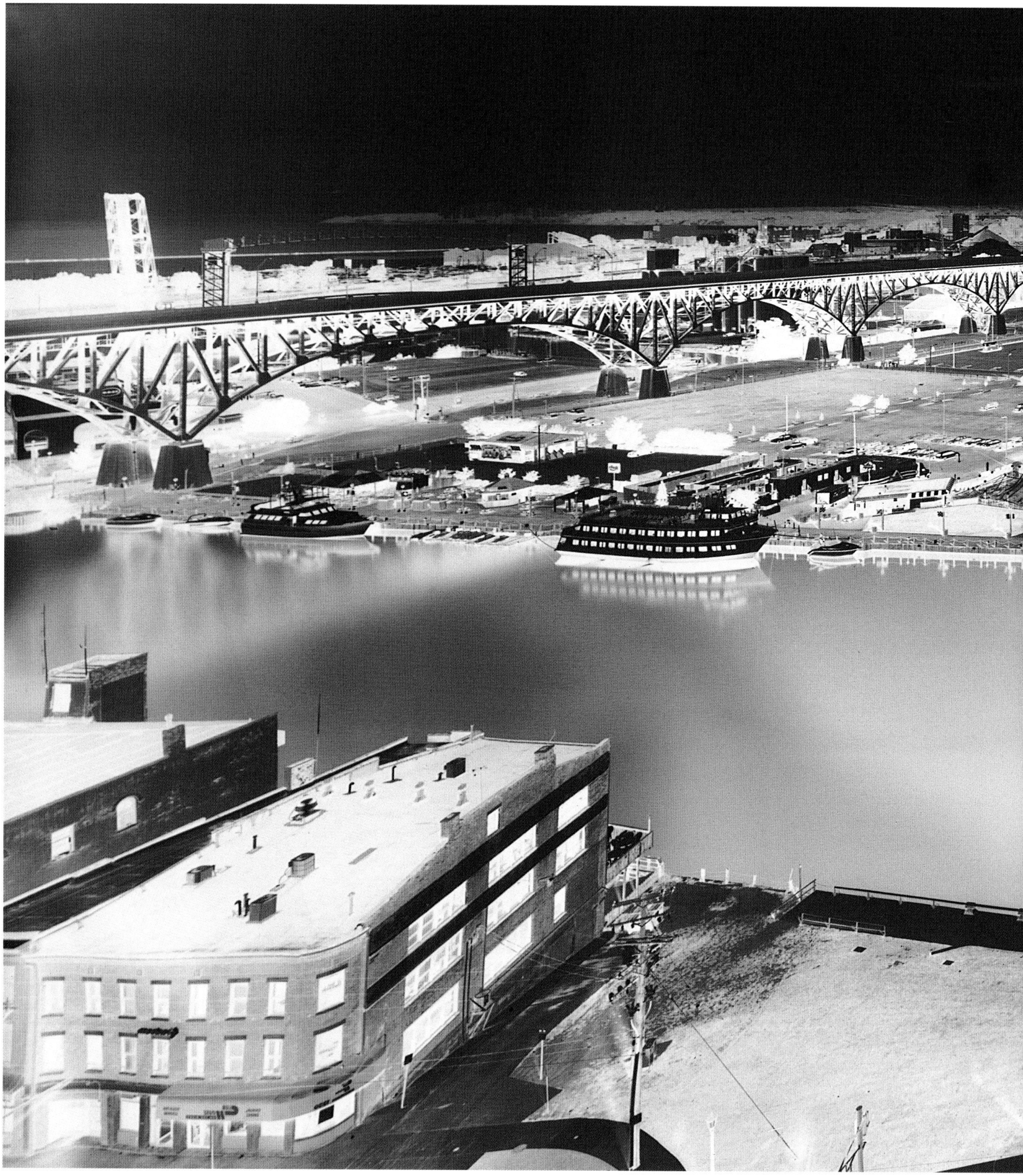

View of Cleveland Flats, V Crittenden Court Apartments, 955 W. St. Clair Ave., 18th Floor, July 6, 1997. 1997. Unique gelatin silver pinhole direct negative print, $57\frac{1}{2}$ inches × 8 feet 5 inches

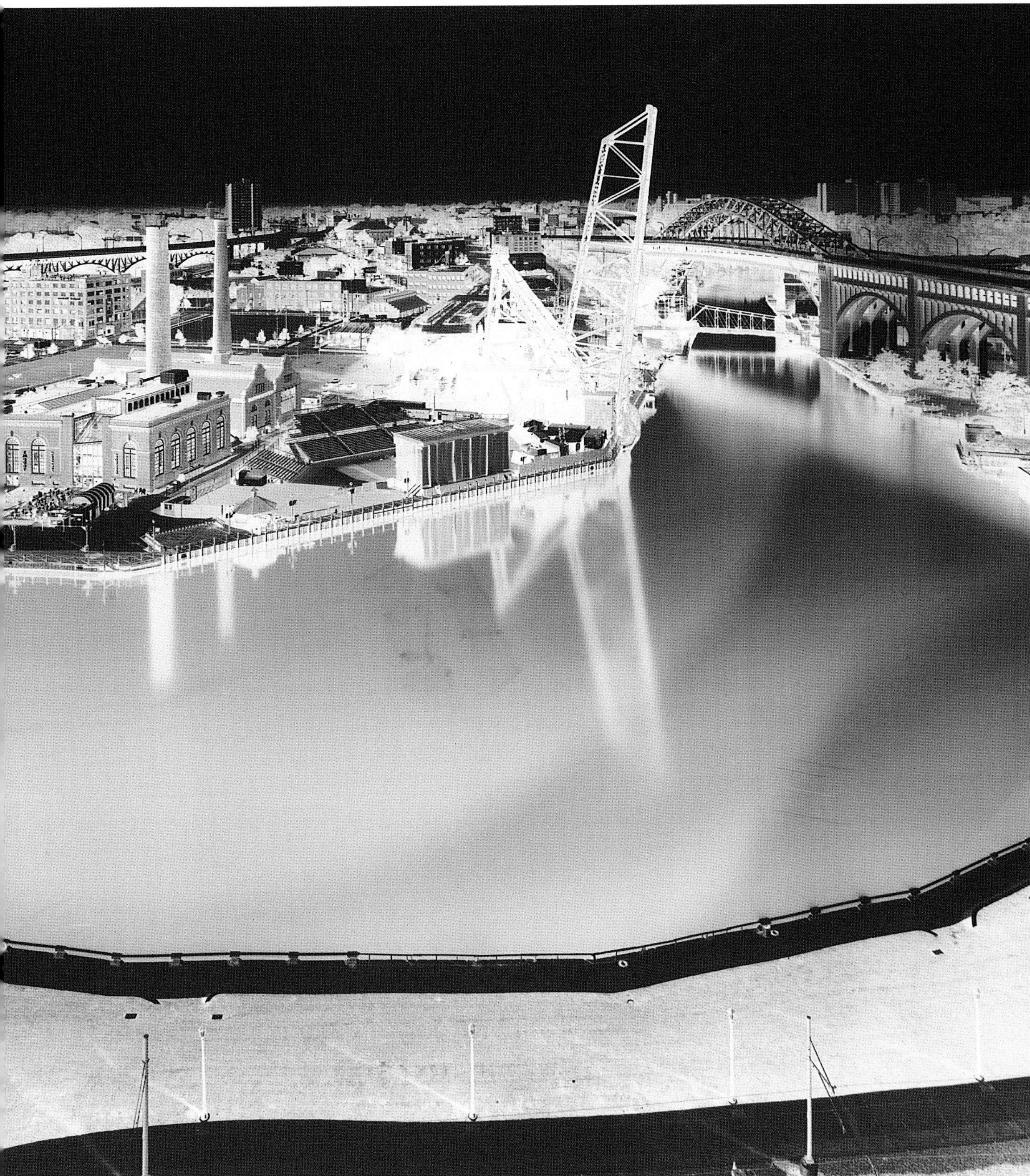

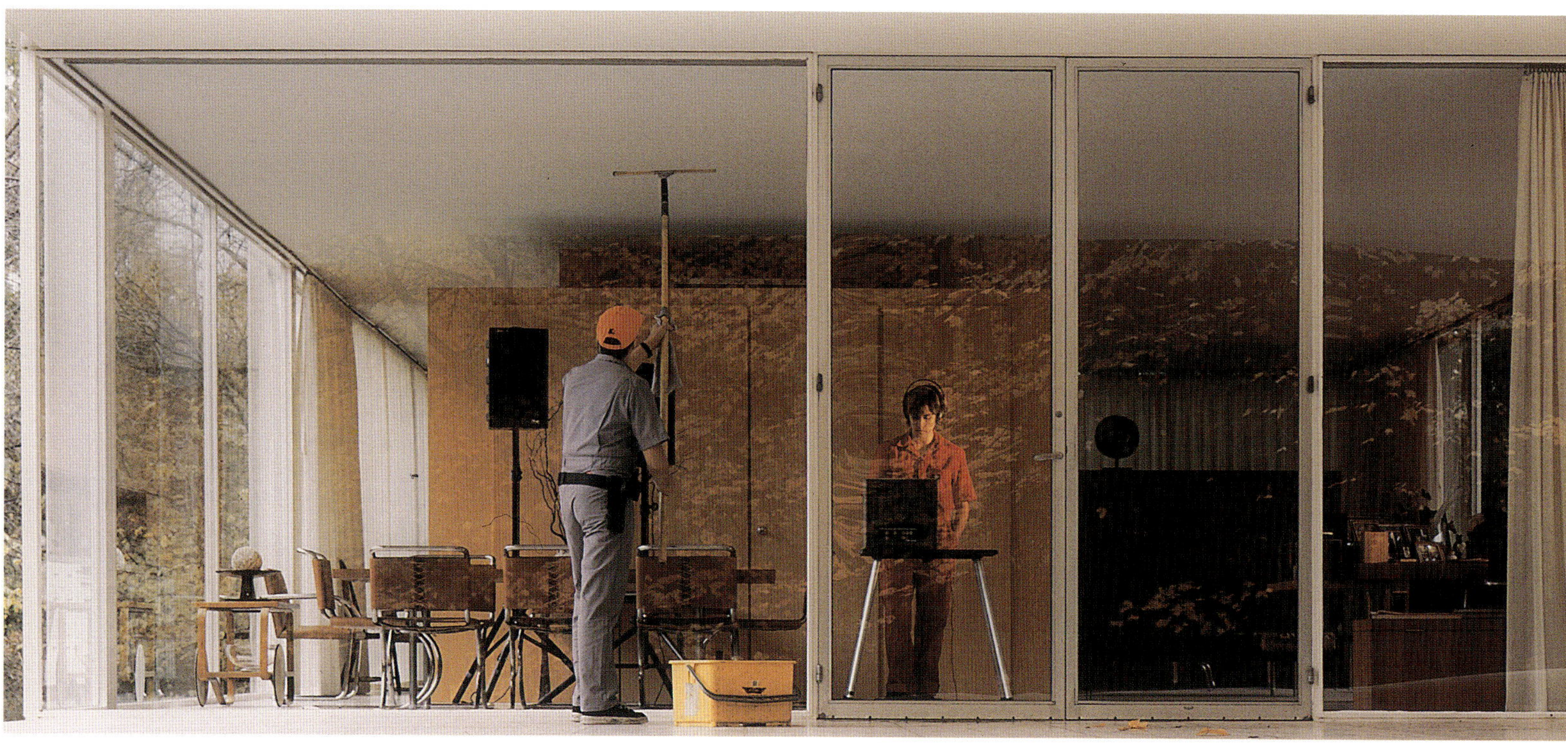

Le Baiser/The Kiss I. 2000. Diptych: chromogenic process prints mounted between plexiglass, 29 inches × 8 feet 10½ inches

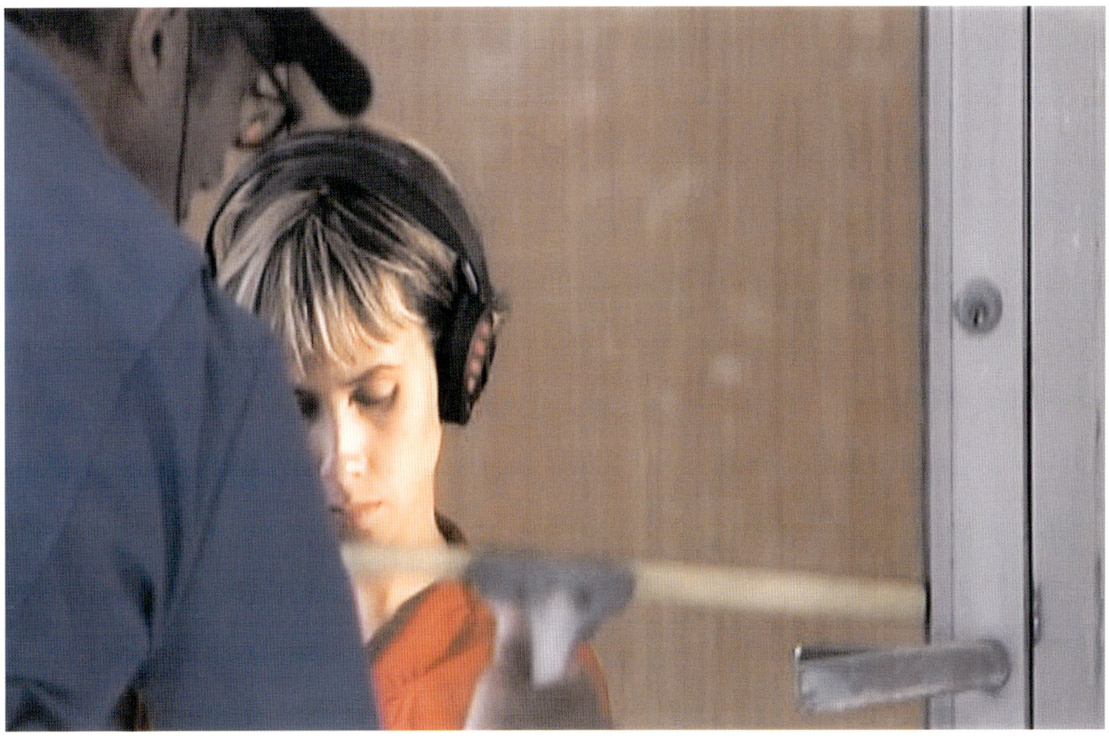

Lake Memphramamagog. 1979. Gelatin silver print, $13^{3}/_{4} \times 13^{3}/_{4}$ inches

Conical Intersect. 1975. Silver dye bleach process print, 31 × 41 inches

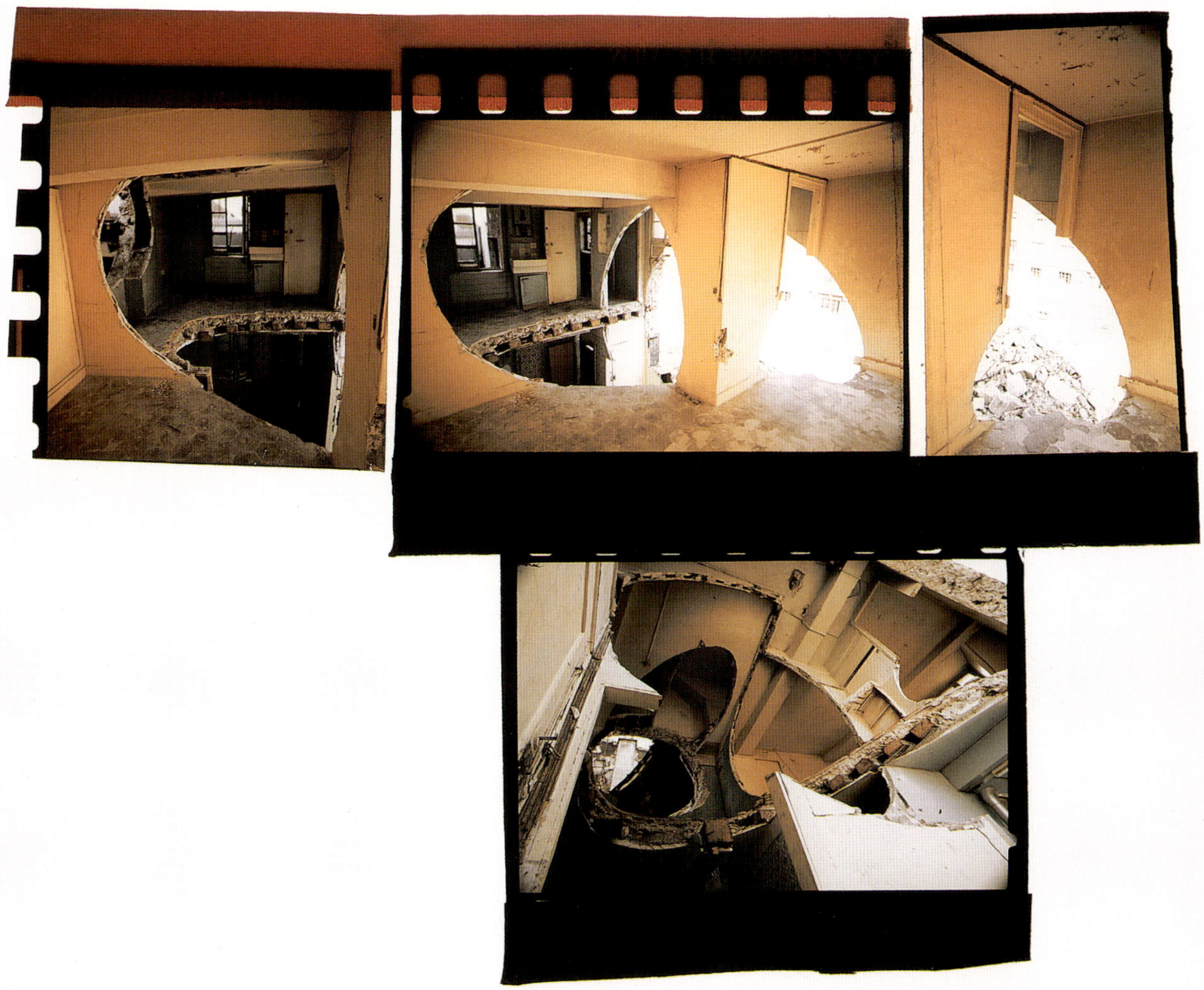

Masks (Small). 1994. Suite of seven chromogenic process prints, $19\frac{1}{2} \times 13$ inches each

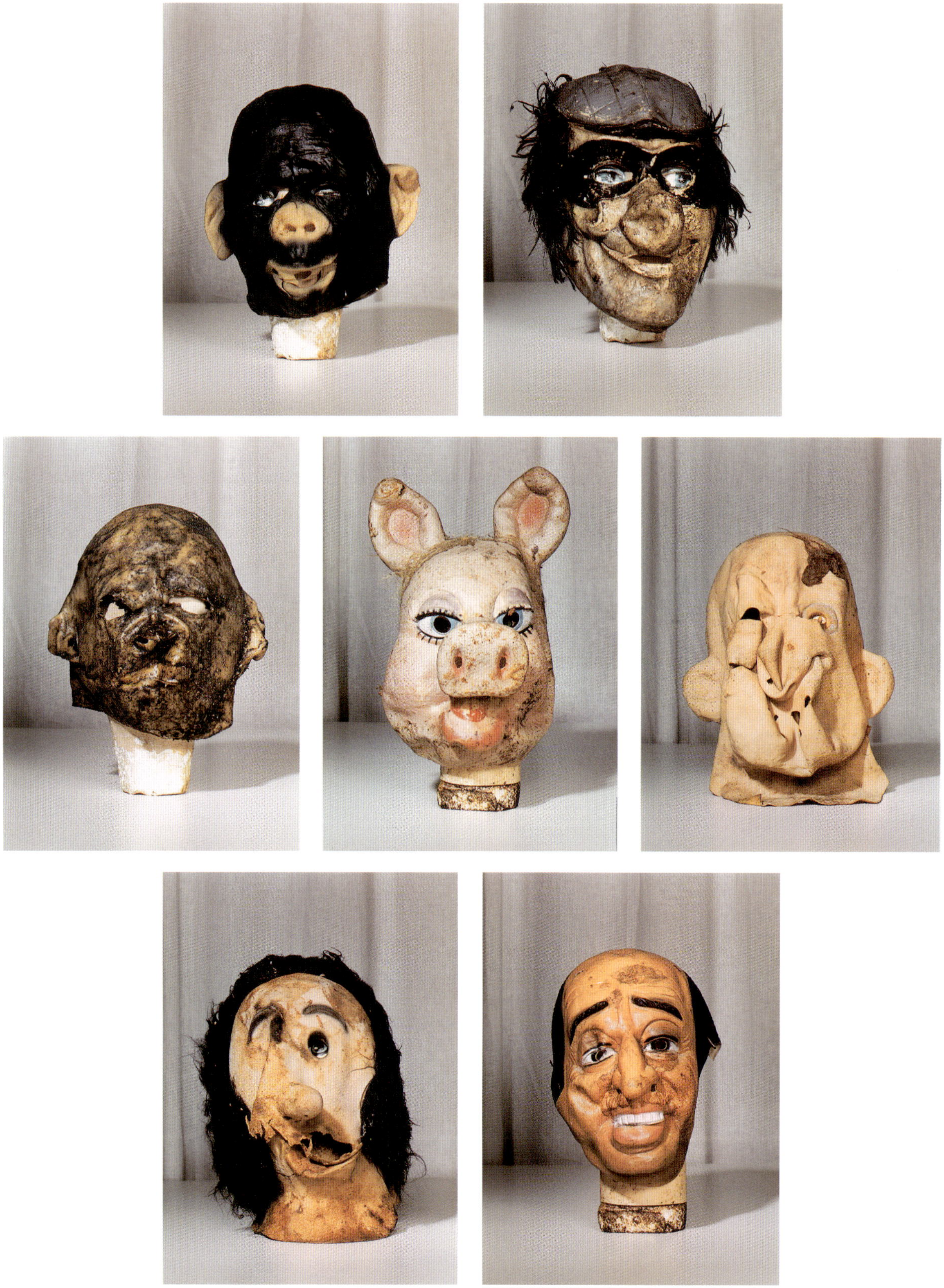

Barrage #50. 1998. Chromogenic process print, mounted between plexiglass, from a series, 18 × 27 inches

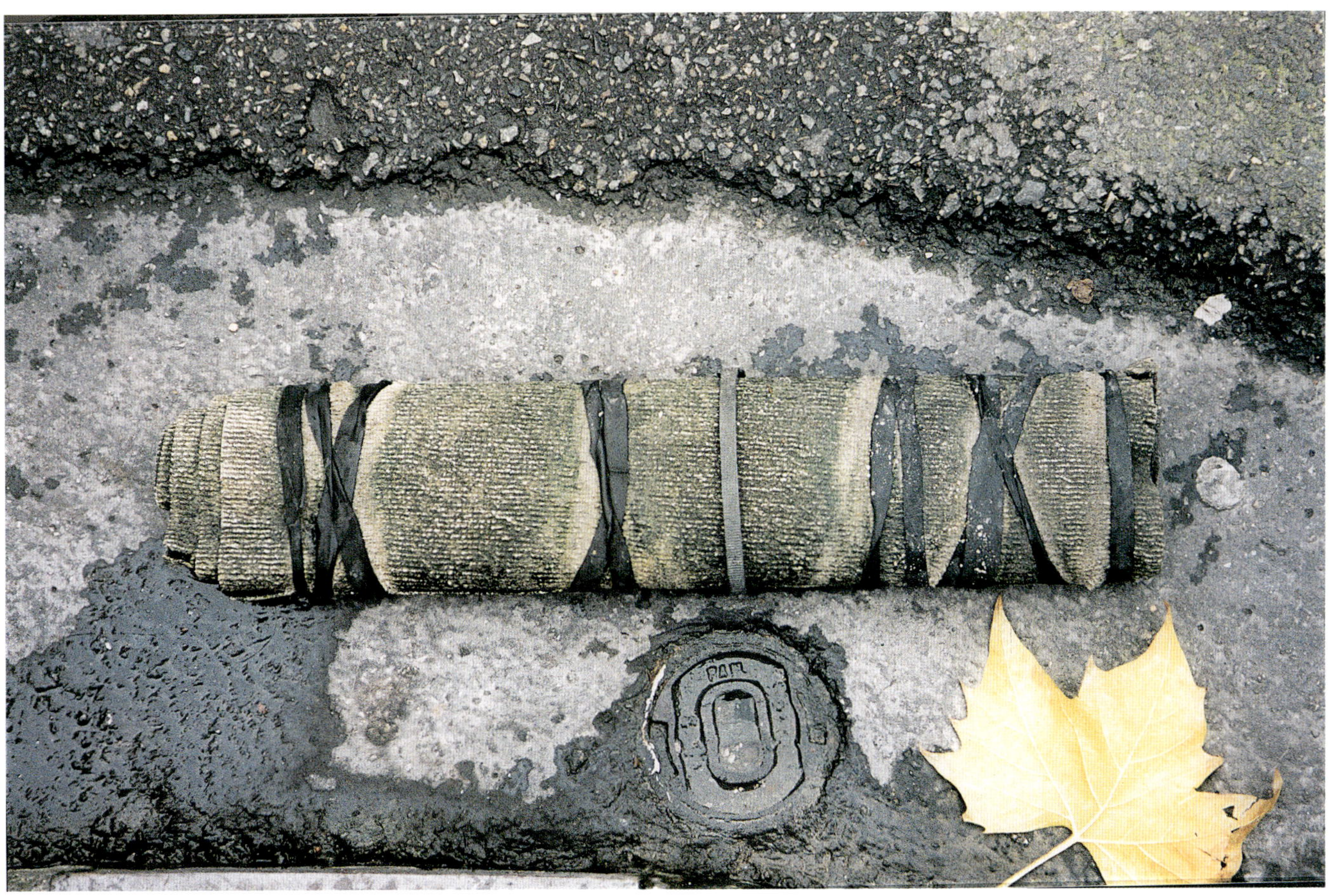

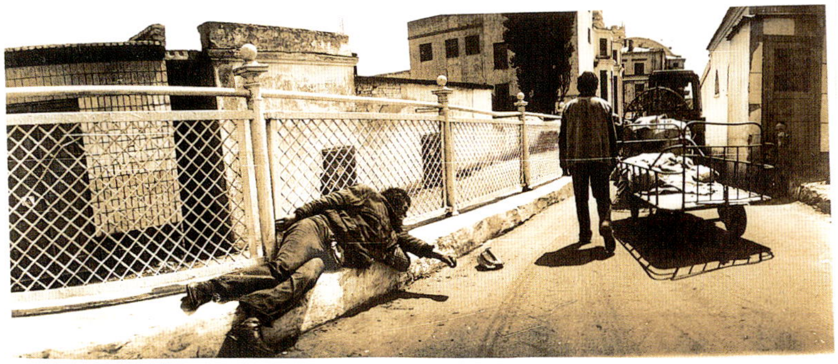

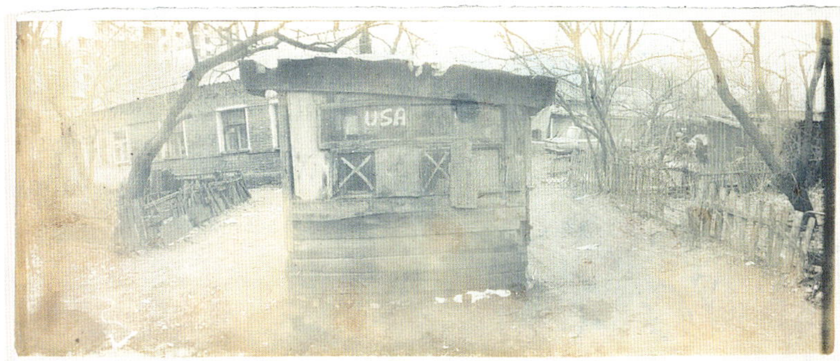
USA

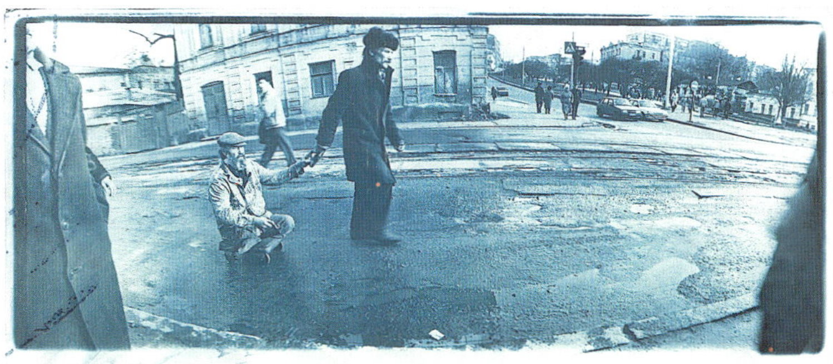

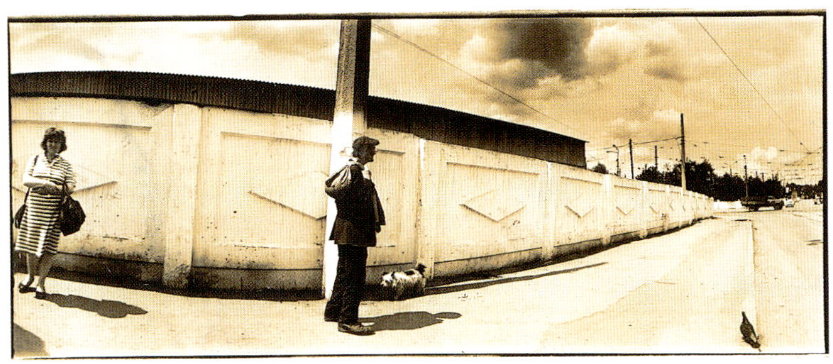

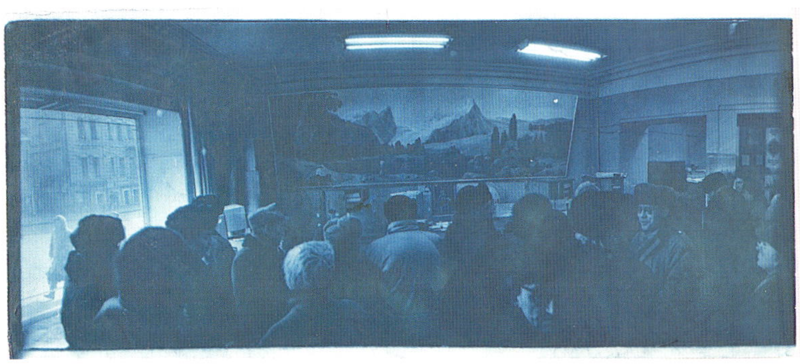

Untitled. From the *Dammerung* series. 1993. Ten toned gelatin silver prints, paper size 5¾ × 11¾ inches each

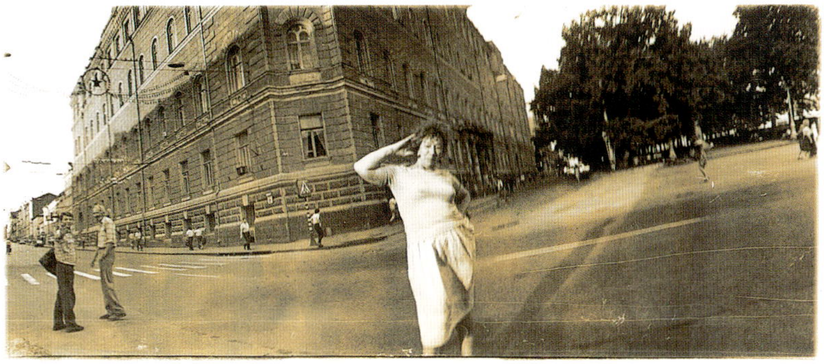

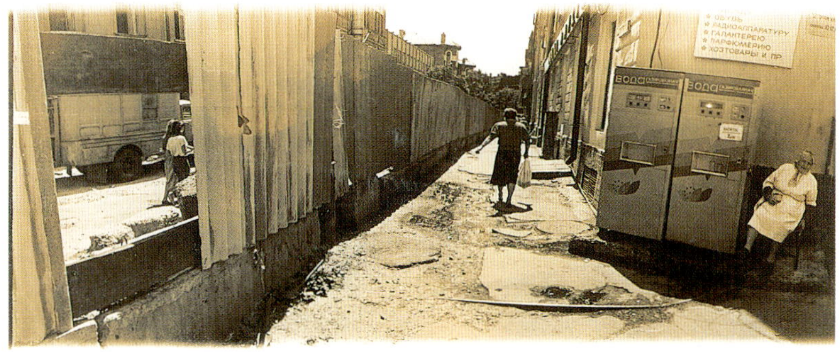

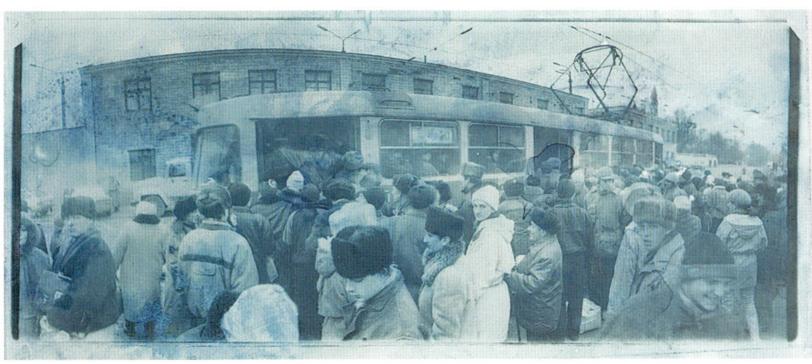

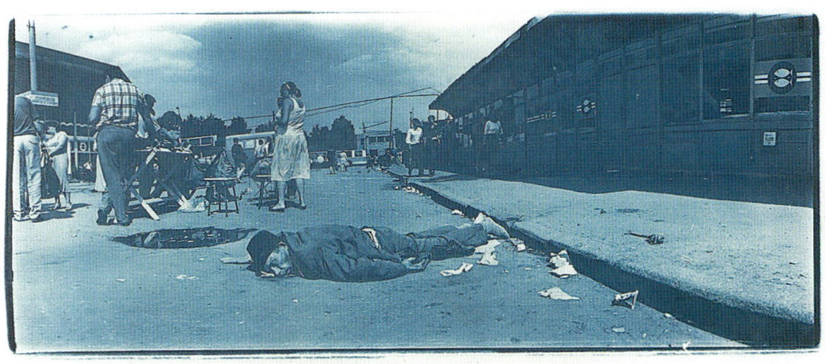

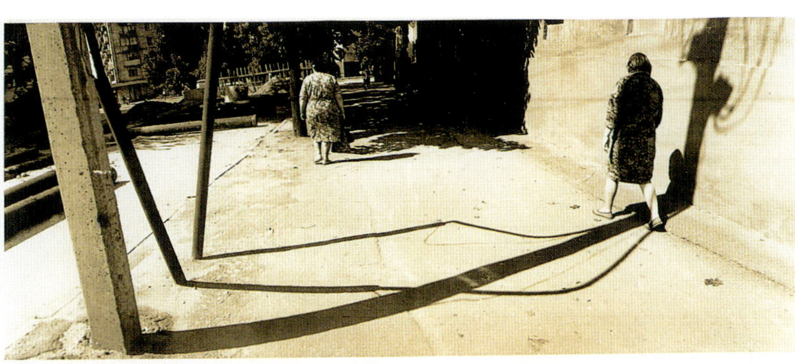

RICHARD MISRACH

Outdoor Dining, Bonneville Salt Flats. 1992. Chromogenic process print, 41 × 51 inches

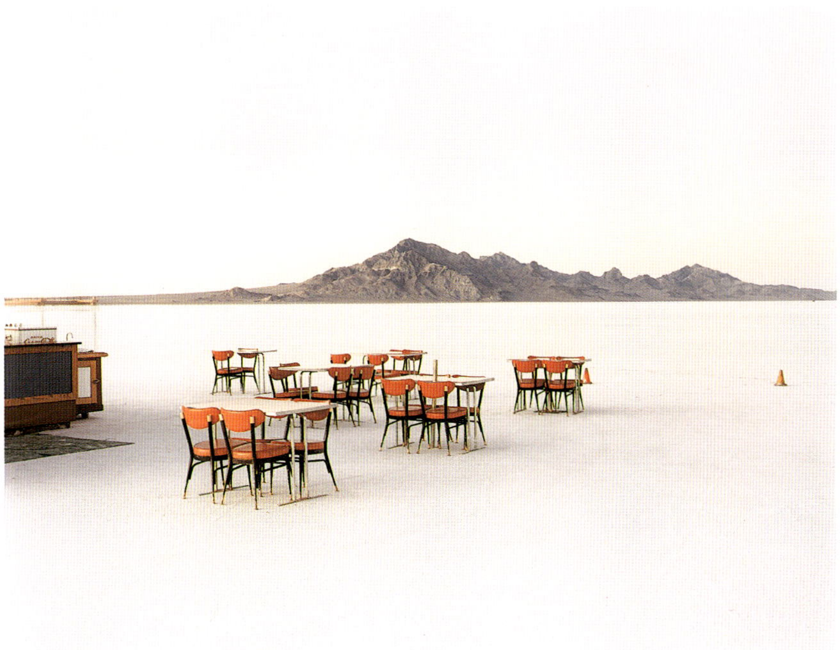

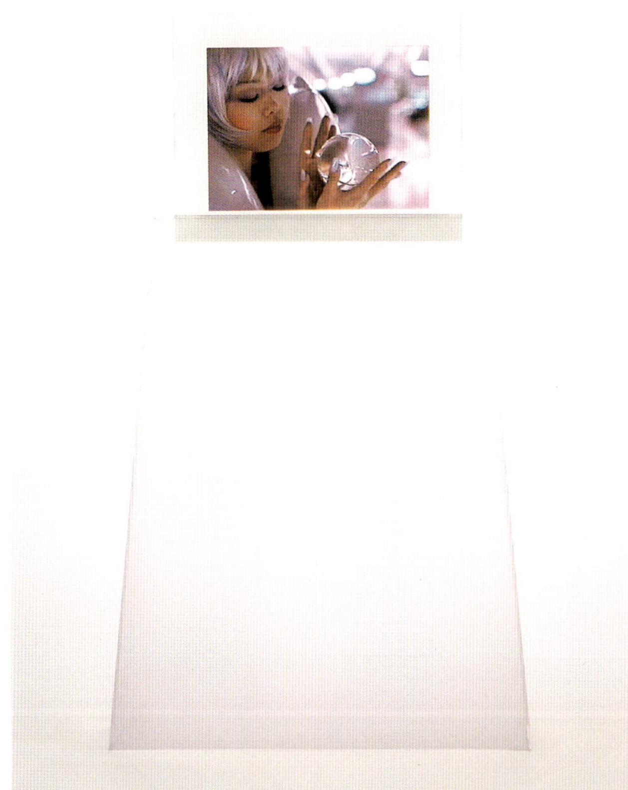

MARIKO MORI

Mirage (Miko no Inori). 1997. Digital video still, sandwiched between etched glass panels with artist's etched plexiglass base, $76\frac{1}{2} \times 43\frac{1}{4} \times 13\frac{3}{4}$ inches

Self-Portrait (Actress) / White Marilyn. 1996.
Silver dye bleach process print, face mounted to plexiglass, 65 1/2 × 81 1/8 inches

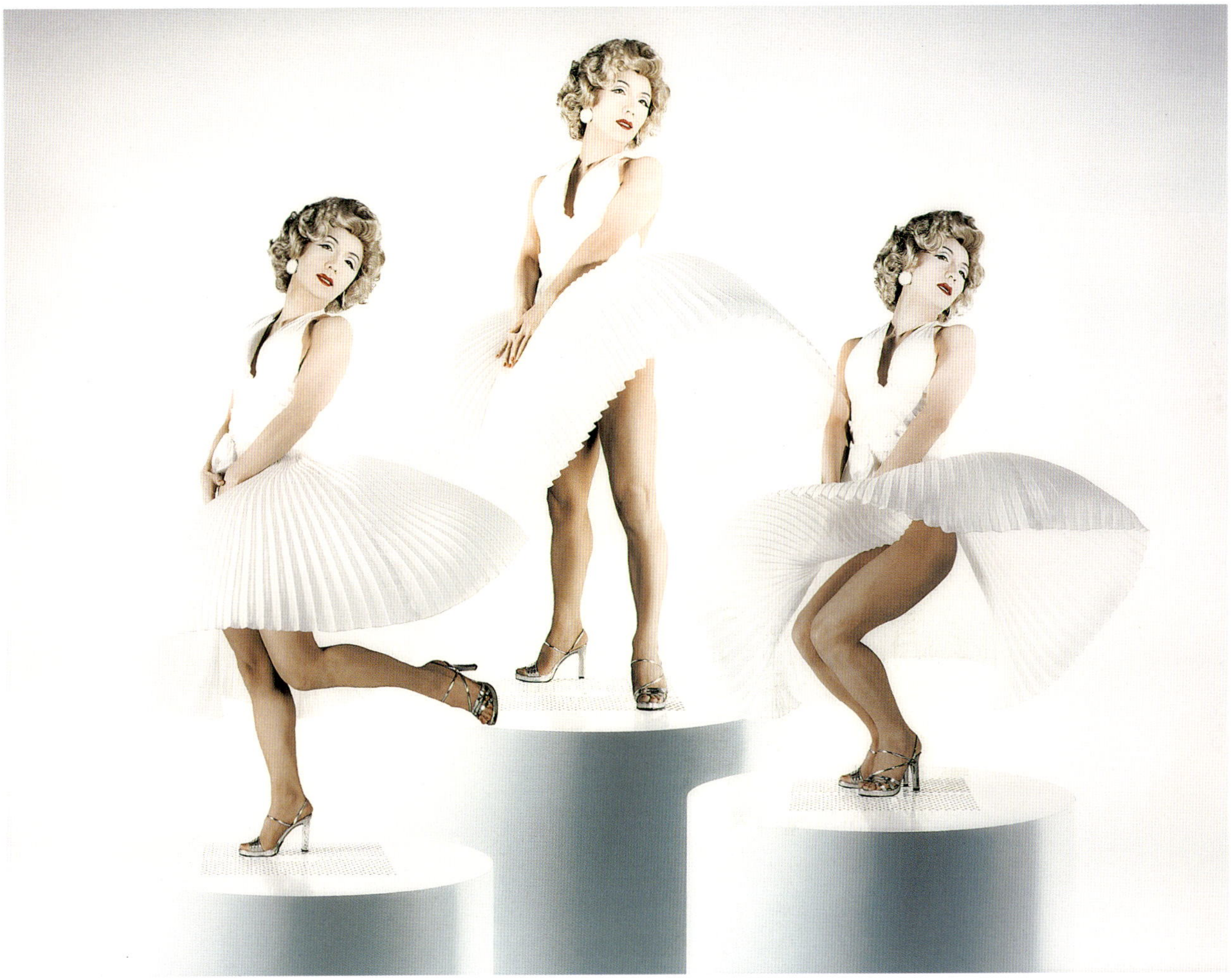

Confession I. 1994. Silver dye bleach process print, face mounted to plexiglass, 36 × 55 inches

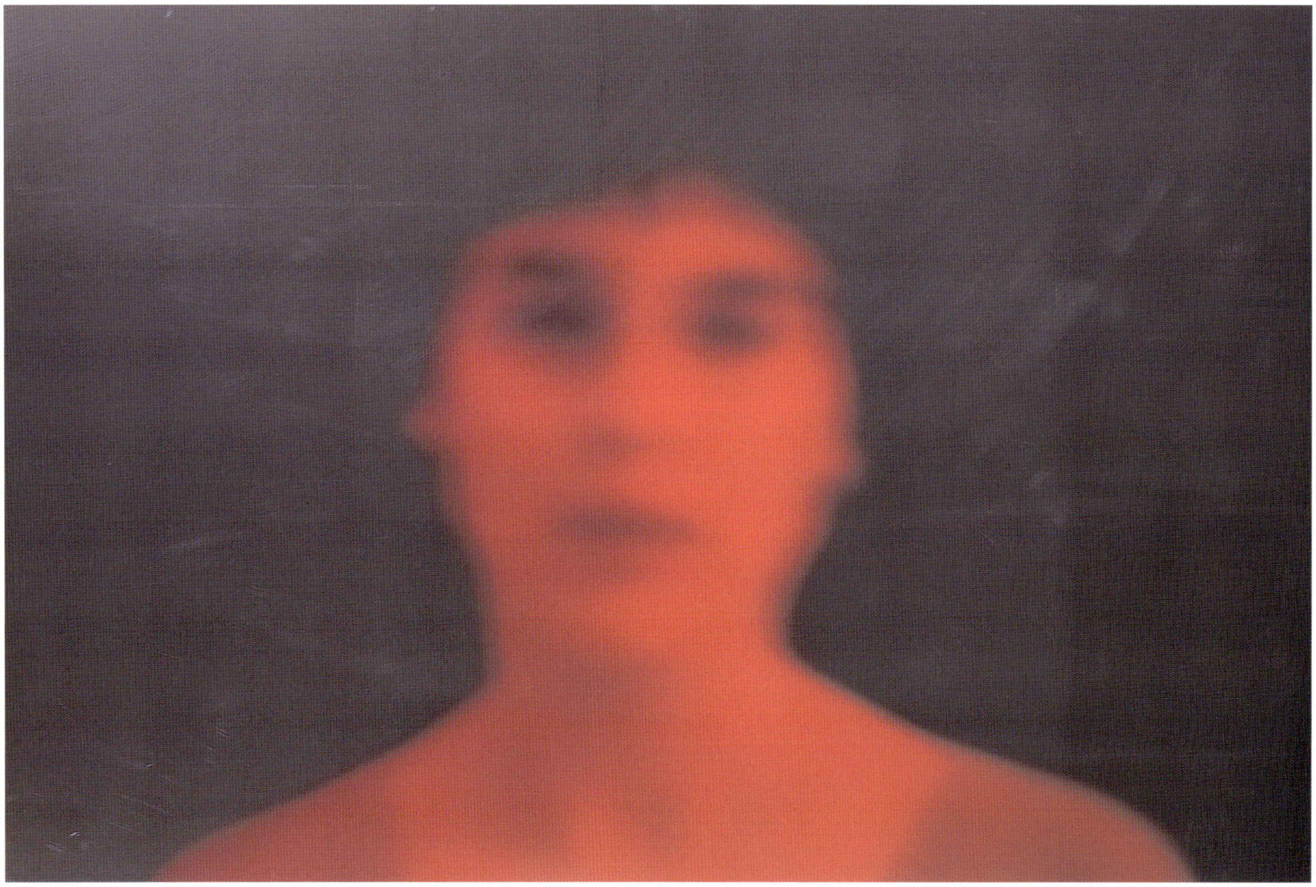

Avoid Tourists. 1998 (1977). Suite of six constructions: gelatin silver prints mounted to cardboard, aluminum, enamel paint on glass, felt, and wire, $50 \times 27\frac{1}{2} \times 2\frac{1}{2}$ inches each

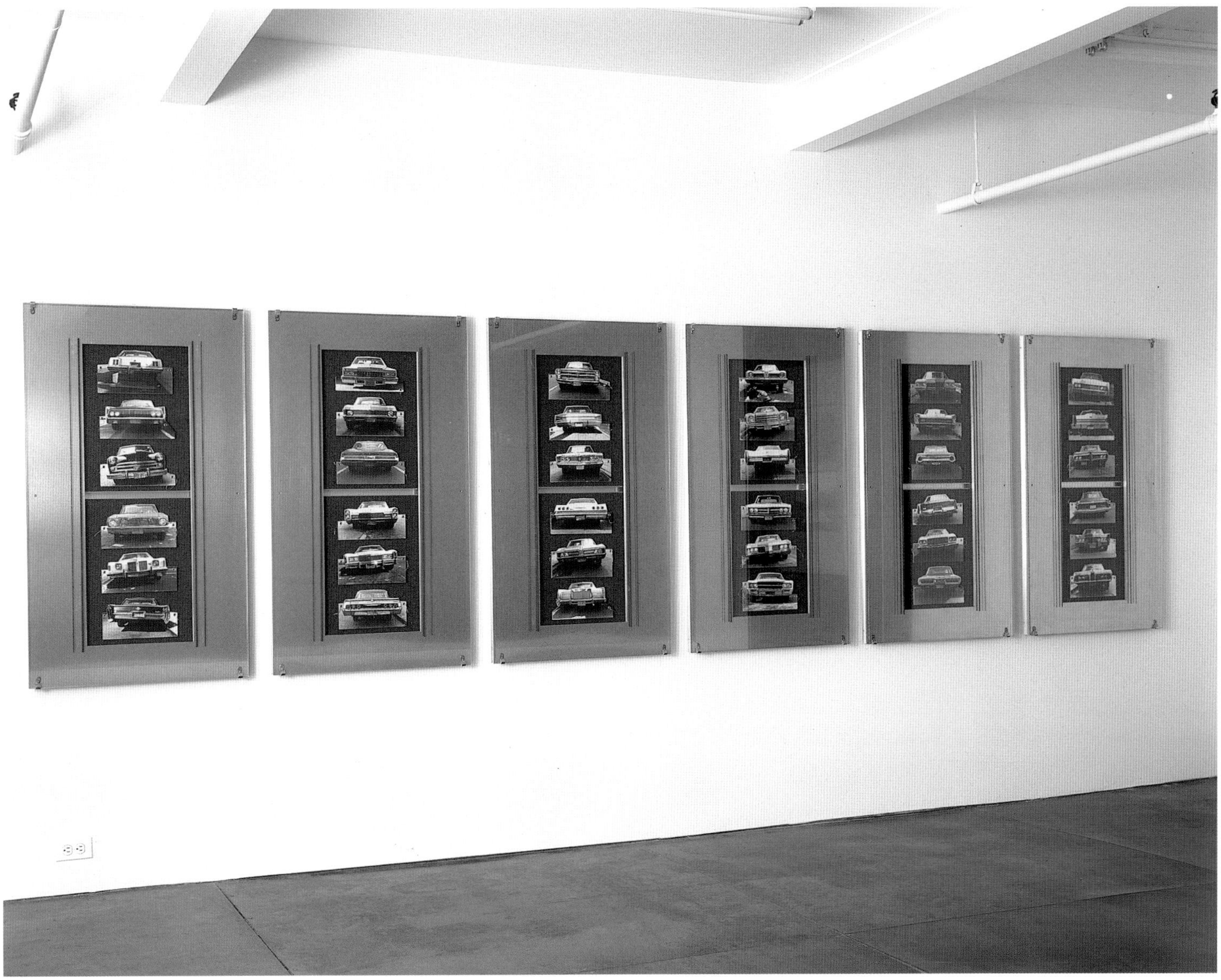

How to Establish Individuality (Mother and Daughter, The Collector, The Entertainer, The Partygirls). 1999. Twenty chromogenic process prints of "props used by Ikea," 49¾ × 61¼ inches

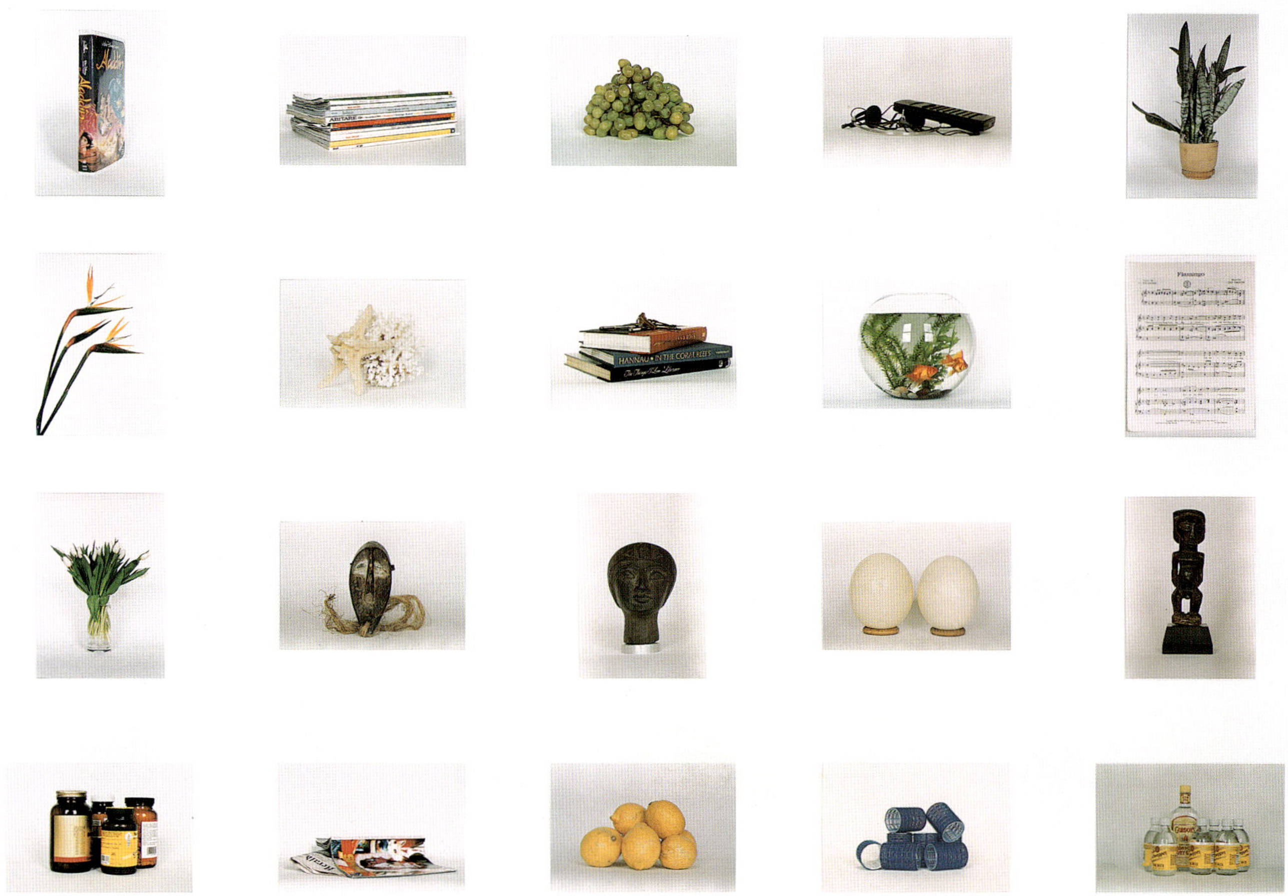

MATT MULLICAN

Untitled. 1990. Color transparency in aluminum lightbox, $36^{3}/_{4} \times 48^{5}/_{8} \times 6^{3}/_{4}$ inches

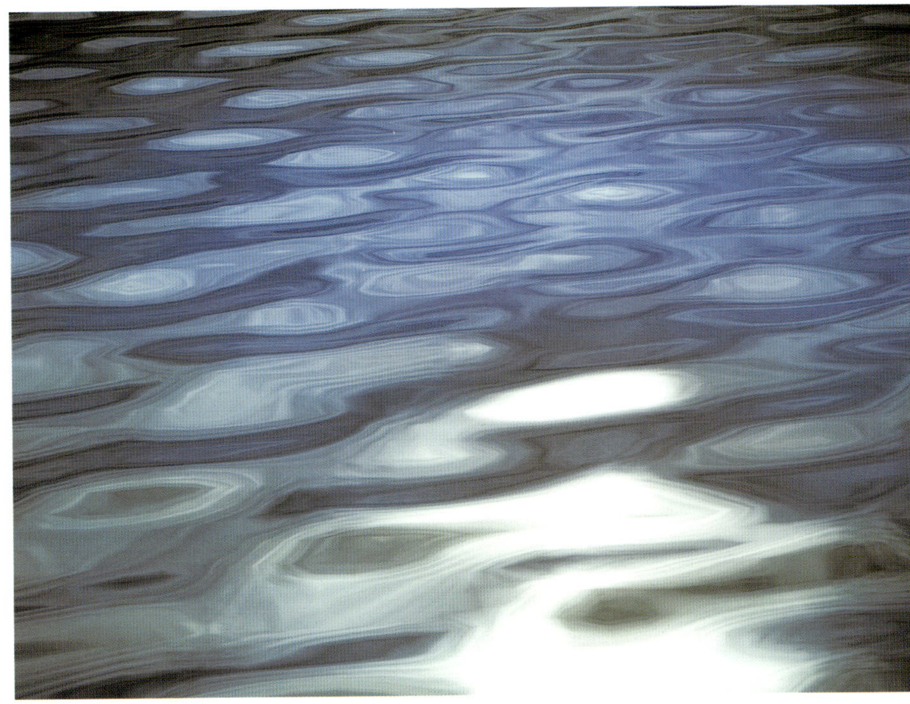

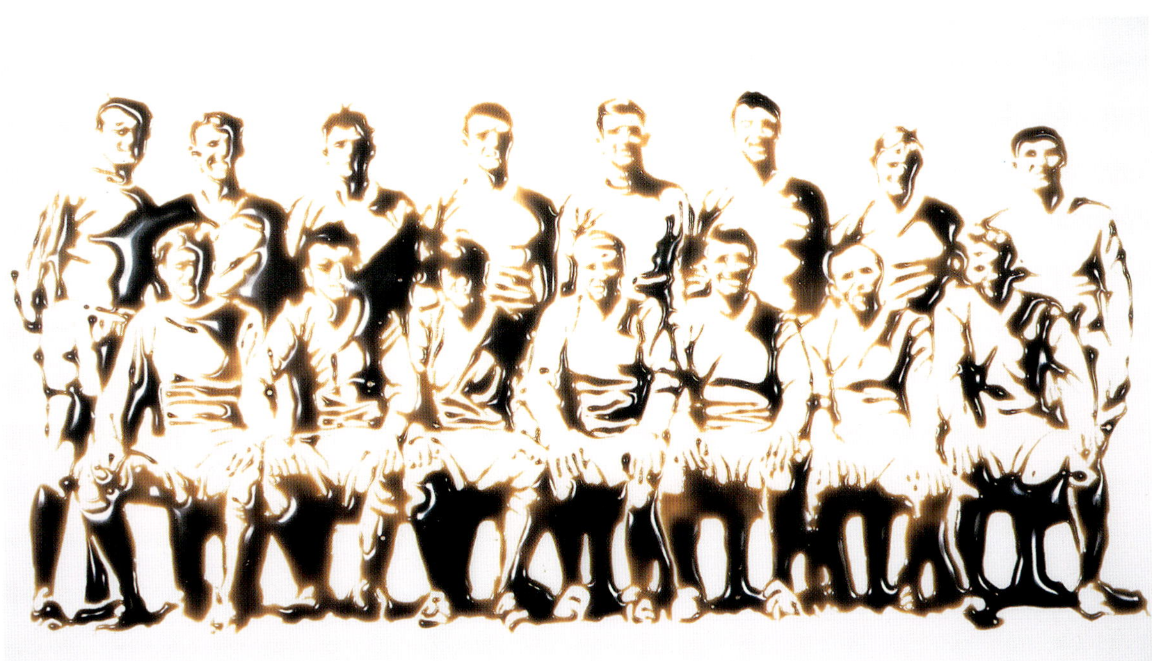

VIK MUNIZ

Team. 1998. Silver dye bleach process print, $51^{1}/_{2} \times 80^{5}/_{8}$ inches

No. 75 (Mars, Avril, Mai) (March, April, May). 1987.
Color photograph from a series, 43 × 43 inches

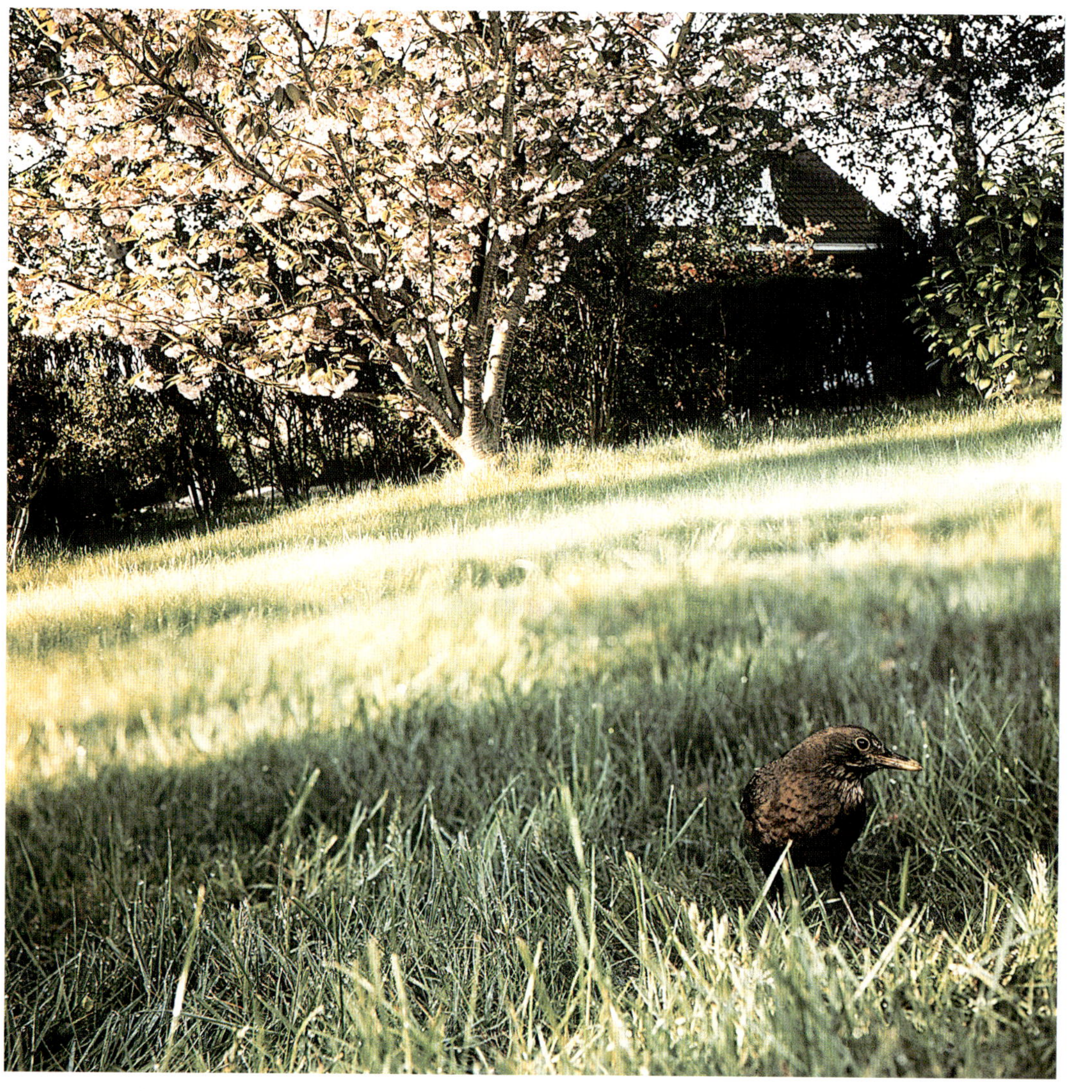

Study for Animal Pyramid. 1989. Gelatin silver prints and tape collaged on rag paper with adhesive residue, 26 × 39½ inches

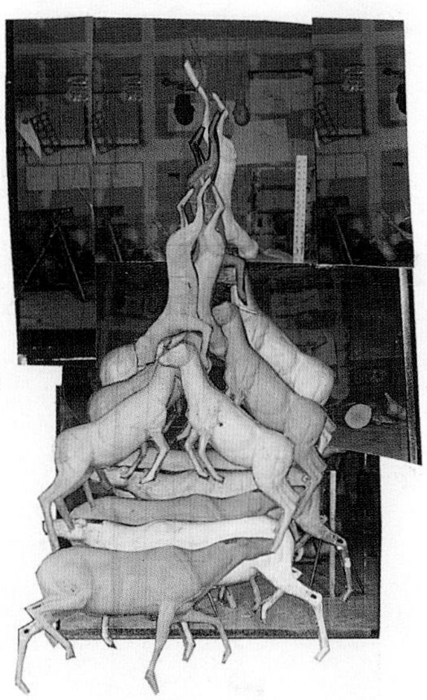

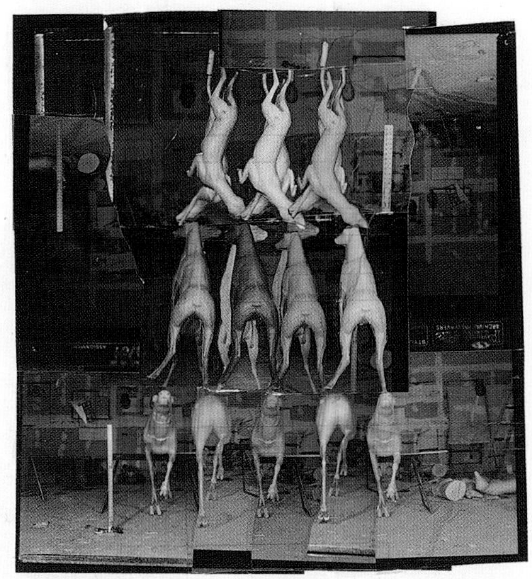

Soliloquy Series. 2000. Silver dye bleach process print, 60 × 44¼ inches

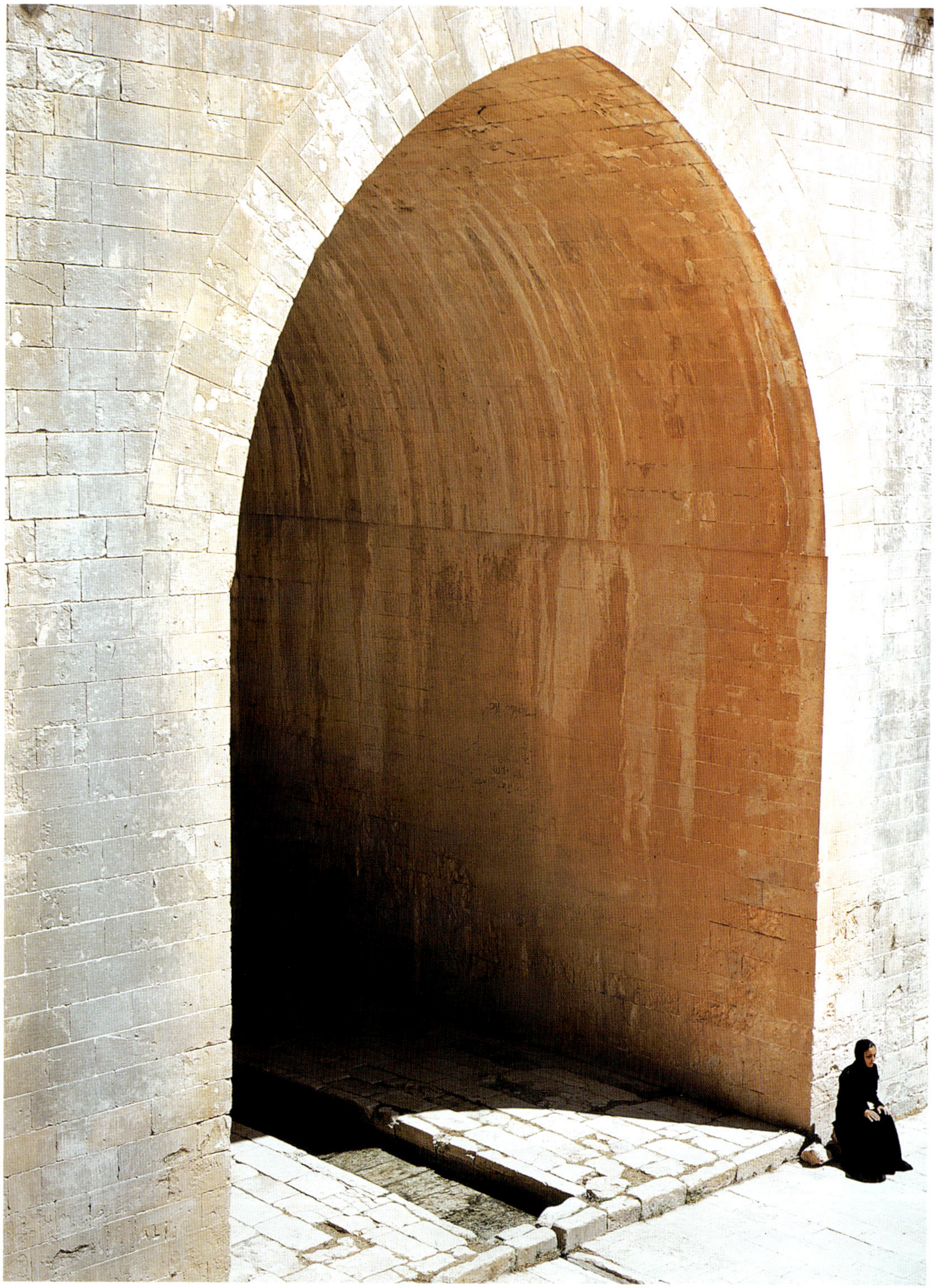

WALTER NIEDERMAYR *Marmolada Punta Rocca IV.* 1994. Diptych: chromogenic process prints, face mounted to plexiglass, $40^{3}/_{8} \times 49^{1}/_{8}$ inches each

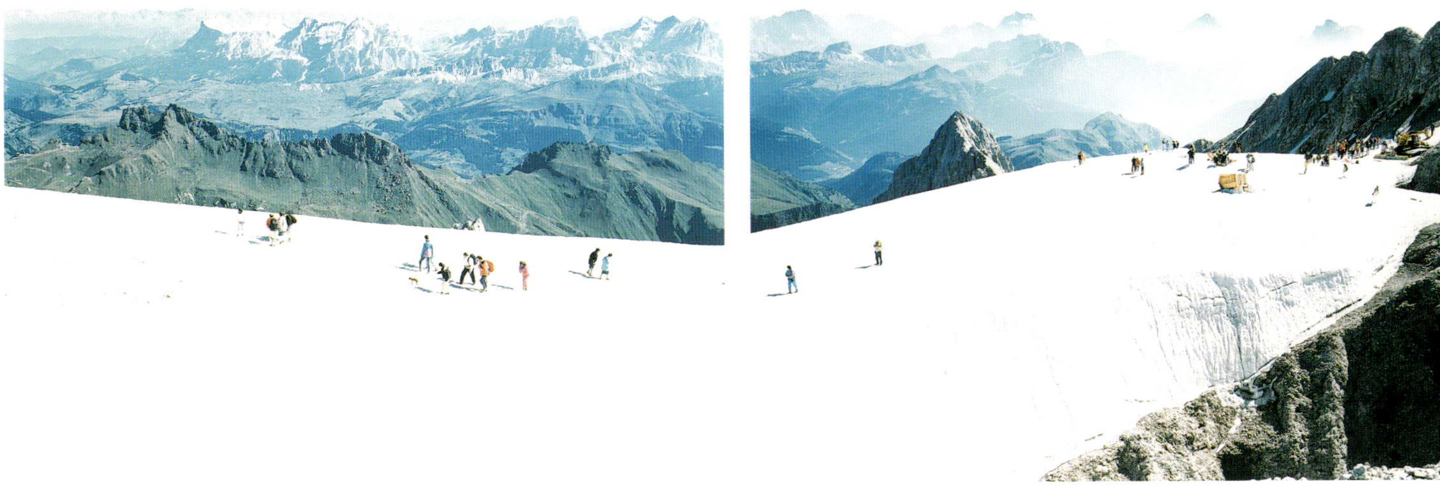

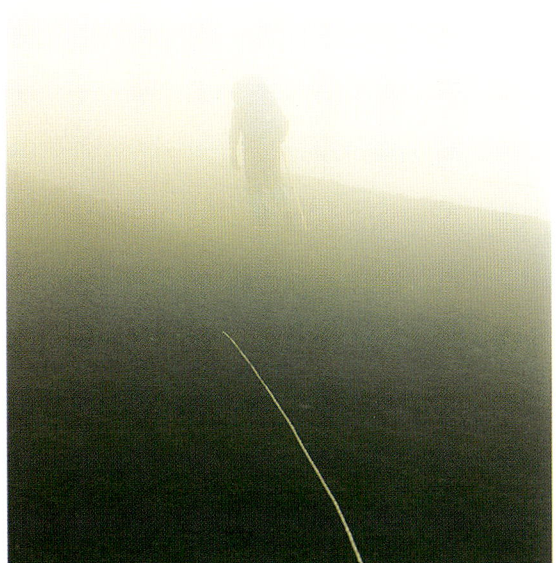

RIKA NOGUCHI *A Prime #12.* 1999. Chromogenic process print from a series, 37 × 26 inches

Folk. 1999. Digitally composited ink jet print, 54 inches × 8 feet $11\frac{1}{4}$ inches

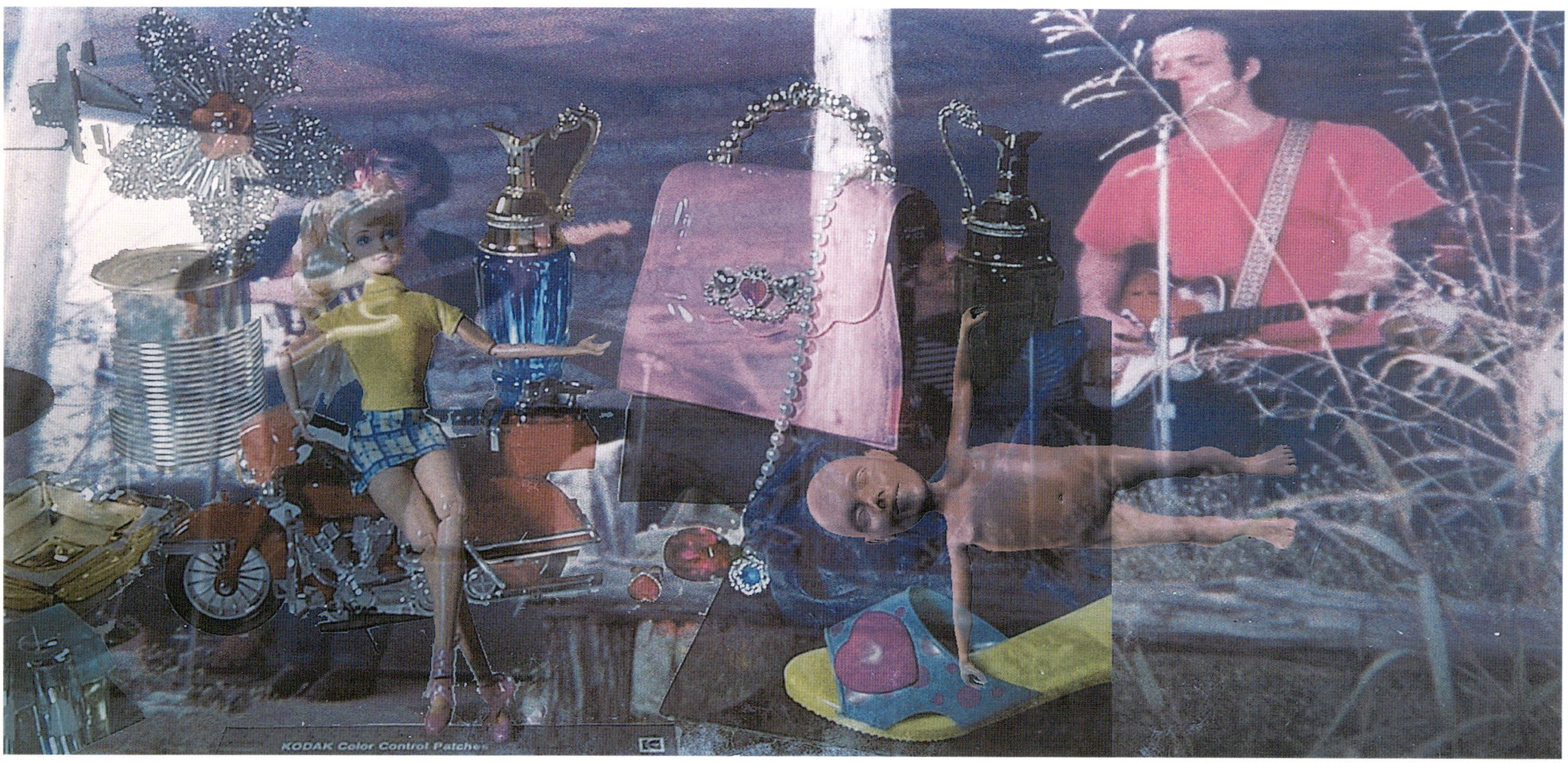

Già Casanova Ontani Roma per le feste 1997 1998 (The Late Casanova Ontani in Rome for the Holidays 1997 1998).
1997–98. Gelatin silver print on paper with watercolor hand tinting in gilded tondo frame, 50½ inches in diameter

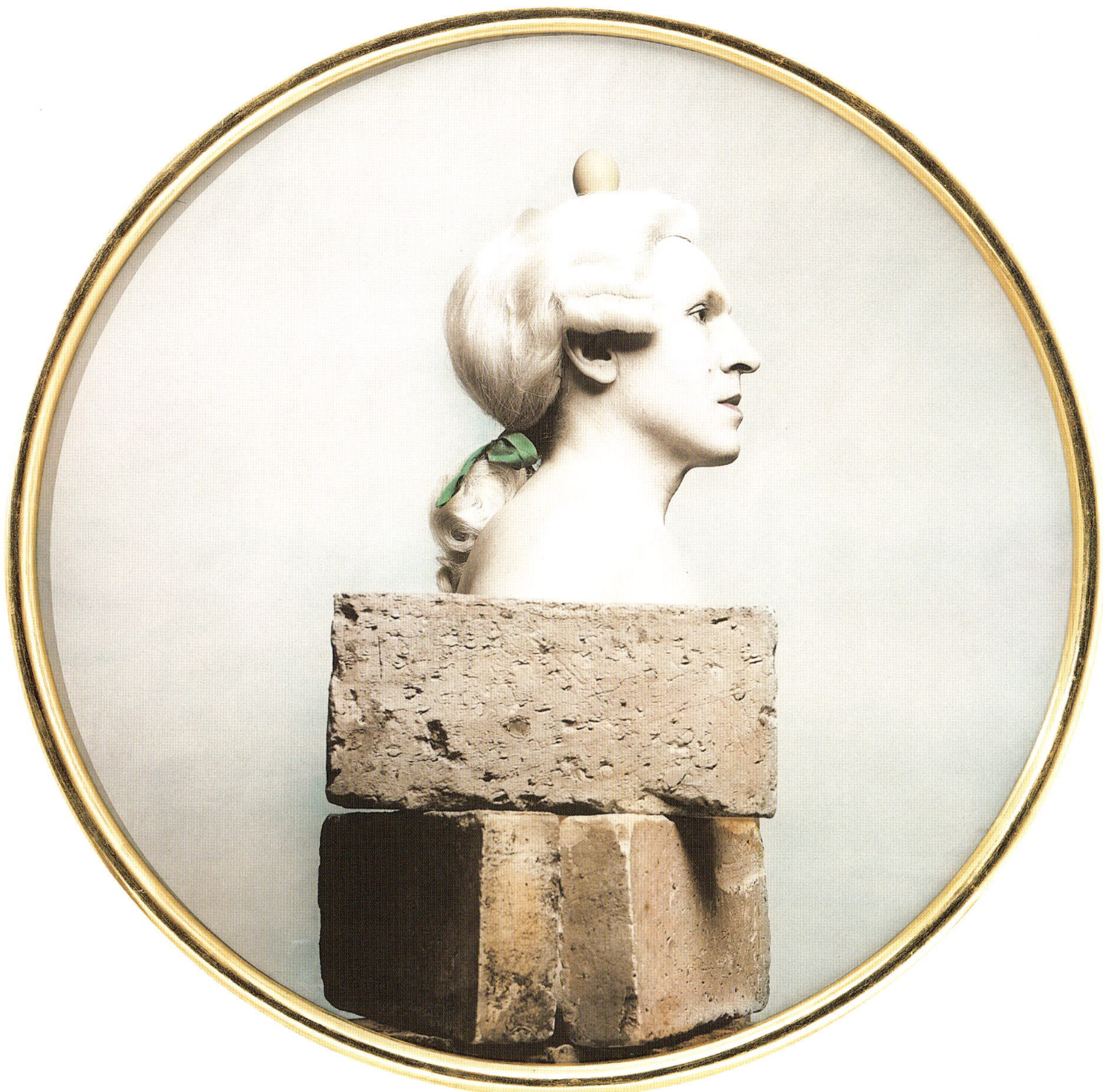

Untitled #13. From the *Freeway* series. 1994.
Platinum print, 2 1/8 × 6 1/2 inches

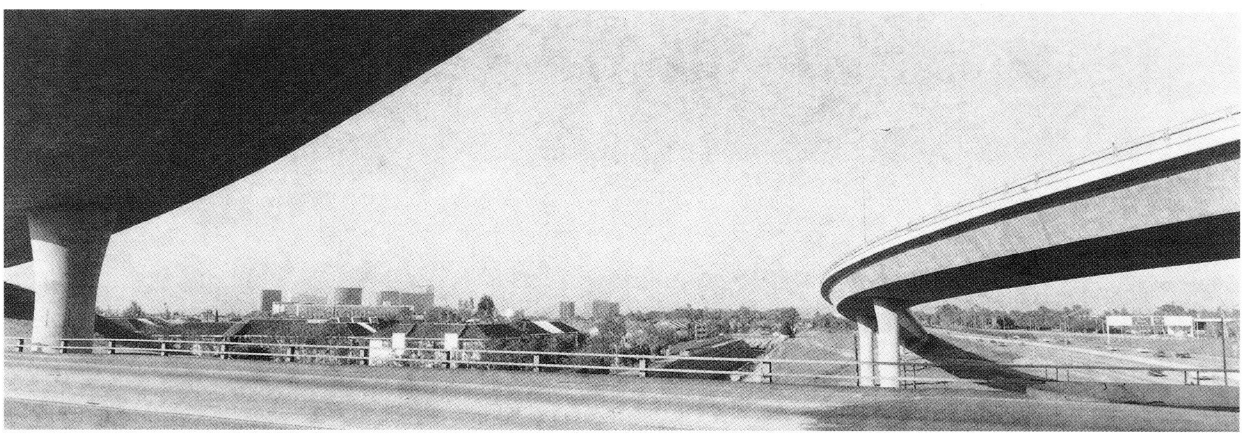

GABRIEL OROZCO

Quatro Parques (Four Parks). 1997. Iris print, $22\frac{7}{8} \times 34\frac{1}{4}$ inches

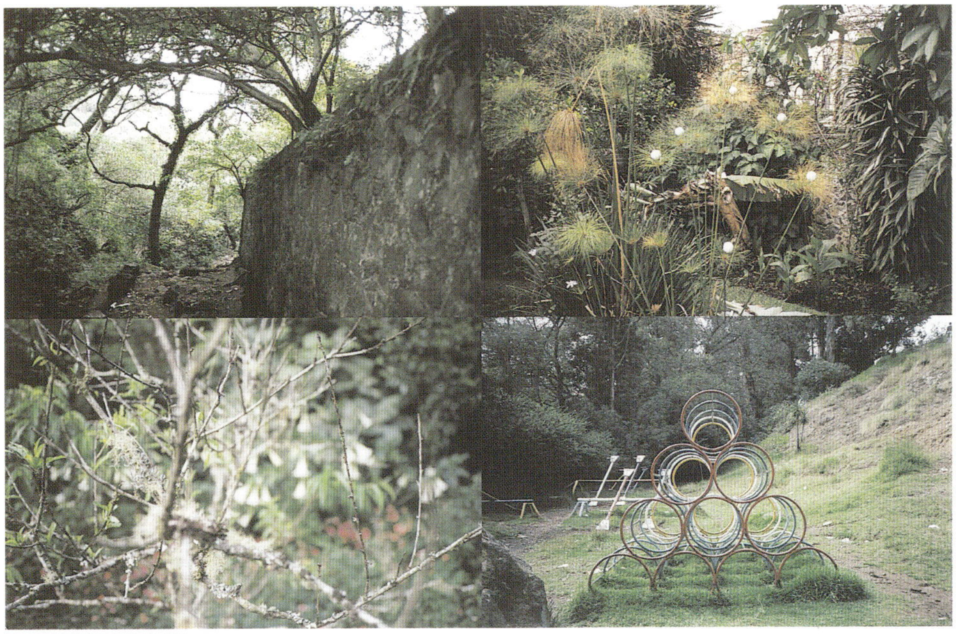

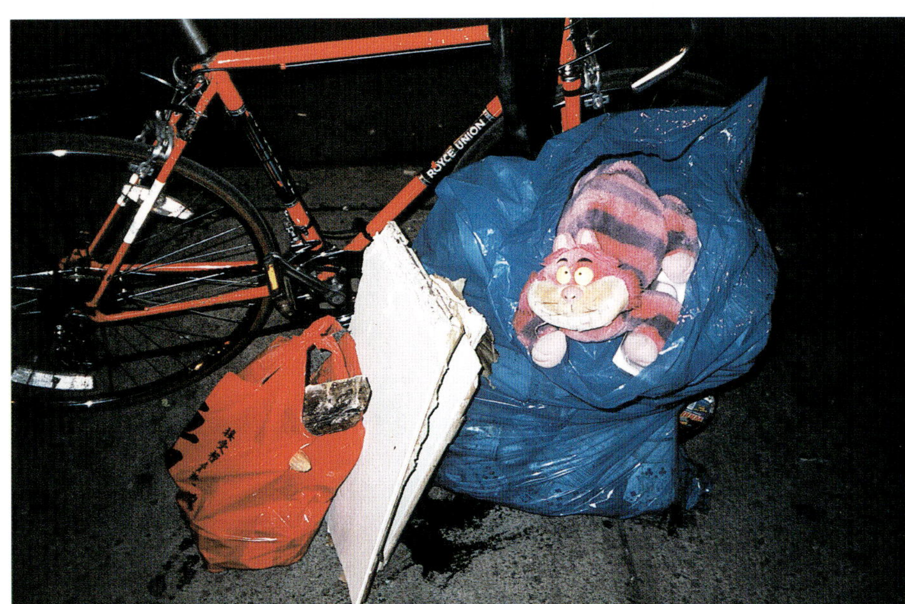

TONY OURSLER

Cheshire Cat from Alice in Wonderland. 1997. Unique laminated silver dye bleach process print, mounted on aluminum, $28\frac{3}{8} \times 35$ inches

Synopsis. 1995–98. Installation: silver dye bleach process print with attached linen panels in plexiglass box frame, and eighteen separate, gessoed linen squares, 72 × 87¾ inches

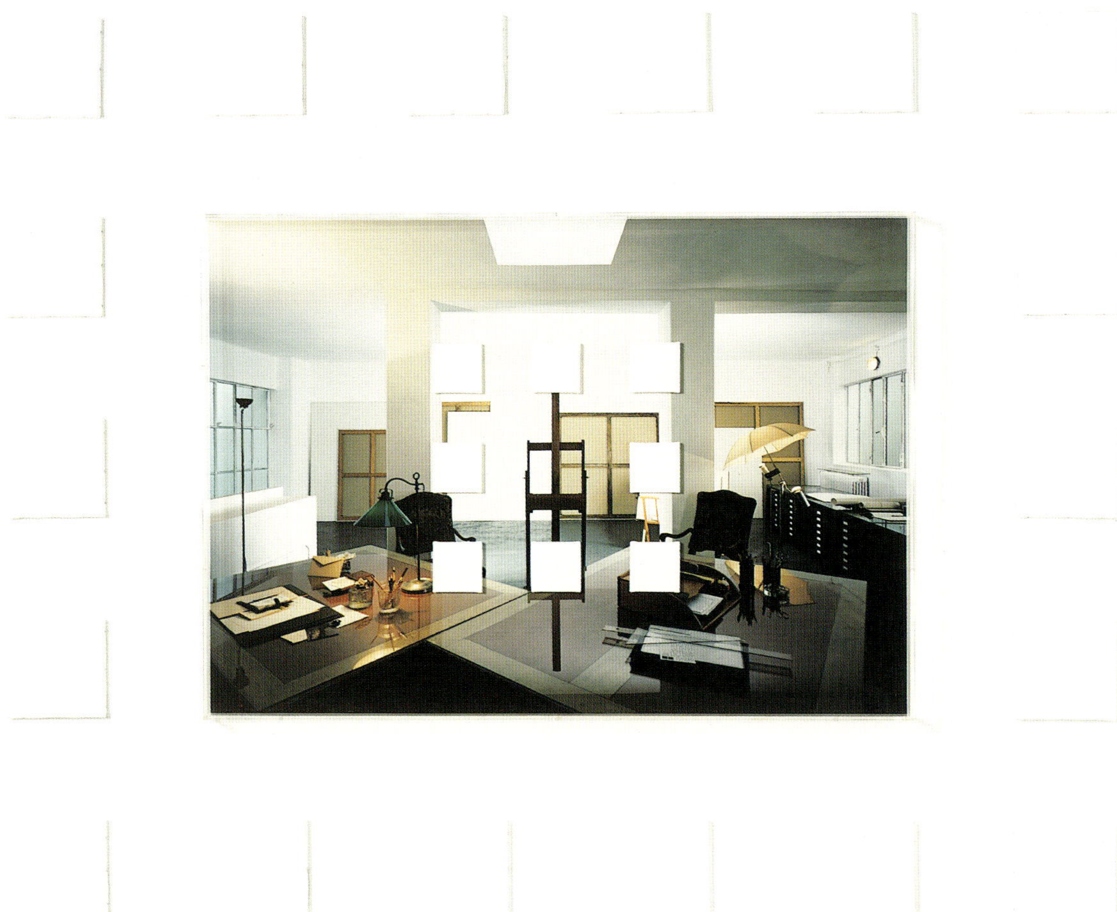

Le Tournant (C,D,G) (The Turning Point [C,D,G]). 1994.
Three color photographs mounted on aluminum, from a larger series, $22\frac{3}{4} \times 34$ inches each

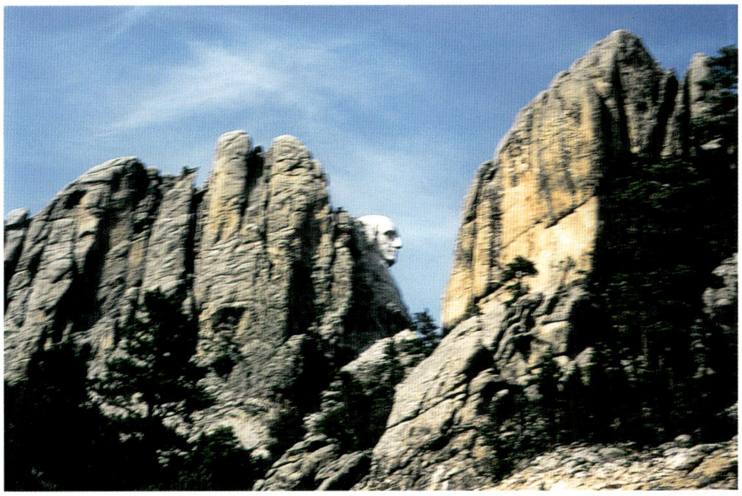

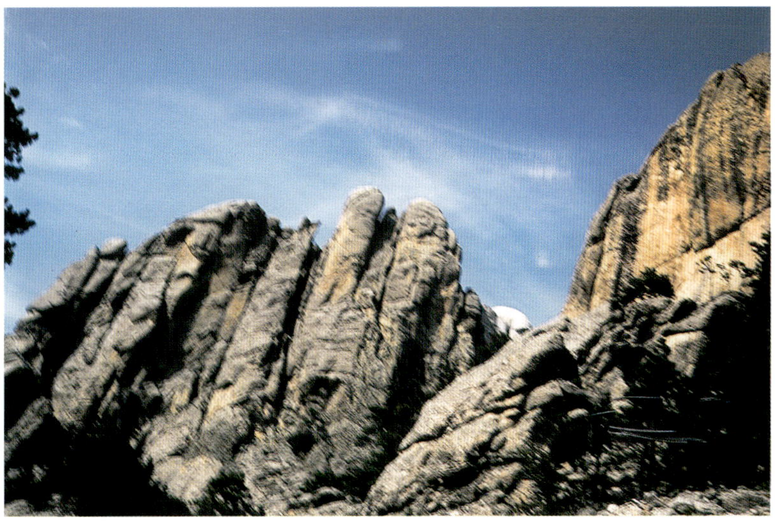

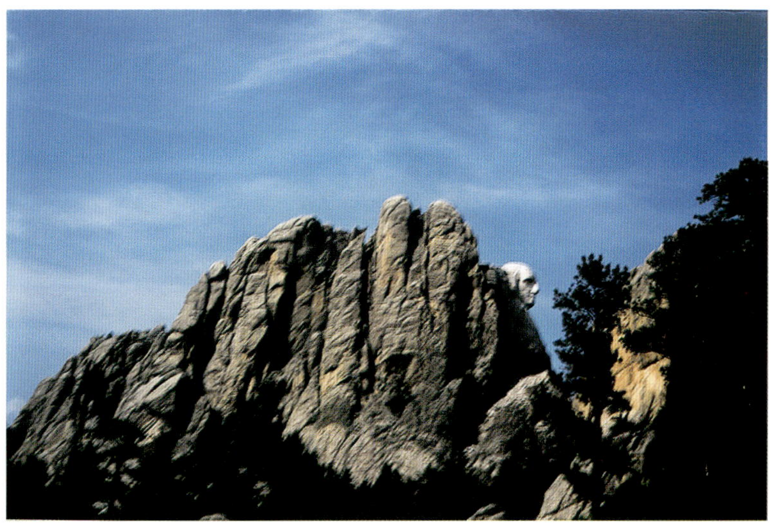

Retaule: Fons del Museu de Pintura de Sant de Mar
(Altarpiece: Paintings from the Museum of Sant de Mar).
1997. Chromogenic process print with original oil paint
retouching, 71 1/2 × 97 3/4 inches

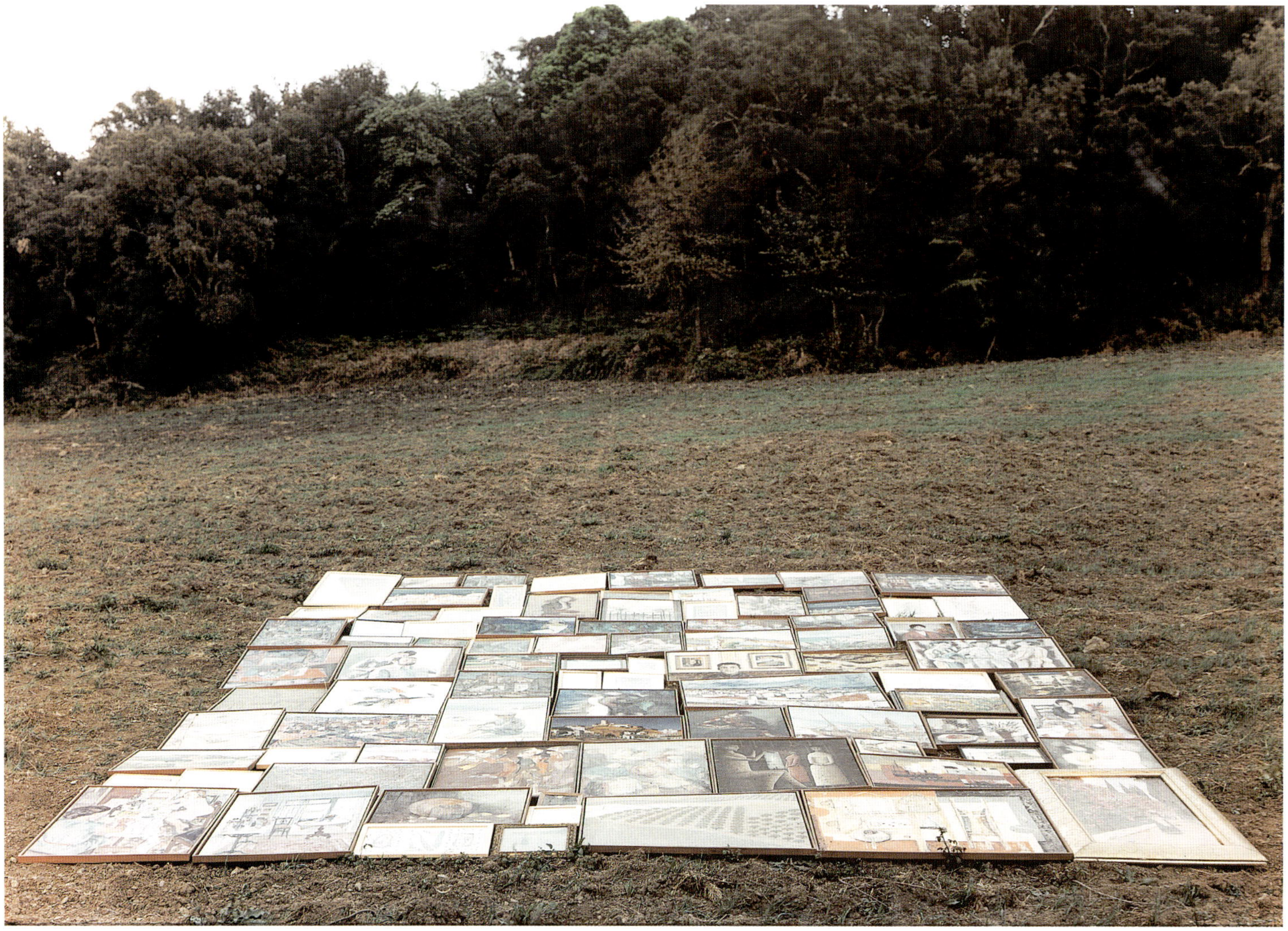

Bridge. 1998. Chromogenic process print, 30 × 40 inches

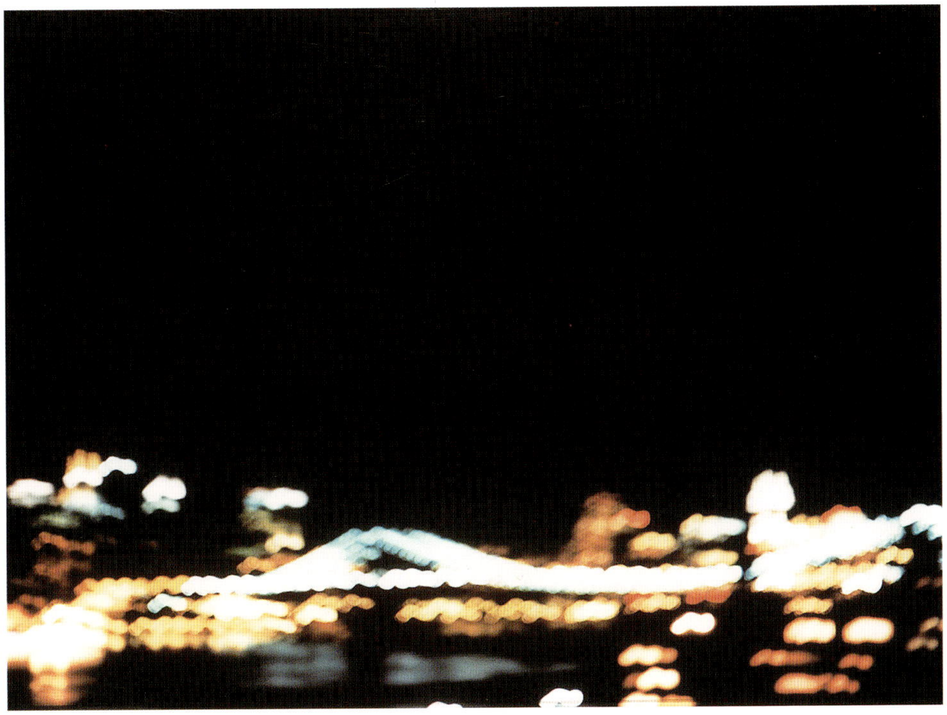

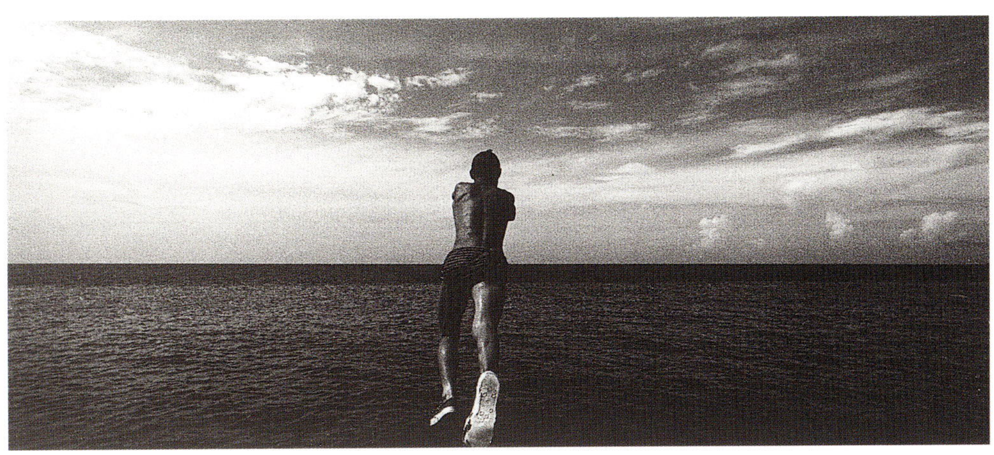

MANUEL PINA

Untitled III. From the *Aguas Baldias (Barren Waters)* series. 1993. Gelatin silver print, 11¼ × 19⅞ inches

Speed Queen Series. 1991. Suite of five gelatin silver contact prints made from negatives exposed and processed with a front loading washing machine, 27 × 28 inches each

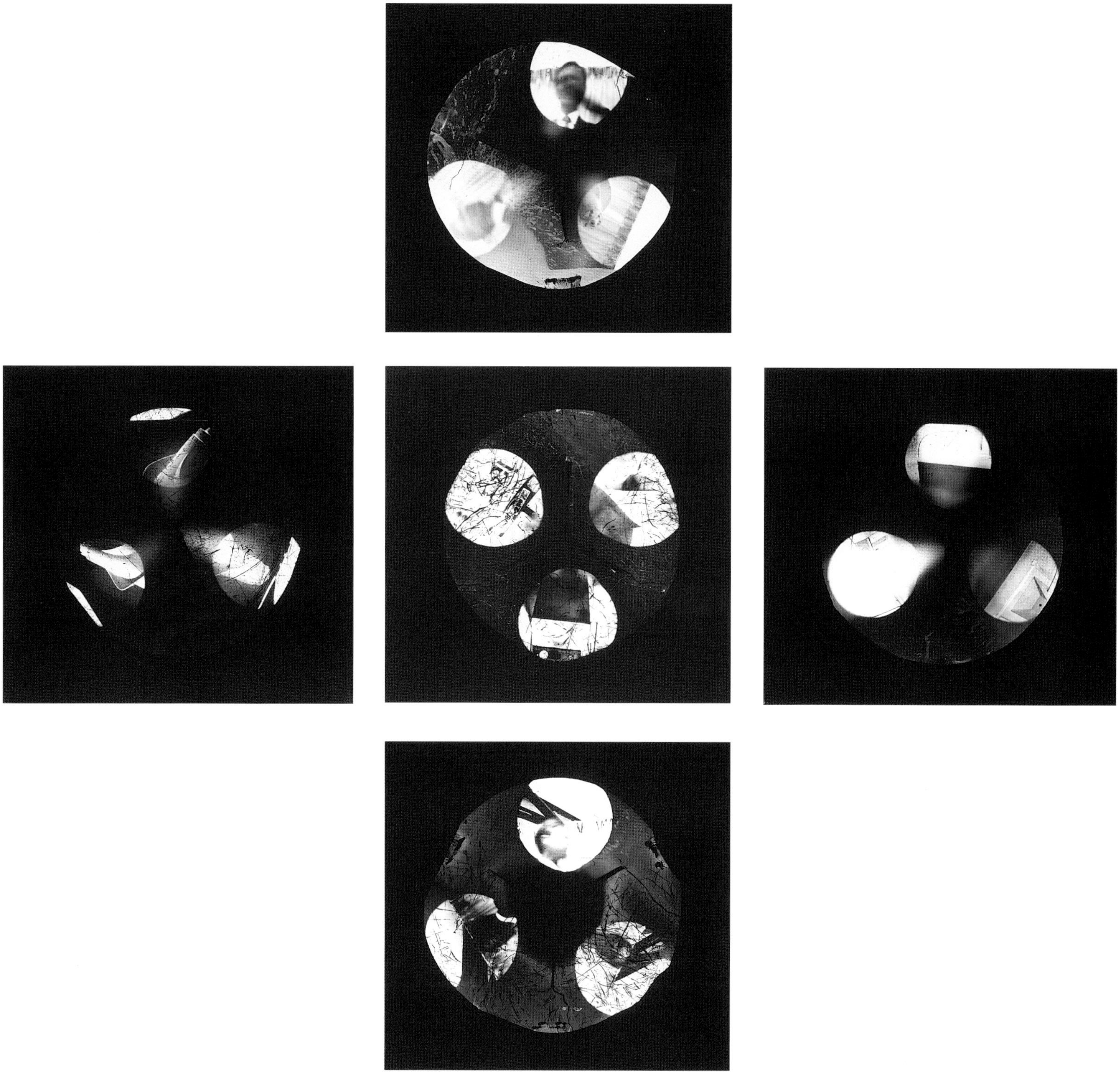

Untitled. 1995. Laminated chromogenic process print, $74\frac{1}{4} \times 74\frac{1}{4}$ inches

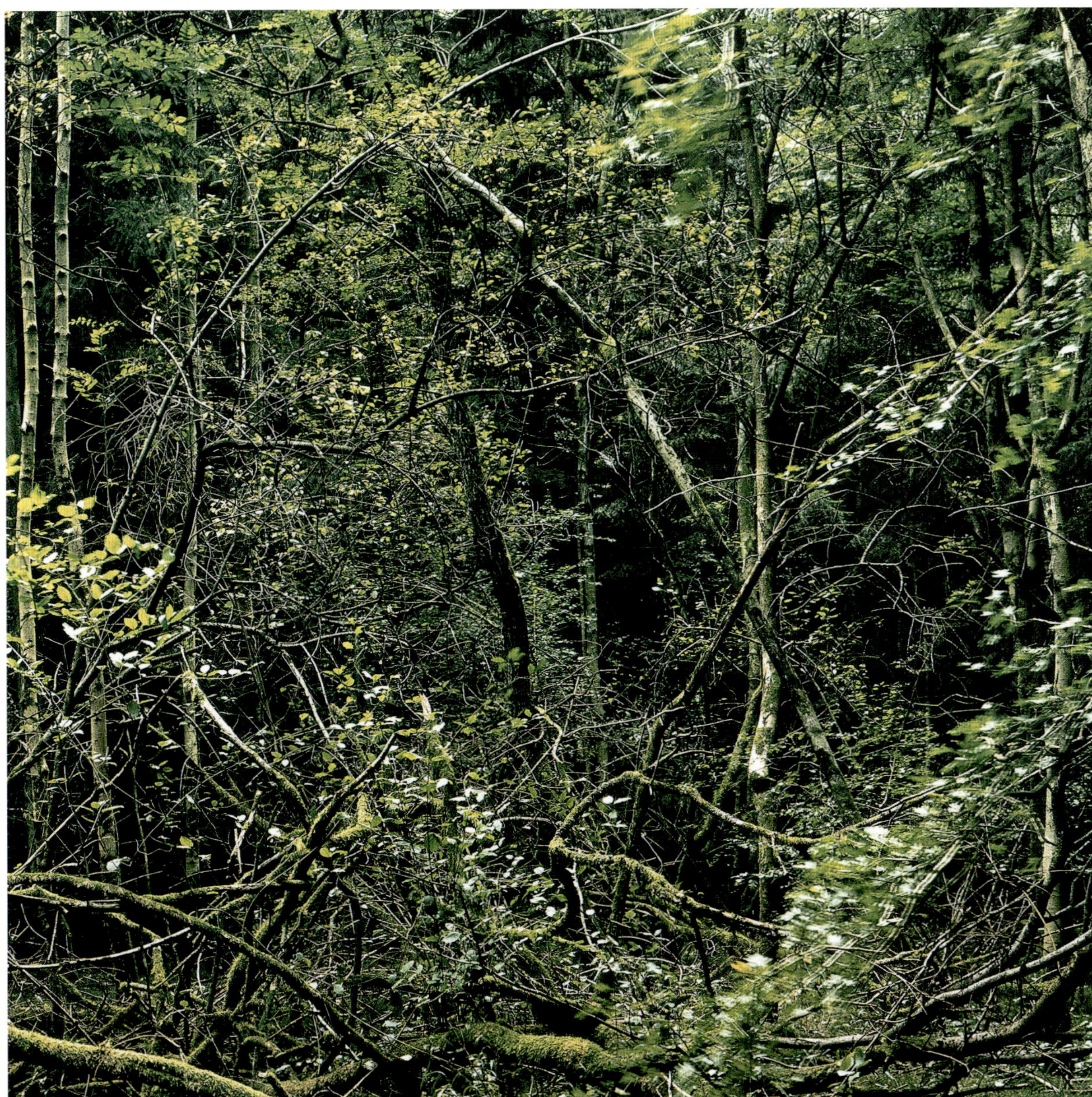

Untitled (Streetscene). 1985. Silver dye bleach process print, 50 × 86 inches

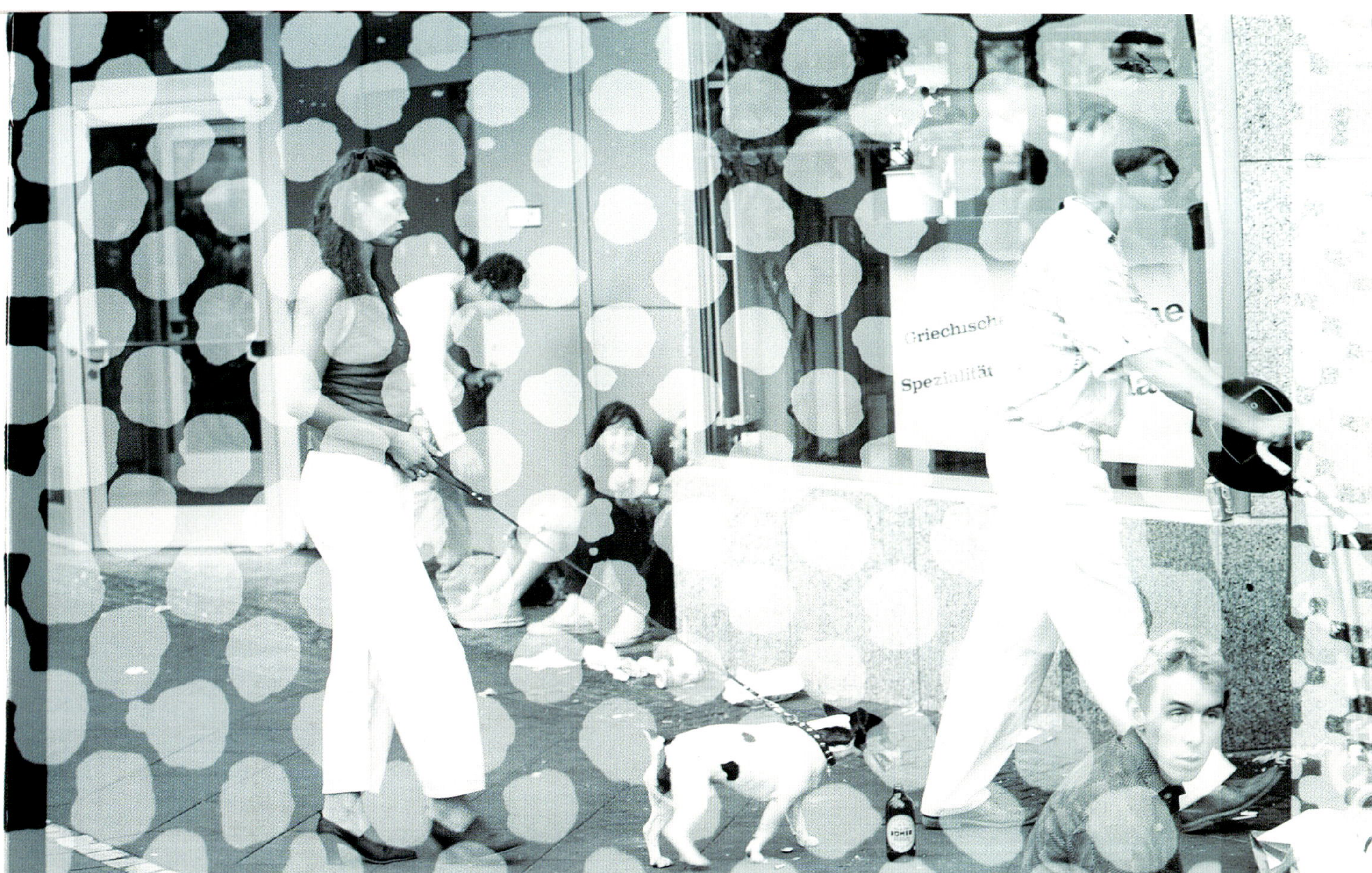

Professional Photography at the Acropolis. 1989–96. Silver dye bleach process print, $23^{3}/_{4} \times 16$ inches

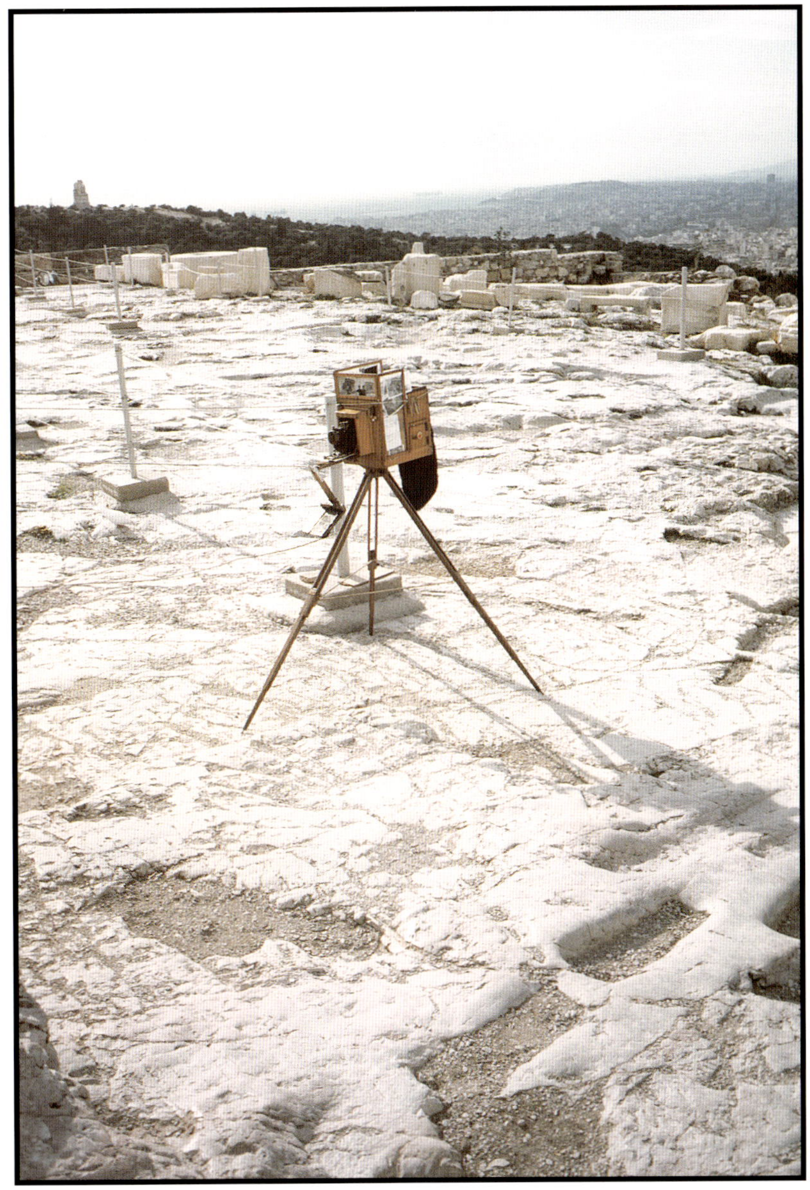

Untitled. From the *Living Rooms* series. 1977. Set of four Ektacolor prints, $23\frac{1}{4} \times 30\frac{7}{8}$ inches each

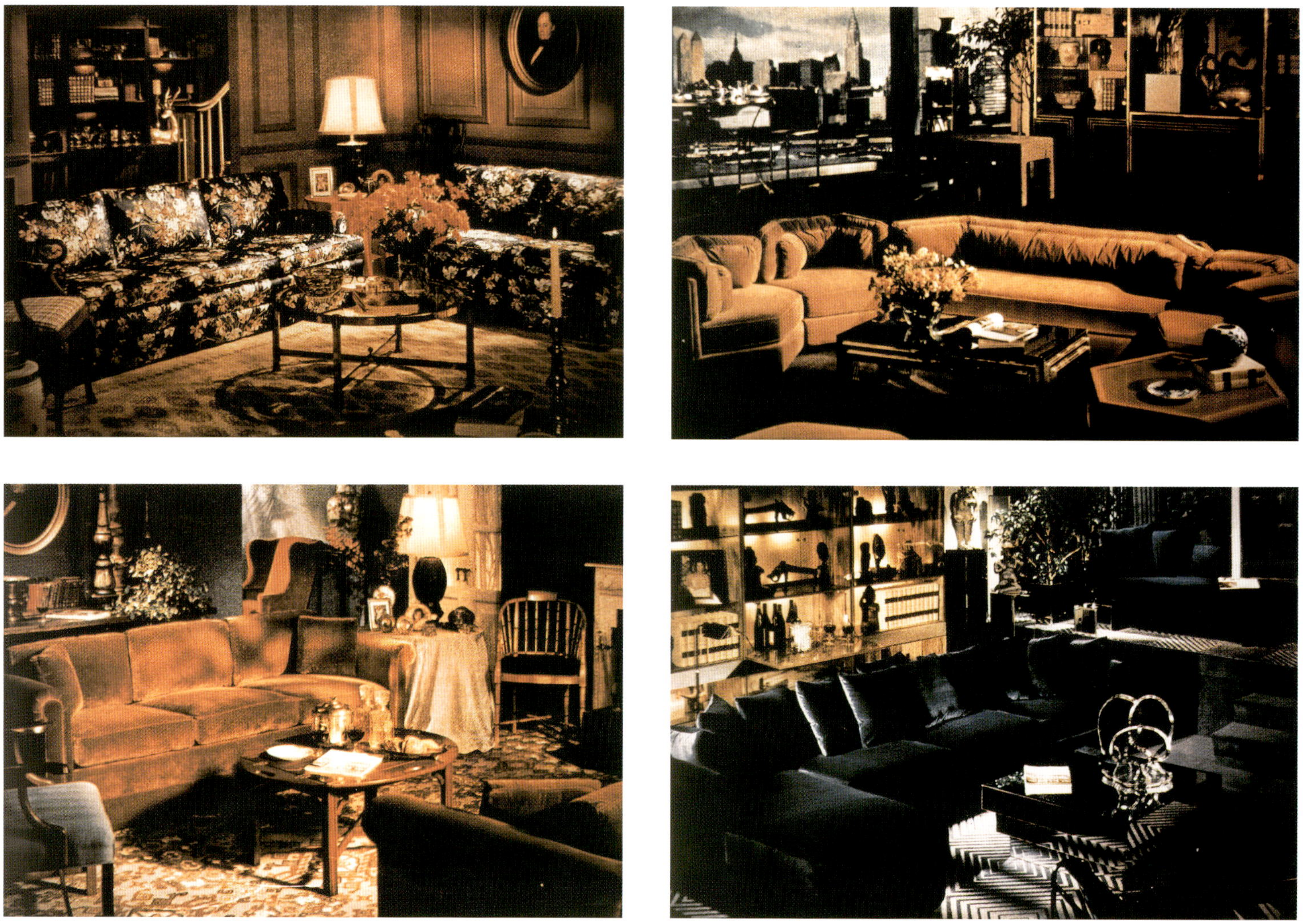

Untitled (Fort Myers, Florida) (Portfolio 2, October Magazine). 1980/1997. Gelatin silver print, $10^3/_4 \times 15^7/_8$ inches

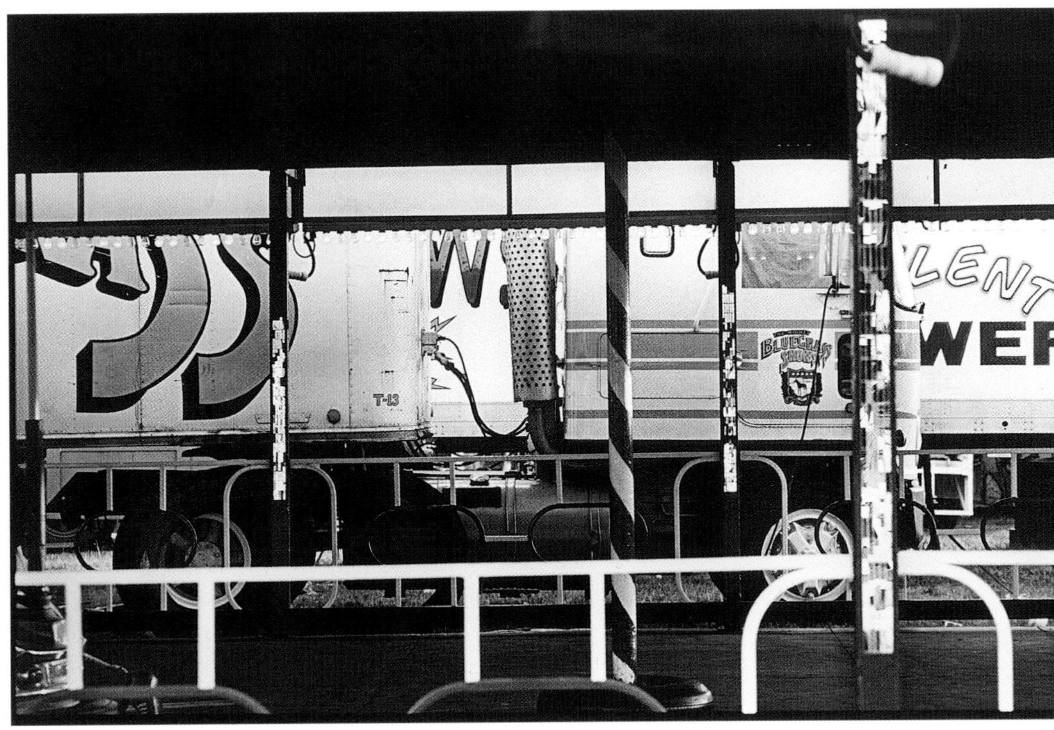

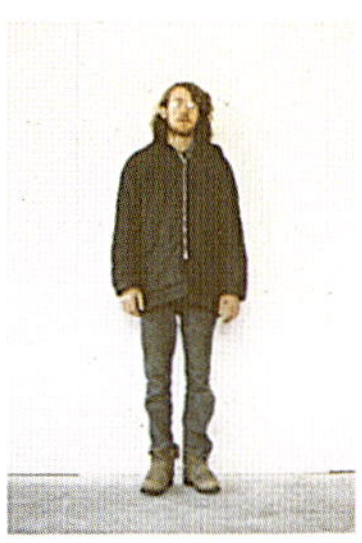 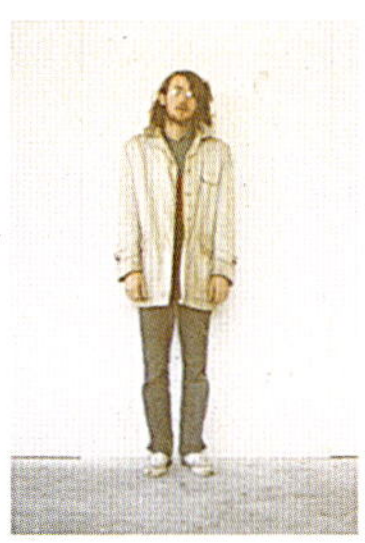 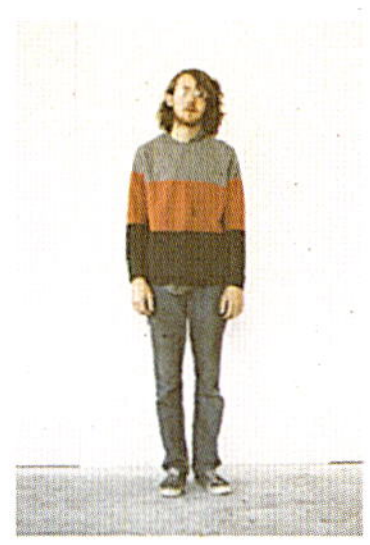 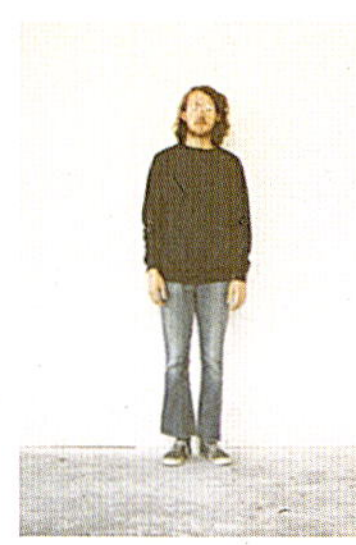 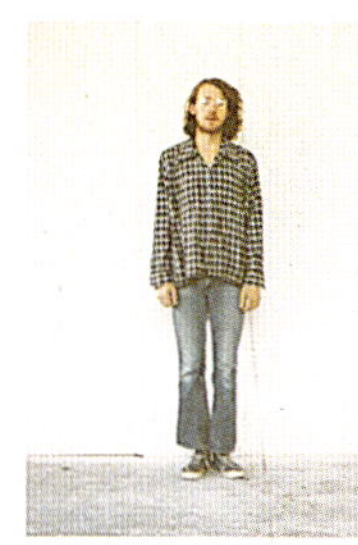 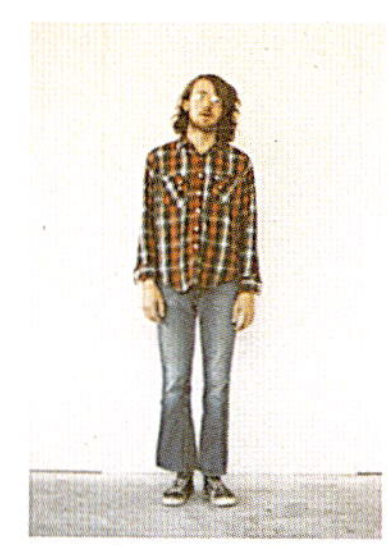 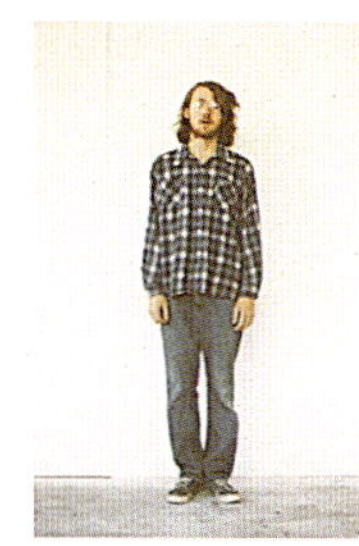 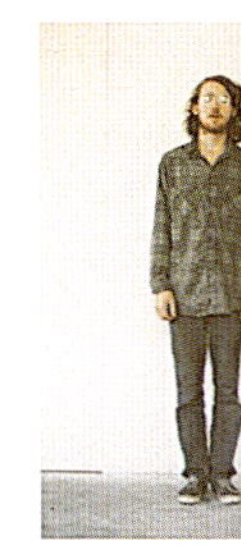

All My Clothes. 1973. Sixteen mounted Polaroids. $9^1/_4 \times 60$ inches

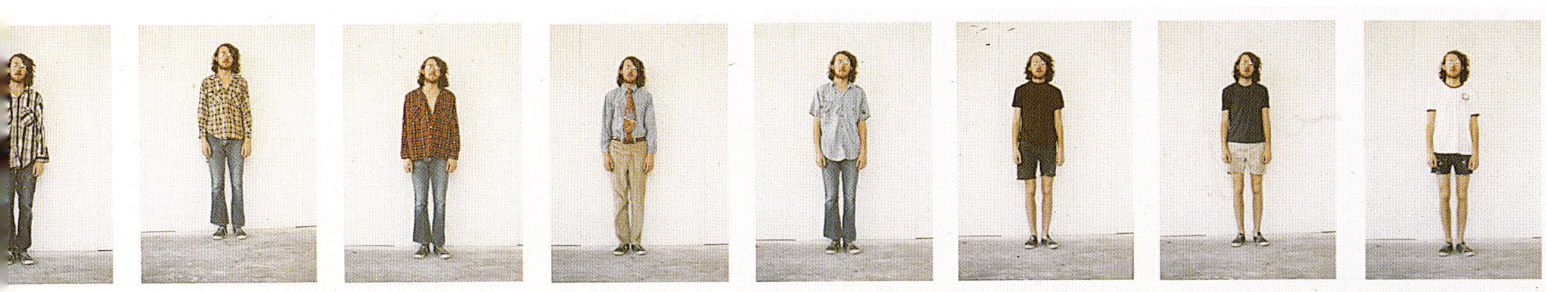

Starship Trooper. 1998. Chromogenic process print, $70\frac{1}{4} \times 50\frac{1}{2}$ inches

Domecke (Corner of a Cathedral). 1998. Silver dye bleach process print, mounted between plexiglass, $30^{3}/_{4} \times 21^{5}/_{8}$ inches

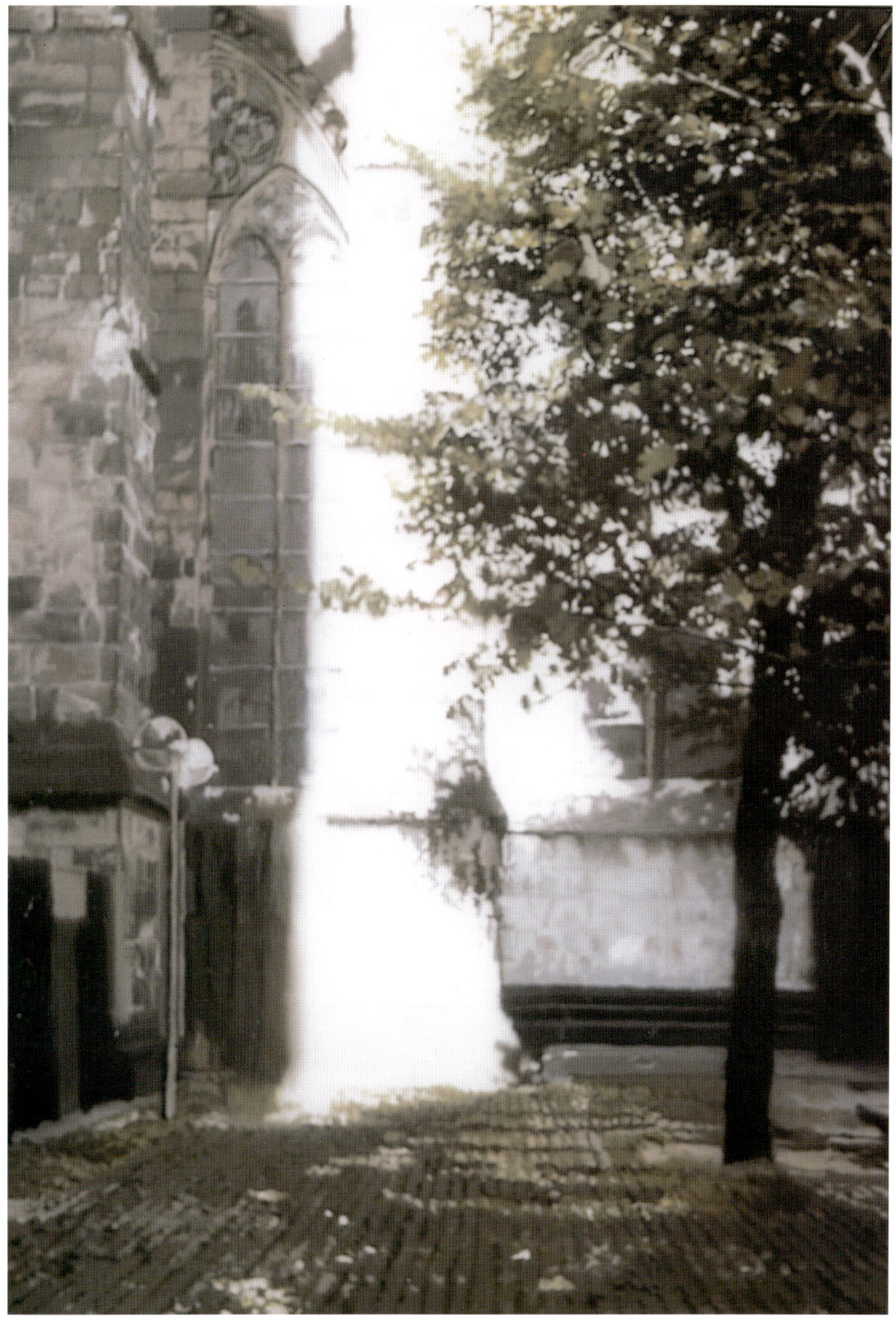

Untitled (The Forest). 1997–98. Lenticular photograph from a series, 26 × 22 inches

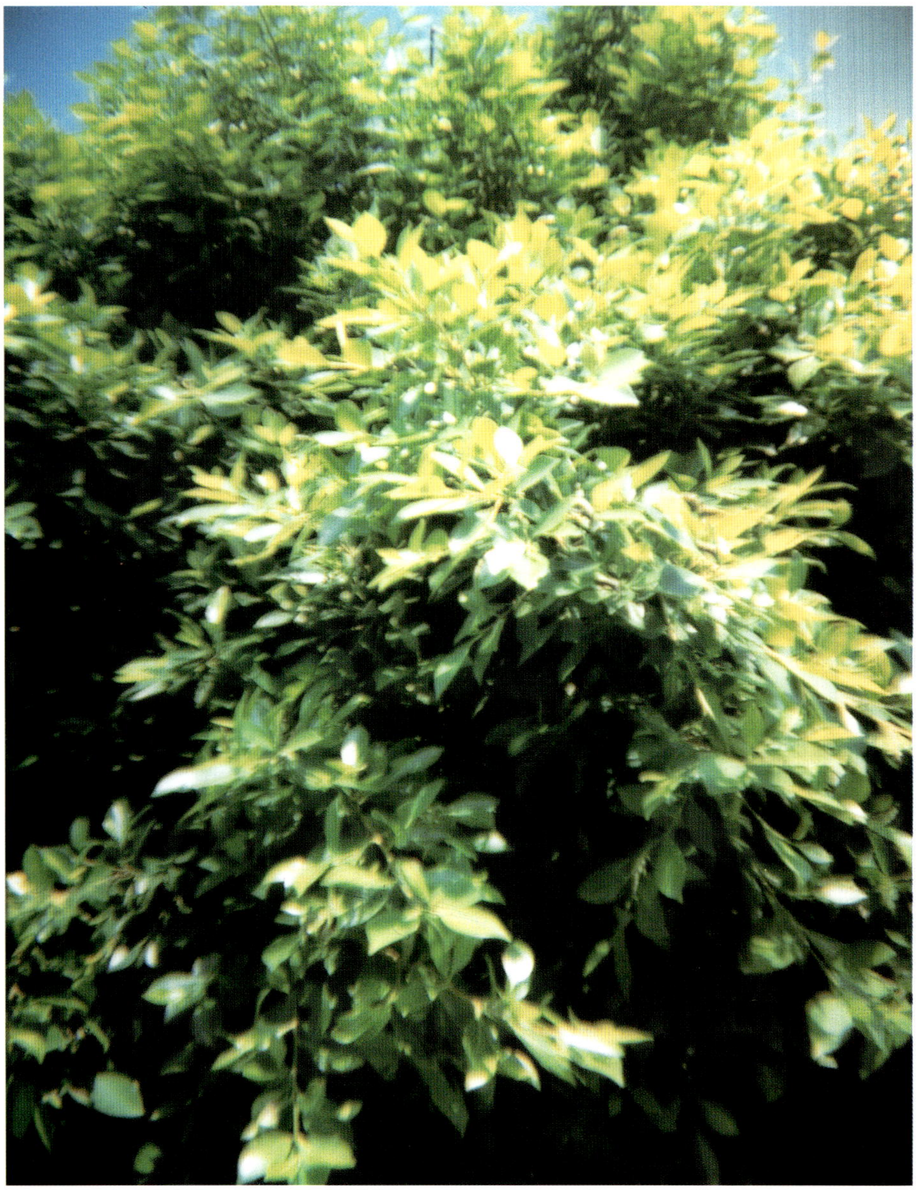

Untitled (Johan Roing). 1988. Chromogenic process print, face mounted to plexiglass, 83 × 65 inches

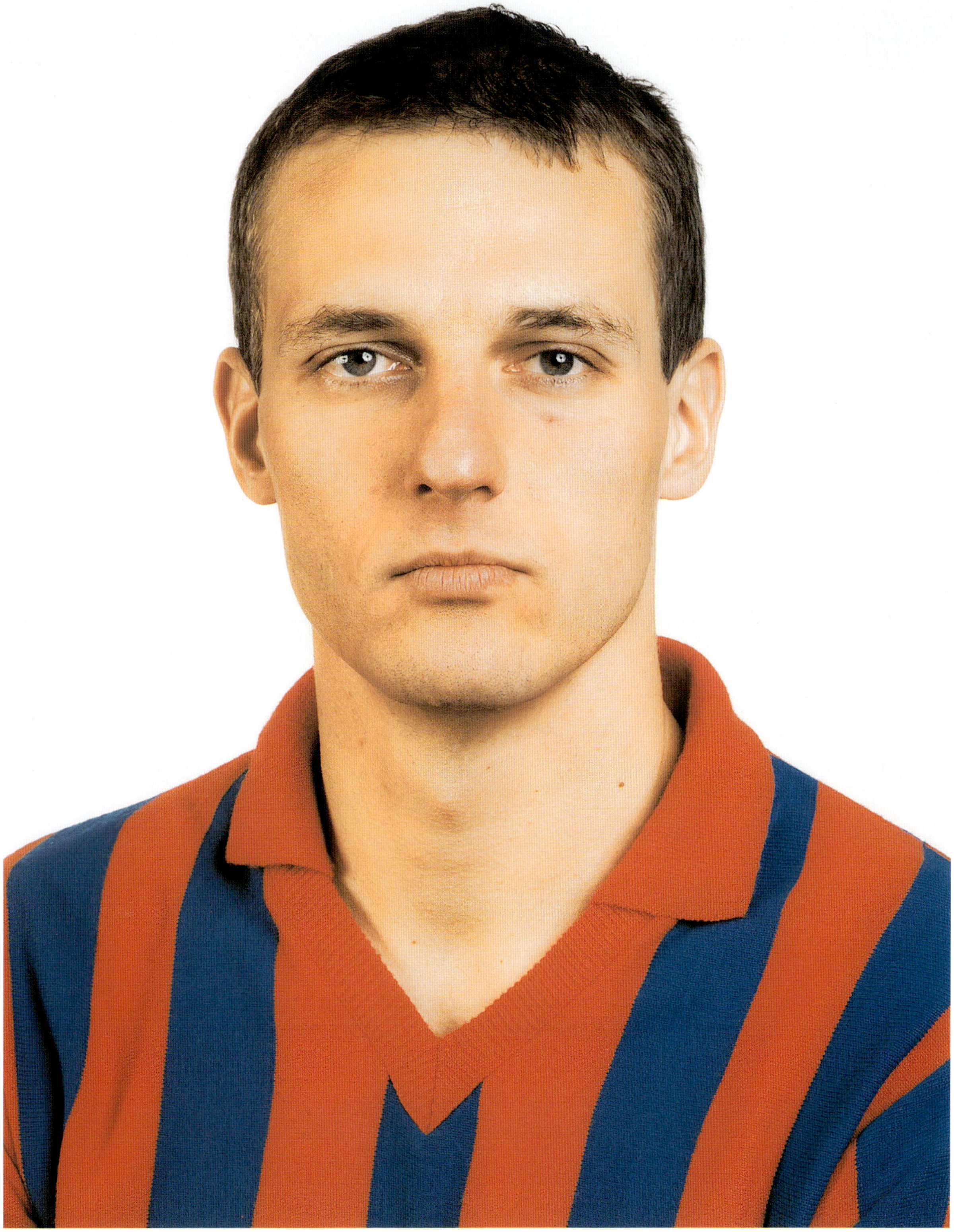

W. B. Yeats. 1972. Sequenced suite of five gelatin silver prints, $26^{5}/_{8} \times 22^{5}/_{8}$ inches each

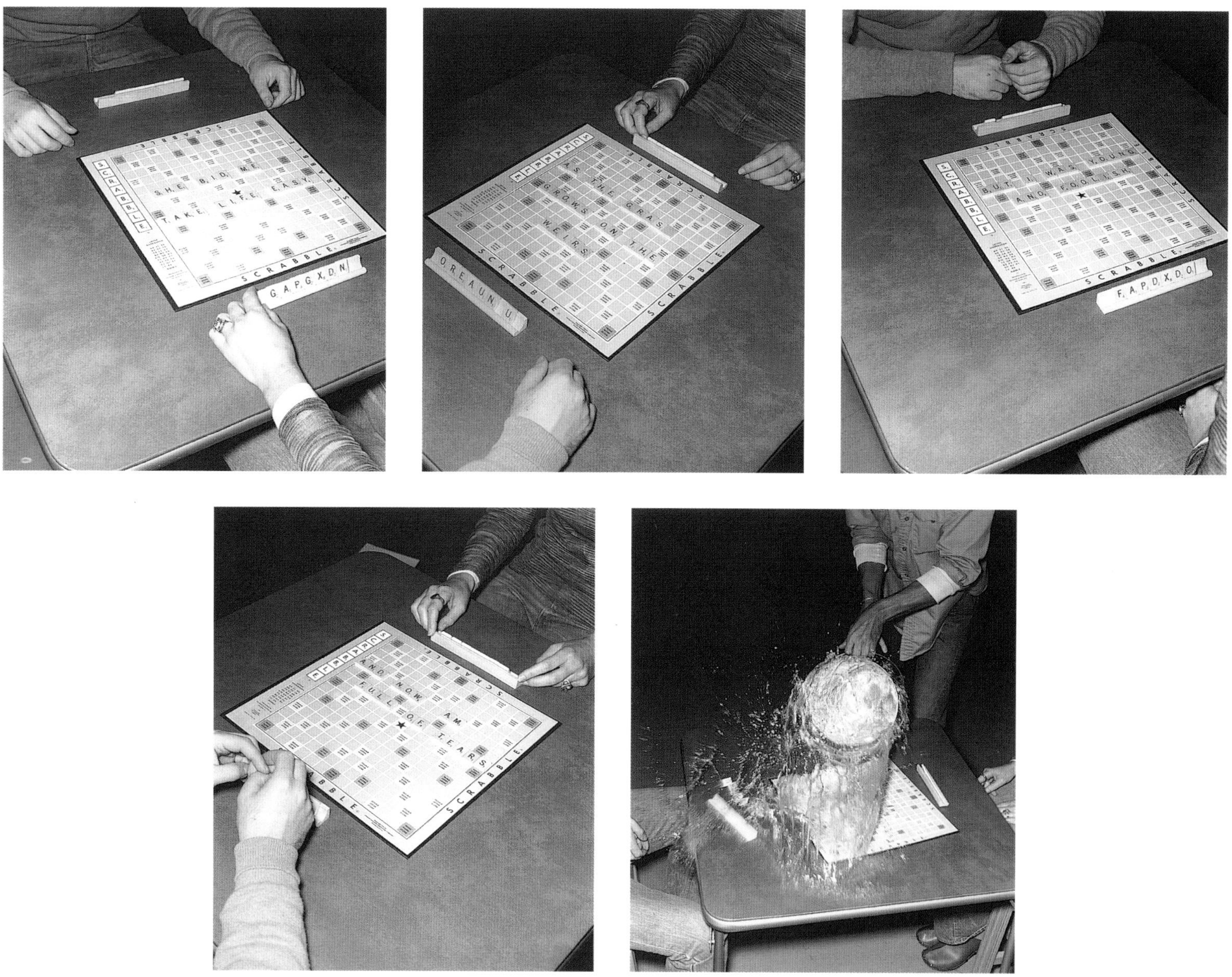

Gasoline Stations. 1962. Portfolio of ten gelatin silver prints, dimensions varied

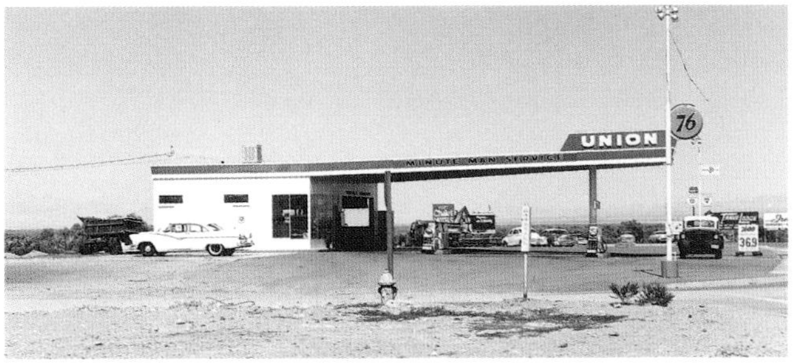

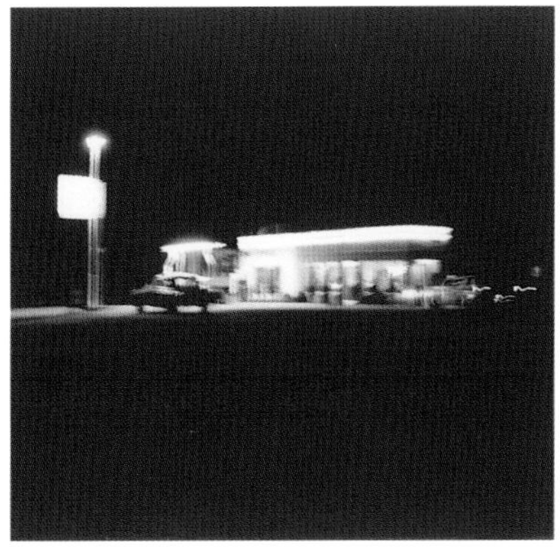

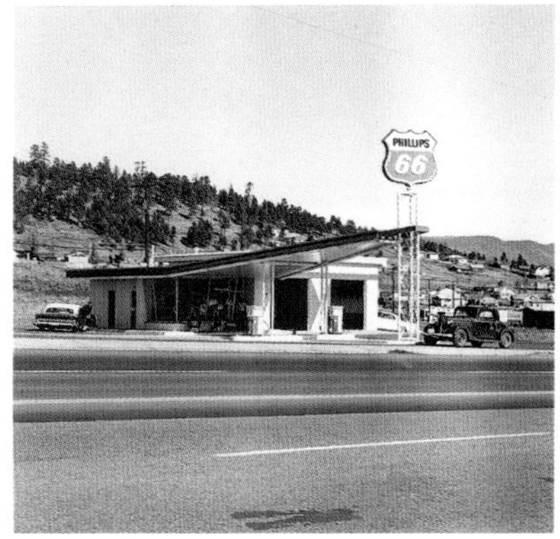

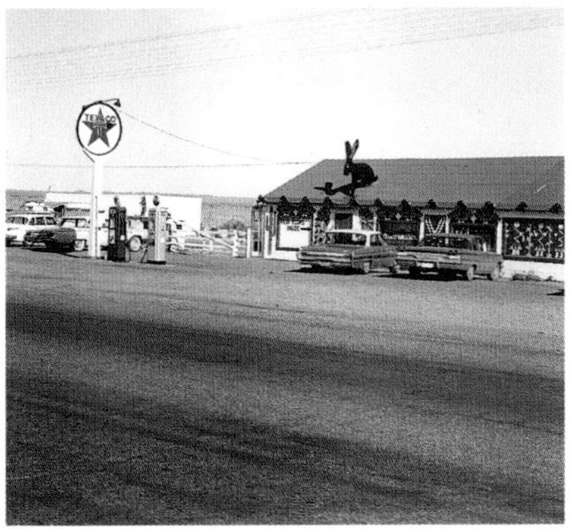

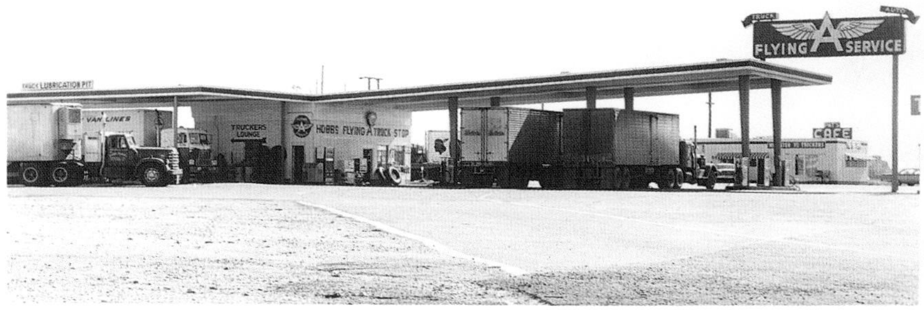

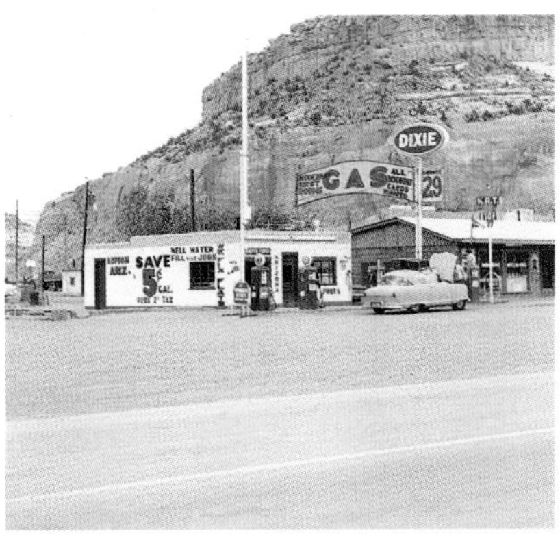

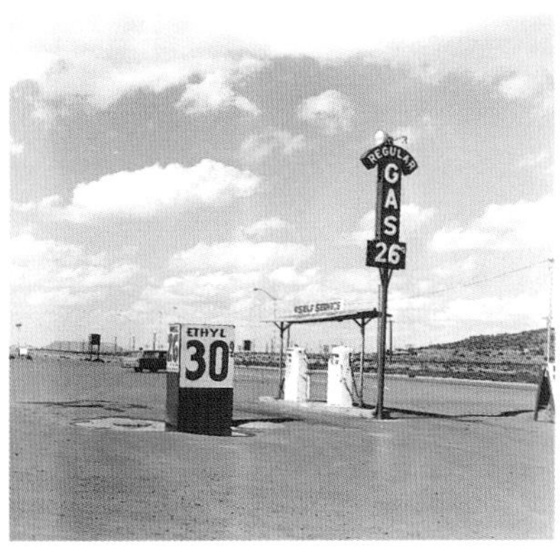

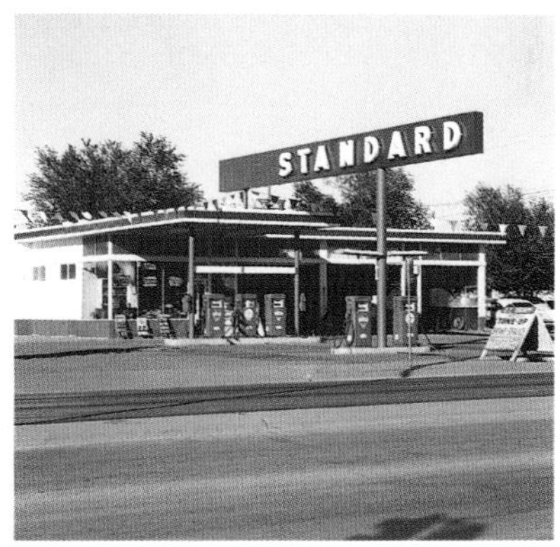

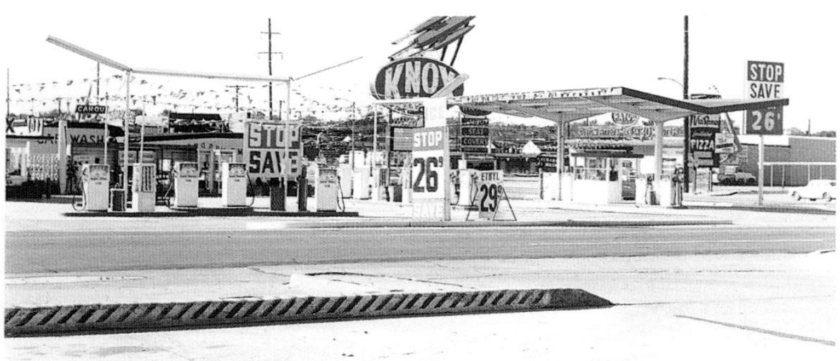

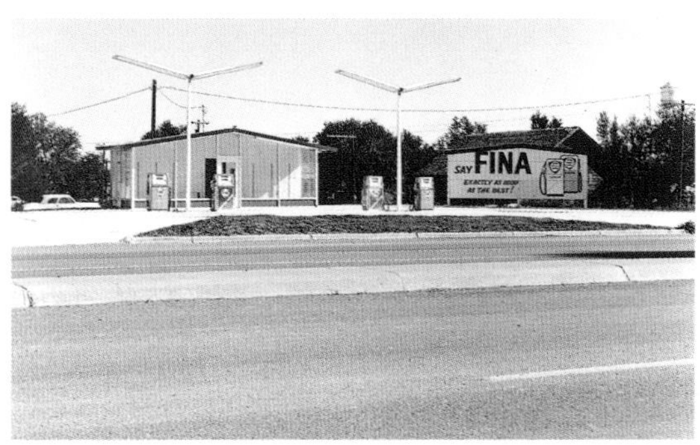

CHRISTOPH RUTIMANN

Waffenlager am Tintensee (Arsenal with Ink Pool). 1985. Silver dye bleach process print of a Polaroid, $15^{3}/_{4} \times 15^{3}/_{4}$ inches

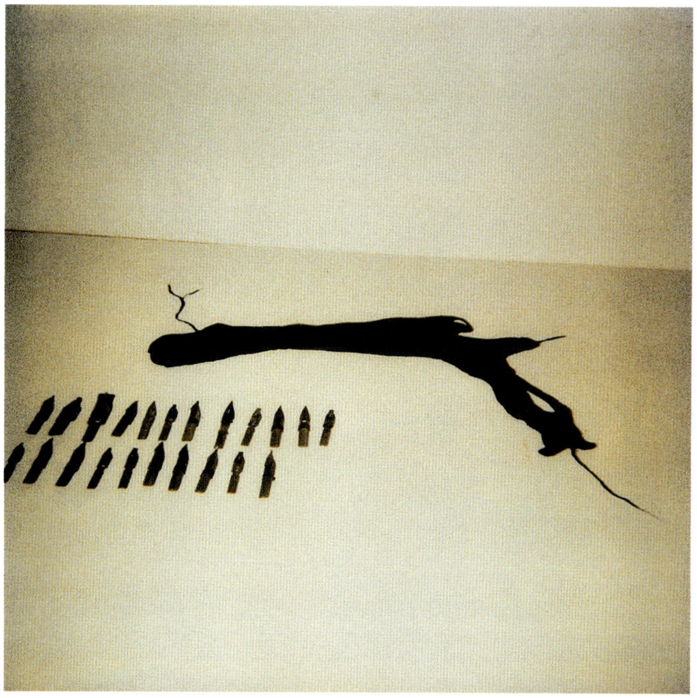

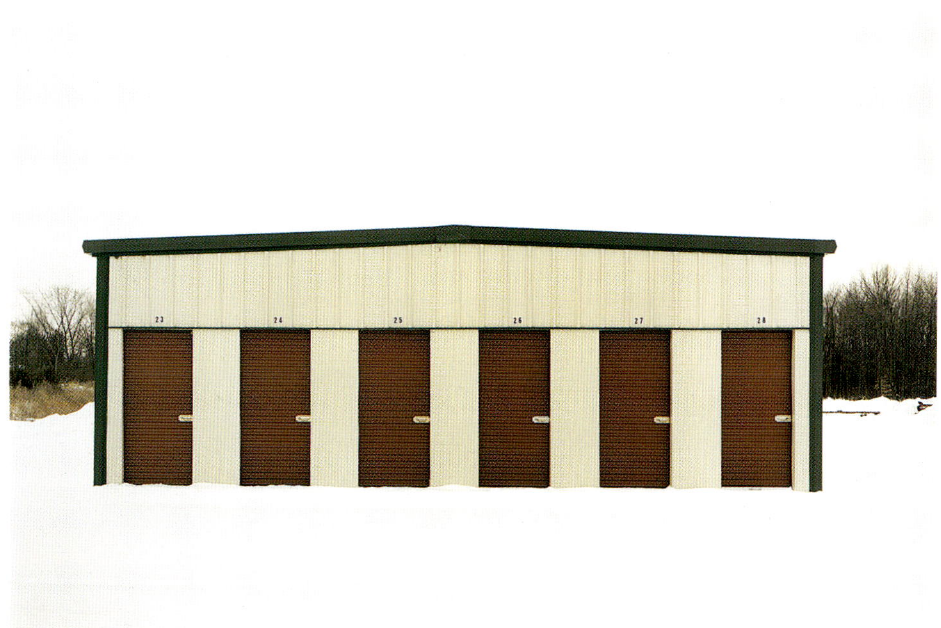

VICTORIA SAMBUNARIS

Untitled. 2000. Silver dye bleach process print, $40^{1}/_{2} \times 56$ inches

5671, 1996. 1996. Chromogenic process print, face mounted to plexiglass, $40^{3}/_{4} \times 70^{3}/_{4}$ inches

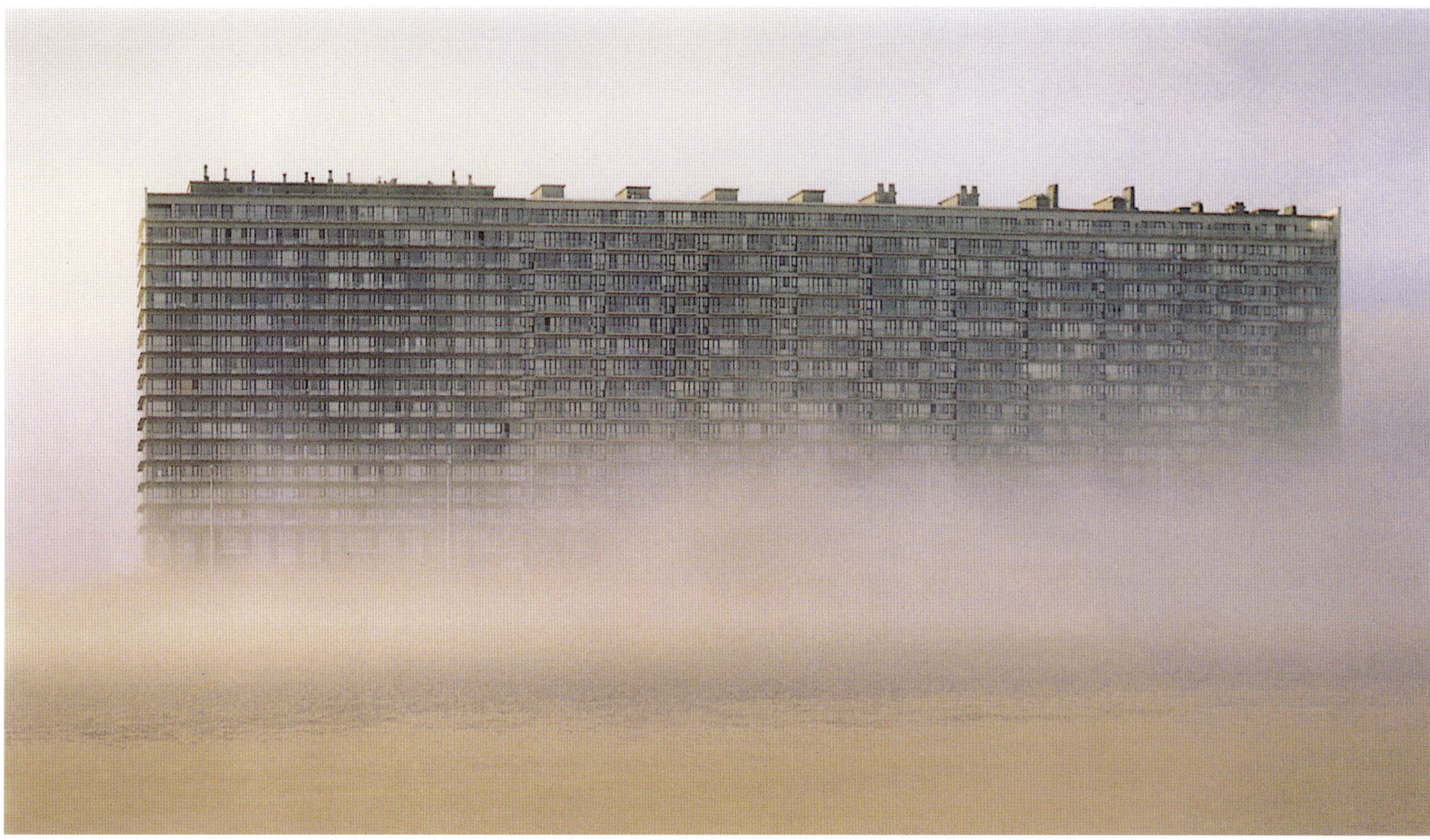

Untitled (Passenger #3). 1994–95. Toned gelatin silver prints from a series, 23 × 19 inches

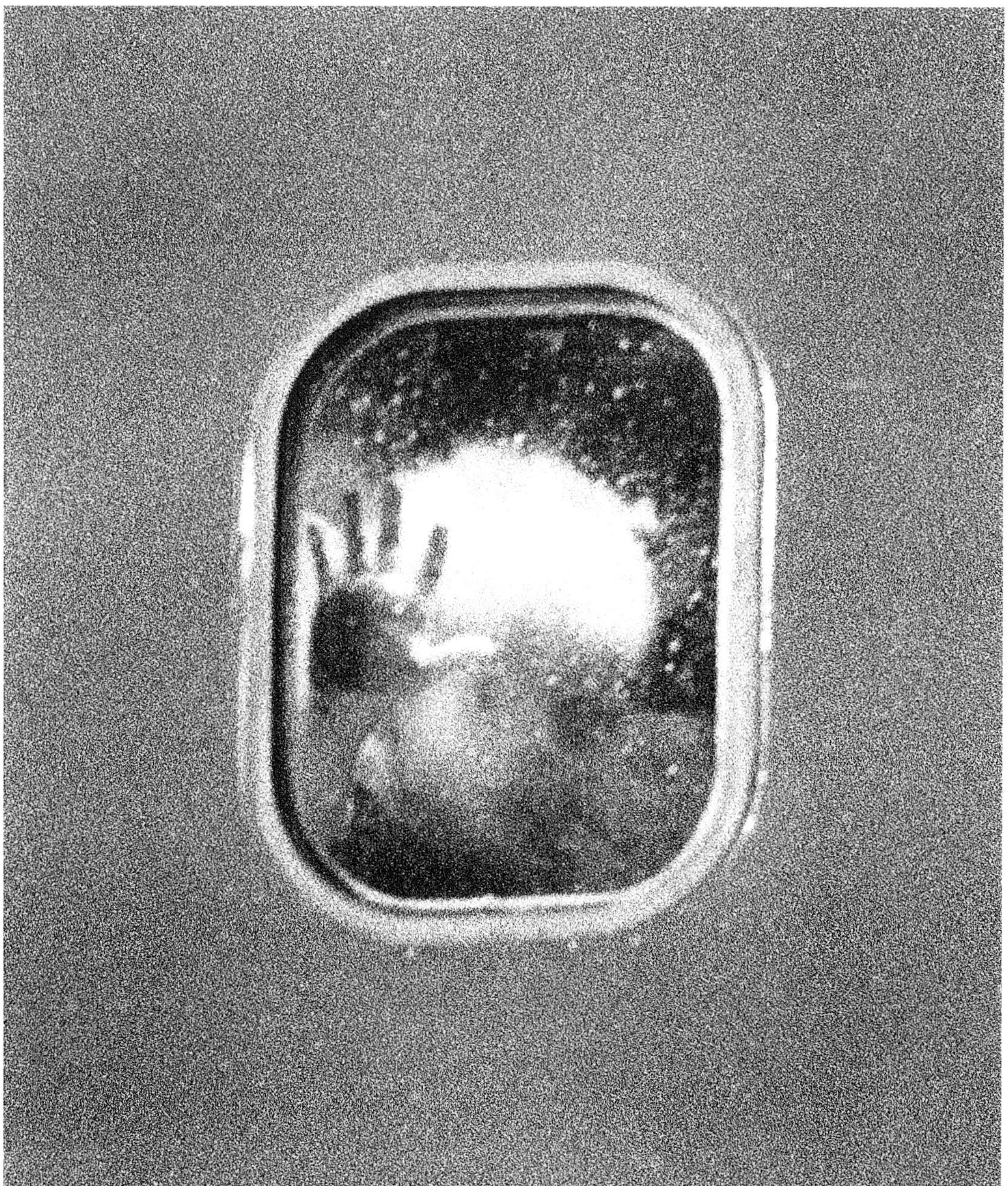

Clockwise from top left:

Raum 20, Haus ur Rheydt '96 (Room 20, "ur" House, Rheydt). 1996

Im Kern Haus ur Rheydt '96 (In the Center, "ur" House, Rheydt '96). 1996

Im Kern Haus ur, Rheydt '96 (In the Center, "ur" House, Rheydt '96). 1996

Das Letzte Loch Haus ur Rheydt '95 (The Last Cavity, "ur" House, Rheydt '95). 1996

Puff aus Berlin Haus ur Rheydt '96 (Berlin Brothel, "ur" House, Rheydt '96). 1996

Liebescaube Haus ur Rheydt '96 (Love Nest, "ur" House, Rheydt '96). 1996

Liebescaube Haus ur Rheydt '96 (Love Nest, "ur" House, Rheydt '96). 1996

Gelatin silver prints in artist's frames from a series, dimensions varied

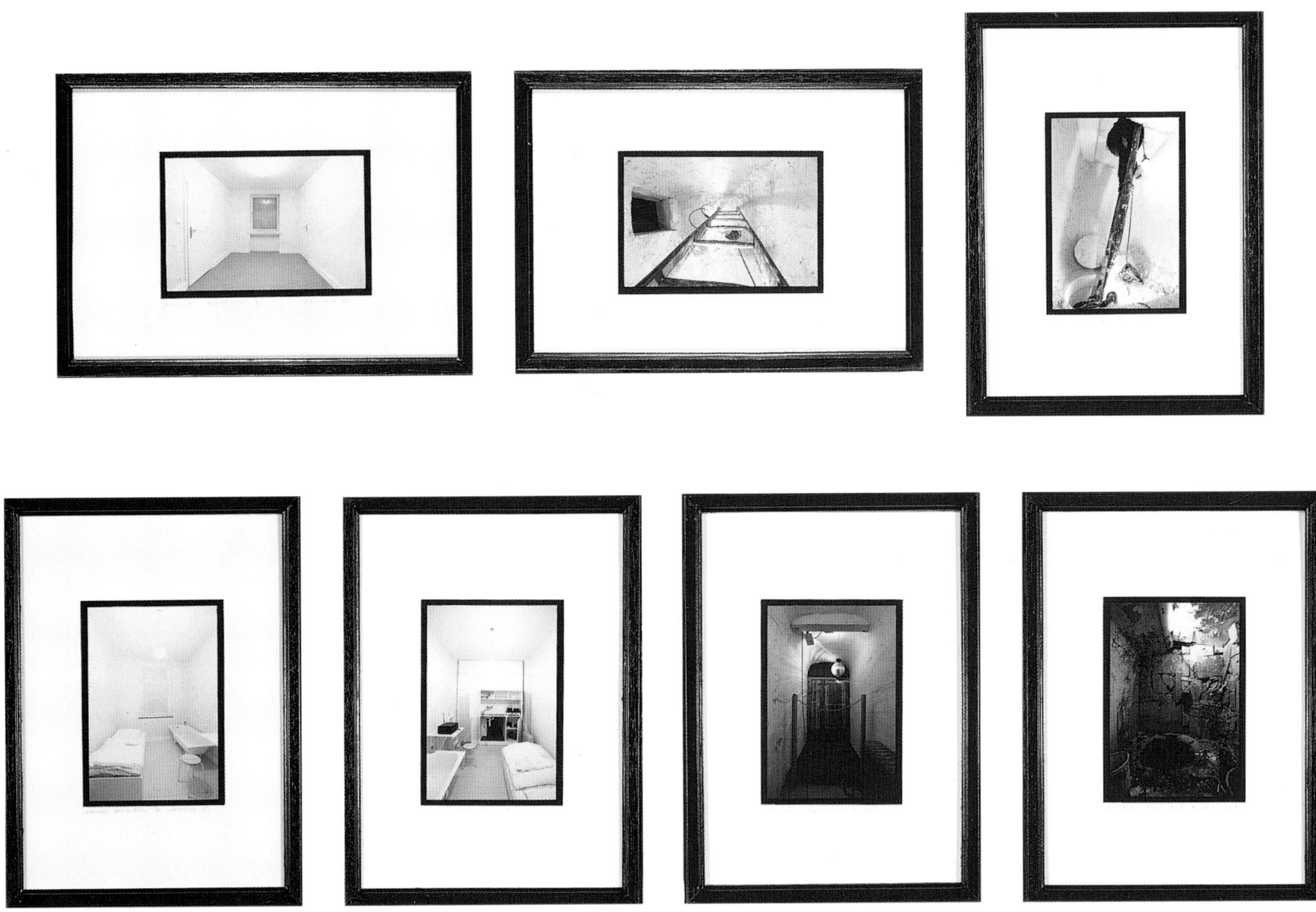

Evangelisch Kirch (Evangelical Church). 1996.
Chromogenic process print, 19¾ × 19¾ inches

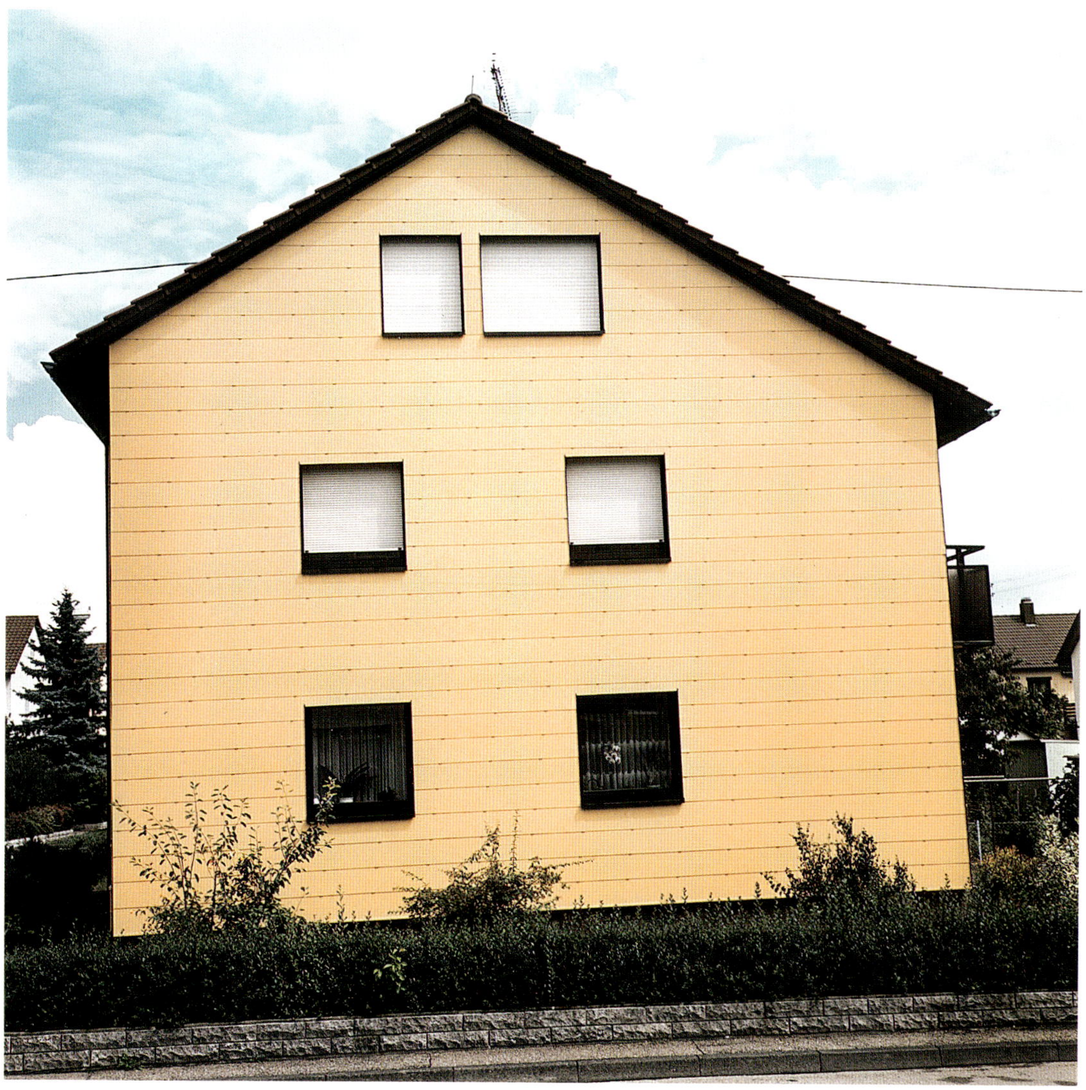

United Enemies—A Play in Ten Scenes. 1994. Three color offset lithographic prints from a series, $25^{1/2} \times 36^{1/4}$ inches each

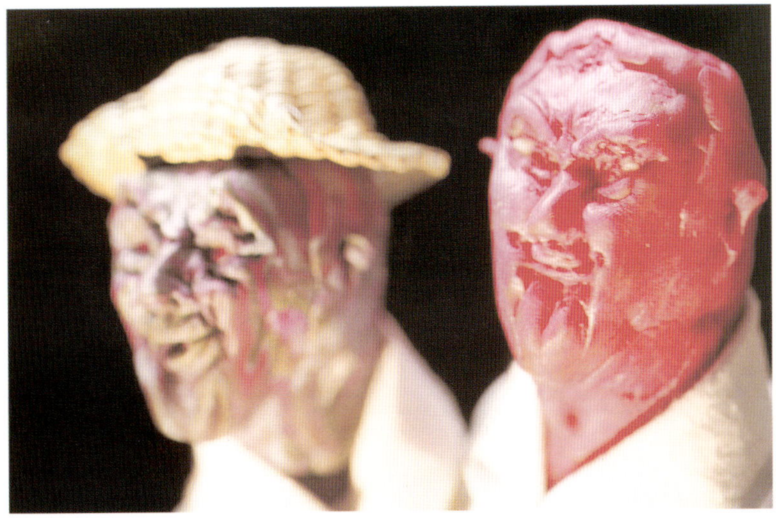

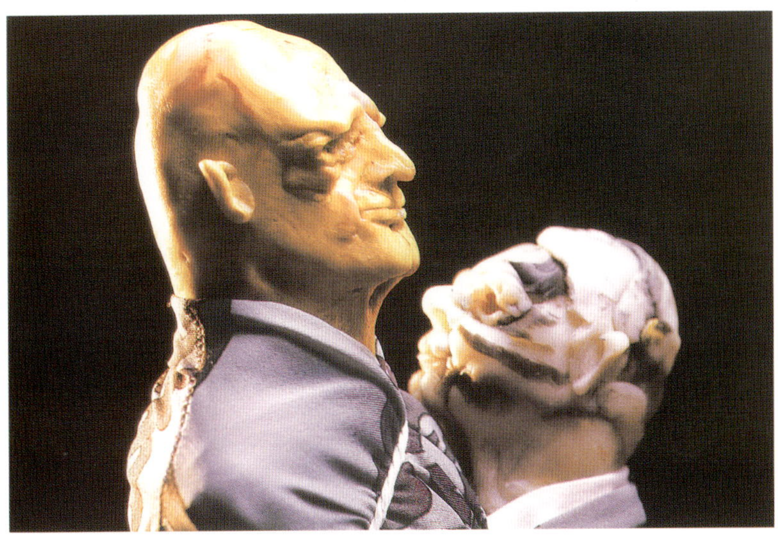

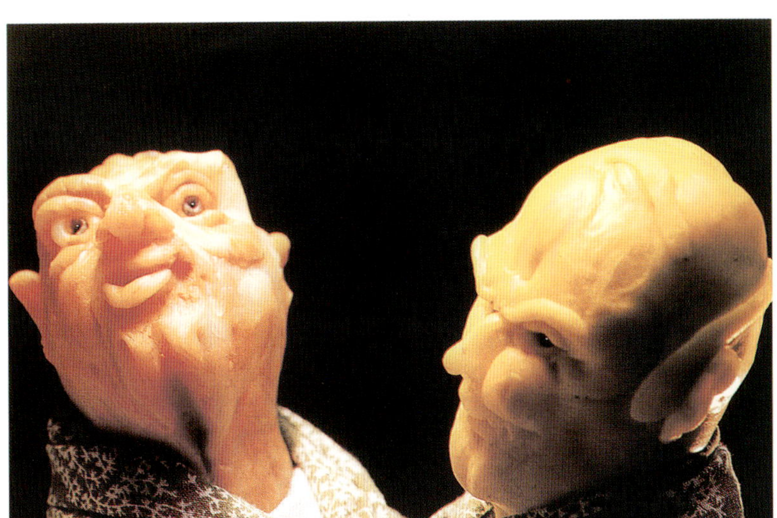

The Church, San Mignato, Florence. 1991. Silver dye bleach process print, $39\frac{1}{2} \times 32$ inches

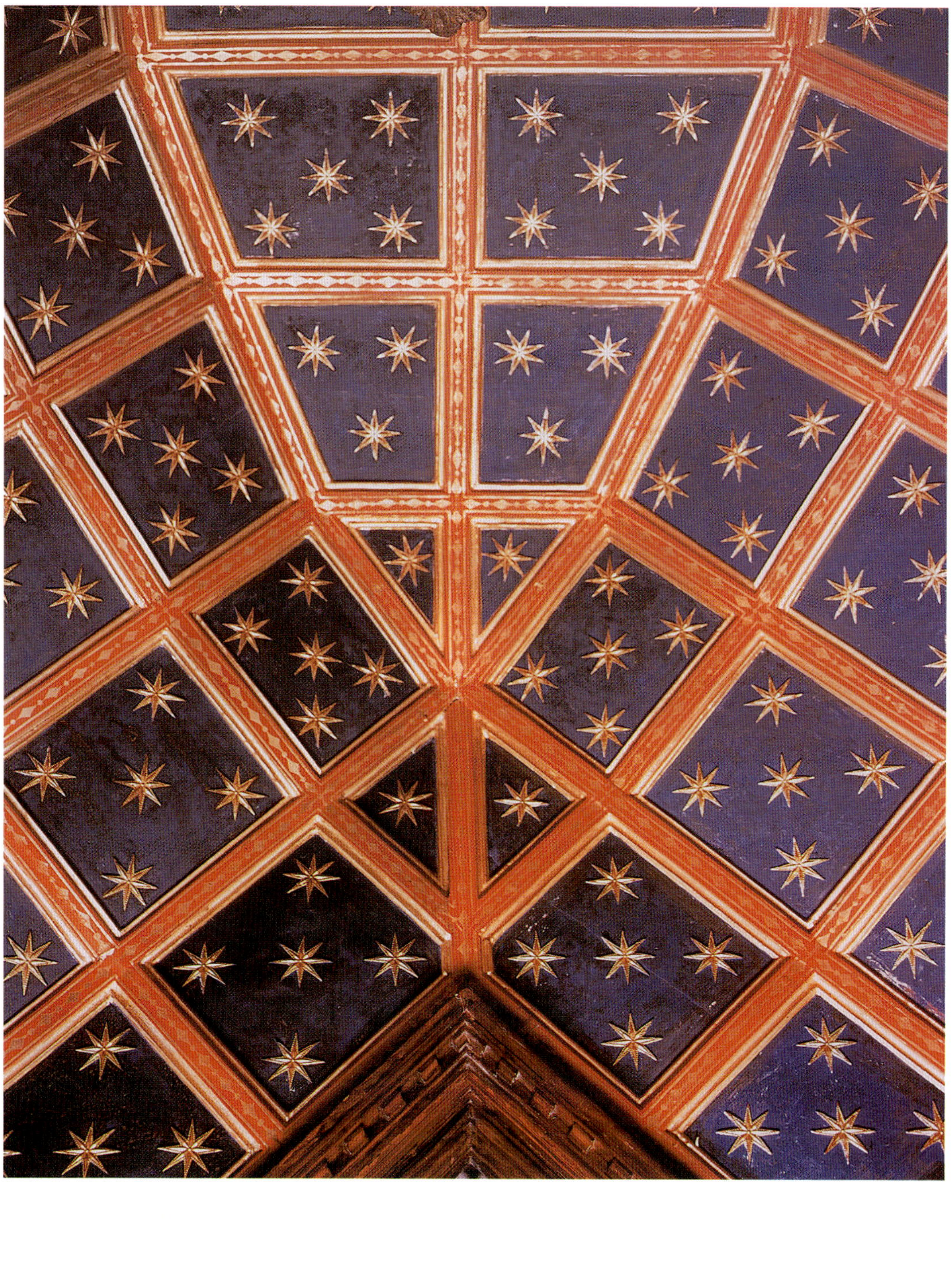

Untitled #214. 1989. Chromogenic process print in artist's frame, 39 × 34 inches

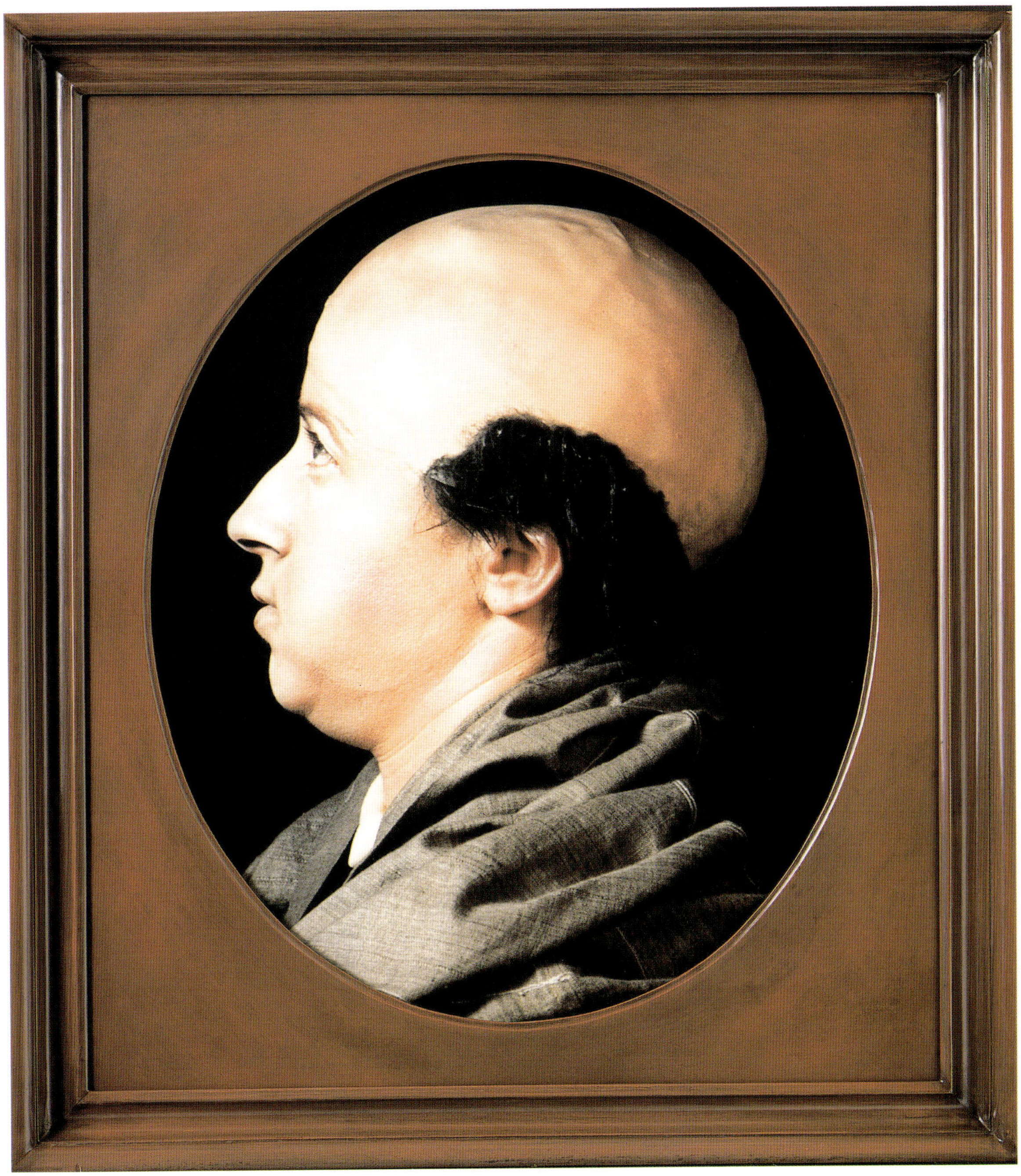

Diary of a Victorian Dandy. Suite of five sequenced chromogenic process prints, laminated in carved and gilded frames, $51\frac{1}{4} \times 75\frac{1}{4}$ inches each

Clockwise from top left:

Diary of a Victorian Dandy: 11:00 hours. 1998

Diary of a Victorian Dandy: 14:00 hours. 1998

Diary of a Victorian Dandy: 19:00 hours. 1998

Diary of a Victorian Dandy: 03:00 hours. 1998

Diary of a Victorian Dandy: 17:00 hours. 1998

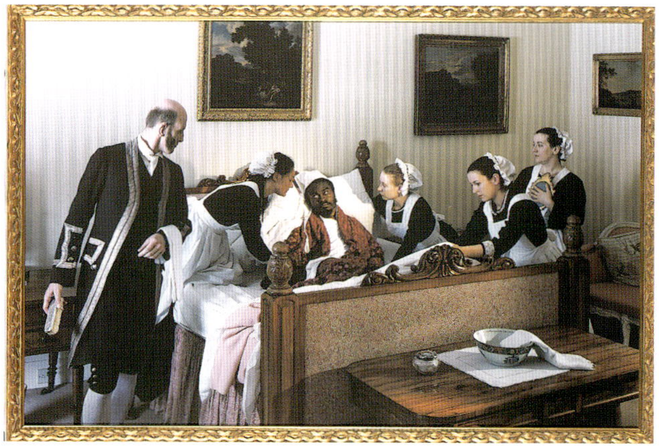

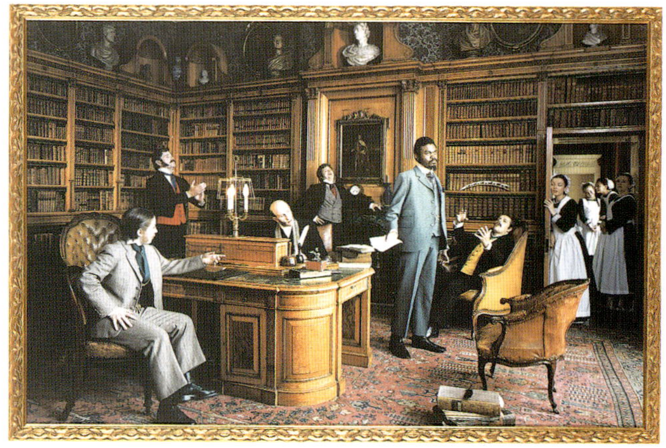

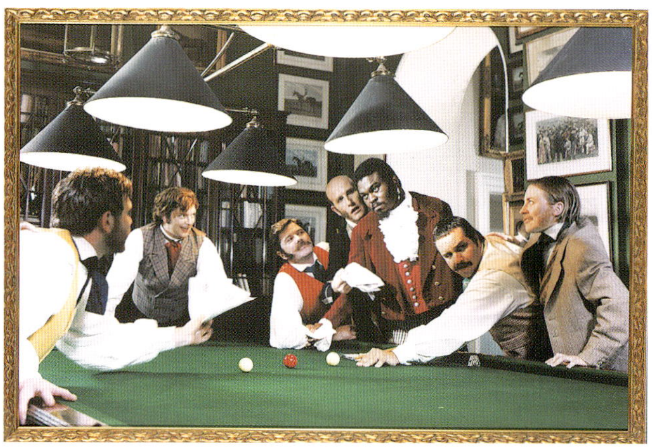

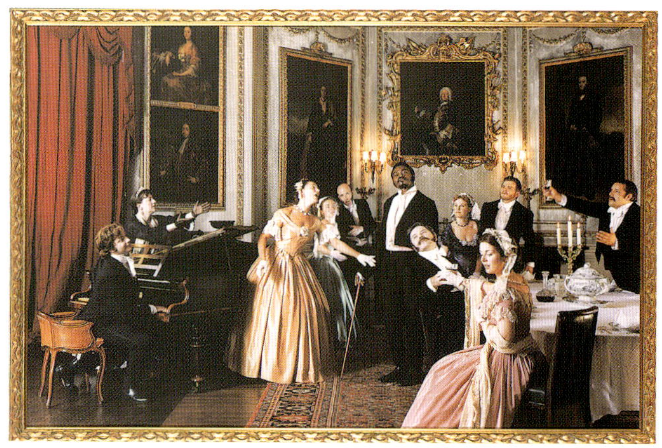

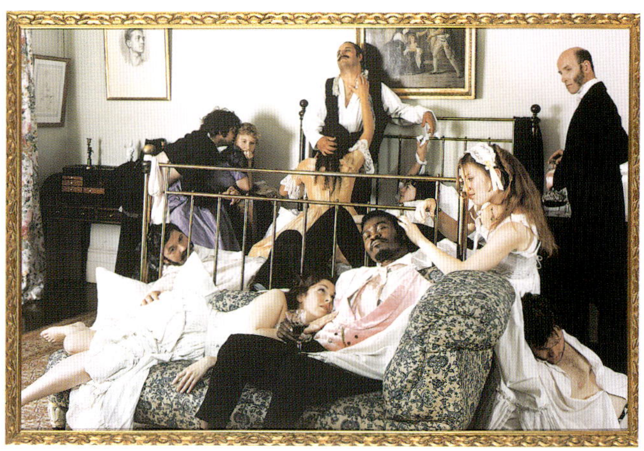

Untitled. 2000. Three chromogenic process prints from 16mm film stills, $5\frac{3}{4} \times 9\frac{7}{8}$ inches each

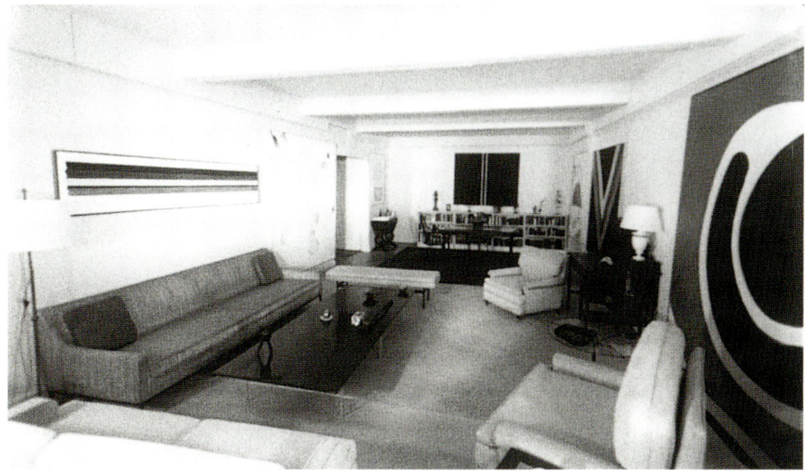

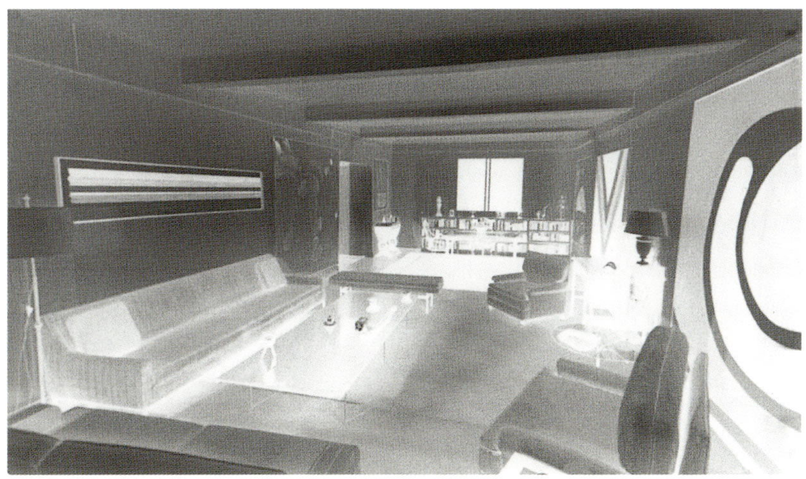

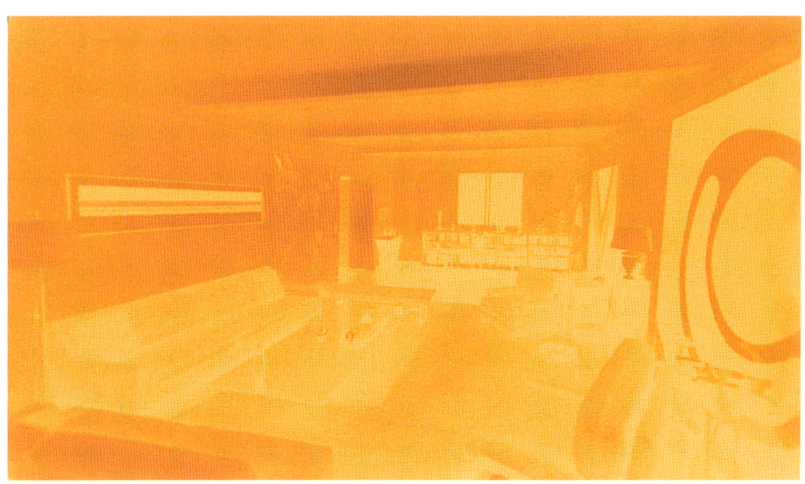

Water Buckets (Sulzer Industrial Hall, Winterthur). 1997.
Suite of four sequenced silver dye bleach process prints,
17 × 21¼ inches each

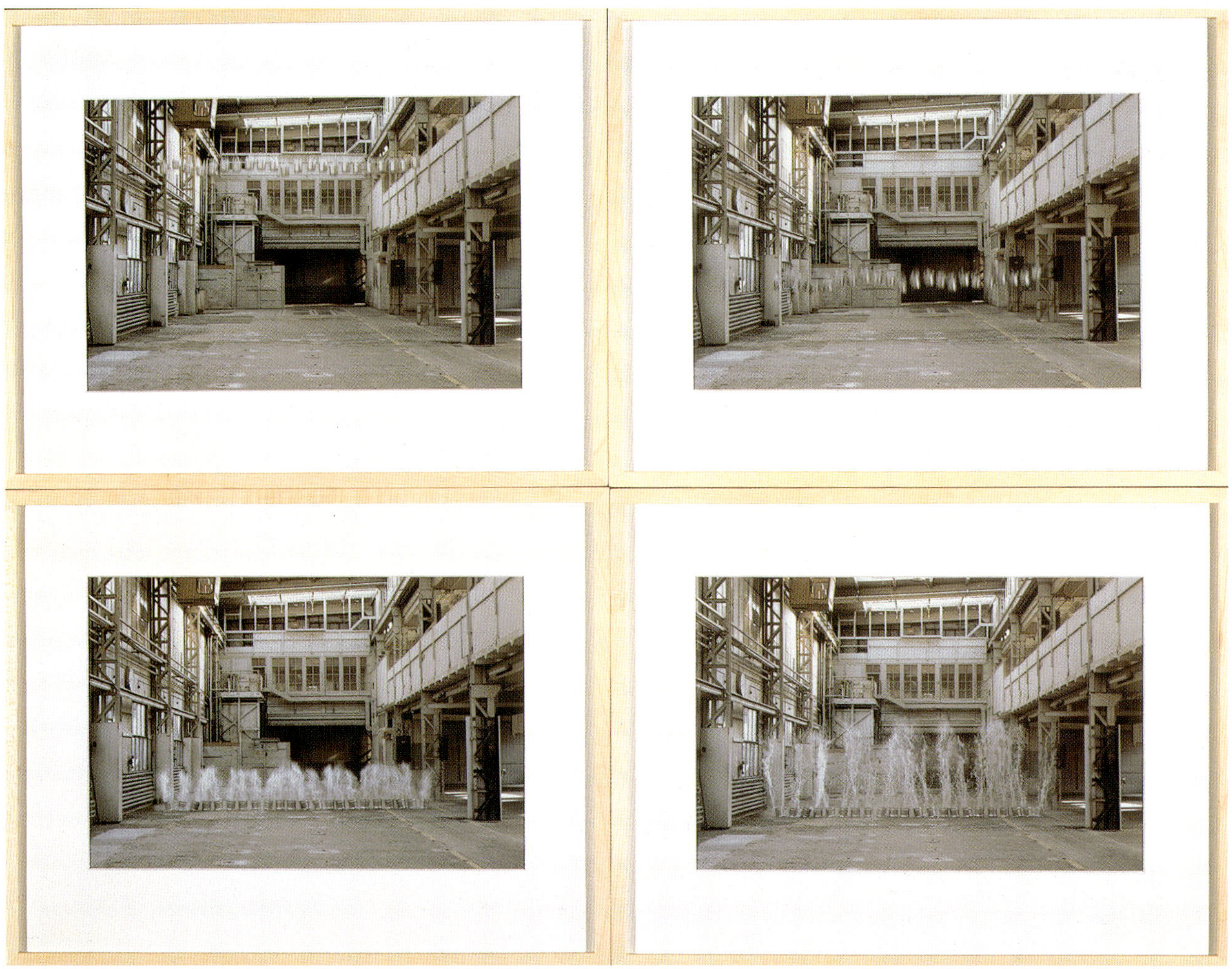

Untitled. 1998. Six unique gelatin silver prints on charcoal paper, dimensions varied

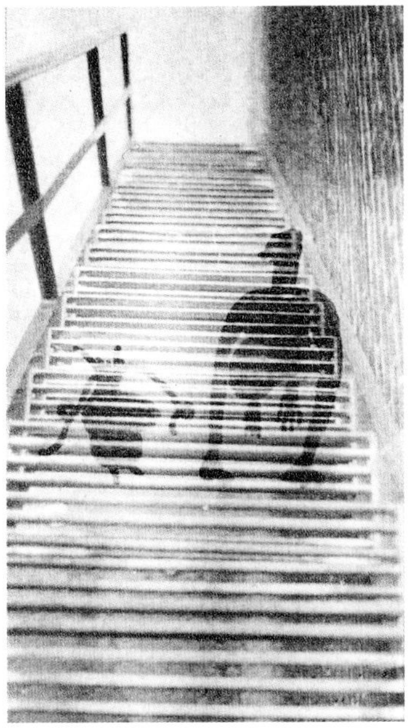
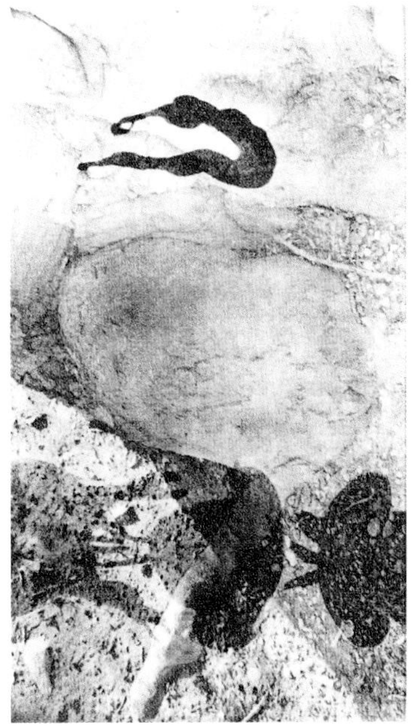
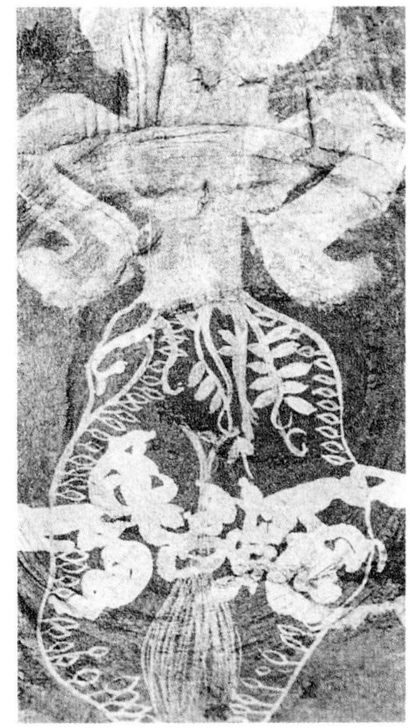
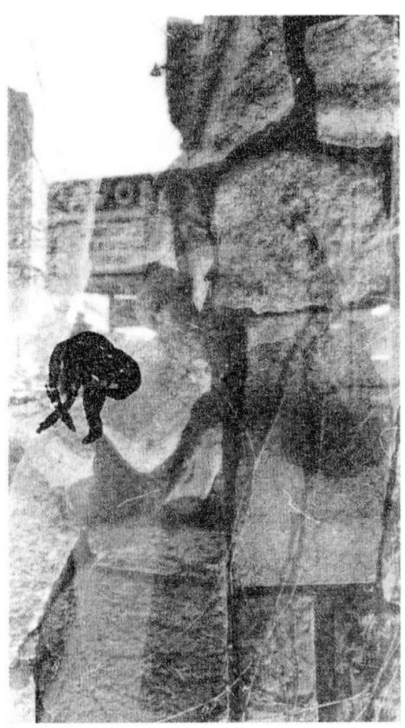
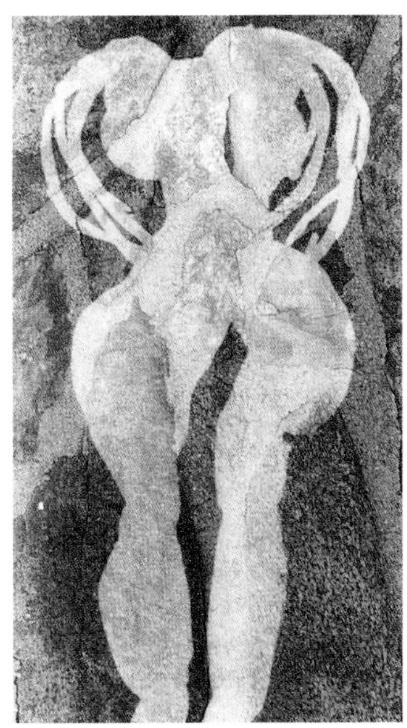
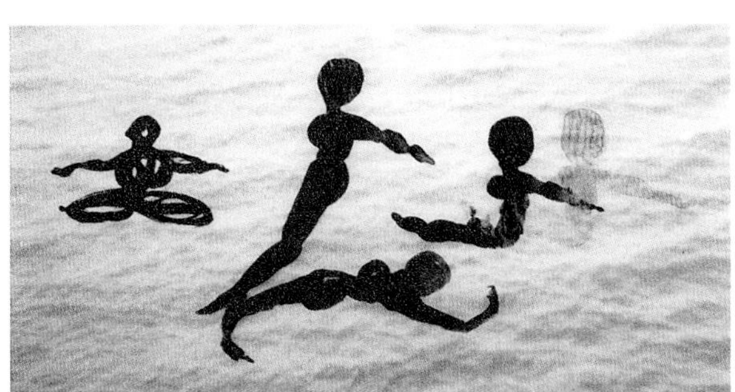

511. 1998. Chromogenic process print, face mounted to plexiglass, 51 × 60⅞ inches

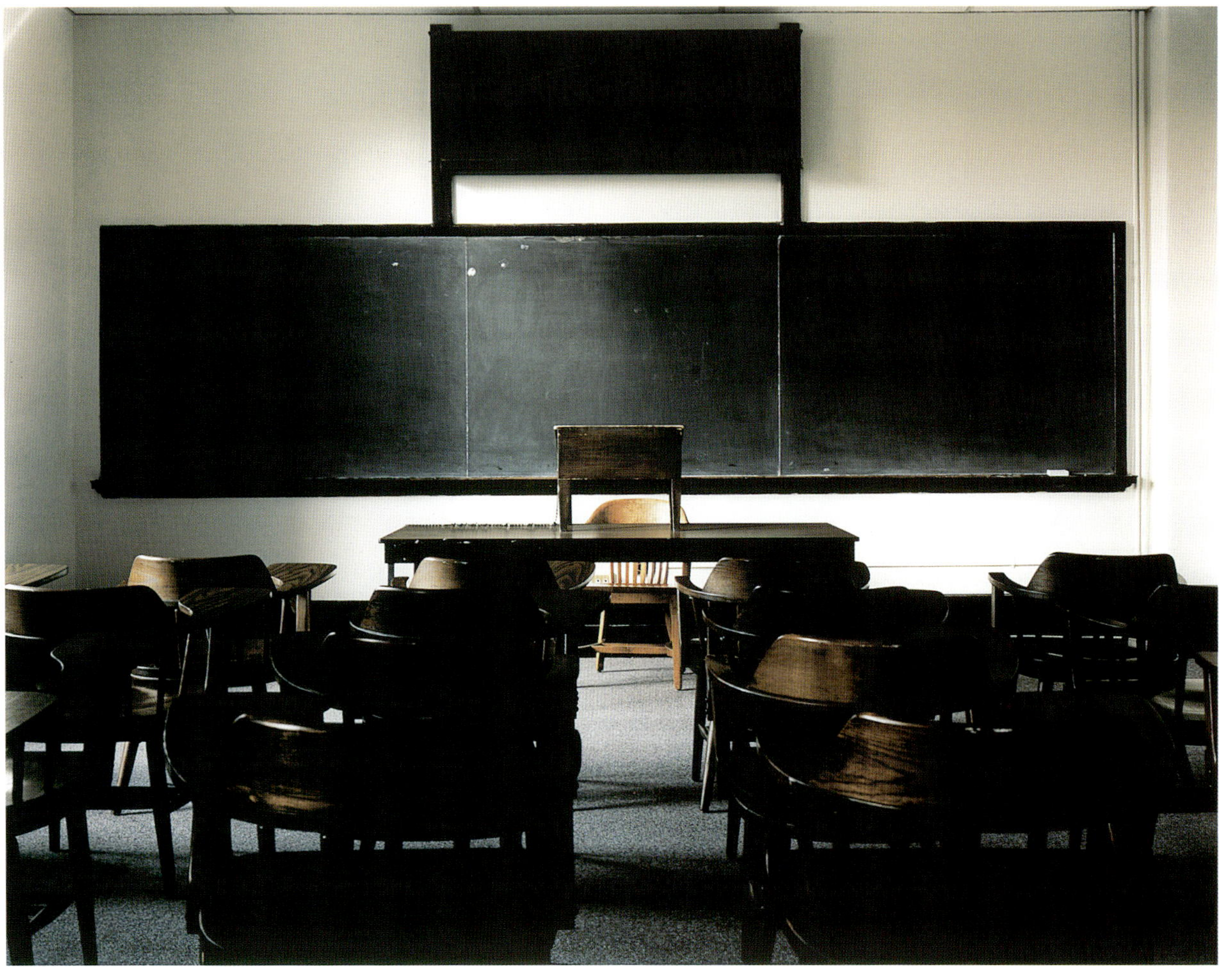

Walking Hourglass. 1989. Silver dye bleach process print, face mounted to plexiglass, 69 × 51 inches

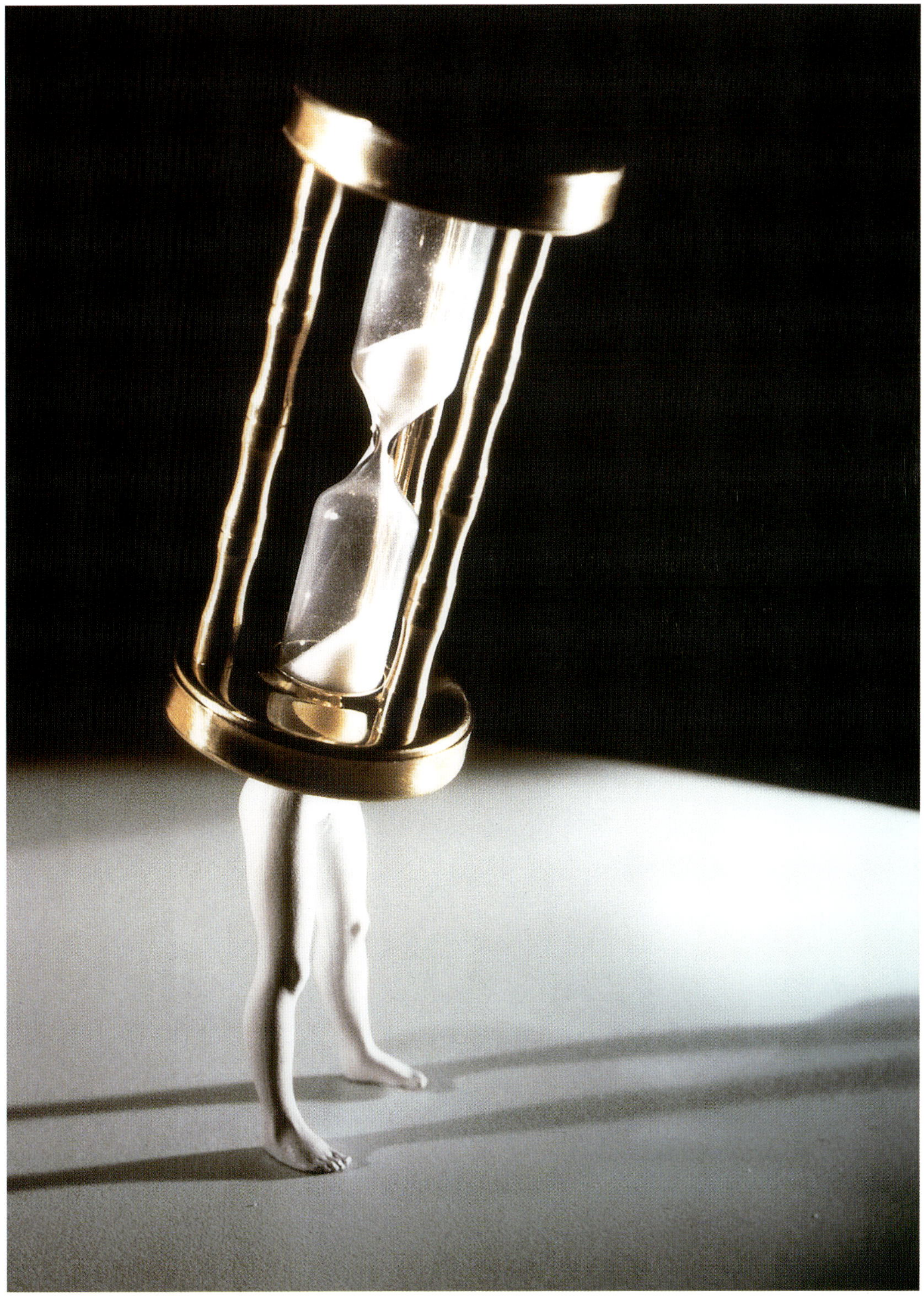

Flipside. 1991. Diptych: gelatin silver prints, engraved plastic plaque, $51\frac{1}{2} \times 70$ inches installed

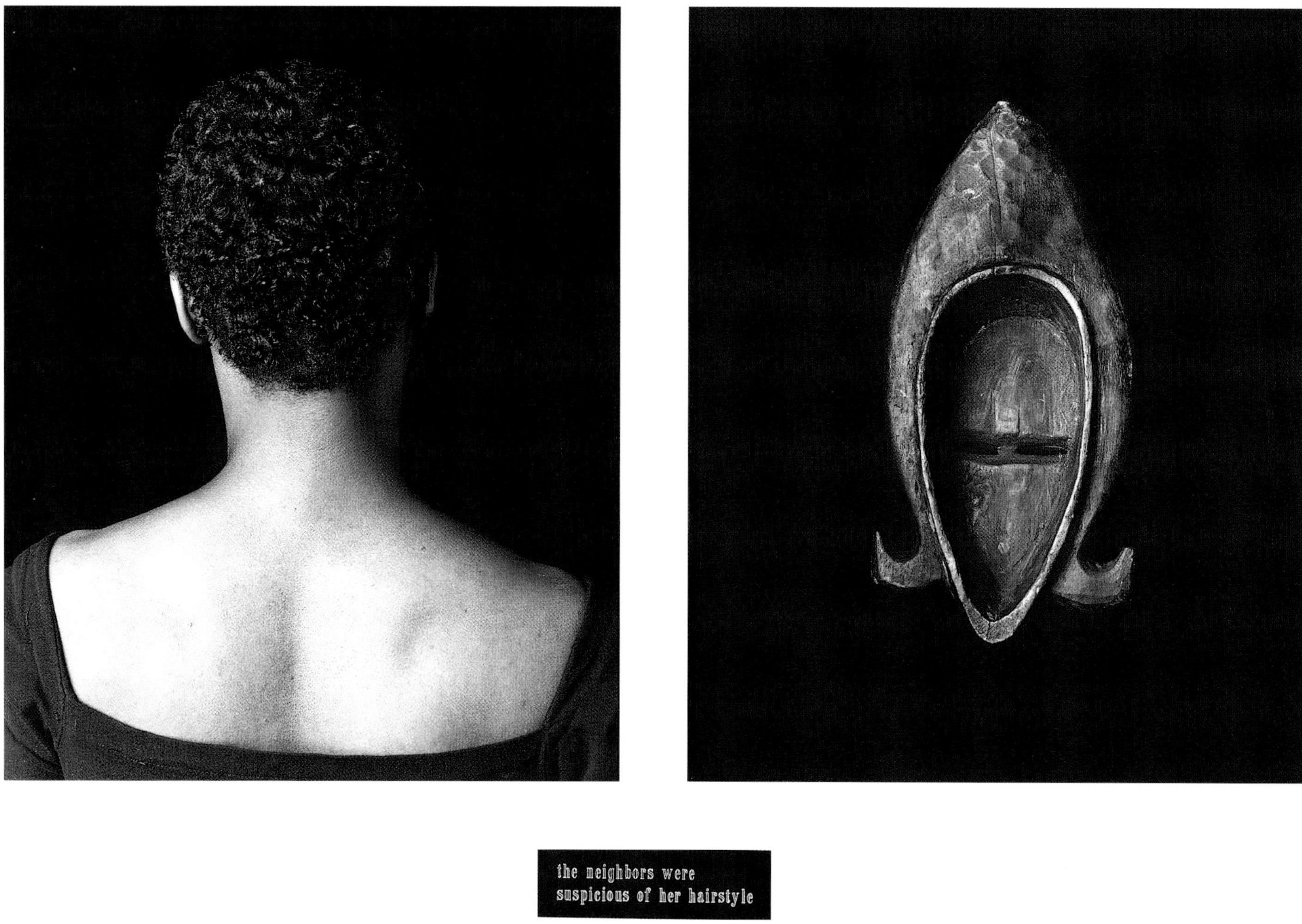

Luxor, Las Vegas. 1996. Chromogenic process print, mounted on aluminum, 47 × 64 inches

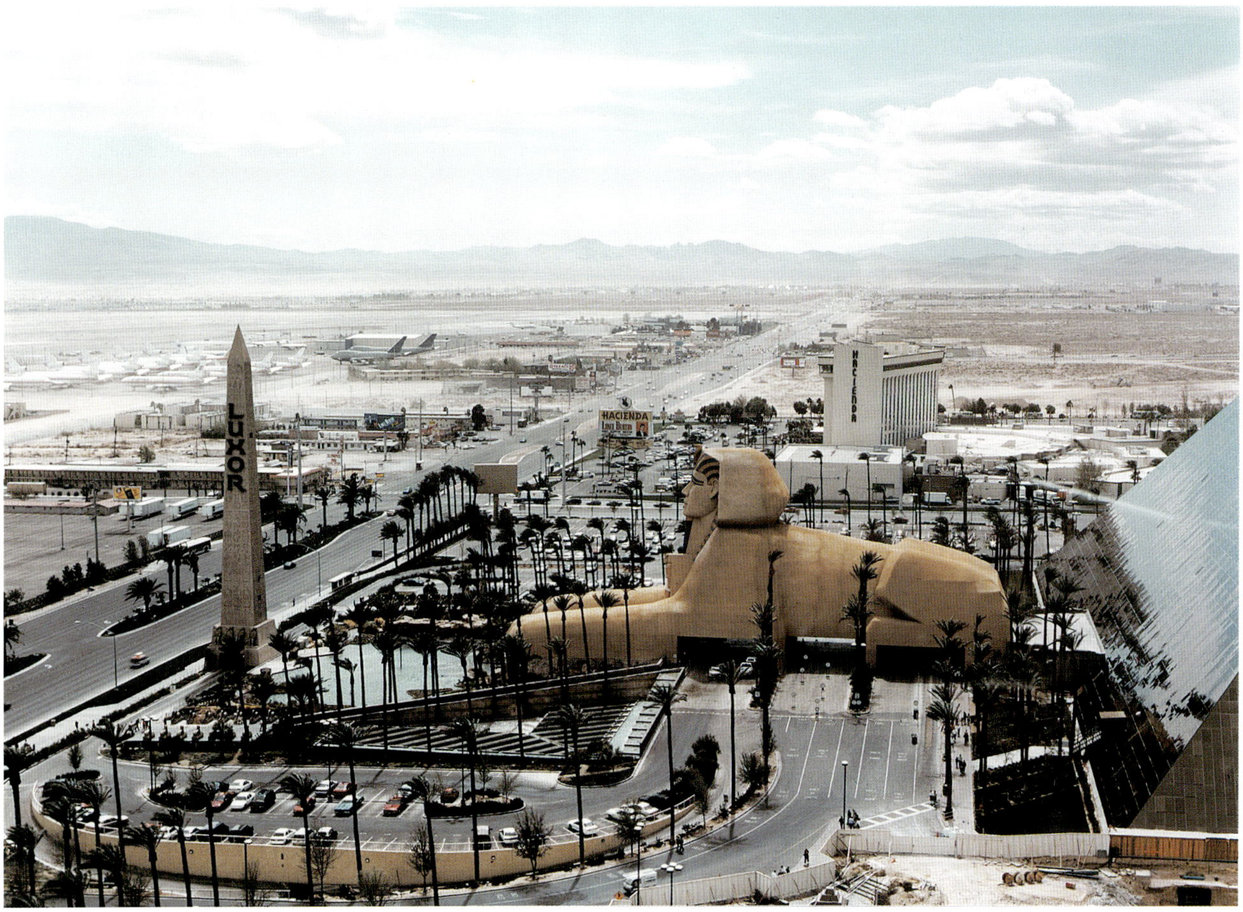

Candle with Black Ground and Fan in Mirror. 1993.
Diptych: silver dye bleach process prints, face mounted to plexiglass, 72 inches × 8 feet 6 inches

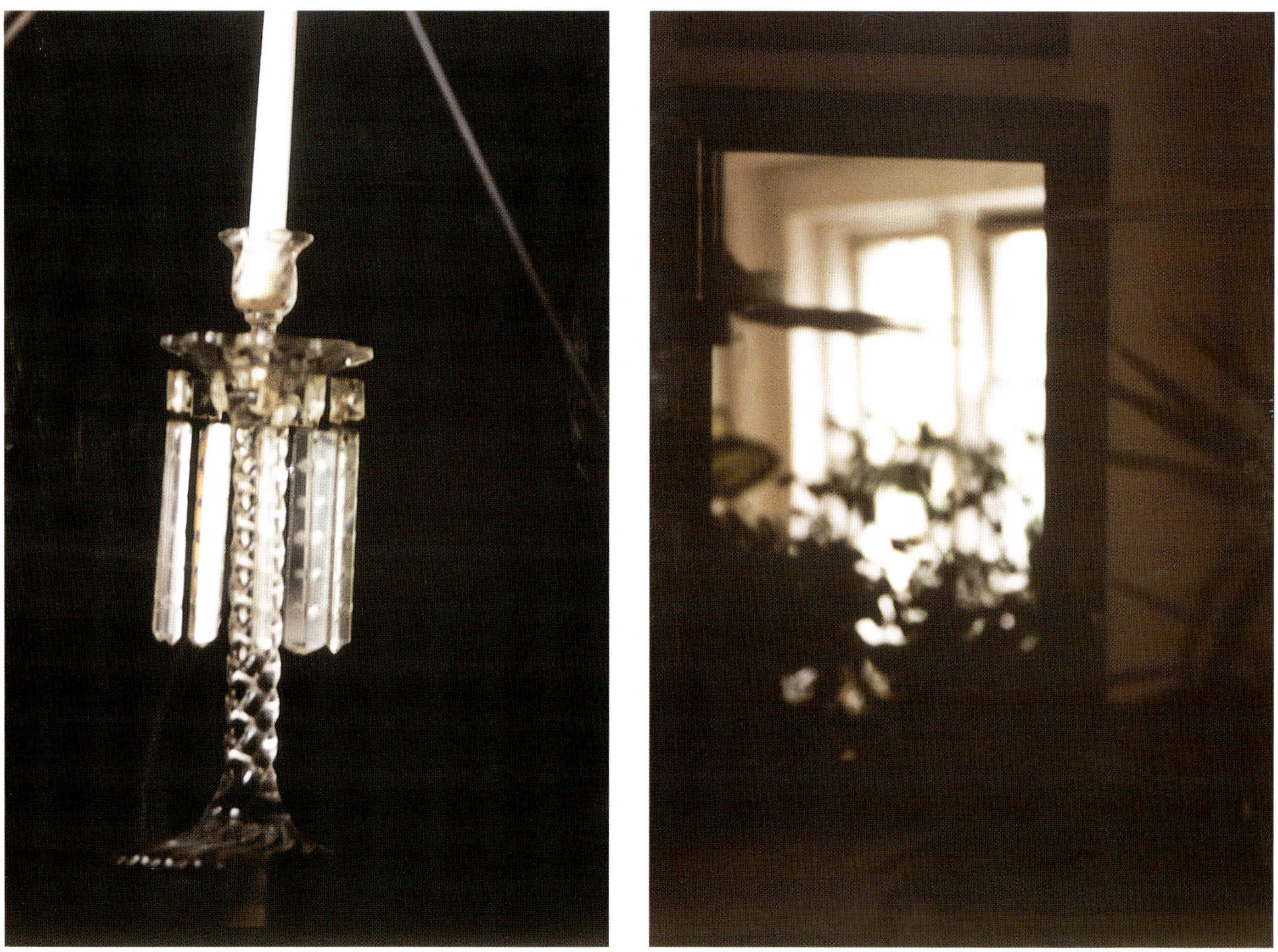

Mirror Displacement. 2000. Three Vibachrome prints from original 35mm slides, 20½ × 20¾ inches each

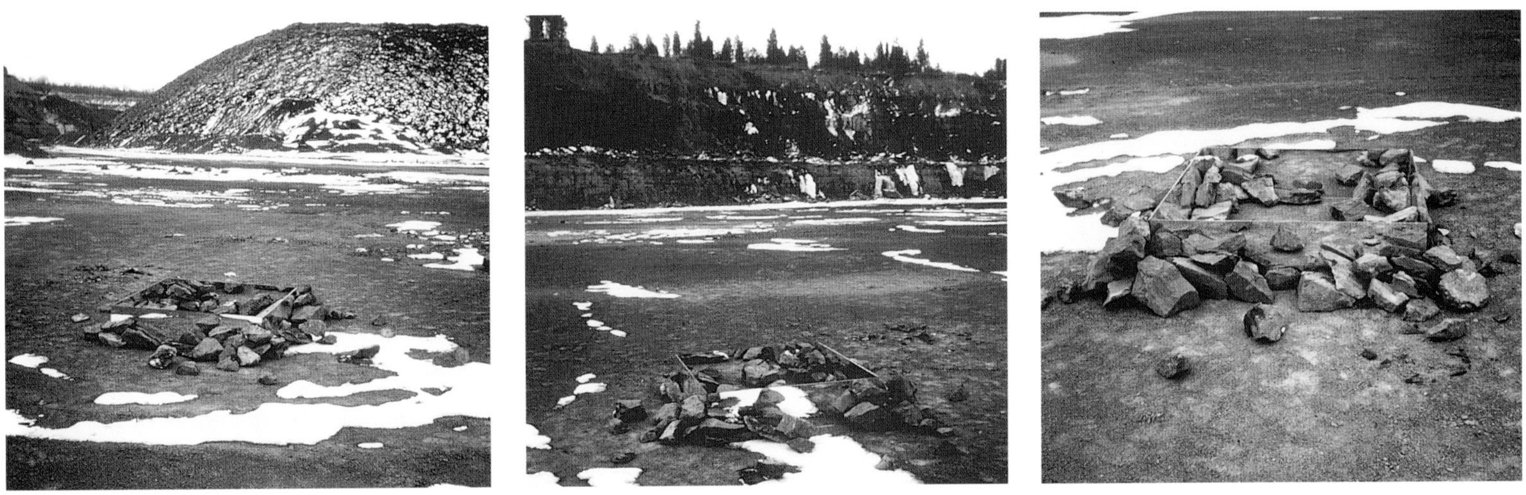

Starvision World. 1997. Installation: nine chromogenic process prints, 75 inches $\times$ 9 feet $2\frac{5}{8}$ inches

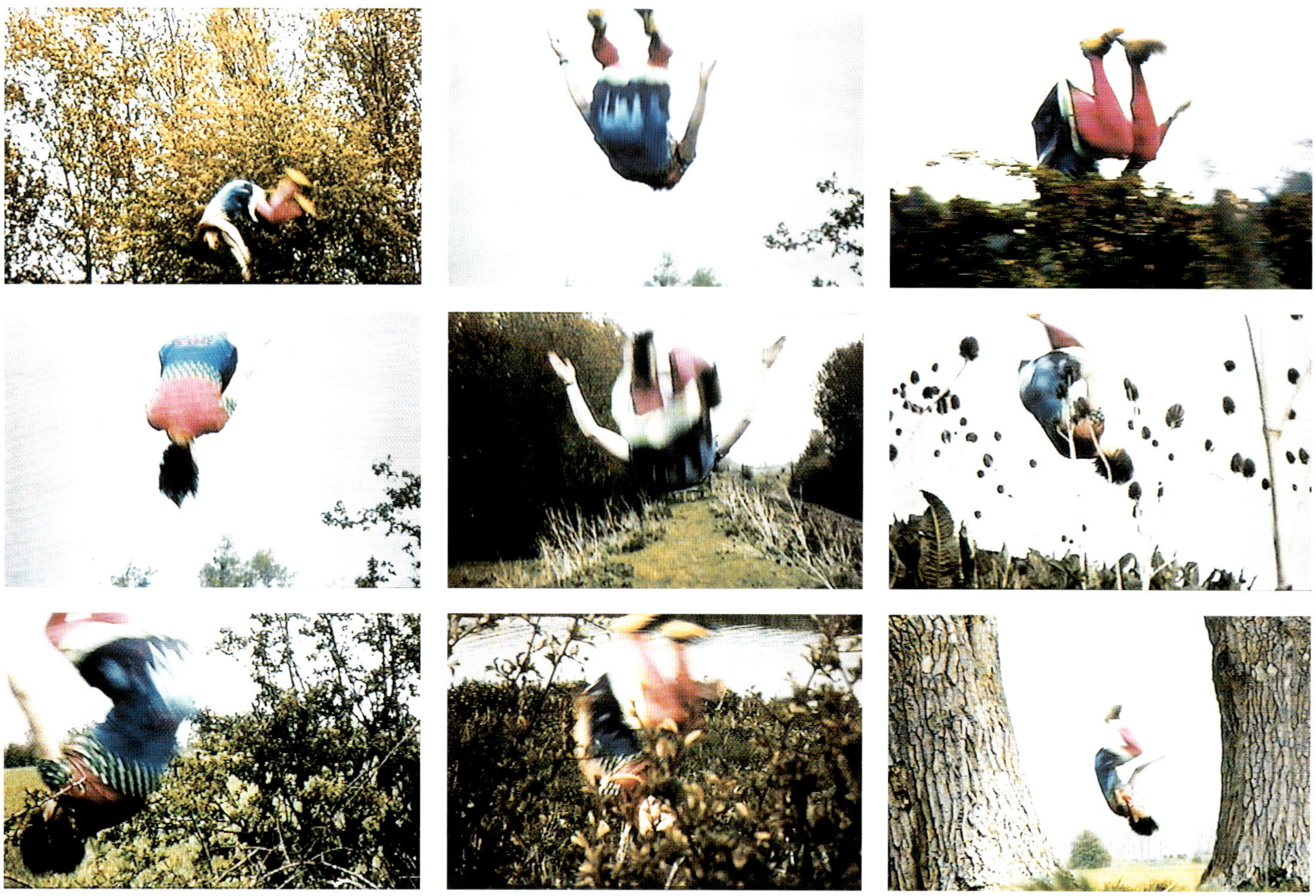

Bondi Beach 99 II. 1999. Chromogenic process print, $71\frac{3}{4} \times 96\frac{1}{2}$ inches

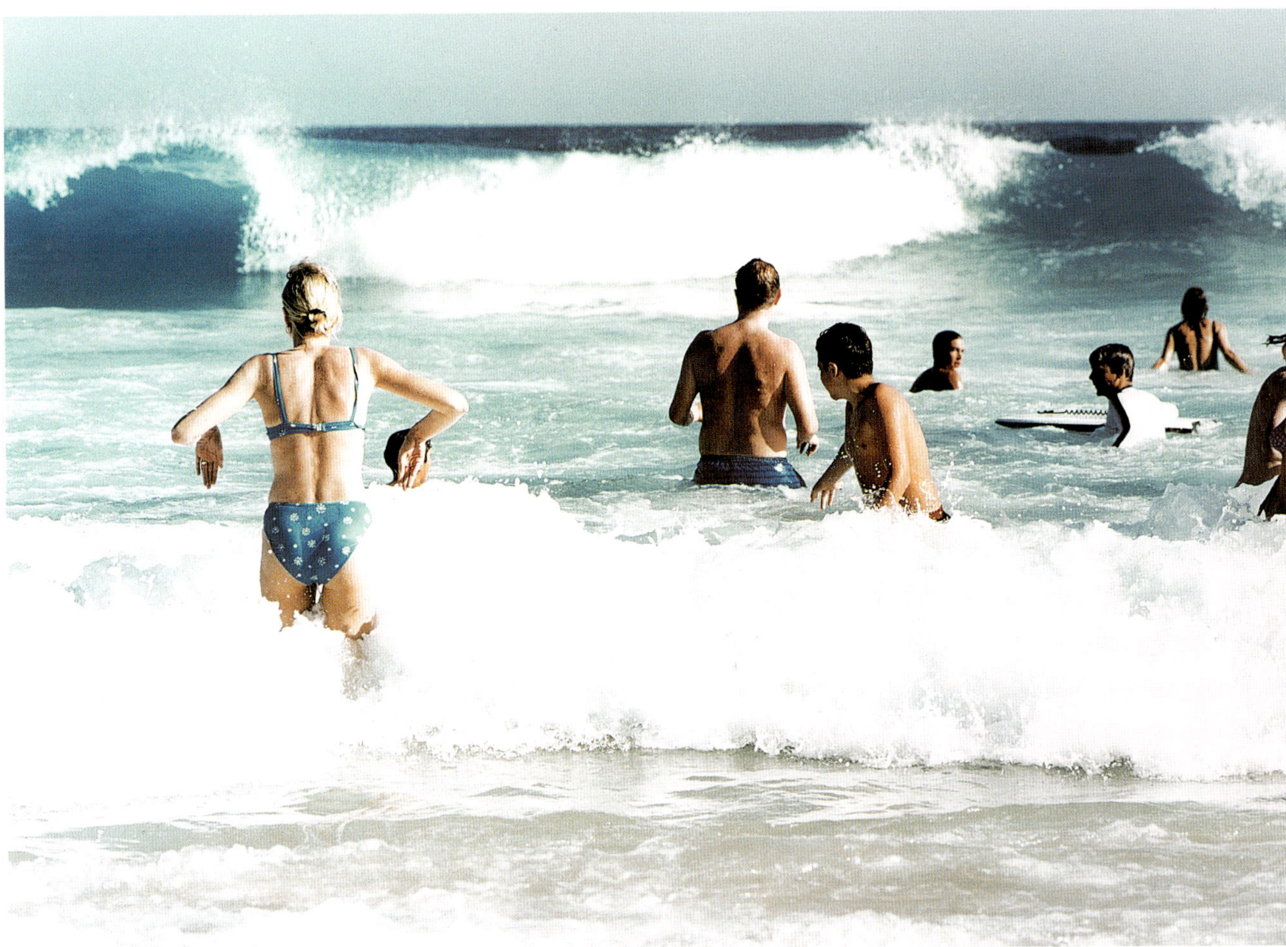

Mailander Dom (Fassade), Mailande, 1998 (Milan Cathedral, [Façade], Milan, 1998). 1998. Chromogenic process print, face mounted to plexiglass, $74\frac{1}{4} \times 92\frac{1}{2}$ inches

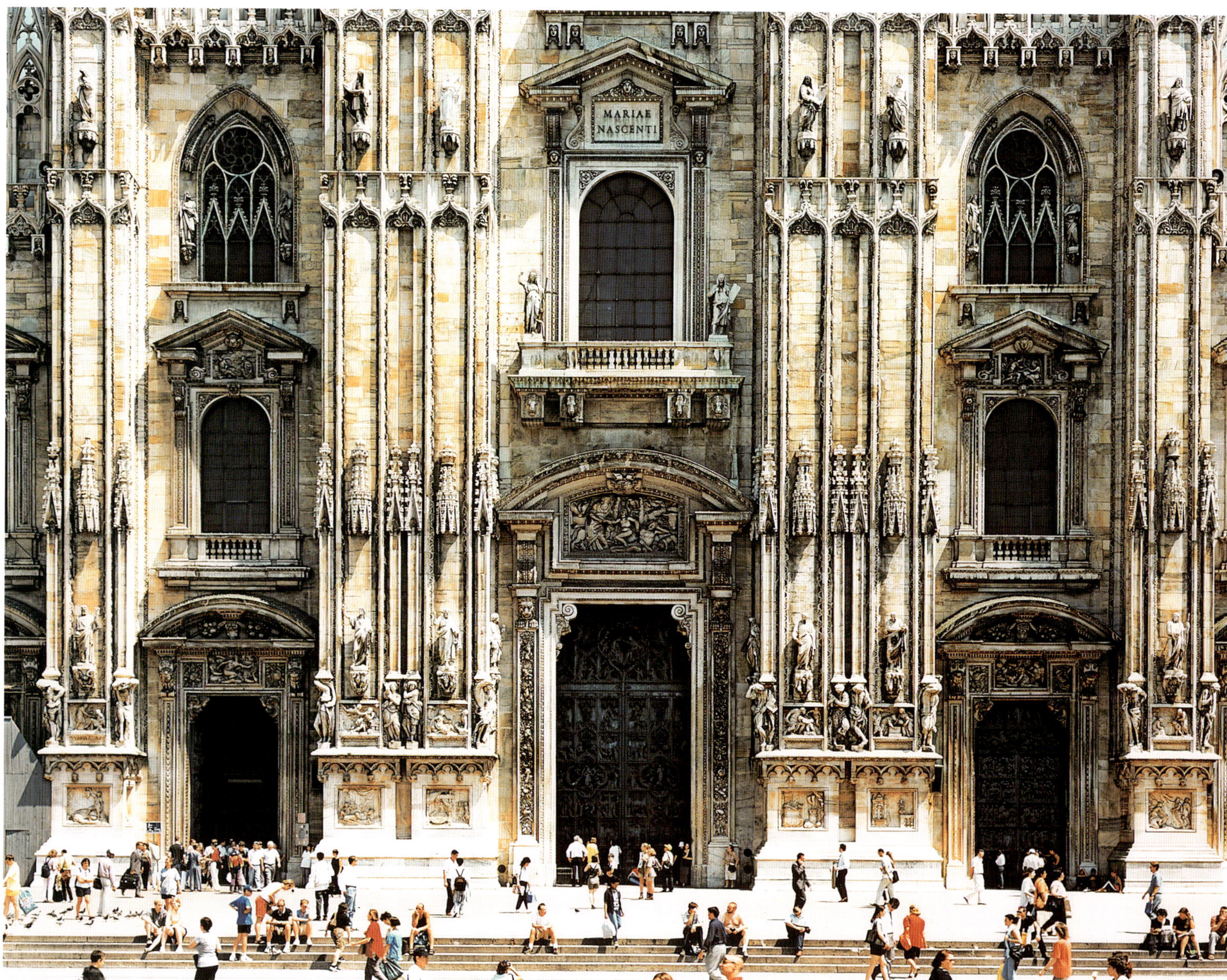

Chrysler Building—William Van Alen. 1997. Gelatin silver print, 23 × 18½ inches

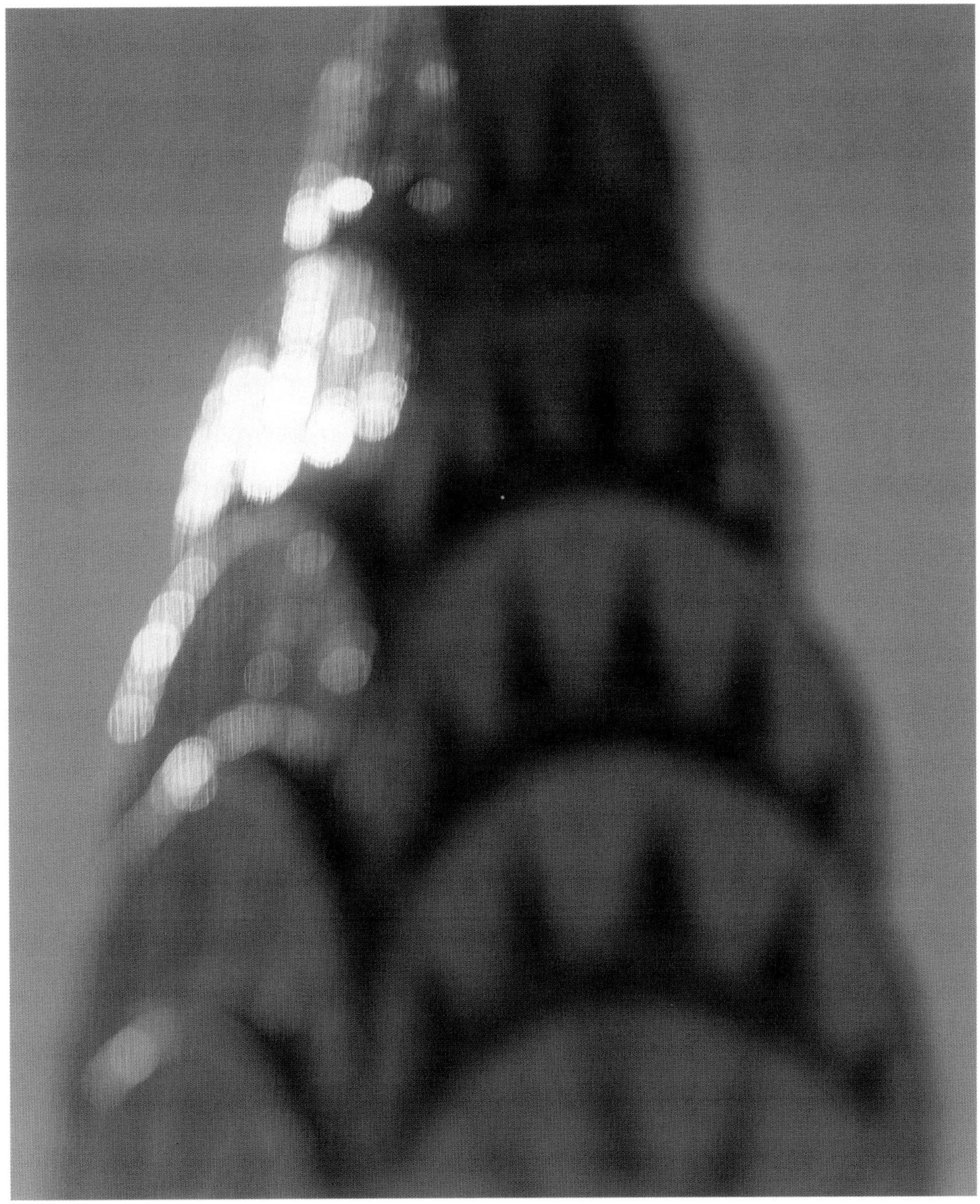

Beach Lane. 1976/1999. Silver dye bleach process print, mounted to aluminum, 20 × 30 inches

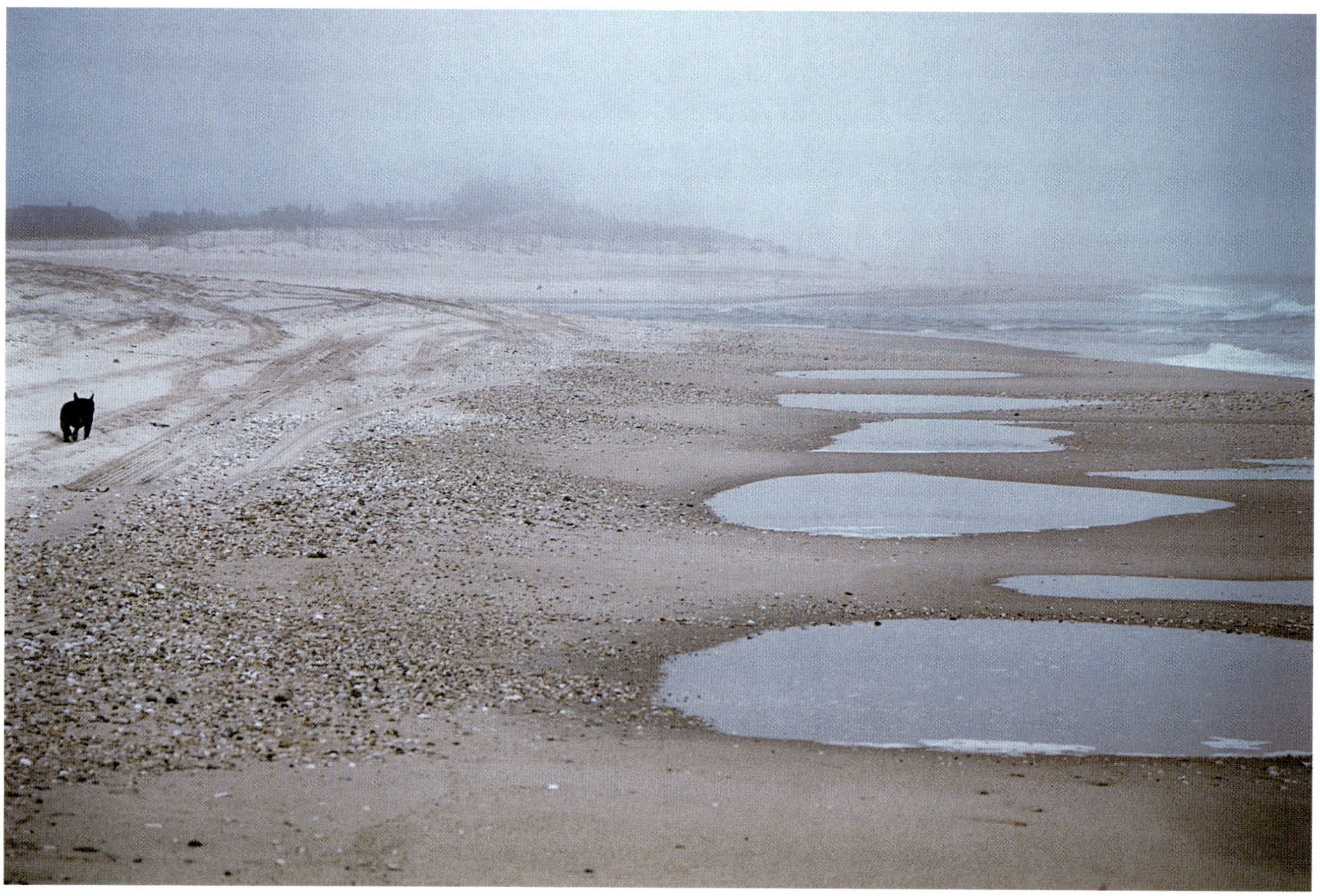

Dad #2. 1999. Digital chromogenic process print from a series, 56 × 42¾ inches

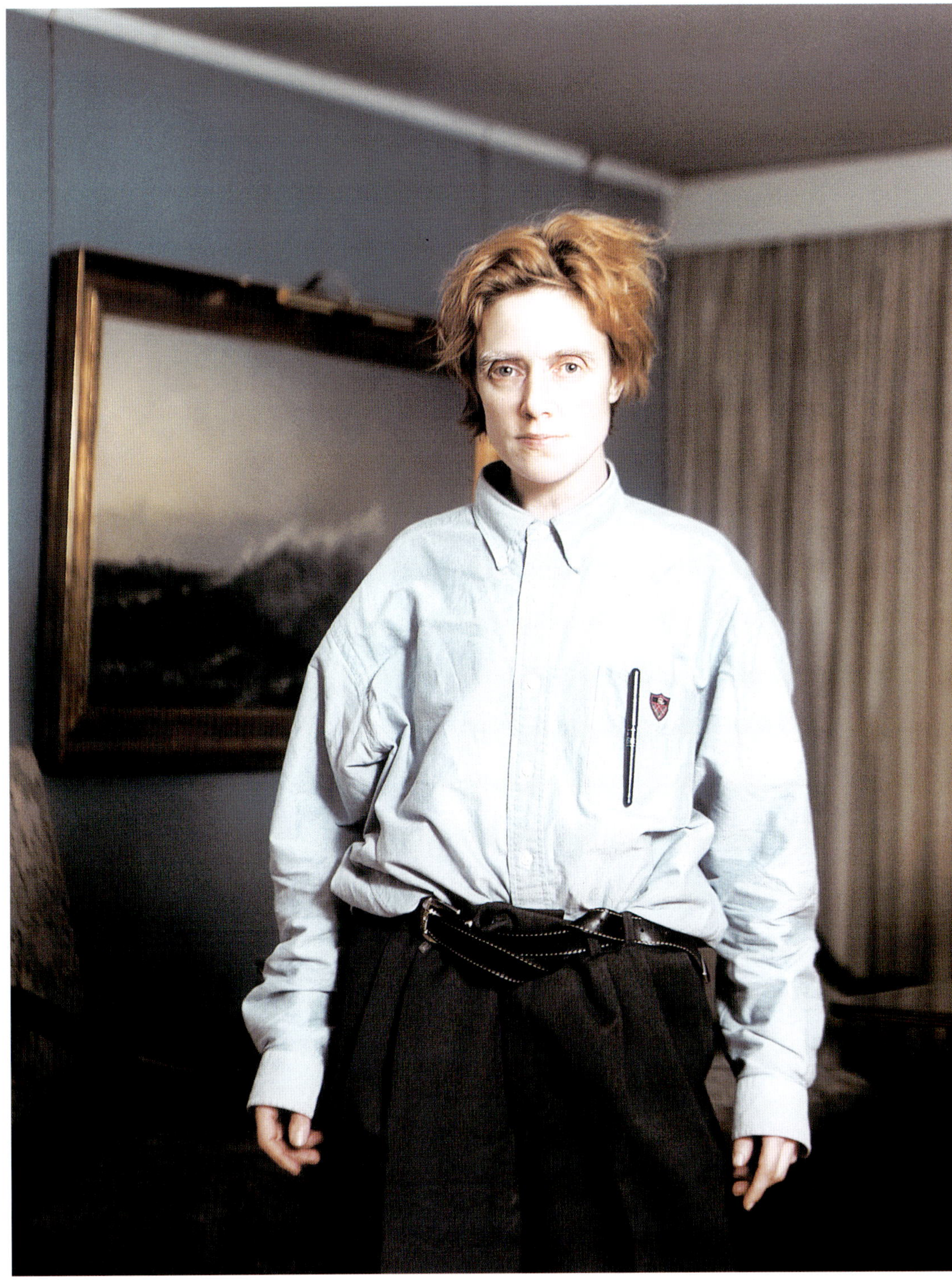

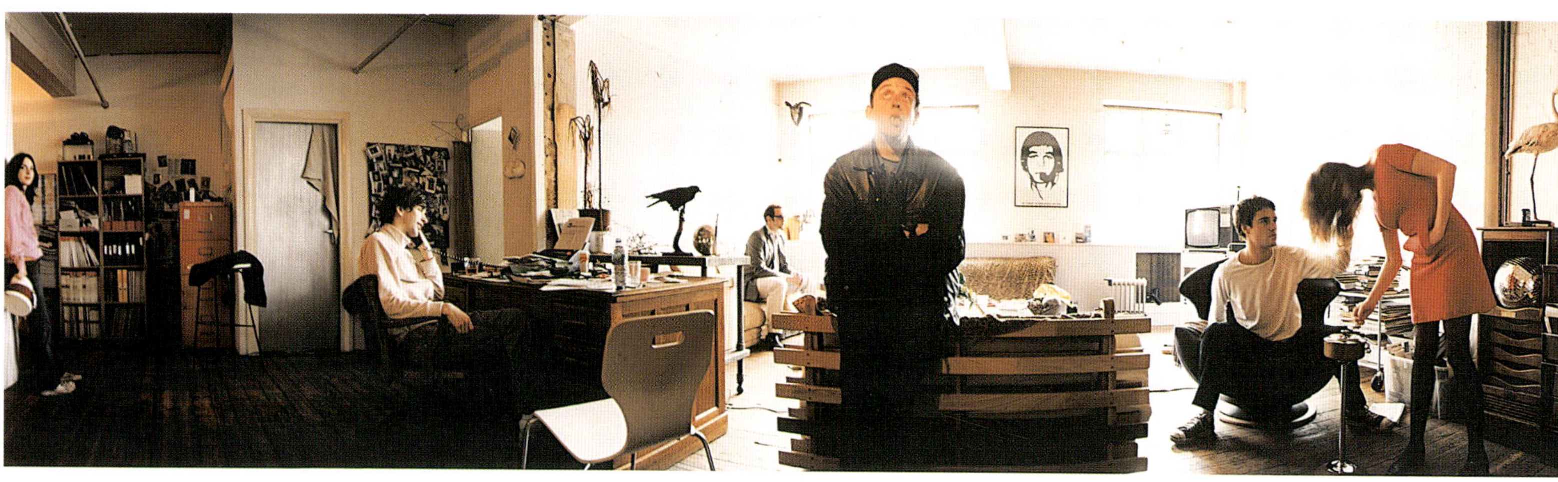

Five Revolutionary Seconds XIV. 1999. Chromogenic process print, 11 × 80 inches

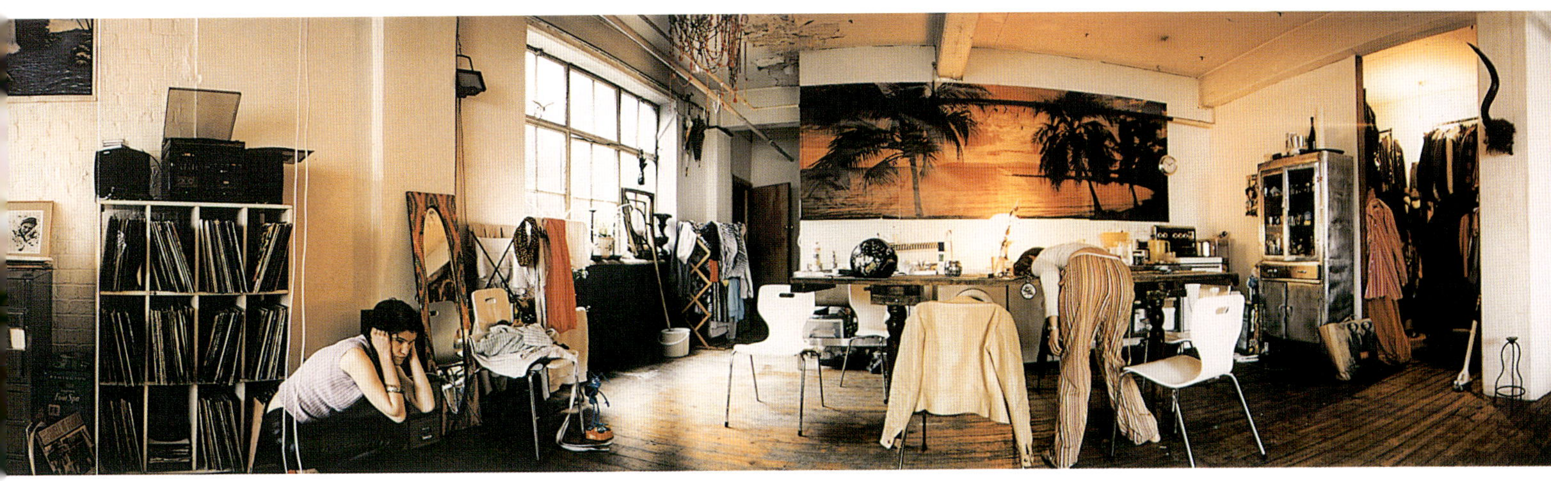

Suzanne & Lutz, White Dress, Army Skirt. 1993.
Chromogenic process print, $23^{1}/_{4} \times 15^{1}/_{2}$ inches

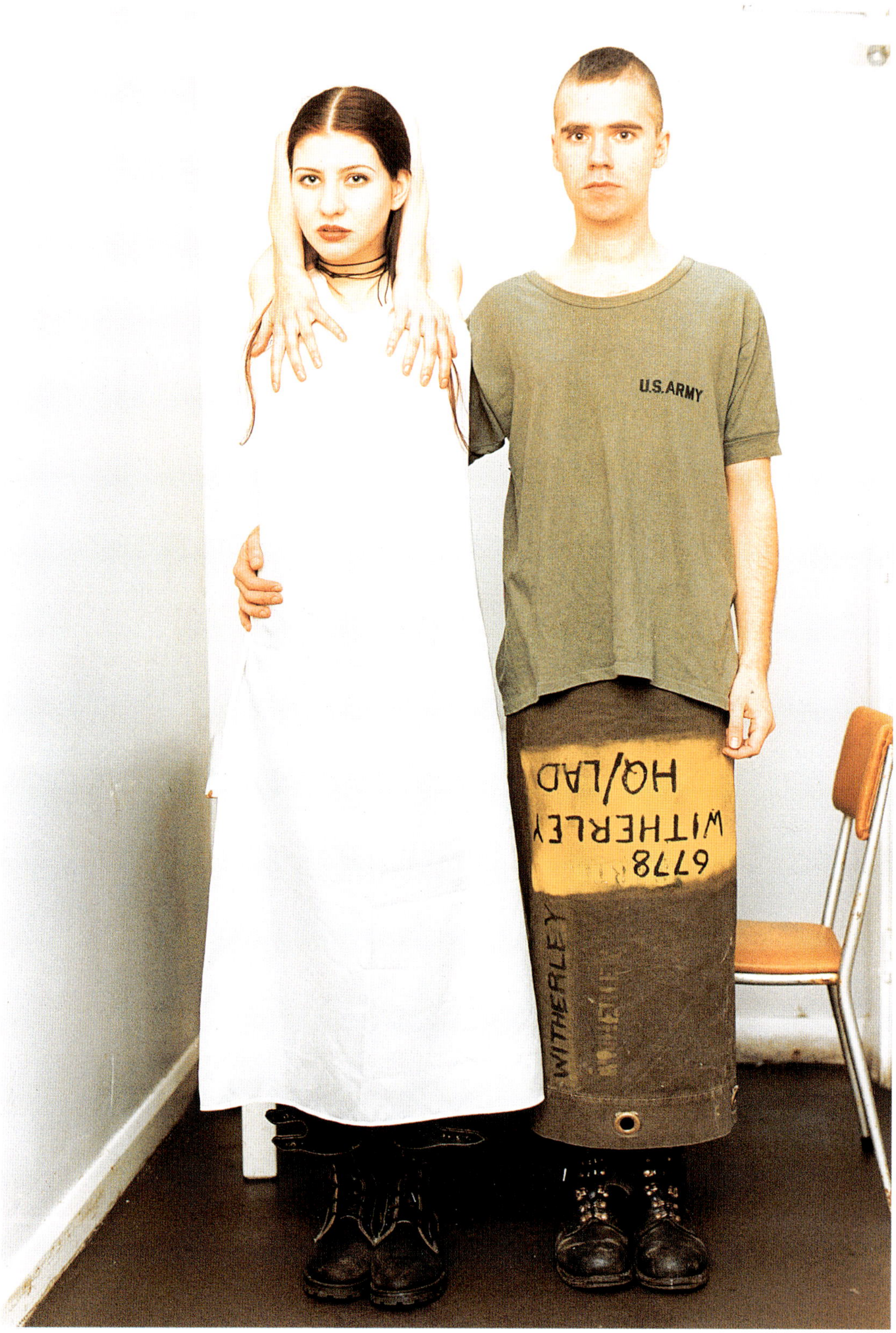

Untitled. 1995. Suite of seven chromogenic process prints, 4 × 6 inches each

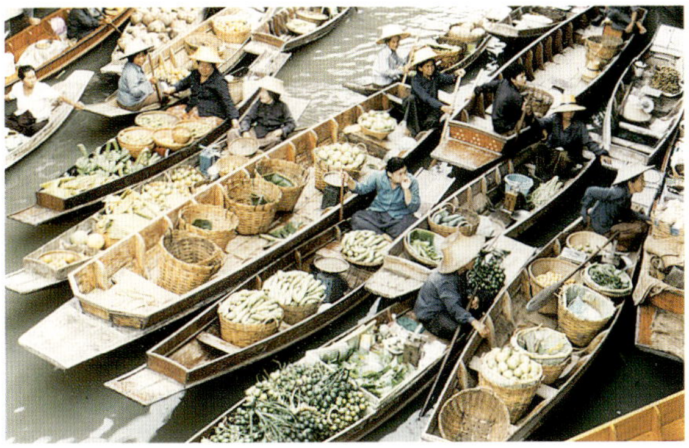

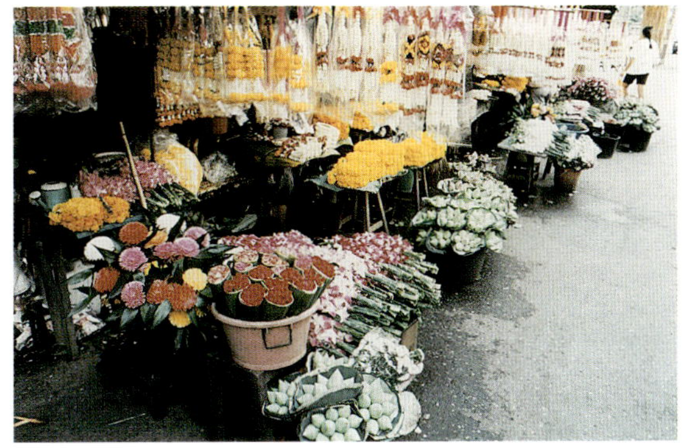

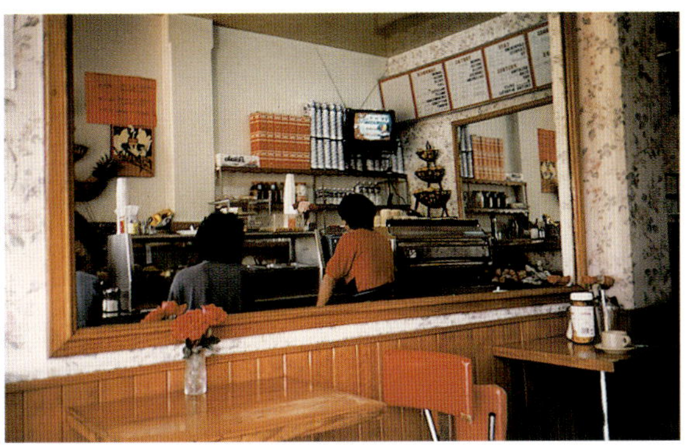

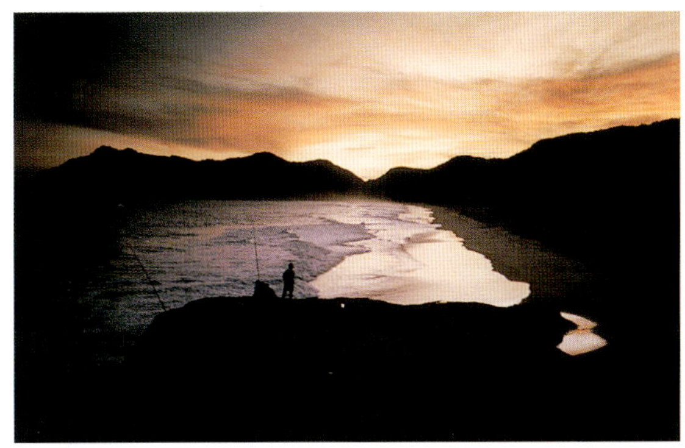

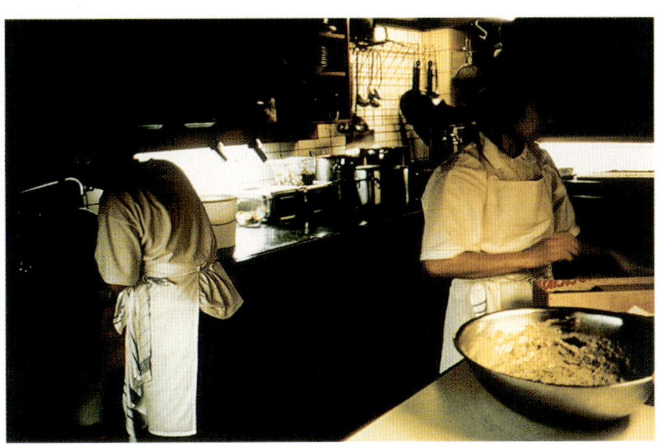

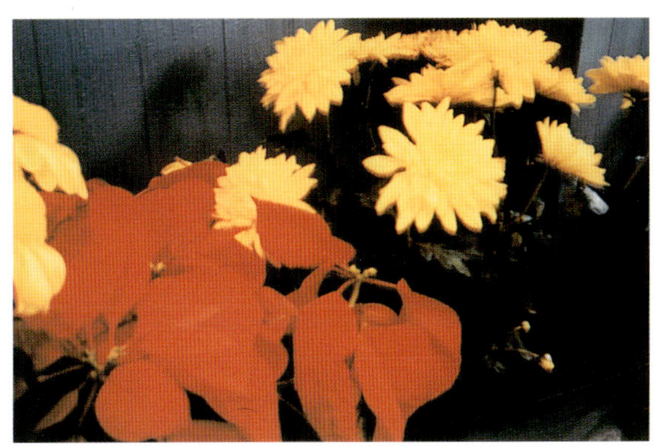

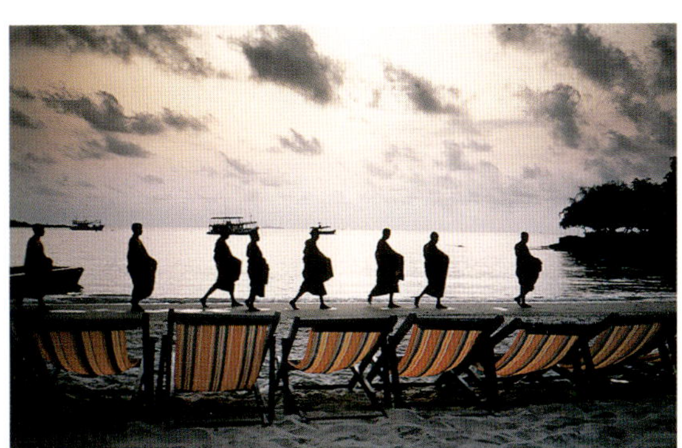

Fritz I. 1993. Silver dye bleach process print, face mounted to plexiglass, $39\frac{1}{4} \times 39\frac{1}{4}$ inches

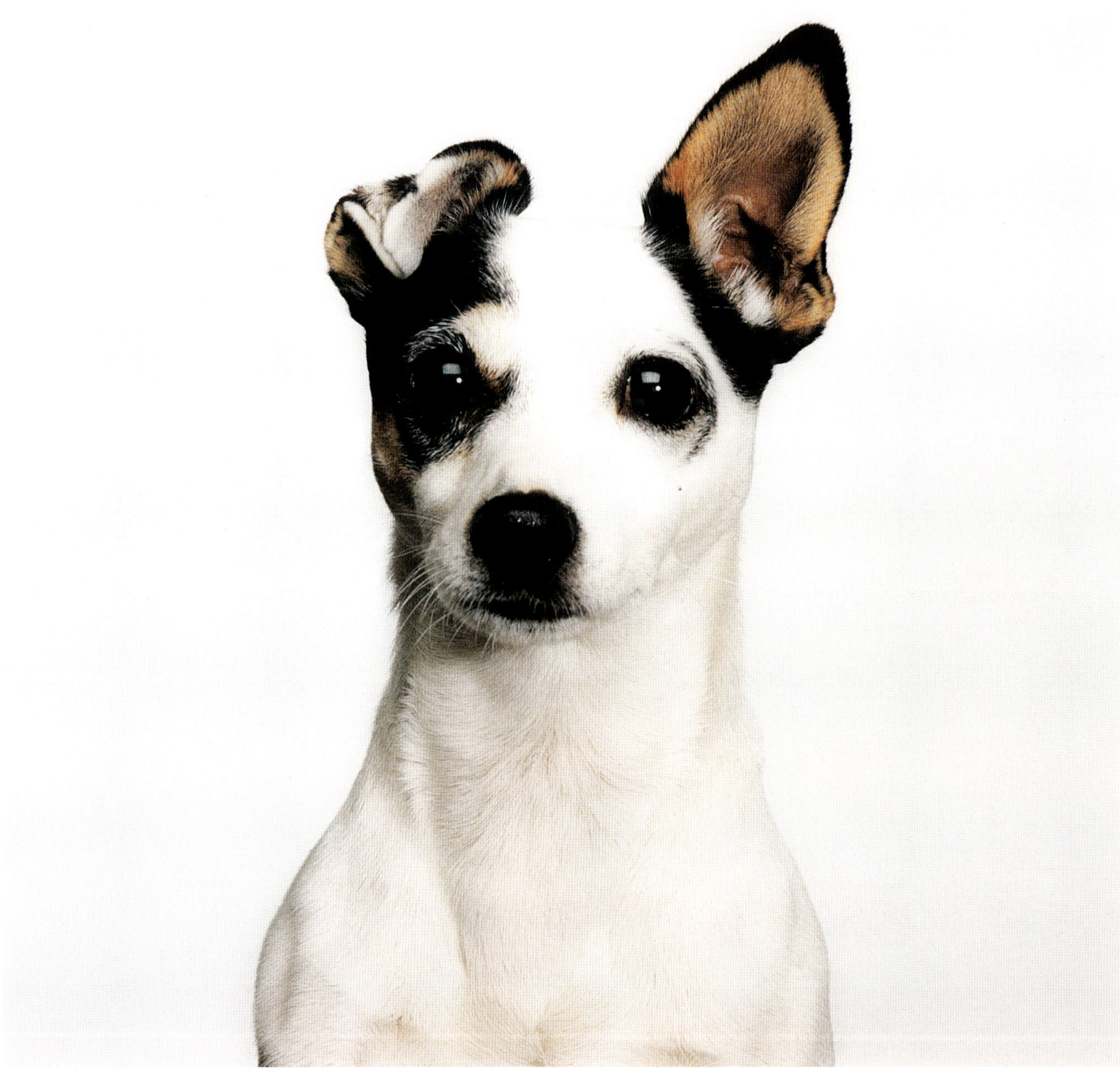

Isortoq Unartoq #7. 1999. Diptych: Chromogenic process prints from a series, face mounted to plexiglass, 29 × 35¼ inches each

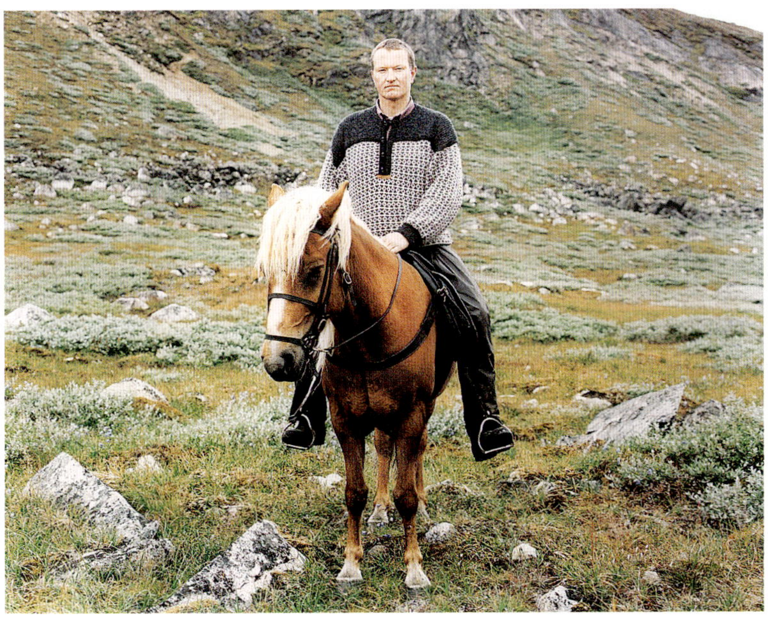

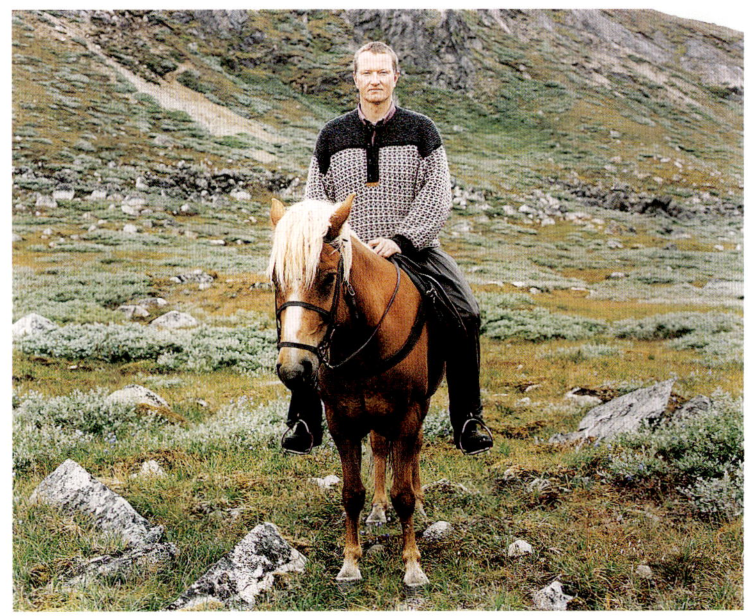

Prague, Refribell, Harbours, Waterloo, Nautilus (details). 1981–82. Suite of eighteen film stills (gelatin silver prints made from Super 8 film) from three films, 17 × 20 inches each

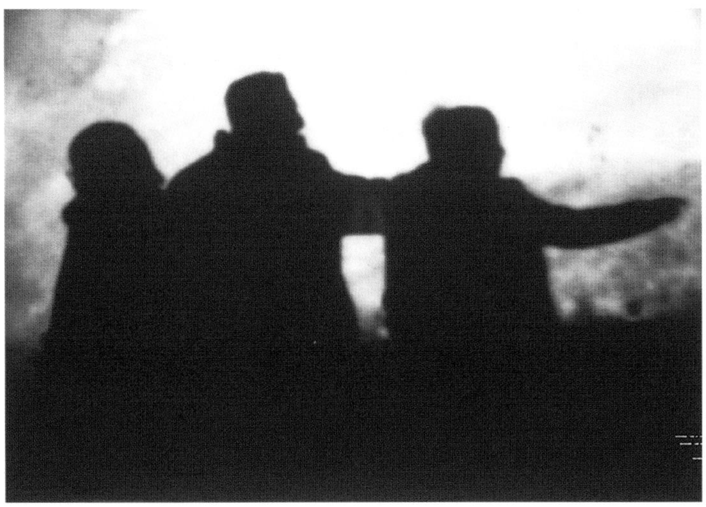

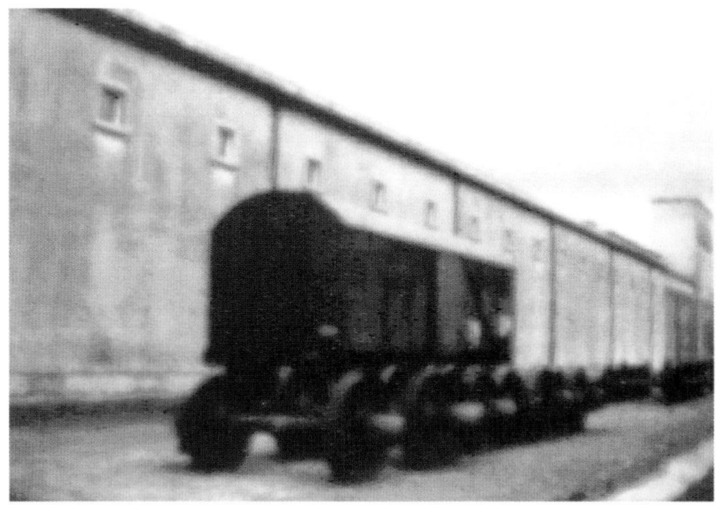

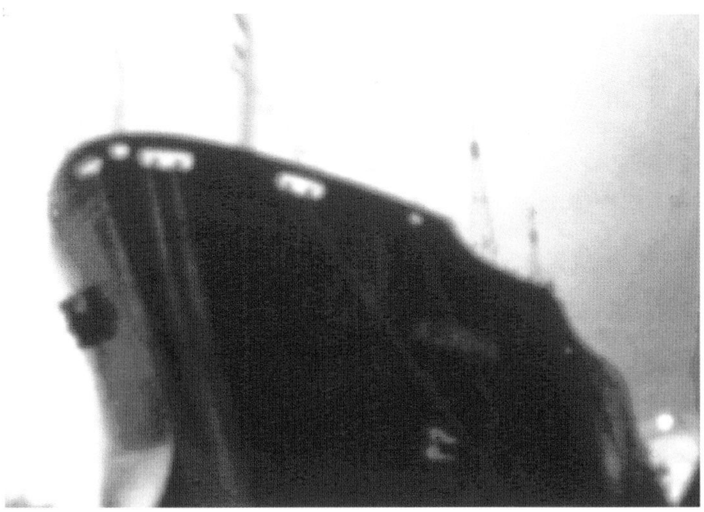

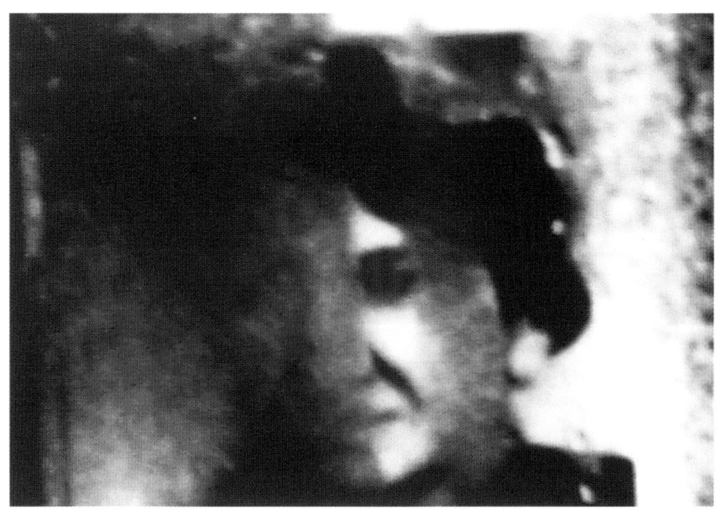

Untitled (Brooklyn Bridge Tail Lights). 1999. Diptych: chromogenic process prints, face mounted to plexiglass, $40^1/_4 \times 40^1/_4$ inches each

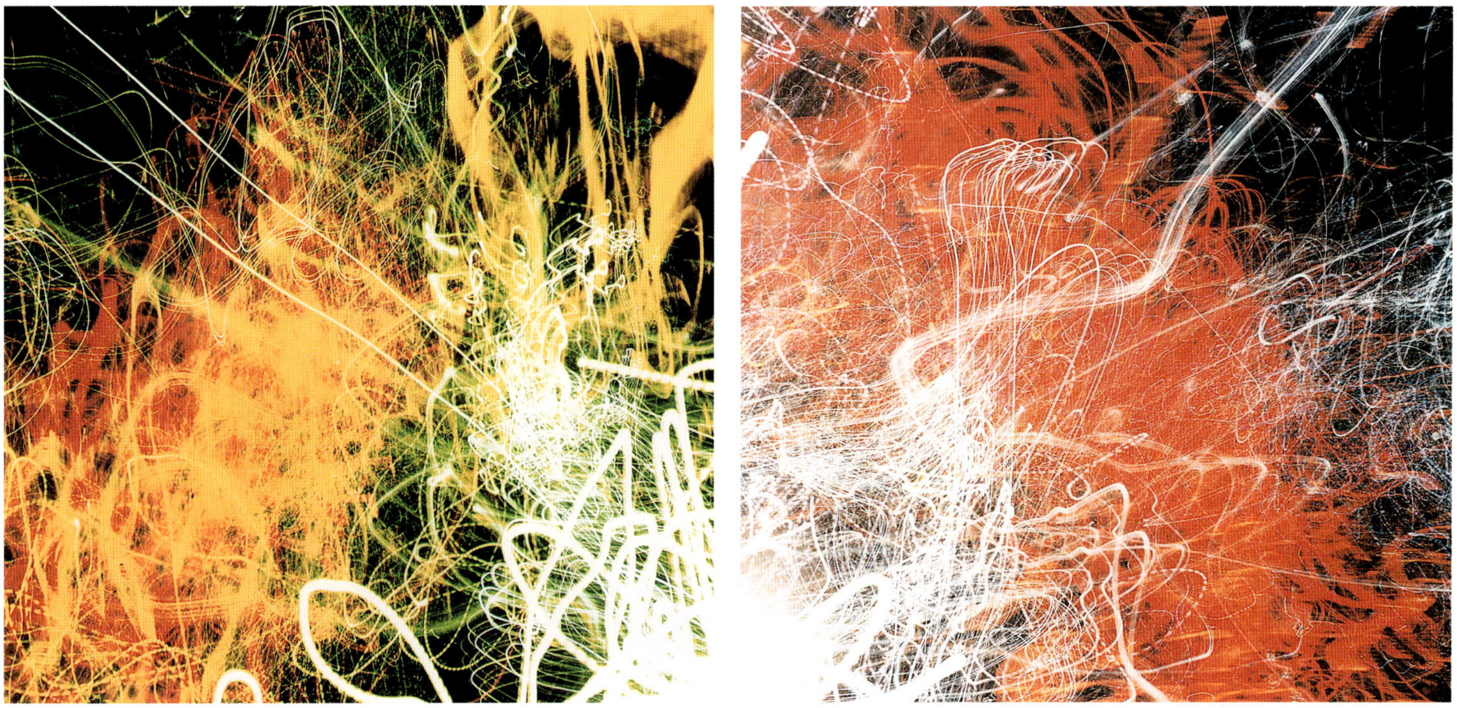

Untitled. 1999. Two chromogenic process prints from a series, 16 × 16 inches each

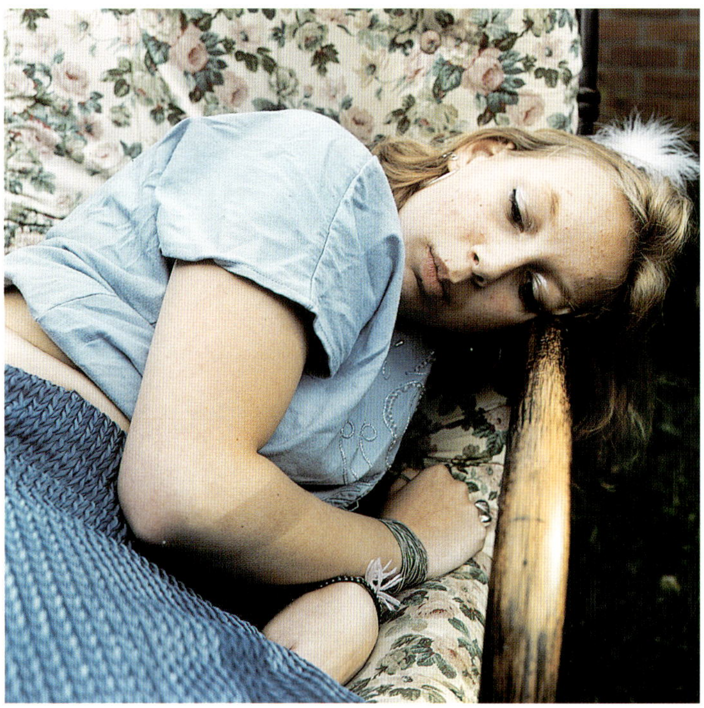

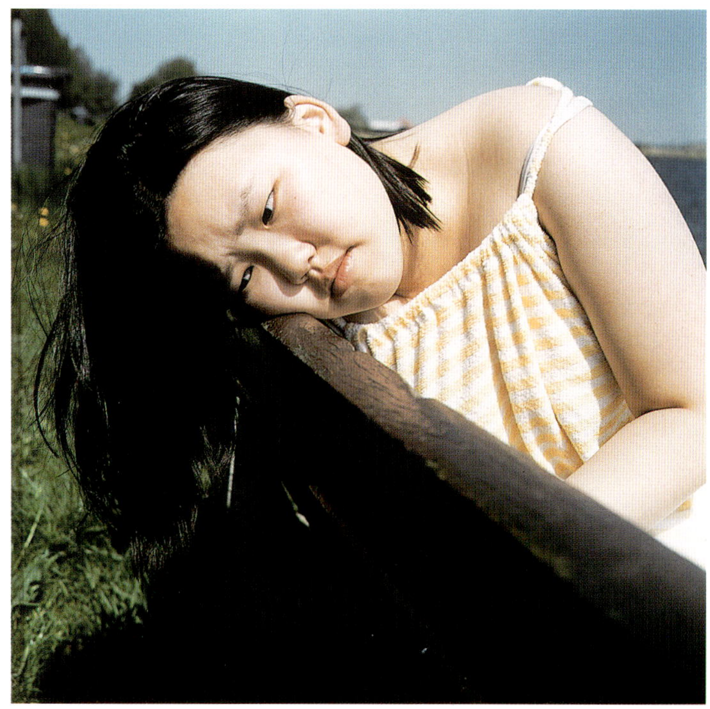

Mêlée de Guerriers nus de Etienne Delann (Scramble of Naked Warriors by Etienne Delann). 1998. Diptych: digital photographs, $18^{1}/_{2} \times 33^{1}/_{8}$ inches each

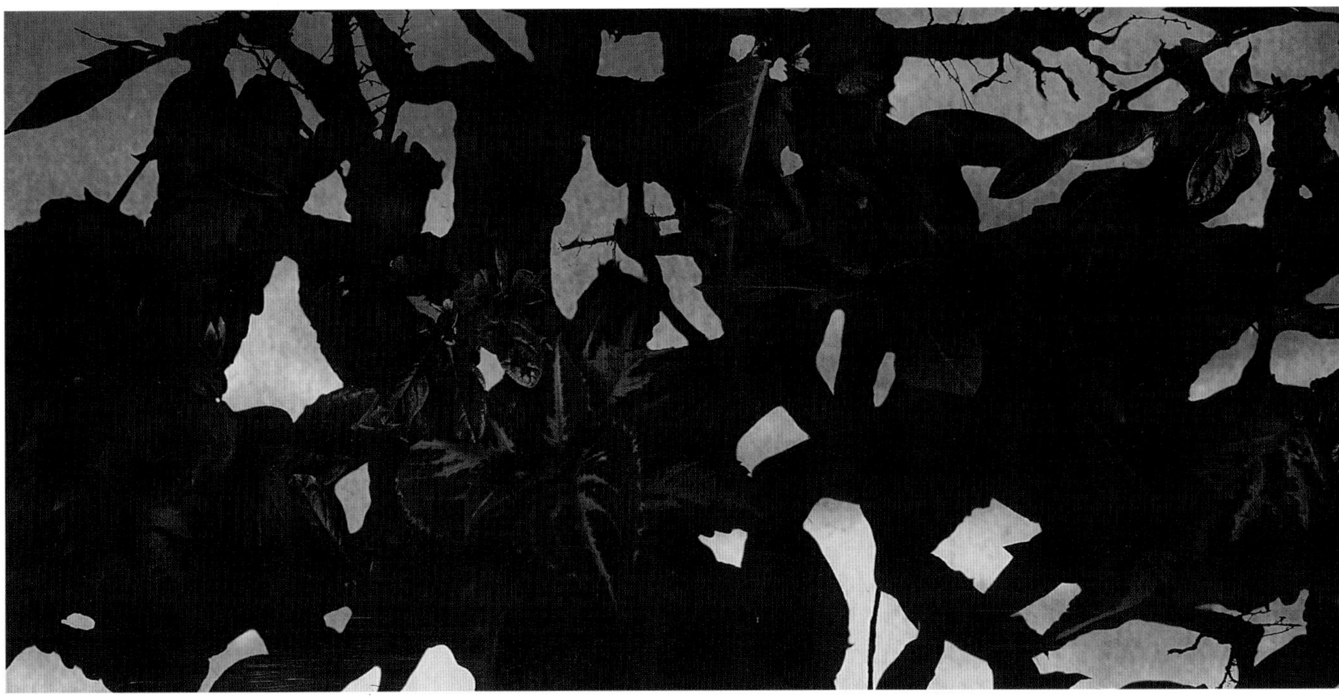

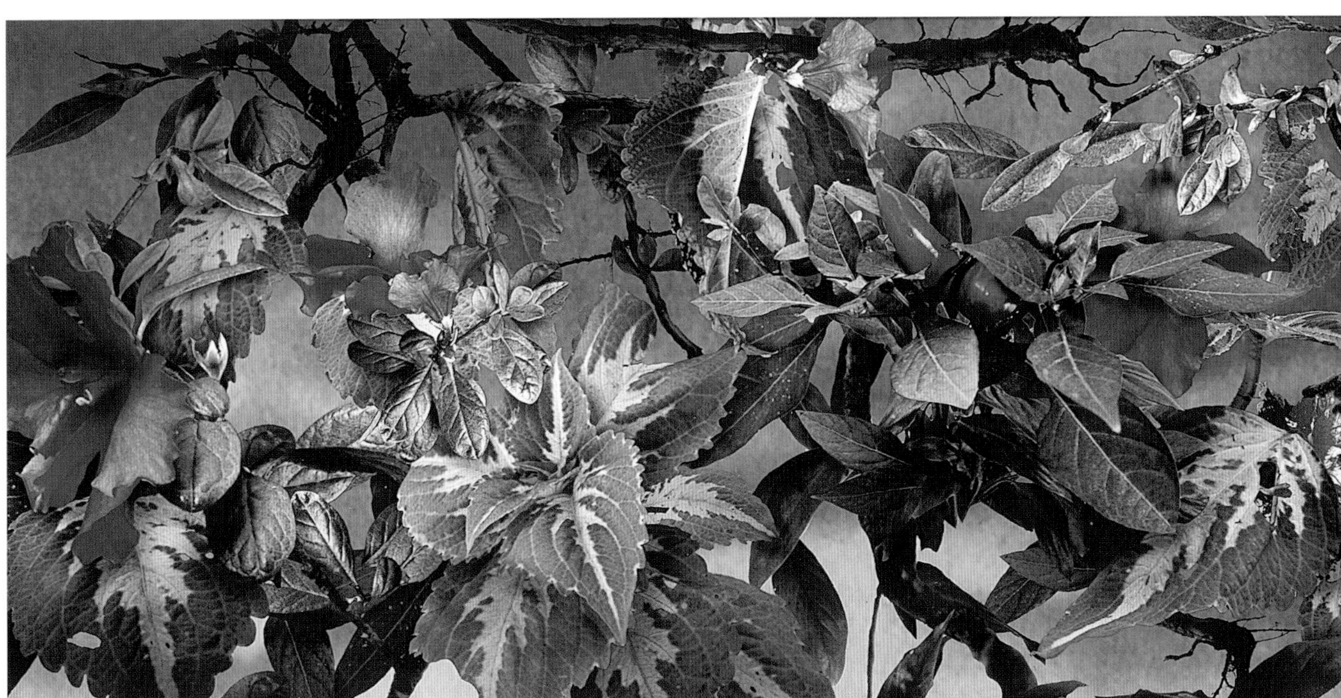

Sea #2. 1999. Chromogenic process print, face mounted to plexiglass, $59^1/_2 \times 72$ inches

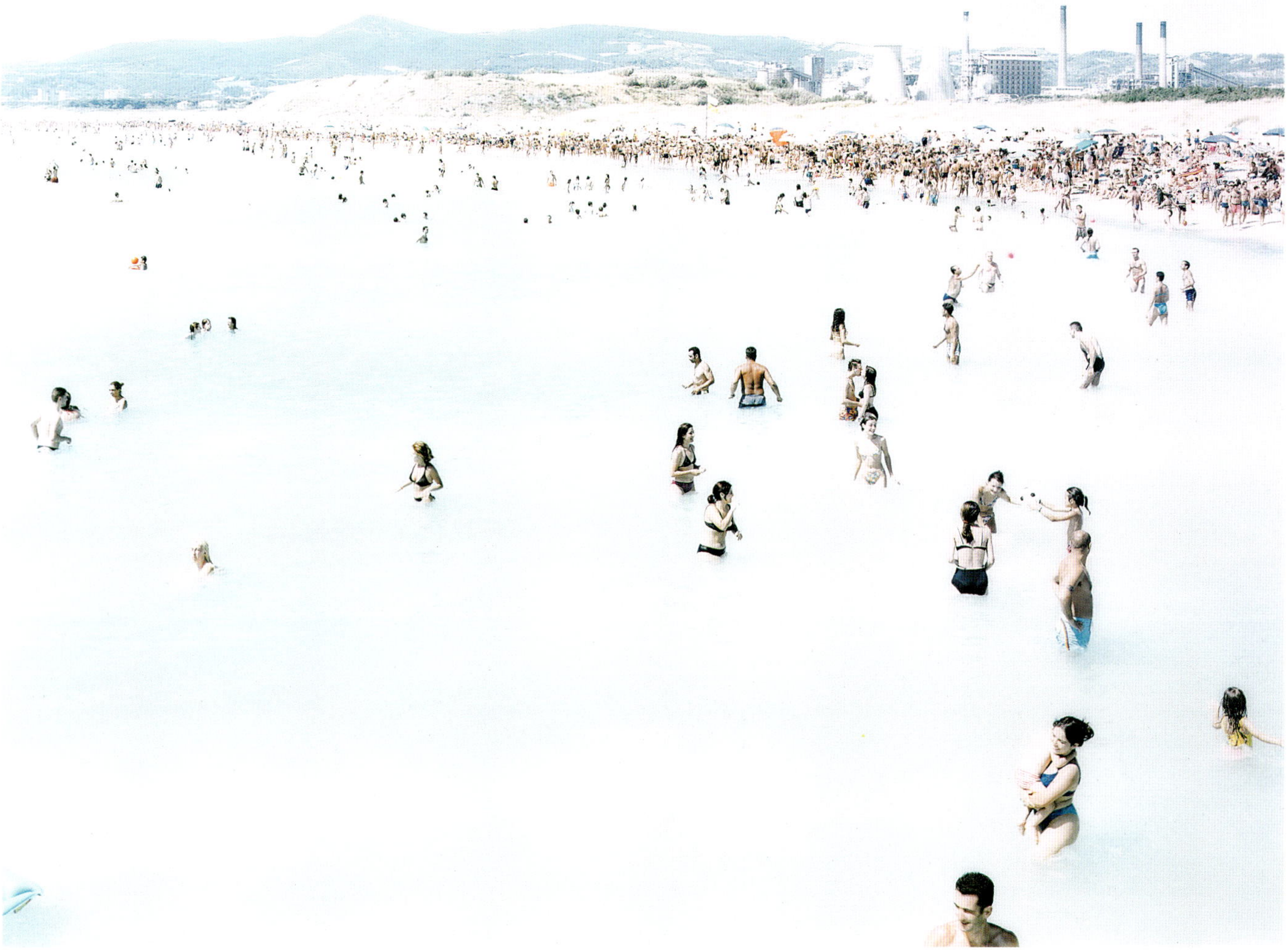

Coastal Motifs. 1989. Silver dye bleach process transparency in an aluminum lightbox, $53^1/_4 \times 64 \times 8^3/_4$ inches

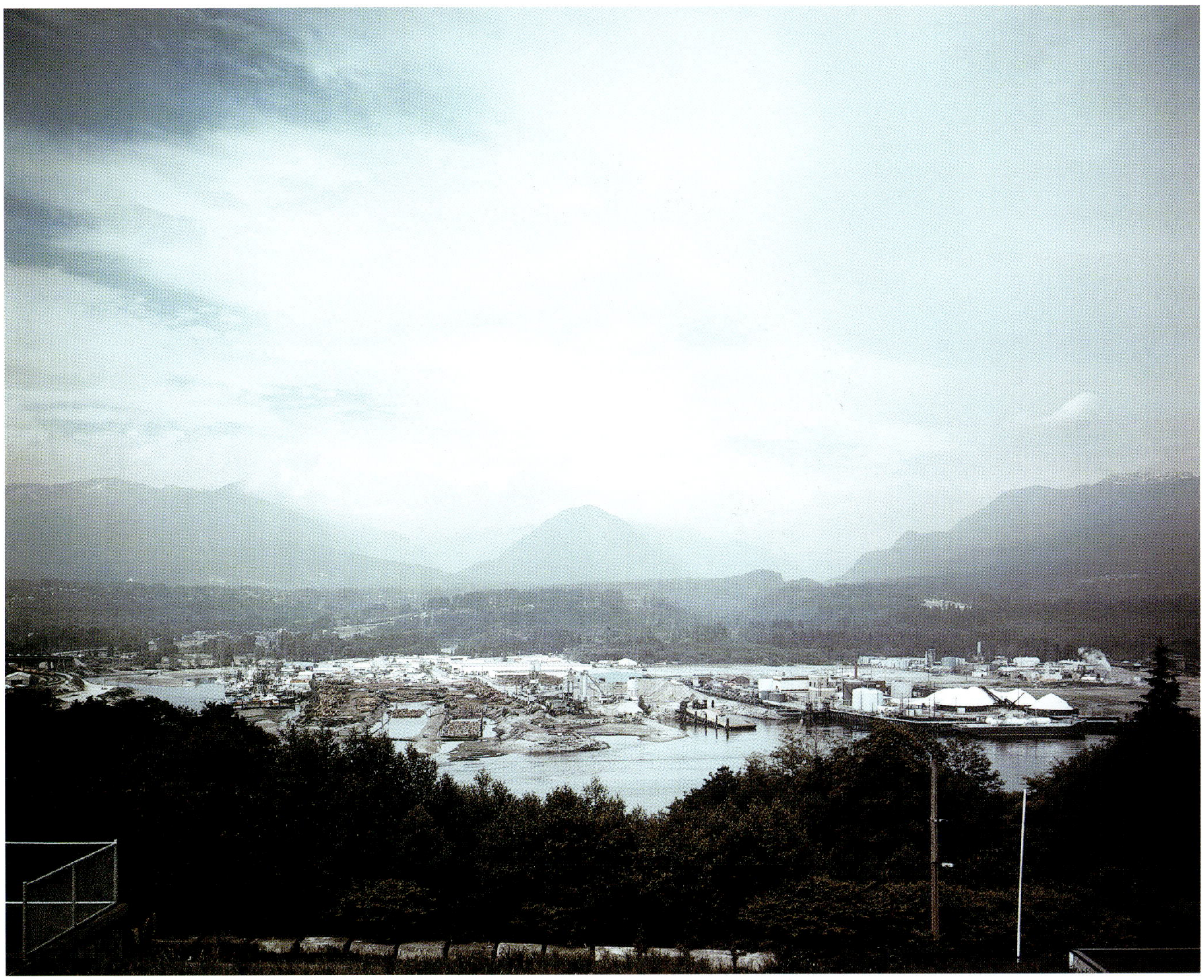

Untitled (Self-Portrait in Drag). 1981. SX 70 Polaroid photograph, $4\frac{1}{4} \times 3\frac{1}{2}$ inches

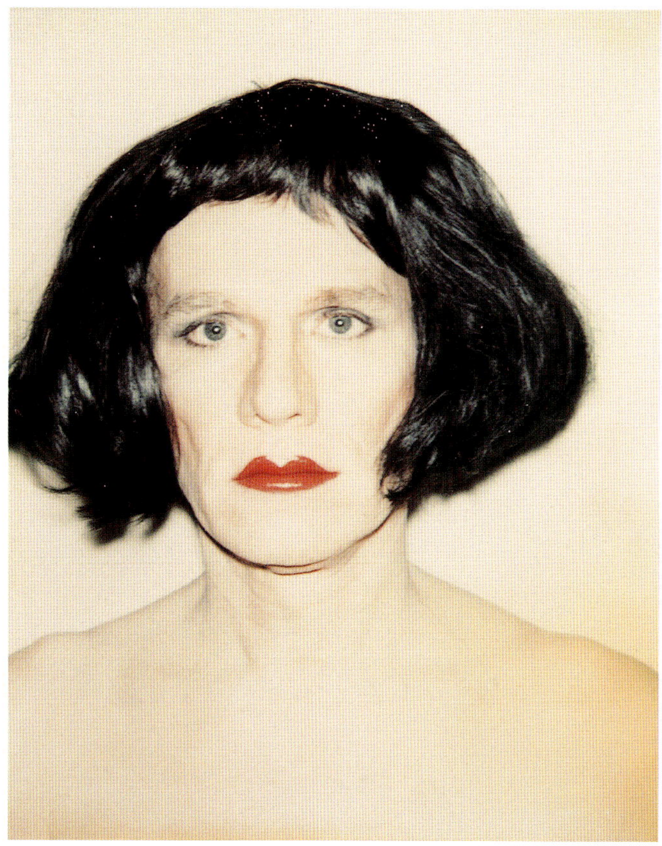

Signs that say what you want them to say not Signs that say what someone else wants you to say—I'm desperate. 1992–93. Chromogenic process print, 47 × 31½ inches

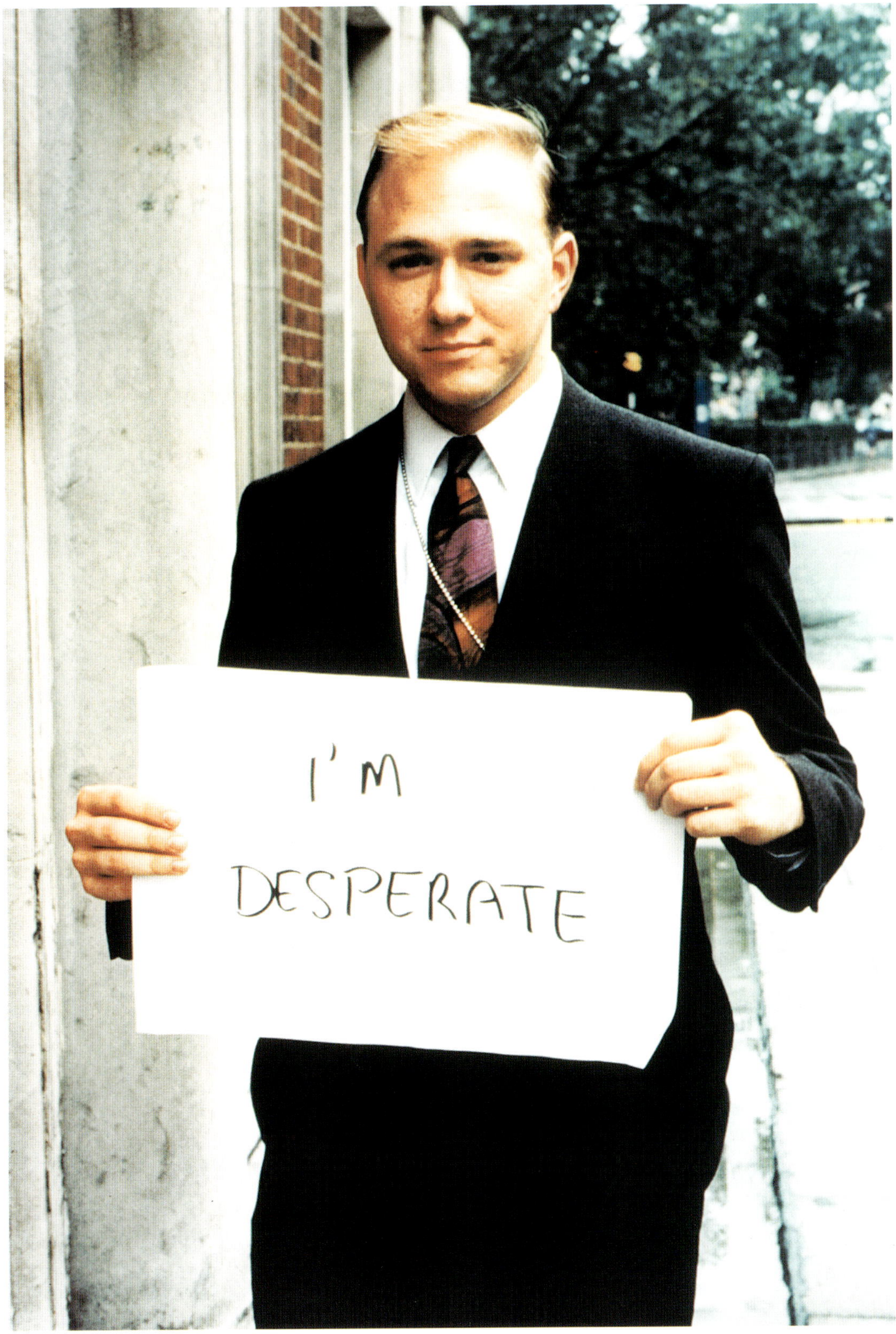

WILLIAM WEGMAN

Building a Box. 1972. Sequenced suite of nine gelatin silver prints in artists's frames, 11 × 11 inches each

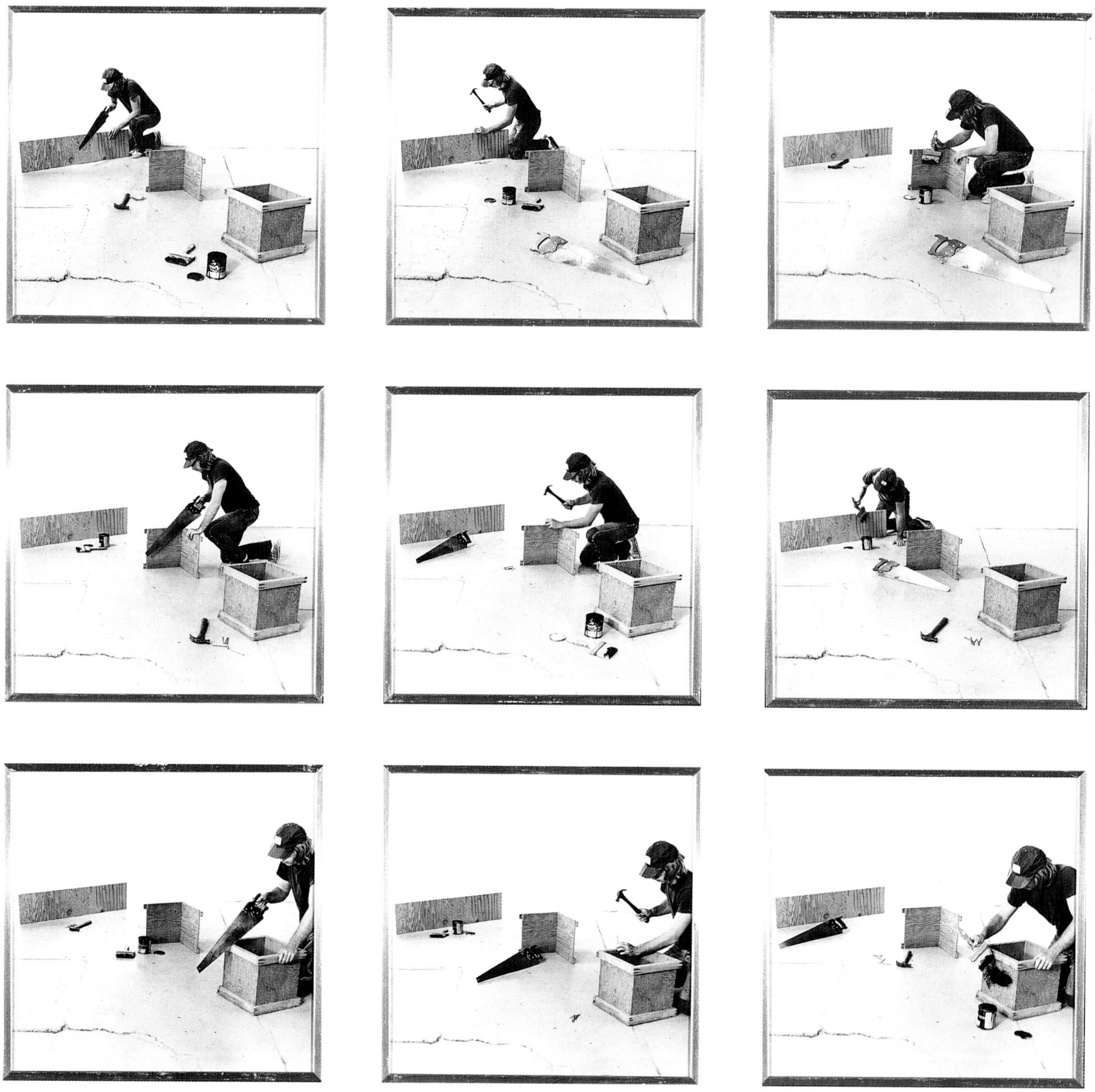

Sky. 1996. Iris print on rag paper, 33 × 26⅝ inches

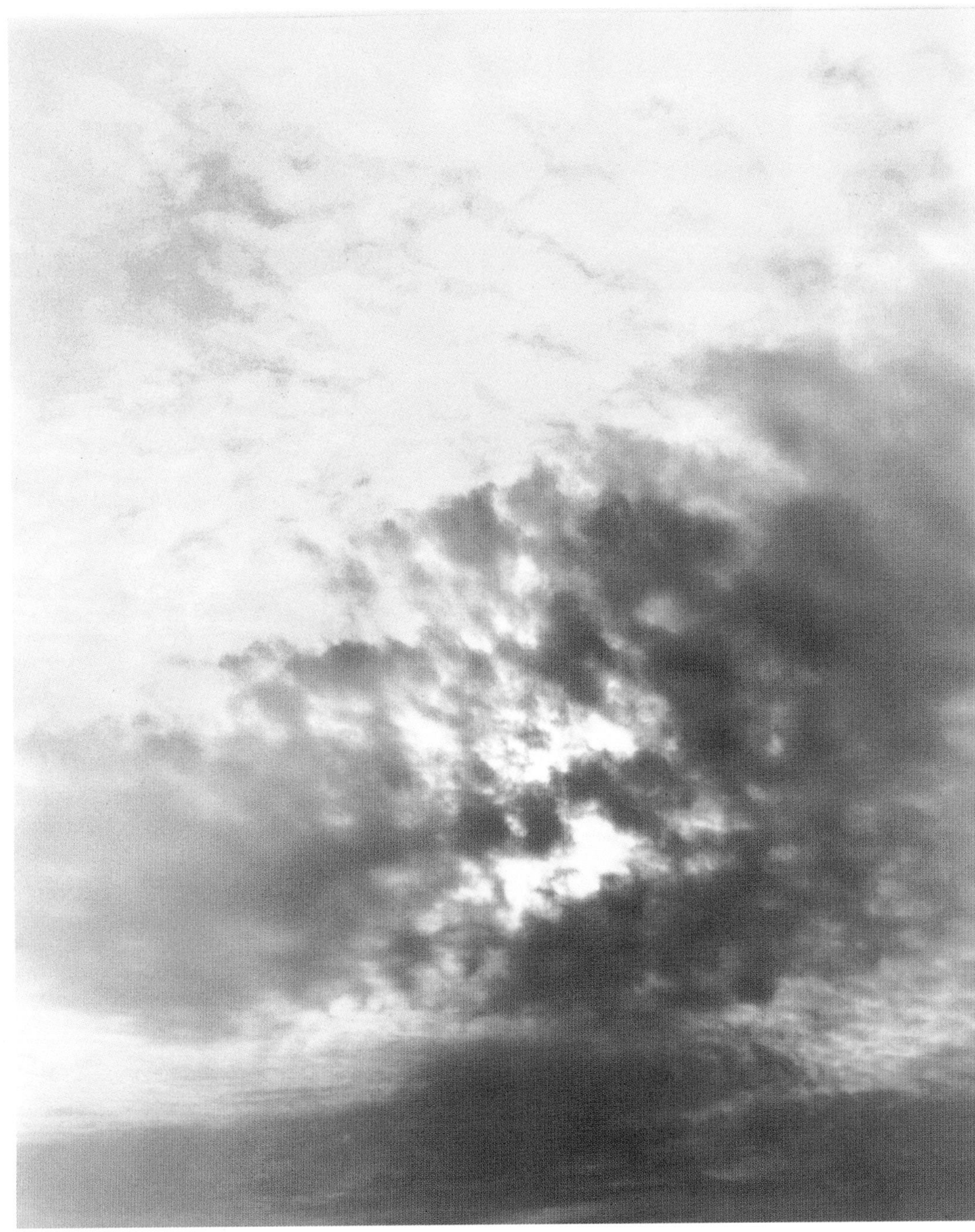

Constructions. 1993–98. Suite of six R-type chromogenic process prints, $6^{1}/_{8} \times 9^{1}/_{2}$ inches each

Clockwise from top left:

Constructions (Concrete Buttress, County Clare, 1996)

Constructions (Construction, Caprese Michelangelo, 1998)

Constructions (Construction, Peloponnese, 1993)

Constructions (Construction, Peloponnese, 1993)

Constructions (Brick Buttress, Arezzo, 1998)

Constructions (Quarry, Carrera, 1998)

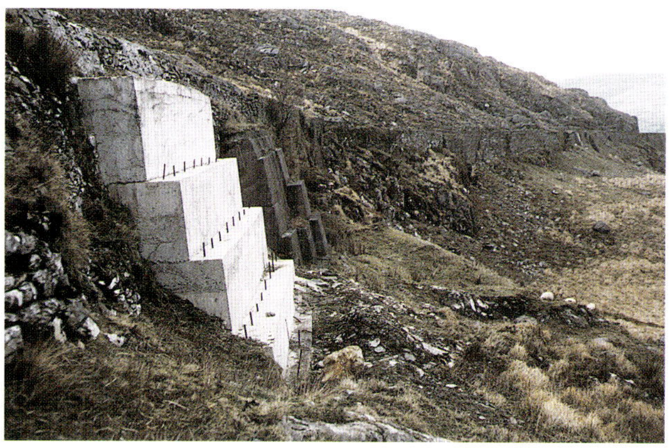

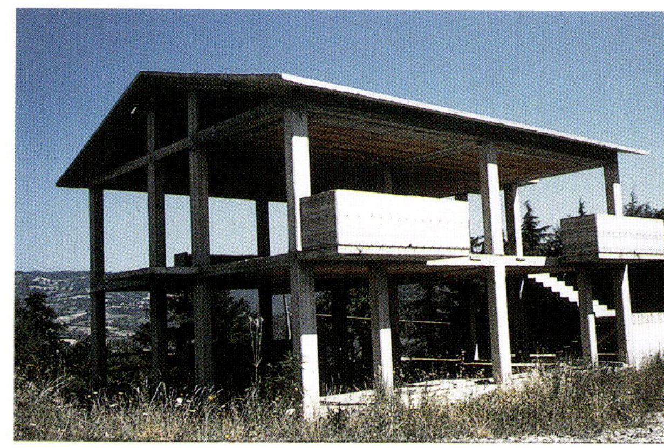

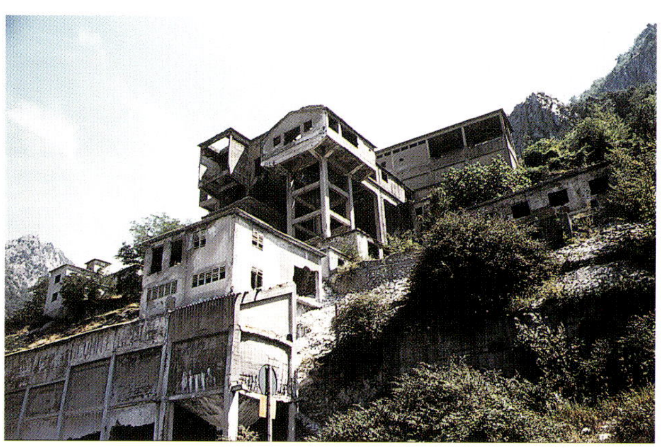

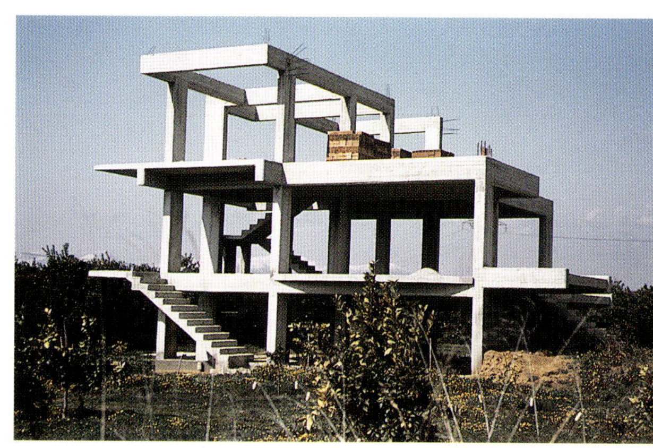

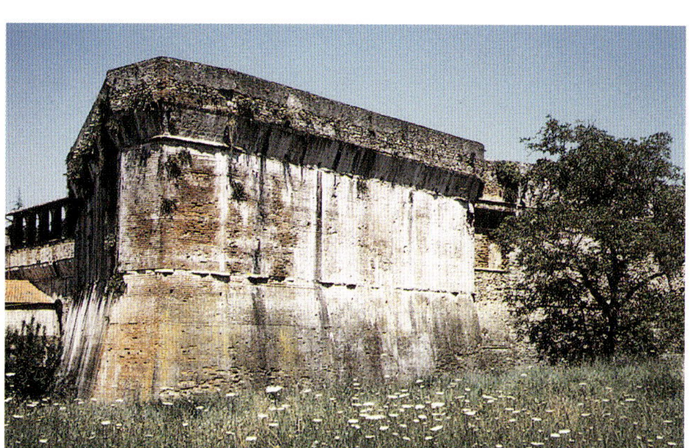

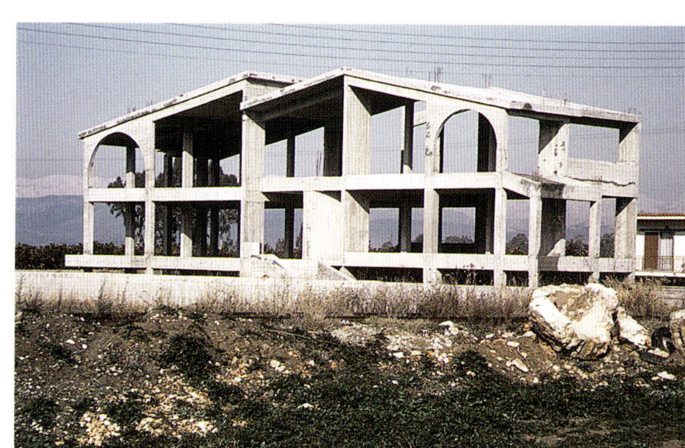

'Valentine' typewriter 1969 plastic (ABS) design Ettore Sottsass jun., Perry King; manufacture Ing. C. Olivetti & Co. SpA, Italy h. 11.5 cm inv. no. V 6.3-393; Nrs. 1–4. 1996. Suite of four silver dye bleach process prints, 26 × 30 inches each

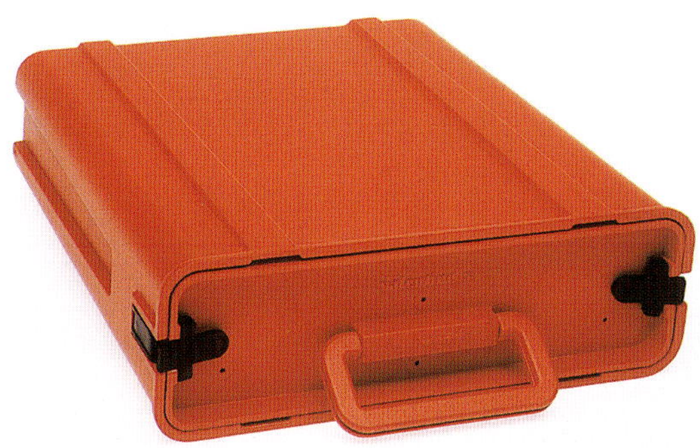

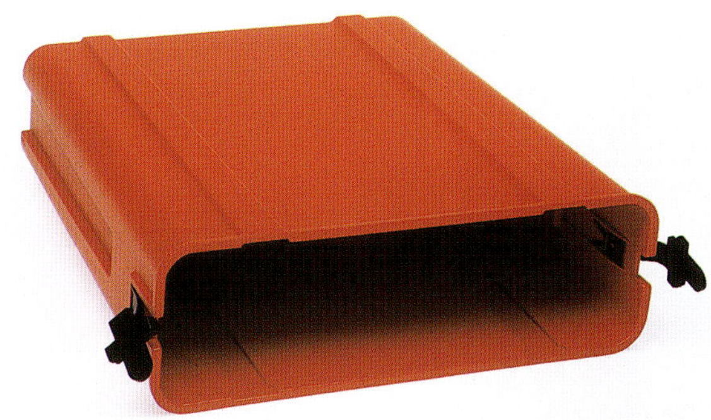

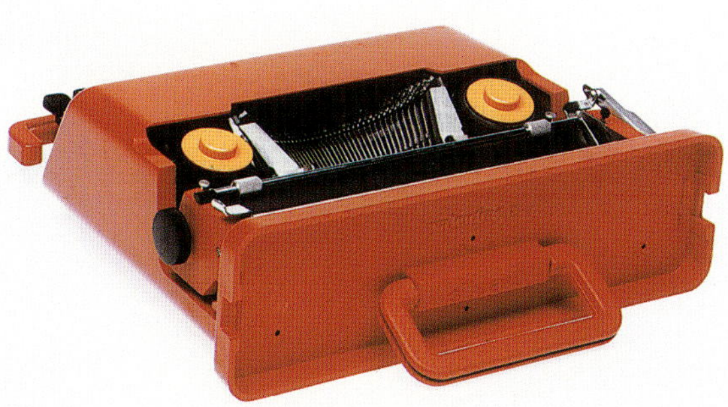

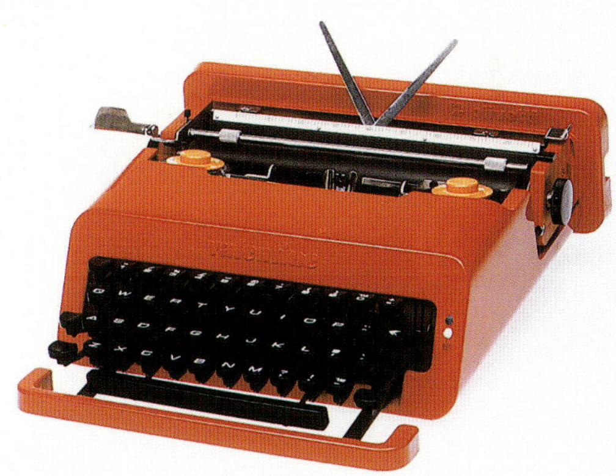

Untitled (Project with Gavin and Lucy) (details). 1992. Installation: twenty-four chromogenic process prints mounted to aluminum, each paired with framed text panel, dimensions varied

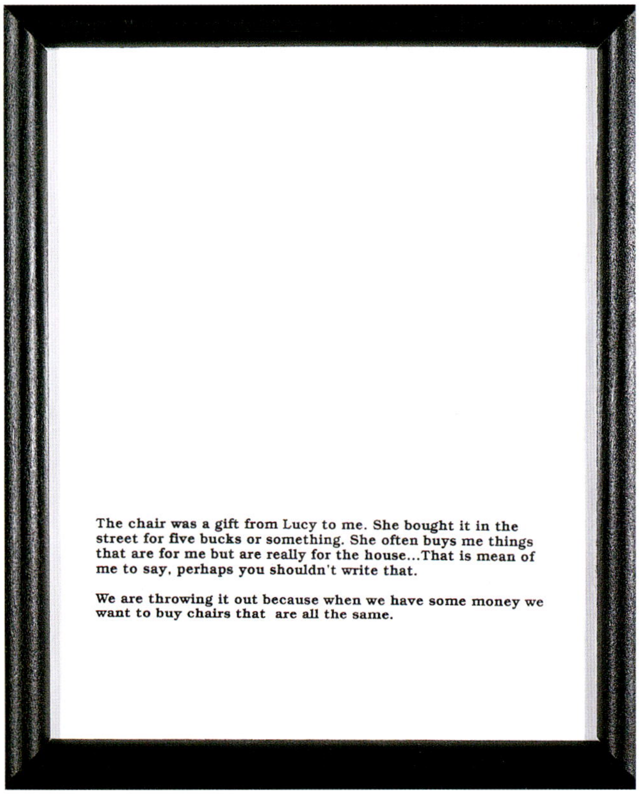

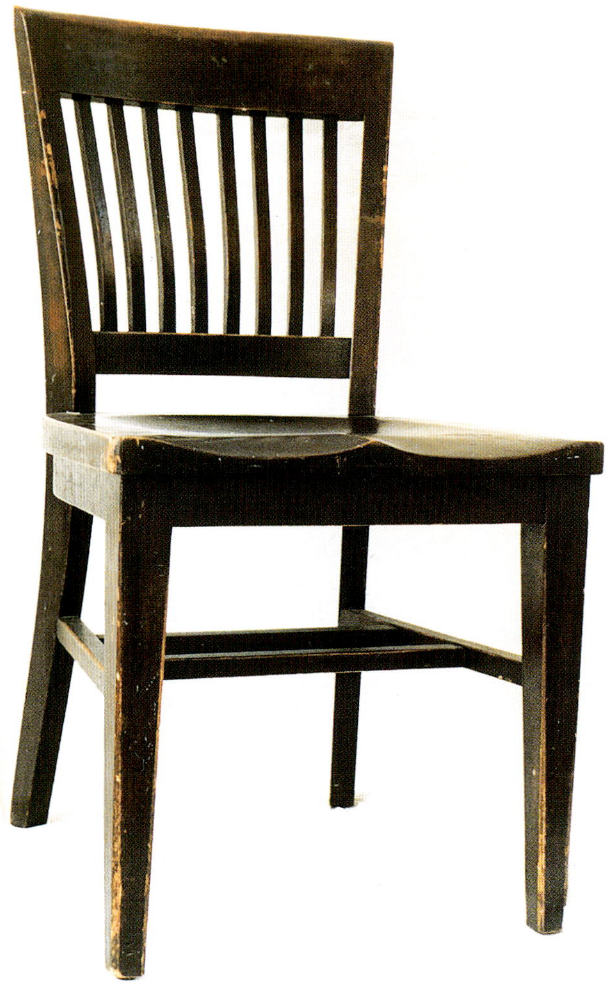

THE COLLECTION

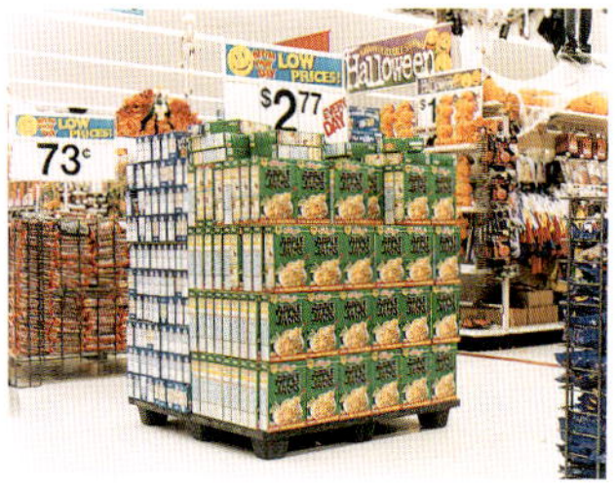

1

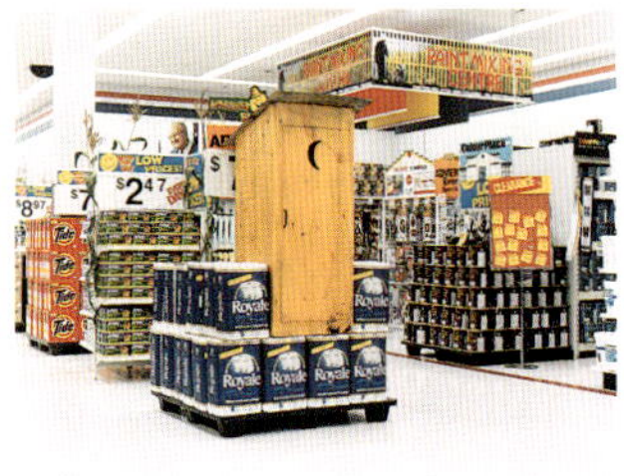

2

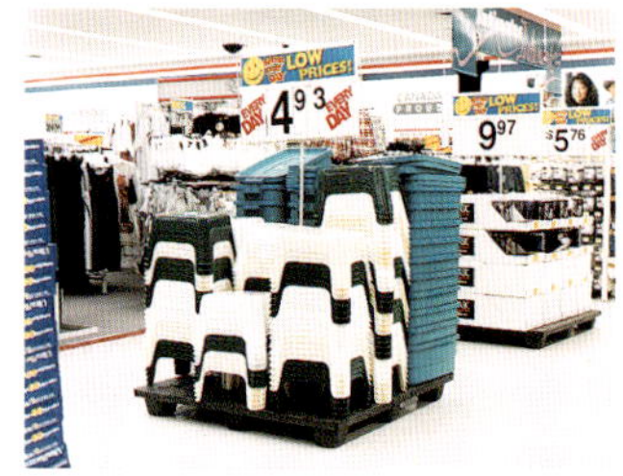

3

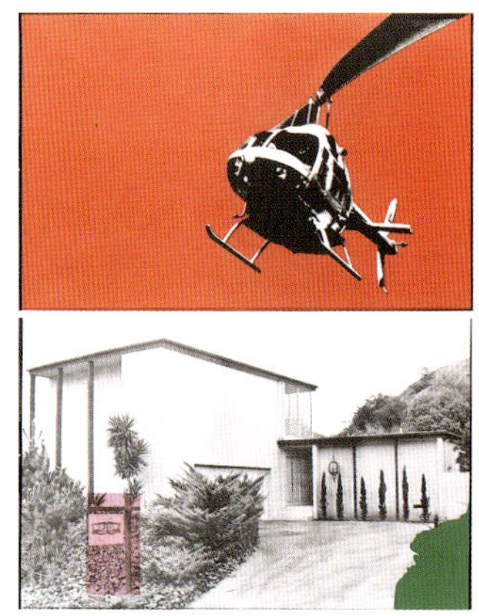

4

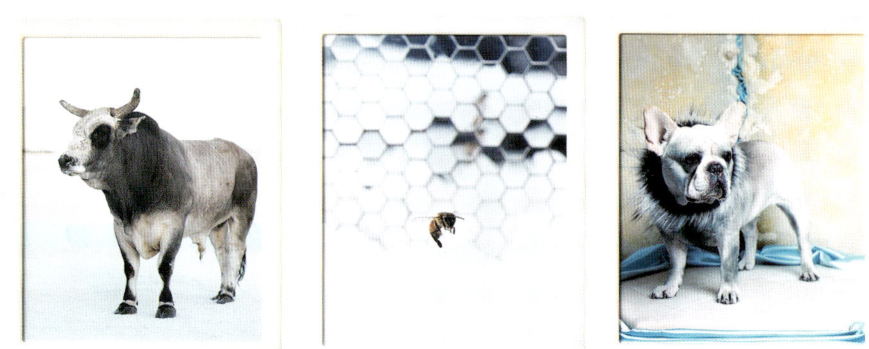

5

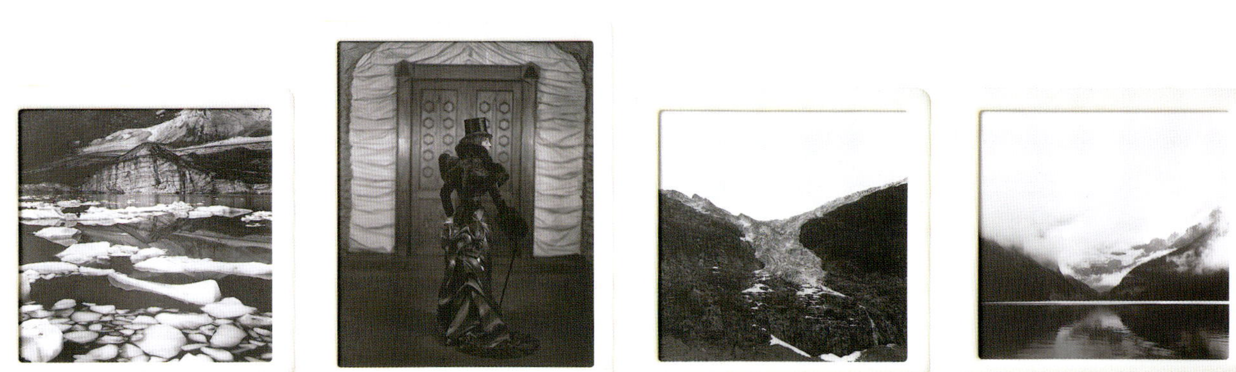

6

ROY ARDEN

1

Wal-Mart Store, Burnaby, B.C. (Applejacks). **1996. Chromogenic process print, $17 \times 21\frac{3}{4}$ inches**

2

Wal-Mart Store, Burnaby, B.C. (Royale). **1996. Chromogenic process print, $17 \times 21\frac{3}{4}$ inches**

3

Wal-Mart Store, Burnaby, B.C. (Plastic Chairs). **1996. Chromogenic process print, $17 \times 21\frac{3}{4}$ inches**

JOHN BALDESSARI

4

Helicopter Over Tract House (With Red Sky). **1990. Stacked diptych: gelatin silver prints, oil tint, and vinyl paint, $96\frac{3}{4} \times 72\frac{1}{4}$ inches**

MATTHEW BARNEY

5

CREMASTER 2: Drone Ensemble. **1999. Three chromogenic process prints in acrylic frames, 42×34 inches each**

6

CREMASTER 2: The Queen's Exposition. **1999. Four gelatin silver prints in acrylic frames, dimensions varied**

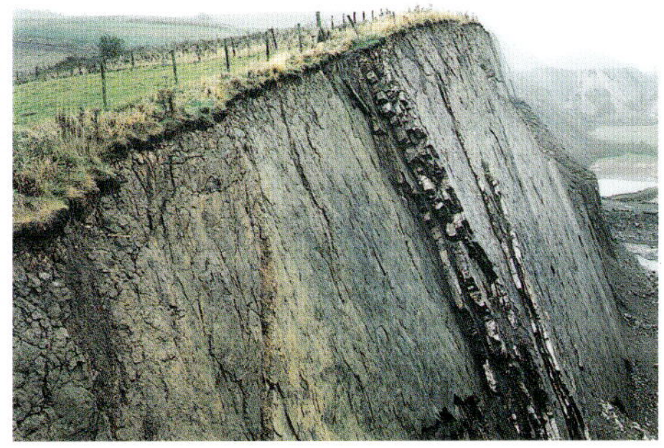

7

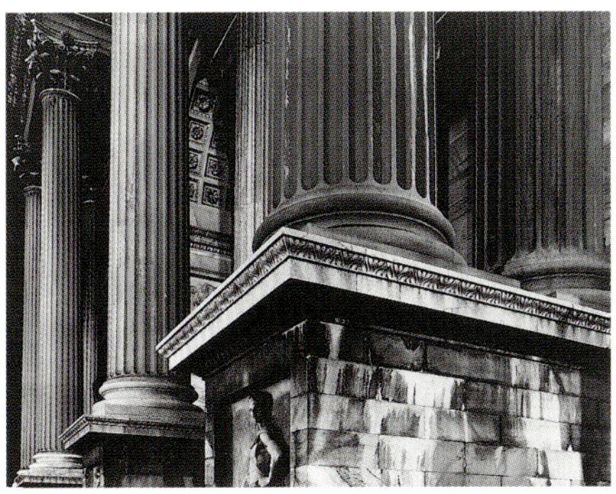

8

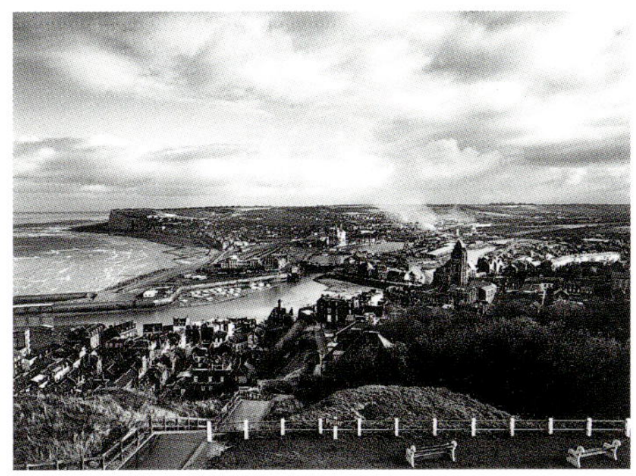

9

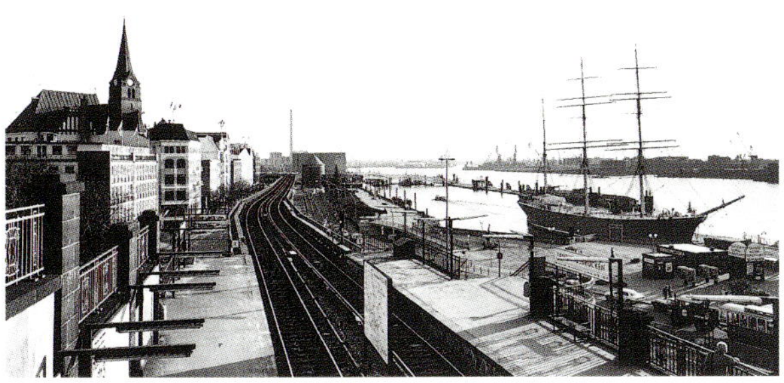

10

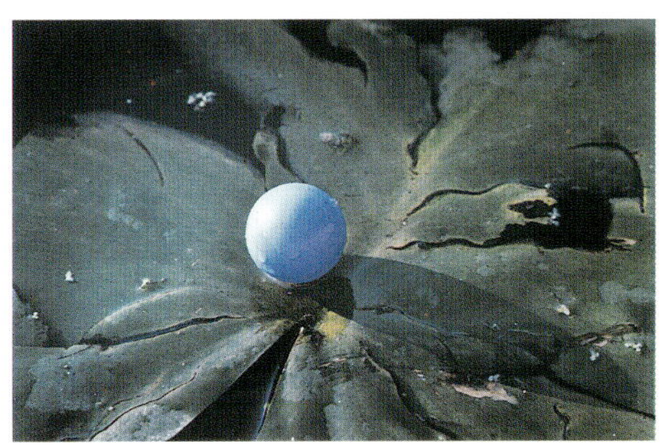

11

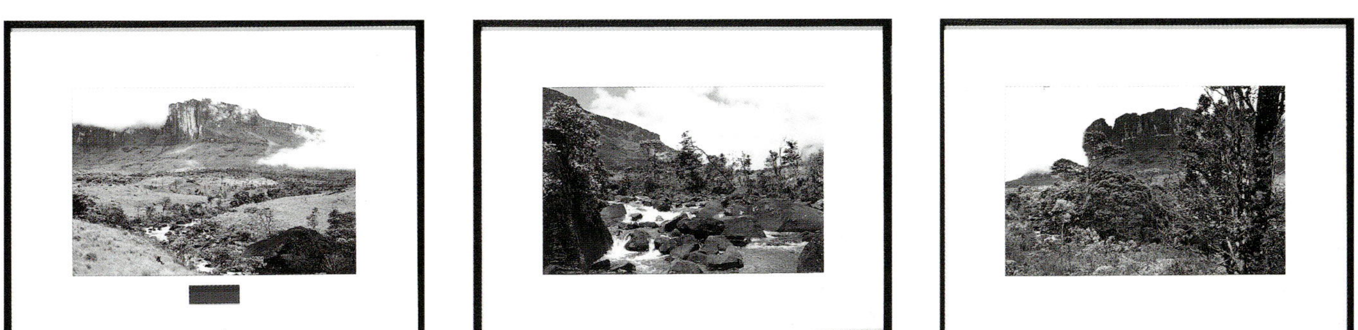

12

JOSEPH BARTSCHERER

7

Canal 4. 1997/98. Chromogenic process print, face mounted to plexiglass, 60 × 85 inches

GABRIELE BASILICO

8

Milano. 1989. Gelatin silver print, 18 × 26 inches

9

Le Tréport. 1985. Gelatin silver print, 18 × 26 inches

10

Hamburg. 1988. Gelatin silver print, $11\frac{1}{2}$ × 23 inches

LOTHAR BAUMGARTEN

11

Pupille (Pupil). 1968. Chromogenic process print, $26\frac{1}{4}$ × $33\frac{1}{4}$ inches

12

Salto Kukenan (Kukenan Falls). 1977–85. Triptych: gelatin silver prints with gouache on mat, $26\frac{1}{4}$ × $33\frac{1}{4}$ inches each

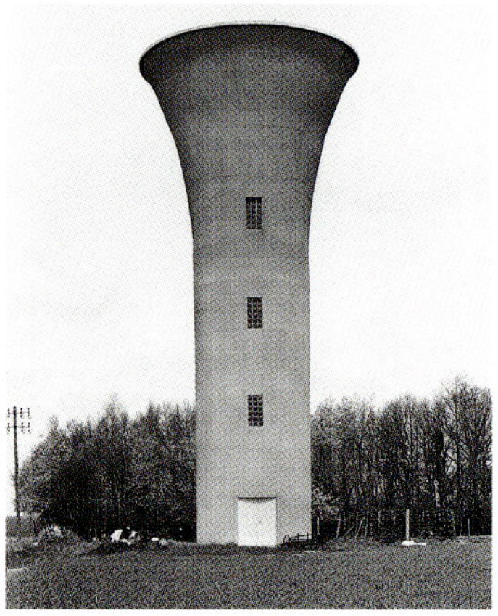

13

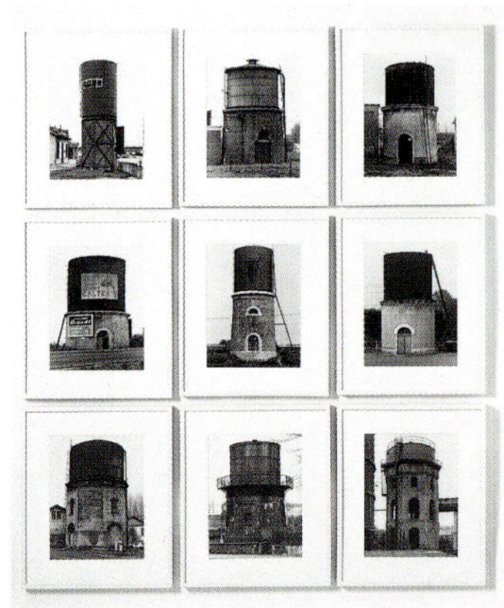

14

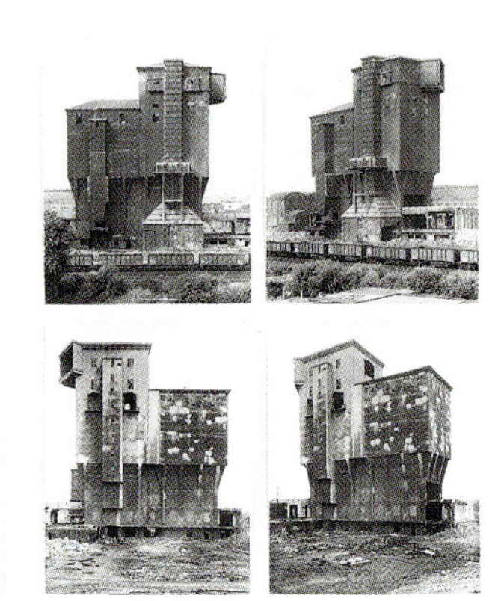

15

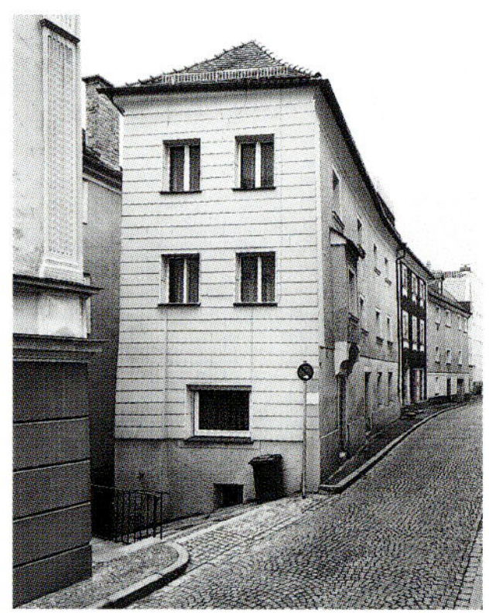

16

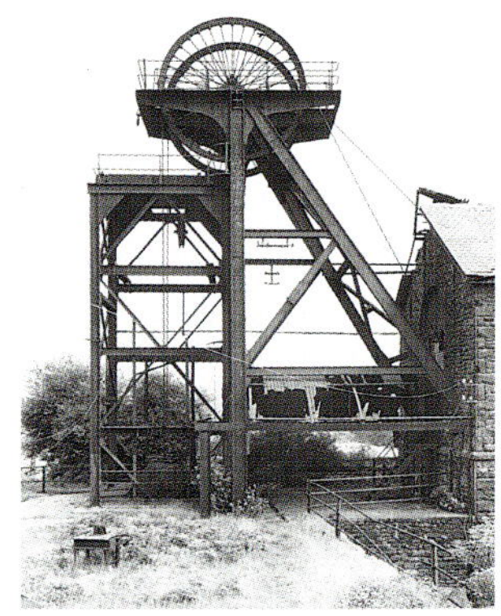

17

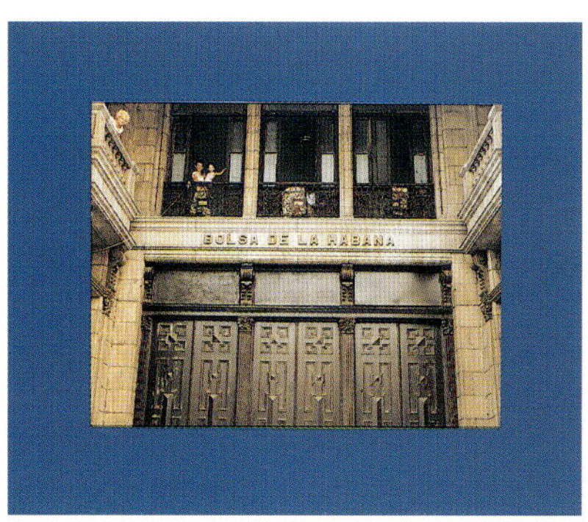

18

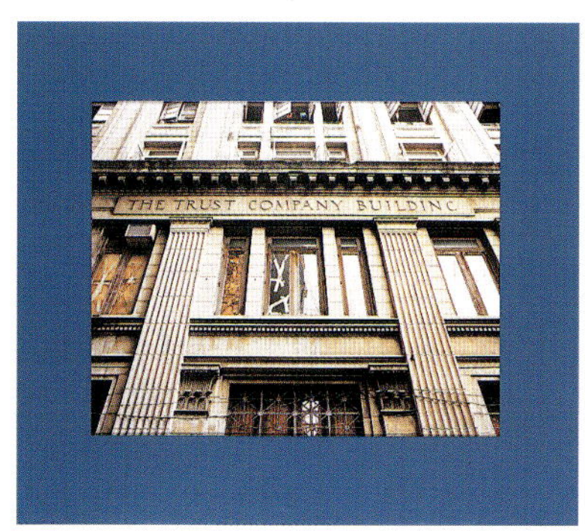

19

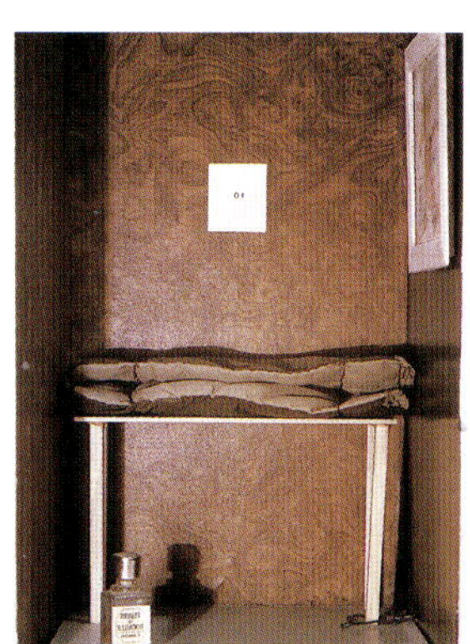

20

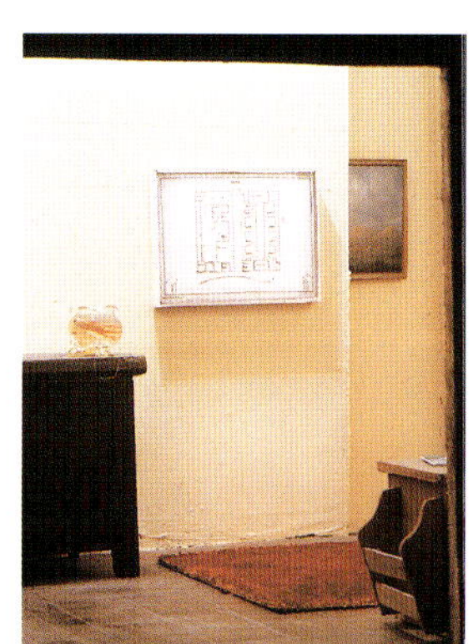

21

BERND AND HILLA BECHER

13
Maisoncelles, Seine-Marne, France. 1972–92. Gelatin silver print, $23\frac{1}{2} \times 19$ inches

14
Watertowers—G. 1988. Installation: nine gelatin silver prints, 69×59 inches

15
Coal Silos. 1971. Four gelatin silver prints, $44 \times 33\frac{3}{8}$ inches

16
Passau, Bavaria, Germany. 1988. Gelatin silver print, $23\frac{1}{8} \times 18\frac{1}{4}$ inches

17
Winding Towers (detail). 1983. Installation: nine gelatin silver prints, $61\frac{1}{2} \times 49\frac{1}{2}$ inches

MAX BECHER AND ANDREA ROBBINS

18
Wall Street in Cuba: The Stock Exchange (La Bolsa). 1993. Chromogenic process print, $28 \times 32\frac{3}{8}$ inches

19
Wall Street in Cuba: Trust Company Building. 1993. Chromogenic process print, $28\frac{3}{4} \times 32\frac{3}{8}$ inches

JULIE BECKER

20
1 of 12 Profiles. 1996–97. Silver dye bleach process print, mounted to aluminum, $39\frac{5}{8} \times 27\frac{3}{8}$ inches

21
Optional Entrance. 1996–97. Silver dye bleach process print, mounted on aluminum, $29\frac{5}{8} \times 27\frac{3}{8}$ inches

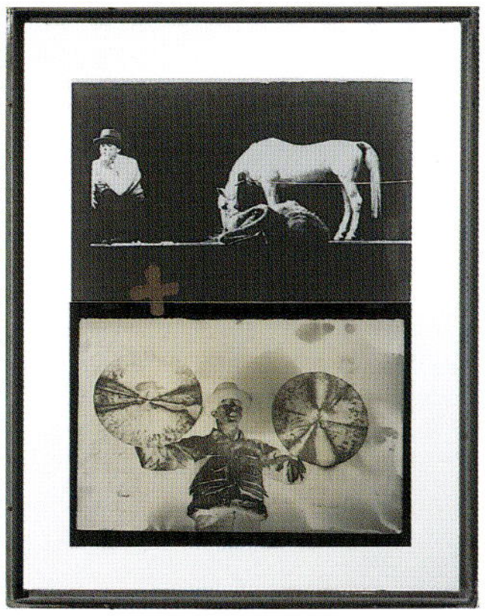
22

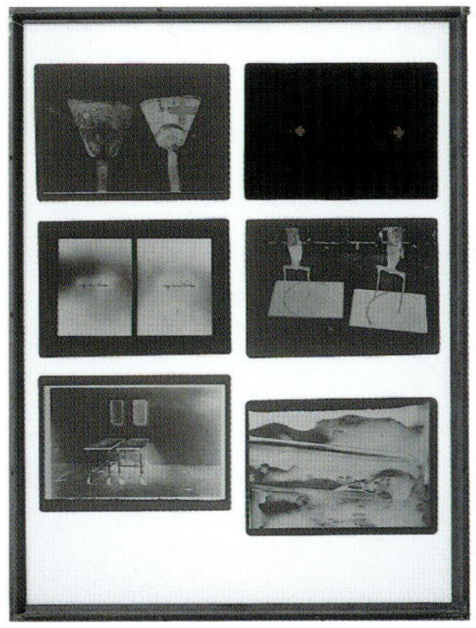
23

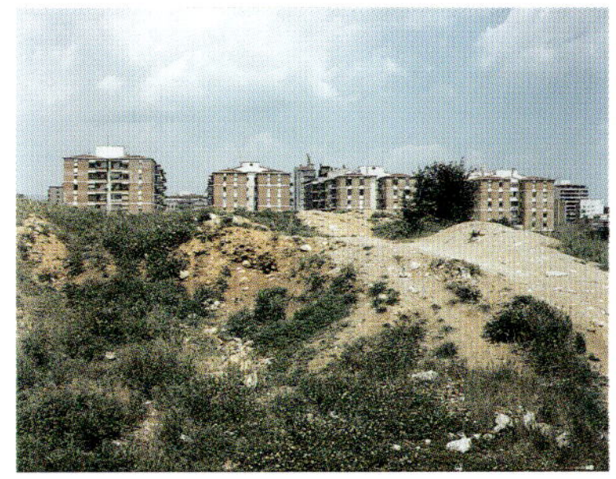
24

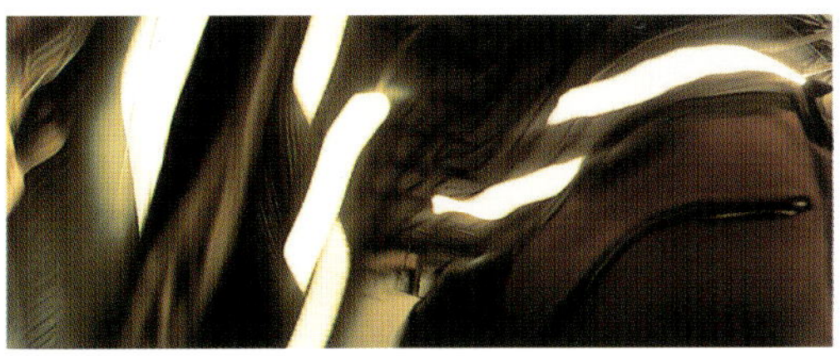
25

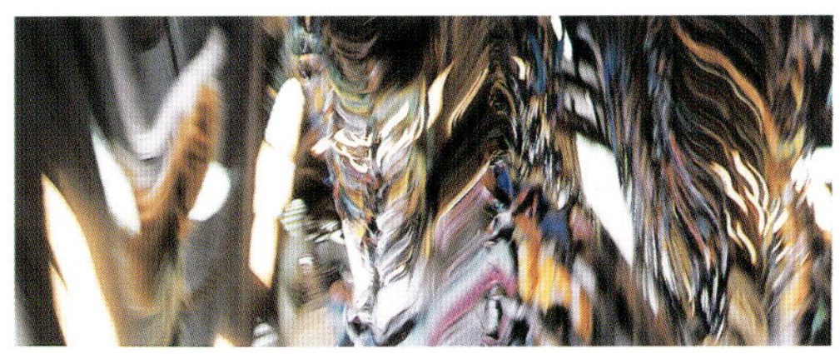
26

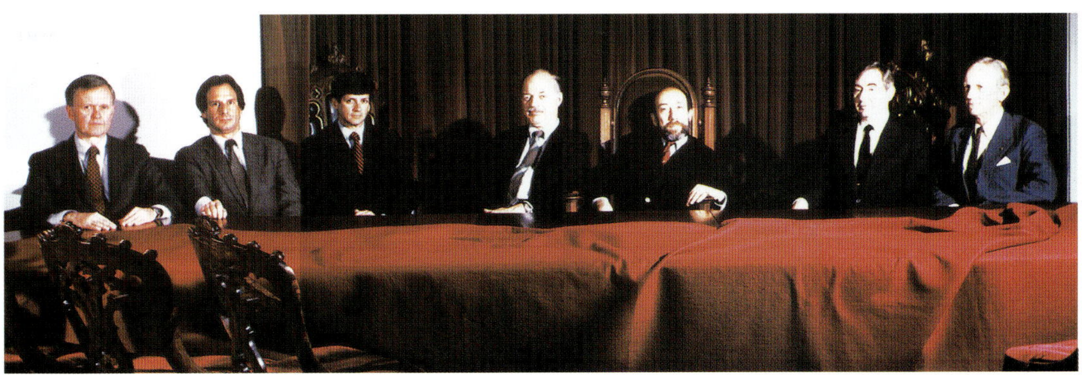
27

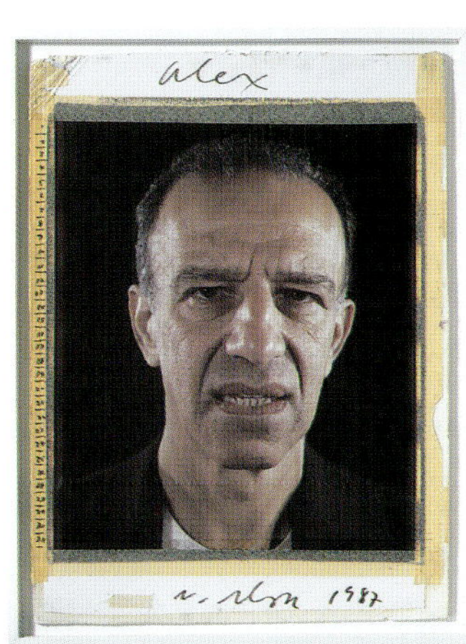

28

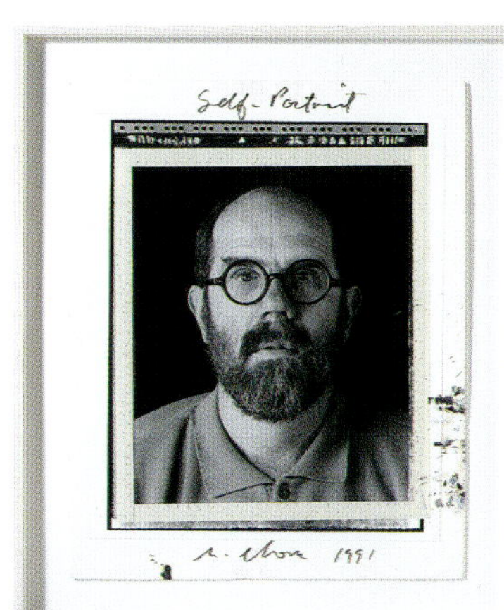

29

JOSEPH BEUYS

22

Iphigenia/Titus Andronicus. 1985. Photopositives and negatives on film, stamped with brown oil paint between glass plates in artist's steel frame with felt, $28\frac{3}{8} \times 21\frac{7}{8}$ inches

23

Zeige Deine Wunde (Show Your Wounds). 1977. Photographic negatives and paint between glass plates in artist's steel frame with felt, $42 \times 31 \times 2$ inches

JEAN-MARC BUSTAMANTE

24

Tableau No. 32. 1980. Chromogenic process print, $43\frac{7}{8} \times 54\frac{3}{8}$ inches

JOHN CHAMBERLAIN

25

Studio Lite IV. 1989. Chromogenic process print, 20×24 inches

26

Untitled. 1997. Chromogenic process print, 20×24 inches

MICHAEL CLEGG AND MARTIN GUTTMANN

27

The Board of Regents. n.d. Installation: four silver dye bleach process prints, face mounted to plexiglass, $56\frac{5}{8}$ inches $\times$ 14 feet 1 inch

CHUCK CLOSE

28

Maquette for "Alex." 1987. Marker, ink, oil paint, and masking tape on Polaroid photograph, on foamcore, $33\frac{1}{2} \times 23\frac{3}{4}$ inches

29

Self-Portrait. 1991. Oil paint, ink, and masking tape on Polaroid photograph, on foamcore, $28 \times 22\frac{3}{8}$ inches

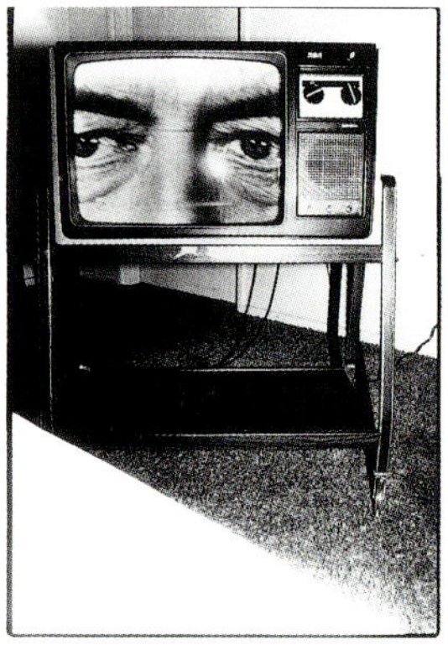
30

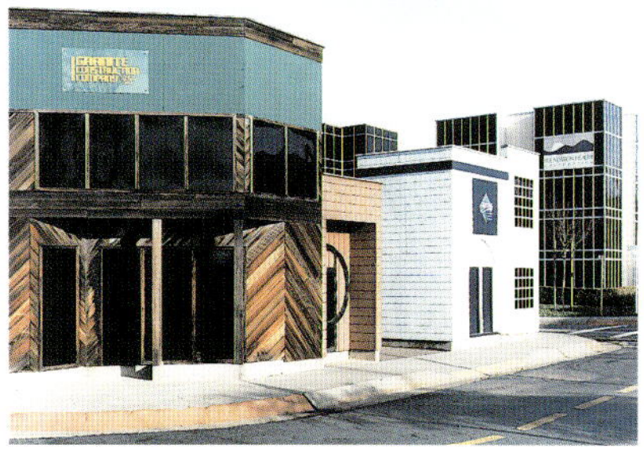
31

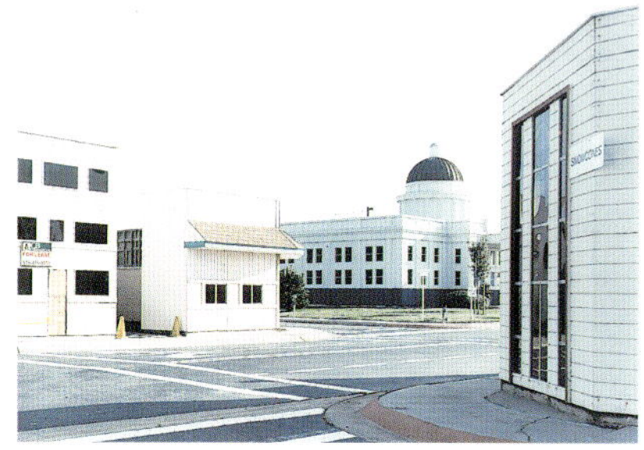
32

33

34

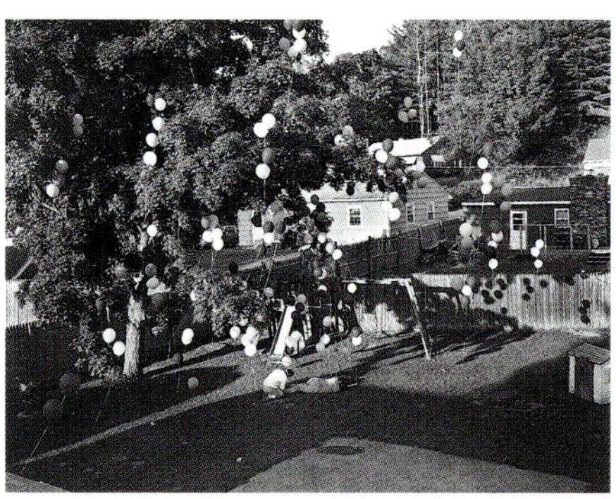
35

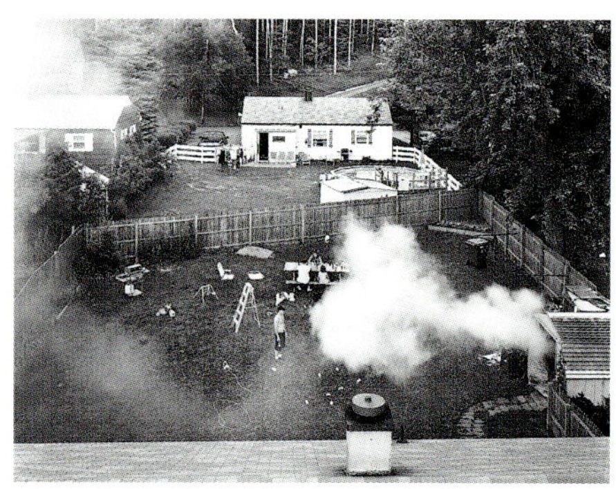
36

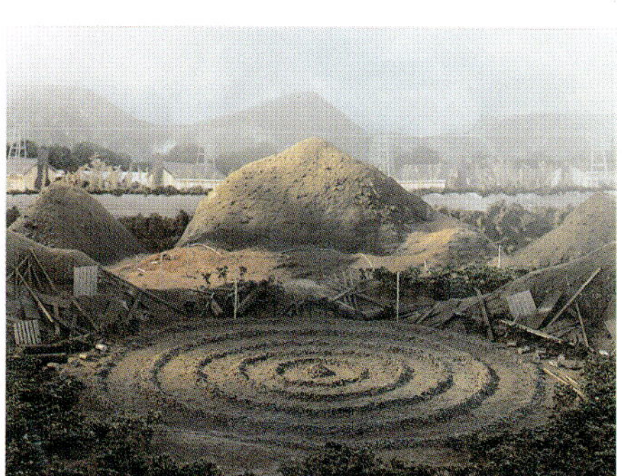
37

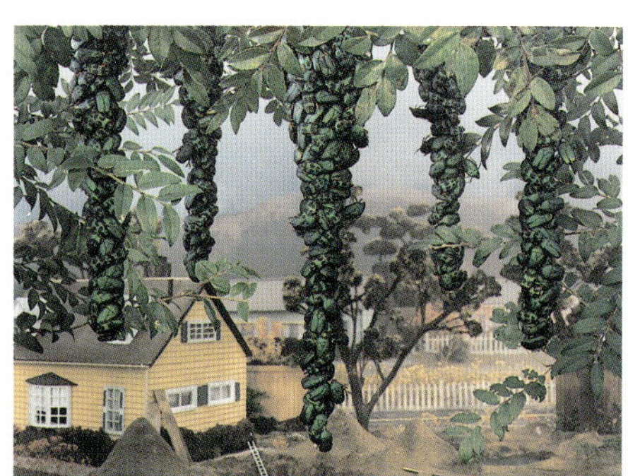
38

BRUCE CONNER

30
The Late Night Movie on TV: June 10, 1978 @ 1:20 to 1:27 am: Sterns Motel in Venice, CA, 1978. 1986. Gelatin silver print $41\frac{1}{2} \times 29$ inches

MILES COOLIDGE

31
Commercial Buildings, Highrise. From the *Safetyville* series. 1994–95. Chromogenic process print, face mounted to plexiglass, $31 \times 39\frac{1}{2}$ inches

32
Unoccupied Storefronts, Denny's Capitol. From the *Safetyville* series. 1994. Chromogenic process print, face mounted to plexiglass, $31 \times 39\frac{1}{2}$ inches

33
Near Hanford 1. From the *Central Valley* series. 1998. Chromogenic process print mounted to galvanized steel coil, $10\frac{1}{4} \times 11$ feet $2\frac{3}{4}$ inches

34
Near Shafter. From the *Central Valley* series. 1998. Chromogenic process print mounted to galvanized steel coil, $10\frac{1}{4}$ inches $\times$ 11 feet 2 inches

GREGORY CREWDSON

35
Untitled. From the *Hover* series. 1996. Gelatin silver print, 28×32 inches

36
Untitled. From the *Hover* series. 1996. Gelatin silver print, 28×32 inches

37
Untitled. From the *Natural Wonder* series. 1993. Chromogenic process print, $27\frac{1}{4} \times 35\frac{1}{2}$ inches

38
Untitled. From the *Natural Wonder* series. 1994. Chromogenic process print, $27\frac{1}{4} \times 35\frac{1}{2}$ inches

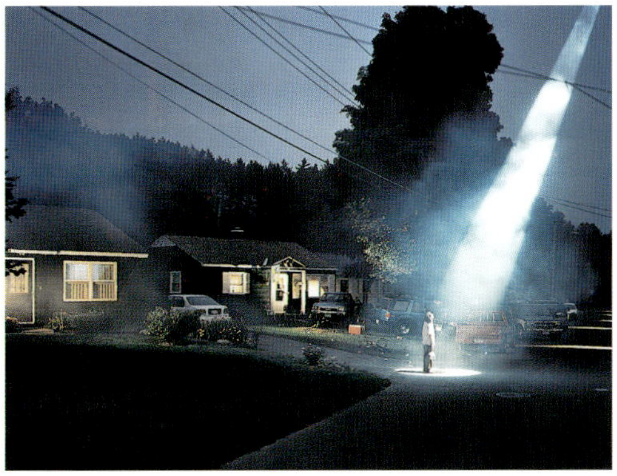

39

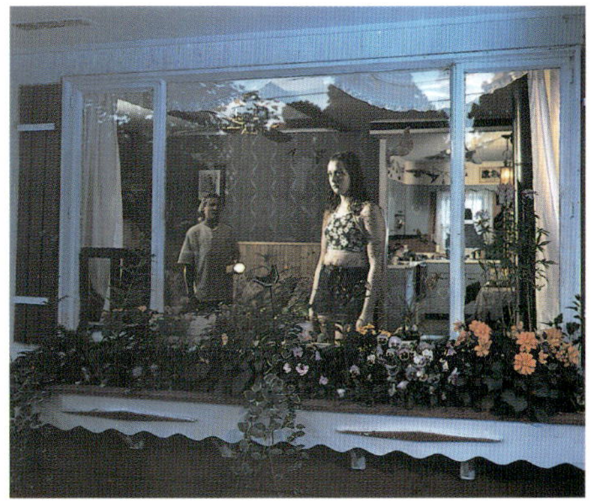

40

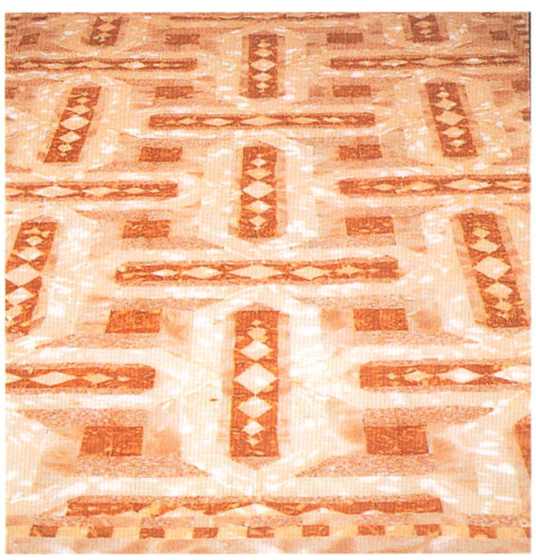

41

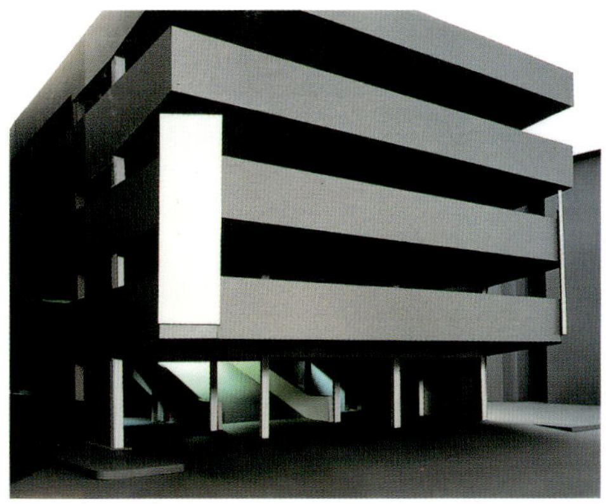

42

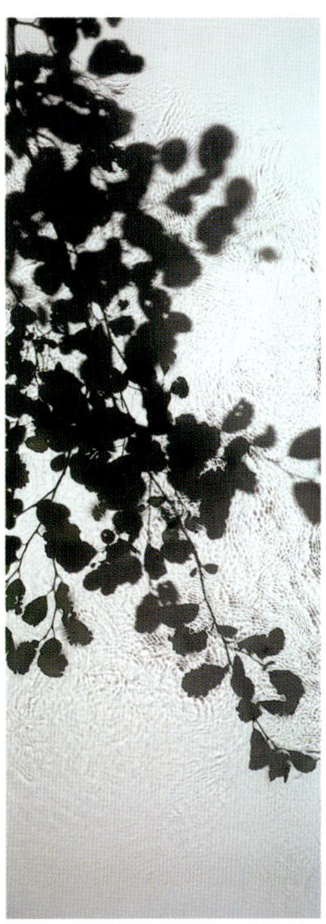

43

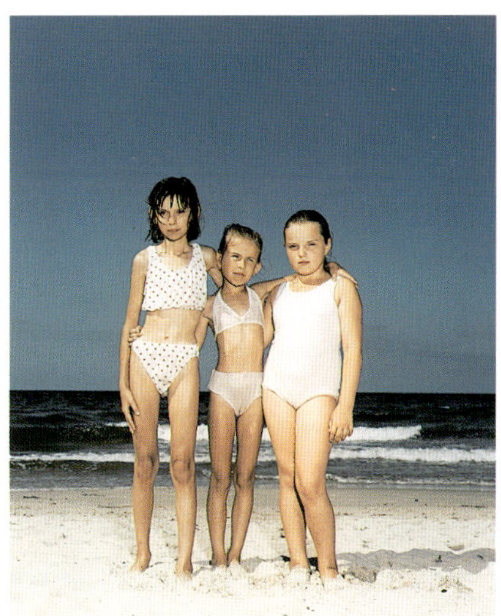

44

39

Untitled. From the *Twilight* series. 1998. Chromogenic process print, 53 × 65 inches

40

Untitled. From the *Twilight* series. 1999. Laser direct chromogenic process print, $53\frac{1}{2} \times 65\frac{1}{2}$ inches

WIM DELVOYE

41

Marble Floor #38. 1999. Silver dye bleach process print, mounted between plexiglass, $52 \times 49\frac{3}{8}$ inches

THOMAS DEMAND

42

Parking Garage. 1996. Chromogenic process print, face mounted to plexiglass, $53\frac{1}{8} \times 64\frac{1}{2}$ inches

SUSAN DERGES

43

The River Taw, 10 June 1997. From the *River Taw* series. 1998. Unique dye destruction photogram, $69\frac{5}{8} \times 27\frac{1}{8}$ inches

RINEKE DIJKSTRA

44

Kolobzeg, Poland, July 23, 1992. 1992. Chromogenic process print, 14 × 11 inches

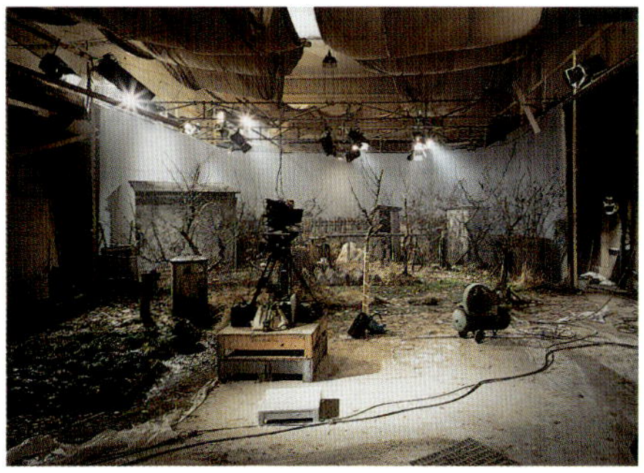

45

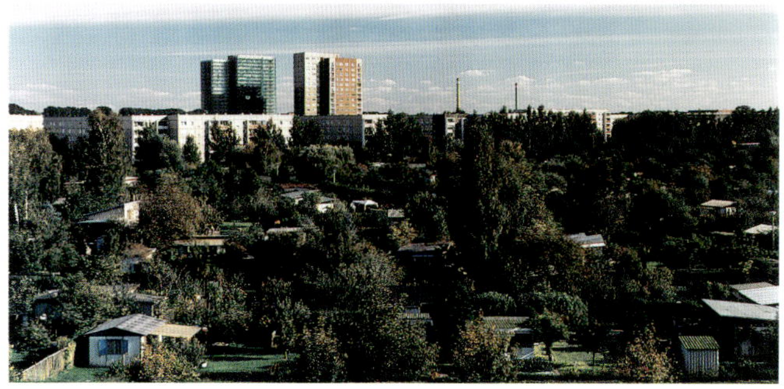

46

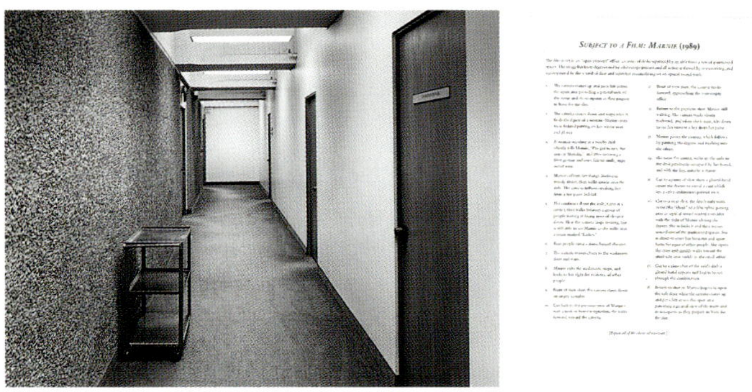

47

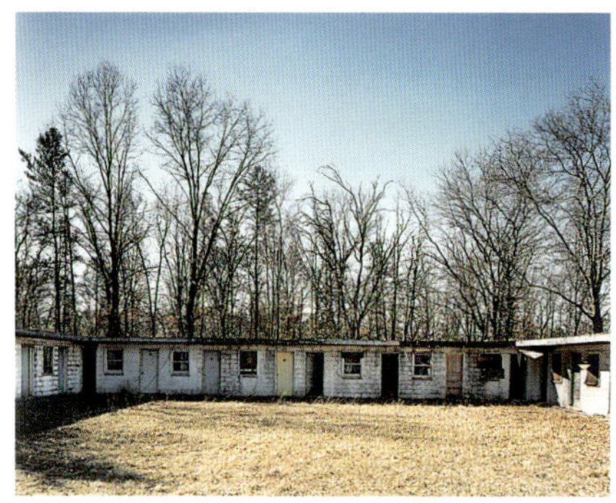

48

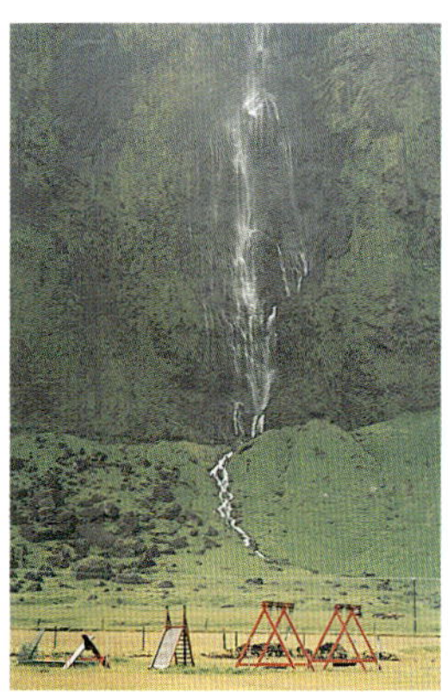

49

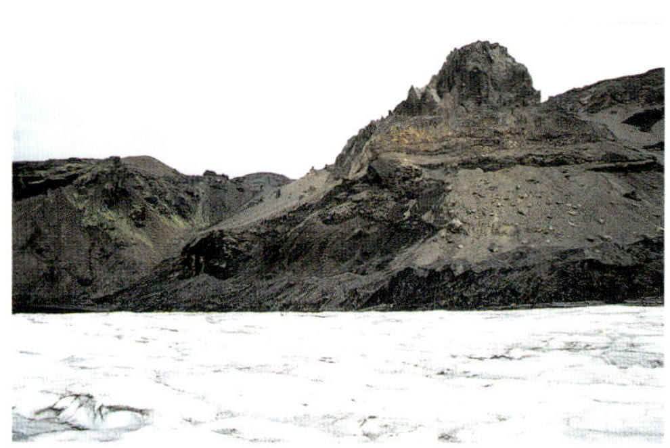

50

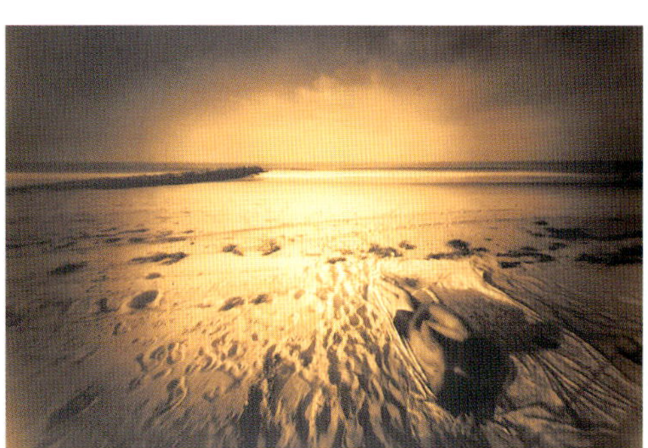

51

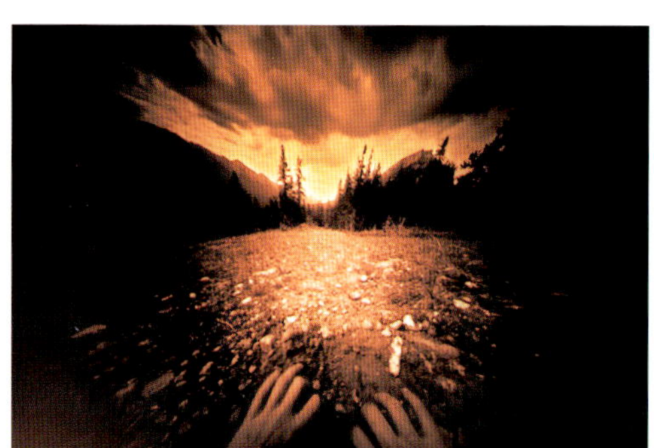

52

STAN DOUGLAS

45
1970's Set for Der Sandmann at DOKFILM Studios, Potsdam, Babelsberg. December 1994. 1994–97. Silver dye bleach process print, 29 × 39 inches

46
Untitled. From the *Berlin Garden Views* series. 1994. Silver dye bleach process print, $18\frac{5}{8} \times 36\frac{5}{8}$ inches

47
Subject to a Film: Marnie (details). 1988–96. Installation: Six gelatin silver prints, including text panel, approximately 64 × 90 inches

48
Abandoned Motel at Idelwild. From the *Detroit* series, part II. 1999. Suite of six chromogenic process prints, $17\frac{3}{4} \times 21\frac{1}{2}$ inches each

OLAFUR ELIASSON

49
Untitled (detail). From the *Waterfall* series. 1996. Sixteen chromogenic process prints from a suite of fifty-eight, $14\frac{3}{4} \times 10$ inches each

50
Untitled (detail). From the *Iceland* series. 1997. Series of seven unique chromogenic process prints, 24 × 36 inches each

BARBARA ESS

51
Untitled. 1986–87. Laminated chromogenic process print, $50\frac{3}{4} \times 69\frac{7}{8}$ inches

52
Untitled. 1988. Laminated chromogenic process print, $52\frac{1}{2} \times 71\frac{1}{2}$ inches

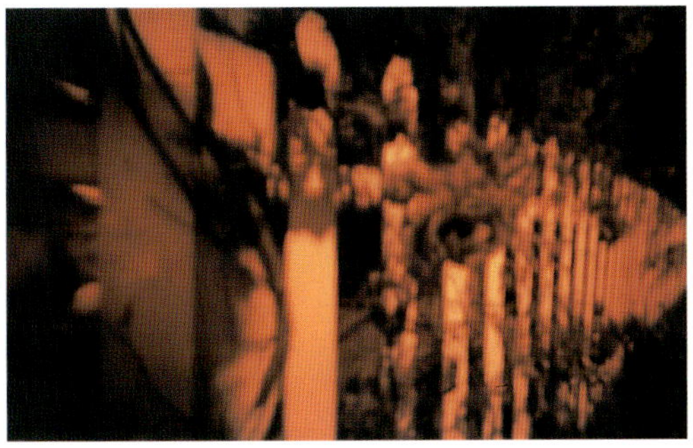

53

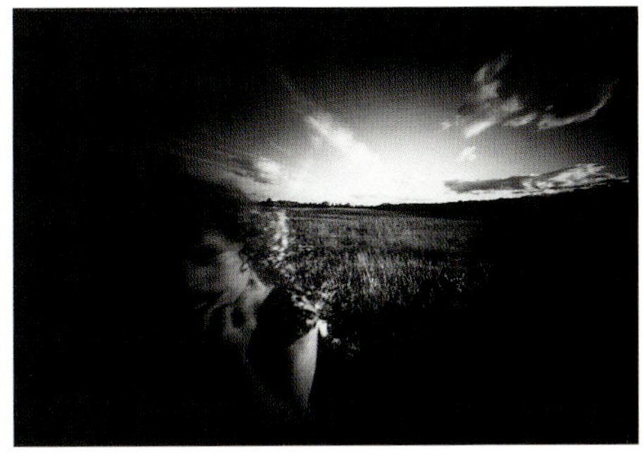

54

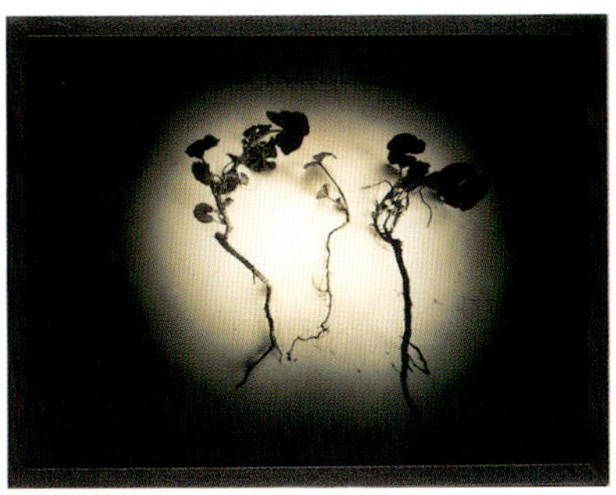

55

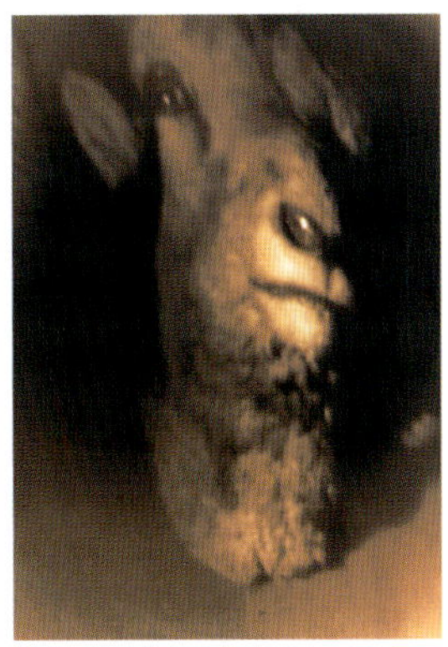

56

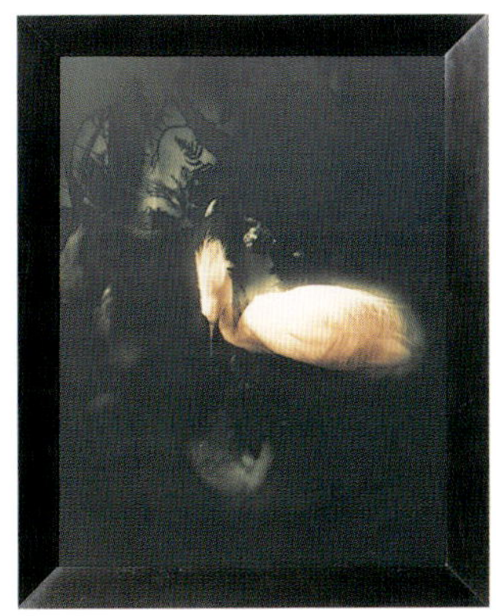

57

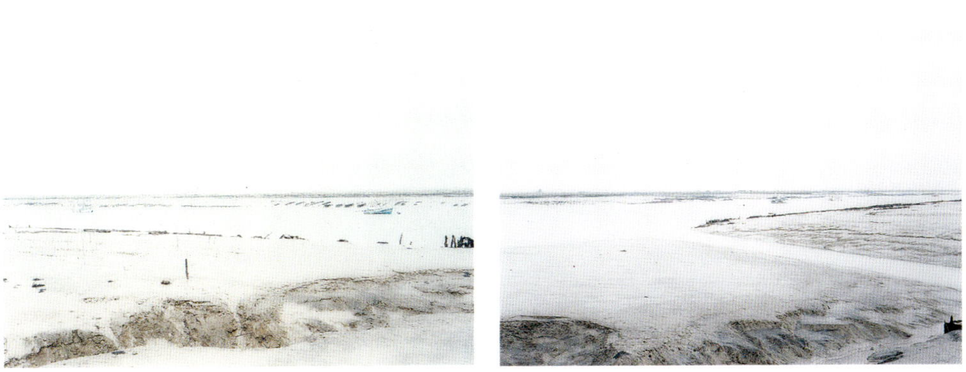

58

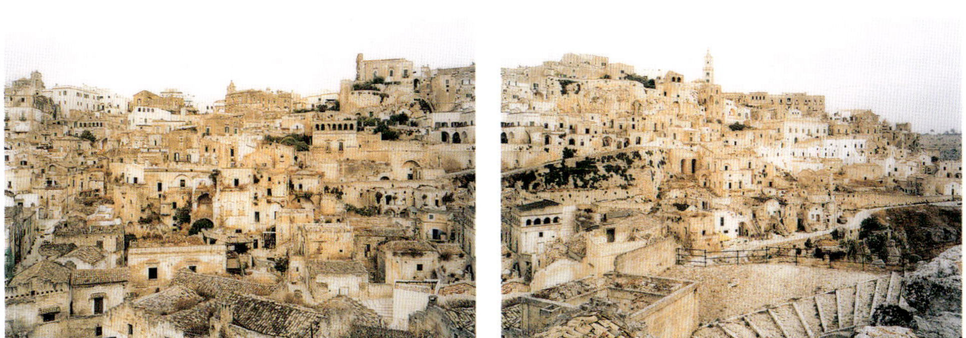

59

5 3

Untitled. 1989. Laminated chromogenic process print, $52\frac{3}{4} \times 76\frac{1}{8}$ inches

5 4

Untitled. 2000. Laminated chromogenic process print, $42\frac{5}{8} \times 57\frac{5}{8}$ inches

5 5

Untitled (Botanical Specimens) (detail). 1997–98. Installation: ten laminated chromogenic process prints in artist's frames, $39\frac{1}{2} \times 57$ inches

5 6

Untitled. 1989. Laminated chromogenic process print, $75\frac{3}{4} \times 52\frac{5}{8}$ inches

5 7

Untitled. 1991. Laminated chromogenic process print in artist's frame, $45\frac{1}{8} \times 36\frac{1}{8}$ inches

ELGER ESSER

5 8

Chattresac I Frankreich 1997 (left). *Chattresac II Frankreich 1997* (right). 1997. Diptych: chromogenic process prints, face mounted to plexiglass, $49 \times 63\frac{1}{2}$ inches each

5 9

Matera I Italien 1998 (left). *Matera II Italien 1998* (right). 1999. Two chromogenic process prints, face mounted to plexiglass, $55\frac{1}{2} \times 71\frac{3}{8}$ inches each

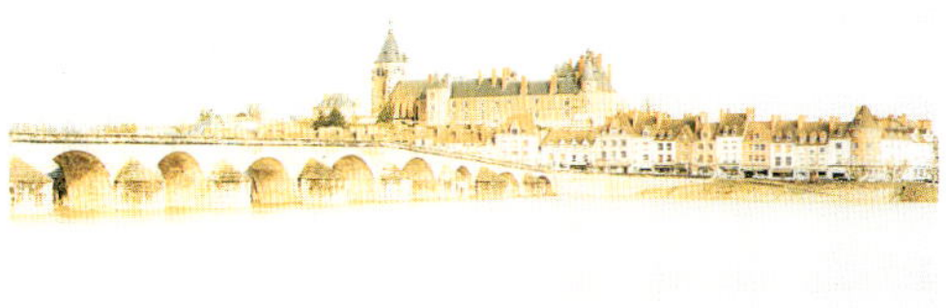

60

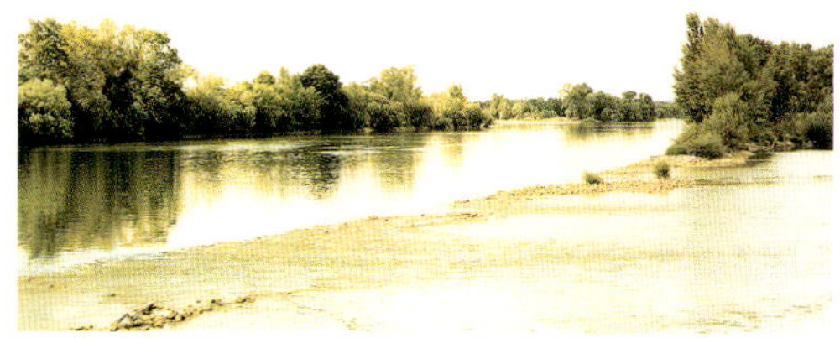

61

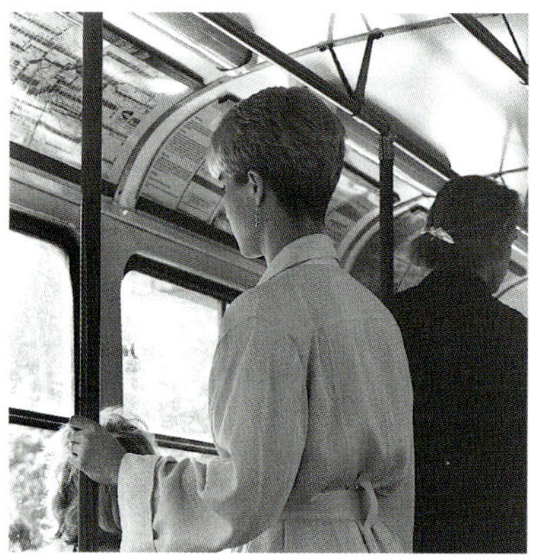

62

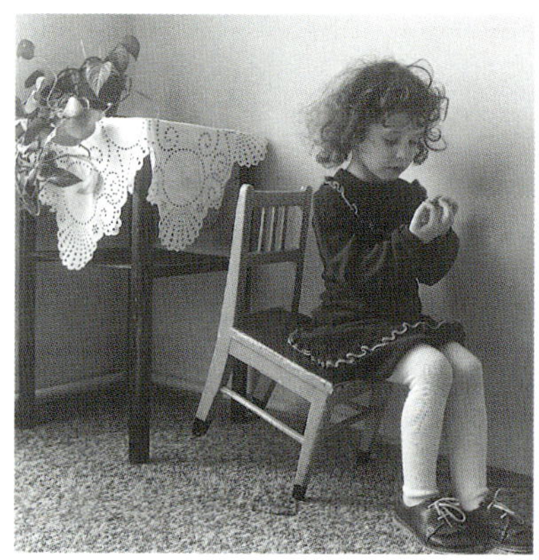

63

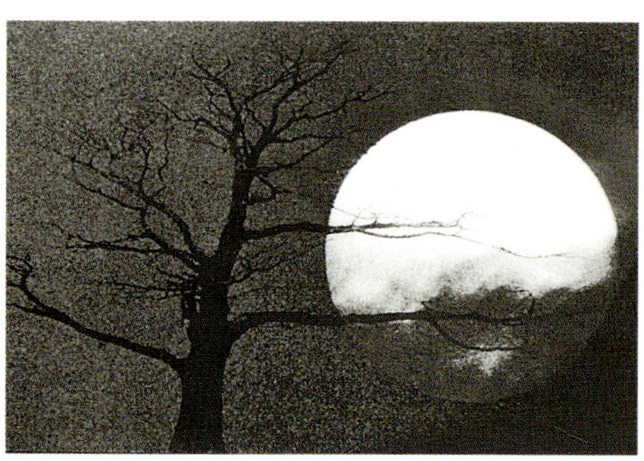

64

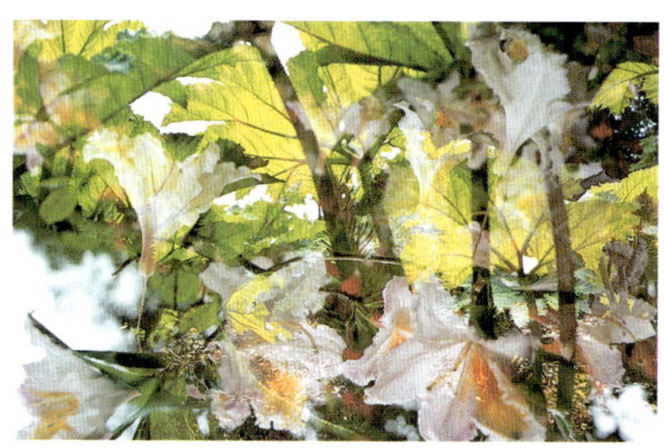

65

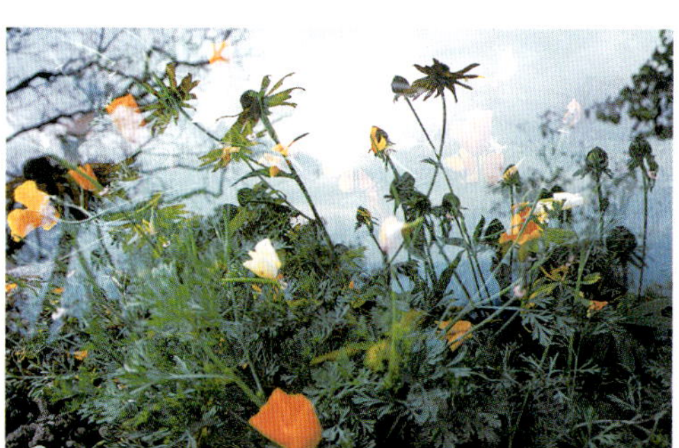

66

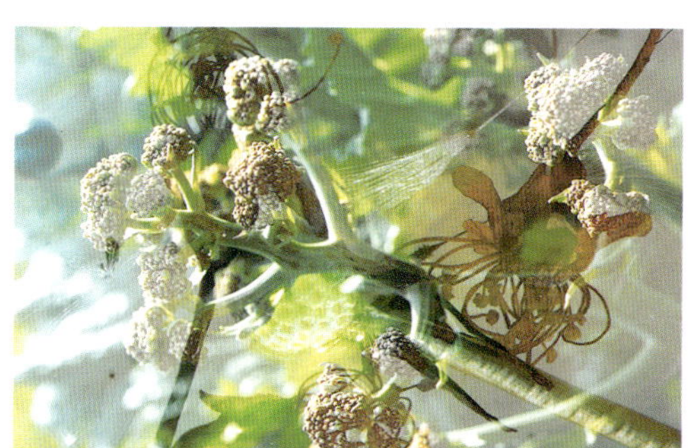

67

ELGER ESSER

60

Gien, Frankreich 1997. 1997. Chromogenic process print, face mounted to plexiglass, $49 \times 63\frac{5}{8}$ inches

61

Chouze, Frankreich 1999. 1999 Chromogenic process print, face mounted to plexiglass $56 \times 71\frac{1}{2}$ inches

PATRICK FAIGENBAUM

62

Untitled. 1994–96. Gelatin silver print, $37\frac{5}{8} \times 36\frac{1}{2}$ inches

63

Untitled. 1994–96. Gelatin silver print, $37\frac{1}{2} \times 36\frac{1}{2}$ inches

HANS-PETER FELDMANN

64

Sonnstagsmotive (detail). 1976–77. Installation: twenty-one offset screen prints on newsprint paper, dimensions varied

PETER FISCHLI AND DAVID WEISS

65

Untitled (FW #2/23). 1997–98. Inkjet print from a series, $29\frac{1}{8} \times 42\frac{1}{8}$ inches

66

Untitled (FW #121). 1997–98. Inkjet print from a series, $29\frac{1}{8} \times 42\frac{1}{8}$ inches

67

Untitled (FW #1/25). 1997–98. Inkjet print from a series, $29\frac{1}{8} \times 42\frac{1}{8}$ inches

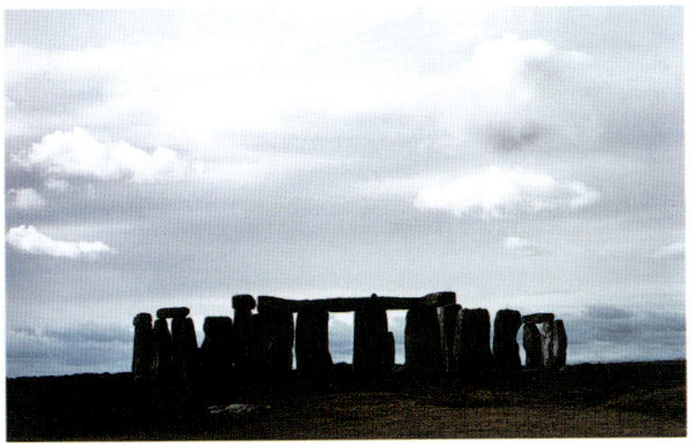

68

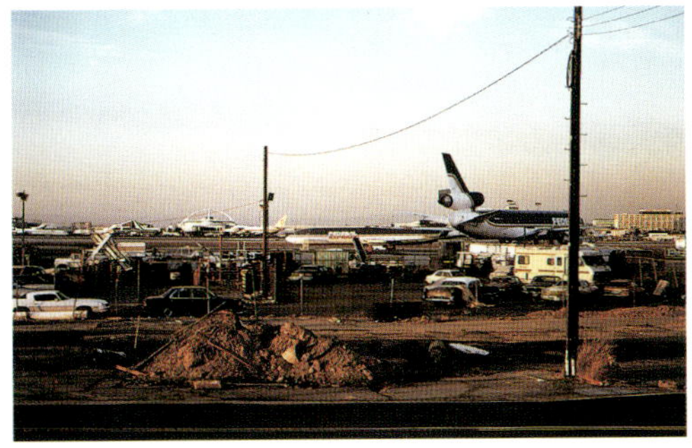

69

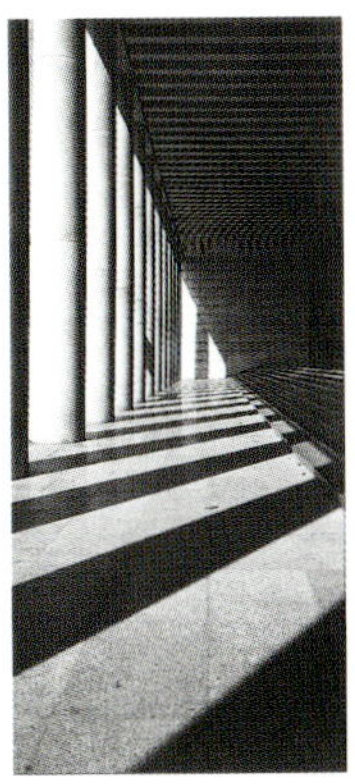

70

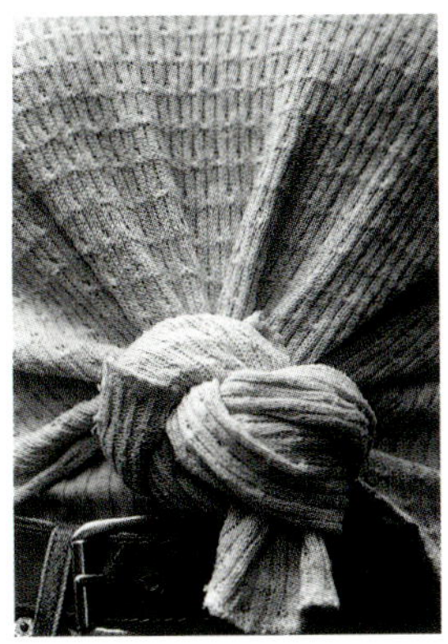

71

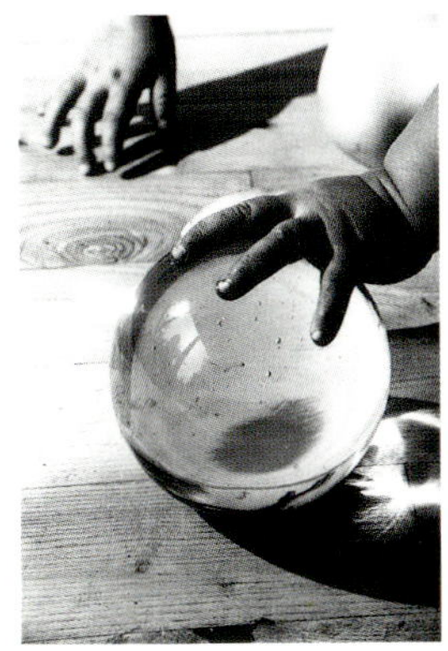

72

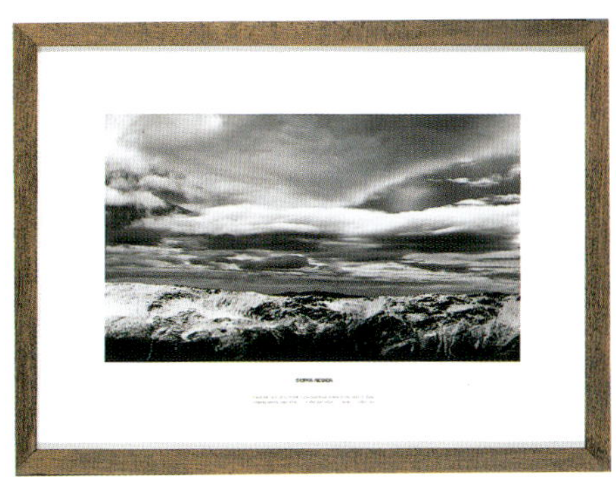

73

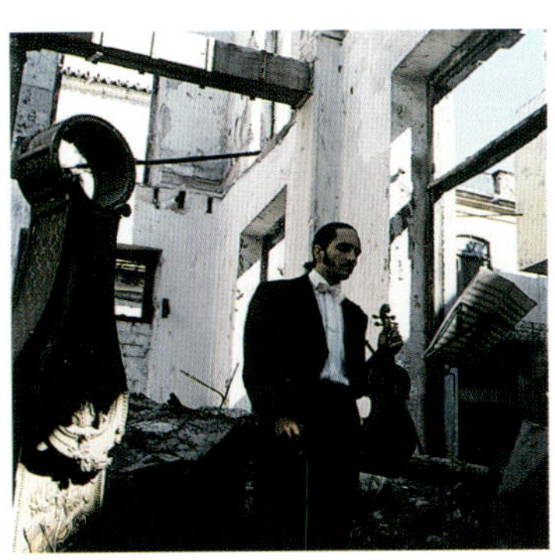

74

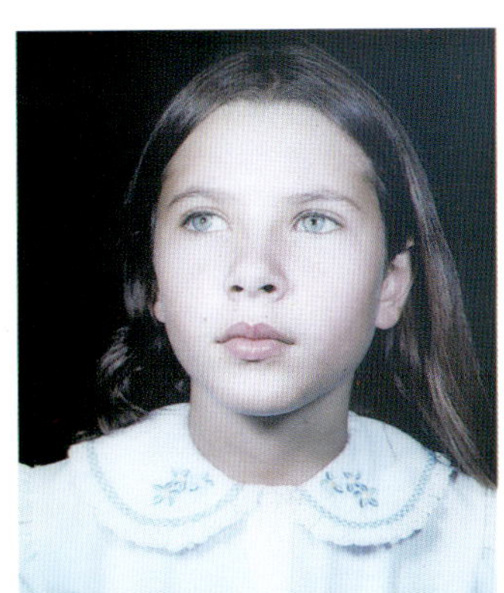

75

68

Stonehenge. 1989. Chromogenic process print, 63¼ × 87 inches

69

Untitled. 1990. Silver dye bleach process print, 63⅓ × 86⅞ inches

GUNTHER FORG

70

Eur, Roma. 1987. Unique gelatin silver print, 9 feet 2⅞ × 51⅝ inches

MICHEL FRANÇOIS

71

Untitled. 1991. Gelatin silver print, 16 × 11 inches

72

Untitled. 1991. Gelatin silver print, 16 × 11 inches

HAMISH FULTON

73

Sierra Nevada. 1979. Bromide print with text in artist's frame, 32⅞ × 43¼ inches

CARLOS GARAICOA

74

About the Grandfather Clock and the Time that...(2). 1995. Silver dye bleach process print, 19 × 18¾ inches

ANNA GASKELL

75

Opening Out. 1996. Chromogenic process print, face mounted to plexiglass, 50⅛ × 40 inches

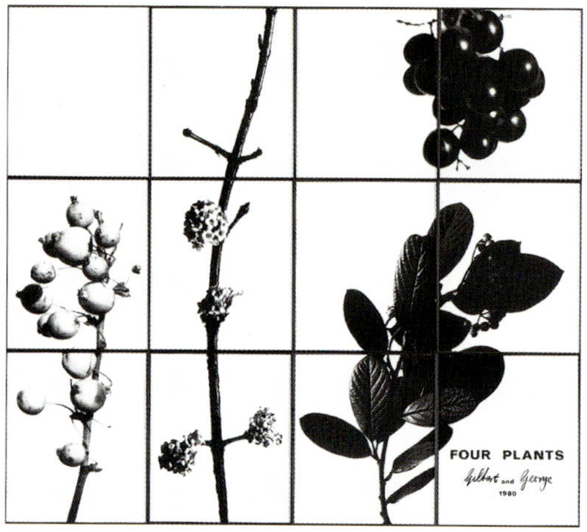

76

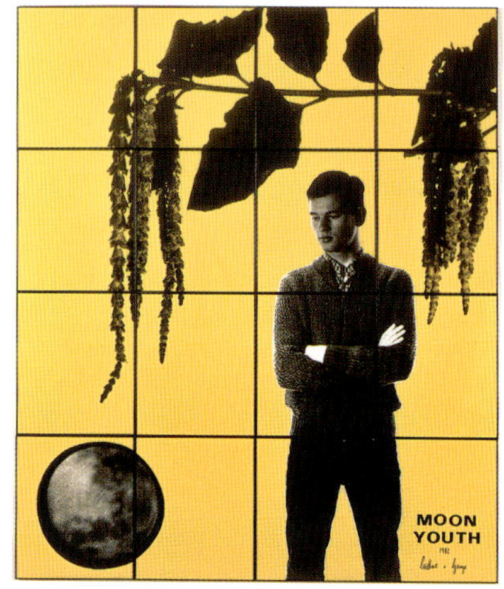

77

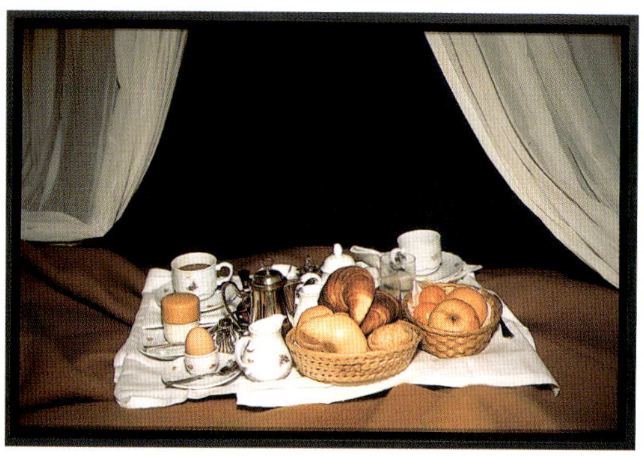

78

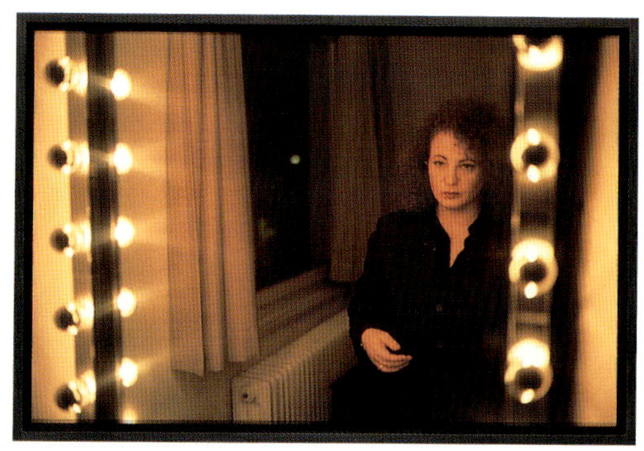

79

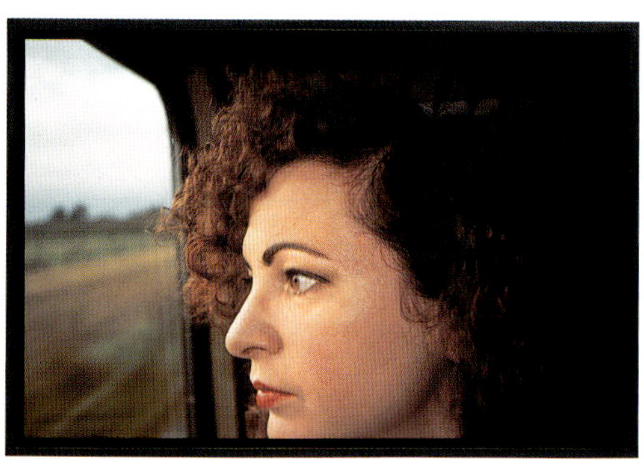

80

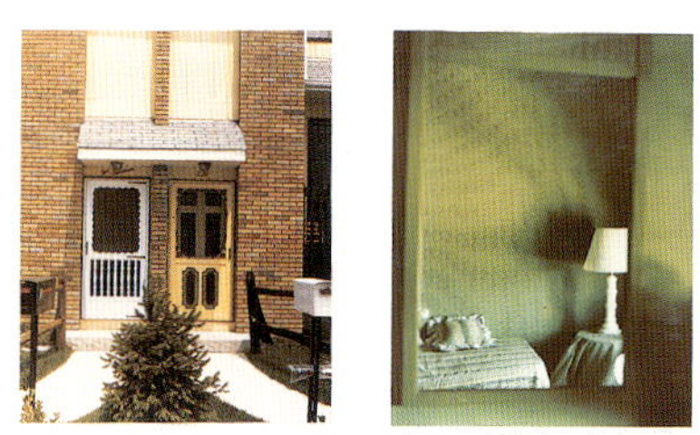

81

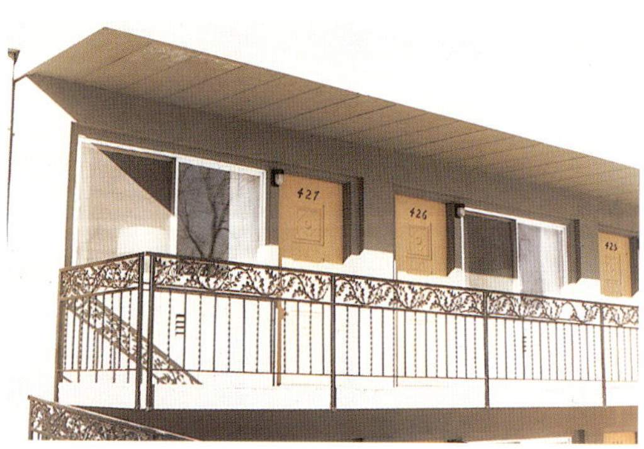

82

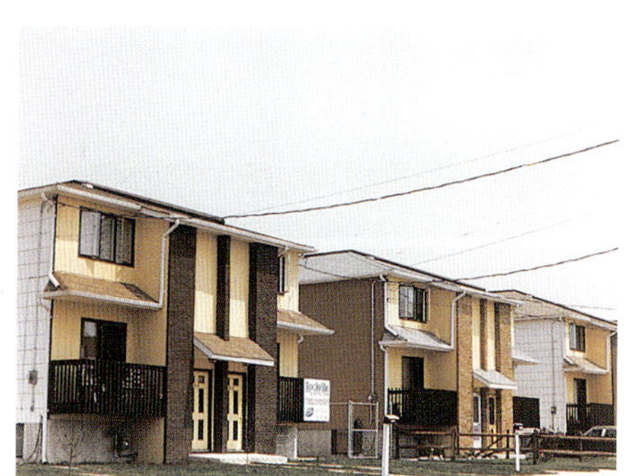

83

GILBERT AND GEORGE

76

Four Plants. 1980. Photopiece: twelve gelatin silver prints in the artists' frames, 72×80 inches

77

Moon Youth. 1982. Photopiece: sixteen hand-colored gelatin silver prints in the artists' frames, 96×80 inches

NAN GOLDIN

78

Breakfast in Bed—Hotel Torre di Bellosguardo, Florence. 1996. Silver dye bleach process print in artist's frame, $28\frac{3}{4} \times 41$ inches

79

Self-Portrait in Hotel Room, Baur au Lac, Zurich. 1998. Silver dye bleach process print in artist's frame, $28\frac{3}{8} \times 41$ inches

80

Self-Portrait on the Train, Germany. 1992. Silver dye bleach process print in artist's frame, $28\frac{3}{4} \times 41$ inches

DAN GRAHAM

81

Entrance with One White and One Yellow Door; Two Home House; Staten Island, N.Y. 1978 (left). *Bedroom with Mirror, Model House; Marin County, California 1974* (right). 1978/1974. Two silver dye bleach process prints mounted on board, $25\frac{1}{4} \times 33\frac{1}{2}$ inches

82

Motel with Yellow Doors, Minneapolis, MN. 1975. Chromogenic process print, $9\frac{3}{8} \times 14$ inches

83

Rockville Estates "Two Home Homes for Sale" Staten Island, New York 1978. 1978. Chromogenic process print, $10\frac{3}{4} \times 13\frac{3}{4}$ inches

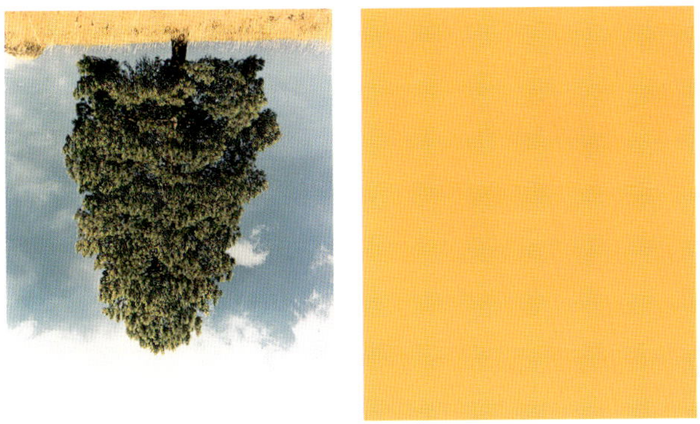

84

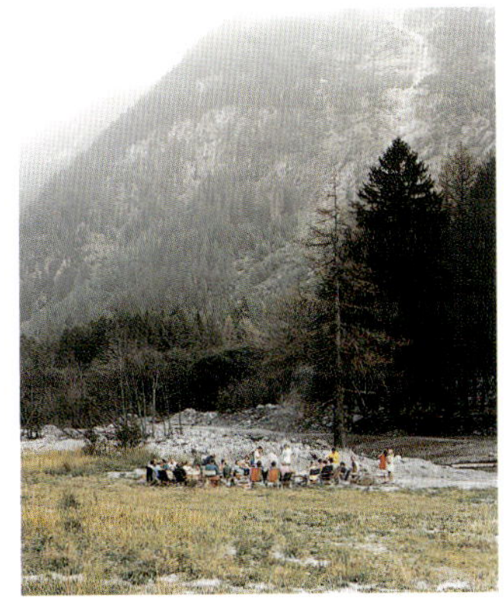

85

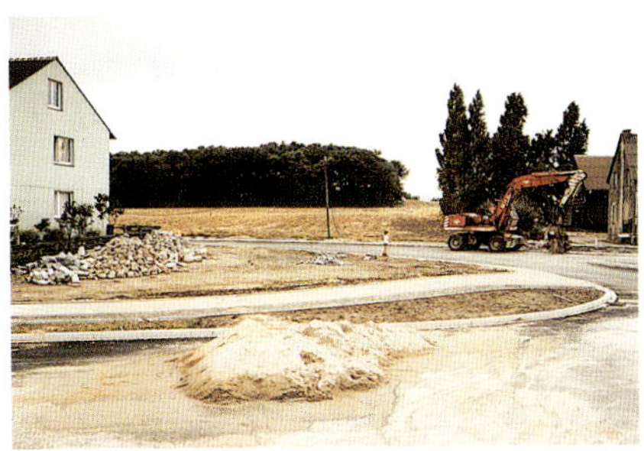

86

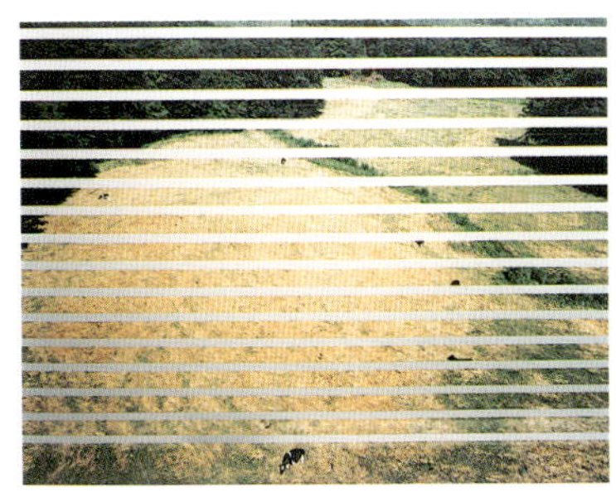

87

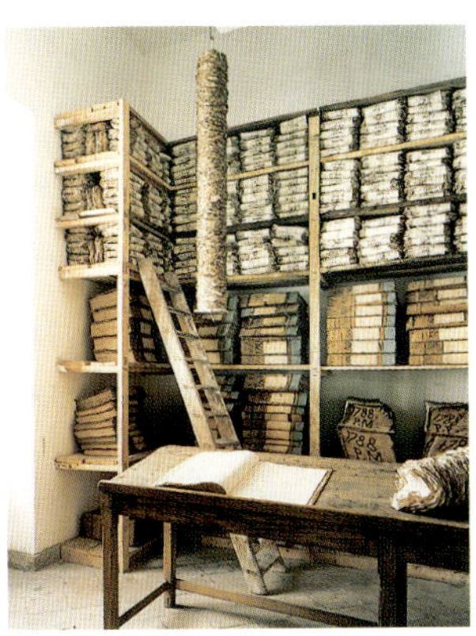

88

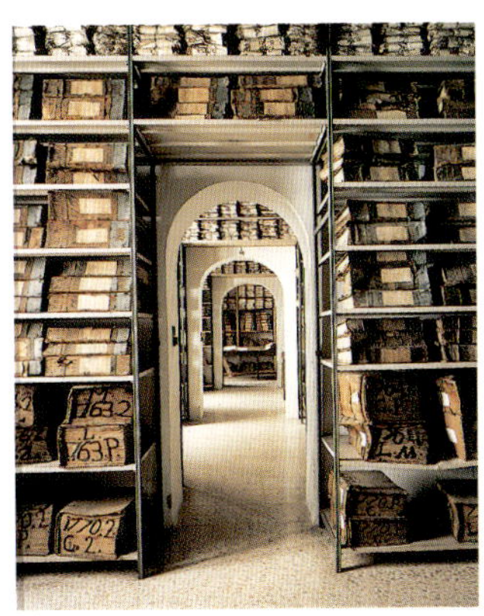

89

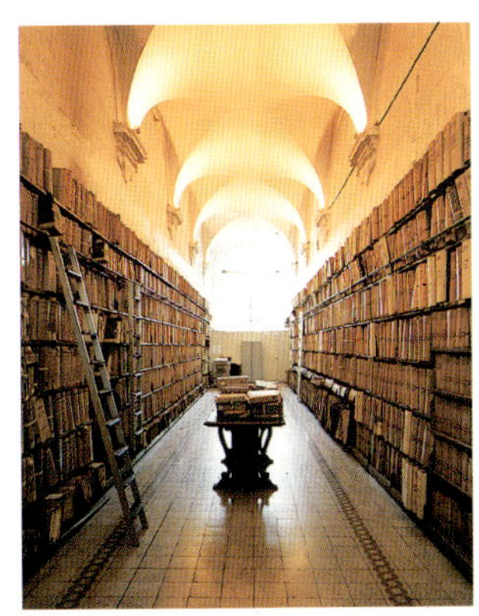

90

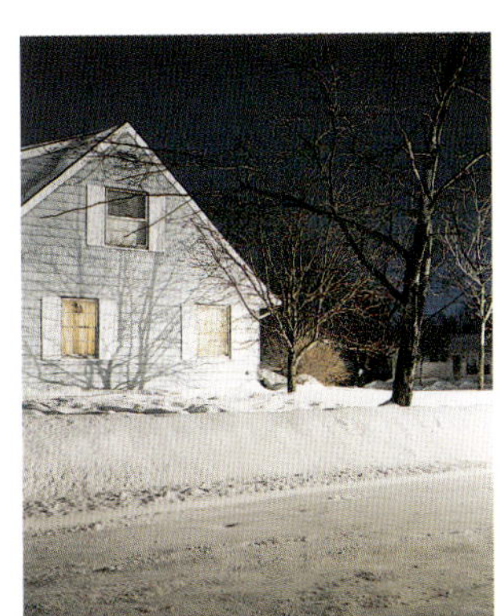

91

RODNEY GRAHAM

84
Ponderosa Pines, BC/CAT hi-way yellow (details). 1992. Installation: five chromogenic process prints, approximately $17\frac{3}{8} \times 100$ inches

ANDREAS GURSKY

85
Moloja. 1989. Chromogenic process print, 83×69 inches

86
Essen. 1984–85. Chromogenic process print mounted between plexiglass and glass, $36\frac{1}{4} \times 31\frac{3}{4}$ inches

87
Autobahn, Mettmann. 1993. Chromogenic process print, $70\frac{7}{8} \times 86$ inches

DOUG HALL

88
Archive of the Bank of Naples. 1997. Chromogenic process print, $62\frac{7}{8} \times 49\frac{3}{4}$ inches

89
Archive of the Bank of Naples, Doorways. 1997. Chromogenic process print, $62\frac{3}{4} \times 49\frac{7}{8}$ inches

90
Main Reading Room, State Archive at Sant' Ivo, Rome. 1997. Chromogenic process print, 63×50 inches

TODD HIDO

91
Untitled #2421. From the *Ohio* series. 1999. Chromogenic process print, $38\frac{7}{8} \times 30\frac{3}{4}$ inches

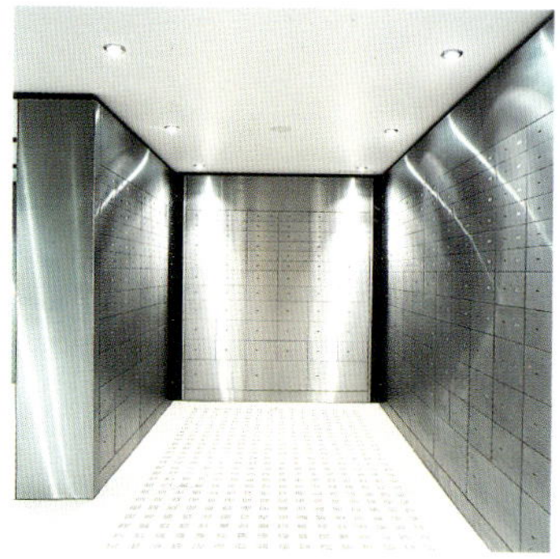
92

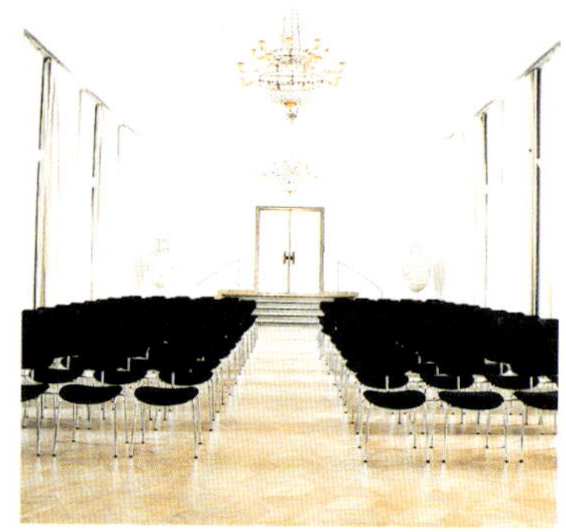
93

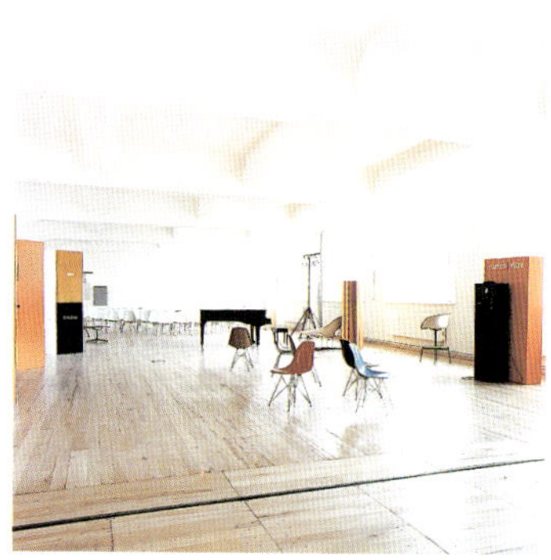
94

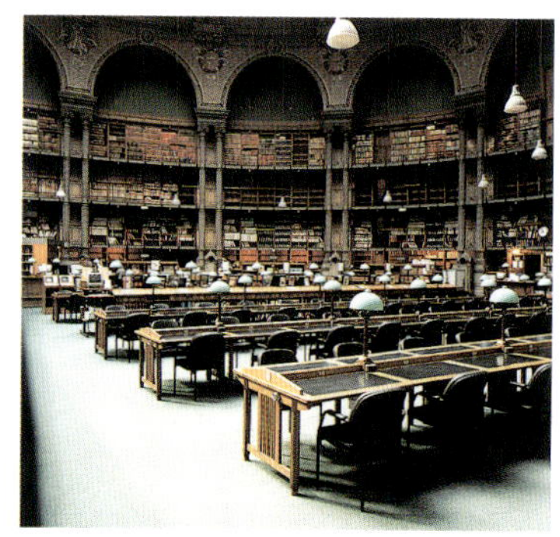
95

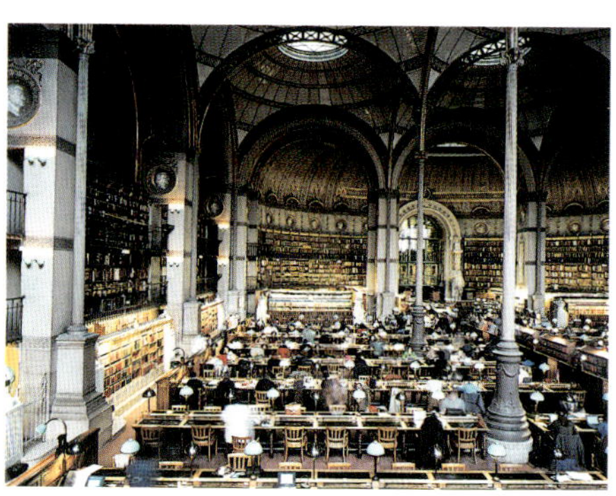
96

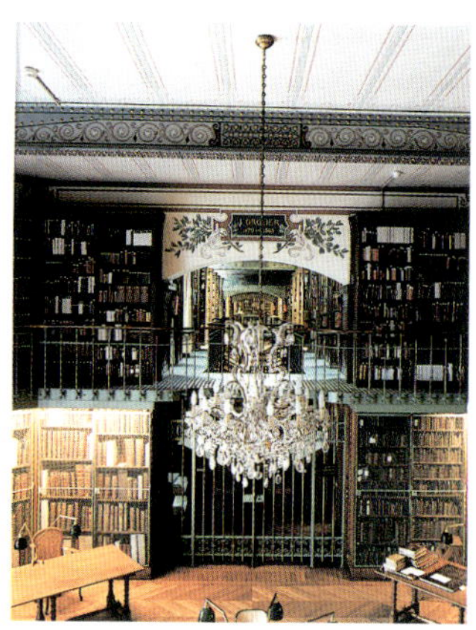
97

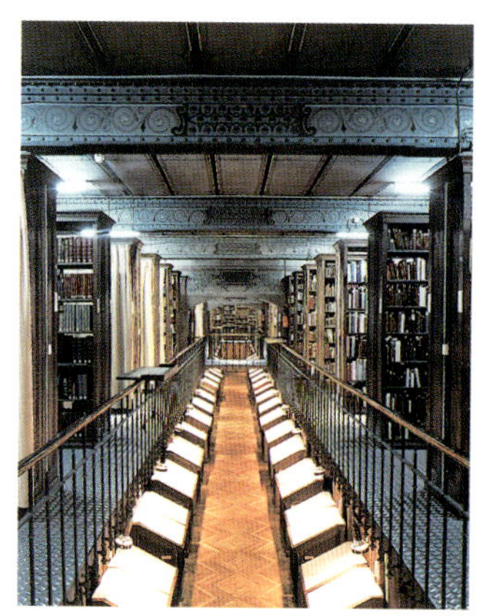
98

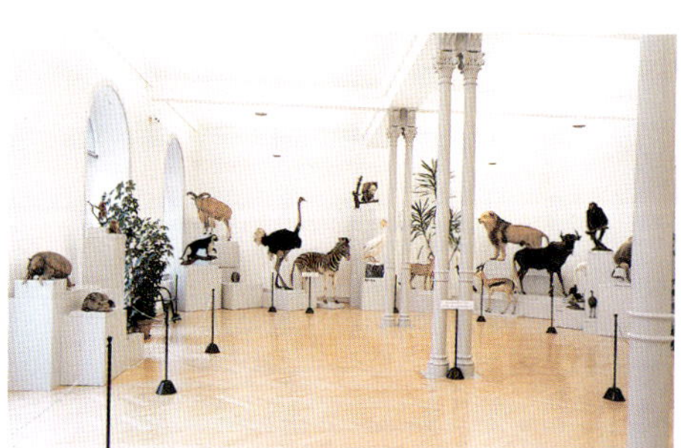
99

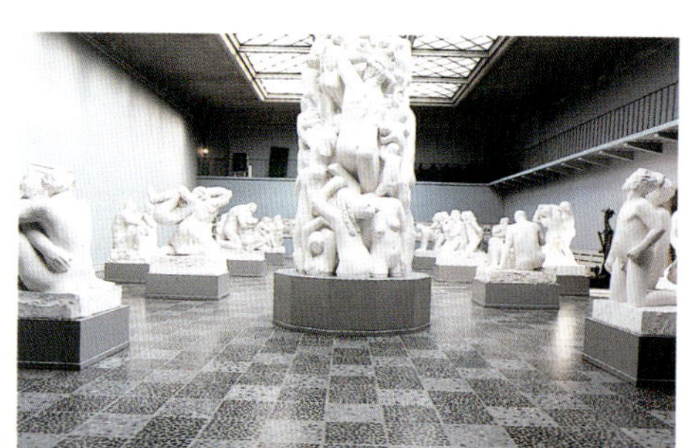
100

C A N D I D A   H O F E R

9 2

Bank Nürnberg, 1999. 1999. Chromogenic process print, 61 × 61 inches

9 3

Schloss Karlsruhe III, 1999. 1999. Chromogenic process print, 61 × 61 inches

9 4

Die Deutschen Werkstätten, Hellerau II. 2000. Chromogenic process print, 60¾ × 60¾ inches

9 5

Bibliothèque Nationale de France, Paris II. 1998. Chromogenic process print from a series, 23 × 23⅜ inches

9 6

Bibliothèque Nationale de France, Paris XIX. 1998. Chromogenic process print from a series, 22½ × 29½ inches

9 7

Bibliothèque Nationale de France, Paris III. 1998. Chromogenic process print from a series, 23 × 17½ inches

9 8

Bibliothèque Nationale de France, Paris IX. 1998. Chromogenic process print from a series, 23 × 17½ inches

9 9

Naturhistorisches Museum, St. Gallen I. 1992. Chromogenic process print, 14 × 21 inches

1 0 0

Viegelandmuseum, Oslo III. 1992. Chromogenic process print, 14 × 21 inches

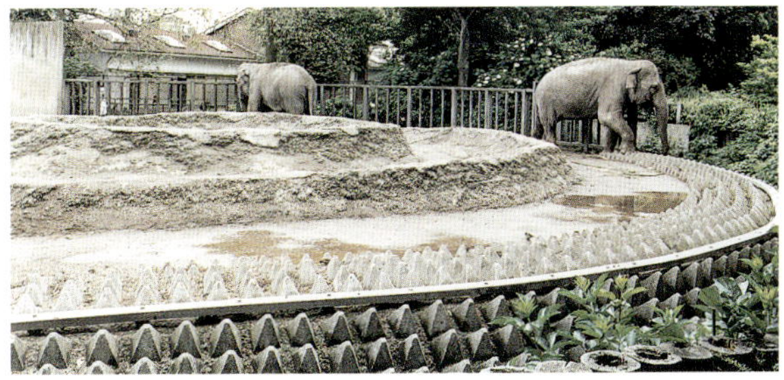

101

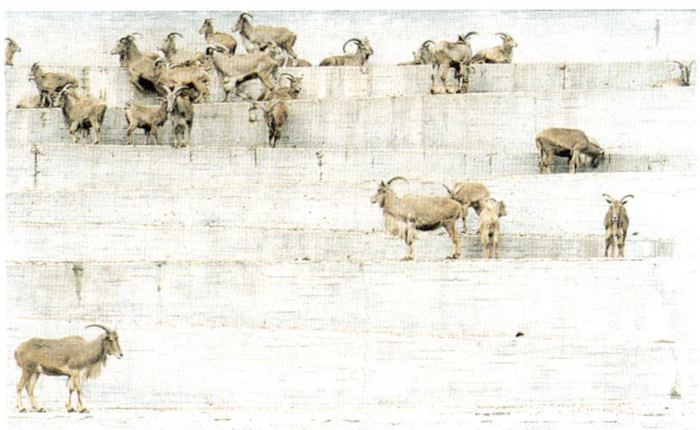

102

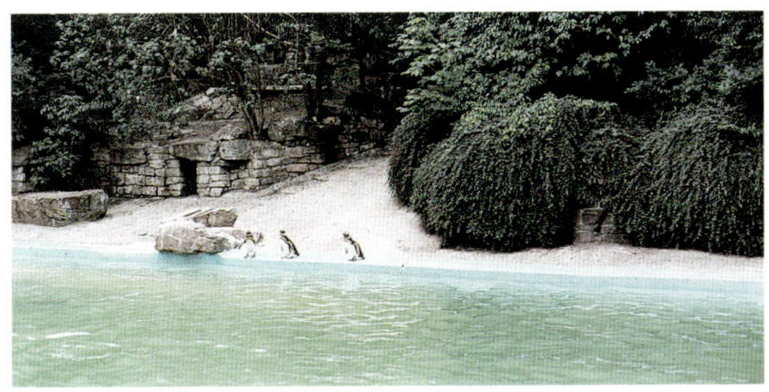

103

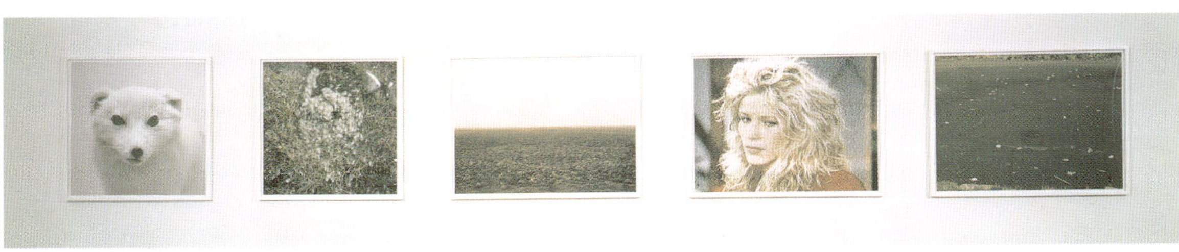

104

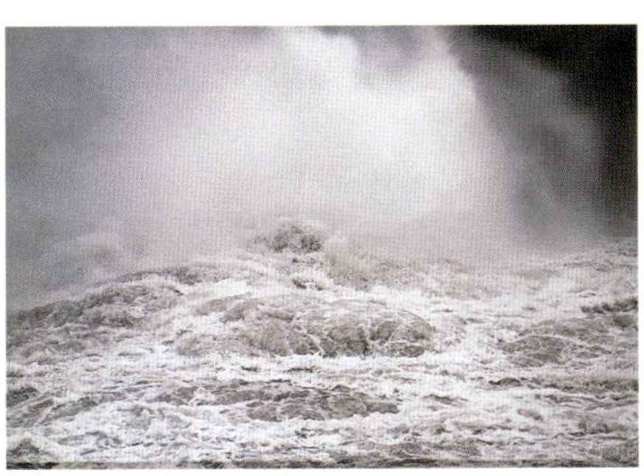

105

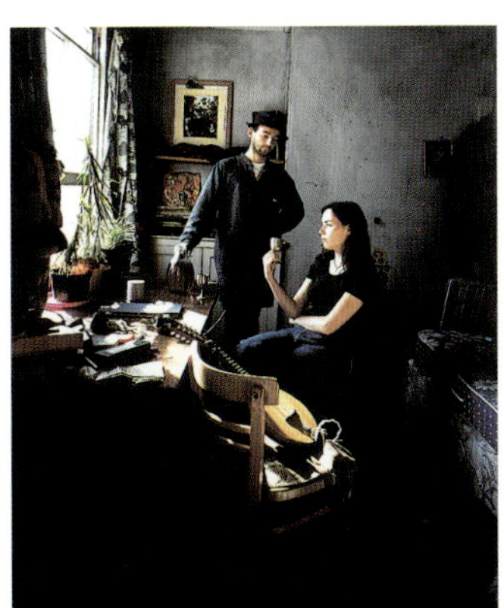

106

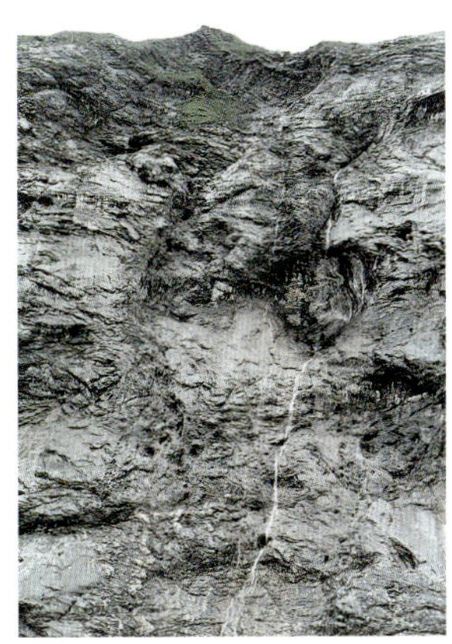

107

1 0 1

Z.G. Amsterdam II. 1992. Chromogenic process print, $10\frac{1}{8} \times 20\frac{3}{4}$ inches

1 0 2

Z.G. Madrid I. 1995. Chromogenic process print, 10×16 inches

1 0 3

Z.G. Karlsruhe II. 1992. Chromogenic process print, $10 \times 20\frac{1}{4}$ inches

R O N I H O R N

1 0 4

Piece (4). 1998. Installation: five iris prints on Somerset paper, 22 inches $\times$ 12 feet $1\frac{1}{4}$ inches

1 0 5

Untitled. 1996. Photolithograph on uncoated paper, $43\frac{1}{8} \times 59$ inches

T O M H U N T E R

1 0 6

The Glass of Wine. 1997. Silver dye bleach process print, $59\frac{1}{4} \times 47\frac{1}{2}$ inches

A X E L H U T T E

1 0 7

Maderaner Tal (Waterfall). 1997. Chromogenic process print, $80\frac{1}{2} \times 58\frac{3}{4}$ inches

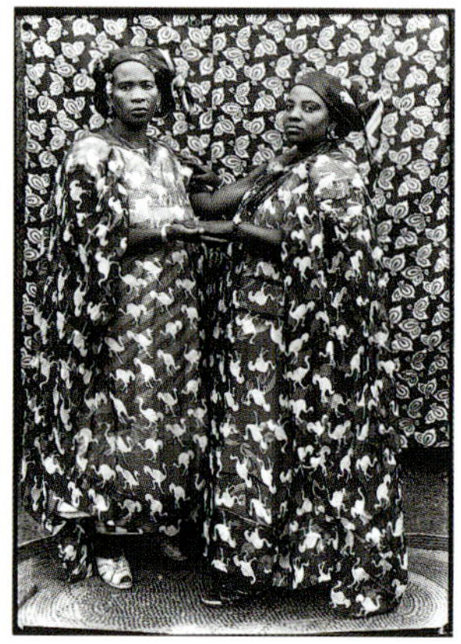

108

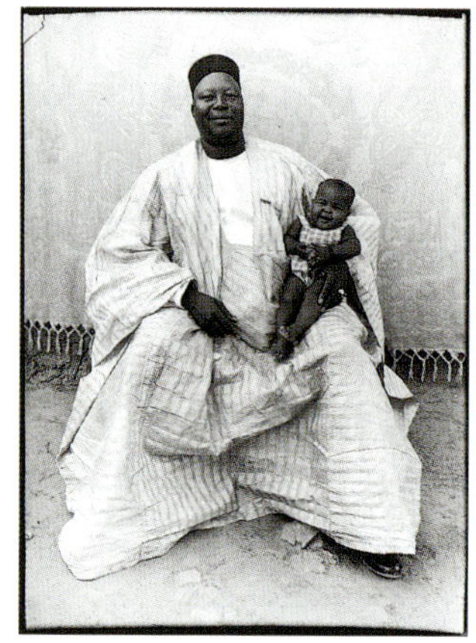

109

SEYDOU KEITA

108

Two Women. 1958/1998. Gelatin silver print, 65 × 46¼ inches

109

Untitled. 1949–51/2000. Gelatin silver print, 77¾ × 49½ inches

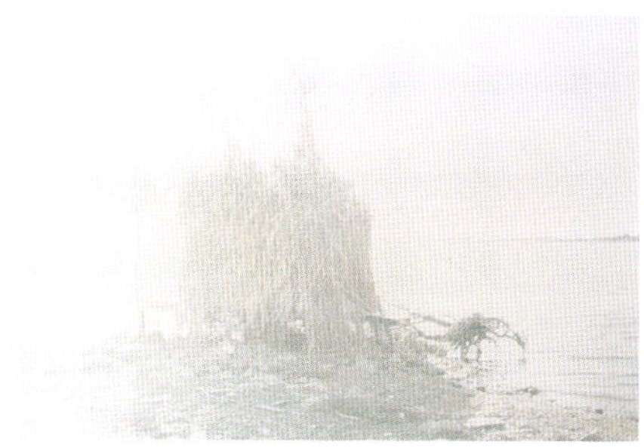

110

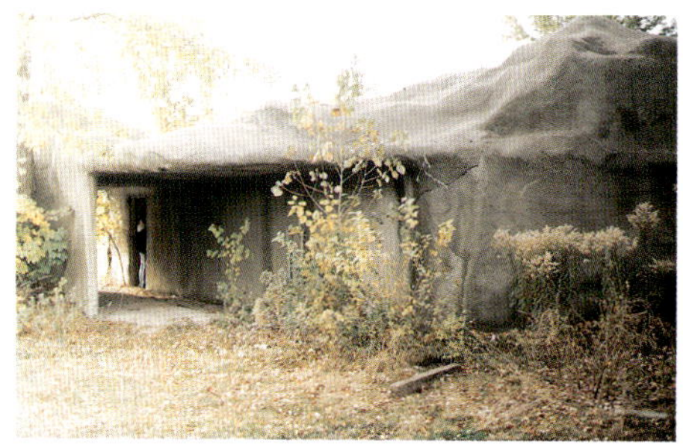

111

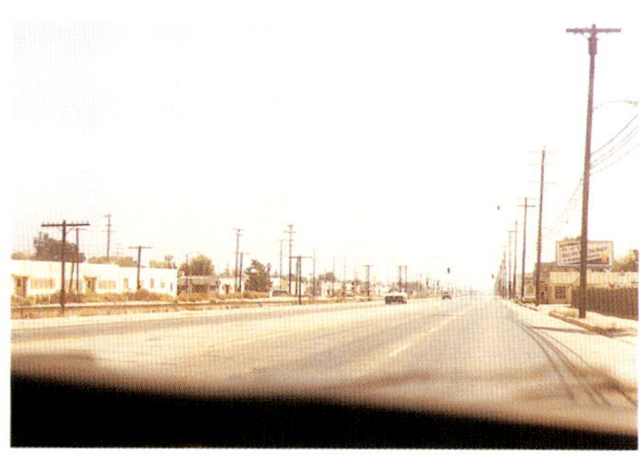

112

MIKE KELLEY

110

Duckblind (Grassy Island Detroit River). 1998. Chromogenic process print, 43¾ × 64¼ inches

111

Abandoned Faux Rock Building. 1998. Chromogenic process print, 43¾ × 64¼ inches

112

Three Valleys (detail). 1980/1998. Suite of twelve chromogenic process prints, 16 × 23½ inches each

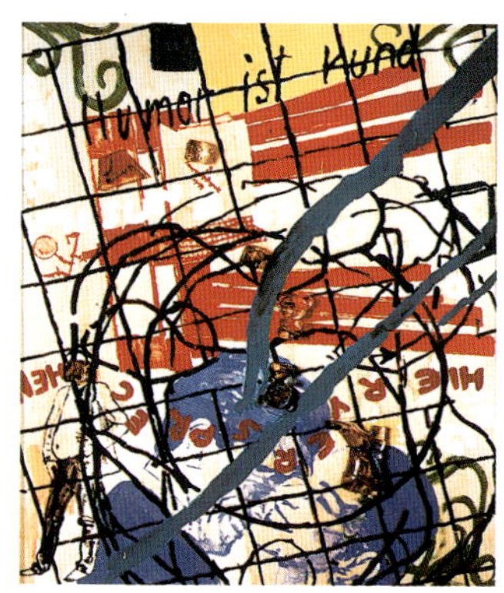

113

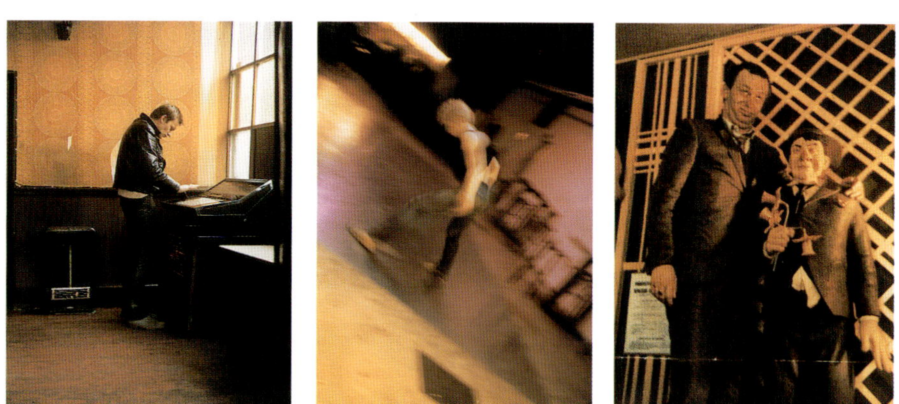

114

MARTIN KIPPENBERGER

113

Untitled (Humor ist rund) (Humour is Round). From the *Heavy Burschi* series. 1989–90. Silver dye bleach process print, 49 × 41¼ inches

114

Untitled. n.d. Three chromogenic process prints from a series, 12¼ × 9 inches each

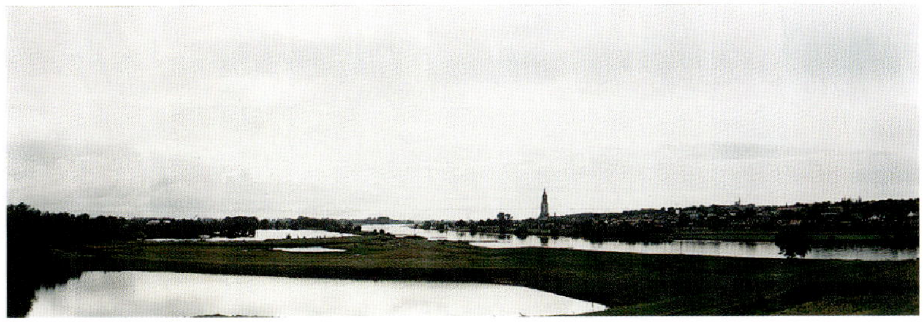

115

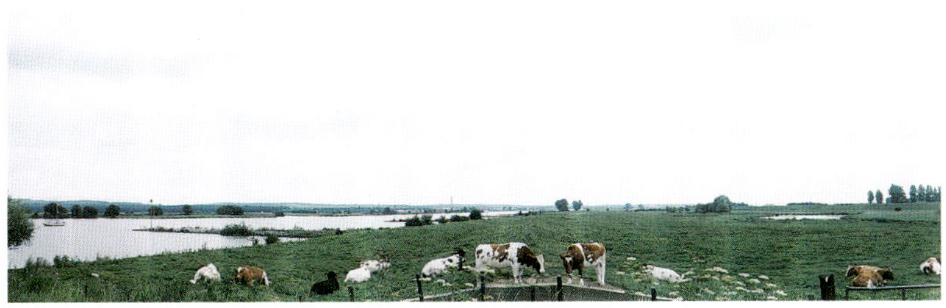

116

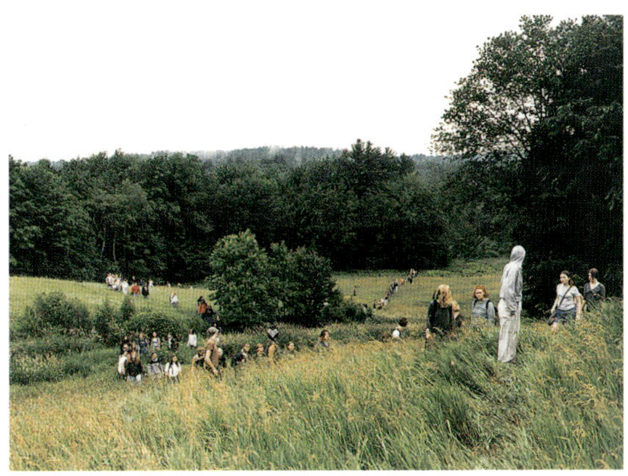

117

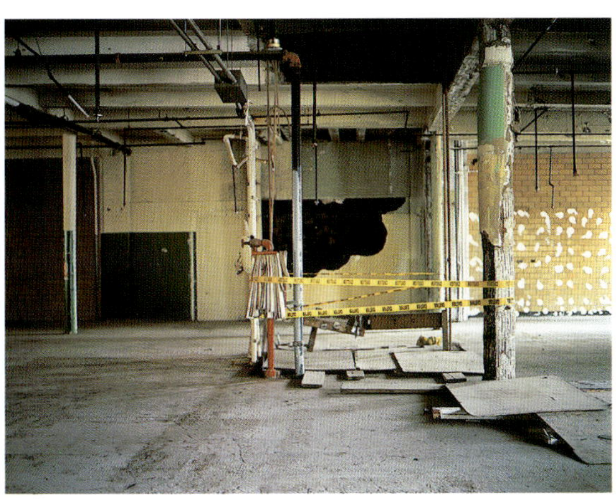

118

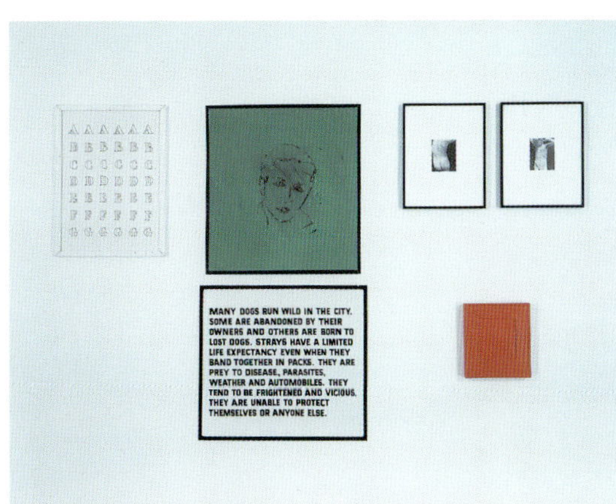

119

JAN KOSTER

115
De Nederrijn bij Eck en Wiel (The Lower Rhine Near Eck en Wiel). **1998. Collage: chromogenic process prints, $14\frac{1}{2} \times 43$ inches**

116
De Nederrijn bij Rhenen (The Lower Rhine Near Rhenen). **1997. Collage: chromogenic process prints, $14 \times 41\frac{1}{2}$ inches**

JUSTINE KURLAND

117
Field Trip. **2000. Laminated chromogenic process print, mounted to aluminum, 30×40 inches**

LOUISE LAWLER

118
Overcast: Caution. **1996. Silver dye bleach process print, mounted to masonite, 48×60 inches**

119
Piero Manzone and Other Artists (Portfolio 1, October Magazine). **1981/1993. Silver dye bleach process print, $5\frac{7}{8} \times 7\frac{1}{4}$ inches**

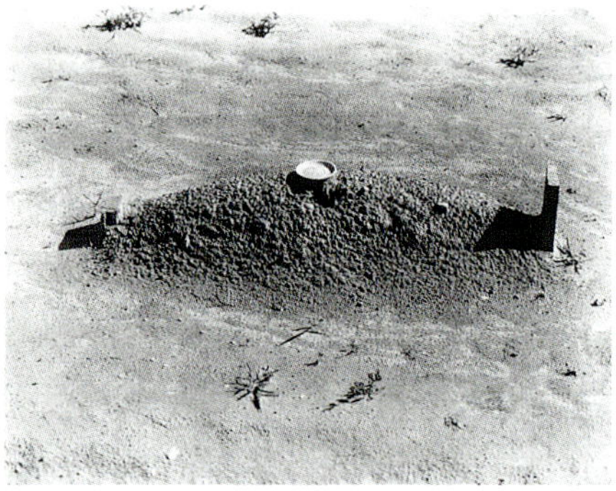

120

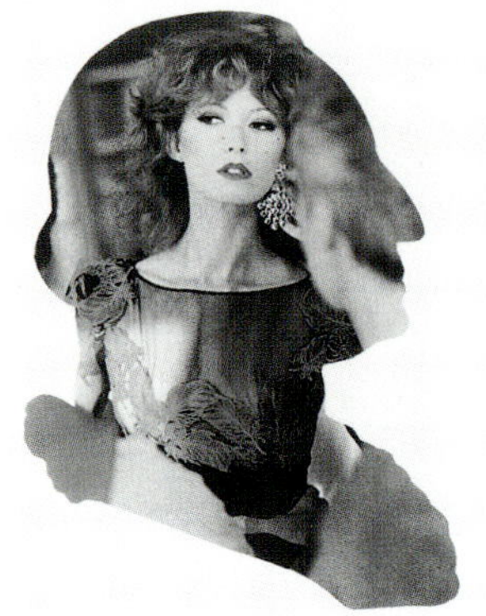

121

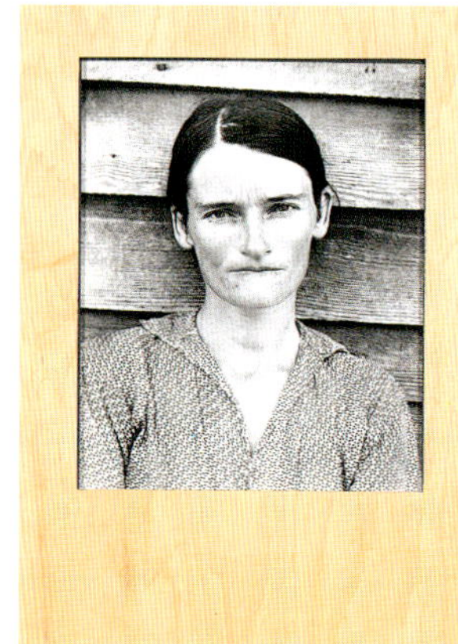

122

SHERRIE LEVINE

120
After Walker Evans. 1981. Gelatin silver print from a series, $7\frac{3}{8} \times 9\frac{1}{2}$ inches

121
President Profile: I (Portfolio 1, October Magazine). 1979/1993. Gelatin silver print, 8×6 inches

122
Untitled (After Walker Evans: Positive #3). 1990. Gelatin silver print in artist's plywood frame, from a series, $29 \times 20\frac{1}{2}$ inches

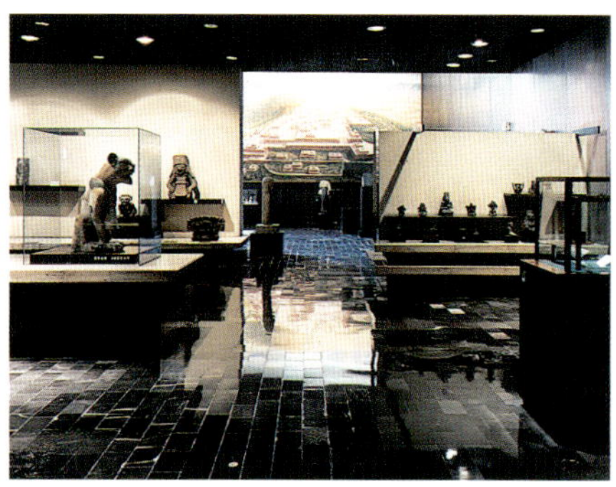

123

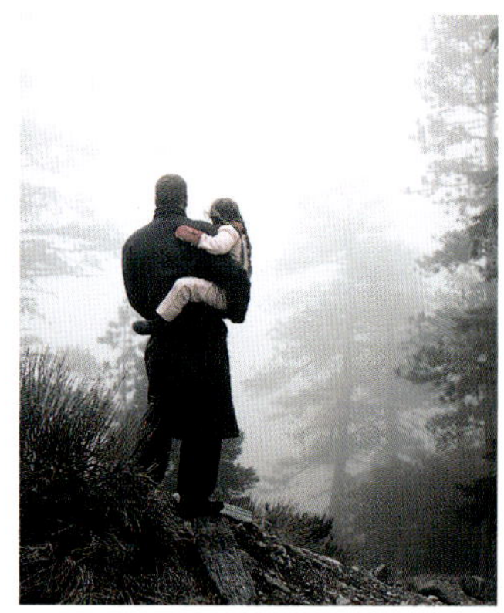

124

SHARON LOCKHART

123
Chronicle of Masonry Work in the Oaxacan Exhibit Hall, National Museum of Anthropology, Mexico City, 1999 (detail). 1999. Suite of nine chromogenic process prints $14\frac{1}{2} \times 18\frac{3}{4}$ inches each

124
Untitled. 1996. Chromogenic process print, 61×49 inches

125
Yuka Koishihara and Eri Kobayashi, Yuka Ishigami, Chinatsu Harui and Hitomi Shibazaki, Kumiko Shirai, 1997. From the *Goshogaoka Basketball Team* series. 1997. Suite of four chromogenic process prints, $22\frac{7}{8} \times 18$ inches each

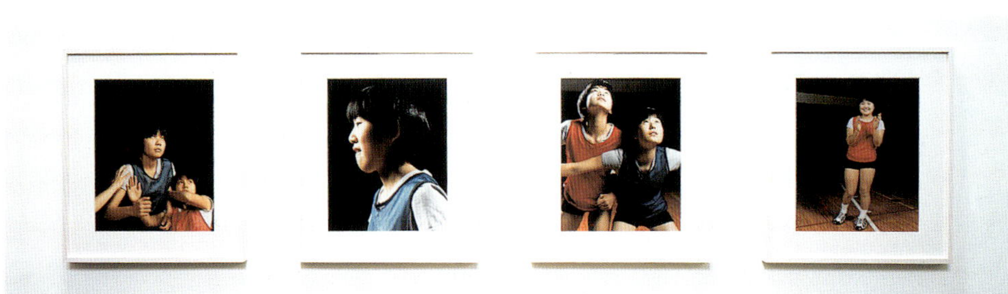

125

SARAH LUCAS

126
Tree Faerie. 1995. Chromogenic process print, $49 \times 37\frac{1}{4}$ inches

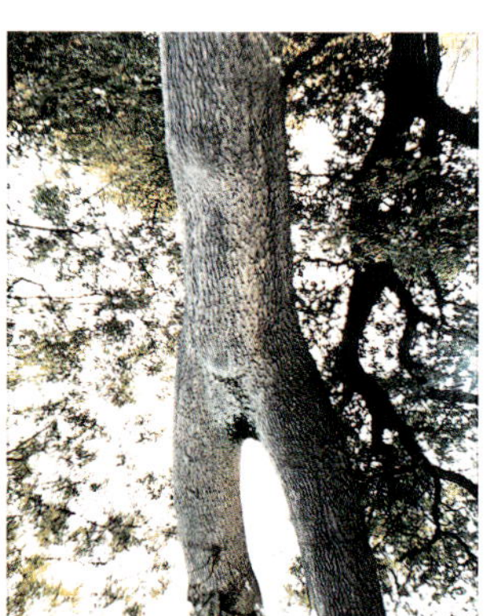

126

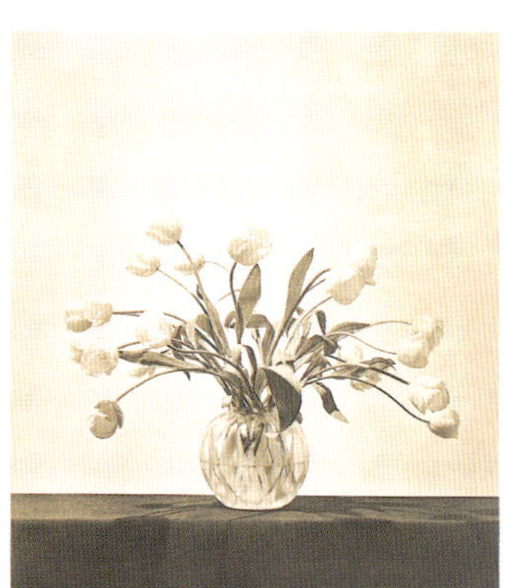

127

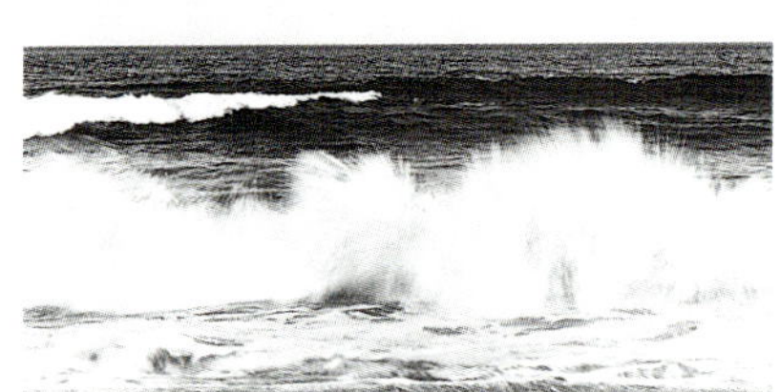

128

ROBERT MAPPLETHORPE

127
Flowers Portfolio (detail). 1983. Portfolio of ten photogravures, $22 \times 17\frac{7}{8}$ inches each

128
Waves. 1979. Gelatin silver print, $13\frac{3}{4} \times 13\frac{3}{4}$ inches

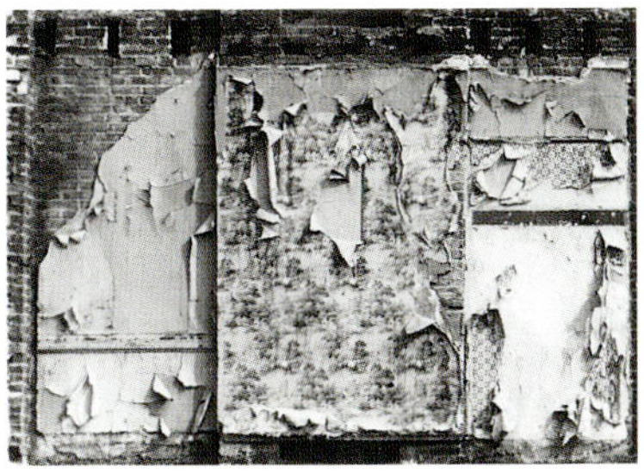
129

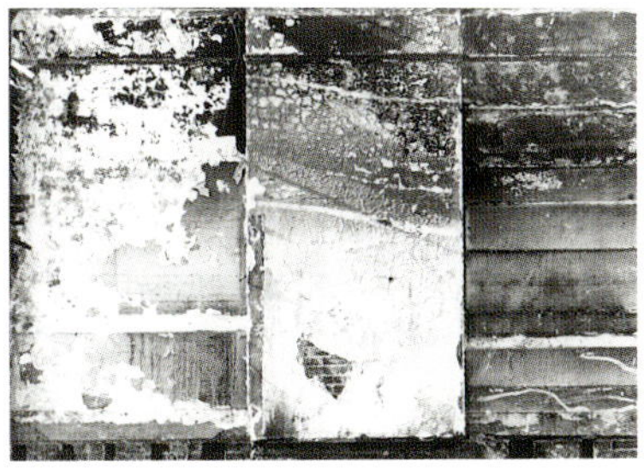
130

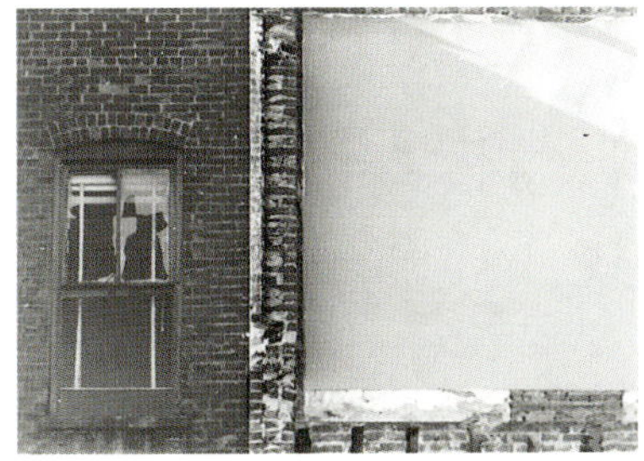
131

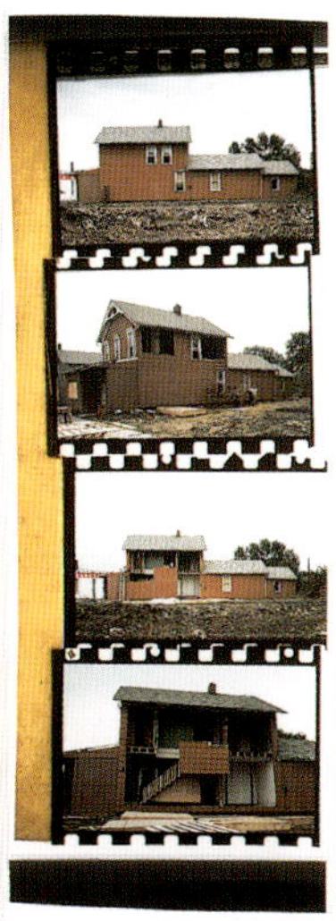
132

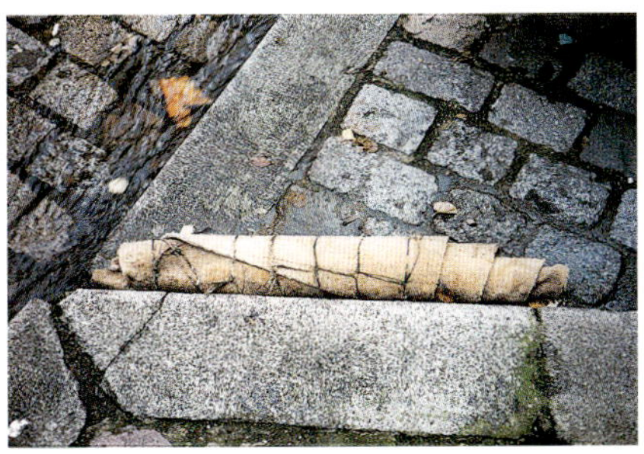
133

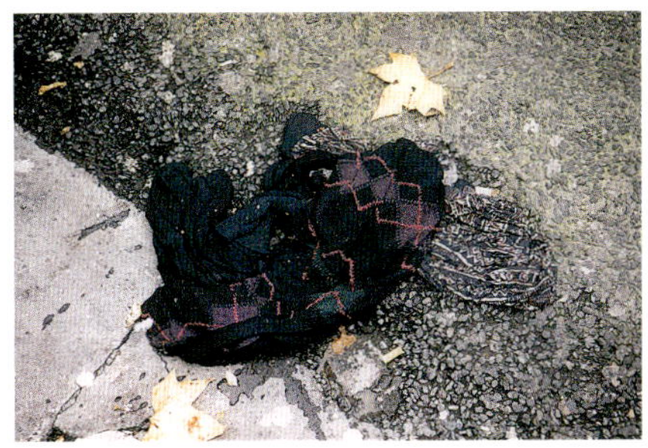
134

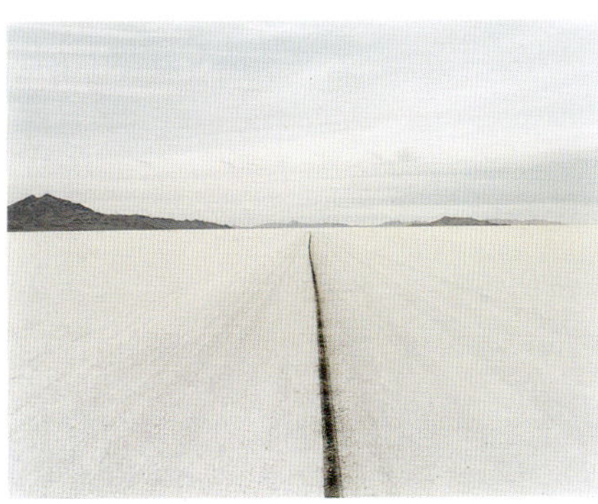
135

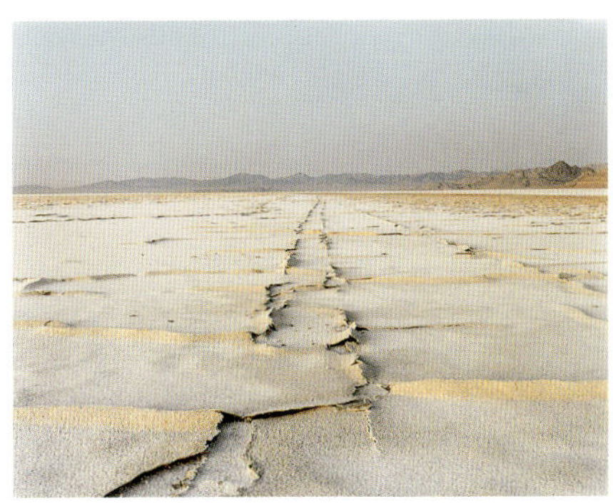
136

137

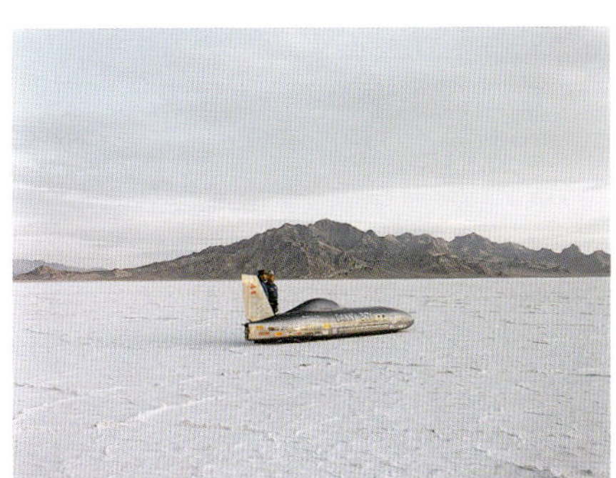
138

GORDON MATTA-CLARK

129
Walls. 1972. Gelatin silver print from a series, 15 × 20$\frac{3}{4}$ inches

130
Walls. 1972. Gelatin silver print from a series, 15 × 20$\frac{3}{4}$ inches

131
Walls. 1972 Gelatin silver print from a series, 15 × 20$\frac{3}{4}$ inches

132
Bingo. 1973. Chromogenic process print, 63$\frac{1}{2}$ × 25$\frac{1}{4}$ inches

STEVE McQUEEN

133
Barrage #44. 1998. Chromogenic process print, mounted between plexiglass, from a series, 18 × 27 inches

134
Barrage #51. 1998. Chromogenic process color print, mounted between plexiglass, from a series, 18 × 27 inches

RICHARD MISRACH

135
Black Line, Bonneville Salt Flats. 1992. Chromogenic process print, 41 × 51 inches

136
Encrusted Tracks, Bonneville Salt Flats. 1992. Chromogenic process print, 41 × 51 inches

137
Carson Sink 10.4.95 6:45 p.m. 1995–97. Unique laminated chromogenic process print in artist's frame, 48$\frac{1}{4}$ × 60$\frac{1}{4}$ inches

138
Danny Boy, Bonneville Salt Flats. 1992. Chromogenic process print, 41 × 51 inches

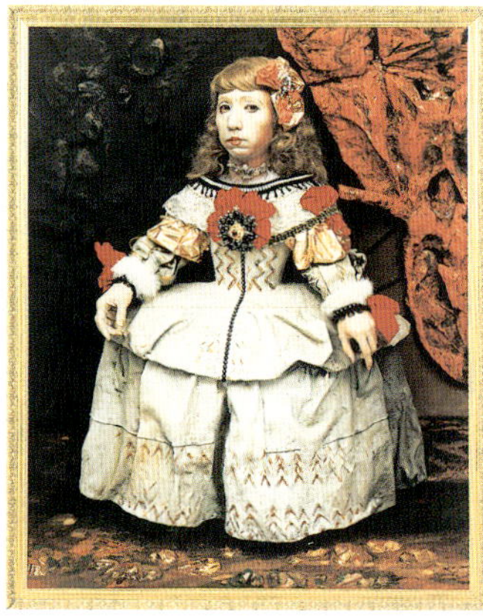

139

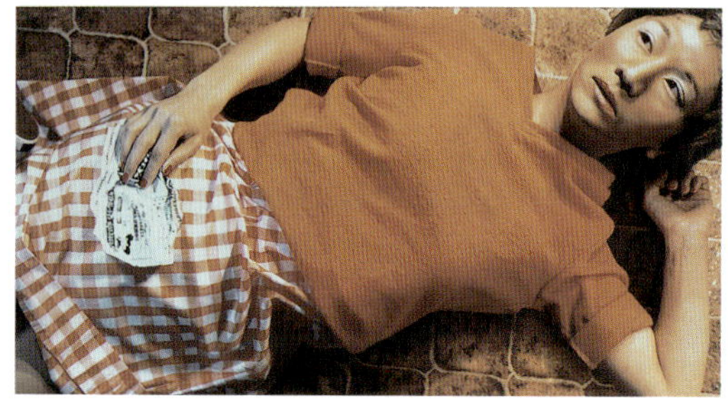

140

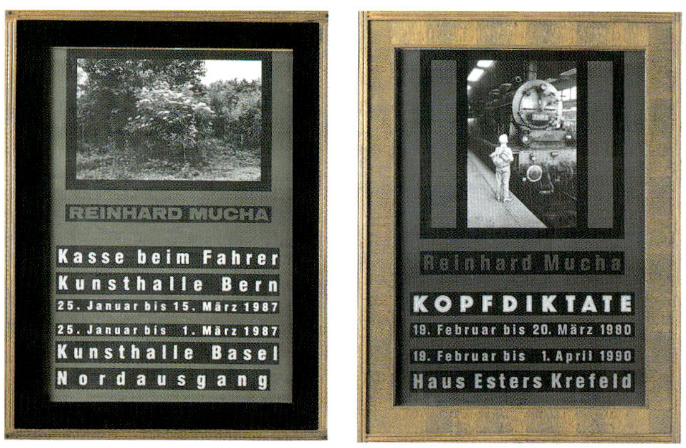

141

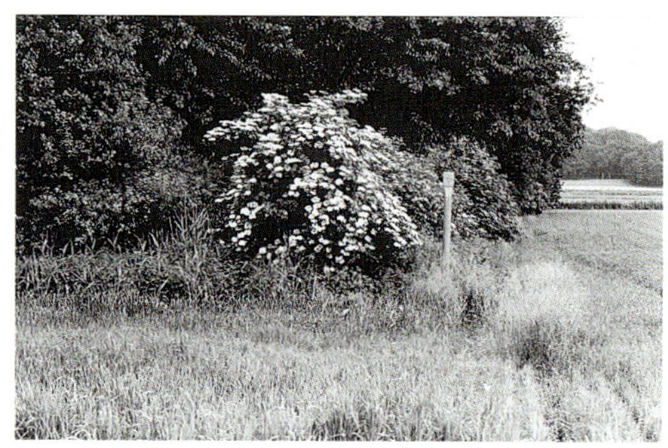

142

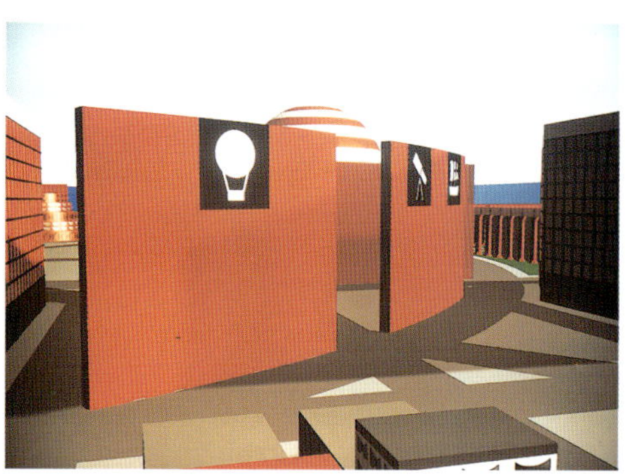

143

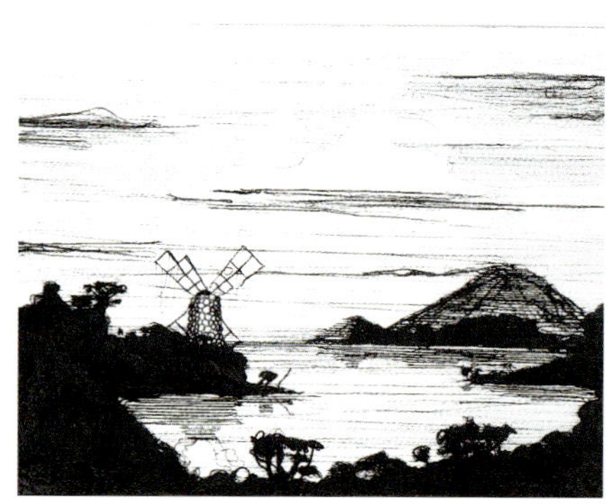

144

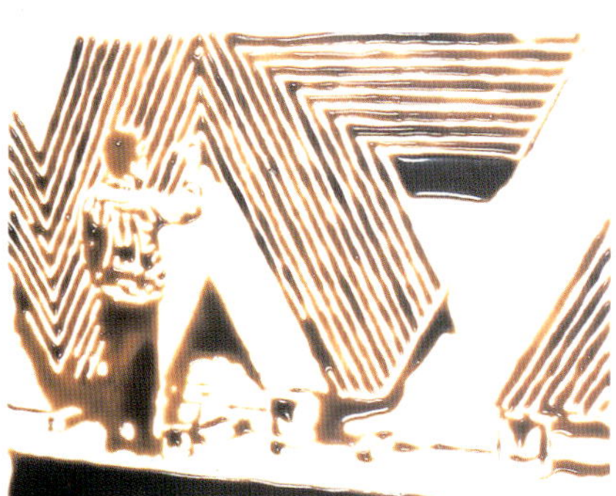

145

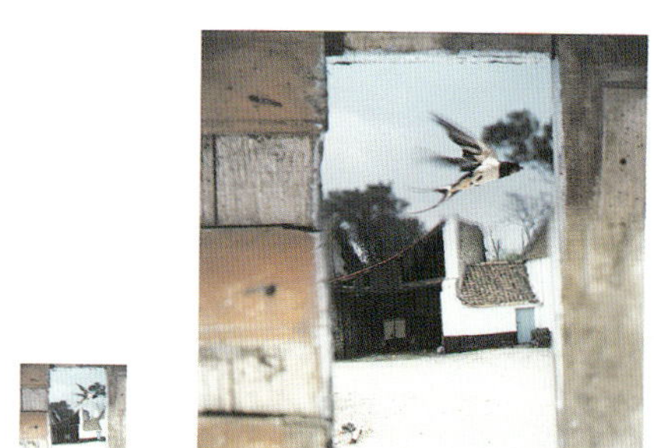

146

YASUMASA MORIMURA

139

Daughter of Art History (Princess A). 1990. Chromogenic process print with acrylic gel medium, in artist's gilded frame, $89\frac{3}{8} \times 71\frac{1}{2}$ inches

140

To My Little Sister, For Cindy Sherman. 1998. Silver dye bleach process print, mounted on aluminum, $25\frac{1}{2} \times 46\frac{1}{4}$ inches

REINHARD MUCHA

141

BBK Edition. 1990. Diptych: offset lithographic prints, artist's oak frames with wood panel construction, and reverse painted glass, $45\frac{1}{4} \times 34\frac{1}{4}$ inches

142

Für Frau Holle (For Frau Holle). 1978. Gelatin silver print, $7\frac{3}{4} \times 11\frac{5}{8}$ inches

MATT MULLICAN

143

Untitled (Wall of History). 1990. Color transparency in aluminum light box, $36\frac{3}{4} \times 48\frac{3}{4} \times 6\frac{3}{4}$ inches

VIK MUNIZ

144

7500 yards (Landscape without an angel after "Hagar and Angel" by Claude Lorrain), 1997. 1997. Toned gelatin silver print, $19 \times 23\frac{1}{4}$ inches

145

Frankstella. 1999. Silver dye bleach process print, $51\frac{1}{2} \times 63\frac{3}{4}$ inches

JEAN-LUC MYLAYNE

146

No. 4 (Juin, Juillet, Août) (June, July, August). 1979. Two silver dye bleach process prints in separate mat windows, from a series, $48\frac{5}{8} \times 64\frac{1}{4}$ inches

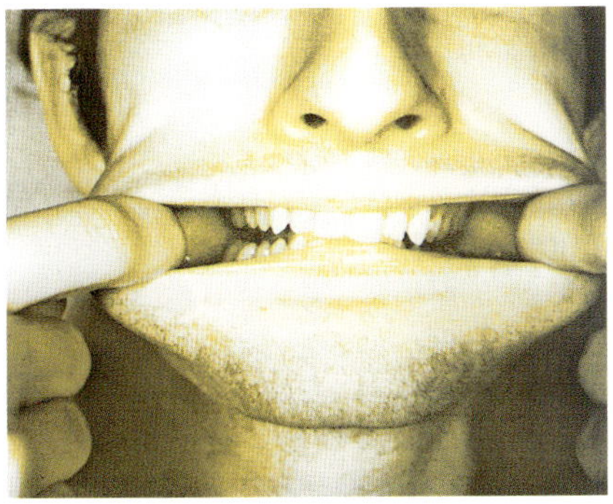

147

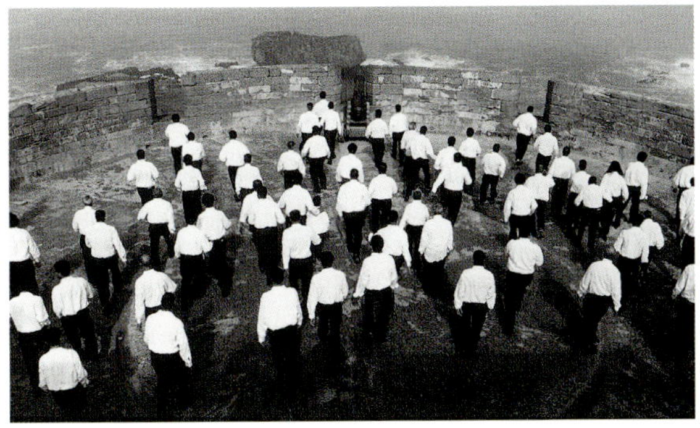

148

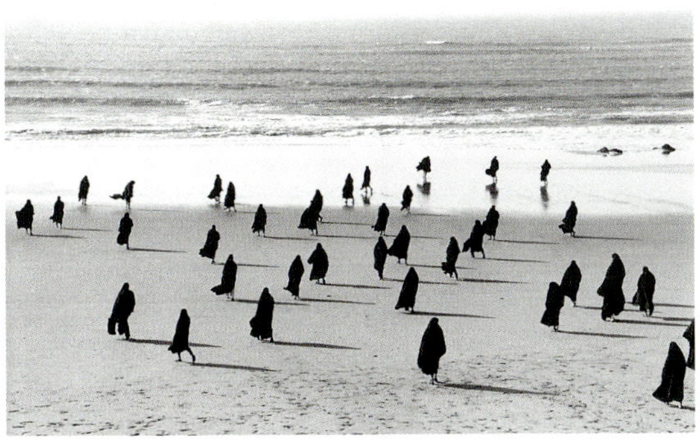

149

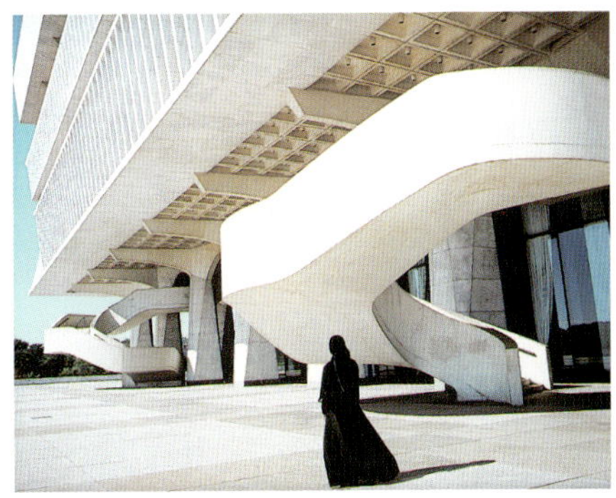

150

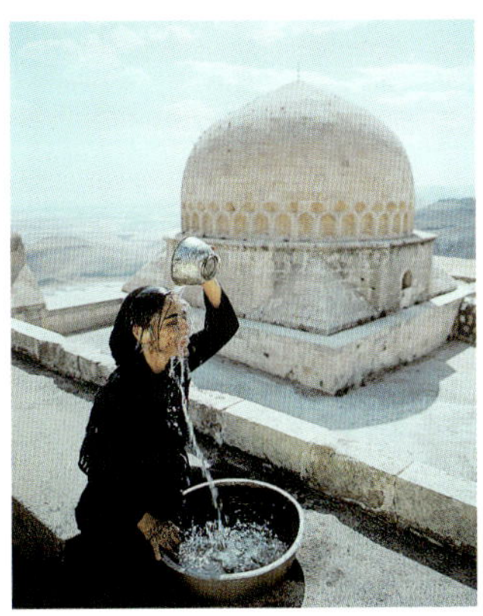

151

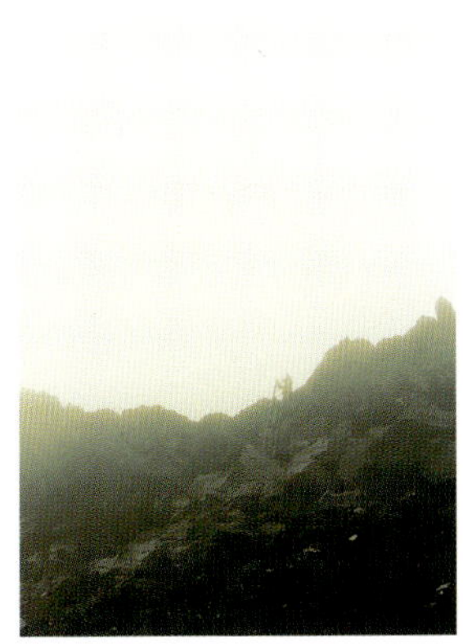

152

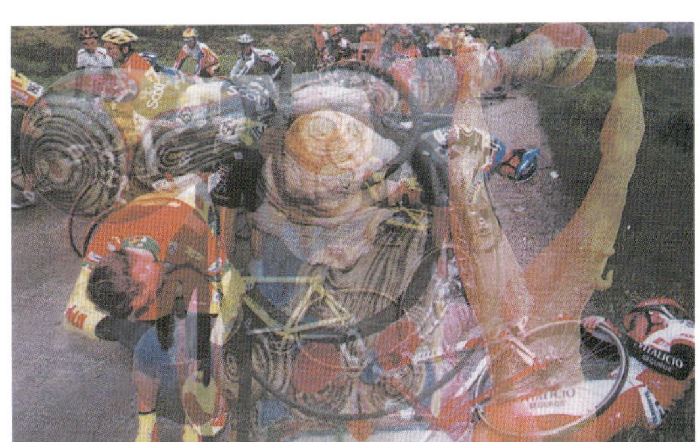

153

BRUCE NAUMAN

147

Studies for Holograms (a–e) (detail). 1970. Suite of five half-tone screened color photographs, 26 × 26 inches each

SHIRIN NESHAT

148

Rapture Series. 1999. Gelatin silver print, 43½ × 70½ inches

149

Rapture Series. 1999. Gelatin silver print, 45½ × 70½

150

Soliloquy Series. 2000. Silver dye bleach process print, 48¼ × 60¼ inches

151

Soliloquy Series. 2000. Silver dye bleach process print, 60¼ × 48¼ inches

RIKA NOGUCHI

152

A Prime #13. 1999. Chromogenic process print from a series, 37 × 26 inches

ALBERT OEHLEN

153

Unfall. 1999. Digitally composited inkjet print, 54 × 80½ inches

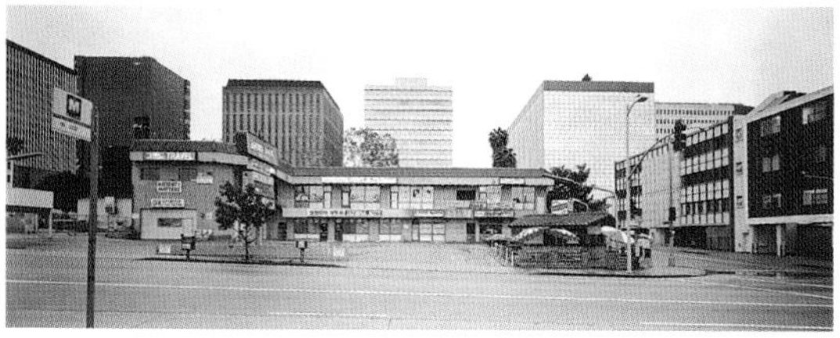
154

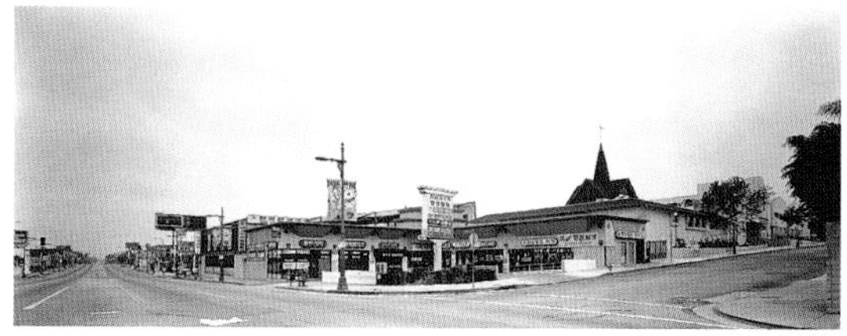
155

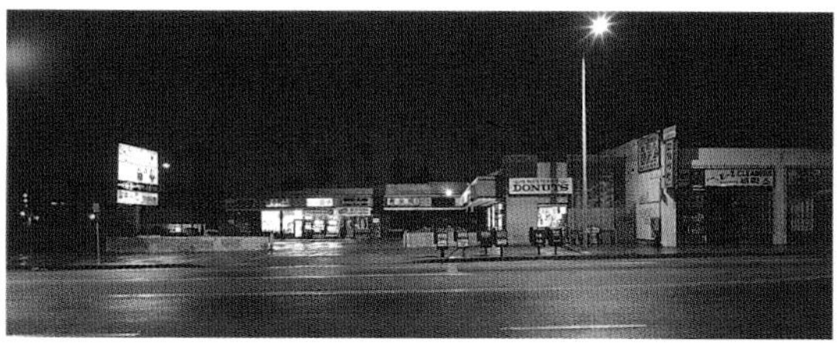
156

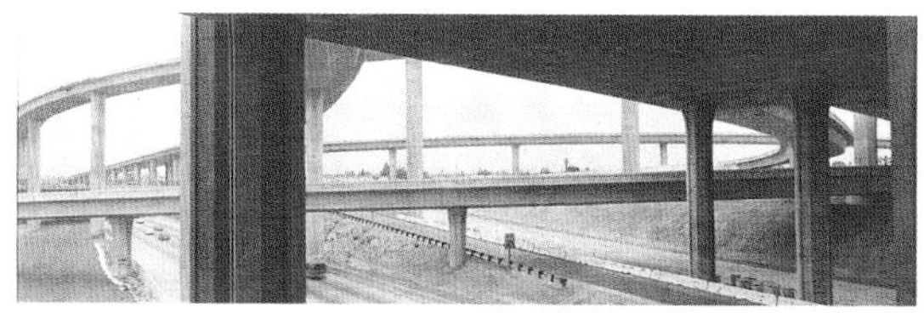
157

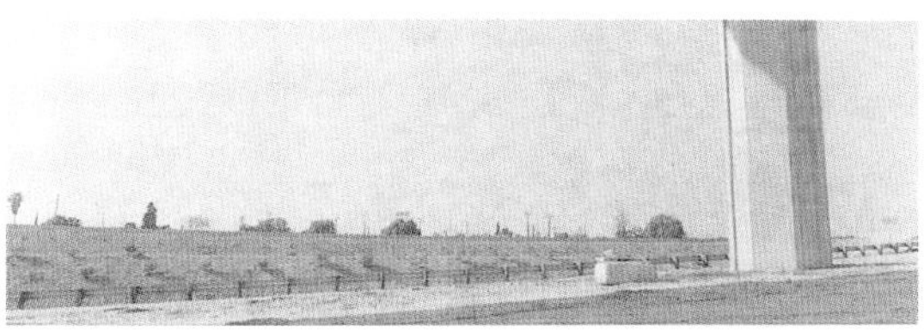
158

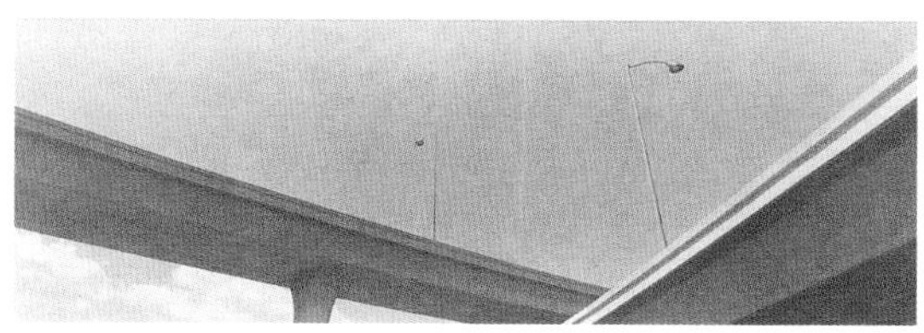
159

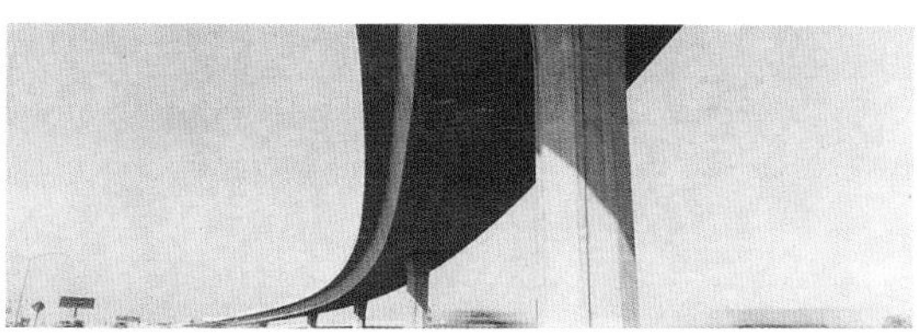
160

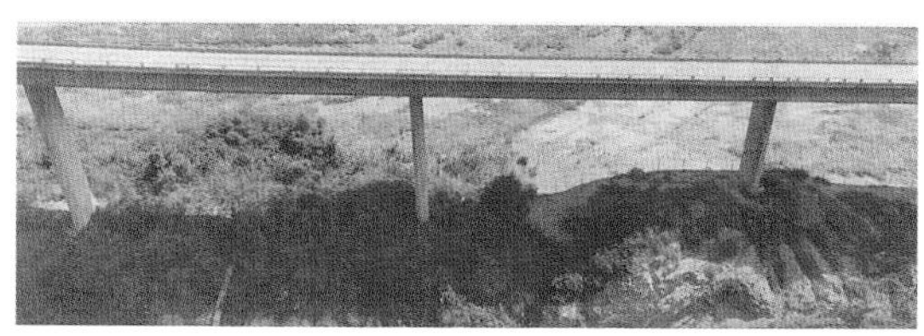
161

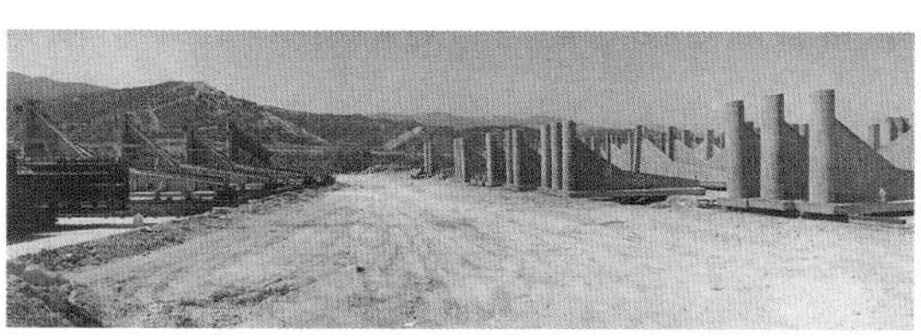
162

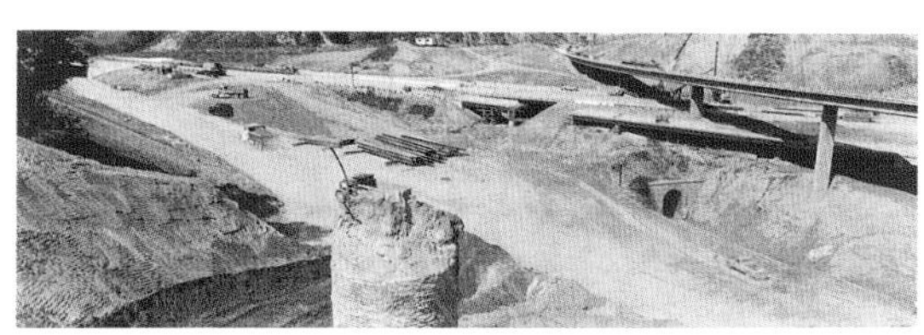
163

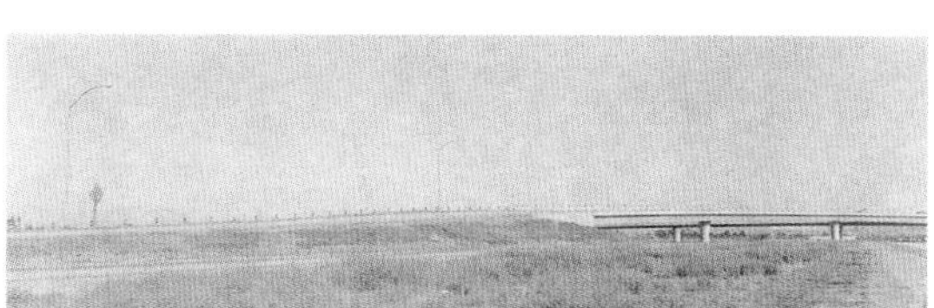
164

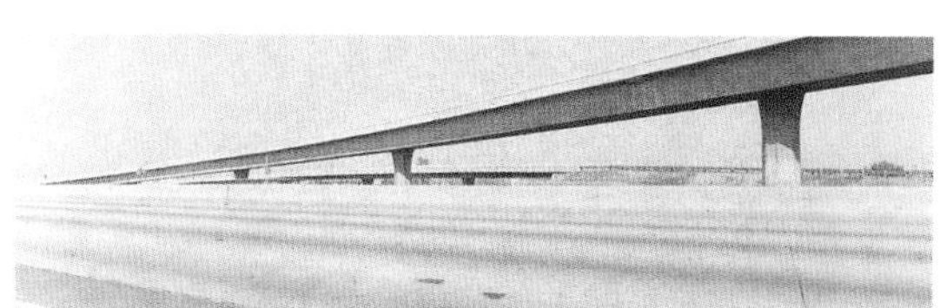
165

CATHERINE OPIE

154
Untitled #1. From the *Mini-mall* series. 1997. Iris print on rag paper, $22 \times 46\frac{3}{4}$ inches

155
Untitled #4. From the *Mini-mall* series. 1997. Iris print on rag paper, $22 \times 46\frac{3}{4}$ inches

156
Untitled #8. From the *Mini-mall* series. 1997 Iris print on rag paper, $22 \times 46\frac{3}{4}$ inches

157
Untitled #11. From the *Freeway* series. 1994. Platinum print, $2\frac{1}{8} \times 6\frac{1}{2}$ inches

158
Untitled #12. From the *Freeway* series. 1994. Platinum print, $2\frac{1}{8} \times 6\frac{1}{2}$ inches

159
Untitled #14. From the *Freeway* series. 1994. Platinum print, $2\frac{1}{8} \times 6\frac{1}{2}$ inches

160
Untitled #20. From the *Freeway* series. 1994. Platinum print, $2\frac{1}{8} \times 6\frac{1}{2}$ inches

161
Untitled #21. From the *Freeway* series. 1994. Platinum print, $2\frac{1}{8} \times 6\frac{1}{2}$ inches

162
Untitled #22. From the *Freeway* series. 1994. Platinum print, $2\frac{1}{8} \times 6\frac{1}{2}$ inches

163
Untitled #23. From the *Freeway* series. 1994. Platinum print, $2\frac{1}{8} \times 6\frac{1}{2}$ inches

164
Untitled #24. From the *Freeway* series. 1994. Platinum print, $2\frac{1}{8} \times 6\frac{1}{2}$ inches

165
Untitled #28. From the *Freeway* series. 1994. Platinum print, $2\frac{1}{8} \times 6\frac{1}{2}$ inches

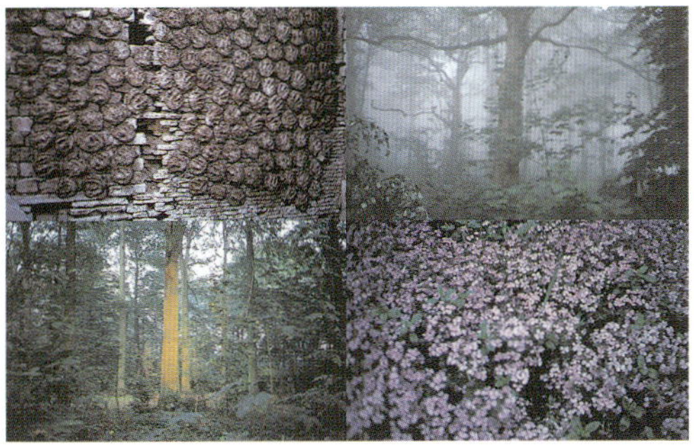
166

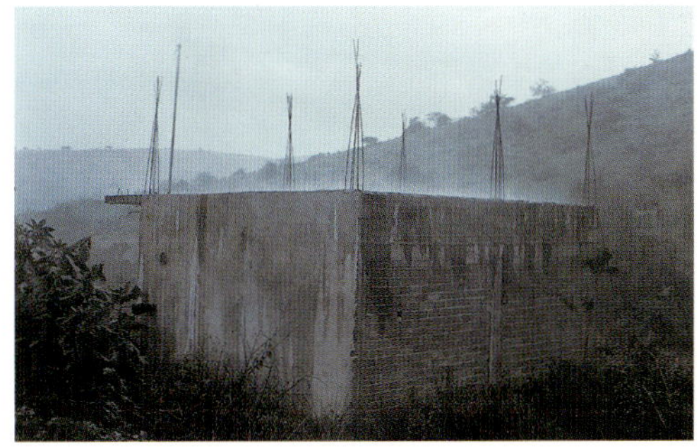
167

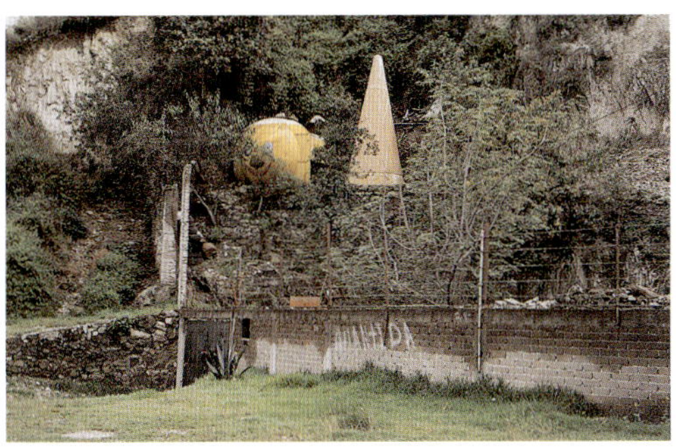
168

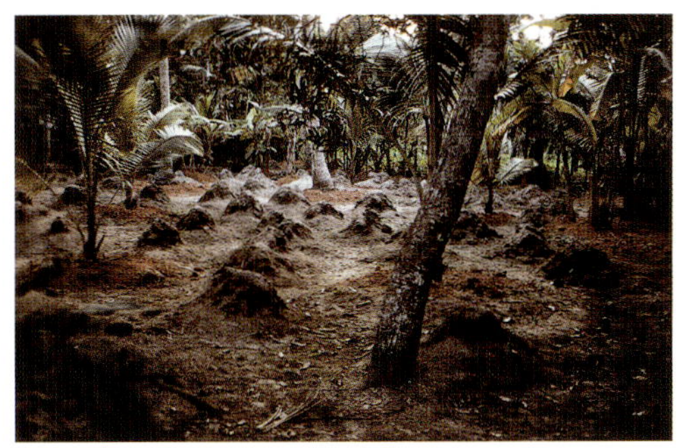
169

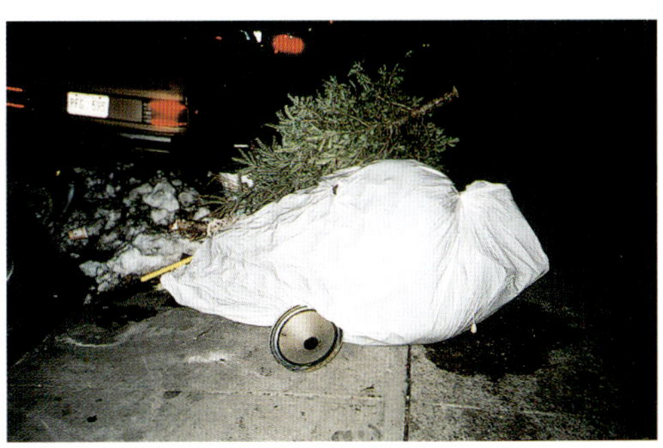
170

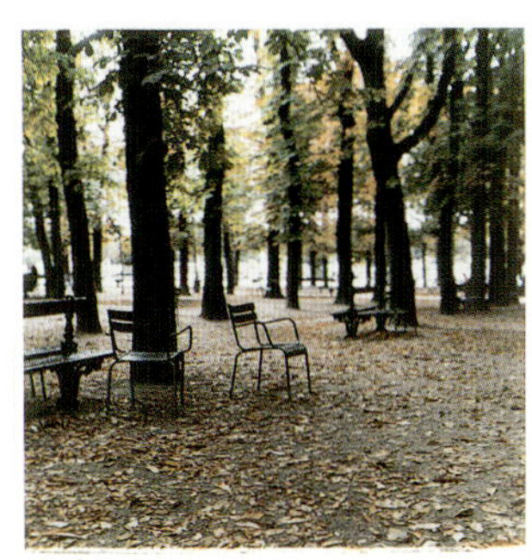
171

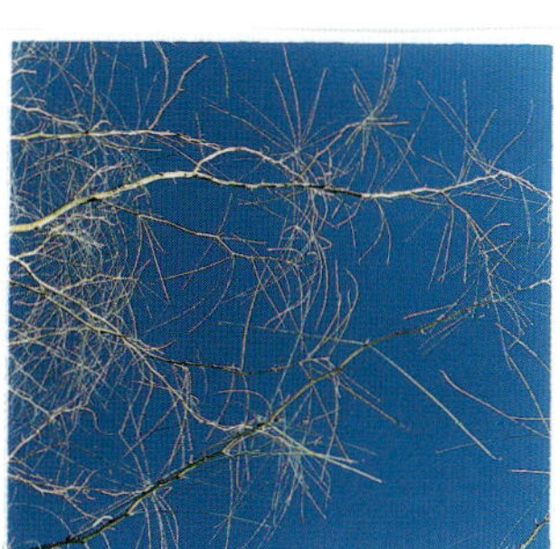
172

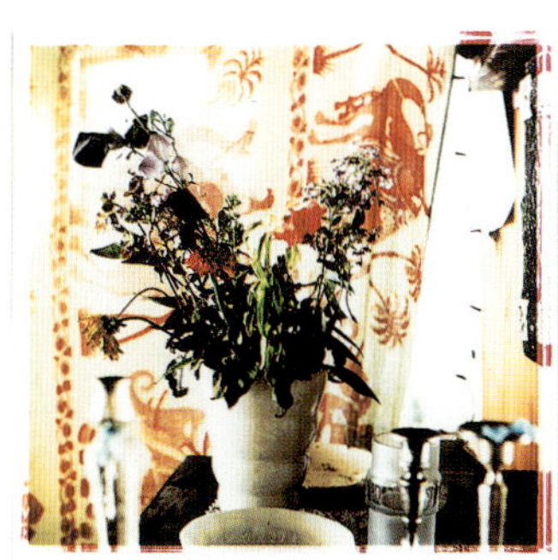
173

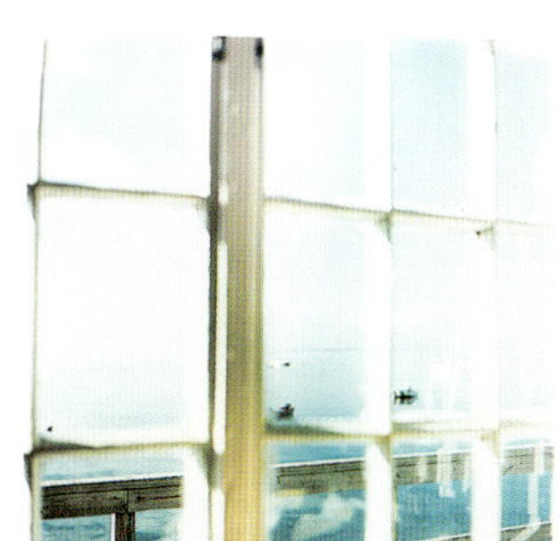
174

GABRIEL OROZCO

166

Follaje (Foliage). 1997. Iris print, 22¼ × 34 inches

167

House and Rain. 1998. Silver dye bleach process print, 12 × 18⅜ inches

168

Ice Cream House. 1995. Silver dye bleach process print, 12 × 18⅜ inches

169

Kerala Garden. 1998. Silver dye bleach process print, 12 × 18⅜ inches

TONY OURSLER

170

Christmas Tree with Speaker. 1997. Unique laminated silver dye bleach process print, mounted on aluminum panel, 23⅜ × 35 inches

JACK PIERSON

171

A Chair. 1993. Chromogenic process print, 43½ × 33½ inches

172

Desert Tree. 1995. Chromogenic process print, 40 × 32 inches

173

Faded Flowers. 1995. Chromogenic process print, 40 × 32 inches

174

Window Panes. 1995. Chromogenic process print, 40 × 32 inches

175

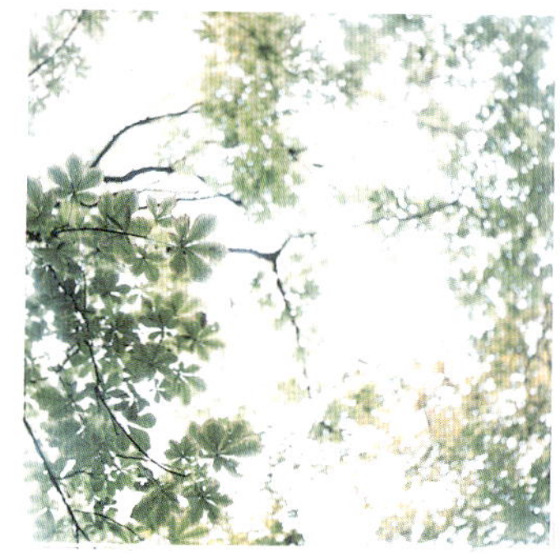

176

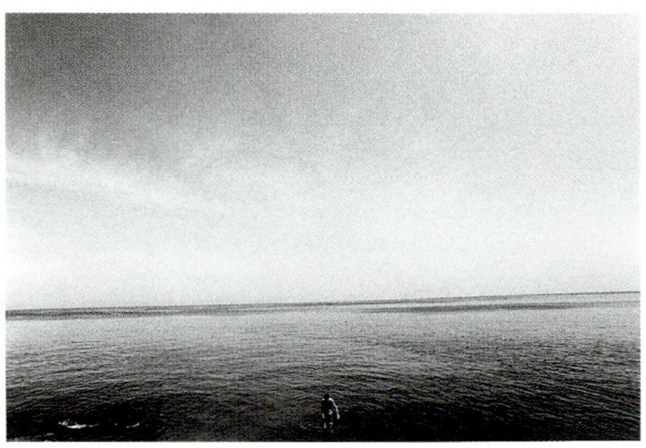

177

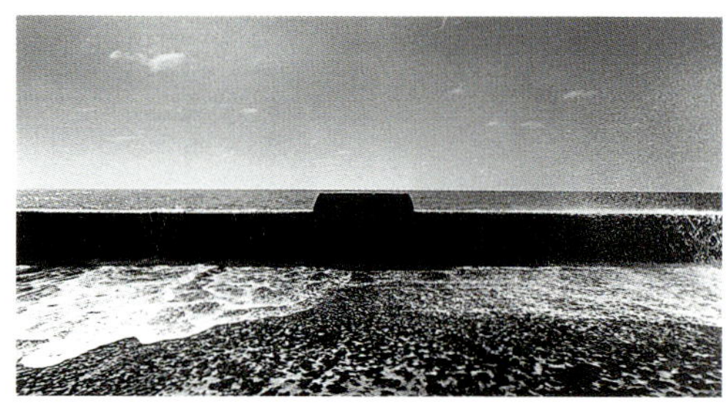

178

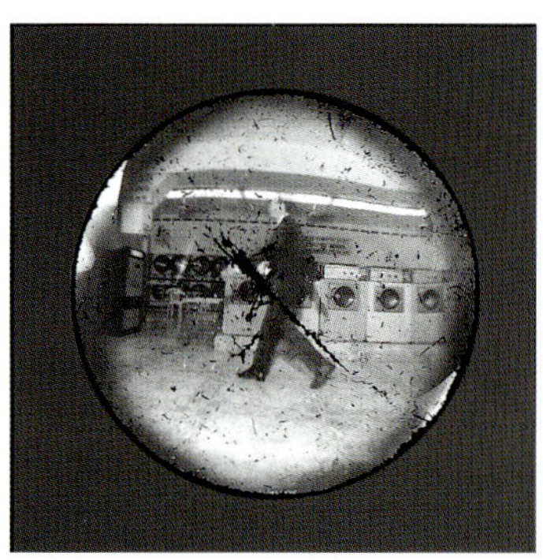

179

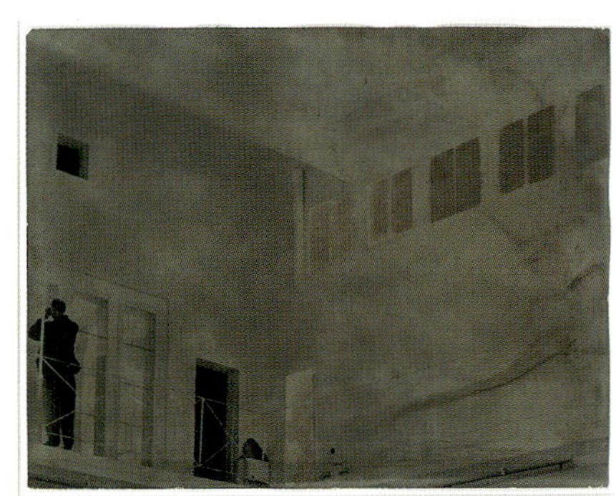

180

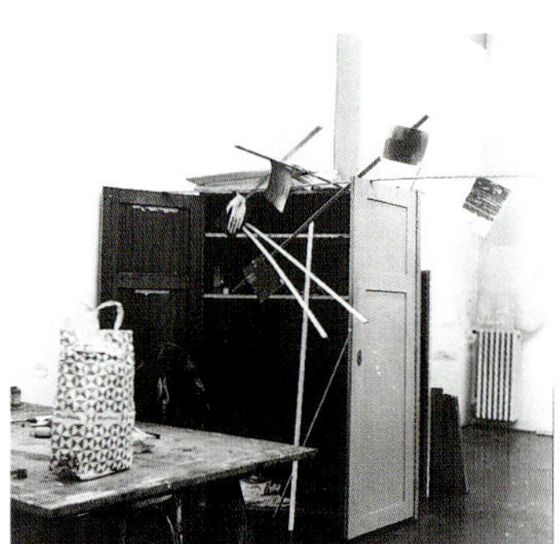

181

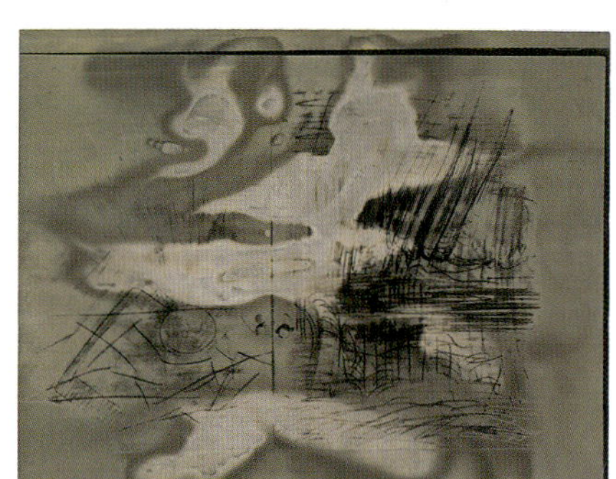

182

JACK PIERSON

175

Red Strip. 1998. Chromogenic process print, mounted on plexiglass, 30×40 inches

176

Trees in Paris. 1993. Chromogenic process print, $43\frac{1}{2} \times 33\frac{1}{2}$ inches

MANUEL PINA

177

Untitled I. From the *Aguas Baldias (Barren Waters)* series. 1993. Gelatin silver print, $11\frac{1}{4} \times 19\frac{7}{8}$ inches

178

Untitled II. From the *Aguas Baldias (Barren Waters)* series. 1993. Gelatin silver print, $10\frac{3}{4} \times 17\frac{3}{4}$ inches

STEVEN PIPPIN

179

Laundromat—Locomotion (Walking Backwards L–L No. 04) (detail). 1997. Suite of twelve gelatin silver contact prints made from negatives exposed and processed with a front loading washing machine, $32\frac{1}{2} \times 32\frac{1}{2}$ inches each

SIGMAR POLKE

180

Biennale de Venise (1). 1986. Unique gelatin silver photograph with manipulated chemistry, $9\frac{3}{8} \times 11\frac{7}{8}$ inches

181

Untitled. 1968/1990. Gelatin silver print, $19\frac{3}{8} \times 19\frac{1}{2}$ inches

182

Untitled. 1988. Unique gelatin silver photogram with manipulated chemistry, $19\frac{1}{2} \times 23\frac{5}{8}$ inches

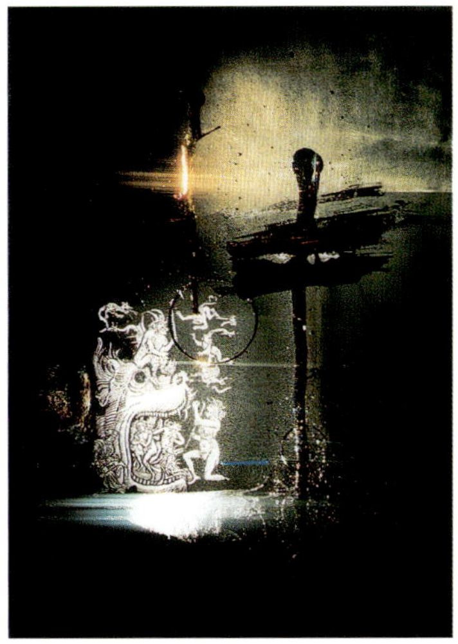
183

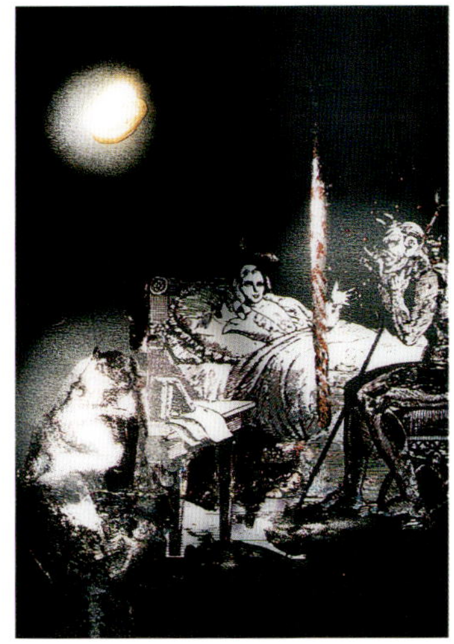
184

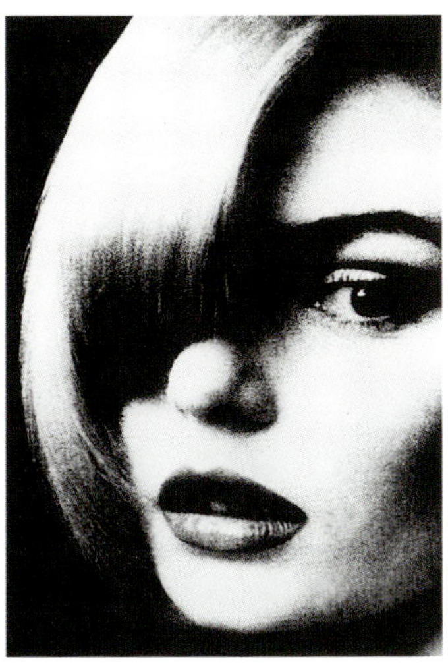
185

186

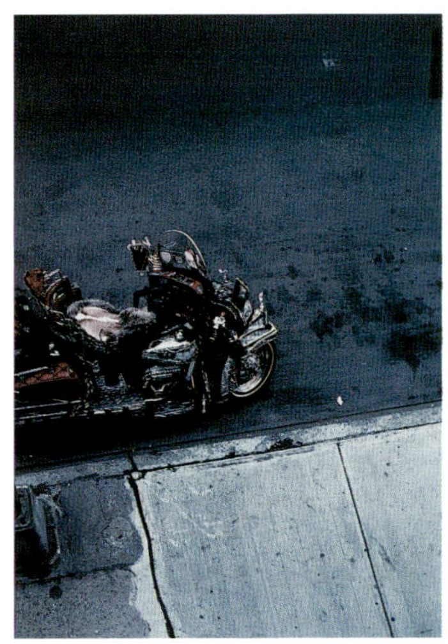
187

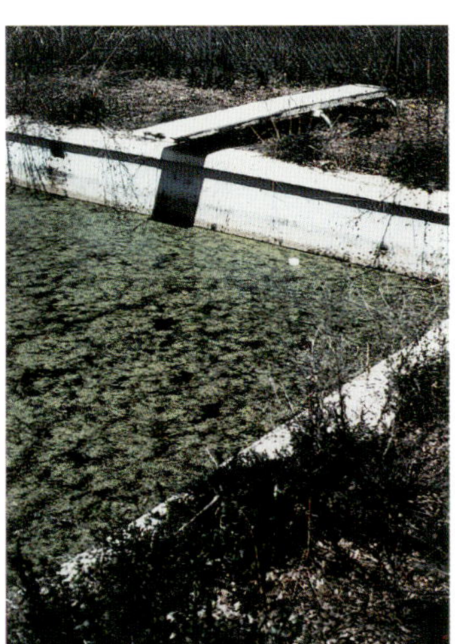
188

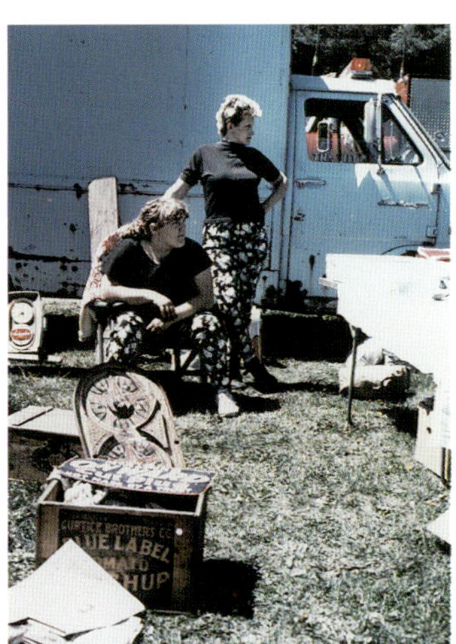

189

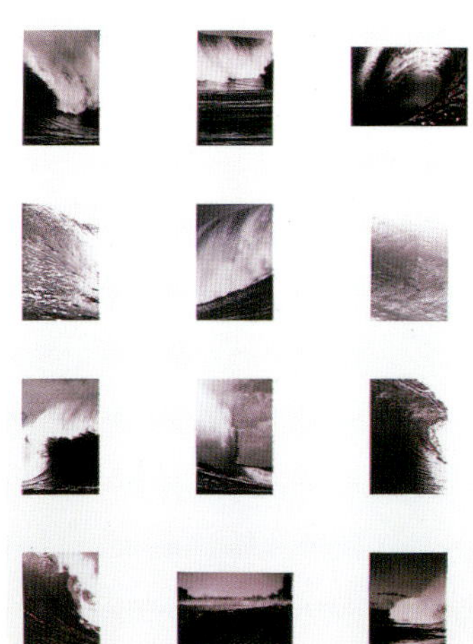
190

SIGMAR POLKE AND AUGUSTINA VON NAGEL

183
Landscape. From the *Aachener Strasse* series. 1995. Chromogenic process print, face mounted to plexiglass $72\frac{1}{2} \times 50\frac{1}{4}$ inches

184
When I Was Young. From the *Aachener Strasse* series. 1995. Chromogenic process print, face mounted to plexiglass, $72\frac{1}{2} \times 49\frac{1}{2}$ inches

RICHARD PRINCE

185
Untitled (Fashion). 1982–84. Ektacolor print, $23\frac{1}{4} \times 15\frac{1}{2}$ inches

186
Untitled (Adult Comedy Action Drama). 1995. Ektacolor print, $19\frac{1}{2} \times 12\frac{3}{8}$ inches

187
Untitled (Adult Comedy Action Drama). 1995. Ektacolor print, $19\frac{1}{2} \times 12\frac{3}{8}$ inches

188
Untitled (Adult Comedy Action Drama). 1995. Ektacolor print, $19\frac{1}{2} \times 12\frac{3}{8}$ inches

189
Untitled (Adult Comedy Action Drama). 1995. Ektacolor print, $19\frac{1}{2} \times 12\frac{3}{8}$ inches

190
The Velvet Beach. 1985. Ektacolor print, 87×48 inches

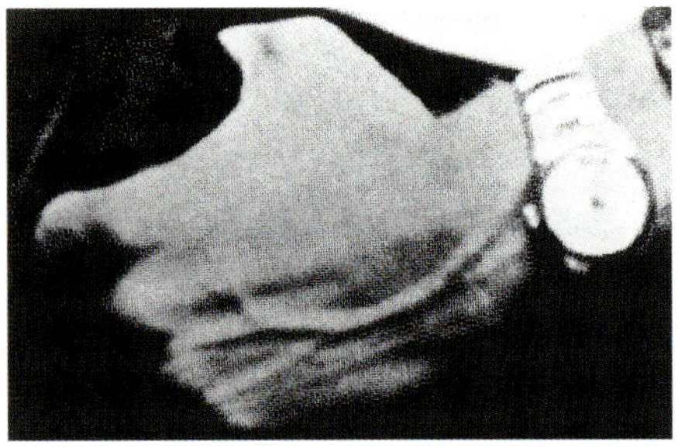

191

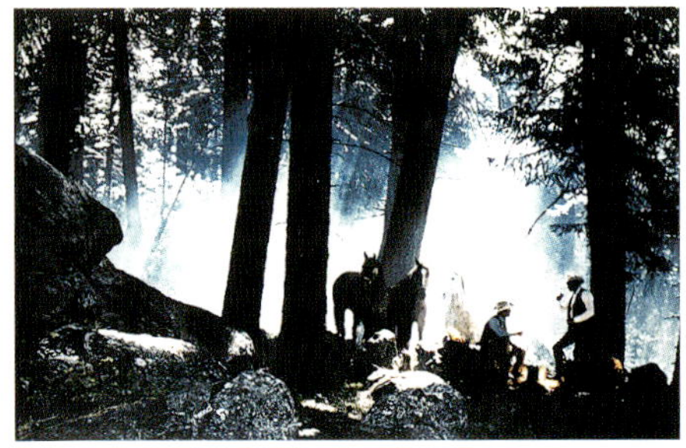

192

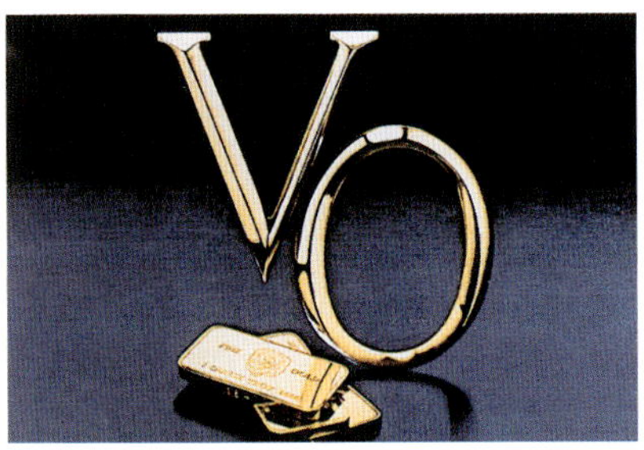

193

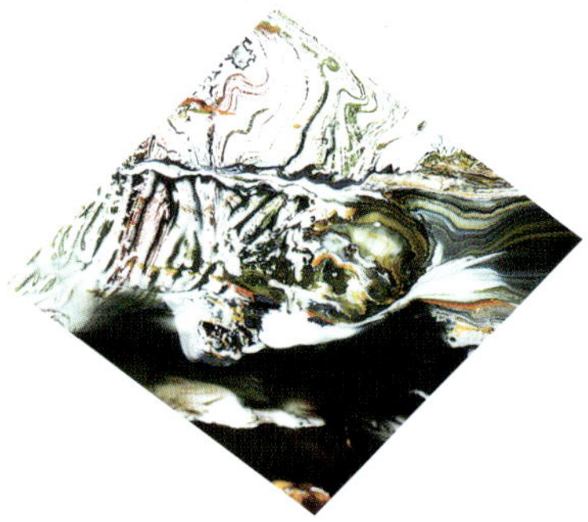

194

195

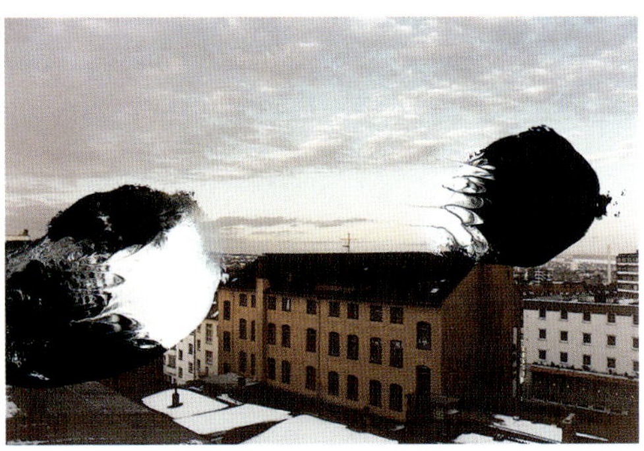

196

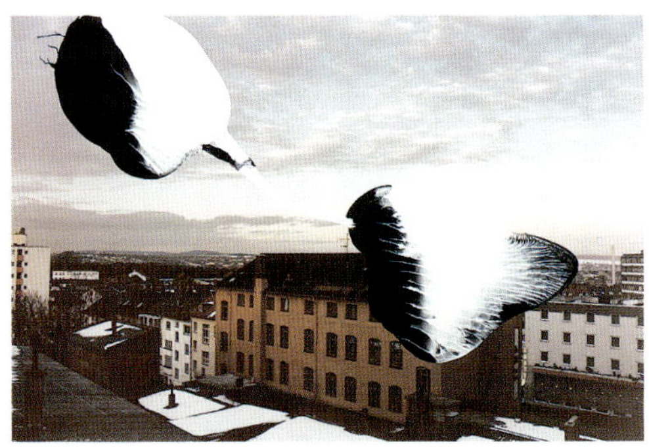

197

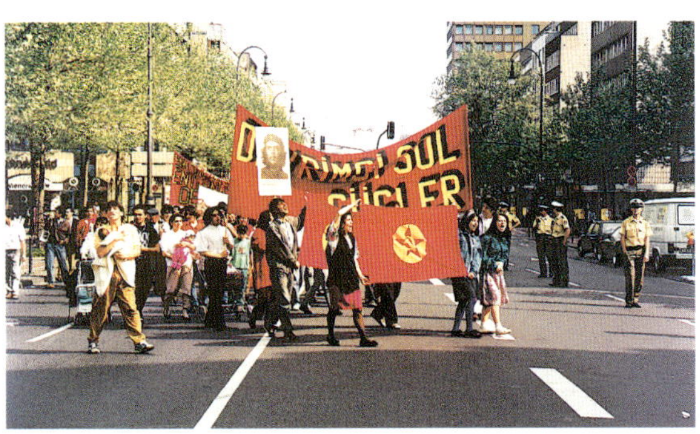

198

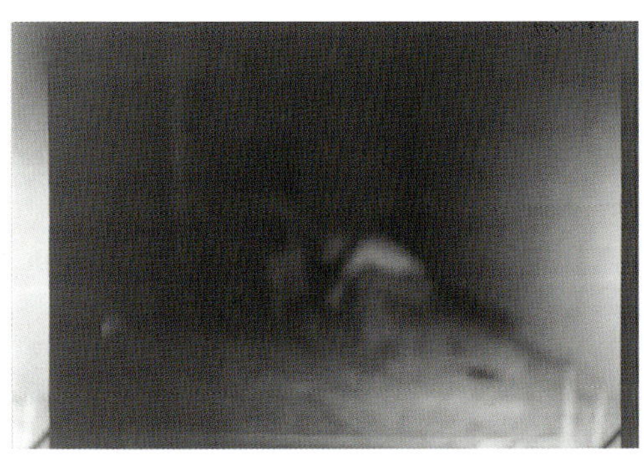

199

RICHARD PRINCE

191

Untitled (Man's Hand with Watch). 1980. Ektacolor print, $39\frac{3}{4} \times 59$ inches

192

Untitled (Cowboy). 1997. Ektacolor print, $56\frac{1}{2} \times 80\frac{1}{4}$ inches

193

Untitled (Portfolio 1, October Magazine). 1977. Ektacolor print, $16\frac{7}{8} \times 20\frac{7}{8}$ inches

GERHARD RICHTER

194

Ophelia. 1998. Silver dye bleach process print, mounted between plexiglass and aluminum board, $40 \times 45\frac{3}{4}$ inches

195

Untitled. 1989. Oil paint on offset print on paper, mounted to plastic, 35×35 inches

196

Untitled. 1992. Oil paint on chromogenic process print, $6\frac{1}{8} \times 9\frac{1}{8}$ inches

197

Untitled. 1992. Oil paint on chromogenic process print, $6\frac{1}{8} \times 9\frac{1}{8}$ inches

198

Demo (Portfolio 2, October Magazine). 1993/1997. Color lithograph, $9\frac{3}{4} \times 16\frac{3}{8}$ inches

199

Sechs Photo (Six Photos) (7.5.89) (detail). 1991. Suite of six sequenced gelatin silver prints, $13\frac{3}{8} \times 19\frac{1}{2}$ inches each

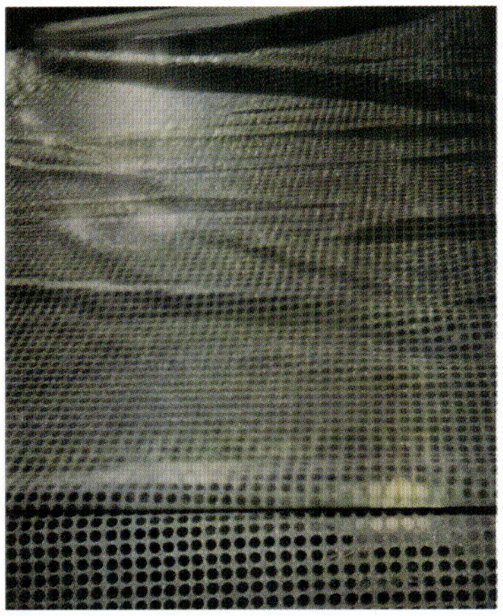

200

201

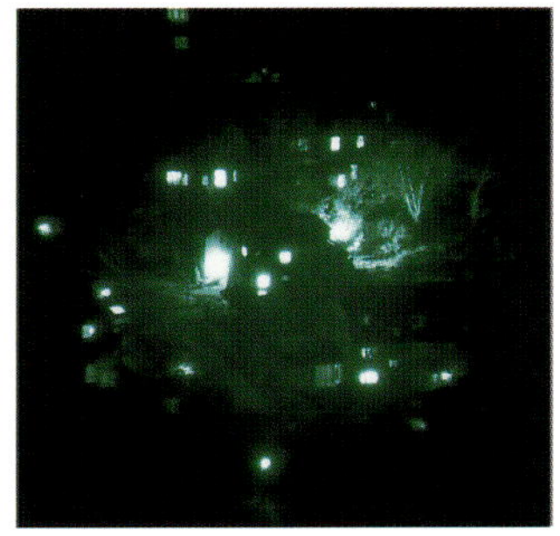

202

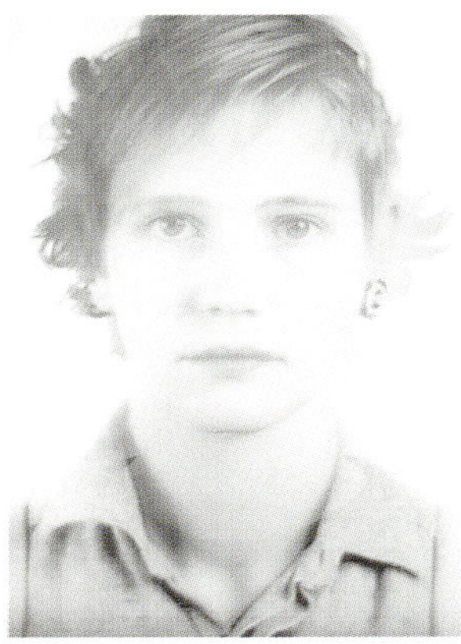

203

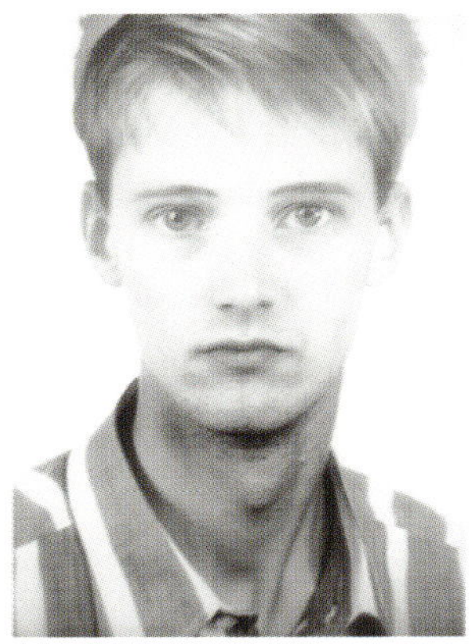

204

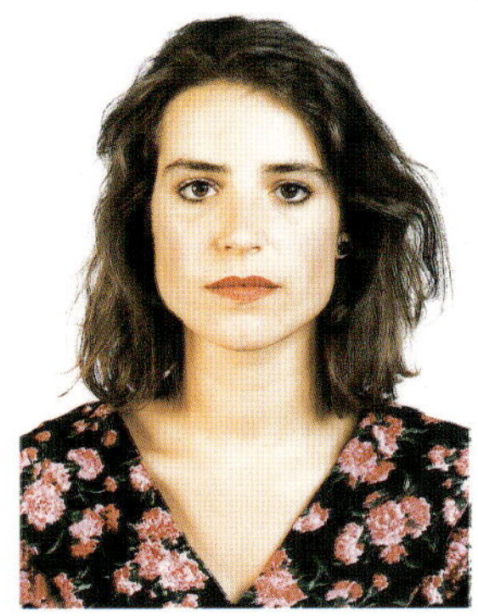

205

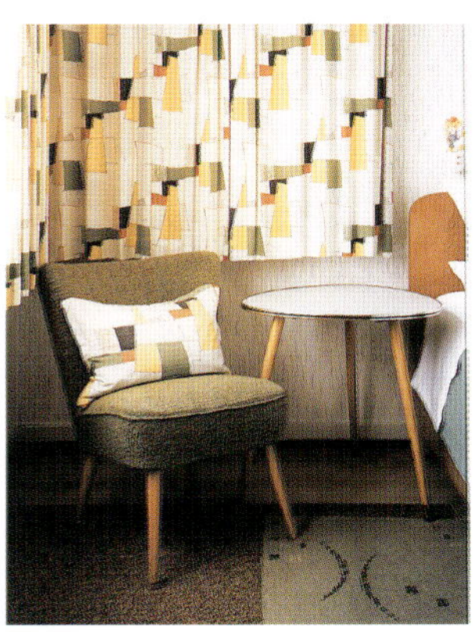

206

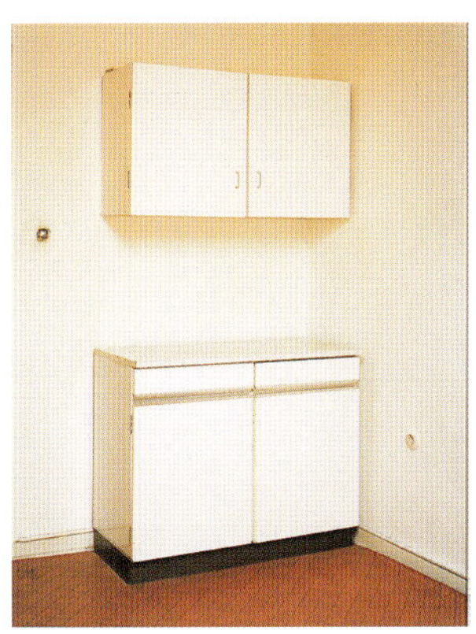

207

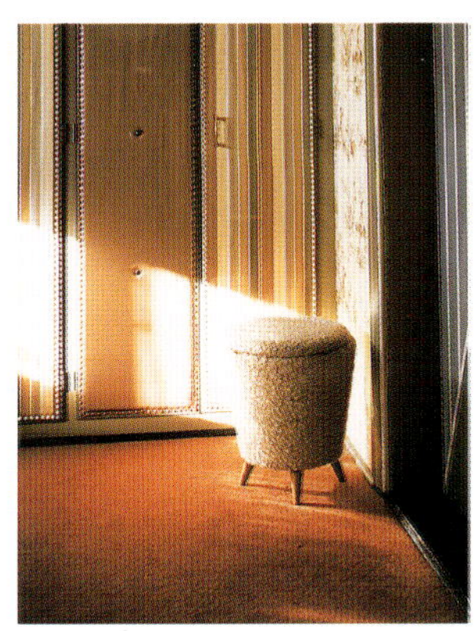

208

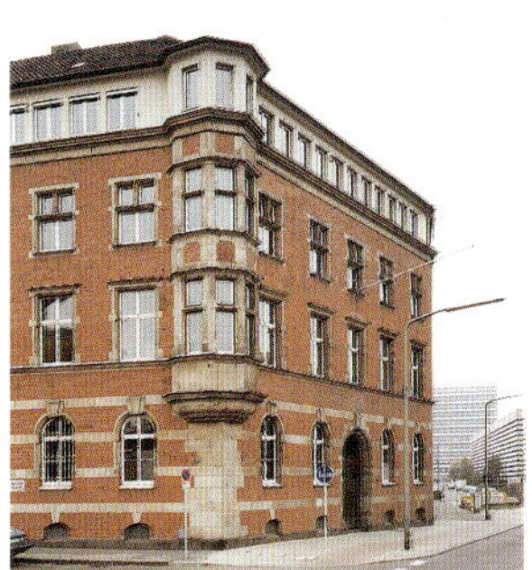

209

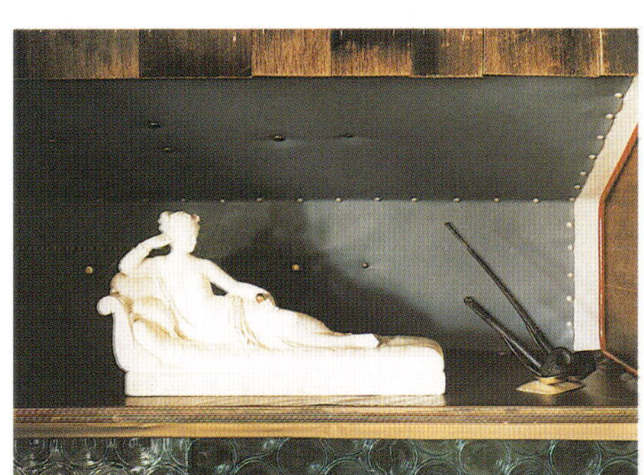

210

MARINA ROSENFELD

200
Untitled (The Sea). **1997–98. Lenticular photograph from a series, 26 × 22 inches**

THOMAS RUFF

201
19h 36m/ -35°. **1992. Chromogenic process print, face mounted to plexiglass, 8 feet $5\frac{3}{4}$ inches × $73\frac{1}{4}$ inches**

202
Nacht (Night) 19 II. **1995. Chromogenic process print, face mounted to plexiglass, $74\frac{3}{8} \times 74\frac{7}{8}$ inches**

203
Anders Portrat (Other Portrait) No. 109/97. **1994–95. Serigraph from a series, $80\frac{3}{4} \times 61\frac{1}{4}$ inches**

204
Anders Portrat (Other Portrait) No. 109A/11. **1995. Serigraph from a series, $80\frac{3}{4} \times 61\frac{1}{4}$ inches**

205
Portrait. **1988. Chromogenic process print, face mounted to plexiglass, $82\frac{3}{4} \times 65$ inches**

206
Interieur (Interior) (1B). **1980. Chromogenic process print, $10\frac{3}{4} \times 8$ inches**

207
Interieur (Interior) (2E). **1983. Chromogenic process print, $10\frac{3}{4} \times 8$ inches**

208
Interieur (Interior) (3D). **1982. Chromogenic process print, $10\frac{3}{4} \times 8$ inches**

209
Haus (House) #7 II. **1986. Chromogenic process print, face mounted to plexiglass, $92\frac{1}{2} \times 73\frac{3}{4}$ inches**

210
Interieur (Interior) (7E). **1983. Chromogenic process print, $8 \times 10\frac{3}{4}$ inches**

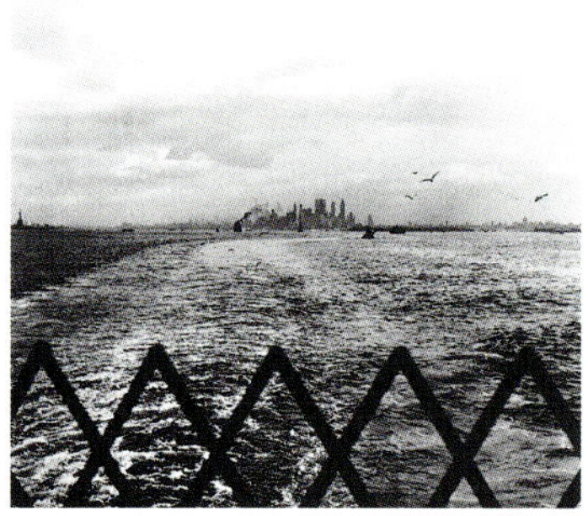

211

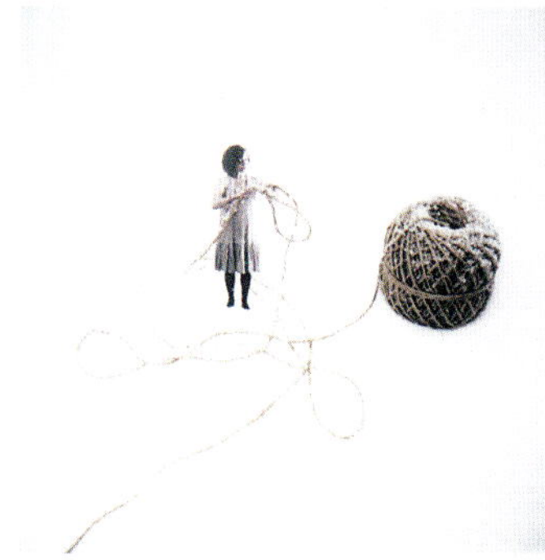

212

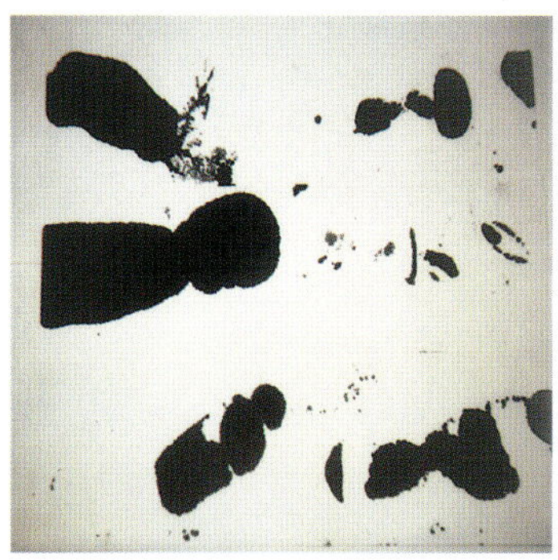

213

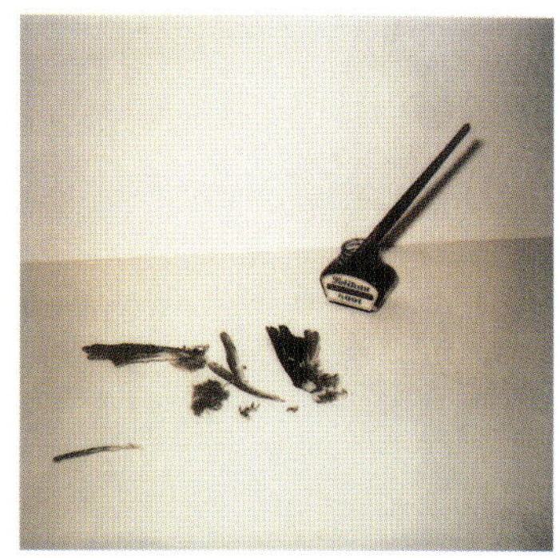

214

215

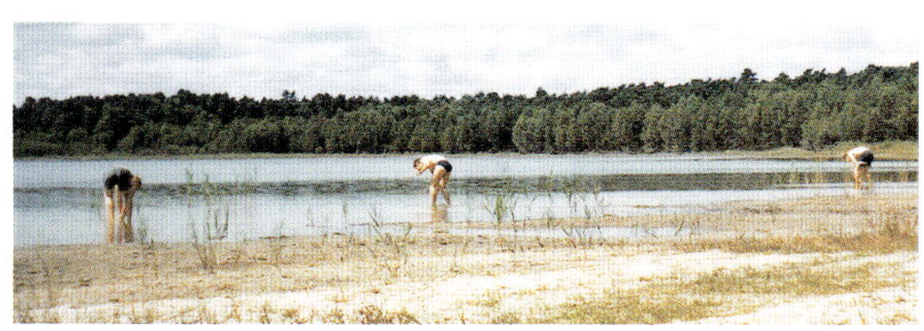

216

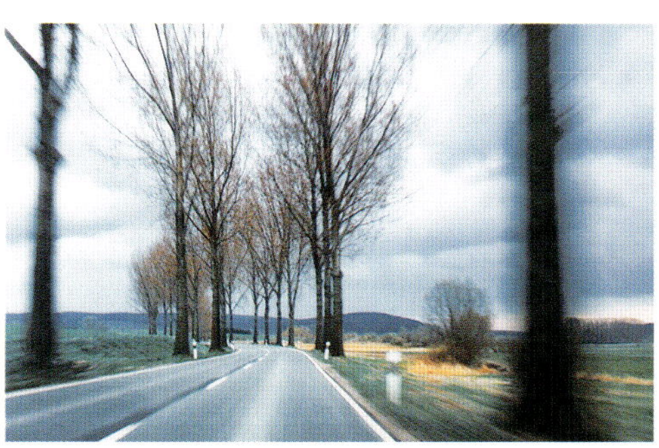

217

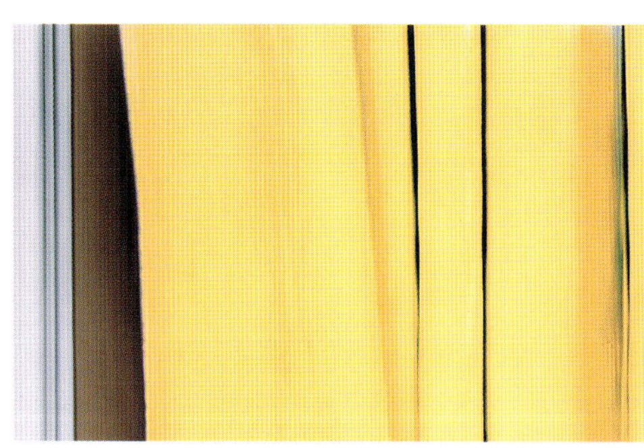

218

EDWARD RUSCHA

211

Manhattan Sea From Staten Island Ferry (Portfolio 2, October Magazine). **1961/1997. Gelatin silver print, $9\frac{7}{8} \times 9\frac{7}{8}$ inches**

CHRISTOPH RUTIMANN

212

Polaroids '95, 1-42 (Nr. 7). **1995. Chromogenic process print of a Polaroid, $19\frac{1}{2} \times 19\frac{1}{2}$ inches**

213

Flecken, die rein nichts Bezwecken (Stains that Achieve Absolutely Nothing). **1985. Silver dye bleach process print of a Polaroid, $15\frac{3}{4} \times 15\frac{3}{4}$ inches**

214

Pelikan und Gefieder (Pelikan and Feathers). **1985. Silver dye bleach process print of a Polaroid, $15\frac{3}{4} \times 15\frac{3}{4}$ inches**

JÖRG SASSE

215

7055, 1998. **1998. Chromogenic process print, face mounted to plexiglass, 36×86 inches**

216

5334, 1998. **1998. Chromogenic process print, mounted to plexiglass, $29\frac{1}{8} \times 86\frac{3}{4}$ inches**

217

5502, 1996. **1996. Chromogenic process print, face mounted to plexiglass, $41\frac{3}{4} \times 62\frac{3}{4}$ inches**

218

9619. **1999. Chromogenic process print, face mounted to plexiglass, $57\frac{1}{2} \times 86\frac{5}{8}$ inches**

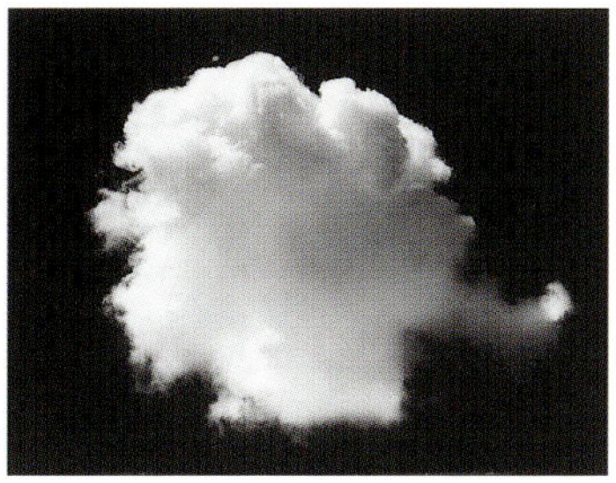
219

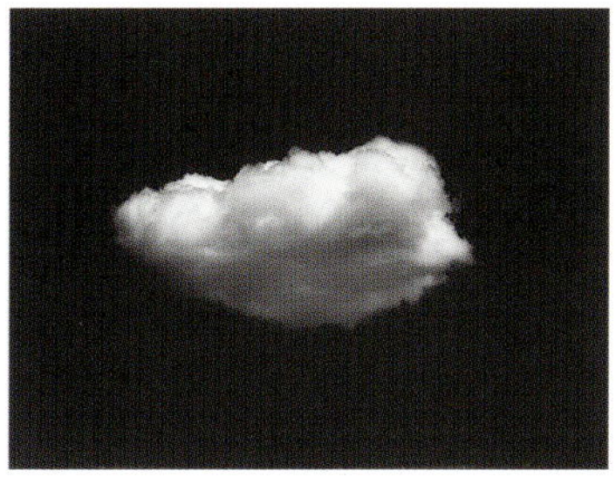
220

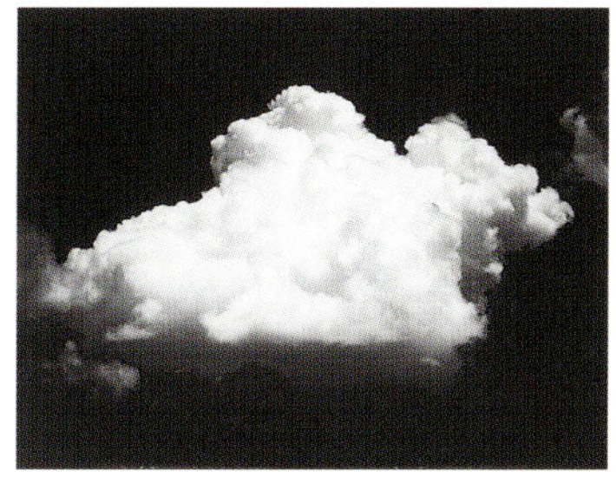
221

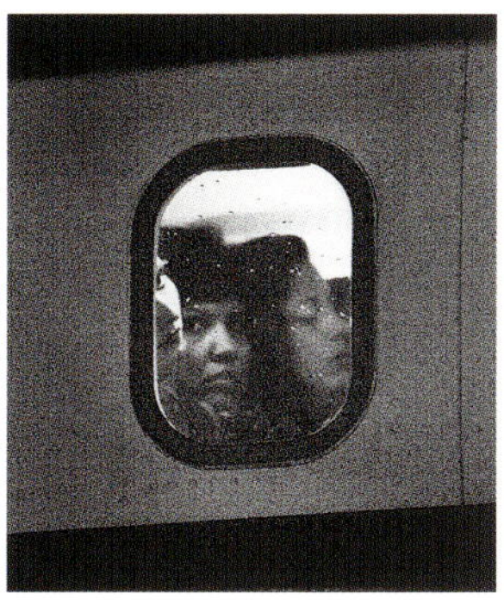
222

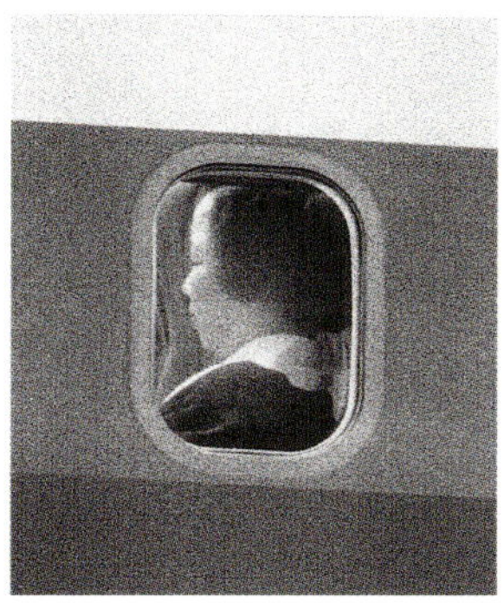
223

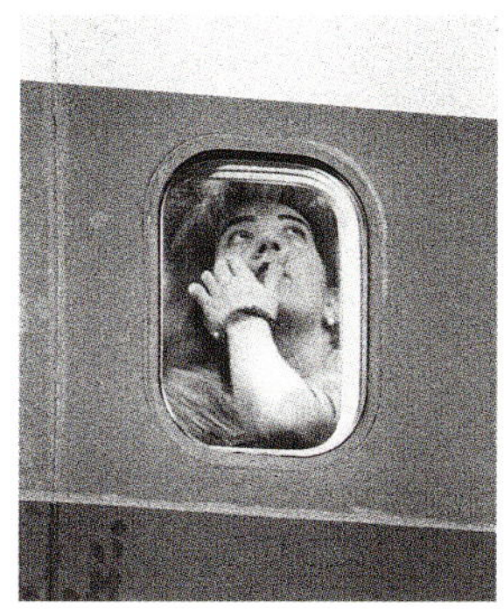
224

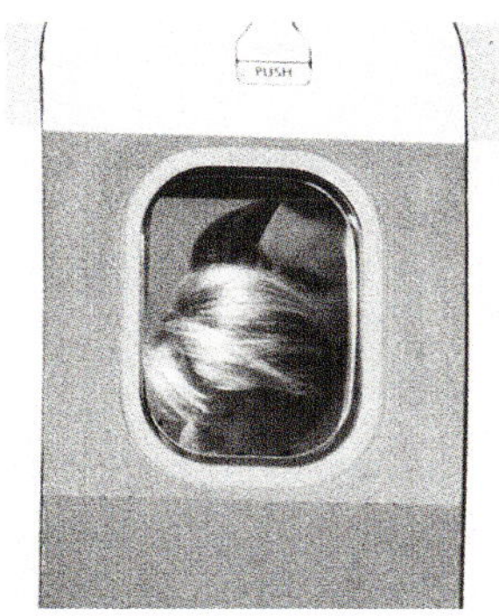

225

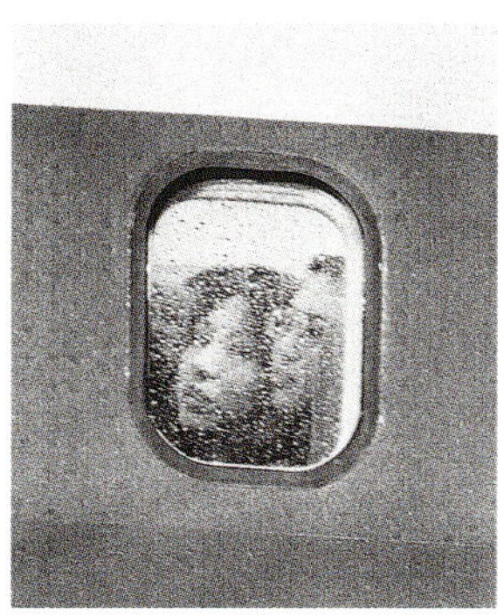
226

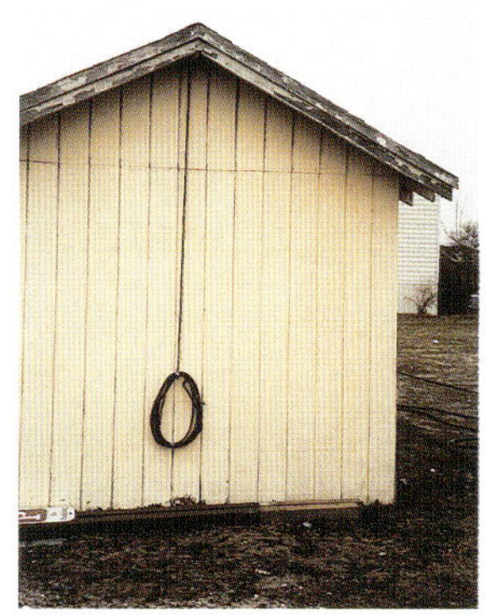
227

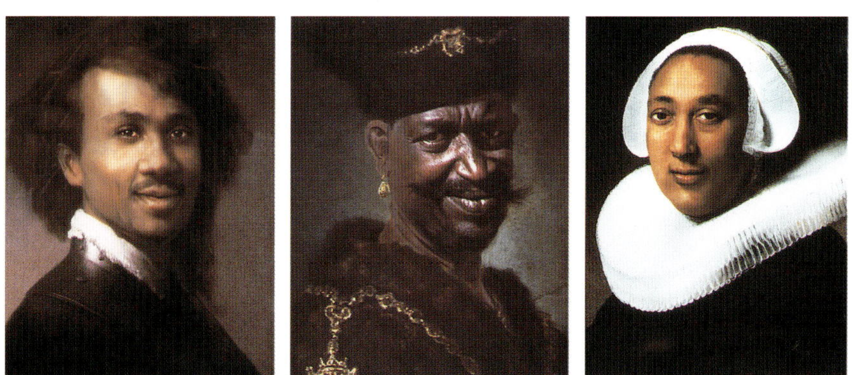
228

JOHN SCHABEL

219
Untitled (Cloud #6). 1996. Gelatin silver print from a series, $14\frac{1}{2} \times 18\frac{3}{4}$ inches

220
Untitled (Cloud #7). 1997. Gelatin silver print from a series, $14\frac{1}{2} \times 18\frac{3}{4}$ inches

221
Untitled (Cloud #8). 1998. Gelatin silver print from a series, $14\frac{1}{2} \times 18\frac{3}{4}$ inches

222
Untitled (Passenger #2). 1994–95. Toned gelatin silver prints from a series, 23×19 inches

223
Untitled (Passenger #4). 1994–95. Toned gelatin silver prints from a series, 23×19 inches

224
Untitled (Passenger #7). 1994–95. Toned gelatin silver prints from a series, 23×19 inches

225
Untitled (Passenger #9). 1994–95. Toned gelatin silver prints from a series, 23×19 inches

226
Untitled (Passenger #11). 1994–95. Toned gelatin silver prints from a series, 23×19 inches

COLLIER SCHORR

227
Fort Tildon, Barracks. 1996. Chromogenic process print, $23\frac{3}{4} \times 15\frac{3}{4}$ inches

ANDRES SERRANO

228
Black Rembrandt. 1991. Triptych: digital silver dye bleach process prints, $16\frac{3}{8} \times 12\frac{3}{8}$ inches each

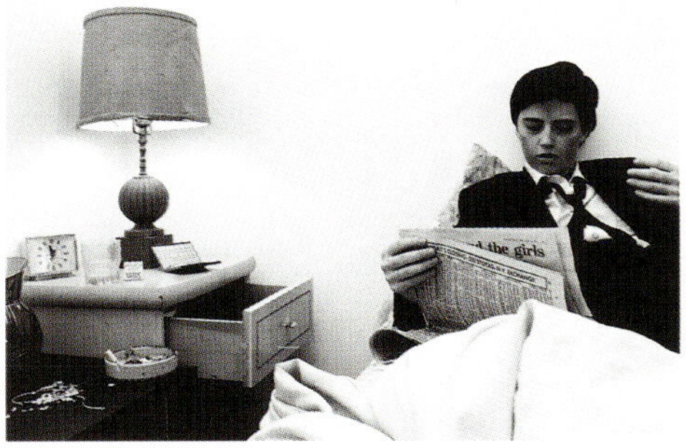

229

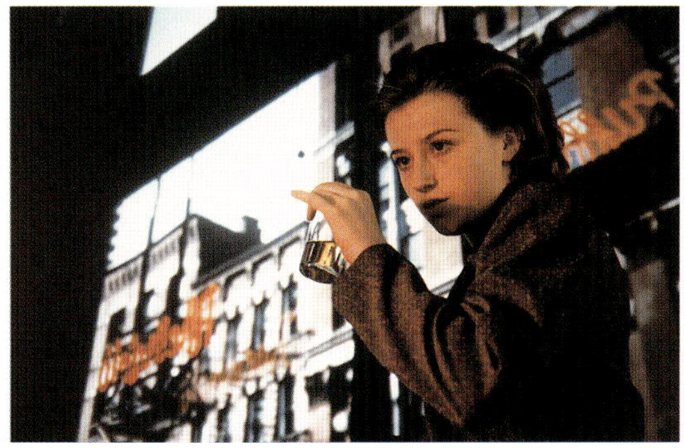

230

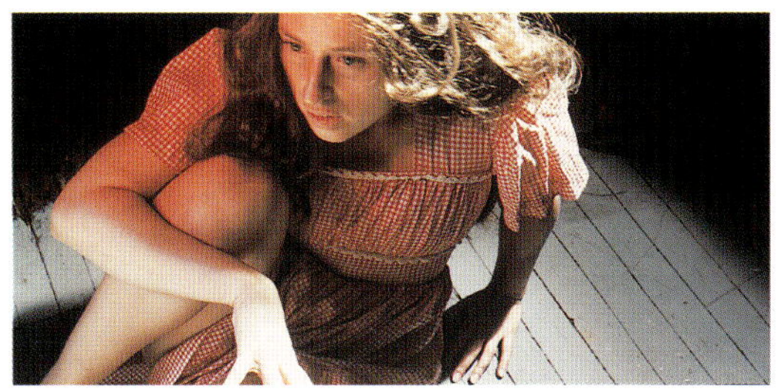

231

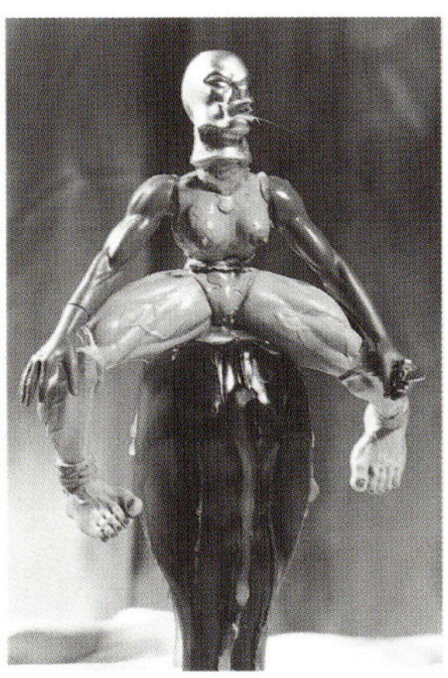

232

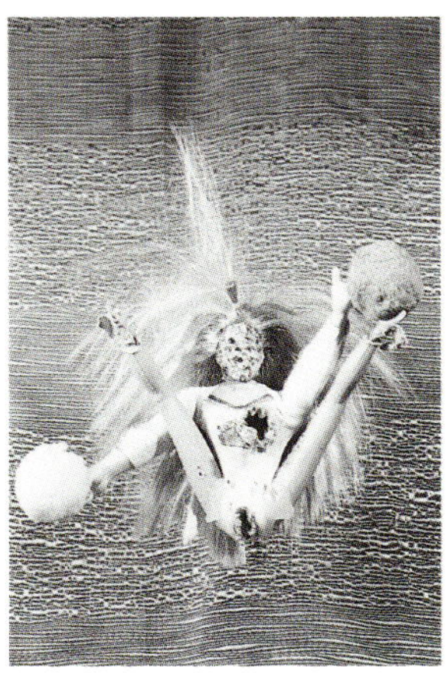

233

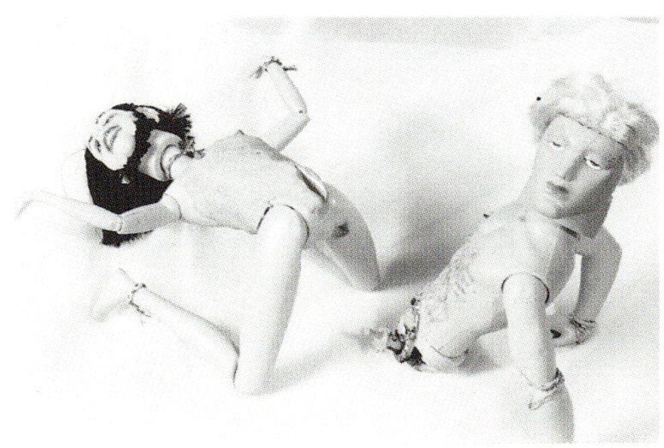

234

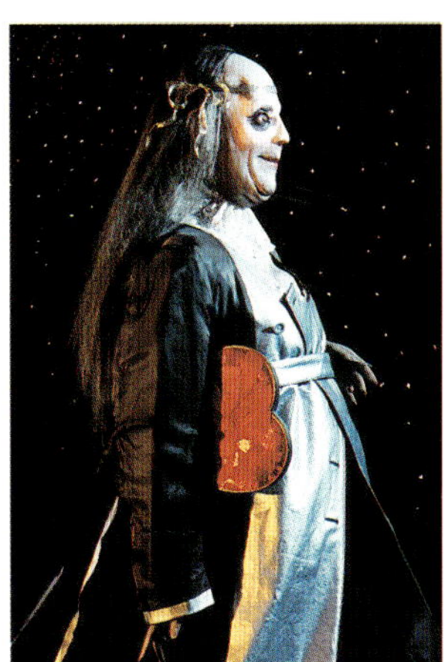

235

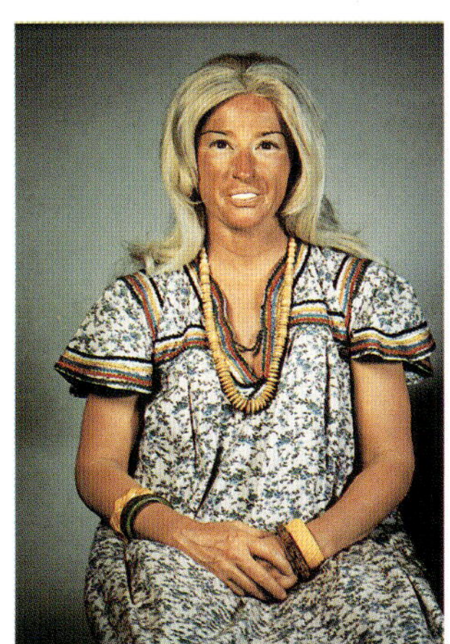

236

CINDY SHERMAN

229
Untitled (Portfolio 1, October Magazine). 1978. Gelatin silver print, $8 \times 10\frac{1}{2}$ inches

230
Untitled #70. 1980. Chromogenic process print, 20×24 inches

231
Untitled #85. 1981. Chromogenic process print, $23\frac{1}{2} \times 47\frac{1}{2}$ inches

232
Untitled. 1999. Gelatin silver print, $47\frac{1}{2} \times 31\frac{1}{2}$ inches

233
Untitled. 1999. Gelatin silver print, $47\frac{1}{2} \times 32$ inches

234
Untitled. 1999. Gelatin silver print, $25\frac{1}{2} \times 38\frac{1}{2}$ inches

235
Untitled. 1994. Chromogenic process print, $50\frac{1}{8} \times 33$ inches

236
Untitled. 2000. Chromogenic process print, 36×24 inches

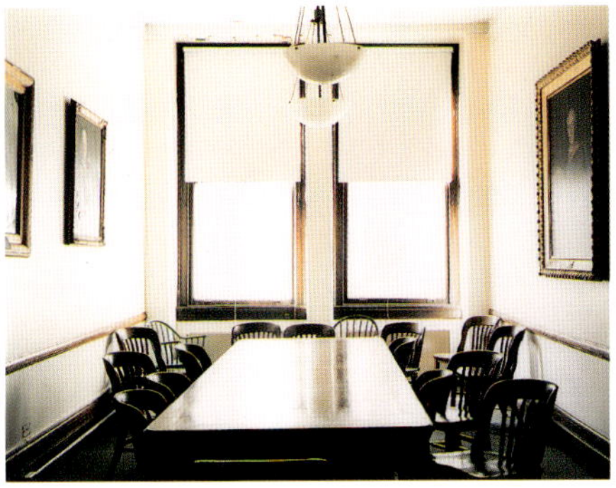

237

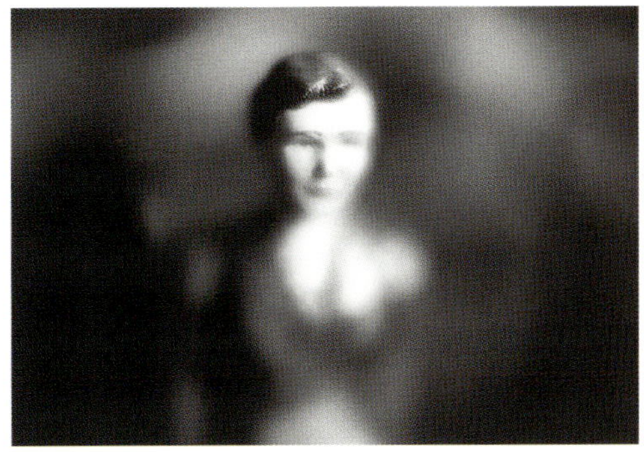

238

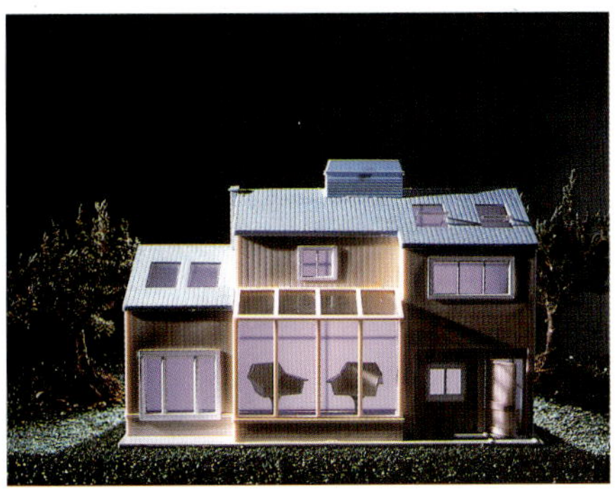

239

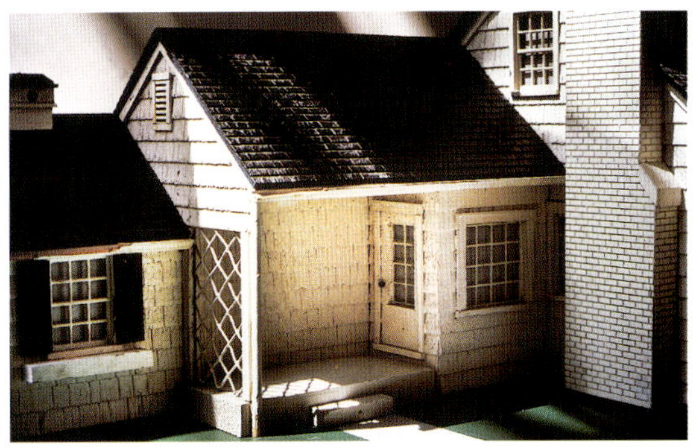

240

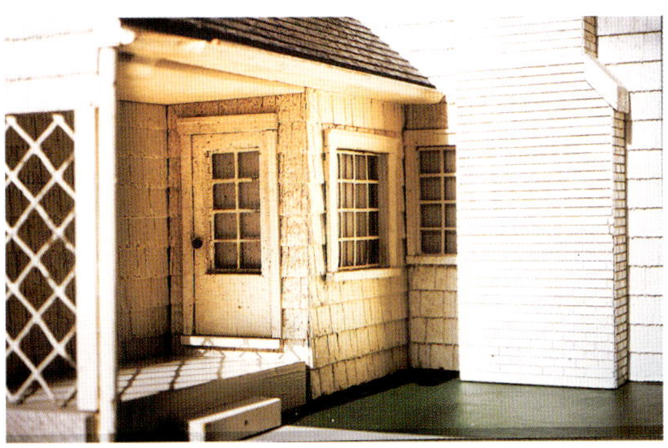

241

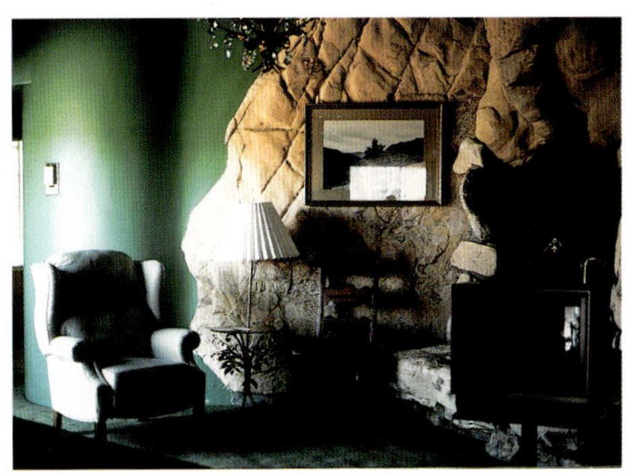

242

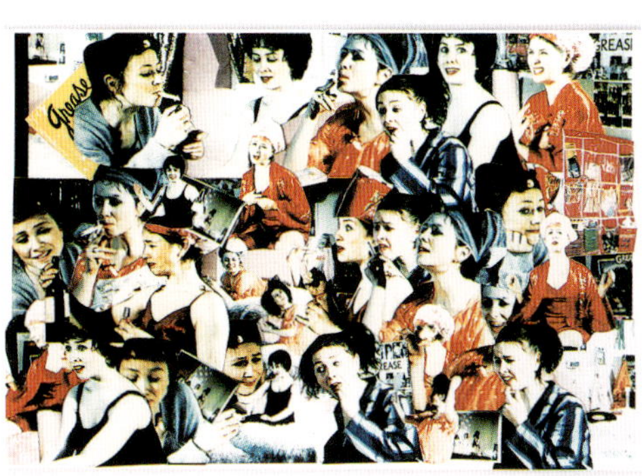

243

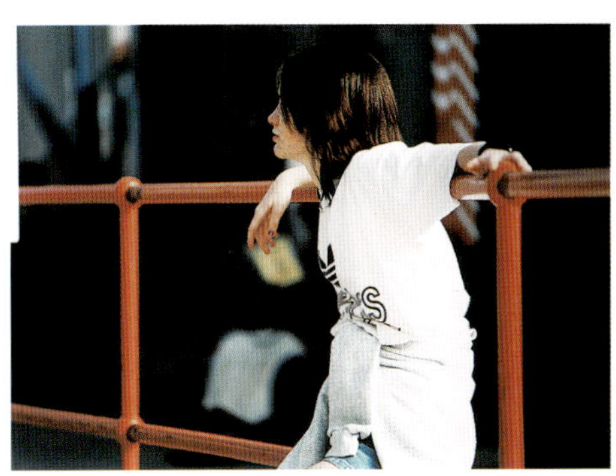

244

GARY SIMMONS

237
612. 1998. Chromogenic process print face mounted to plexiglass, $51 \times 60\frac{7}{8}$ inches

LAURIE SIMMONS

238
Untitled/Woman's Head (Portfolio 1, October Magazine). 1976. Gelatin silver print, $17\frac{1}{2} \times 20\frac{1}{2}$ inches

239
Pink House. 1998. Silver dye bleach process print, $52\frac{1}{2} \times 65$ inches

240
White House/Green Lawn (View 1). 1998. Silver dye bleach process print from a series, 22×32 inches

241
White House/Green Lawn (View 3). 1998. Silver dye bleach process print from a series, 22×32 inches

BRIDGET SMITH

242
Highway Suite. 1996. Chromogenic process print, mounted to aluminum, 47×64 inches

GEORGINA STARR

243
Hypnodreamdruff-Frenchy. 1996. Chromogenic process print, 43×62 inches

BEAT STREULI

244
Oxford Street 97 (34/12). 1998. Chromogenic process print, $69\frac{3}{4} \times 79\frac{1}{2}$ inches

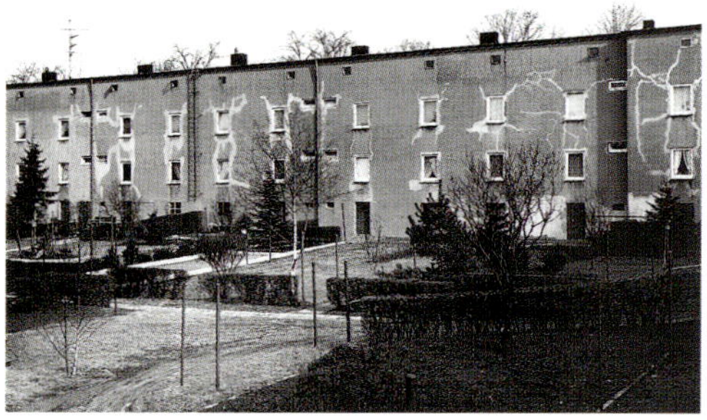

245

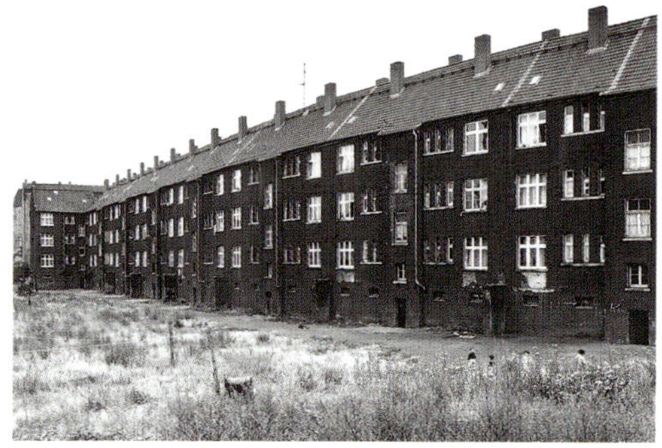

246

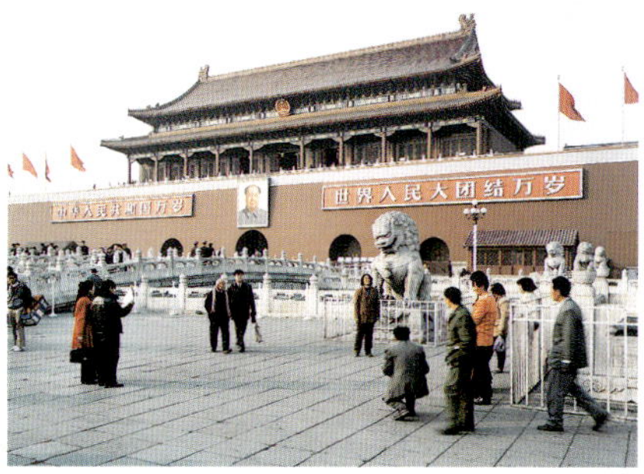

247

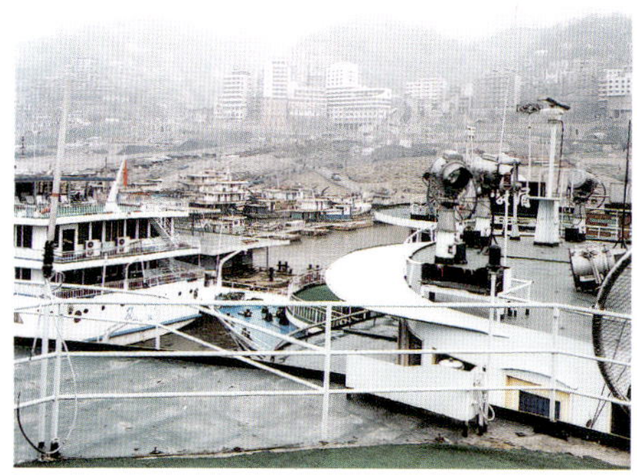

248

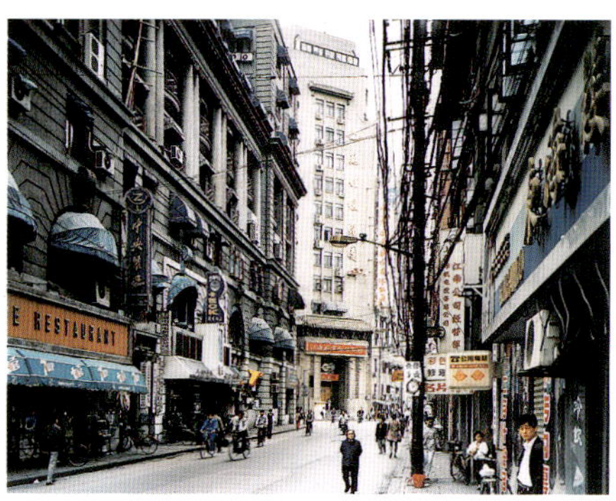

249

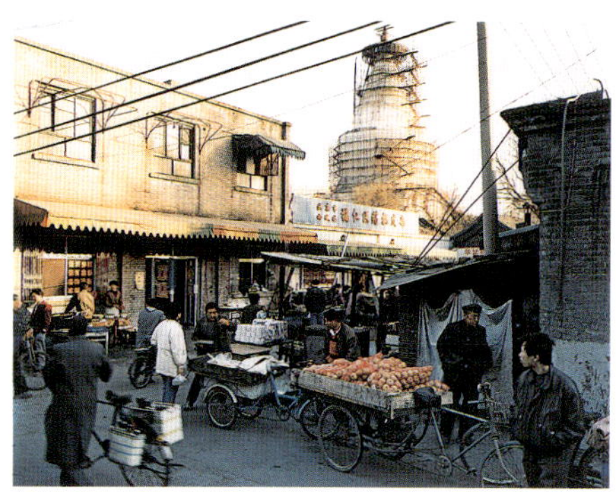

250

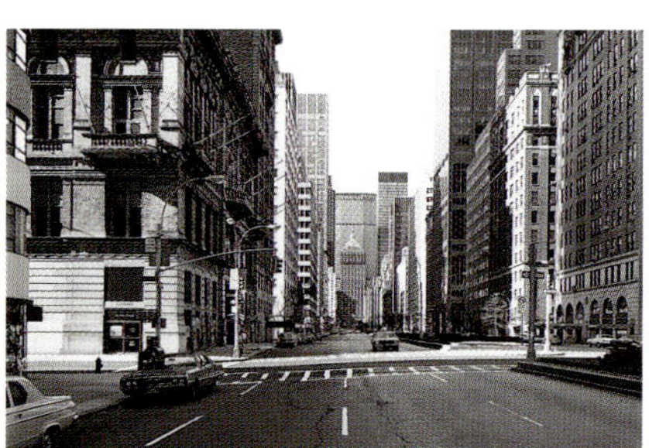

251

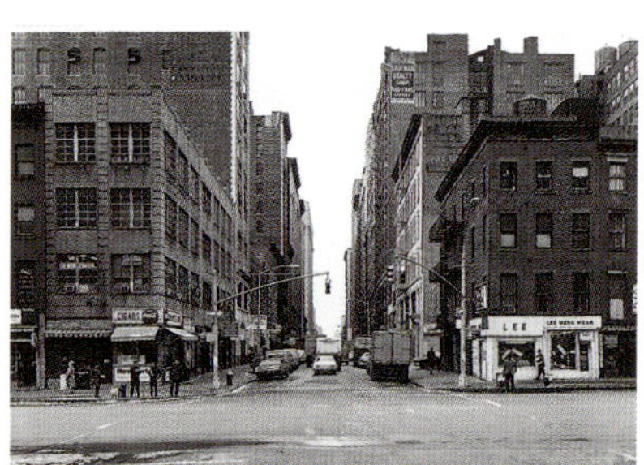

252

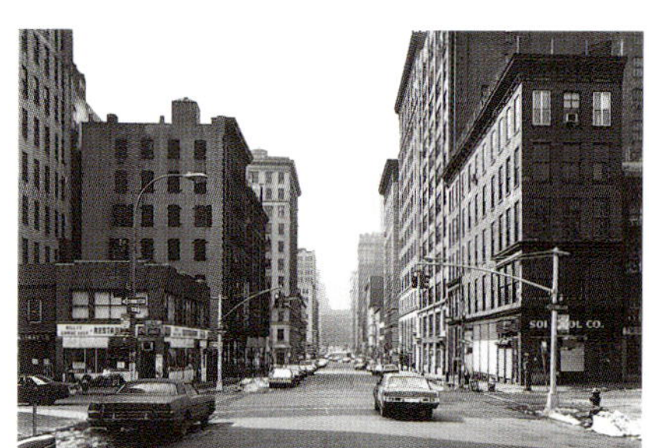

253

THOMAS STRUTH

245

Am Kreuzacker, Duisburg. 1985. Gelatin silver print, $15\frac{7}{8} \times 22\frac{1}{8}$ inches

246

Hubertusstasse, Duisburg. 1989. Gelatin silver print, $17 \times 23\frac{3}{4}$ inches

247

Tein An Men, Beijing, 1997. 1997. Chromogenic process print, face mounted to plexiglass, $74\frac{1}{2} \times 91\frac{1}{2}$ inches

248

Boats at Wushan, Yangtse River, Wushan, 1997. 1997. Chromogenic process print, face mounted to plexiglass, $74\frac{1}{4} \times 89$ inches

249

Jaingxi Zhong Lu, Shanghai, 1996. 1996. Chromogenic process print, face mounted to plexiglass, $49\frac{1}{2} \times 57\frac{3}{4}$ inches

250

Markt mit Stupa, Beijing, 1996 (Market with Stupa, Beijing). 1996. Chromogenic process print, face mounted to plexiglass, $50\frac{5}{8} \times 59\frac{1}{4}$ inches

251

Park Avenue (Mit Auto) (with Car), New York/Midtown, 1978. 1978. Gelatin silver print, $15\frac{1}{2} \times 23$ inches

252

West 25th Street, New York/Chelsea, 1978. 1978. Gelatin silver print, $15\frac{1}{2} \times 23$ inches

253

Lafayette Street (Grand Street) New York/ Soho, 1978. 1978. Gelatin silver print, $15\frac{3}{4} \times 22$ inches

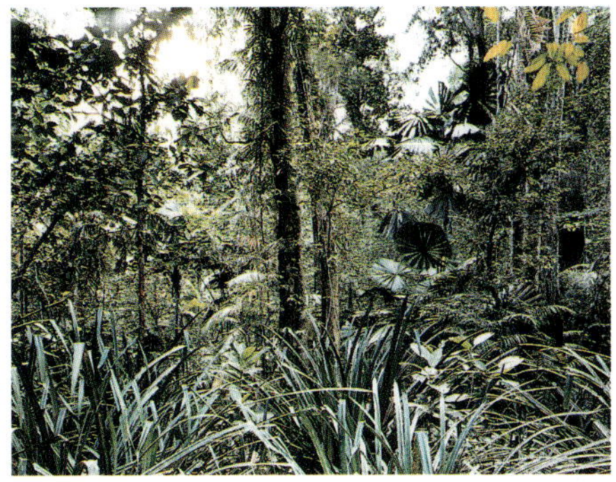

254

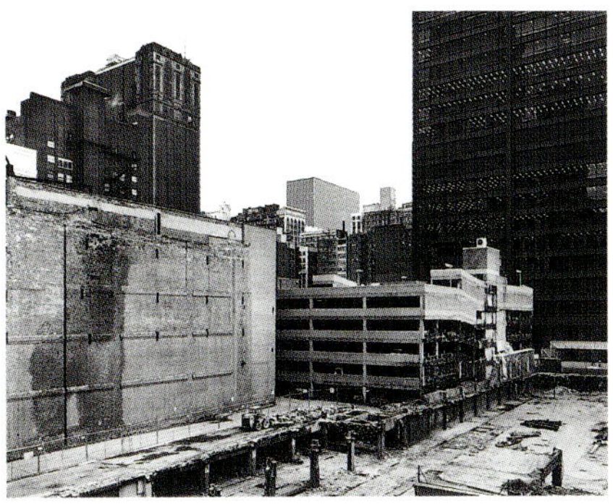

255

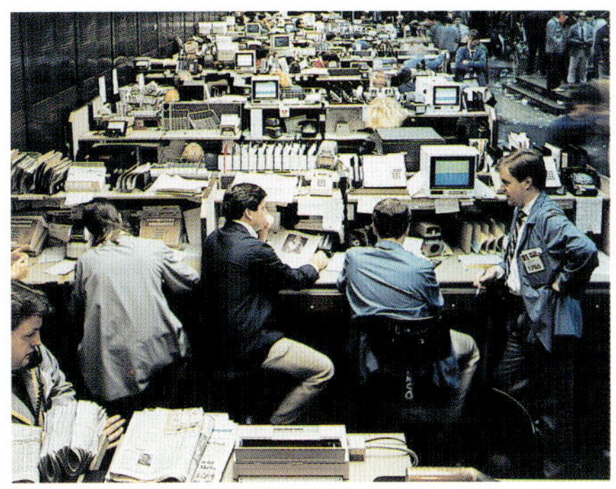

256

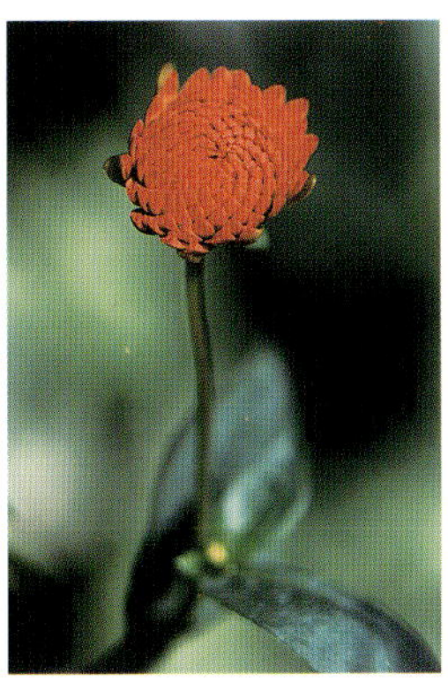

257

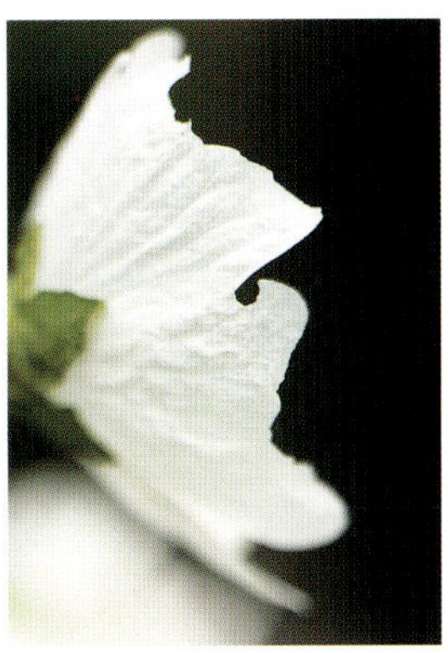

258

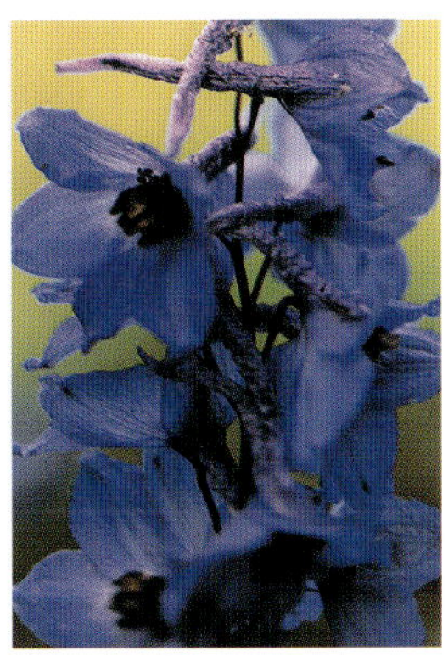

259

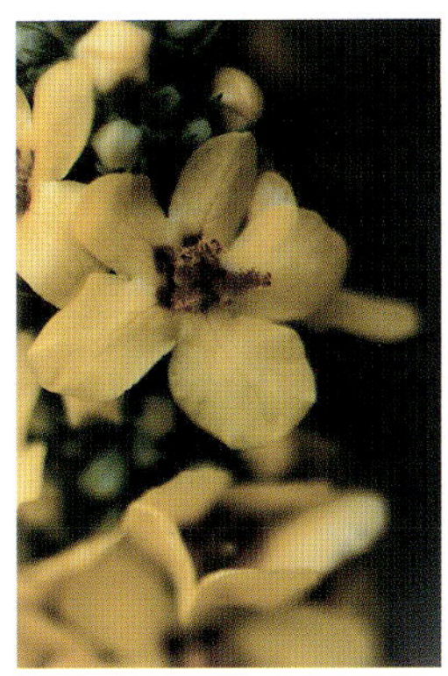

260

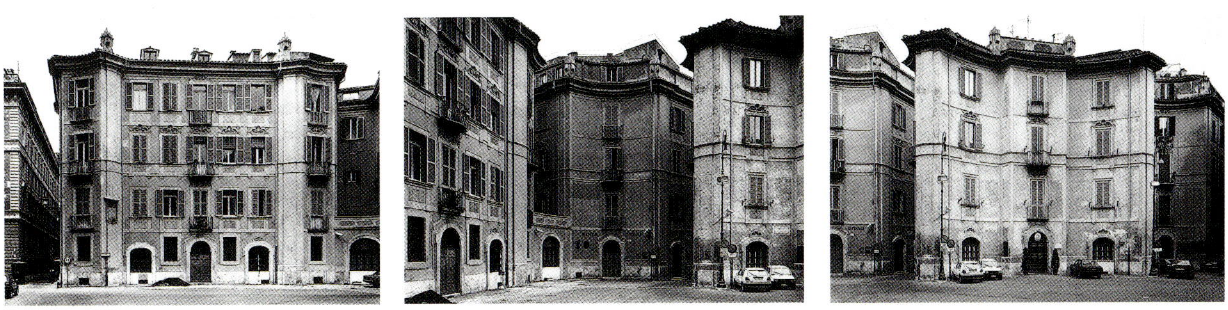

261

254
Paradise 7, Daintree, Australia, 1998. **1998. Chromogenic process print, face mounted to plexiglass, $74\frac{3}{4} \times 93\frac{3}{8}$ inches**

255
The Loop (Looking Towards Dearborn Street). **1990. Gelatin silver print, $18\frac{1}{4} \times 22\frac{1}{2}$ inches**

256
Chicago Board of Trade II. **1990. Chromogenic process print, 24×30 inches**

257
Plant Number 21, Dahlia, Winterthur, 1992. **1992. Chromogenic process print from a series, $22\frac{5}{8} \times 15\frac{1}{8}$ inches**

258
Plant Number 6, Mallow, Winterthur, 1992. **1992. Chromogenic process print from a series, $22\frac{3}{4} \times 15\frac{3}{4}$ inches**

259
Plant Number 7, Violet Larkspur, Winterthur, 1992. **1992. Chromogenic process print from a series, $22\frac{5}{8} \times 15\frac{1}{8}$ inches**

260
Plant Number 8, Yellow Mullein, Winterthur, 1992. **1992. Chromogenic process print from a series, $22\frac{5}{8} \times 15\frac{1}{8}$ inches**

261
Piazza di San Ignazio I **(from the *Rome* series). 1990. Three gelatin silver prints, 17×24 inches each**

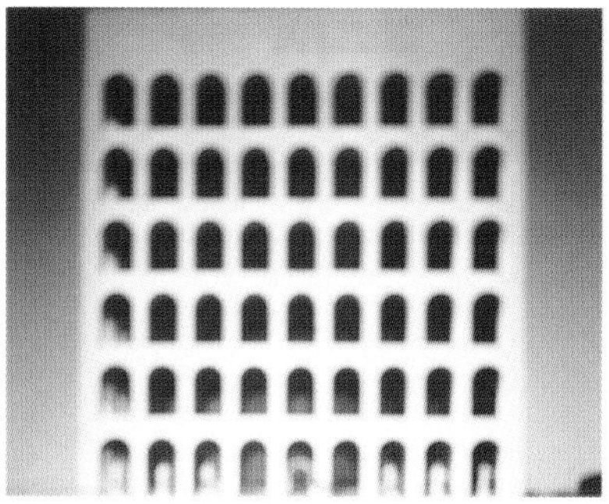
262

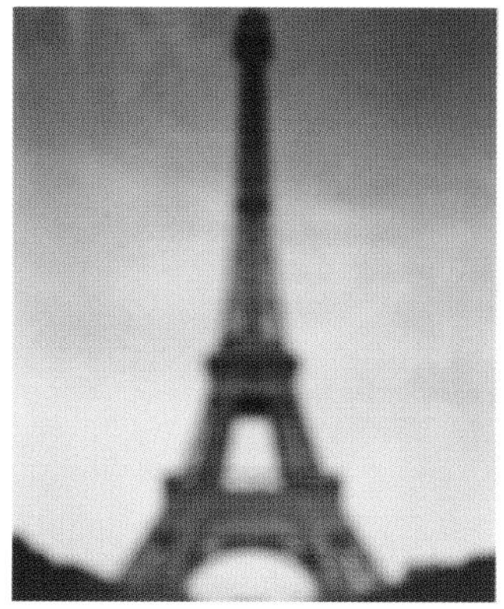
263

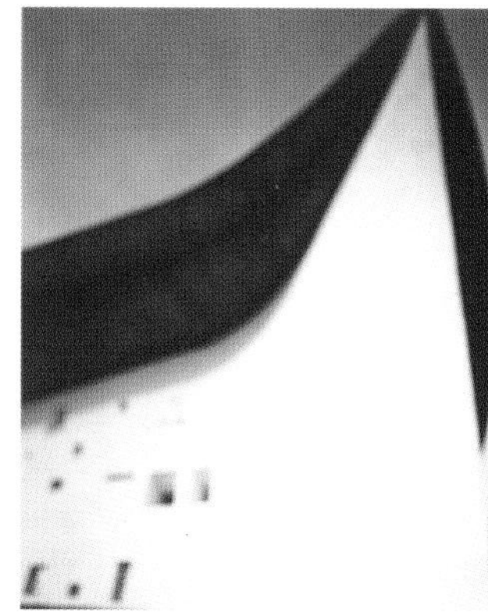
264

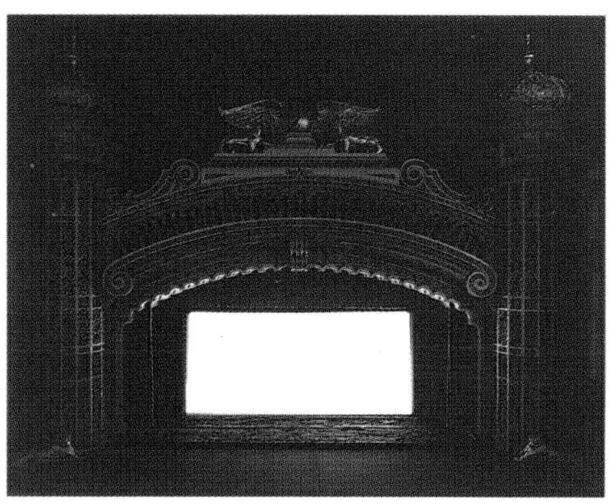
265

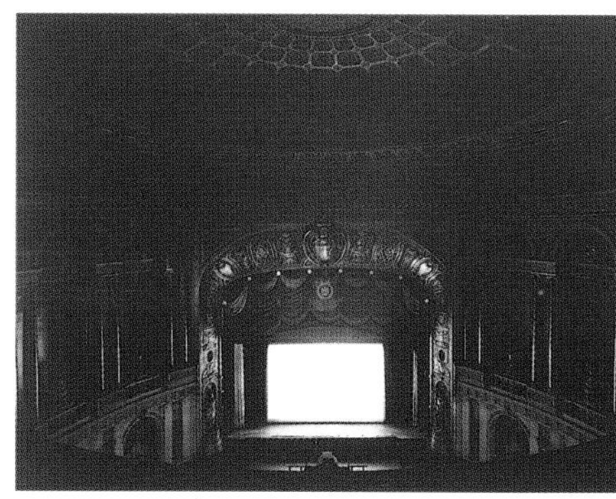
266

267

268

269

270

HIROSHI SUGIMOTO

262

EUR Palazzo della Civilta Romana. **1997. Gelatin silver print, $18\frac{1}{2} \times 23$ inches**

263

Eiffel Tower—Gustave Eiffel. **1998. Gelatin silver print, $23 \times 18\frac{1}{2}$ inches**

264

Chapel of Nôtre Dame du Haut—Le Corbusier. **1998. Gelatin silver print, $23 \times 18\frac{1}{2}$ inches**

265

Civic, New Zealand. **1991. Gelatin silver print, $16\frac{1}{2} \times 21\frac{1}{4}$ inches**

266

Palms, Michigan. **1980. Gelatin silver print, $16\frac{1}{2} \times 21\frac{1}{4}$ inches**

267

Black Sea, Ozuluce. **1991. Gelatin silver print, $16\frac{5}{8} \times 21\frac{1}{8}$ inches**

268

Ionian Sea, Santa Cesarea III. **1990. Gelatin silver print, $16\frac{1}{2} \times 21\frac{3}{8}$ inches**

269

Pacific Ocean, Oregon I. **1985. Gelatin silver print, $16\frac{5}{8} \times 21\frac{1}{8}$ inches**

270

Tyrrhenian Sea, Scilla. **1993. Gelatin silver print, $16\frac{5}{8} \times 21\frac{1}{8}$ inches**

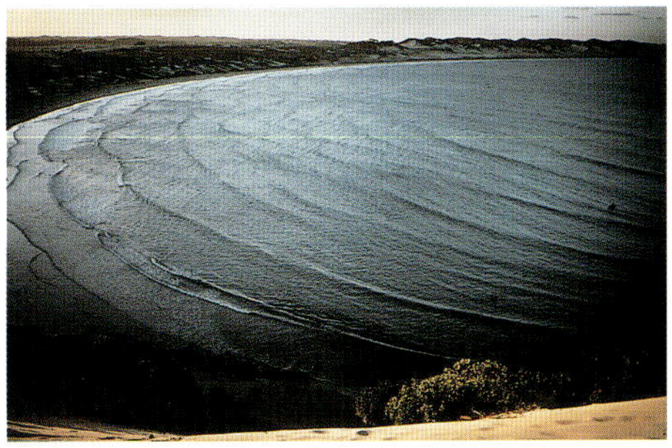

271

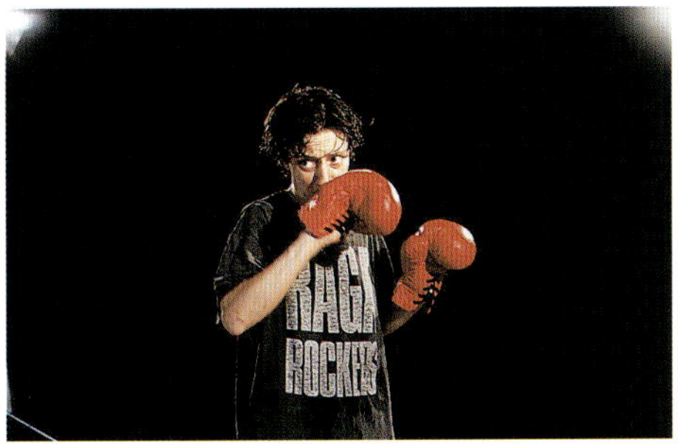

272

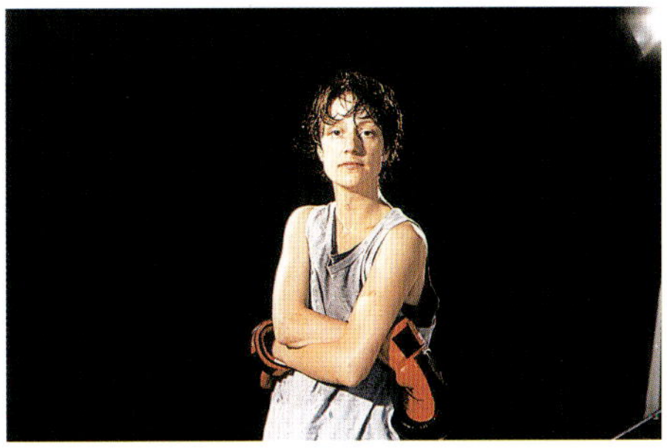

273

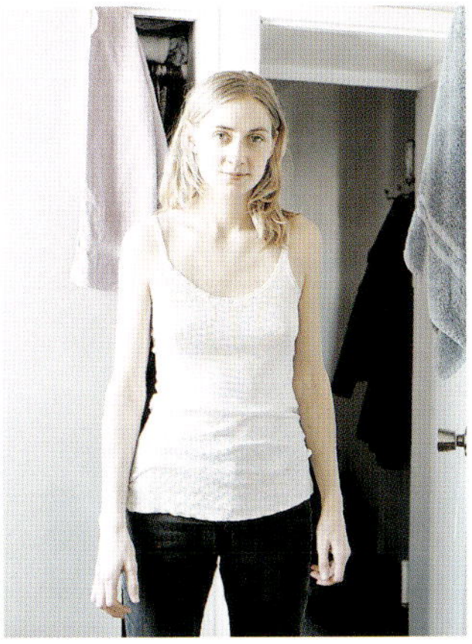

274

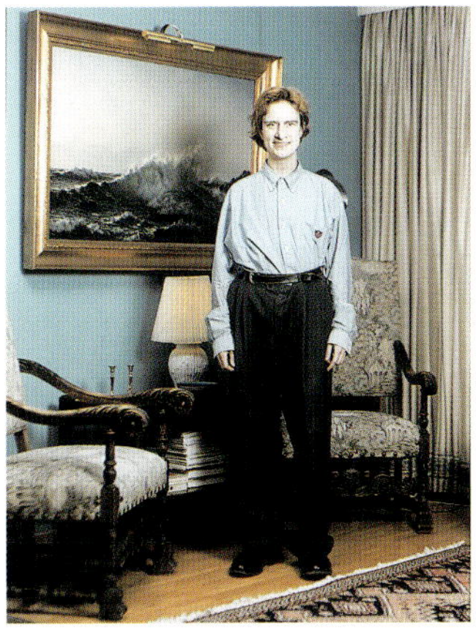

275

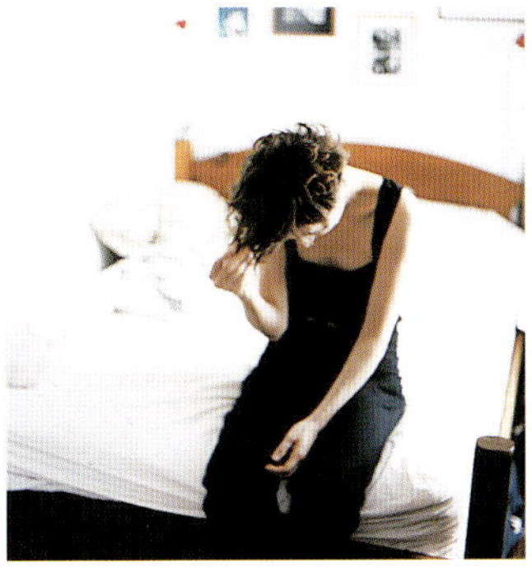

276

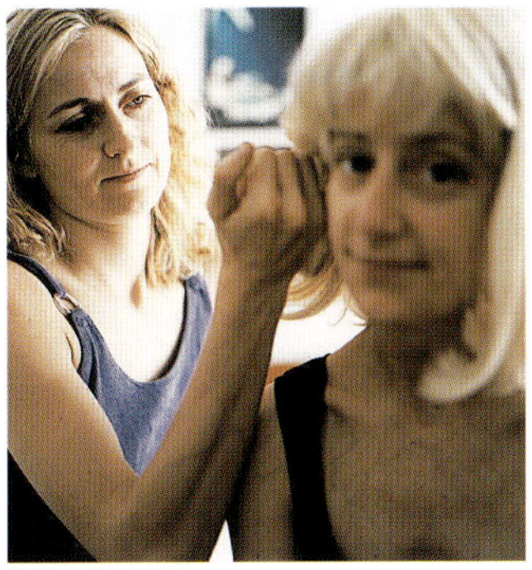

277

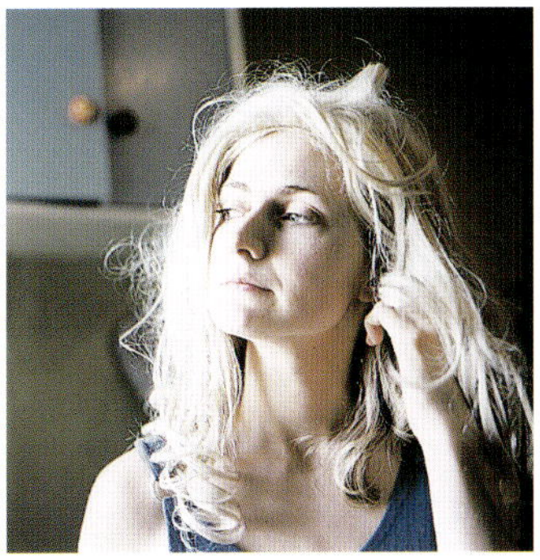

278

BILLY SULLIVAN

271
Ponte Negra. 1976/1999. Silver dye bleach process print mounted to aluminum, 20 × 30 inches

VIBEKE TANDBERG

272
Boxer #2. 1998. Chromogenic process print, 37 × 54$\frac{1}{2}$ inches

273
Boxer #1. 1998. Chromogenic process print, 37 × 54$\frac{1}{2}$ inches

274
Line #4. 1999. Digital chromogenic process print, 53 × 40$\frac{1}{2}$ inches

275
Dad #3. 1999. Digital chromogenic process print from a series, 56 × 42$\frac{3}{4}$ inches

276
Untitled (Line #6). 1999. Chromogenic process print from a series, 15$\frac{1}{4}$ × 14$\frac{7}{8}$ inches

277
Untitled (Line #5). 1999. Chromogenic process print from a series, 15$\frac{1}{4}$ × 14$\frac{7}{8}$ inches

278
Untitled (Line #9). 1999. Chromogenic process print from a series, 15$\frac{1}{4}$ × 14$\frac{7}{8}$ inches

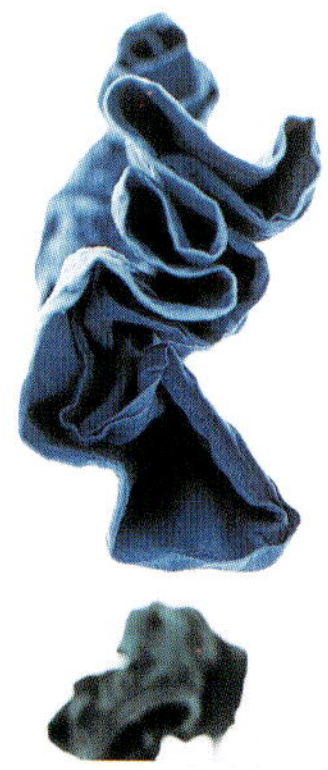

279

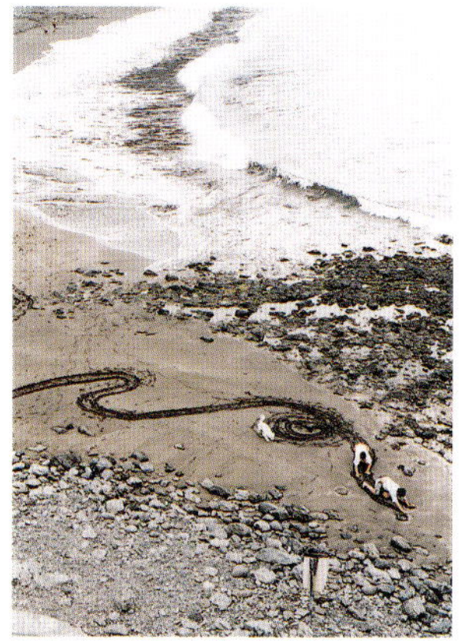

280

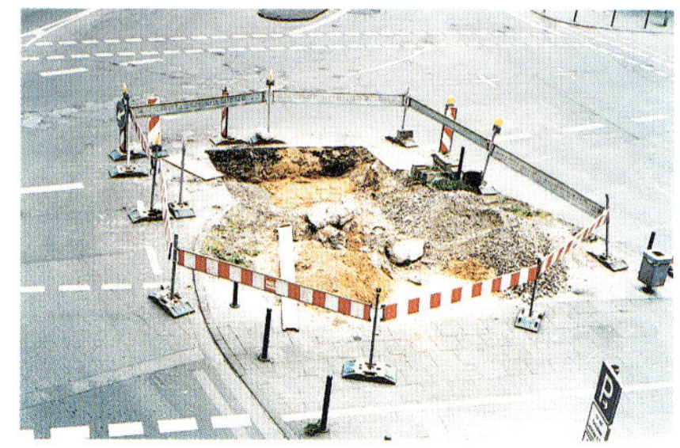

281

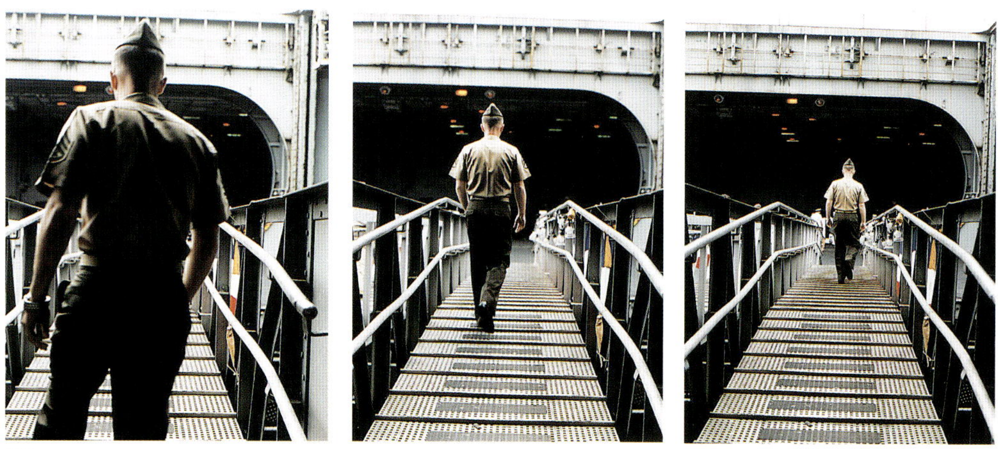

282

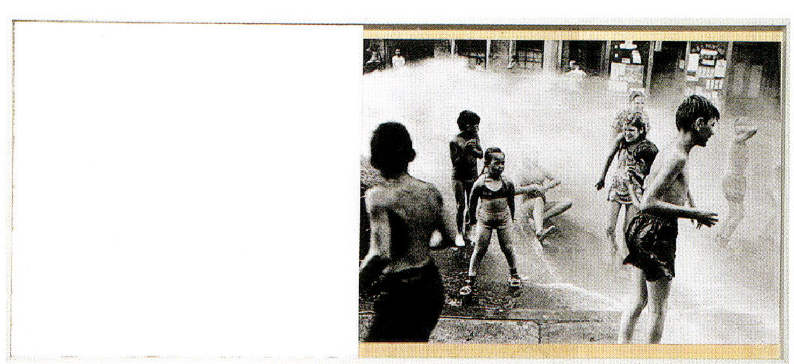

283

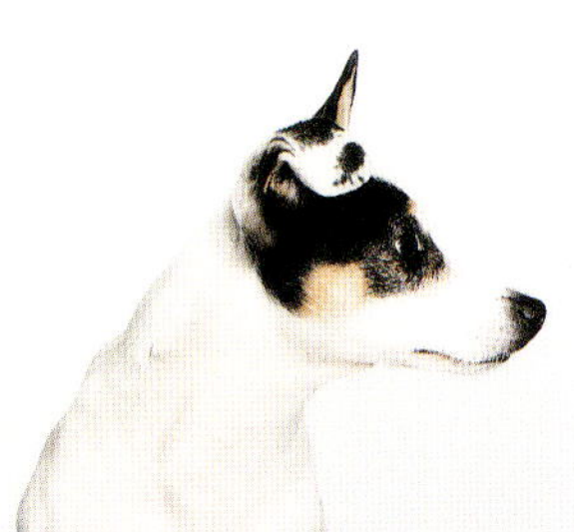

284

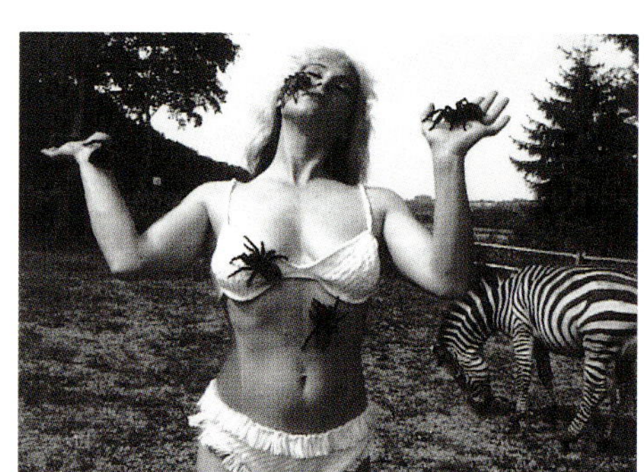

285

WOLFGANG TILLMANS

279

Faltenwurf (Blau) (Drapery [Blue]). 1998. Chromogenic process print, $73\frac{3}{8} \times 56\frac{1}{4}$ inches

280

Untitled (La Gomera). 1997. Unique chromogenic process print, face mounted to plexiglass, $70 \times 48\frac{3}{8}$ inches

281

Roadworks 98. 1998. Chromogenic process print, $58\frac{1}{4} \times 83\frac{3}{4}$ inches

282

Soldier, Gangway I, II, III. 1995. Triptych: chromogenic process prints, $25\frac{3}{8} \times 21\frac{3}{8}$ inches each

ROSEMARIE TROCKEL

283

Untitled. 1988. Gelatin silver print, mounted on plywood panel, plexiglass, reverse painted with acrylic paint in artist's frame, $41 \times 92\frac{1}{4}$ inches

284

Fritz II. 1993. Silver dye bleach process print, face mounted to plexiglass, $39\frac{1}{4} \times 39\frac{1}{4}$ inches

285

Yvonne (detail). 1997. Suite of ten iris print video stills on rag paper, $6\frac{3}{4} \times 9$ inches each

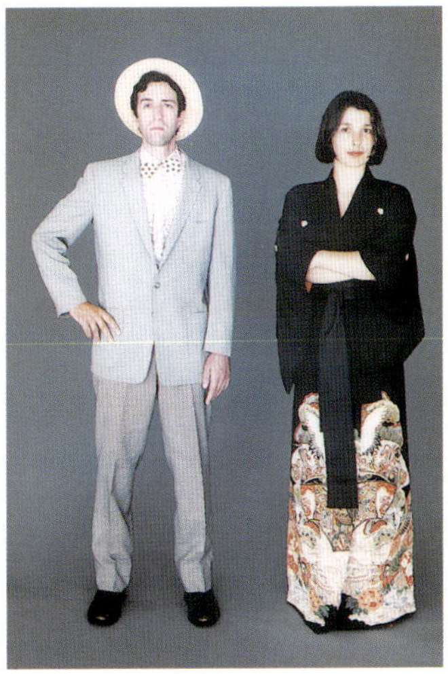
286

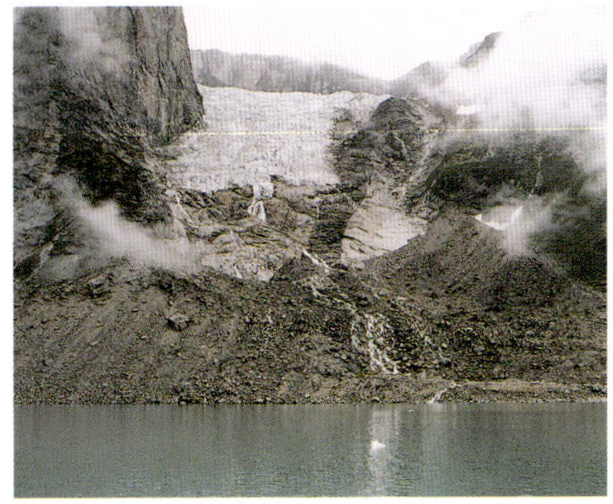
287

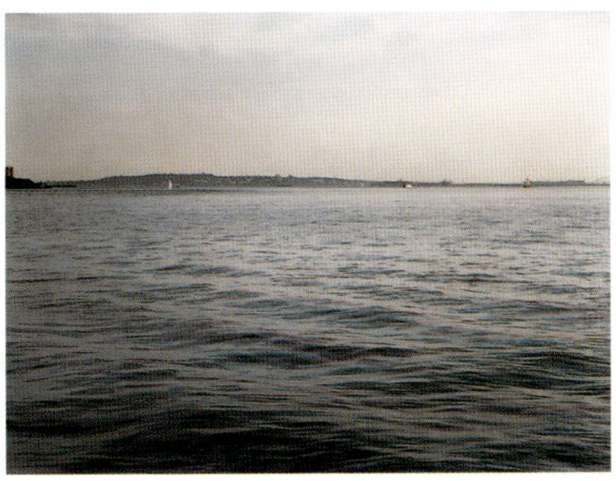
288

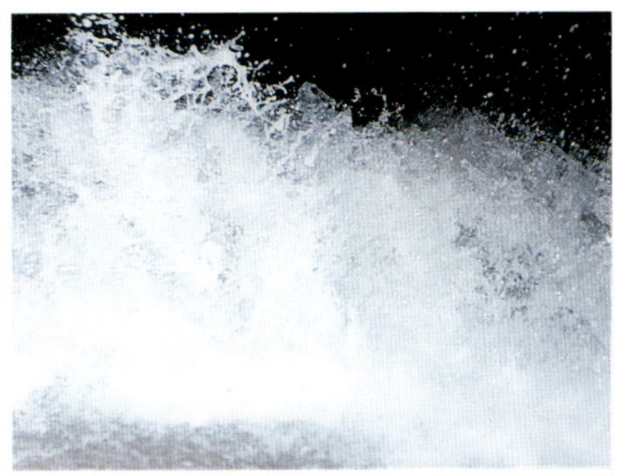
289

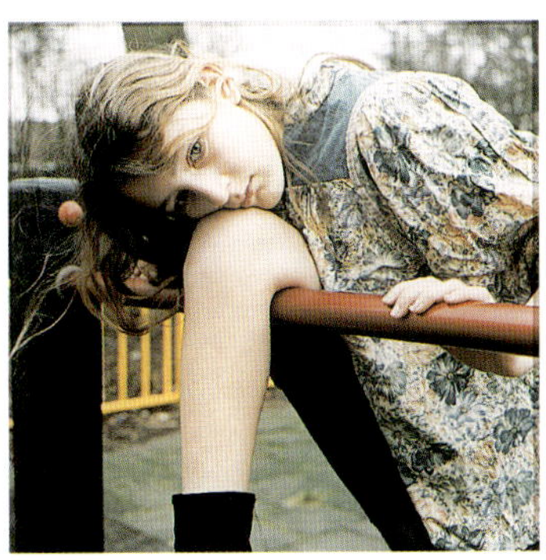
290

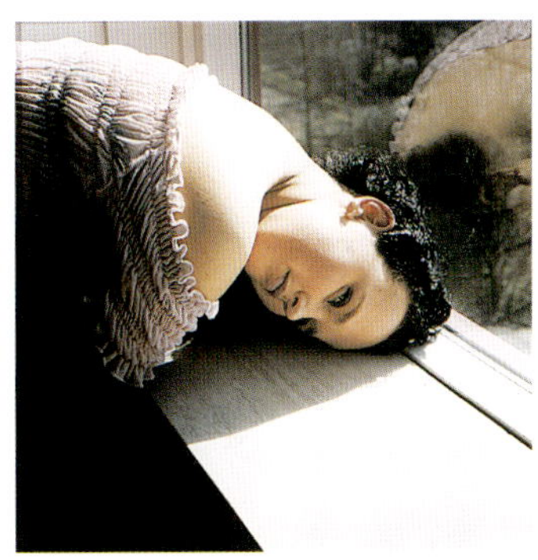
291

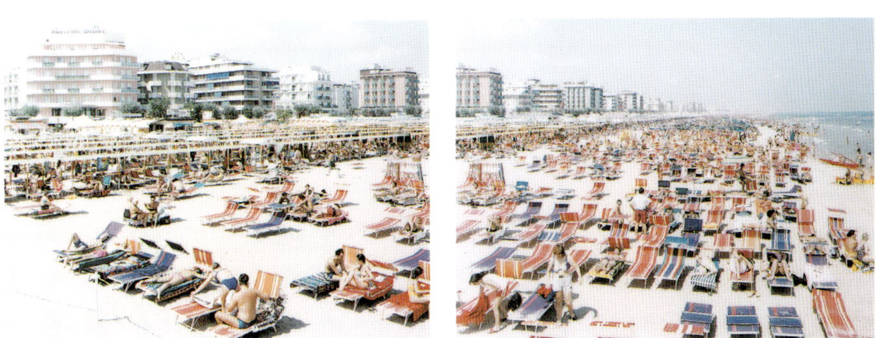
292

METTE TRONVOLL

286

Vincent Katz, Vivien Bittencourt. **1996. Chromogenic process print, face mounted to plexiglass, $86\frac{5}{8} \times 57$ inches**

287

Isortoq Unartoq #14. **2000. Chromogenic process print from a series, $73 \times 83\frac{5}{8}$ inches**

PIOTR UKLANSKI

288

Untitled (Staten Island). **1999. Chromogenic process print, mounted between plexiglass and aluminum, $46\frac{1}{4} \times 60$ inches**

289

Untitled (Wave). **1997. Chromogenic process print, mounted between aluminum and plexiglass, $18 \times 23\frac{1}{2}$ inches**

HELLEN VAN MEENE

290

Untitled. **1999. Chromogenic process print from a series, 16×16 inches**

291

Untitled. **1999. Chromogenic process print from a series, 16×16 inches**

MASSIMO VITALI

292

Riccione Diptych. **1997. Diptych: chromogenic process prints, $59\frac{1}{8}$ inches $\times$ 11 feet 10 inches**

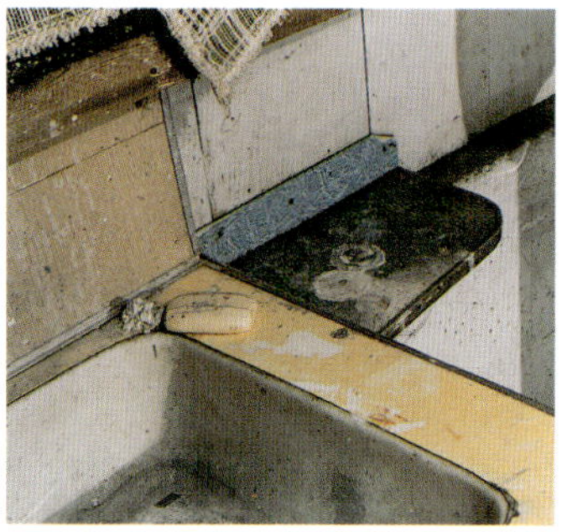
293

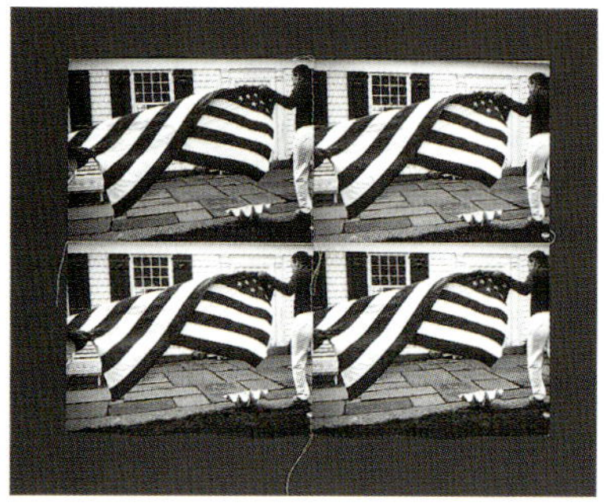
294

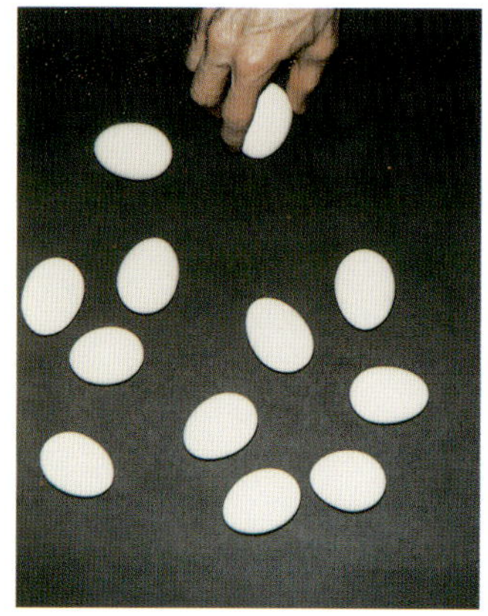
295

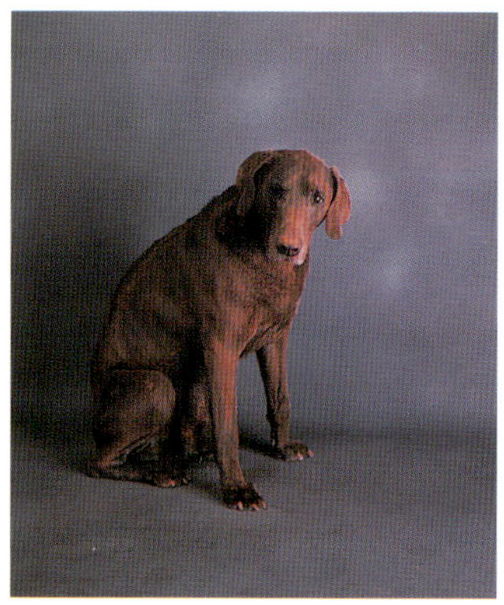
296

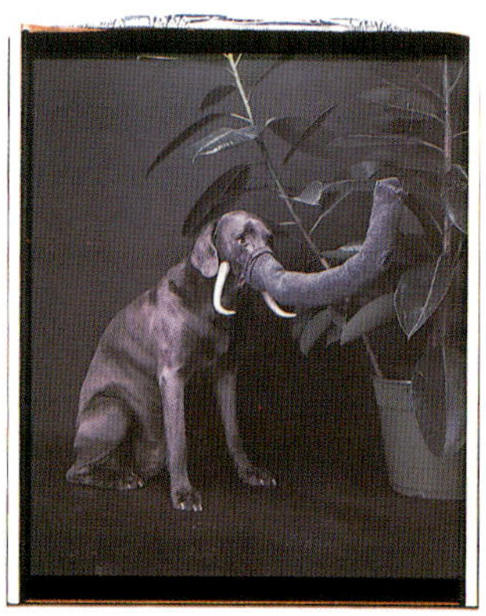
297

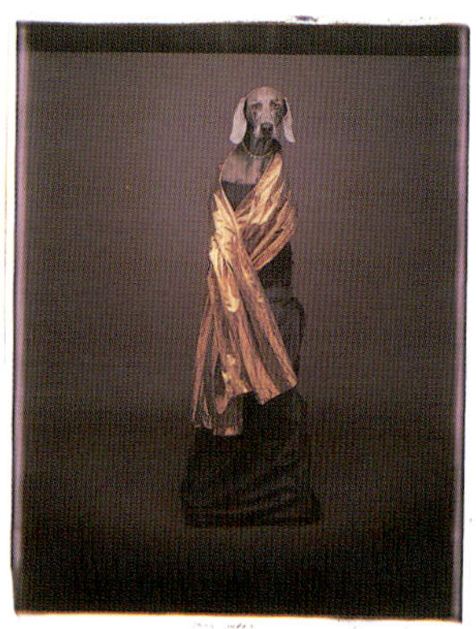
298

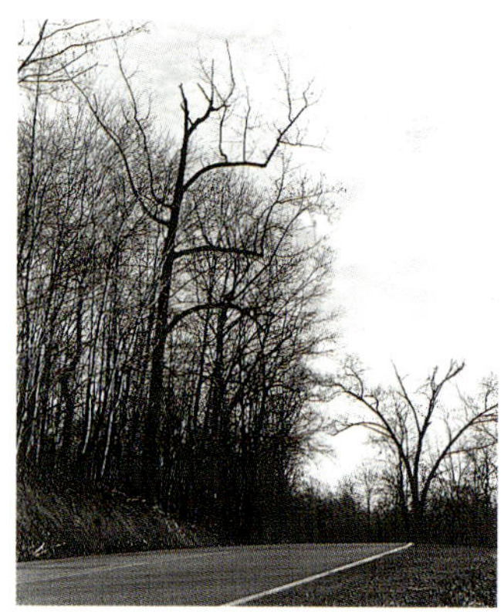
299

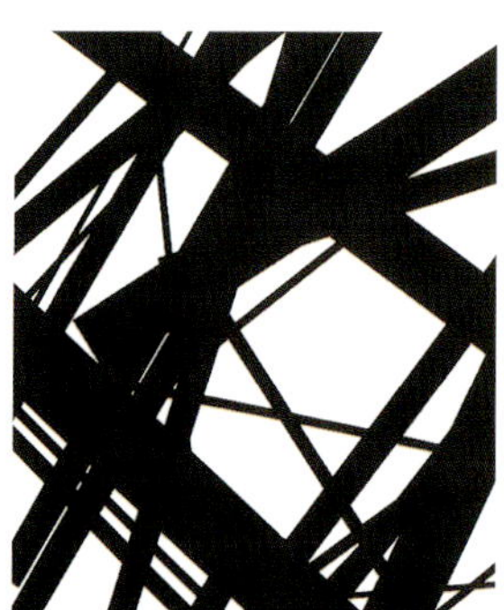
300

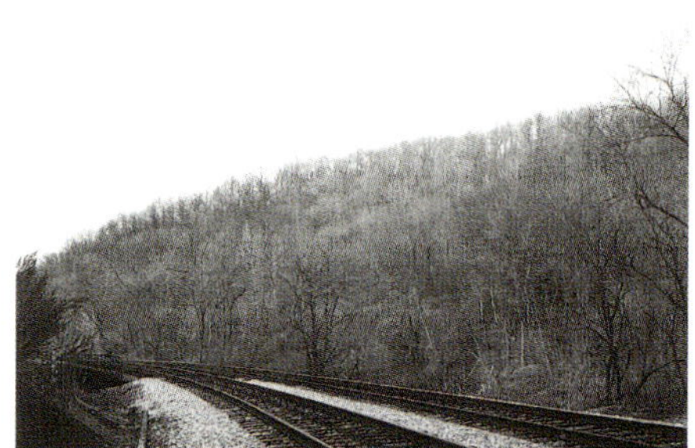
301

JEFF WALL

293

Diagonal Composition. 1992–93. Unique chromogenic process print, $16\frac{1}{2} \times 17\frac{3}{4}$ inches

ANDY WARHOL

294

American Flag. 1976–86. Four gelatin silver prints, machine stitched, $21\frac{3}{8} \times 27\frac{3}{8}$ inches

295

Untitled (Eggs). 1981. Polaroid photograph, $3\frac{5}{8} \times 2\frac{7}{8}$ inches

WILLIAM WEGMAN

296

Red/Gray Gray/Red. 1982. Two Polaroid prints, 32×50 inches

297

Elephant. 1980. Polaroid print, $28\frac{1}{2} \times 21\frac{3}{4}$ inches

298

Sash Grudge. 1990. Polaroid print, 29×22 inches

JAMES WELLING

299

Edge of the Road, Morgantown, WV. 1993. Unique toned gelatin silver print, 22×18 inches

300

#25. 1998. Gelatin silver print, $38\frac{1}{2} \times 26\frac{1}{2}$ inches

301

CSX Tracks Panther Hollow, Pittsburgh, Pa. 1998. Iris print on rag paper, 27×34 inches

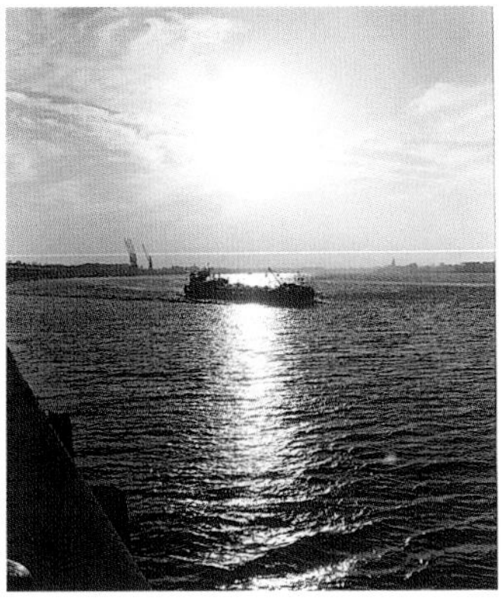

302

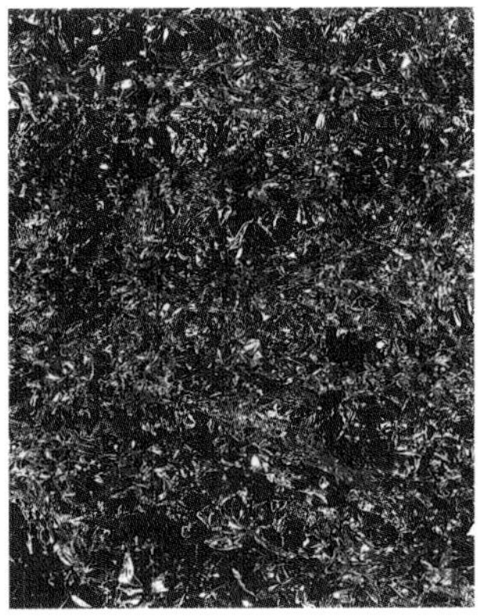

303

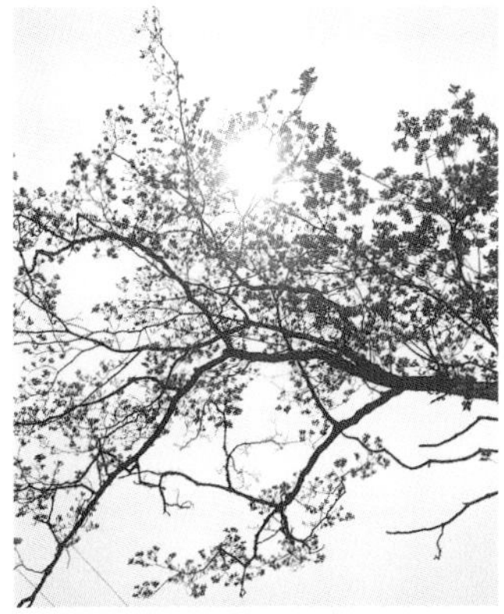

304

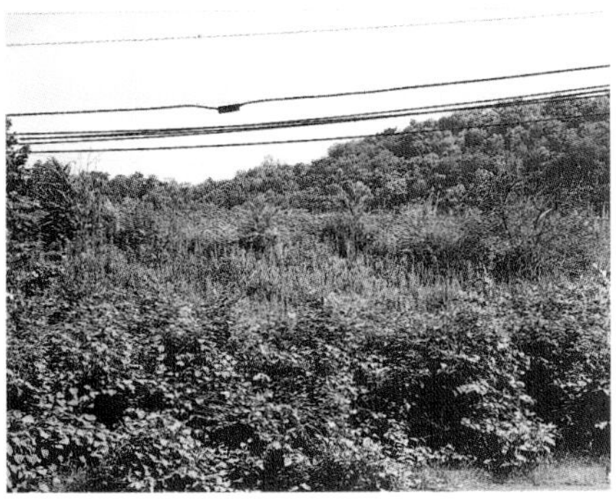

305

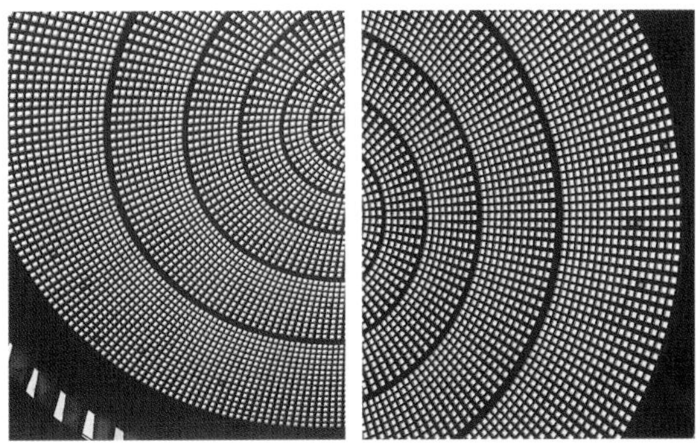

306

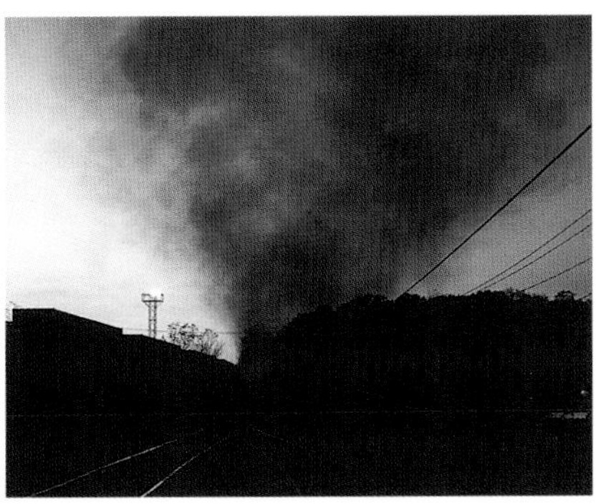

307

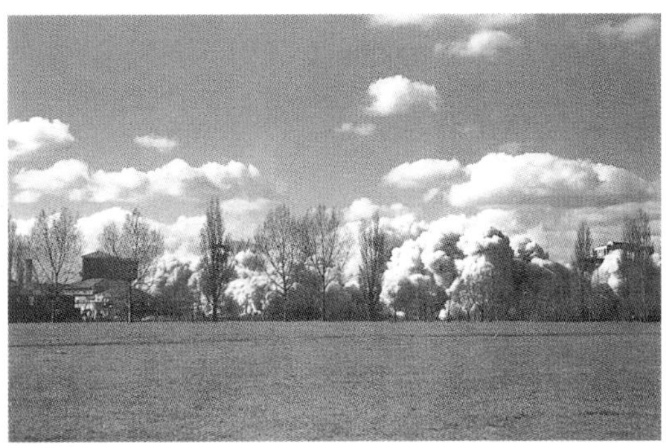

308

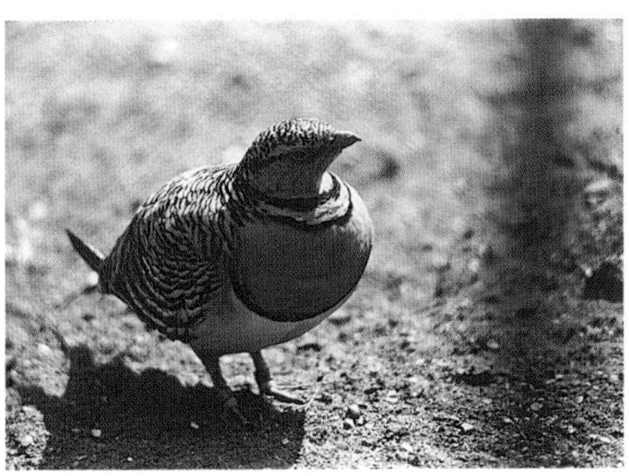

309

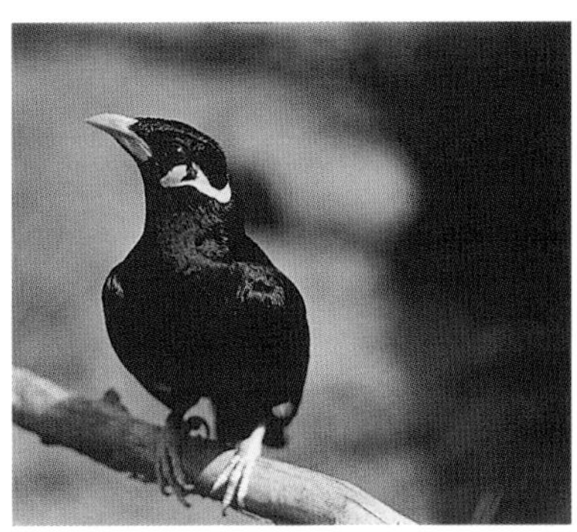

310

3 0 2

The Schelde. 1994. Unique toned gelatin silver print, 22 × 18 inches

3 0 3

Untitled (42) (Portfolio 1, October Magazine). 1980. Gelatin silver print, 6 × 4$^3/_4$ inches

3 0 4

Meriden. 1992. Iris print on rag paper, 33$^3/_8$ × 26$^5/_8$ inches

3 0 5

Songbird. 1998. Iris print on rag paper, 27 × 34 inches

3 0 6

Ravenstein 3. 1998. Diptych: iris print on rag paper, 33$^1/_2$ × 26$^1/_2$ inches each

3 0 7

Westbound Departure. 1993. Unique toned gelatin silver print, 18 × 22 inches

RACHEL WHITEREAD

3 0 8

Demolished (B3) (detail). 1996. Installation: twelve duotone screen prints on Somerset paper, 21$^3/_4$ × 31$^7/_8$ inches each

CHRISTOPHER WILLIAMS

3 0 9

Supplement (5. Morocco). 1990. Gelatin silver print from a series, 17 × 23 inches

3 1 0

Supplement (6. Nepal). 1990. Gelatin silver print from a series, 17 × 23 inches

INDEX OF ARTISTS

Page numbers in *italics* refer to illustrations.

Abramovic, Marina
Born in 1946, Belgrade, Yugoslavia. Resides in Amsterdam, The Netherlands. *35*

Ahtila, Eija-Liisa
Born in 1959, Hämeenlinna, Finland. Resides in Helsinki, Finland. *36*

Aitken, Doug
Born in 1968, Redondo Beach, California. Resides in Los Angeles. 29–30, *37*

Almond, Darren
Born in 1971, Wigan, England. Resides in London. *38*

Anselmo, Giovanni
Born in 1934, Borgofranco d'Ivrea, Italy. Resides in Torino, Italy. *39*

Antoni, Janine
Born in 1964, Freeport, Bahamas. Resides in New York City. *40*

Arden, Roy
Born in 1957, Vancouver, British Columbia. Resides in Vancouver, British Columbia. *41, 224*

Artschwager, Richard
Born in 1923, Washington, D.C. Resides in Hudson, New York. *42*

Ashton Harris, Lyle
Born in 1965, New York. Resides in New York City. *43*

Baldessari, John
Born in 1931, National City, California. Resides in Santa Monica, California. 14–15, *15*, 18, *44, 224*

Barney, Matthew
Born in 1967, San Francisco. Resides in New York City. 23–24, *45, 224*

Barth, Uta
Born in 1958, Berlin. Resides in Los Angeles. *46*

Bartscherer, Joseph
Born in 1954, New York City. Resides in New York City. *47, 225*

Basilico, Gabriele
Born in 1944, Milan. Resides in Milan. *48, 225*

Baumgarten, Lothar
Born in 1941, Rheinsberg, Germany. Resides in Berlin and New York City. *48, 225*

Becher, Bernd
Born in 1931, Siegen District in Germany. Resides in Düsseldorf, Germany. *10*, 11, 18, 31, 32, *49, 226*

Becher, Hilla
Born in 1934, Berlin. Resides in Düsseldorf, Germany. *10*, 11, 18, 31, 32, *49, 226*

Becher, Max
Born in 1964, Düsseldorf, Germany. Resides in New York City. *50, 226*

Becker, Julie
Born in 1972, Los Angeles. Resides in Los Angeles. *51, 226*

Beecroft, Vanessa
Born in 1969, Genoa, Italy. Resides in New York City. 24, 25, *52*

Behrend, Ute
Born in 1961, Berlin. Resides in Cologne, Germany. *53*

Beuys, Joseph
Born in 1921, Krefeld, Germany. Died in 1986. *54, 227*

Billingham, Richard
Born in 1970, Birmingham, England. Resides in West Midlands, England. *55*

Birchler, Alexander
Born in 1962, Baden, Switzerland. Resides in Austin, Texas. *111*

Boberg, Oliver
Born in 1965, Kreis Recklinghausen, Germany. Resides in Fürth, Germany. *56*

Bock, John
Born in 1965, Gribbohm, Germany. Resides in Berlin. *57*

Boltanski, Christian
Born in 1944, Paris. Resides in Malakoff, France. *58*

Bustamante, Jean-Marc
Born in 1952, Toulouse, France. Resides in Paris. *59, 227*

Calle, Sophie
Born in 1953, Paris. Resides in Paris. *60*

Casebere, James
Born in 1953, Lansing, Michigan. Resides in New York City. *61*

Castella, Vincenzo
Born in 1952, Naples, Italy. Resides in Milan. *62*

Chamberlain, John
Born in 1927, Rochester, Indiana. Resides in Sarasota, Florida. *62, 227*

Clegg, Michael
Born in 1957, Dublin, Ireland. Resides in New York City and San Francisco. *63, 227*

Close, Chuck
Born in 1940, Monroe, Washington. Resides in New York City. 17, *64–65, 227*

Cohen, Lynne
Born in 1944, Racine, Wisconsin. Resides in Ottawa, Ontario. *66*

Collins, Hannah
Born in 1956, London. Resides in Barcelona. *66*

Collishaw, Mat
Born in 1966, Nottingham, England. Resides in London. *67*

Conner, Bruce
Born in 1933, McPherson, Kansas. Resides in San Francisco. *68, 228*

Coolidge, Miles
Born in 1963, Montreal, Quebec. Resides in Los Angeles. *69, 228*

Coppes, Martino
Born in 1965, Como, Switzerland. Resides in Mendrisio, Switzerland. *69*

Crewdson, Gregory
Born in 1962, Brooklyn, New York. Resides in New York City. 28–29, *29, 70, 228, 229*

Darboven, Hanne
Born in 1941, Munich, Germany. Resides in Hamburg, Germany. *71*

Delvoye, Wim
Born in 1965, Wervik, Belgium. Resides in Ghent, Belgium. *72, 229*

Demand, Thomas
Born in 1964, Munich, Germany. Resides in Munich, Germany. *73, 229*

Derges, Susan
Born in 1955, London. Resides in Devon, England. *74, 229*

Dibbets, Jan
Born in 1941, Weert, The Netherlands. Resides in Amsterdam, The Netherlands. 12, *12*, 18, 28, *75*

diCorcia, Philip-Lorca
Born in 1953, Hartford, Connecticut. Resides in New York City. 27–28, *76*

Dijkstra, Rineke
Born in 1959, Sittard, The Netherlands. Resides in Amsterdam, The Netherlands. 27, 28, *77, 229*

Doherty, Willie
Born in 1959, Derry, Northern Ireland. Resides in Derry, Northern Ireland. *78*

Doig, Peter
Born in 1959, Edinburgh, Scotland. Resides in London. *79*

Douglas, Stan
Born in 1960, Vancouver, British Columbia. Resides in Vancouver, British Columbia. *80, 230*

Eliasson, Olafur
Born in 1967, Copenhagen, Denmark. Resides in Berlin. *81, 230*

Ess, Barbara
Born in Brooklyn, New York. Resides in New York City. *82, 230, 231*

Esser, Elger
Born in 1967, Stuttgart, Germany. Resides in Düsseldorf, Germany. *83, 231, 232*

Faigenbaum, Patrick
Born in 1954, Paris. Resides in Paris and Italy. 19–20, 27, *83, 232*

Fairhurst, Angus
Born in 1966, Kent, England. Resides in London. *84*

Feldmann, Hans-Peter
Born in 1941, Germany. Resides in Düsseldorf, Germany. *85, 232*

Fischli, Peter
Born in 1952, Zürich, Switzerland. Resides in Zürich, Switzerland. 27, *86–87, 232, 233*

Forg, Gunther
Born in 1952, Füssen, Germany. Resides in Switzerland. *88, 233*

François, Michel
Born in 1956, Saint Trond, Belgium. Resides in Brussels, Belgium. *89, 233*

Fulton, Hamish
Born in 1946, London. Resides in Canterbury, England. 13, *89, 233*

Fuss, Adam
Born in 1961, London. Resides in New York City. *90*

Gabellone, Giuseppe
Born in 1973, Brindisi, Italy. Resides in Milan. *90*

Garaicoa, Carlos
Born in 1967, Havana. Resides in Havana. *91, 233*

Gaskell, Anna
Born in 1969, Des Moines, Iowa. Resides in New York City. 24, 27, 28, *92, 233*

Gilbert and George
(see Passmore, Gilbert and Proesch, George)

Goldin, Nan
Born in 1953, Washington, D.C. Resides in Paris and New York City. 18, 19, *19*, 23, 27, *94, 234*

Gonzalez-Torres, Felix
Born in 1957, Guaimaro, Cuba. Died in 1996. *95*

Gordon, Douglas
Born in 1966, Glasgow, Scotland. Resides in Glasgow, Scotland. *96, 97*

Gorgoni, Gianfranco
Born in 1941, Rome, Italy. Resides in New York City, Milan, and Havana. *98*

Graham, Dan
Born in 1942, Urbana, Illinois. Resides in New York City. 12–13, *99, 234*

Graham, Rodney
Born in 1949, Vancouver, British Columbia. Resides in Vancouver, British Columbia. *100, 235*

Groover, Jan
Born in 1943, Plainfield, New Jersey. Resides in Montpon, France. *101*

Gursky, Andreas
Born in 1955, Leipzig, Germany. Resides in Düsseldorf, Germany. 31, 32–33, *102–3, 235*

Guttmann, Martin
Born in 1957, Jerusalem, Israel. Resides in New York City and San Francisco. *63, 227*

Hall, Doug
Born in 1944, San Francisco. Resides in San Francisco. *104, 235*

Hanson, Chris
Born in 1964, Montreal, Quebec. Resides in New York City. *104*

Hido, Todd
Born in 1968, Kent, Ohio. Resides in San Francisco. *105, 235*

Hirakawa, Noritoshi
Born in 1988, Fukuoka, Japan. Resides in New York City. *106*

Hodges, Jim
Born in 1957, Spokane, Washington. Resides in New York City. *107*

Hofer, Candida
Born in 1944, Eberswalde, Germany. Resides in Cologne, Germany. 31, 32, *33, 108, 236, 237*

Horn, Roni
Born in 1955, New York City. Resides in New York City. *109, 237*

Horsfield, Craigie
Born in 1949, Cambridge, England. Resides in London. *110*

Hubbard, Teresa
Born in 1965, Dublin, Ireland. Resides in Austin, Texas. *111*

Hume, Gary
Born in 1962, Kent, England. Resides in London. *111*

Hunter, Tom
Born in 1965, Bournemouth, England. Resides in London. *112, 237*

Hutte, Axel
Born in 1951, Essen, Germany. Resides in Düsseldorf, Germany. *113, 237*

Jeong-a, Koo
Born in 1967, Seoul, Korea. Resides everywhere. *114*

Jetelova, Magdalena
Born in 1946, Semily, Czechoslovakia. Resides in Düsseldorf, Germany. *115*

Jones, Sarah
Born in 1959, London. Resides in London. *116*

Keita, Seydou
Born in Bamako, Mali. Resides in Bamako, Mali. *117, 238*

Kelley, Mike
Born in 1954, Detroit, Michigan. Resides in Los Angeles. *118–19, 238*

Kersels, Martin
Born in 1960, Los Angeles. Resides in Sierra Madre, California. *120*

Kiefer, Anselm
Born in 1945, Donaueschingen, Germany. Resides in France. *121*

Kippenberger, Martin
Born in 1953, Dortmund, Germany. Died in 1997. *122, 238*

Koons, Jeff
Born in 1955, York, Pennsylvania. Resides in New York City. 22, *23, 123*

Koster, Jan
Born in 1959, Kampen, The Netherlands. Resides in Amsterdam, The Netherlands. *124, 239*

Kounellis, Jannis
Born in 1936, Piraeus, Greece. Resides in Rome and Düsseldorf, Germany. *124*

Kurland, Justine
Born in 1969, Warsaw, New York. Resides in New York City. *125, 239*

Lafont, Suzanne
Born in 1949, Nîmes, France. Resides in Paris. *126*

Lane, Abigail
Born in 1967, Penzance, England. Resides in London. *127*

Lawler, Louise
Born in 1947, Bronxville, New York. Resides in New York City. *128, 239*

Le Va, Barry
Born in 1941, Long Beach, California. Resides in New York City. 23, *129*

Lemieux, Annette
Born in 1957, Norfolk, Virginia. Resides in Boston. *130–31*

Levine, Sherrie
Born in 1947, Hazleton, Pennsylvania. Resides in New York City. 24–25, *25, 132, 240*

LeWitt, Sol
Born in 1928, Hartford, Connecticut. Resides in Chester, Connecticut. 17, *133*

Lockhart, Sharon
Born in 1964, Norwood, Massachusetts. Resides in Los Angeles. *135–36, 240*

Long, Richard
Born in 1945, Bristol, England. Resides in Bristol, England. 13, *136*

Lucas, Sarah
Born in 1962, London. Resides in London. *137, 240*

Lutter, Vera
Born in 1960, Kaiserslautern, Germany. Resides in New York City. *138–39*

Manglano-Ovalle, Inigo
Born in 1961, Madrid, Spain. Resides in Chicago. *140–41*

Mapplethorpe, Robert
Born in 1946, New York City. Died in 1989. 25–26, 27, *142, 240*

Matta-Clark, Gordon
Born in 1943, New York City. Died in 1978. *143, 241*

McCarthy, Paul
Born in 1945, Salt Lake City, Utah. Resides in Los Angeles. *144*

McQueen, Steve
Born in 1969, London. Resides in Amsterdam, The Netherlands. *145, 241*

Mihailov, Boris
Born in 1938, Kharkov, Ukraine. Resides in Kharkov, Ukraine. *146–47*

Misrach, Richard
Born in 1949, Los Angeles. Resides in Berkeley, California. *148, 241*

Mori, Mariko
Born in 1967, Tokyo, Japan. Resides in New York City. 22–23, *148*

Morimura, Yasumasa
Born in 1951, Osaka, Japan. Resides in Osaka, Japan. *149, 242*

Mossman, Anna
Born in 1963, London. Resides in London. *150*

Mucha, Reinhard
Born in 1950, Düsseldorf, Germany. Resides in Düsseldorf, Germany. *151, 242*

Muller, Christian Philipp
Born in 1957, Biel, Switzerland. Resides in New York City. *152*

Mullican, Matt
Born in 1951, Santa Monica, California. Resides in New York City. *153, 242*

Muniz, Vik
Born in 1961, São Paulo, Brazil. Resides in New York City. *153, 242*

Mylayne, Jean-Luc
Born in 1946, Amiens, France. Resides in France. *154, 242*

Nauman, Bruce
Born in 1941, Fort Wayne, Indiana. Resides in New Mexico. 14, 15, 18, 20, 23, 24, 29, *155, 243*

Neshat, Shirin
Born in 1957, Qazvin, Iran. Resides in New York City. 30, *31, 156, 243*

Niedermayr, Walter
Born in 1952, Bolzano, Italy. Resides in Bolzano, Italy. *157*

Noguchi, Rika
Born in 1971, Saitama, Japan. Resides in New York City. *157, 243*

Oehlen, Albert
Born in 1954, Krefeld, Germany. Resides in Cologne, Germany. *158, 243*

Ontani, Luigi
Born in 1943, Vergato, Italy. Resides in Italy. *159*

Opie, Catherine
Born in 1961, Sandusky, Ohio. Resides in Los Angeles and New York City. 20, *21*, 23, 27, *160, 244*

Orozco, Gabriel
Born in 1962, Jalapa, Vera Cruz, Mexico. Resides in Mexico and New York City. *161, 245*

Oursler, Tony
Born in 1957, New York City. Resides in New York City. *161, 245*

Paolini, Giulio
Born in 1940, Genova, Italy. Resides in Torino, Italy. *162*

Paradeis, Florence
Born in 1964, Anthony, France. Resides in Paris. *163*

Passmore, Gilbert
Born in 1943, Dolomites, Italy. Resides in London. 13–14, 28, *93, 234*

Perejaume
Born in 1957, Sant Pol de Mar, Spain. Resides in Sant Pol de Mar, Spain. *164*

Pierson, Jack
Born in 1960, Plymouth, Massachusetts. Resides in New York City and Provincetown, Massachusetts. 18–19, *165, 245, 246*

Pina, Manuel
Born in 1958, Havana. Resides in Havana. *165, 246*

Pippin, Steven
Born in 1960, Redhill, England. Resides in London and Berlin. 29, 30, *166, 246*

Poitevin, Eric
Born in 1961, the Meuse, France. Resides in the Meuse, France. *167*

Polke, Sigmar
Born in 1941, Oels, Germany (now Olesnica, Poland). Resides in Cologne, Germany. *16,* 16–17, 18, *168, 246, 247*

Prina, Stephen
Born in 1954, Galesburg, Illinois. Resides in Los Angeles. *169*

Prince, Richard
Born in 1949, Panama Canal Zone. Resides in upstate New York. 25, *25, 170, 247, 248*

Proesch, George
Born in 1942, Devon, England. Resides in London. 13–14, 28, *93, 234*

Rauschenberg, Robert
Born in 1925, Port Arthur, Texas. Resides in New York City and Captiva Island, Florida. 9–11, 13, 18, *171*

Ray, Charles
Born in 1953, Chicago, Illinois. Resides in Los Angeles. 21, 22, *172–73*

Rehberger, Tobias
Born in 1966, Esslingen, Germany. Resides in Frankfurt, Germany. *174*

Richter, Gerhard
Born in 1932, Dresden, Germany. Resides in Cologne, Germany. 15–16, *16,* 18, *175, 248*

Robbins, Andrea
Born in 1963, Boston. Resides in New York City. *50, 226*

Rosenfeld, Marina
Born in 1968, New York City. Resides in New York City. *176, 249*

Ruff, Thomas
Born in 1958, Harmersbach, Germany. Resides in Düsseldorf, Germany 31–32, *177, 249*

Ruppersberg, Allen
Born in 1944, Cleveland, Ohio. Resides in New York City. *178*

Ruscha, Edward
Born in 1937, Omaha, Nebraska. Resides in Los Angeles. 13, *179, 250*

Rutimann, Christoph
Born in 1955, Zürich, Switzerland. Resides in Mullheim TG, Switzerland. *180, 250*

Sambunaris, Victoria
Born in 1964, Lancaster, Pennsylvania. Resides in New York City. *180*

Sasse, Jörg
Born in 1962, Bad Salzuflen, Germany. Resides in Düsseldorf, Germany. *181, 250*

Schabel, John
Born in 1957, Great Falls, Montana. Resides in New York City. *182, 251*

Schneider, Gregor
Born in 1969, Rheydt, Germany. Resides in Rheydt, Germany. *183*

Schorr, Collier
Born in 1963, New York City. Resides in Brooklyn, New York. *184, 251*

Schutte, Thomas
Born in 1954, Oldenburg, Germany. Resides in Düsseldorf, Germany. *185*

Serrano, Andres
Born in 1950, New York City. Resides in New York City. *186, 251*

Sherman, Cindy
Born in 1954, Glen Ridge, New Jersey. Resides in New York City. 21–22, 23, 24, 27, 28, *187, 252*

Shonibare, Yinka
Born in 1962, London. Resides in London. *188*

Sietsema, Paul
Born in 1968, Los Angeles. Resides in Los Angeles. *189*

Signer, Roman
Born in 1938, Appenzell, Switzerland. Resides in St. Gall, Switzerland. *190*

Sikander, Shahzia
Born in 1969, Lahore, Pakistan. Resides in New York City. *191*

Simmons, Gary
Born in 1964, New York City. Resides in New York City. *192, 253*

Simmons, Laurie
Born in 1949, Long Island, New York. Resides in New York City. 27, *193, 253*

Simpson, Lorna
Born in 1960, Brooklyn, New York. Resides in Brooklyn, New York. *194*

Smith, Bridget
Born in 1966, Essex, England. Resides in London. *195, 253*

Smith, Seton
Born in 1955, Newark, New Jersey. Resides in Paris and New York City. *196*

Smithson, Robert
Born in 1938, Rutherford, New Jersey. Died in 1973. 13, *197*

Sonnenberg, Hendrika
Born in 1963, Toronto, Ontario. Resides in New York City. *104*

Starr, Georgina
Born in 1968, Leeds, England. Resides in London. *198, 253*

Streuli, Beat
Born in 1957, Altdorf, Switzerland. Resides in Düsseldorf, Germany. *199, 253*

Struth, Thomas
Born in 1954, Geldern, Germany. Resides in Düsseldorf, Germany. *6,* 31, *200, 254, 255*

Sugimoto, Hiroshi
Born in 1948, Tokyo, Japan. Resides in New York City. 25, *26,* 26–27, *201, 256*

Sullivan, Billy
Born in 1946, New York City. Resides in New York City. *202, 257*

Tandberg, Vibeke
Born in 1967, Oslo, Norway. Resides in Oslo, Norway and New York City. *203, 257*

Taylor-Wood, Sam
Born in 1967, London. Resides in London. *204–5*

Tillmans, Wolfgang
Born in 1968, Remscheid, Germany. Resides in London. 29, 30, *206, 258*

Tiravanija, Rirkrit
Born in 1961, Buenos Aires, Argentina. Resides in New York City. *207*

Trockel, Rosemarie
Born in 1952, Schwerte, Germany. Resides in Cologne, Germany. *208, 258, 264*

Tronvoll, Mette
Born in 1965, Trondheim, Norway. Resides in Berlin, Germany. *209, 259*

Tuymans, Luc
Born in 1958, Mortsel, Belgium. Resides in Antwerp, Belgium. *210*

Uklanski, Piotr
Born in 1968, Warsaw, Poland. Resides in New York City and Warsaw, Poland. *211, 259*

Van Meene, Hellen
Born in 1972, Alkmaar, The Netherlands. Resides in Alkmaar, The Netherlands. *212, 259*

Varejao, Adriana
Born in 1964, Rio de Janeiro, Brazil. Resides in Rio de Janeiro, Brazil. *213*

Vitali, Massimo
Born in 1944, Como, Italy. Resides in Lucca, Italy. *214, 259*

von Nagel, Augustina
Born in 1952, Germany. Resides in Cologne, Germany. *247*

Wall, Jeff
Born in 1946, Vancouver, British Columbia. Resides in Vancouver, British Columbia. 28, *215, 260*

Warhol, Andy
Born in 1928, Pittsburgh, Pennsylvania. Died in 1987. 9, *10,* 10–11, 12, 18, 21, 24, *216, 260*

Wearing, Gillian
Born in 1963, Birmigham, England. Resides in London. *217*

Wegman, William
Born in 1943, Long Meadow, Massachusetts. Resides in New York City. *218, 260*

Weiss, David
Born in 1946, Zürich, Switzerland. Resides in Zürich, Switzerland. 27, *86–87, 232, 233*

Welling, James
Born in 1951, Hartford, Connecticut. Resides in Los Angeles. 29, 30, *30, 219, 260, 261*

Whiteread, Rachel
Born in 1963, London. Resides in London. *220, 261*

Williams, Christopher
Born in 1956, Los Angeles. Resides in Los Angeles. *221, 261*

Zittel, Andrea
Born in 1965, Escondido, California. Resides in Joshua Tree, California and Brooklyn, New York. *2–3, 222*

Photograph Credits

All photographs courtesy the Metropolitan Bank & Trust except the following: page 49 Courtesy Sonnabend Gallery, New York; page 57 Courtesy Marian Goodman Gallery, New York; page 70 Courtesy Barbara Gladstone Gallery, New York; page 79 Courtesy Neuger/Riemschneider, Berlin; page 81 (top) Courtesy Sonnabend Gallery, New York; page 93 Courtesy James Cohan Gallery, New York; page 150 Courtesy Murray Guy, New York; page 181 Courtesy of Lehmann Maupin, New York; page 190 Courtesy Galerie Hauser & Wirth. Photograph by Stefan Rohner; page 201 Courtesy Sonnabend Gallery, New York; page 218 Courtesy William Wegman Studio; page 226 (#14) Courtesy Sotheby's, New York; page 234 (#77) Courtesy Sotheby's, New York; page 237 (#104) Courtesy Matthew Marks Gallery, New York; page 240 (#125) Courtesy Blum & Poe, New York

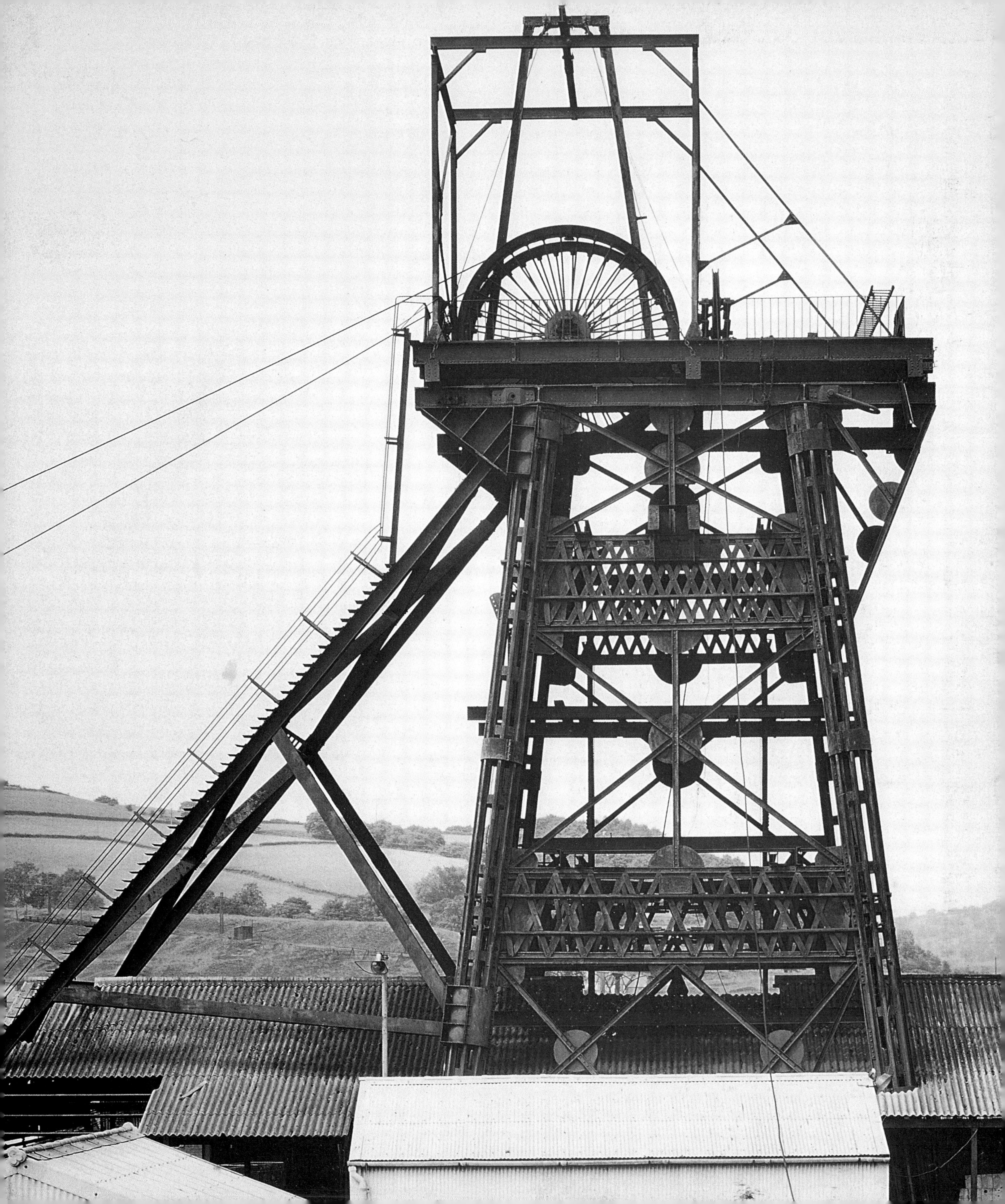